Cyberstyle!

The Writer's Complete Desk Reference

James L. Clark

Professor, Business Department, Pasadena City College

Lyn R. Clark

Professor, Computer Applications and Office Technologies Department,
Los Angeles Pierce College

THOMSON LEARNING™

Cyberstyle!; The Writer's Complete Desk Reference, by James L. Clark and Lyn R. Clark

First trade edition, 2001

ISBN:0-324-07073-X

Printed in the United States of America
1 2 3 4 5 03 02 01 00

For more information contact South-Western College Publishing, 5101 Madison Road, Cincinnati, Ohio, 45227 or find us on the Internet at http://www.swcollege.com.

For permission to use material from this text or product, contact us by
- **telephone: 1-800-730-2214**
- **fax: 1-800-730-2215**
- **web: http://www.thomsonrights.com**

Library of Congress Cataloging-in-Publication Data
Clark, James Leland, 1929–
Cyberstyle!: The writer's complete desk reference / James L. Clark, Lyn R. Clark.
p. cm.
Includes bibliographical references and index.
ISBN 0-324-07073-X (pbk. : alk. paper)
1. Commercial correspondence—Handbooks, manuals, etc. I. Title: Cyberstyle!. II. Clark, Lyn. III. Clark, James Leland, 1929– IV. Title.

HF5726.C55 2001
808'.06665—dc21 00-034439

This book is printed on acid-free paper.

Contents

Preface

Cyberstyle! The Writer's Complete Desk Reference, has been designed for the Internet Age to provide assistance in the preparation of all types of written business communications. Its content and style focus upon the needs of office personnel, business writers, and other business professionals to produce suitable documents for success in a highly competitive, fast-paced global economy. *Cyberstyle!* presents detailed and precise information for writing, formatting, and transmitting business documents. It serves as a reference book to answer specific questions regarding language conventions, business formats, and document transmission as they relate to the preparation of E-mail messages, business letters, memorandums, reports, manuscripts, proposals, bulletins, résumés, faxes, agendas, itineraries, and meeting minutes.

Cyberstyle! serves as a reference for all persons in business who are responsible for communicating through the written word. Similar to the indispensable dictionary, this handbook compresses other essential reference information into a single source for producing effective business documents. It is targeted for use in businesses by managers, administrative assistants, secretaries, word processors, and all others who have responsibility for producing effective written communications. Persons in all fields of business, education, government, law, and medicine will benefit from using *Cyberstyle!* as a reference in preparing written documents for their professional position and their personal business circumstances.

A Comprehensive Reference Manual for Business

Cyberstyle! is succinct, yet comprehensive. It covers thoroughly the principles of grammar, punctuation, capitalization, number usage, word hyphenation and division, and abbreviation format in simple, easy-to-understand language. Each rule is illustrated with examples or example sentences related to business circumstances or conditions. In addition, nearly 200 word confusions—ones such as *affect/effect, ensure/insure,* and *principal/principle*—are differentiated by simple definitions and discriminating examples.

Content and formats for various business documents are covered thoroughly in *Cyberstyle!* All the major parts of a business letter, forms of address for domestic and foreign correspondence, and commonly used letter styles are discussed and illustrated, along with the basic formats for writing memorandums. Report writers will find helpful the expanded guidelines for citing sources, preparing visuals, setting up listings, providing main and text headings, compiling preliminary pages and bibliographies, and formatting a report in general. Instructions and examples for preparing E-mail messages, itineraries, agendas, and meeting minutes further enhance the usability of this book as a business writer's resource. To assist readers with the entire document processing cycle, *Cyberstyle!* provides detailed procedures for preparing business documents on computer-based equipment and accessing the Internet to collect information.

Up-to-the-Minute Features:

The following features make *Cyberstyle!* timely and informative:

- A chapter on connecting to the Internet, accessing the World Wide Web, and using search sites to locate information (see Chapter 9).
- A chapter on fax transmissions and E-mail messaging—purpose and function, features, templates, procedures, message preparation, and E-mail netiquette (see Chapter 10).
- Information on accessing and using Internet career centers as well as specific instructions and examples for preparing résumés to be placed on-line (see Chapter 13).
- Extensive listing (addresses and descriptions) of Internet sites—reference, news, business, government, directory, career center, and travel (see Chapter 15).
- A section on organizing and managing computer files and folders using Windows Explorer (see Chapter 16).
- A glossary that provides definitions of commonly used computer and Internet terms (see Glossary B).

Easy-to-Use Guides

Several features, besides the table of contents and the extensive index, increase the functional use of *Cyberstyle!* as a reference book:

1. **Solution Finders**—comprehensive topic indexes at the beginning of each chapter enable readers to locate easily solutions to their problems.
2. **Two-color format**—rules are printed in red and examples are printed in black so that principles may be located, read, and understood quickly.
3. **Example headings**—boldfaced headings differentiate aspects of each rule so that specific examples and applications may be located immediately.
4. **Spiral binding**—the lie-flat feature of spiral binding permits readers to compare readily their problems with the examples.
5. **Glossary of grammatical terms**—a listing with definitions and examples of all the grammatical terms used in this book may be accessed for further clarification of any language principle.

Fast Solutions to Problems

Information you need may be located easily and quickly in *Cyberstyle!* by using a four-step process.

1. Find the chapter you need by viewing the list of contents shown on the back cover.
2. Turn to the Solution Finder at the beginning of that chapter by using the page-edge chapter divider tab.

3. Locate the information you need in the Solution Finder. Each main topic is listed alphabetically followed by subsections of that topic and their corresponding section numbers.
4. Turn to the appropriate section within the chapter by referring to the page guide references (the section numbers shown at the top right corner of the odd-numbered pages).

If information cannot be located by surveying the contents listed on the back cover, use the comprehensive index at the end of the book to find the appropriate section.

Acknowledgments

We thank the following reviewers for their assistance in the preparation of this reference book:

Dr. Shirley A. Mixon, East Central University
Barbara B. Foti, Washington Business School
John L. Waltman, Ph.D., Eastern Michigan University
Joyce Harlow, Rogue Community College
Dr. Marilee Knapp, Mott Community College
Paul R. Sawyer, Southeastern Louisiana University
Carolena Lyons-Lawrence, Ph.D., San Diego State University

James and Lyn Clark
E-mail: ClarksHOW@aol.com

Comma

1–1 Series

a. **In a sentence containing a series of three or more equally ranked parts (words, phrases, or short clauses), place a comma after each part except the last one. Be sure to use a comma before the conjunction (*and, or, nor*).[1]**

words

Three of the most popular Internet search sites are Yahoo!, AltaVista, and Excite.

Our $5.99 luncheon special includes a salad, sandwich, beverage, and dessert.

Next year's budget will permit us to hire in this branch office an accountant, a network administrator, and an additional administrative assistant.

phrases

A new manager was hired to improve customer service, computerize our records management system, and implement more cost-effective procedures.

short clauses

Karen Jones made the sale, Chris Lopez approved the contract, and Ralph Harris directed me to ship the computers immediately.

b. **Commas are not used when the parts of a series are all joined by conjunctions.**

words

Only checks **or** bankcards **or** purchase orders are acceptable.

phrases

For the past year we have contracted with A-Z Building Services to clean the offices nightly **and** maintain the grounds weekly **and** provide general repairs as needed.

c. **Although generally avoided, *etc.* is sometimes used to indicate "and so forth" at the end of a series. If used, *etc.* is set off by commas; it is not preceded by the word *and.***

---

[1]Some periodicals and literary writers prefer to omit the comma before the conjunction in a series. For business writing, however, use the comma before the conjunction to promote ease of reading and clarity.

within a sentence

Checking accounts, savings accounts, money market accounts, certificates of deposit**, etc.,** are available through our Internet banking service.

end of a sentence

We plan to visit all our branch offices this year—Dallas, Los Angeles, Chicago, London, Paris, Rome**, etc.**

d. **A comma is not used before an ampersand (&) in an organizational name unless the organization officially uses the comma in its name.**

no comma

Her first interview is with Gates, Hamilton **&** Gates.

comma

Augner, Haight, Liggett**, &** Phelan is a long-established accounting firm in the Chicago area.

1–2 Parenthetical Expressions

a. **Transitional words and expressions that are considered unnecessary for the grammatical completeness of a sentence and that *interrupt its natural flow* are set off with commas. A partial list of such parenthetical expressions follows:**

according to our records
accordingly
after all
all in all
all things considered
also
as a matter of fact
as a result
as a rule
at any rate
at the same time
besides
between you and me
by the way
consequently
even so
finally
for example
fortunately
furthermore
hence
however
in addition
incidentally
in conclusion
indeed
in effect
in essence
in fact
in general
in my opinion
in other words
instead
in summary
in the first place
in the meantime
likewise
moreover
namely
needless to say
nevertheless
no
no doubt
obviously
of course
on the contrary
on the other hand
on the whole
otherwise
perhaps
periodically
secondly
so
that is
then
therefore
thus
too
under the circumstances
unfortunately
what is more
without a doubt
yes

beginning of a sentence

Needless to say, our company was one of the first to establish an Internet site.

end of a sentence

The store will be closed over the Labor Day weekend, **without a doubt**.

within a sentence

A large crowd, **nevertheless,** attended the art exhibit.

b. **Sometimes words and phrases used as parenthetical expressions *do not interrupt* the flow of a sentence. In such cases no commas are used with the expression.**

beginning of a sentence

Perhaps the package will arrive in Denver by Monday.

end of a sentence

Our manager is planning to visit New York City **too**.

within a sentence

She was **indeed** concerned about the omissions in the financial analysis.

c. **Exclamations at the beginning of a sentence are parenthetical expressions that require a comma.**

Oh, what a surprise to see Ms. Hilton in court again!

Ah, we will have difficulty transferring these holdings into liquid assets!

d. **Enumerations or explanations used as parenthetical expressions *within a sentence* are set off by commas, dashes, or parentheses. Use commas when the enumerated or explanatory information has no internal commas, dashes when the information contains commas within it, or parentheses when the information is considered to be only incidental to the rest of the sentence.**

commas

Only one company, **namely, Consolidated Enterprises,** bid on the contract.

dashes

He reported income from several sources—**namely, salary, interest, dividends, and rentals**—on his last income tax return.

parentheses

Our vice president toured several Ohio cities **(Cleveland, Columbus, and Toledo)** to find a suitable plant site.

e. **A parenthetical expression introducing an enumeration or explanation *after a complete thought* may be set off with either (1) commas or (2) a semicolon and a comma. If the enumeration or explanation itself is a complete thought or contains internal commas, use a semicolon and a comma. Otherwise, use commas.**

commas

We are expecting two exceptionally large orders next week, **namely,** from Reed's Department Store and Payco.

There are several ways we can cut our expenses during the next quarter, **for example,** by reducing our advertising budget.

semicolon and comma

This customer ordered new furniture for her living room; **namely, a sofa, two chairs, two lamp tables, and an occasional table**.

f. **Short introductory prepositional phrases essential to the meaning of a sentence should not be mistaken for parenthetical expressions. These phrases answer specifically questions such as *when, where, why,* or *how*. Introductory prepositional phrases containing fewer than five words (but not containing a verb form) generally flow smoothly into the sentence and are *not* followed by a comma.**

when?

In the future please place your orders with our Eastern Washington office.

At your convenience please fill out and return the enclosed form.

where?

At this conference we met agents from all parts of the United States, Canada, and Mexico.

In this case we are able to grant only a partial refund of the purchase price.

why?

For that reason we have turned over your account to our attorney for collection.

On this basis we have decided to expand our operations to South America.

how?

In this way you will be able to cut your travel costs significantly.

With this software you can speed up the operation of any desktop computer by at least 20 percent.

g. **Adverbs used as parenthetical expressions do not require commas.**

However brilliant his work may be, Mr. Rogers will not be promoted until his disposition improves.

Obviously concerned about the drop in sales, our manager called a meeting of all sales personnel.

Too many agents have not yet submitted their monthly sales summary.

1–3 Direct Address

When calling a person by name, title, or affiliation, use commas to set off the reference. Speaking directly to individuals or groups requires their names be set off by commas because these names are used in direct address. For words used in direct address within a sentence, capitalize only (1) proper nouns and (2) personal and professional titles.

beginning of a sentence

Ladies and gentlemen, congratulations on your achievements!

Ms. Phelps, you have been promoted to assistant vice president.

within a sentence

Will you please, **Dr. Jones,** send us your check for $150 by March 30.

The book you have ordered, **Professor,** is presently out of stock.

Please examine for yourselves, **ladies and gentlemen,** how this proposal will affect you.

You, **fellow golfer,** will now be able to cut strokes from your game with this new Leading Edge driver.

end of a sentence

You are certainly a competent assistant, **Ms. Boyer**.

You also should be concerned about this issue, **fellow American**.

1–4 Appositives

a. **Appositives are word groups that rename or explain the nouns or pronouns they follow. These descriptive words usually add extra information and are set off by commas. (See 1-4b and 1-4c for exceptions.)**

within a sentence

All the reports were submitted to Ms. Hartford, **our sales manager,** for approval.

Our vice president, **Mr. Voddon,** will be in Belgium all next week.

end of a sentence

At your suggestion we contacted a representative in your nearest branch office, **the Hillsdale office**.

She had reservations on the 5:30 p.m. flight, **the last flight to Seattle that day**.

b. **Restrictive appositives—descriptive word groups that are *needed to identify* the person or thing further described—are not set off by commas. These restrictive appositives tell *which one* or *which ones* and are essential to the meaning of the sentence.**

necessary for identification—tells which one or which ones

The book ***Procedures for the Automated Office*** will be released next week.

Your student **Larry Green** has an appointment to see you tomorrow.

We **board members** are responsible for ensuring that each child in our community receives a quality education.

unnecessary for identification

His latest book, ***College English,*** was released last December.

Your best student, **Ann Freeman,** has an appointment to see you next week.

c. **Closely related one-word appositives or those forming parts of proper names do not require commas.**

closely related one-word appositives

My sister **Ellen** has received two promotions within the last year.

I **myself** plan to attend the organizational meeting in Memphis.

In this area the state legislation sets forth only general guidelines for us **teachers**.

proper name

His last two novels dealt with the lives of Alexander **the Great** and Richard **the Lionhearted**.

d. **College degrees and abbreviations written after individuals' names are set off by commas; the abbreviations *Jr.* and *Sr.* and Roman numerals, however, are not set off by commas unless an individual chooses to include them.**

Abbreviations such as *Inc.* and *Ltd.* after company names are also set off by commas if a particular company elects to include them.

commas with college degree or abbreviation after name of individual

Marilyn Drengson, **Doctor of Divinity,** will deliver the main graduation address.

Caroline R. Ryan, **Ph.D.,** is the author of *Executive Decision Making*.

Our firm will be represented by Alan Moskley, **Esq.**[2]

Please schedule an appointment with Neal F. Kirby, **D.D.S., M.D.,** to have your wisdom teeth extracted.

---

[2]Courtesy or professional titles are not used with the abbreviation *Esq. Esq.* may be used after the name of a lawyer. It replaces the courtesy title (*Mr., Mrs.,* or *Ms.*) and the professional title *Attorney-at-Law*.

no commas with "Jr.," "Sr.," or Roman numeral after name of individual

Mr. Lowell T. Harrison **Jr.** will be our new sales representative in South Africa.

Please send copies of the contract to David Warburton **Sr.** and the other names listed in the attached letter.

Donald J. Ellington **III** has just been appointed secretary of state.

commas with abbreviations after company names

A. G. Edwards & Sons**, Inc.,** has moved its offices to Wilshire Boulevard.

Clothiers**, Ltd.,** is one of the largest jobbers on the West Coast.

no commas with abbreviations after company names

We have contracted with Ricon MED **Inc.** to install the wheelchair lifts in our hospital vans.

Most of the stocks in this estate are held by PaineWebber **Inc.**

Your crystal order from Cash & Co. **Ltd.** will be shipped from Ireland within the next week.

e. **Words or expressions referred to simply as words or expressions should be written in italics rather than set off by commas. If an italic font is not available, underscore or place in quotation marks the words or expressions.**

italics

Too many writers use ***insure*** when they should use ***ensure***.

underscored

The word **convenience** is often misspelled in business documents.

quotation marks

The phrase **"Thanking you in advance"** is an outdated expression that should not be used in business letters.

1–5 Dates and Time Zones

a. **Dates containing combinations of weekday, calendar date, and year require commas. Place a comma *after each element* used unless, of course, the element concludes a sentence. Remember *always* to place a comma *after* the year when a calendar date and year appear within the sentence.**

Commas are not used with a calendar date expressed alone.

calendar date expressed alone

On **February 28** our books were audited by the Internal Revenue Service.

calendar date and year

On **February 28, 2001,** our books were audited by the Internal Revenue Service.

weekday and calendar date

On **Tuesday, February 28,** our books were audited by the Internal Revenue Service.

weekday, calendar date, and year

On **Tuesday, February 28, 2001,** our books were audited by the Internal Revenue Service.

b. **Expressions of month and year are written without commas.**

The Internal Revenue Service audited our books in **February 2001**.

In **March 2003** we will release our new line of products.

c. **Set off by commas any time zones used with clock times.**

Our flight will leave Denver at 9:35 a.m., **MST,** and arrive in New York City at 3:18 p.m., **EST**.

We received your fax from Japan at 10:40 a.m., **PDT**.

1–6 Addresses

a. **The parts of an address written in sentence form are separated by commas.**

name and complete address

Please send the check to **Ms. Harriet Buckley, Manager, Accounting Department, American Paper Company, 2996 Grandview Avenue, N.E., Suite 312, Atlanta, Georgia 30305-3245,** by May 1.

complete address only

Mr. Livingston may be reached at **740 Gayley Avenue, Apt. 3, Los Angeles, California 90025**.

b. **Use commas to set off a state following the name of a city. Likewise, use commas to set off a country following the name of a city. Remember to use the second comma after the state or country name when it appears in the middle of a sentence.**

within a sentence

The letter was sent to Kansas City, **Missouri,** in error.

Please confirm this order from Frankfurt, **Germany,** at the company's E-mail address.

end of a sentence

On our tour we will visit Boston, **Massachusetts**.

Next month we will be opening new offices in Brisbane, **Australia**.

1–7 Coordinating Conjunctions

a. **The words *and, but, or,* and *nor* are coordinating conjunctions. Place a comma before any of these words that separate two independent clauses (complete thought units) in a compound sentence. No comma is used if both clauses are not totally independent and could not stand alone as separate sentences. (See Section 1–18 for use of a semicolon instead of a comma.)**

two independent clauses

Several of our staff members should reach their sales goals by the end of this month**, and** they will then be eligible to win a bonus vacation to Hawaii.

There are still 43 orders to fill**, but** we will close for vacation as scheduled.

You may have the interest added to your account**, or** we can send you a monthly check for the interest earned.

We have not purchased any appliances from this distributor within the past three months**, nor** have we requested an extension of our credit line.

You may, Mr. Villano, obtain up-to-date flight schedules from our Web site on the Internet**, and** you can make your reservations at the same time.

Over one hundred of our clients indicated an interest in attending our free seminars**, but** we can, unfortunately, accommodate only half of them in this series.

no second independent clause

I plan to complete this project by Wednesday but cannot promise that it will reach your desk before Monday.

We are aware of the growth and increased sales potential in your district and that another salesperson should be assigned to your territory.

b. **In imperative sentences (command statements), the subject *you* is understood. Separate with a comma two independent clauses, whether one or both are in the imperative form.**

Ship the books to me at Grant Occupational Center**, but** send the invoice to the bookstore manager at Eastern College.

Please call Dr. Greenberg's office tomorrow morning**, and** his nurse will let you know what time the doctor is expected to finish surgery.

c. **When a simple adverb, an introductory phrase, or a dependent clause precedes and applies equally to two clauses, the second clause is not**

a totally separate thought unit. Consequently, no comma is placed before the conjunction.

simple adverb

Please call the doctor's office tomorrow morning and arrange to have your appointment changed to next week. (The adverb *please* refers to both *call* and *arrange*. Therefore, the second clause is not an independent thought unit and a comma is not required.)

introductory phrase

During the next month our board members will visit several sites in Memphis and they will select one for our new branch office. (*During the next month* applies equally to both clauses. Consequently, the second clause is not an independent thought unit and a comma is not required.)

dependent clauses

When Mr. Howard calls, ask him for his new address and send him 100 copies of our revised price list. (Subject *you* is understood in both clauses. *When Mr. Howard calls* applies to both clauses. Therefore, the second clause is not an independent thought unit and no punctuation mark is required.)

As soon as we receive your E-mail response, we will notify our distributor and he will ship your order the next day. (In this case *As soon as we receive your E-mail response* applies to both clauses; therefore, no punctuation mark is needed before the conjunction *and*.)

d. **Omit the comma in short compound sentences connected by *and*. For simplicity, "short" in these cases *may be* interpreted as those compound sentences containing up to 12 or 13 words.**

Format five additional disks and use them to back up this subdirectory.

John wrote the letter and his supervisor signed it.

I received the inquiry yesterday and my assistant contacted the client immediately.

1–8 Independent Adjectives

Use commas to separate two or more independent adjectives that modify a noun. No commas are needed, though, when the first adjective modifies the second adjective and the noun as a unit. To identify independent adjectives, (1) reverse the adjectives, (2) read the adjectives independently, and (3) read the sentence with the word *and* between the adjectives. If the sentence makes sense and means the same thing with the adjectives read in these ways, then commas should be placed between them.

independent adjectives

Be sure to enclose a **stamped, addressed** envelope with your inquiry.

The president had surrounded herself with **efficient, intelligent** assistants.

We received a **demanding, discourteous, unprecedented** letter from your company.

first adjective modifies second adjective and noun

The posters were lettered in **large bold print**.

He received several **attractive business offers**.

The room was filled with **old local newspapers** dating back to the 1970s.

Does the press release describe Liza's **dazzling blue evening gown**?

1–9 Introductory Clauses

a. An introductory dependent clause is separated from the rest of the sentence by a comma. Introductory dependent clauses contain a subject and a verb and usually begin with one of the words listed below:

as, if, when — are most common	after	provided	until
	although	since	whenever
	because	so	while
	before	unless	

When Mr. Jones received his $30,000 inheritance, he invested the money in mutual funds.

So that we may reach a decision by March 14, please fax us your bid within the next two days.

b. A shortened form of an introductory clause is separated from the rest of the sentence by a comma.

If so, the delivery of these materials may be delayed. (If that is so, ...)

As agreed, we will offer the contract to the lowest qualified bidder. (As we agreed, ...)

Whatever the reason, without a sales receipt we cannot accept returned merchandise at a higher price than the current selling price. (Whatever the reason may be, ...)

c. Occasionally an introductory clause may follow another introductory word group. In such cases place a comma only after the introductory clause.

Mrs. Jones said that **when these accounts are paid,** we will reinstate their credit privileges.

I hope that **before you file your income tax return,** you will check with our tax attorneys on this issue.

d. When an introductory clause is followed by two main clauses, place a comma only after the introductory clause.

When Gerald addresses prospective clients, he speaks clearly and he answers all questions courteously.

If you wish employment with our company, visit our Web site at www.remco.com and complete our on-line application form.

e. When a sentence contains two introductory clauses, place a comma only after the second clause.

If you decide to purchase this system and after you have received the president's authorization, please submit all the specifications on our standard purchase order form.

1–10 Introductory Phrases

a. An introductory infinitive phrase (a verb preceded by *to*) is followed by a comma.

To arrive at an immediate decision, the Board of Directors called an emergency stockholders' meeting.

To carry out the original plans, Ms. Morii hired two additional employees.

b. An introductory participial phrase (a verb form used as an adjective—verb ending in *ing* or *ed*) is followed by a comma.

Starting in late 1998, networks in selected cities across the United States began to deliver digital television (DTV) broadcasts in addition to all existing analog broadcasts.

Concerned about the sudden decrease in sales, Ms. Alexander flew to the West Coast office.

c. An introductory prepositional phrase (a word group that begins with a preposition and ends with an object) is separated from the rest of the sentence by a comma if it contains a verb form *or* five or more words.[3] After an introductory prepositional phrase that contains no verb form and fewer than five words, use a comma only if it is necessary for clarity.

A partial list of prepositions used to begin introductory prepositional phrases follows:

about	among	behind	during	on	until
above	around	below	for	over	up
after	at	between	from	through	upon
along	before	by	in	under	with

[3]Some authorities suggest four words.

verb form

Upon receiving the papers, Swift & Company filed suit against its former parent company.

After reviewing the case, the judge decided in favor of the defendant.

By enrolling today, you are assured of receiving a place in the class that begins on March 1.

After calling you, I notified our insurance company of the theft.

five words or more

During the past few days of litigation, both sides have made significant concessions.

Between July 1 and August 31, all our stores will be closed on Mondays.

Within the next few days, you should receive a written confirmation from the Hawaiian Village Hotel.

no verb form and fewer than five words

About three months ago our laboratories released to the press information about several new medical breakthroughs.

Through your efforts we have been able to locate new customers for our towels and linens.

For over two weeks our offices have been without air-conditioning.

On September 30 we will open our new branch office in London.

comma necessary for clarity

After the class, discussion on this issue will continue until 3 p.m. in Conference Room 14.

In my office, files dating back to 1992 are stored in three of the cabinets.

Until next Monday, morning deliveries will be accepted only between 8:30 and 10 a.m.; afternoon deliveries, between 3 and 5 p.m.

d. **An introductory phrase that follows another introductory word group is treated as if the opening introductory word group were not included. In other words, mentally omit the opening expression, and punctuate the introductory phrase according to the rules in Section 1–10a–c.**

infinitive phrase

Mr. Wilson explained that **to meet our production deadline,** we would have to work overtime for the remainder of the week.

participial phrase

Ms. Winston expressed concern over the poor handling of complaints by our customer service representatives; and **speaking calmly and empathetically,** she demonstrated how they should handle irate customers.

prepositional phrase, fewer than five words

We were notified that **on Monday** we will resume our regular schedule.

May we assure you that **within the next week** your order will be shipped from our warehouse.

prepositional phrase, five or more words

I hope that **in view of the urgency of the situation,** we will obtain the full cooperation of our staff.

We expect that **during this rapid growth period,** many investors will attempt to acquire our on-line company.

e. Any phrase that acts as the subject or is part of the predicate is not followed by a comma.

phrase that acts as a subject

To answer your question would require several days' research on the part of our staff.

Helping his employees prepare for advancement does not rank high among Mr. Green's management attributes.

phrase that is part of the predicate

From the intensive police investigation came some new evidence that led to the apprehension of the suspected arsonists.

1–11 Restrictive and Nonrestrictive Phrases and Clauses

Restrictive phrases and clauses modify and contribute substantially to the main idea of a sentence and are essential to its meaning. They tell *who, what,* or *which one* and are not set off with commas.

Nonrestrictive phrases and clauses add an additional idea and do not significantly change or contribute to the main idea of a sentence. They are unessential word groups; that is, they are not needed by the main clause to tell *who, what,* or *which one*. Set off nonrestrictive phrases and clauses from the rest of the sentence with commas. Notice that phrases and clauses directly following proper nouns are nonrestrictive.

a. Relative clauses (those beginning with *who, whose, whom, which,* or *that*) are either restrictive (no comma) or nonrestrictive (comma required).

restrictive and essential to meaning

Office employees **who are able to use a spreadsheet program such as Excel or Lotus** can obtain well-paying jobs. (Tells *which kind* of office employee.)

nonrestrictive and not essential to meaning

Ms. Kennedy, **who readily uses both Excel and Lotus,** can obtain a well-paying job. (Additional idea. Clause following a proper noun.)

In the first example the clause "who are able to use a spreadsheet program such as Excel or Lotus" limits the type of office employees who "can easily obtain well-paying jobs." In the second example "who readily uses both Excel and Lotus" is of no assistance in *identifying* Ms. Kennedy but is merely an additional idea. Therefore, this example is a nonrestrictive clause that is set off by commas.

restrictive and essential to meaning

All students **who are enrolled in history classes** will take part in organizing World Affairs Day. (Tells *which* students.)

nonrestrictive and not essential to meaning

Joseph, **who is enrolled in a history class,** will take part in organizing World Affairs Day. (Additional idea. Clause following a proper noun.)

b. Careful writers will use *that* for restrictive clauses (no comma) and *which* for nonrestrictive clauses (comma required).

restrictive

The stores **that are located in the Flintridge Mall** are sponsoring a free parking lot carnival this weekend.

All our insurance programs **that appeal to young adults** should be featured in this new brochure.

nonrestrictive

Unlike HTML (Hypertext Markup Language), **which is a fairly rigid set of standards,** XML (Extensible Markup Language) is designed for flexibility.

We have canceled our winter sales meeting, **which was scheduled from December 11–13 in Miami**.

c. Dependent adverbial clauses (ones that begin with words such as *if, as, when, since, because,* etc.) that follow the main clause may be restrictive (no comma) or nonrestrictive (comma required). Restrictive clauses (1) answer such questions as *when, why, how,* or *whether* or (2) limit the main idea of the sentence. Nonrestrictive clauses add an additional idea that does not, however, alter the meaning of the main clause.

restrictive and essential to meaning

We will ship your order **as soon as your account is approved**. (Tells *when*.)

National Food Products has doubled its monthly sales **since the advertising campaign began**. (Tells *when*.)

Please send us this information by March 1 **so that we may update our records.** (Tells *why*.)

Our company president retired last month **because his doctor recommended a six-month leave of absence**. (Tells *why*.)

You can receive this handsome carrying case free of charge **if you will fill out and return the enclosed questionnaire**. (Tells *how*.)

We can still promise you the discount price **if we receive your order on or before July 15**. (Tells *whether*.)

We cannot install the additional equipment you requested **unless we receive an authorization from your main office**. (Limits main idea.)

You may order these sale items from our Web site **as long as our current supply of merchandise lasts**. (Limits main idea.)

nonrestrictive and not essential to meaning

He has written his letter of resignation, **although I do not believe he will submit it**. (Additional idea.)

We will continue with our plans to introduce new voice-recognition software, **whatever the competition might be**. (Additional idea.)

Next week our Board of Directors will tour our new South Haven plant, **where we will be hiring several hundred new employees**. (Additional idea.)

d. A dependent clause or a short independent clause used to provide an extra idea within a sentence is nonrestrictive and is set off with commas (or dashes for emphasis).

interrupting dependent clause

Sales figures for last year, **as you can see from the financial reports,** were nearly 10 percent higher than we had projected.

On Tuesday morning, **when you arrive for the meeting,** please give the manuscript to my assistant.

We can, **as I see the situation,** complete this project at least a month before its deadline date.

This year's line of holiday greeting cards—**although the cards are larger and more exquisite**—is less expensive than last year's.

interrupting short independent clause

Ms. Moore is, **I believe,** the only applicant who presently resides out of the state.

We will, **I hope,** be able to supply you with this information by July 1.

e. Participial, infinitive, or prepositional phrases appearing within a sentence may be restrictive (no comma) or nonrestrictive (comma required), depending on whether or not they tell *who, what, what kind,* or *which one*. Phrases that answer these questions are restrictive (no comma).

participial restrictive

All employees **planning to participate in the stock option program** must sign up by July 1. (Tells *which ones.*)

participial nonrestrictive

Mr. Daly, **planning to participate in the stock option program,** has agreed to conduct seminars on this employee benefit. (Additional idea. Phrase following a proper noun.)

infinitive restrictive

We are planning **to sign up for the program** by July 1. (Tells *what.*)

infinitive nonrestrictive

The stock option plan offers employees an excellent investment opportunity, **to mention only one company fringe benefit**. (Additional idea.)

prepositional restrictive

The advertising brochures **for our August sale** will be ready June 30. (Tells *which ones.*)

Manufacturers **like us** find themselves in financial difficulty today. (Tells *what kind.*)

Clients **like the Atkinsons** make the real estate business a pleasure. (Tells *what kind.*)

prepositional nonrestrictive

We are planning, **in response to numerous requests,** to open our city ticketing agencies on Sundays as well. (Additional idea.)

Small appliance manufacturers, **like us,** are in financial difficulty today. (Additional idea.)

1–12 Contrasting, Limiting, and Contingent Expressions

Contrasting, limiting, or contingent expressions are set off with commas. Words often used to introduce contrasting and limiting expressions include *not, never, but, seldom,* and *yet.*

contrasting expression

She had considered selling her stocks, **not her rental property,** to increase her liquid assets.

limiting expression

The association will give us four tickets, **but only for members of our sales staff.**

contingent expression

The sooner we are able to contact our investors in Chicago, **the sooner** we will be able to finance this new project.

The more money you can invest, **the greater the return** you can expect.

The more lines of resolution a monitor can display, **the sharper the detail** you will observe in the picture.

1–13 Omitted Words

Commas are often used to indicate the omission of words when the context of the sentence makes the omitted words clearly understood.

Four new assistants were hired in the Accounting Department; three, in the Policy Issue Department. (Three *new assistants were hired* in the Policy Issue Department.)

Last week Mr. Higgins used voice-recognition software to prepare three long reports; this week, two long reports. (This week *Mr. Higgins used voice-recognition software to prepare* two long reports.)

Our B-124 contract expired on June 14; the B-127 contract, June 16; and the B-132, June 21. (The B-127 contract *expired on* June 16, and the B-132 *contract expired on* June 21.)

1–14 Punctuation for Clarity

a. **Two identical verbs that appear together in a sentence are separated by a comma.**

Whoever **wins, wins** a trip to Hawaii.

Whoever **travels, travels** at his own risk.

Whatever irregularities **occurred, occurred** without the knowledge of the president.

b. **Words repeated for emphasis are separated by a comma.**

Many, many years ago this company was founded by Bernard Harris.

It has been a **long, long** time since one of our vice presidents has visited the East Coast offices.

c. A word or phrase at the beginning of a sentence that could be read incorrectly with the words that follow is set off by a comma.

Ever since, she has been employed by the Hirschell Corporation of Boston.

The month before, the corporation expanded its operations to Brazil.

From the beginning, students are expected to proofread their own work carefully.

In our business, letters are written primarily to sell goods and services and to collect money.

d. A name written in inverted form is separated by a comma between the last name and the first name.

Irwin, Carl   Luers, Barbara R.

1–15 Short Quotations

a. A short quoted sentence is set off from the rest of the sentence by a comma. When the quoted sentence is broken into two parts, commas are required before and after the interjected thought.

beginning quotation

"All employees will receive two days' paid vacation after the contract is completed," said Mr. Adams.

interrupted quotation

"All employees will receive two days' paid vacation," said Mr. Adams, **"after the contract is completed."**

ending quotation

Mr. Adams said, **"All employees will receive two days' paid vacation after the contract is completed."**

b. Unless a beginning quotation is interrupted, omit any separating commas when the quoted sentence is a question or an exclamation.

question

"When will the bids for this contract be opened?" asked Ms. Snow.

interrupted question

"When," asked Ms. Snow, **"will the bids for this contract be opened?"**

exclamation

"What a wonderful opportunity you have given our staff!" exclaimed Mr. Stevens.

interrupted exclamation

"What a wonderful opportunity," exclaimed Mr. Stevens, **"you have given our staff!"**

c. No comma is needed to set off a quotation or part of a quotation that is woven into a complete sentence or one that is not a complete thought.

woven into sentence

The chairperson operated on the premise that **"a stitch in time saves nine."**

John is reported to have said that **". . . no vacancies will be filled until June 1."**

incomplete sentence

Please mark the top of this package **"This Side Up."**

The human resources manager advised me **"to e-mail my application as soon as possible."**

He merely answered **"yes"** to all the questions.

d. When a comma and a quotation mark fall at the same point in a sentence, *always* place the comma inside the closing quotation mark. Periods, too, are *always* placed inside the closing quotation mark.

"We intend to give customers access to our services over wireless," reported Dawn Chambers, E-Trade's chief information officer.

Her last magazine article, "Western Travel," appeared in *Automotive Digest*.

John said, "Be sure to e-mail your response by June 11."

e. For placement of question marks and exclamation marks with closing quotation marks, see Sections 1–44a and 1–46c.

1–16 Numerals

a. Expressed in United States format, numerals of more than three digits require commas.

1,320 63,481 963,481 1,293,070 23,092,946 450,500,000

b. Two independent figures appearing consecutively in a sentence are separated by a comma.

Two consecutive numbers that act as adjectives modifying the same noun are *not* separated by a comma. Instead, write the first number in words and the second one in figures. If the first number cannot be expressed in *one or two words,* place it in figures also.

independent figures

Of this **$123,000, $112,000** is secured by real property.

During **2000, $876,000** worth of sales were financed through this plan.

By October **1, 43** people had submitted on-line résumés for this position.

two numbers modifying a noun, word-figure form

I will need **thirty 12-inch** rulers for my drafting class.

Each package contains **twelve 2-inch** nails.

Be sure to order **twenty-four 100-watt** bulbs for the lamps in the doctors' waiting rooms.

two numbers modifying a noun, figure-figure form

While you are at the post office, please purchase **125 33-cent** stamps.

The prescription was for **250 10-milligram** tablets.

When the carton fell, **127 40-watt** bulbs were broken.

c. **Commas are omitted in years, house numbers, zip codes, telephone or fax numbers, decimal fractions, metric measurements, and any label-numeral combinations. In metric measurements use a space to separate all numerals containing more than four digits.**

year

1998 1780 2007

house number

9732 Porter Street 19573 Bestor Boulevard

zip code

Northridge, CA 91324 Bothell, WA 98041-3011

telephone or fax number

(212) 482-9768, Ext. 4412 *or* 212-482-9768, Ext. 4412

decimal fraction

0.2873

metric measurement

1200 kilometers 10 200 kilometers

label-numeral combination

Serial No. 83621 page 1276 Room 1890 Invoice 43798

d. **Volume numbers and page references are separated by commas.**

Please refer to Volume XI**,** page 9.

The article appeared in Volume X**,** July 1999**,** page 23.

e. **Measurements (such as weights, capacities, dimensions, etc.) are treated as single units and are not interrupted by commas.**

weight

Their new baby weighed **8 pounds 7 ounces**.

dimension

He is **5 feet 10 inches** tall.

The room measurements are **20 feet 6 inches** by **18 feet 4 inches**.

time period

Our flight time was estimated to be **2 hours 40 minutes**.

Semicolon

1–17 Independent Clauses Without Coordinating Conjunctions

a. **A semicolon is used between two or more closely related independent clauses (complete thoughts that could stand alone as separate sentences) that are not connected with a coordinating conjunction (*and, but, or, nor*).**

two independent clauses

Several orders were delayed in the Milwaukee office last month; Ms. Williams will check into our shipping procedures there.

Plan to attend the next meeting of the American Management Association International; you will find this association to be well worth your time.

three independent clauses

Mr. Horowitz drafted the contract specifications last week; Ms. Ames consulted the firm's attorneys on Monday; Mr. Dotson signed and mailed the company's offer on Wednesday.

b. **Short and closely related independent clauses may be separated by commas.**

two short independent clauses

Pittsburgh Bank issued the checks, TSI mailed them to clients.

three short independent clauses

The monitor flashed, it emitted sparks, it went blank.

He came in, he looked around, he left.

1–18 Independent Clauses With Coordinating Conjunctions

Two independent clauses linked by a coordinating conjunction (*and, but, or, nor*) are generally separated with a comma. Lengthy, complicated sentences containing internal commas in either or both clauses,

however, may be punctuated with a semicolon between the two clauses.

clauses separated with a comma

She planned to attend the Chicago meeting, **but** several important matters interfered with her plans.

Yes, Mr. Dale, we have on hand your current order, **but** we can ship it only after your account is up-to-date.

We were pleased with the results of the survey, **and** you will, of course, receive a copy of the summary.

Yes, you may mail in your monthly payment, **or** you may take it to one of our fast, convenient pay stations.

clauses separated with a semicolon

Several large orders were recently placed through the Dayton office; **and** Ms. Baca, our national sales manager, has commended the sales staff for its diligent efforts in making such rapid progress in a new office.

You, of course, need not attend the committee meeting scheduled for June 4; **but** I believe, Mr. Plotkin, you will find reading the minutes of this meeting helpful before you address the Board of Directors next week.

1–19 Independent Clauses With Transitional Expressions

Two independent clauses (complete thoughts) separated by a transitional expression require a semicolon. A partial list of common transitional expressions follows. In addition, those words and phrases listed in Section 1–2a may be considered transitional expressions when they separate two closely related complete thoughts.

accordingly	indeed	notwithstanding	then
besides	in fact	on the contrary	therefore
consequently	in other words	on the other hand	thus
furthermore	likewise	otherwise	yet
hence	moreover	so	
however	nevertheless	still	

A comma is used after a transitional expression of more than one syllable or where a strong pause is needed after a one-syllable expression.

transitional expression with one syllable

The library will have difficulty obtaining a budget increase this year; **thus** members of your staff should not plan to receive all the books specified on this requisition.

transitional expression containing more than one syllable

New catalogs will be shipped to our customers the first week in February; **therefore,** we expect a 20 percent sales increase for the months of February, March, and April.

1–20 Series Containing Internal Commas or Complete Thoughts

a. **Items in a series are usually separated by commas. When, however, one or more of the parts contain internal commas, use semicolons to separate the items.**

Representatives from Boston, Massachusetts; Los Angeles, California; and Denver, Colorado, were not present at the conference.

Among those present at the convention were Mr. Harmon Fieldcrest, president of Fieldcrest Steel Industries; Dr. Joyce Morton, research director for the University of Wisconsin; Mr. Garland Hansen, vice president of Wisconsin State Bank; and Ms. Donna Anderson, secretary-treasurer of CRA Consultants, Inc.

b. **Three or more independent clauses (complete thoughts) comprising a series are separated by semicolons. Only very short clauses are separated by commas.**

series of independent clauses

Nearly 7,000 circulars were mailed to prospective clients in 1994; over 15,000 circulars were mailed in 1999; and next year we plan to mail over 10,000 new brochures as well as 20,000 circulars.

series of independent clauses with internal commas

Mr. John Harris, our company president, will arrive on Saturday; Mrs. Olga Williams, one of our vice presidents, will arrive on Monday; and Ms. Carol Watson, our company treasurer, will arrive on Tuesday.

series of short independent clauses

The tenant called yesterday, we investigated his complaint immediately, and the roof will be repaired next week.

1–21 Enumerations and Explanations

a. **Certain words and phrases are used to introduce enumerations or explanations that follow an independent clause (complete thought). Some common introductory expressions follow:**

for example (e.g.)	for instance	that is (i.e.)
namely (viz.)	that is to say	

If the enumeration or explanation following the introductory expression *contains commas* or *forms another complete thought,* use a semicolon after the opening independent clause and a comma after the introductory expression.

enumeration containing commas

Many factors have contributed to the sharp increase in production costs during the past three months; **namely,** price increases in raw materials, wage increases for electrical workers, and overtime salaries for the entire production staff.

explanation forming another complete thought

To open its Syracuse office, Caldwell Industries advertised for a number of new employees; **that is to say,** not all its employees were willing to transfer to the new location.

b. Some independent clauses followed by expressions that introduce enumerations and explanations require a comma, not a semicolon, after the independent clause. If the enumeration or explanation that follows the introductory expression does *not* contain commas or form another complete thought, use commas after the independent clause and the introductory expression.

enumeration without internal commas

As a member of our user group, you are eligible to purchase additional computer peripherals through our discount program, **for instance,** a scanner or a CD read/write drive.

explanation forming an incomplete thought

You may wish to call Ms. Hendrix for further advice, **for example,** to inquire what kind of database software would be appropriate for your office.

c. Enumerations or explanations used as parenthetical expressions within a sentence are not set off by semicolons. Use commas when the enumerated or explanatory information has no internal commas; use dashes or parentheses when the information contains internal commas.

commas

Your accounting procedures, **for example, posting customer deposits,** can be streamlined with our software.

dashes

Because of current economic conditions, we must find new vendors for some of our multimedia equipment—**e.g., computer video cameras, digital still cameras, and portable data projectors**—to stay within our budget allocations.

parentheses

Your recommendations **(namely, downsizing our human resources staff, scanning all incoming résumés, and computerizing our testing program)** were approved unanimously by the board.

d. **Complete thoughts that introduce enumerations or explanations without an introductory expression are followed by a colon, not a semicolon.**

Several new items were introduced in this popular line: gloves, scarves, and hosiery.

The following people were present at the sales managers' meeting: Roberta Adams, Horace Brubaker, Phillip Haledon, and Susan McCloskey.

Only 82 teachers attended the ARTA state conference: apparently many of our members did not receive their brochures in time to plan for this event.

1–22 Semicolon Placement

Always place the semicolon outside closing quotation marks and parentheses.

quotation marks

Last month Mr. Harrison promised, "I will mail you a check the 1st of next month"**;** but we have received no money or explanation from him.

parentheses

Several members of the Accounting Department were ill last week (with the flu)**;** consequently, our end-of-month reports will reach the home office a week late.

Colon

1–23 Formally Enumerated or Listed Items

a. **Use a colon after an independent clause (complete thought) that introduces a formal listing or an enumeration of items. Words commonly used in introductory independent clauses include *the following, as follows, these,* and *thus*. Sometimes, however, the introduction is implied rather than stated directly. Use a colon following both direct and implied introductions.**

direct introduction

Mrs. Robinson ordered the following new furniture and equipment for her offices: three desks, six chairs, two sofas, two microcomputers, and one laser printer.

These rules should be observed for a successful job interview:

1. Dress appropriately.
2. Obtain beforehand information about the company and its products or services.

3. Appear interested in the company and the job.
4. Answer questions courteously.
5. Thank the interviewers for their time.

implied introduction

Several kinds of desktop computers were on display**:** IBM, Compaq, DEC, Apple, Hewlett-Packard, Dell, and Sony.

In determining whether to use a colon or semicolon for introducing enumerated items, use the colon when the enumeration is not preceded by a transitional introductory expression such as *namely, for example, e.g., that is,* or *i.e.* If an introductory expression immediately precedes the listing, use a semicolon before the expression and a comma after it. (See Section 1–21a for examples.)

b. The colon is *not* used to introduce listings of items in the following situations: (1) when an intervening sentence separates the introductory sentence and the enumerated items, (2) when the enumerated items follow a "being" verb or are the object of a verb, (3) when the enumerated items are the object of a preposition, and (4) when the listing is immediately preceded by an enumerating expression.

no colon: intervening sentence

The following new stemware patterns will be available January 1. They will be introduced to our dealers next month.

1. Fantasia
2. Sunburst
3. Apollo
4. Moonglow

no colon: following a "being" verb or acting as the object of a verb

The words most commonly misspelled **were** *convenience, occasionally, commodity, consequently,* and *accommodate.* (Not: ". . . were: *convenience, ...*")

Examples of popular Web browsers **include** Netscape Navigator, Microsoft Internet Explorer, and America Online. (Not: ". . . include: Netscape . . . .")

no colon: object of a preposition

The first lesson introduces the user **to** the Menu Bar, the Standard Toolbar, and the Formatting Toolbar. (Not: ". . . to: the Menu . . . .")

Sales meetings are scheduled **for** January 3, February 4, March 7, and April 9. (Not: ". . . for: January 3, ...")

no colon: listing after enumerating expression

Please order some additional supplies**, namely,** 8½- by 11-inch white copy paper, legal-size envelopes, and letter-size manila file folders.

1–24 Explanatory Sentences

Separate two sentences with a colon when the second sentence explains, illustrates, or supplements the first.

explanation

During the next three months, we will gross approximately 50 percent of our annual sales: major toy purchases occur during September, October, and November.

illustration

Our new advertising campaign will be directed toward buyers of economy cars: we will stress efficient gas mileage, low maintenance costs, and reliability.

supplement

Several new customers complained about the delay in receiving their charge cards: they wished to have them in time to complete their holiday shopping.

1–25 Long Quotations

Long one-sentence quotations and quotations of two or more sentences are introduced by a colon.

For long quotations of two or more sentences (and usually more than three lines), omit the quotation marks and format them as separate paragraphs. They are indented from the left and right margins and separated from the main text by single blank lines at the beginning and the end of the quotation.

long one-sentence quotation

Ms. Judy Dolan, human resources manager of Hartnell Corporation, reported in her annual summary: "Graduates from the University of Southern California's School of Business have been placed in a number of our divisions, and they have risen to middle-management positions within a three-year period."

long quotation of two or more sentences

The following item of importance was noted from the board minutes of March 16:

> A new product, which will revolutionize word processing, will be introduced on July 1. Trade journal publicity will be the major vehicle for distributing information about this product. Efforts by the sales staff for July will be directed specifically at marketing the new Model AB 2782 communication network.

As you can see from the board minutes, our company will soon . . . .

1–26 Special-Purpose Uses for the Colon

a. **In business letters a colon is placed after the salutation when the mixed punctuation format is used (see Section 12–23).**

Dear Bill: Dear Ms. Corrigan: Gentlemen:

b. **Use the colon to separate hours and minutes in expressions of time.**

We will arrive at **8:30 a.m.** on Tuesday, March 24.

At **12:15 p.m.** Ms. Hardesty is scheduled to address the Compton Chamber of Commerce.

c. **In expressing ratios, use the colon to represent the word *to*.**

The label instructions recommend proportions of **4:1**.

The union members voted **2:1** against accepting the new contract.

d. **The colon is often used to separate elements in literary references.**

between title and subtitle

Dr. Susan Cornner's latest book, *Business Communication: Theory and Applications*, 3rd ed., is now in stock in our college bookstore.

between place of publication and publisher in footnotes and bibliographies

Clark, James L., and Lyn R. Clark. *HOW 9: A Handbook for Office Workers*. 9th ed. Cincinnati: South-Western College Publishing, 2001. (bibliography)

between volume and page number in footnotes and bibliographies

---

[10]Virginia C. Beauchamp and Robert M. Dougherty, "Organizational Communications: Frameworks for Making Yours 'People Oriented,'" *The Bulletin for the Association of Business Communication* 60 (March 1997): 36–38. (footnote)

biblical citation

As an introduction to his sermon, the minister quoted Isaiah **24:1** (Chapter 24, verse 1).

1–27 Colon Format and Use With Other Punctuation Marks

a. **In computer-generated (or typewritten) copy, space once or twice after a colon. Placing two spaces after a colon promotes ease of reading for business documents.**

May I please have the following documents by next week: a copy of the rental agreement, the returned check, and the 30-day notice to move.

b. **Place the colon outside closing quotation marks and parentheses.**

closing quotation mark

Please distribute to the following staff members copies of Lynn Haile's latest article, "Closing the Sale Effectively"**:** Mina Balejian, Charles Ballesteros, Paul Kellogg, and Kyung Kim.

closing parenthesis

Several contractors are being considered for the new project (Mountain Hills)**:** Wyeth & Sons, Burnside Developers, and Hartman and Associates.

c. **In vertical listings introduced by a colon, conclude each item in the listing with a period only if the items are complete sentences.**

Single-space the items in a vertical listing. If any item in the listing occupies more than one line, double-space between the items. If all the items in the listing consist of a single line, you *may either* leave one blank line between each item *or* just single-space the listing. Always place one blank line before and after a listing.

In business letters and memorandums, vertical listings may be indented from the left and right margins *or* may assume the margins of the main text.[4] Items in a listing may or may not be numbered.

complete sentences, numbered items, standard margins

We have discontinued manufacturing our Model 1040A microwave oven for the following reasons:

1. The popularity of our smaller ovens has decreased continually during the past eighteen months.

2. Manufacturing costs and prices differ only slightly from those for our standard-size ovens.

3. Two other models smaller than our standard-size ones have been more popular.

incomplete sentences, unnumbered items, indented left and right margins

Effective July 1 new premium rates will be in force for the following types of policies:

Jewelry riders on home owners' policies
Liability coverage for drivers under 25 and over 80 years of age
Earthquake riders on all casualty policies
Term life insurance for males 65 and older

---

[4]See Section 13–9 for guidelines governing the format and preparation of horizontal and vertical listings in reports and manuscripts as well as in business letters and memorandums.

1–28 Capitalization With Colons

a. **When a colon is used to introduce a horizontal listing of items, the first letter after the colon is not capitalized unless it begins a proper noun. Capitalize the first letter of each item in a vertical listing.**

lowercase letter in horizontal listing

Place the following items in the tray: **t**he original invoice, the duplicate invoice, and the shipping copy.

proper noun capitalized

Four employees were promoted last week: **T**eresa Caruana, Sue Rigby, Lloyd Bartholome, and Arthur Rubin.

capitalized letters in vertical listing

You may pay for your Empress Vacation Time-Share package in a number of ways:

> **P**ersonal check
>
> **C**redit card—Visa, MasterCard, or American Express
>
> **E**ighteen monthly installments of $637.50

Do not miss the opportunity to get in on the ground floor of this . . . .

b. **Do not capitalize the first letter after a colon when the second sentence explains or supplements the first unless the letter begins a proper noun.**

lowercase letter begins second sentence

Your account has been temporarily frozen: **o**utstanding bills for $327 still remain unpaid.

proper noun capitalized

The $1,000 award was given to Andrew Schultz: **D**r. Schultz's Web site was judged to be the best by a panel of three experts in Web page design.

c. **Capitalize the first word after a colon when the colon introduces a formal rule or principle stated as a complete sentence.**

Apply the following rule in preparing all your E-mail messages: **A**lways use a subject line to identify the content of your message.

Mr. Wilson emphasized the importance of strict adherence to the following policy: **I**n case of absence all employees must notify their immediate supervisor by 8:30 a.m. that day.

d. **When two or more sentences follow a colon, capitalize the first letter of each sentence.**

Several suggestions emerged from the discussion: **T**o begin with, an engineering firm should be consulted to determine the extent of damage to the property. **T**hen a building contractor should be contacted for estimates to repair the damage. **F**inally, financial institutions should be surveyed to obtain the best terms for reconstructing the property.

e. **Capitalize the first letter of sentences or phrases introduced by words such as *Note, Attention, Warning, Caution, For Rent,* or *For Sale.***

Warning: **A**ll cars parked illegally will be towed away at vehicle owner's expense.

Caution: **P**lease hold children by hand.

For Rent: **L**arge three-bedroom home with family room, fireplace, air-conditioning, and pool. Phone (617) 555-3542.

f. **Capitalize the first word of quoted material that follows a colon.**

Mr. Rosen informed the board about expansion plans for this year: **"S**ince property on the corner of Tampa and Nordhoff has already been purchased, construction of our new branch office will begin early this spring so that we can open this office in September or October."

Dash

1–29 Parenthetical Elements, Appositives, and Summaries

a. **Parenthetical elements and appositives are usually set off from the rest of the sentence by commas. When the parenthetical element or appositive contains internal commas, however, substitute dashes (or parentheses) for the separating commas.**

Where possible, use an em dash—a character that appears as a solid line and is twice the length of a hyphen. In keyboarding material that does not allow access to the em dash through an extended character set,[5] form the dash by typing two hyphens with no space before, between, or after (see Section 1–32).

parenthetical element with internal commas

Last month Ms. Arntson**—**with the hope of increasing sales, recruiting new employees, and establishing sources of supply**—**made several trips to the Middle East.

---

[5]Word processing programs provide access to extended character sets. Extended characters are letters, number styles, symbols, and foreign language characters that are not on the standard keyboard but are needed to produce documents that simulate printed material. These extended characters may be accessed through the menu bar, a keyboard command, or a toolbar.

appositive with internal commas

Several Internet sites—Amazon.com, Schwab.com, and eToys.com—have set a revolutionary pattern for American purchasing trends in the twenty-first century.

b. **Use a dash to set off a brief summary from the rest of the sentence.**

Thanksgiving, Christmas, and New Year's Day—these are the only holidays the store will be closed.

White, black, navy, red, and tan—you have your choice of these five colors.

c. **To achieve greater separation, use dashes instead of commas to set off abrupt parenthetical elements or those requiring emphasis. Appositives requiring emphasis may also be separated from the rest of the sentence with dashes instead of commas.**

abrupt parenthetical element

Her main concern—notwithstanding her interest in job security—was finding employment in an organization where opportunities for advancement were numerous.

emphatic parenthetical element

Several orders were rerouted to the Milwaukee office—not to the Salt Lake City branch.

emphatic appositive

Additional heavy-duty equipment—bulldozers and graders—was needed to complete the project.

d. **For emphasis use a dash in place of a comma or a semicolon to introduce an example or explanation.**

example requiring emphasis

Insurance coverage adequate five years ago may no longer fulfill the purpose for which it was designed—for example, if current inflationary trends continue, fire and theft insurance may not cover the replacement costs of the insured properties.

explanation requiring emphasis

Our sales of greeting cards have increased 25 percent since 1999—namely, from $1 million to $1.25 million.

e. **Afterthoughts or side thoughts generated from the text, but not necessarily part of it, may be separated from the rest of the sentence by dashes.**

afterthought

Mrs. Wilson had planned to finish installing the new software this afternoon—at least John thought she had planned to do it then.

side thought

All members of our staff were invited to the conference on simplifying communication procedures—only Ms. Harris was unable to attend the session.

1–30 Hesitations in Verbal Reports

Use dashes to indicate hesitations, faltering, or stammering in reports of conversations, testimonies, or speeches.

Ms. Morrow: Yes, Mr. President—we expect perhaps oh—a—35 percent increase in sales during the next year.

Mr. Schatz: Well—perhaps a new inventory-control system will solve some of the current problems.

1–31 Source of Quotations

A dash is placed before the source of a quotation when the source is listed after the quotation.

"We can expect a great decrease in our unemployment rate during the next ten months."

—H. J. Scott

"The difference between the right word and the almost right word is the difference between lightning and the lightning bug."

—Mark Twain

1–32 Format and Placement of Dash

a. **In printing, in desktop publishing, or with word processing programs, use an em dash (not a hyphen or an en dash) to form the dash; leave no space before or after the em dash. The em dash is the length of two hyphens and may be accessed through the extended character set of most word processing programs.[6]**

Form the dash on a typewriter (or in computer software without access to an extended character set) by typing two hyphens consecutively; leave no space before, between, or after the hyphens.

A dash never begins a new line, but it may appear at the end of a line.

em dash

Several influential community organizations—the Kiwanis Club, the Chamber of Commerce, and the Rotary Club—sponsored Marian C. Crawford for the vacant seat on the board of education.

---

[6]Extended characters are letters, number styles, symbols, and foreign language characters that are not on the standard keyboard but are needed to produce documents that simulate printed material. These extended characters may be accessed through the menu bar, a keyboard command, or a toolbar.

typewritten dash

Three cities--Atlanta, New Orleans, and Fort Worth--are still under consideration for our new plant site.

end of line

Contract negotiations—after reaching an impasse on December 20—were resumed on January 5.

b. **The only punctuation mark that may precede an opening dash is a period in an abbreviation. Closing dashes may be preceded by a period in an abbreviation, a question mark, or an exclamation mark.**

opening dash after abbreviation

Prices quoted on all Eastern furniture were f.o.b.—freight charges from Pennsylvania to Los Angeles amounted to $834.

closing dash after question mark

A new kind of after-dinner mint—do you know which one I mean?—was introduced by the Sweitzer Candy Company last month.

Period

1–33 End of Sentence

Place a period at the end of a declarative sentence, an imperative statement or command, an indirect question, and a polite request.

Polite requests end with a period even though they may appear to have the format of a question. A polite request (1) asks the reader to perform a specific action and (2) is answered by the reader's compliance or noncompliance with the request. (See Section 1–41e for additional information and examples.)

declarative sentence

We have received free introductory offers from America Online, CompuServe, and Prodigy.

Several new products were introduced to the stockholders at the April 5 meeting.

imperative statement

Fill in and mail your application for admittance by April 30.

Please check to ensure you have locked all entrances and engaged the security system before leaving the store.

indirect question

She asked who was responsible for planning and coordinating the sales meeting.

Most of the telephone calls have been inquiries asking where we have moved our store.

polite request

Will you please send us your check for $174.55 by May 1.

May I have your E-mail address so that I can send you this information today.

1–34 End of Independent Phrase

Independent phrases, those phrases representing implied complete thoughts not directly connected to the following thought, are concluded with a period.

Now, to get to the point. Will you be able to accept responsibility for conducting a sales campaign during June?

Yes, for the most part. Our salespeople have increased their sales since the new incentive program was established.

1–35 Abbreviations and Initials

a. Abbreviations are usually concluded with periods. However, after abbreviations for business and governmental organizations, associations, radio and television stations, federal agencies, and certain professional designations (*CLU, CPA, CPS, PLS*), the periods are omitted. (See Section 1–39a for spacing following the period.)

period after abbreviation

Fletcher, Hagan, and Company **Inc.** released several new stock issues.

periods after abbreviations

Mr. Haynes requested that all orders be sent on a **c.o.d.** basis.

Most of these products were manufactured in the **U.S.A.**

no periods with certain abbreviations

I hope the educational project director for **NASA** will be able to address our convention.

Did you purchase additional **IBM** stock?

b. Place a period after an initial. Leave one space between the period and the next word.

Ms. Roberta **D.** Holt accepted the invitation to address the convention participants.

We have tried for several days to contact **A. F.** Elliot.

1–36 Outlines

a. Word processors have an outline feature that automatically supplies listing characters before each item in an outline. The software offers several models from which to choose. The setup and amount of space between the listing character and the item are determined by the kind and location of the tabs set in the document.

Use periods after letters and numbers in alphanumeric outlines, except those enclosed in parentheses. Leave the equivalent of two blank spaces before beginning the contents of the item.

Use periods after whole numbers in decimal outlines. Leave the equivalent of two blank spaces after the last typed character before beginning the contents of the item.

alphanumeric outline

I. Xxxxxx
  A. Xxxxxx
  B. Xxxxxx
    1. Xxxxxx
    2. Xxxxxx
      a. Xxxxxx
      b. Xxxxxx
        (1) Xxxxxx
        (2) Xxxxxx
          (a) Xxxxxx
          (b) Xxxxxx
            1) Xxxxxx
            2) Xxxxxx
              a) Xxxxxx
              b) Xxxxxx
II. Xxxxxx
III. Xxxxxx
IV. Xxxxxx

decimal outline

1. Xxxxxx
  1.1 Xxxxxx
  1.2 Xxxxxx
    1.21 Xxxxxx
    1.22 Xxxxxx
      1.221 Xxxxxx
      1.222 Xxxxxx
        1.2221 Xxxxxx
        1.2222 Xxxxxx
          1.22221 Xxxxxx
          1.22222 Xxxxxx
            1.222221 Xxxxxx
            1.222222 Xxxxxx
2. Xxxxxx

b. **Use periods after complete sentences in outlines and listings. No punctuation mark is placed after an incomplete thought.**

periods—complete sentences

A. Two new processes were developed as a result of the experiments.
   1. Lamination of fiberglass to wooden surfaces contributes to vessel buoyancy.
   2. Sealing of surfaces prevents excessive moisture absorption.

no periods—incomplete sentences

A. Two types of digital broadcasts
   1. HDTV (High Definition TV)
      a. Offers extremely high resolution
      b. Shows film-like pictures
      c. Provides CD-quality sound
      d. Uses a wide-screen format
   2. SDTV (Standard Definition TV)
      a. Offers good quality digital pictures
      b. Provides CD-quality sound

1–37 Decimals

Use periods to signify decimals.

Of the customers responding to our survey, only **34.7** percent rated our service as “Excellent.”

Last year Mr. Phoenix paid $120 for the 2,000 sale announcements; this year he paid **$145.50** for the same kind and number.

1–38 Ellipses

An ellipsis (a series of three periods with a space before, between, and after the series) is used for emphasis in advertising material or for showing omissions in quoted material. In showing omissions, indicate the completion of a thought with an additional period or other closing punctuation mark. (See Section 1–52 for further information on the use of ellipses.)

emphasis

Place your order today... for relief from tension headaches . . . for ending miserable aches and pains ... for a happier, tension-free you.

omission

The president read from the consulting company’s report: “Basically, operations for the next year should be conducted according to the attached plan .... Several of your current operations personnel should ... implement the recommended procedures.”

1–39 Period Format

a. **No space is placed between a decimal point and a number or after a period within an abbreviation. However, within a sentence one space follows an initial or the concluding period in an abbreviation. In copy prepared on a word processor, allow one or two spaces after a period at the end of a sentence.[7] Always allow two spaces in typewritten copy.**

decimal—no space

Since 1999 costs of manufacturing materials have risen **18.5** percent.

period within abbreviation—no space

All prices quoted are **f.o.b.**

initial—one space

John **R.** Gardner was elected chair of the committee.

abbreviation within sentence—one space

Dr. Sussman has scheduled **Mrs.** Johnson for surgery at 9 **a.m.** on June 23 in Encino Hospital.

end of sentence—one space

Please submit proof that the property taxes have been **paid.** As soon as we receive copies of your canceled check, we can close escrow.

end of sentence—two spaces

Please submit proof that the property taxes have been **paid.** As soon as we receive copies of your canceled check, we can close escrow.

b. **Use only one period to end a sentence, even though the sentence may end with an abbreviation.**

She is scheduled to arrive between 9 and 10 a.m.

Mr. Kirk's mail is to be forwarded to him in Washington, D.C.

c. **A period is always placed inside the closing quotation mark.**

Ms. Allison promptly replied, "No funding requests will be honored after July 1."

Our editor was pleased with your magazine article, "New Ideas for Home Builders."

d. **A period is placed inside the closing parenthesis when the words in parentheses are a complete sentence. When words in parentheses are not a complete thought and are part of another sentence, place the period outside the closing parenthesis.**

---

[7]For desktop publishing some authorities recommend one space after a period that concludes a sentence. To promote ease of reading in documents written for business, others use two spaces after a period that concludes a sentence. Spacing after a concluding period is discretionary, and word processing software can be defaulted to permit one or two spaces.

complete sentence in parentheses

Several executives left the company after the merger. (They were disappointed with the new leadership.)

incomplete sentence in parentheses

Only three items were discontinued after the consulting analysts completed their investigation (last March).

Question Mark

1–40 Direct Questions

Conclude a direct question that requires an answer with a question mark.

How many times have you tried to contact Ms. Cates?

Of all the people at the board meeting, how many would you estimate were disappointed with the salary proposal?

1–41 Statements With Questions

a. **When a sentence contains a statement followed by a direct question, conclude the sentence with a question mark. Separate the statement from the question with a comma, dash, or colon, depending upon the nature of the statement.**

question mark with comma

I would recommend that we contact at least three other vendors before selecting a permanent source of supply, wouldn't you agree?

question mark with dash

They were satisfied with the report—weren't they?

question mark with colon

Each of us should consider the following question: what can we do to improve the profit picture for next year?

b. **Conclude a statement that contains a short, direct question with a question mark.**

You have filed your income tax return, have you not, for the last taxable year?

Our rental payments are current—aren't they—for the leased offices in the Bradley building?

c. **Conclude with a question mark a statement that is meant as a question.**

You still expect to leave for Cleveland tomorrow morning?

The conference has been delayed until April?

d. Place a period, rather than a question mark, after an indirect question.

Mr. Joyner asked when we expected our Albany office to release the information.

Ms. Casavilca inquired about the possibility of her placing several students in our Accounting Department as trainees in an internship program.

e. Polite requests phrased as questions are followed by periods rather than question marks because they are considered to be commands or "please do" statements. A polite request (1) asks the reader to perform a specific action and (2) is answered by having the reader either take or ignore the action requested instead of responding with a "yes" or "no." Both components *must* be present for a period to be used; otherwise, a question mark is correct.

polite request requiring period

Will you please send us three copies of your latest financial report.

May I please have this information by the end of the month.

Won't you take a few minutes now to fill out the questionnaire and return it in the enclosed envelope.

May we count on your support with a "yes" vote on Proposition 11.

direct question requiring question mark

Would you be willing to address envelopes for the senator's reelection campaign? (Requires "yes" or "no" response.)

May we call on you next week for a demonstration? (Requires "yes" or "no" response.)

Wouldn't you like to be the proud owner of a new Supra 28 laptop computer? (Does not require reader to return a "yes" or "no" response, but no *specific* action is requested.)

May we have your support in the future? (Does not require reader to return a "yes" or "no" response, but no *specific* action is requested.)

May I compliment you on your outstanding performance in meeting this year's sales quota? (No "yes" or "no" response is required; however, no *specific* action is requested.)

1–42 Expressions of Doubt

Doubt in expressing statements of fact may be signified by enclosing a question mark in parentheses.

His last visit to the South was in 1998 **(?)**.

She earns $2,900 **(?)** a month.

1–43 Series of Questions

When a sentence contains a series of questions, place a question mark at the end of each question. Only the first letter of the sentence is capitalized unless a question in the series begins with a proper noun or is a complete thought. Leave one space after a question mark that appears within a sentence; leave one or two spaces after the concluding question mark (depending upon the style used throughout the document).[8]

series of incomplete questions

What are the primary responsibilities of the president? the executive vice president? the treasurer?

Who requested copies of the report—the judge? the insurance company? the plaintiff's attorney?

series of proper noun questions

Will the new flight route stop in San Diego? Los Angeles? San Francisco?

series of independent questions

Several important issues were discussed at the conference last week: What style trends will be popular during the next decade? What comfort demands will the public make on furniture manufacturers? How much will price influence consumer furniture purchases?

1–44 Question Mark Placement and Format

a. Question marks may be placed either inside or outside the closing quotation mark or parenthesis.

When a complete question is contained within the quotation or parenthetical remark, place the question mark inside the closing quotation mark or parenthesis. If the entire sentence, not just the quotation or parenthetical remark, comprises the question, place the question mark outside the closing quotation mark or parenthesis.

Use only one concluding punctuation mark at the end of a sentence.

complete question contained in quotation marks

"Will the entire original cast be present for the opening night in Philadelphia?" asked a local reporter.

The governor then inquired, **"Who is in charge of this committee?"**

---

[8]Some desktop publishing authorities recommend only one space after the concluding punctuation mark; others use two spaces to promote ease of reading in business documents. The use of one or two spaces after a concluding punctuation mark is governed by the preference of the document originator.

complete question contained in parentheses

We received official notification last week **(did your notice arrive yet?)** that we must vacate our offices by the 1st of the month.

The committee informed me that J. Wilson Edwards has been appointed manager of the Phoenix office. **(Did you approve this appointment?)**

question encompasses entire sentence

Have you finished reading the article "Investment Opportunities Abroad"?

Will you be able to ship this order by May 15 (earlier if possible)?

b. **If an entire sentence and a quotation within the sentence are both questions, use only the first question mark—the one appearing inside the closing quotation mark.**

Did the president ask, "When will the directors hold their next meeting**?**"

c. **In word processing copy leave one space after a question mark that appears within a sentence and one or two spaces after a question mark that appears at the end of a sentence.[9] In typewritten copy leave two spaces after a question mark at the end of a sentence.**

one space after questions within sentence

Should I place these supplies on the desk**?** in the cabinet**?** in the storeroom**?**

one space after ending question mark

What time should we leave for the airport**?** When is your flight scheduled to depart**?** What time do you expect to arrive in Atlanta**?** May I please have answers to these questions by this afternoon.

two spaces after ending question mark

What time should we leave for the airport**?** When is your flight scheduled to depart**?** What time do you expect to arrive in Atlanta**?** May I please have answers to these questions by this afternoon.

Exclamation Mark

1–45 Use of Exclamation Mark

To express a high degree of emotion, use an exclamation mark after a word, phrase, clause, or sentence.

[9]Some desktop publishing authorities suggest using only one space after a concluding punctuation mark; others use two spaces in business documents to promote ease of reading. The choice of one or two spaces remains with the document originator, and word processing software may be defaulted to implement this choice.

word

What! You mean the new software will not arrive until next week?

phrase

How beautiful! The designer certainly used a great deal of color and imagination in creating this pattern.

clause

If he attends! He'd better attend, or Mr. Ramirez will get a new assistant.

sentence

Yes, she finally got an interview!

1–46 Exclamation Mark Placement and Format

a. In word processing copy leave one or two spaces after the exclamation mark before beginning the next word.[10] In typewritten copy use two spaces after the exclamation mark.

b. The exclamation mark should be used sparingly in business documents, and placing exclamation marks in two consecutive sentences or thought units should be avoided. Instead, use commas, periods, or question marks to complete an exclamatory thought.

exclamation with comma

Oh, I don't see how we can possibly meet the contract deadline without working overtime!

exclamation with period

No! Mr. Jones has not resigned.

exclamation with question mark

What! You expected the completed analysis last week?

c. Exclamation marks may be placed before or after the closing quotation mark or parenthesis.

When a complete exclamatory remark is a quotation or is enclosed in parentheses, place the exclamation mark inside the closing quotation mark or parenthesis. If the entire sentence, not just the quotation or parenthetical element, comprises the exclamatory expression, place the exclamation mark outside the closing quotation mark or parenthesis.

Use only one concluding punctuation mark at the end of a sentence.

---

[10] Some desktop publishing authorities recommend only one space after an ending punctuation mark; others use two spaces to foster reading ease. Document originators may use either style as long as they are consistent throughout the document.

complete exclamatory expression in quotation marks

At the time of the emergency, one of the employees shouted, **"Break down the door!"**

complete exclamatory expression in parentheses

He obtained the help of several advisors **(what a mistake that was!)** to assist him in selecting the project subcontractors.

Management was shocked at the employees' reactions to the new process. **(Only 14 percent of the staff welcomed the new procedures!)**

exclamatory expression encompasses entire sentence

I cannot believe Marie Huffinger's statement, **"Only 3 percent of the merchandise was returned"!**

If you wish to take advantage of these bargains, you will have to act now **(today)!**

Quotation Marks

1–47 Direct Quotations

Direct quotations contain the exact wording used by a writer or speaker. In business documents place one-sentence quotations and short two-sentence quotations within quotation marks.

Use commas to introduce most one-sentence quotations. Long one-sentence quotations and quotations of two sentences or more are introduced by a colon.

Quotation marks are not used for indirect quotations that do not use the exact wording of the reference.

direct quotation

"The economy cannot help slowing down by next year," said Dr. Roger Watson, a renowned economist.

"Although this stock has split three times since 1984," explained Ms. Mooneyhan, **"you cannot anticipate that it will continue to do so."**

One of the reporters shouted, **"Look out! The building is collapsing."**

Mr. Goldman explained in his February 8 memo: **"Because my wife became ill Monday morning and was hospitalized that afternoon, I was unable to attend the meeting. Please send me a copy of the minutes."**

indirect quotation

Kriss Powell, our production manager, said that our manufacturing costs per unit will increase at least 30 percent within the next year.

1–48 Long Quotations

In business documents long quotations of two sentences or more (and usually more than three lines) are written without the quotation marks and appear as separate paragraphs. They are indented from the left and right margins and separated from the main text by single blank lines at the beginning and the end of the quotation.

The speaker brought out the importance of effective management communication when she made the following statement:

> To exercise the function of leadership, there must be effective communication. If a leader cannot communicate, there is no leader because information cannot pass between the two groups. For instance, in management one cannot delegate duties and authority without effective communication.

Effective communication is paramount to effective leadership in . . . .

1–49 Short Expressions

a. **When short expressions—such as jargon, words used in humor, technical words used in a nontechnical way, coined expressions, slang words, or other phrases—need to be emphasized or clarified for the reader, they are placed in quotation marks. These same words are often shown in italics instead.**

words used for emphasis

The FCC (Federal Communications Commission) has set 2006 as a **"reasonable date"** for broadcasters to give back their analog channels. (or *reasonable date*)

slang words

Mr. Rhodes has difficulty working with others on the production team because he always wants to be **"in the driver's seat."** (or *in the driver's seat*)

technical words used in a nontechnical way

Mr. Rollins announced that **"all systems are go"** for the new golf course and condominium project in Scottsdale. (or *all systems are go*)

b. **Place in quotation marks the definitions of words or expressions. Italicize (or underscore if italics are not available) the word or expression defined.**

defined word

According to some economists, a ***recession*** is actually a **"little depression."**

defined expression

The French term ***faux pas*** means **"a social blunder."**

c. References to the words *marked, labeled, stamped,* or *signed* are placed in quotation marks.

Be sure to mark all packages **"Glass—Handle With Care."**

The envelope was stamped **"Addressee Unknown, Return to Sender."**

The letter was signed **"Philip Armstrong"** but contained no return address on either the letter or the envelope.

1–50 Literary Titles

Titles of various kinds of literary or artistic works such as magazine or newspaper articles, chapters of books or pamphlets, unpublished manuscripts, episodes in television series, acts in plays or musicals, short poems, lectures, songs, and themes are placed within quotation marks.

Names of books, magazines, pamphlets, newspapers, and other complete published or artistic works that contain subdivisions, however, are placed in italics (or underscored if italics are not accessible). (See Section 3–6 for further information and examples of titles placed in italics or underscored.)

book and chapter title

The chapter **"Webmaster Responsiblities"** contained in ***Web Site Design and Maintenance*** was helpful in specifying the duties and responsibilities of our Webmaster.

musical and song title

Of all the songs from the musical production ***Man of La Mancha***, **"The Impossible Dream"** is probably the most well recognized.

episode in television series

For the past four years, **"To Serve Man"** has been aired on our network's Thanksgiving Day marathon of selected episodes from the ***Twilight Zone***.

lecture title

Her last lecture, **"Combating Inflationary Trends,"** was very well attended.

1–51 Quotations Within Quotations

Use single quotation marks to signify a quotation within a quotation. If your software does not support single quotation marks, use the apostrophe key.

For quoted material within single quotation marks, return to using double quotation marks.

quotation within a quotation

The report stated, "According to the U.S. Chamber of Commerce, **'The problem of air and water pollution must be solved within the next decade if our cities are to survive.'** "

quotation within single quotation marks

The newspaper quoted the attorney as saying, "When I asked the defendant, 'Did you endorse the check **"Robert S. Parry"**?' he replied, 'No, I did not.' "

1–52 Ellipses

An ellipsis (a series of three periods with a space before, between, and after the series) is used to show an intentional omission of quoted material:

(1) If the omission begins the quoted sentence, use an ellipsis to begin the quotation.

(2) If the omission occurs within a sentence, use an ellipsis to substitute for the omitted words.

(3) If the omission occurs at the end of a sentence, use an ellipsis and then add the closing punctuation mark for the sentence.

(4) If one or more sentences have been omitted after the quoted sentence or sentences, first conclude the last sentence with the appropriate punctuation mark and then follow with an ellipsis to show the omission.

omission at beginning of quotation

The instructions stated, "**. . .** and turn knob in clockwise direction." (Remember to leave one space between the opening quotation mark and the first period in the ellipsis, one space between the periods, and one space after the closing period in the ellipsis.)

omission within sentence

The new sign was worded to discourage nonresidents from parking in the private lot: "Violators will be towed **. . .** cars will be released only upon payment of a $500 fine."

end-of-sentence omission

The guarantee reads: "All repairs that are not covered under the warranty will be made at a 25 percent discount **. . . .**"

One of the directors inquired, "How many miles is the home office from our various branch offices; i.e., Houston, Dallas, Oklahoma City, Atlanta, **. . . ?**"

one or more sentences omitted

The directive stated specifically: "Please ship our international orders by September 1. . . . Our European distributors must have their merchandise by October 1." (Close the sentence with a period. Place one space before each period in the ellipsis; place one or two spaces after the final period in the ellipsis before beginning the next sentence.)

The marketing manager wrote in her August 1 memo, "Will you be able to attend the conference in Baltimore? . . . We will need to set up our display booths on September 9." (Use a closing punctuation mark followed by an ellipsis with a space before, between, and after each period. Place one or two spaces after the final period in the ellipsis before beginning the next sentence.)

1–53 Capitalization With Quotation Marks

a. **Capitalize the first word of a complete sentence enclosed in quotation marks.**

"**P**lease call me before 10 a.m. tomorrow," requested Mrs. Edwards.

Andrew replied, **"Yes,** I will be able to attend the conference on July 28."

b. **Capitalize incomplete thoughts enclosed in quotation marks only if the quoted words themselves are capitalized. First, last, and main words[11] in quoted expressions preceded by "stamped" or "marked" are usually capitalized.**

capitalized

His check was returned from the bank marked **"Insufficient Funds."**

"Handle With Care" was stamped on the package.

Did you mark the invoice **"Paid in Full"**?

not capitalized

Mrs. Atkins asked us to spend **"as little time as possible"** on this project.

1–54 Quotation Mark Placement

a. **Periods and commas are always placed inside the closing quotation mark; semicolons and colons, outside the closing quotation mark.**

[11] *Main* words are all words *EXCEPT* (1) the articles *a, an,* and *the;* (2) the coordinating conjunctions *and, but, or,* and *nor;* (3) the word *to* in an infinitive (*to* write); and (4) prepositions with three or fewer letters (e.g., *of, for, in, on, by*).

period

The purchase requisition stipulates, "Cancel this order if the merchandise cannot be delivered by the 1st of July."

comma

"Our operating costs must be lowered," said Mr. Collins.

semicolon

The consultant's report stated emphatically, "A thorough analysis of the company's data and information processing system should be undertaken"; however, no steps have been taken to initiate such an analysis.

colon

Mrs. Cox recommended that the following vacation policy be adopted "unless a better one can be formulated": (1) Employees should select their vacation time on the basis of seniority and (2) conflicts should be resolved by the employees themselves, whenever possible.

b. When a complete question or exclamation is contained within the quotation, place the question mark or exclamation mark inside the closing quotation mark. If the entire sentence comprises the question or exclamation, then place the appropriate mark outside the closing quotation mark. If both the quotation and the entire sentence are questions, use only the first question mark.

complete question within quotation

He asked, **"Where are the annual reports filed?"**

entire sentence comprises question

Do you have a copy of her latest article, "Air Pollution Control"?

complete exclamation within quotation

"Do not," exclaimed Mr. Rey, **"leave the lights burning all night again!"**

entire sentence comprises exclamation

Our new sales manager is a real "go-getter"!

question within a question

Did Mr. Heinze inquire, "What time will our flight depart?"

Apostrophe

1–55 Possessives

a. When a noun, singular or plural, does not end with a pronounced *s*, add an apostrophe and *s* (*'s*) to form the possessive case.

singular noun

Yes, I found the requisition on my **assistant's** desk.

Lisa's father owns these three restaurants.

Most of the **company's** profits were earned during the first quarter of this year.

plural noun

Women's fashions are much more colorful this year.

Most of our discounted **children's** toys have already been sold.

This garment is made from 100 percent **sheep's** wool.

b. **When a noun, singular or plural, ends with a pronounced *s*, generally add an apostrophe (') to form the possessive case. However, an apostrophe and *s* ('*s*) may be added to singular nouns ending in a pronounced *s* if an additional *s* sound is also pronounced.**

singular noun—add ' only

Mrs. Simons' attendance record during the past five years has been perfect.

Most of these museum pieces were found among **Athens'** ruins.

plural noun—add ' only

Our staff reviews **customers'** accounts every 60 days.

Yesterday one of our agents sold the **Simonses'** home.

singular noun with additional s sound—add 's

We have been invited to our **boss's** home for dinner on April 27.

The **class's** scores on this examination were exceptionally high.

Ask **Mr. Jones's** assistant for a copy of the report.

Were you present in court during the **witness's** testimony?

c. **Use an apostrophe to show possession with nouns that represent people, animals, and other living entities (animate objects) or nouns related to time, distance, value, or celestial bodies. For other types of nouns (inanimate objects), show possession with an *of* phrase.**

animate possessive

The **employees'** representatives will meet with us on July 15.

Were the **horse's** hooves lacerated during the race?

Preserve your **hair's** color and luster with Richman's Protein$^+$ conditioning shampoo.

How can we be assured that the **tree's** roots will not crack the walls of the swimming pool?

Our **company's** steadily declining profits eventually led to the replacement of all its executive officers. (The word *company* is animate because it is composed of animate objects—people.)

time possessive

This **year's** profit and loss statement showed a gain of nearly 12 percent.

Enclosed is a check for three **months'** rent.

Yesterday's mail was still lying on her desk unopened when this **morning's** mail arrived.

distance possessive

Our office is just a **stone's** throw from the airport.

The thief rushed by within **arm's** length.

value possessive

She ordered several thousand **dollars'** worth of laser printer paper.

You owe me 50 **cents'** change.

celestial possessive

During the summer months the **sun's** rays can be extremely harmful if one is not careful.

Is **Mars'** atmosphere suitable for human survival?

inanimate possessive

The **terms of the loan** were extended another six months. (Not *loan's terms*)

Who broke the **base of the pot**? (Not *pot's base*)

d. **Form the possessive of compound nouns by having the last word show possession.**

She was designated her **father-in-law's** beneficiary.

Our next holiday party will be held at the **chairman of the board's** home.

My two **sisters-in-law's** business is doing well.

e. **When two or more nouns have joint ownership, only the last noun shows possession. When the nouns represent individual ownership, however, each noun must show possession.**

joint possession

Bill and Sheryl's new assistant has worked at ABCO Corporation for three years. (Bill and Sheryl share the same assistant—joint possession.)

The Harrises and the Bradys' new boat was damaged in the storm. (The Harrises and the Bradys own the same boat—joint possession.)

individual possession

Mary's and Henry's offices have been relocated to the new wing of our building. (Mary and Henry have different offices—individual possession.)

The Schaeffers' and the Gonzalezes' houses are on the same street. (The Schaeffers and the Gonzalezes live in different houses—individual possession.)

f. **The possessive of indefinite pronouns such as *anyone, everyone, someone, anybody, everybody, somebody,* and *nobody* is formed by using the same rules that apply to possessive nouns.**

It is **anyone's** guess when we will be able to resume production.

Somebody's car, which was parked illegally in a handicapped space, has been towed away.

g. **The possessive forms of personal or relative pronouns (such as *its, yours, hers, theirs,* or *whose*) do not include apostrophes. These pronouns are often confused with verb contractions, all of which contain apostrophes.**

possessive pronoun

Although the company had **its** greatest sales volume last year, it still failed to show a profit.

I met Ralph, **whose** father is a major stockholder in our company.

contraction

It's (It is) one of our most profitable lines.

I met with Pamela, **who's (who is)** the acquisitions editor on this project.

h. **Possessives of abbreviations are formed by using the same rules that apply to possessive nouns (Sections 1–55a and 1–55b).**

***abbreviation not ending with pronounced* s**

The **CPA's** report was comprehensive.

NASA's new space project is scheduled for a 2004 launching.

***abbreviation ending with pronounced* s**

Barker Bros.' annual sale will be held next week.

All **R.N.s'** badges are to be turned in at the end of each shift.

You may wish to follow the **IRS's** advice in this instance. (Use *'s* instead of just an apostrophe because of the extra pronounced *s* sound.)

i. **Use the possessive case of a noun or a pronoun before a gerund (an *-ing* verb used as a noun).**

noun

Don's accounting of his last business trip to Japan is incomplete.

pronoun

We would appreciate **your** returning the enclosed form by March 31.

j. **When a possessive noun is followed by an explanatory expression (an appositive), use an apostrophe only in the explanatory expression. When this form of writing sounds awkward, as it does in most cases, show possession by using an *of* phrase.**

apostrophe

Ms. Madden, **our production manager's**, office is being remodeled.

of *phrase*

The office **of our production manager,** Ms. Madden, is being remodeled.

k. **Many organizations with plural possessives in their names have omitted the apostrophe; organizations with singular possessives have tended to retain the apostrophe. The precise format used by the organization itself should be followed.**

plural possessive

We have just received loan approval from **Farmers** Bank and Trust.

singular possessive

The contract was issued to **Linton's** Manufacturing Company.

l. **Sometimes the possessed item is not explicitly stated in a sentence, but it is understood or clearly implied. In such cases the ownership word still uses an apostrophe to show possession.**

This year the holiday party will be held at **Steve's**.

Be sure to meet me at the **doctor's** by 2 p.m.

The wallet found in the corridor was **Mr. Lopez's**.

Deliver this floral arrangement to the **Briggses**'.

This month's sales are considerably higher than last **month's**.

1–56 Additional Uses of the Apostrophe

a. **Use the apostrophe to form contractions.**

single-word contraction

acknowledged **ack'd** national **nat'l** cannot **can't**

two-word contraction

you would **you'd** is not **isn't** I have **I've**

b. **The apostrophe is used for clarity to form the plural of all isolated lowercase letters and the single capital letters *A, I, M,* and *U*.**

plural of lowercase letter

Be sure to dot your **i's** and cross your **t's**.

How many times have I reminded you to watch your **p's** and **q's**?

plural of capital letters "A," "I," "M," and "U"

Mr. Craig's daughter received three ***A's*** on her report card.

Avoid using too many ***I's*** in the business documents you write.

c. **The apostrophe may be used for the single quotation mark to signify a quotation within a quotation.**

Terry reported, "The president opened the forum with **'We're going to drive QuickWrite's sales back up to and beyond its former high!'**"

d. **Use the apostrophe to signify the omission of figures in expressing a year.**

Job prospects for the class of **'02** look favorable—especially in the computer industry.

e. **In technical material the apostrophe may be used as a symbol for *feet*.**

12' × 15' (room)   5' 3" (height)   80' × 110' (area)

Parentheses

1–57 Nonessential Expressions

Parentheses are used to set off and subordinate nonessential expressions that would otherwise confuse the reader because (1) they give supplementary information that has no direct bearing on the main idea or (2) they call for an abrupt change in thought. References and directions are two examples of expressions that are often enclosed in parentheses.

abrupt change in thought

I wrote to Mr. Furstman **(I tried to call him, but there was no answer)** and asked him to contact us before October 4.

reference

All major repairs over $3,000 must first be cleared through proper channels. **(See Bulletin 8 dated March 2.)**

directions

Please send 500 copies of our annual report to each of our European offices. **(Send them by air M-Bag mail.)**

1–58 Numerals

Numerals in legal, business, and professional documents are often shown in parentheses to confirm a spelled-out figure.

All work is guaranteed for ninety **(90)** days.

Compensation for services rendered will not exceed three thousand dollars **($3,000)**.

The committee may not consider any bid over nine thousand nine hundred ninety-nine dollars **($9,999)**.

On March 4 our client received a check for two thousand eight hundred forty-three dollars and seventy-five cents **($2,843.75)**.

1–59 Enumerated Items

Enclose in parentheses numbers or letters used to enumerate lists of items within a sentence.

See Section 1–36a for the use of parentheses with alphanumeric outlines.

numbers

Please supply me with the following information for the current year: the number of **(1)** new employees, **(2)** people who retired, **(3)** people who resigned, and **(4)** people terminated by the company.

letters

This report supplies the following current information for Marengo County: **(a)** salary trends, **(b)** unemployment statistics, and **(c)** placement requests.

1–60 Parentheses With Other Punctuation Marks

a. **Words, phrases, and clauses enclosed in parentheses in the middle of a sentence function as part of the sentence in applying rules of punctuation and capitalization.**

word

We will fly to Fort Lauderdale **(Florida)** for our annual convention.

phrase

Ms. Haven will gross nearly $800,000 **(as compared to a $500,000 average)** in sales this year.

clause

Our new manager **(several members of our staff met him last week)** will conduct a communications seminar in the spring.

b. **When an incomplete thought enclosed in parentheses ends a sentence that requires a period, place the period outside the closing parenthesis.**

According to our legal counsel, this procedure violates laws in only two states **(Minnesota and Wyoming).**

Several members of the committee will meet in Kansas City this weekend **(if possible).**

c. **When a complete thought enclosed in parentheses ends a sentence that requires a period, the two parts are treated separately. Place a period at the end of each sentence, with the final period appearing inside the closing parenthesis.**

Yes, your order was shipped on April 17. **(You should receive it within five to six working days from the shipment date.)**

Several members of our staff attended the ATLW conference this year. **(This year's conference was held in Honolulu.)**

d. **If an interrupting word, phrase, or clause shown in parentheses requires a question mark or exclamation mark, use such a mark of punctuation only if the sentence ends with a different mark.**

parenthetical question

Our new vice president **(do you know Colleen Merrell?)** will arrive in Los Angeles tomorrow.

Were you informed that our new price list **(has your copy arrived yet)** will go into effect on October 1?

parenthetical exclamation

Have you heard about the recent enormous price increases **(I can't believe them!)** in single-family dwellings?

Living conditions **(you can scarcely call them that)** are absolutely deplorable in this section of the city!

e. **Place commas, semicolons, and colons outside the closing parenthesis.**

comma

If you plan to attend the president's retirement banquet (on May 16**),** please send your reservations to Terry Thomsen by Monday, May 12.

semicolon

His report deals primarily with the importance of our country's major transportation systems (railroads, inland waterways, motor trucks, pipelines, and air transportation**);** therefore, little emphasis was given to rising transportation costs.

colon

On February 15 Ms. Haddad will introduce two new product lines (for women's fashion departments**):** the Sportswoman Series and the Sun and Surf Coordinates.

Brackets

1–61 Use of Brackets

a. Use brackets to insert an explanation, a correction, or a comment in quoted material.

To show that an error in quoted material appeared in the original document, enclose the term *sic* (meaning "so" or "this is the way it was") in brackets.

Mr. Gilmer stated in his report: "With new equipment to speed up the production process **[he did not specify what new equipment was needed]**, substantial savings can be mad **[sic]** in both material and labor costs."

b. Brackets may be used within parentheses to indicate yet another subordinate idea.

The auction of Rita Rothchild's possessions **(**including jewelry, furs, furniture, movie costumes **[from 1945 through 1975]**, china, silverware, and other memorabilia**)** is scheduled for July 17 and 18.

1–62 Use of Angle Brackets

In footnotes or bibliographical citations, some authorities use angle brackets to enclose the addresses (URLs) of Internet sites.

---

[5]Ellen Neuborne, "Time for Retailers to Face Their Web 'Terror,'" *BusinessWeek Online: BusinessWeek e.biz*, 5 July 1999, <http://www.businessweek.com/ebiz/index.html> (5 July 1999).

1–63 Brackets With Other Punctuation Marks

The placement of other punctuation marks with brackets follows the same principles outlined for parentheses in Section 1–60.

Asterisk

1–64 Use of Asterisk

Asterisks may be used to call the reader's attention to footnotes in a document when they appear infrequently and occur at widely spaced intervals. The asterisk follows other punctuation marks, except the dash, closing parenthesis, or closing bracket.

after most punctuation marks

A recent government report states, "Air traffic is expected to double within the next decade.**"***

before dash, closing parenthesis, or closing bracket

We are studying the works of Ray Bradbury***—**one of our leading contemporary science fiction writers.

Companies that have hired outside consultants to develop cost-cutting procedures have reported good results. (Several articles supporting the effectiveness of outside consultants have recently appeared in leading professional journals.***)**

Many national magazines (such as *Time*, *Newsweek*, and *Business-Week* [May and June issues*****]) have published informative, interesting articles on using the Internet.

Diagonal

1–65 Use of Diagonal

Use a diagonal (also called a "solidus," "slash," or "virgule") between (1) letters in some abbreviations, (2) numerals in fractions, and (3) the expression *and/or* to show that the terms are interchangeable. No space appears before or after the diagonal.

abbreviation

Please address the envelope as follows: Mrs. Maureen Savage, **c/o** Mr. George Martin, Display Manager, Wilson Disc Company, 1141 Western Avenue, Los Angeles, California 90024.

fraction

Costs have increased ½ percent since last week.

To reupholster the reception room sofa will require **12 5/8** yards of fabric.

and/or

Authorizations for future purchases may be obtained from Ms. Jorgensen **and/or** Mr. Kline.

Underscore

1–66 Use of the Underscore

The underscore is generally not used in computer-generated or printed copy. Other font attributes—italics, bolding, bolded italics, and varying font sizes—have been substituted for the underscore.

In typewritten copy the underscore is used to emphasize such items as headings; words that would normally be italicized; and titles of books, magazines, newspapers, pamphlets, and various other published or artistic works (See Section 3–6). Continuous lines, with no spacing

between words, are used for underscoring. Except for periods with abbreviations, punctuation marks immediately following underscored material are not underscored.

italicized word

He always misspells the word **convenience**.

magazine title

According to an article in **BusinessWeek**, most movies are currently being filmed outside the United States.

television show with subdivision

"Jack the Ripper" was the first episode on this season's television series **Unsolved Mysteries**.

abbreviation

Be sure to place **a.m.** in lowercase letters.

punctuation mark following standard underscored material

Did the bookstore order sufficient copies of **Merriam-Webster's Collegiate Dictionary**?

Ampersand

1–67 Use of the Ampersand

a. The ampersand (&), a symbol that represents the word *and,* is used primarily to express the official name of some business organizations.

ampersand in company name

Johnson **&** Johnson was the subcontractor for the project.

A. G. Edwards **&** Sons, Inc., is handling the sale of this new stock issue.

use of* and *in company name

All merger talks with Merritt **and** Sons have been delayed until the end of our fiscal period.

b. When the ampersand represents *and* in a series, use a comma before the ampersand only if the organization does so in its official name.

no comma before the ampersand

The law offices of Levitt, Myers **&** Cohen represented the plaintiff in this case.

comma before the ampersand

Fall fashions from Liz, Lee**,** **&** Co. should arrive in our store by the middle of July.

Chapter 2

Hyphenating and Dividing Words

pre/

Hyphenating and Dividing Words Solution Finder

End-of-Line Divisions

Hyphenating Words

Hyphenating Words

2–1 Compound Nouns and Verbs

Often two or more words act as one idea. Nouns and verbs in this class may be written as separate words, written as single words, or hyphenated. Consult an up-to-date dictionary to determine the exact form of compound nouns and verbs.[1]

separate words, nouns

sales tax	editor in chief	life insurance	charge account
data processing	air conditioner	port of entry	voice mail

single words, nouns

checkbook	workforce	salesperson	paycheck
spreadsheet	database	stepfather	moneymaker

hyphenated words, nouns

brother-in-law	attorney-at-law	by-product	self-interest
double-talk	face-lift	go-around	air-conditioning

separate words, verbs

to set up	to mark down	to step down	to call in
to stand out	to trade in	to slip up	to double up

single words, verbs

to upgrade	to keyboard	to downsize	to landscape
to videotape	to download	to handpick	to mastermind

hyphenated words, verbs

to tape-record	to air-condition	to triple-space	to cross-examine
to ill-treat	to e-mail	to double-check	to piece-dye

2–2 Compound Adjectives

When two or more words appearing together act as a single idea to describe a noun or pronoun, these words function as a compound adjective. In many cases compound adjectives are hyphenated; in other cases they are not. Use the following guidelines to determine whether or not a compound adjective should be hyphenated.

a. A number of compound adjectives are listed and shown hyphenated in the dictionary. These adjectives may be considered *permanent* compounds. They are hyphenated whenever they are used as adjectives in a sentence, no matter where they appear in the sentence—before or after the nouns or pronouns they modify.

---

[1]All spellings and hyphenations used in this manual are based upon *Merriam-Webster's Collegiate Dictionary*, 10th ed. (Springfield, Mass.: Merriam-Webster, Incorporated, 1999).

permanent compound adjective before a noun or pronoun

up-to-date	**up-to-date** equipment
well-known	**well-known** brands
part-time	**part-time** employment
snow-white	**snow-white** mountains
smooth-tongued	**smooth-tongued** salesperson
small-scale	**small-scale** operation
hands-off	**hands-off** policy
machine-readable	**machine-readable** text
no-fault	**no-fault** insurance
public-spirited	**public-spirited** citizens

permanent adjective compound following noun or pronoun

All the software installed on these computers is **up-to-date**.

If your job is **part-time**, please check the appropriate box on the enclosed form.

These clothing brands are **well-known** throughout the world.

Mailing addresses on envelopes from major corporations are usually **machine-readable**.

You cannot deny that this community is **public-spirited**.

b. **Sometimes compound nouns are used as single-thought adjectives to describe other nouns or pronouns. When these combinations are shown as *open compounds* (not hyphenated) in the dictionary, they are not hyphenated when they are used as compound adjectives.**

compound noun	***compound noun used as compound adjective***
data processing	**data processing** center
life insurance	**life insurance** policy
money market	**money market** account
human resources	**human resources** management
finance company	**finance company** records
charge account	**charge account** customer
high school	**high school** teacher
word processing	**word processing** software
income tax	**income tax** return
department store	**department store** personnel
mobile home	**mobile home** sales
real estate	**real estate** commission

c. **Many single-thought word groups that function as compound adjectives are not shown in the dictionary. Such word groups are known as *temporary compounds*. These temporary compounds are hyphenated and written in singular form (where applicable) when they appear *before* the nouns or pronouns they describe. They are not hyphenated, however, when they appear after the words they modify.**

temporary compound before noun or pronoun—hyphenated

We have already installed **voice-activated** software in several of our computers.

All **city-owned** property is exempt from these county taxes.

A **well-established** legal firm has been retained to represent our interests.

Capture that **never-to-be-forgotten** moment with pictures by Mardell!

The mayor's **not-too-cordial** attitude toward the press was evident.

temporary compound in singular form before noun or pronoun—hyphenated

This property has a **123-foot** driveway leading up to the house.

The Holtzes are interested in purchasing a **four-bedroom** home.

The Walters' **7-pound-12-ounce** son was born yesterday at 5 a.m.

All vehicles are expected to abide by the **65-mile-an-hour** speed limit on this highway.

temporary compound following noun or pronoun

We have investigated using software that is **voice activated**.

None of the properties in this section are **city owned**.

This firm has been **well established** in the Houston area for nearly thirty years.

Your wedding should be a day that is **never to be forgotten**.

Mr. Simms' greetings this morning were certainly **not too cordial**.

The driveway leading up to the house is **123 feet** long.

The Holtzes' new home has **four bedrooms**.

At birth the Walters' baby weighed **7 pounds 12 ounces**.

The speed limit on this highway is **65 miles an hour**.

d. **When *two separate* proper nouns or *two separate* common nouns are combined to form single-thought adjectives before other nouns or pronouns, these compounds are hyphenated.**

separate proper nouns used as an adjective

This morning's issue of the newspaper carried several articles on **Chinese-American** relations.

Your **Chicago-London** flight has been delayed until tomorrow.

separate common nouns used as an adjective

Today's training session will deal with **union-management** relations.

Most of the classes offered by our institute maintain a 15:1 **student-teacher** ratio.

e. The components of a *single* proper noun are not hyphenated when they are used as an adjective.

We have been negotiating with a **Far Eastern** firm for the last three months.

How many **University of Nebraska** alumni have you been able to locate in Salt Lake City?

f. Adverbs ending in *ly* that are combined with adjectives to form a single modifier are not hyphenated.

I understand that your session sparked the most **hotly debated** issues at the conference.

Dr. Stevens is an **exceptionally gifted** nuclear physicist.

g. Two separate colors stated in a compound modifier are hyphenated. Other adjectives, however, used in conjunction with colors are not hyphenated unless the combination is a permanent compound shown in the dictionary.

two separate colors

This **blue-green** fabric was selected for upholstering the sofas in the hotel lobby.

The artist used **red-orange** hues effectively in portraying the Hawaiian sunset.

adjective combined with color

The **bluish green** water magnified the size of the iridescent, colorful fish.

The **bright red** flag can easily be seen from a distance.

Ask all our sales representatives to wear **dark gray** suits to the exhibition.

The **emerald green** cover of your new book stands out quite visibly.

Place these artists' prints against a **snow-white** background to accentuate their deep color contrasts. (The adjective *snow-white* is shown hyphenated in the dictionary.[2])

h. When a series of hyphenated adjectives has a common ending, use suspending hyphens.

Have these announcements printed on **8½- by 11-inch** bond paper.

Please order a supply of **1/16- and 1/8-inch** drill bits.

Most of the awards were given to **tenth- and eleventh-grade** students.

All construction bids for this hillside are based on **one-, two-, and three-level** family dwellings.

---

[2]*Merriam-Webster's Collegiate Dictionary,* 10th ed. (Springfield, Mass.: Merriam-Webster, Incorporated, 1999), 1113.

i. **Amounts in the millions and billions, percentages, and words used with numerals or letters are *not* hyphenated when they function as compound adjectives.**

amounts in the millions and billions

How will the president deal with the projected **$1 billion** decline in the Gross Domestic Product?

Nearly **160 million** people worldwide are connected to the Internet.

percentages

You will receive a **10 percent** discount on all orders placed through our Web site.

There will be a ½ **percent** increase in our state sales tax effective July 1.

words used with numerals or letters

Will our new employee be rated in as a **Grade 1** administrative assistant?

How many **Vitamin C** tablets are in each container?

Please ship these **Model 85A** wall units by October 1.

j. **Simple fractions are hyphenated *only* when they are used as compound adjectives.**[3]

compound adjective

John sold his **one-fourth** ownership in the company for $575,000.

Amendments to our bylaws require a **two-thirds** majority approval by our voting membership.

simple fraction as noun

Only **one third** of the stockholders responded to the questionnaire.

The Board of Directors voted to reinvest **one half** of this year's profits in additional research and development projects.

2–3 Prefixes

a. **Words beginning with *ex* (meaning "former") and *self* are hyphenated; those beginning with *pre, re,*[4] and *non* are generally not hyphenated. Words beginning with *co* and *vice* may or may not be hyphenated. Use**

[3]"Table of Numbers," Footnote 5, *Merriam-Webster's Collegiate Dictionary,* 10th ed. (Springfield, Mass.: Merriam-Webster, Incorporated, 1999), 798.

[4]The words *re-collect* meaning "to collect again," *re-cover* meaning "to cover anew," *re-create* meaning "to create again," *re-lease* meaning "to lease again," *re-present* meaning "to present again," *re-press* meaning "to press again," *re-sign* meaning "to sign again," *re-sort* meaning "to sort again," and *re-tread* meaning "to tread again" are exceptions to this rule. Note that without the hyphens these words would have completely different meanings.

your dictionary to check the hyphenation of words with these two beginnings.

ex and self

Bob Hubbard, the **ex-baseball** star, is now in the real estate business.

Our **ex-chairman** still has all the committee records in his files.

To be successful in sales, a person should have an outgoing personality and project **self-confidence**.

Employee **self-satisfaction** contributes to raising both morale and productivity.

pre, re, and non

All the floppy disks we use have been **preformatted**.

Where will the **preemployment** interviews be held?

Please **recheck** all the total columns carefully.

We should have the wheels on this truck **realigned**.

Tuition **reimbursements** will not be made for classes taken at **nonaccredited** educational institutions.

You may wish to initiate legal proceedings against Phillips Bros. for **nonpayment** of its account.

co

co-edition
co-owner
co-occurrence

coauthor
codefendant
coinsurance

vice

vice-chancellor
vice-consul

vice admiral
vice president

b. When a prefix is added to a proper noun, place a hyphen between the prefix and the proper noun.

We found that many firms operating in the South today date back to **pre-Civil War** times.

If you cannot promise a **mid-August** delivery date, cancel the order.

To some people a 4th of July without fireworks would be **un-American**.

2–4 Numbers

a. Compound numbers from *21* to *99* are hyphenated when they appear in word form.

Ninety-six of our agents responded to the questionnaire, but we are still awaiting replies from **twenty-four** more.

b. **In numbers over *99* expressed in word form, components other than compound numbers are not hyphenated.**

The lessee shall pay a sum of **Two Thousand Eight Hundred Seventy-five Dollars and Twenty-four Cents** ($2,875.24) to the lessor.

c. **Simple fractions not used with units of measure are expressed in word form. These fractions are hyphenated *only* when they function as compound adjectives.**

simple fraction used as noun

Over **two thirds** of our employees voted to ratify the new contract.

Only **three fourths** of our company cars are presently equipped with cellular phones.

simple fraction used as compound adjective

Our company wishes to purchase a **one-fourth** interest in the new shopping mall planned for the Pinehurst area.

A **two-thirds** majority vote is needed to pass this proposition, which will appear on the November ballot.

d. **When a number-word combination functions as a *single unit* (a compound adjective) to describe a noun, (1) express the word part of the compound adjective in singular form and (2) separate the parts of the compound adjective with a hyphen. Only in percentages, amounts in the millions and billions, and capitalized word-numeral combinations are the hyphens omitted.**

hyphen—number-word compound adjective

We have a **three-year** lease on this building.

Our highways have a **65-mile-an-hour** speed limit.

Drivers are charged **50-cent** tolls along this turnpike.

He just started a **$2,800-a-month** job.

The Joneses' **7-pound-8-ounce** baby girl was born on December 25.

no hyphen—percentage

We experienced a **25 percent** sales increase this year.

no hyphen—amount in the millions

Ridgewood Inc. announced a **$3 million** profit for the year.

no hyphen—capitalized word-numeral combination

Your Evansdale **Model 380** curio cabinet should arrive in our store within the next three weeks.

e. **In word processing copy use an en dash (if possible) to represent the terms *to* or *through* between two numerals. In typewritten copy, though, use the hyphen to replace these terms.**

As you requested, your vacation this year has been scheduled from July **3–18**.

Refer to pages **70–75** for further instructions.

End-of-Line Word and Word-Group Divisions

Where possible, avoid dividing words at the end of a computer-generated or typewritten line because complete words are easier to read, easier to understand, and neater in appearance. Sometimes, however, word divisions at the end of a line are necessary to avoid overly uneven line lengths or, in justified copy, awkward-appearing lines with large spaces between words.

Observe the following rules to divide words and certain word groups correctly at the end of a line. Some of these rules should be adhered to strictly; others are flexible in their application, especially in desktop published copy. The following sections address (1) words and word groups *never* to be divided, (2) word divisions to be avoided, if possible, and (3) rules and guidelines for proper end-of-line word and word-group divisions.

2–5 Words and Word Groups Never to Be Divided

Some words and certain word groups may not be divided under any circumstances:

a. Do not divide one-syllable words, including those that end in *ed*.

one-syllable words

freight straight threats thought through bread

one-syllable ed *words*

called changed weighed planned striped shipped

b. Do not set off a single-letter syllable at either the beginning or the end of a word.

beginning of a word

i tinerary a warded e nough
i dentify o mitted u niform

end of a word

radi o bacteri a health y photocop y criteri a rati o

c. Do not set off a two-letter syllable at the end of a word. At least three characters of a divided word must appear on the next line.

present ed compa ny month ly
build er week ly debt or

d. **Do not divide abbreviations unless a hyphen already appears within the abbreviation. Hyphenated abbreviations may be divided after the hyphen.**

not divided

UNESCO	AMSLAN	U.S.A.	AOL	UCLA	Ph.D.
Ed.D.	B.A.	Sept.	bdrm.	c.o.d.	equiv.

may be divided

AFL-CIO KMET-TV NBEA-WBITE

e. **Do not divide month and day; *a.m., p.m., noon,* or *midnight* from clock time; percentages from the word *percent*; page numbers from page references; or other such closely related word-and-numeral combinations.**

If you are using a word processor, place a nonbreaking space between the components of the combination to keep all parts on the same line.

month and day

November 25 January 5 May 1

a.m., p.m., noon, *or* midnight *with clock time*

10 a.m.	6:30 a.m.	2 p.m.
4:05 p.m.	12 midnight	12 noon

***percentage with the word* percent**

0.5 percent	1 percent	8.25 percent
42.5 percent	100 percent	

page number with page reference

page iv page 23 page 241 page 1073

other word-and-numeral combinations

7 ounces	Room 341	Model 4A	No. 437892
Check 873	6 inches	210 miles	43 yards
33 cents	Suite 310	Chapter 3	size 12

f. **Do not divide contractions or numerals.**

contractions

wouldn't	doesn't	haven't
should've	you're	o'clock

numerals

$15,487 1,240,500 3 billion 4,500 $2.5 million

g. **Do not divide the last word in more than two consecutive lines.**

h. **Do not divide *the last word in a paragraph* or *the last word on a page.***

2–6 Words to Avoid Dividing, If Possible

Although observing the following rules is desirable, situations may occur where end-of-line word divisions are unavoidable. Apply these rules—unless doing so would result in an extremely ragged right margin.

a. Avoid dividing words containing six letters or fewer.

forget   person   better   number   listen   filter

b. Avoid dividing a word after a two-letter prefix.

en large   re warding   im portant
de pendent   un necessary

c. Avoid dividing a word at the end of the first line of a paragraph in typewritten copy. Desktop published copy and copy generated by word processing software are generally not governed by this guideline.

2–7 Rules and Guidelines for Dividing Words

Divide words *only* between syllables. Use an up-to-date dictionary or a word division manual to locate the correct syllabication of words to be divided. All word divisions shown in this reference manual are based on the syllabication shown in *Merriam-Webster's Collegiate Dictionary,* 10th ed., the 1999 printing, published by Merriam-Webster, Incorporated.

Words containing several syllables often require forethought to determine the appropriate place to separate the word. Use the following guidelines to determine where to divide a word:

a. Divide hyphenated and single-word compounds at their natural breaks.

hyphenated compound

vice-/chancellor[5]   self-/esteem   Governor-/elect   brother-/in-/law

single-word compound

common/place   hand/made   break/down   sales/person

b. Where possible, divide words after a prefix or before a suffix.

prefix

anti/body   super/intendent   mis/fortune   sub/stantiate

suffix

evasive/ness   corpora/tion   employ/ment   conscien/tious

c. Divide words between double letters *except* when the root word itself ends with the double letters and is followed by a suffix.

divided between double letters

bul/letin   accom/modate   neces/sarily
vacil/late   mil/len/nium

---

[5]The slash (/) as used here and in the following sections of this chapter signifies appropriate places for dividing words at the end of a line.

divided after double letters

business/like   fulfill/ment   helpless/ness   install/ing

d. Divide words between two vowels pronounced separately.

continu/ation   experi/ence   gradu/ation   influ/ential

e. Divide words *after*, not before, a single vowel pronounced as a syllable except when the vowel is part of a suffix.

single vowel

clar**i**/fication   apol**o**/gize   congrat**u**/lations   ben**e**/ficial

suffix vowel

accept/able   collaps/ible   forc/ible   collect/ible   allow/able

2–8 Guidelines for Dividing Word Groups

Certain word groups are preferably divided in specific places. Use the following guidelines to separate dates, names of individuals, addresses, numbered items, copy containing dashes, and copy containing ellipses. If you are using a word processor, place a nonbreaking space between any parts in the word group that should appear on the same line.

a. Divide dates between the day and the year, but *not* between the month and the day.

January 7, / 1999   *not* January / 7, 1999
April 15, / 2003   *not* April / 15, 2003

b. Full names of individuals are ideally divided directly before the last name, but they may be divided before a middle name. Do not, however, divide a name after a courtesy title, before a middle initial, or before an abbreviation.

Names preceded by long professional titles *may also be* divided between the title and the first name or between words in the title.

divided before last name

Ms. Marilyn / Farrar	*not*	Ms. / Marilyn Farrar
Dr. Roberta P. / Rosenberg	*not*	Dr. / Roberta P. Rosenberg Dr. Roberta / P. Rosenberg
Mr. William / Harrison Jr.	*not*	Mr. / William Harrison Jr. Mr. William Harrison / Jr.

divided before middle name or last name

Lorraine / Hoover / Clark   Khristopher / William / Savage

divided after long title or between words in a long title

Lieutenant / Harvey / Petrowski

Assistant / Professor / Alice H. / Duffy

c. **Avoid, where possible, dividing a street address directly after the house number. Street addresses are preferably divided between the street name and the street designation (*Street, Avenue, Boulevard, Lane,* etc.). If the street name contains more than one word, the address may also be broken between words in the street name.**

division of single-word street name

1138 Monogram / Avenue
One Park / Street
20 Wilshire / Boulevard
3624 59th / Place

division possibilities of street name containing more than one word

6800 Coldwater / Canyon / Avenue
218 East / Hawes / Street
17325 San / Fernando / Mission / Boulevard
849 North / 73rd / Street

d. **Geographical locations in addresses may be divided between the city and state and the state and zip code. They may also be divided between words in cities and states containing more than one word.**

Dubuque, / Iowa / 52001
San / Diego, / California / 92109-2134
Poughkeepsie, / New / York / 12601-1032

e. **Divide a numbered or lettered horizontal listing directly before the number or letter, but not directly after.**

At the seminar an affirmative action officer gave these reasons: (1) fewer job openings in the teaching profession, (2) enrollment declines in the student population, and (3) an increase in the mandatory retirement age for teachers.

f. **A sentence with a dash may be broken after the dash, but not directly before it.**

The Board of Directors surely agrees that your policies are excellent—
a step in the right direction.

When our peak sales subside at the end of the year—in December—
we plan to move our offices to San Francisco.

g. **A sentence may be divided directly after an ellipsis, not directly before. At least one word of the sentence must appear on the same line before the ellipsis.**

If you are using a word processor, place a nonbreaking space before and between the periods in an ellipsis to prevent the periods from word wrapping incorrectly to the next line.

As the article stated, "The mayor's campaign issues focus on . . .
crime prevention in our city."

According to the *Newsweek* article, "As the number of network access providers continues to grow, prices for these services will drop. . . .
Such factors will result in substantially fewer providers."

Chapter 3

Capitalization

u.S.

Capitalization Solution Finder

Capitalization Solution Finder *(continued)*

3–1 Beginning Words

a. Capitalize the beginning words of sentences, quoted sentences, independent phrases, lines of poetry, and items in an outline.

sentence

Learn how you can save on commission charges by doing all your stock transactions on-line.

quoted sentence

The guarantee states, **"Defective** parts will be replaced free of charge."

independent phrase

Now, to the important point.

poetry

By the rude bridge that arched the flood,
Their flag to the April's breeze unfurled,
Here once the embattled farmers stood,
And fired the shot heard round the world.
—Emerson

outline

1. **Specific** instructions
   a. **Type** of product
   b. **Tools** needed for assembly
   c. **Diagrams** illustrating assembly

b. The initial letter of an incomplete quoted thought that is woven in with the rest of the sentence is not capitalized unless the first word is (1) a proper noun, (2) preceded by identification words such as *marked* or *stamped,* or (3) capitalized because of another rule of capitalization.

lowercase

Mr. Reyes was directed to **"take** care of this situation immediately."

proper noun

Mr. Stone's response was simply **"General** Motors common stock."

***preceded by identification words* marked *or* stamped**

This package should be stamped **"Fragile—Handle With Care."**

Your check was returned by the bank marked **"Insufficient Funds."**

another rule of capitalization

Be sure to read **"The** 700 Club" in this week's issue of *Time*.

c. In standard salutations used for correspondence, capitalize the first word and any nouns contained in the salutation. For salutations

directed to undetermined individuals, capitalize the first word and all *main* words[1] that follow.

Capitalize only the first word of a complimentary close.

standard salutation—first word and all nouns

Dear **M**r. **J**ones: **G**entlemen: **M**y dear **F**riend:

Dear fellow **A**merican: **L**adies and **G**entlemen:

salutation to undetermined individual—first word and all main words

To **W**hom **I**t **M**ay **C**oncern:

To **S**tockholders of **R**ecord on **M**ay 1, 2003:

complimentary close

Sincerely yours, **C**ordially yours, **Y**ours very truly,

d. **The first word following a colon is generally not capitalized. Capitalize the first word, however, when the words following the colon (1) begin with a proper noun, (2) consist of two or more sentences, (3) begin a vertical listing, (4) present a formal rule, or (5) require emphasis.**

first word not capitalized

Our maintenance crew has requested us to order the following garden supplies: **lawn** seed, liquid fertilizer, and insect spray.

We are experiencing a two months' delay in our production schedule: **the** warehouse fire set us back considerably.

proper noun following colon

Three colleges are involved in the project: **DeKalb** Community College, MiraCosta College, and the City College of New York.

two or more sentences following colon

Here are two important questions to consider: **Will** enlarging our facilities at this time be economically feasible? **Is** the current market able to assimilate any increased production?

vertical listing following colon

Please send us copies of the following items:

1. **Lease** agreement with Property Management Associates
2. **Statement** of income and expenses for 2001
3. **Budget** of projected income and expenses for 2002

---

[1] *Main* words are all words except the articles *a, an, the;* the conjunctions *and, but, or, nor;* the word *to* used with an infinitive; and prepositions containing two or three letters (*of, for, on,* etc.)

formal rule following colon

Please use the following format in preparing all correspondence: **Prepare** letters in modified-block style with blocked paragraphs and mixed punctuation.

item of special emphasis following colon

Note: **Several** of our employees were listening to the World Series during working hours.

Wanted: **Student** to work weekends and holidays.

e. **Unless the word is a proper noun, the first word of a complete thought contained in parentheses *within a sentence* is not capitalized. A complete thought contained in parentheses that appears immediately after a sentence is treated as a separate unit, and the first word is capitalized.**

first word not capitalized within sentence

Several minor changes (**these** were recommended by Mr. Lloyd) will be made in the final draft.

parentheses within sentence—proper noun capitalized

Your recommendations (**Ms.** Williams approved all of them) will be incorporated into the marketing survey.

parentheses after end of sentence—first word capitalized

A group of marketing students wishes to tour our main plant in Atlanta. (**The** students will arrange for their own transportation.)

3–2 Proper Nouns and Adjectives[2]

a. **Proper nouns (words that name a particular person, place, or thing) and adjectives derived from proper nouns are capitalized. Capitalize the names of persons, cities, states, countries, rivers, mountains, streets, parks, colleges, buildings, shopping centers, malls, developments, organizations, ships, airplanes, specific events, etc.**

proper noun

We have opened a new branch office in **Austin, Texas**.

Our offices are in the **Atlantic Richfield Building** on **Fifth Street**.

The **Orange County Fair** will be held in **Petit Park** this year.

When will the **Brownsville Shopping Mall** be ready for occupancy?

We flew to **Florida** on a **Boeing 757** to meet our cruise ship, the **Song of Norway**.

Next month **John** and **Lisa** will take a raft down the **Colorado River**.

---

[2]The capitalization principles that follow are based primarily on those suggested by *The Chicago Manual of Style*, 14th ed. (Chicago: The University of Chicago Press, 1993).

How much is the toll for the **Golden Gate Bridge**, which crosses **San Francisco Bay**?

adjective derived from proper noun[3]

Football and baseball are typical **American** sports.

Be sure to order **Roquefort** dressing and grated **Swiss** cheese for the salad bar.

The **Socratic** method is often used in debates.

Where can I find a listing of **Internet** access providers for our area code?

How much **Canadian** money do you have in your wallet?

The use of the **Heimlich** maneuver has saved many people from choking to death.

Our store, the Furniture Guild, always carries an extensive inventory of **Victorian** furniture.

b. **When well-known descriptive terms, such as nicknames, are used in place of proper nouns, they are capitalized.**

My territory includes all sales districts west of the **Rockies**. (Rocky Mountains)

Most of his business trips have been to the **Windy City**. (Chicago)

Old Hickory was particularly popular with the frontiersmen. (Andrew Jackson)

Several of our colleagues from the **Big Apple** will attend the convention. (New York City)

c. **Sometimes proper nouns, such as the names of widely used commercial products, become common nouns through popular usage.[4] As a result, they are not capitalized. Always capitalize, however, specific brand or trade names of products. Any words that describe the type or kind of product (such as *refrigerator, vacuum cleaner, television, computer,* or *printer*) are not capitalized unless they represent a coined derivative that is considered part of the trade name.**

common noun meaning

Be sure that each address on this mailing list has a **zip code**.

Before computer-aided design these drawings were all done in **india** ink.

---

[3]The capitalization of all adjectives derived from proper nouns is based on entries shown in *Merriam-Webster Collegiate Dictionary,* 10th ed. (Springfield, Mass.: Merriam-Webster, Incorporated, 1999).

[4]Check an up-to-date dictionary to determine which proper nouns have become common nouns and are no longer capitalized. The examples shown here are based on entries from *Merriam-Webster's Collegiate Dictionary,* 10th ed. (Springfield, Mass.: Merriam-Webster, Incorporated, 1999).

Our restaurant serves **french** fries with all sandwiches.

Copies of the **braille** alphabet may be obtained from the Foundation for the Junior Blind.

Reproductions of this statue can easily be made from plaster of **paris.**

How many **china** patterns does Regency carry in its line?

The old-fashioned **venetian** blinds in our reception area should be replaced with attractive vertical blinds.

Did the **thermos** break when it fell off the shelf?

You will find dining at Adagio's Ristorante an **epicurean** delight.

The demand for cars with **diesel** engines is declining steadily.

brand or trade name with common noun product

Did you order a **Sony portable television**?

Our new **Frigidaire freezer** was delivered today.

Please install a tape backup system in this **Compaq computer** for our client.

The **Xerox copier** in our office produces photographic-like colored images.

Does your pharmacy chain carry **Kleenex tissues** exclusively?

product name part of trade name

Your **Amana Radarange** will give you many years of service.

Contact your nearest **Griffin Press-Tiles** dealer for pricing information.

Almost every day for lunch Mr. Rosen orders either a **Filet-O-Fish** or **Chicken McNuggets** from McDonald's.

3–3 Abbreviations

Most abbreviations are capitalized only if the words they represent are capitalized. Exceptions to this rule are the abbreviations of academic degrees and certain coined business expressions. Refer to Section 6–11 for the proper format of abbreviations commonly used in business.

lowercase words represented by lowercase abbreviations

Please send 5 **doz.** hammers **c.o.d.** (*dozen* and *collect on delivery*)

You may contact me anytime after 5:30 **p.m.** (*post meridiem*)

capitalized words represented by capitalized abbreviations

She sat for the **CPA** examination last May. (*Certified Professional Accountant*)

Mrs. Johnson was awarded a bachelor of arts degree from **UCLA** in 1996. (*University of California, Los Angeles*)

exceptions

Our university offers **B.S.** and **M.S.** degrees in psychology through the College of Letters, Arts, and Sciences. (*bachelor of science* and *master of science*)

On this application form please include any other names by which you may be known and precede them with the initials **AKA**. (*also known as*)

3–4 Numbered or Lettered Items

Capitalize word-numeral and word-letter combinations except in the case of page, paragraph, line, size, and verse references.

The word *number* is abbreviated except when it appears at the beginning of a sentence.

capitalized word-numeral and word-letter combinations

A reservation is being held for you on **Flight** 487 to Chattanooga.

Please check **Invoice** B3721 to verify that all items have been shipped.

Did you receive our order for your **Model** D china case?

The meeting is scheduled to be held in **Room** 132 of the Barnard Business Building.

lowercase word-numeral and word-letter combinations

Refer to **page** 3, **paragraph** 2, of the contract for the schedule of project completion.

We are sold out of **size** XL in our Style 483 blazer.

the word* number *abbreviated within a sentence

Have you had an opportunity to restock our supply of **No.** 10 white envelopes?

I believe that my policy, **No.** 68341, covers this kind of injury.

This invoice was paid with our Check **No.** 1253 dated January 25.

the word* number *written out at the beginning of a sentence

Number 145-MD has been out of stock for over three months.

3–5 Personal and Professional Titles[5]

a. **Capitalize the courtesy titles *Mr., Ms., Mrs., Miss, Master,* and *Dr.* when they precede and are used in conjunction with persons' names.**

[5]The principles presented here are based upon those contained in *The Chicago Manual of Style*, 14th ed. (Chicago: The University of Chicago Press, 1993), 240–244.

Capitalize also a title representing a person's profession, company position, military rank, service rank, religious station, or political office when it precedes and is used directly with a person's name *in place of a courtesy title.*

A title representing family relationship or nobility is capitalized when it appears before the name of an individual and is used directly with the name.

courtesy title

Please send copies of this report to **Mr.** Donald Curry and **Dr.** Scot Ober.

Both **Ms.** Bielich and **Mrs.** Scher-Padilla have agreed to serve on the selection committee for this position.

Please inform **Master** Todd Jaffarian that he has been selected as one of the finalists in the "eight-year-old" category of our children's contest.

professional title

The meeting will be chaired by **Professor** Wanda Stitt.

title indicating company position

Although **President** Newton attended the stockholders' meeting, he asked **Vice President** Eleanor Chu from our Minneapolis branch to present the earnings report for this year.

military or service rank title

All medical problems should be referred to **Major** Michael Zimmerman.

These kinds of police matters are under **Captain** Murillo's jurisdiction.

religious title

Please ensure that **Archbishop** Lucatorto receives copies of these financial reports.

The **Reverend** William Trump will be the guest minister for next Sunday's services.

The family has requested that **Rabbi** Cogan conduct the service.

political title

We are looking forward to meeting with **Mayor** Charles Bowshier next Friday.

Please ask **Senator** Rhodes to authorize payment of this invoice.

What time will the networks air **Governor** Reece's address?

title showing family relationship

As soon as **Aunt** Elizabeth's house is sold, her attorney will set up the trust fund.

These U.S. Savings Bonds were given to the children by **Grandpa** Fairbanks.

title of nobility

Several of the recent articles in this magazine have dealt with the life of **Prince** Charles.

This style of furniture dates back to the era of **Queen** Victoria.

b. **A person's title—professional, business, military, service, religious, political, family, or one pertaining to nobility—is not capitalized when it is followed by the person's name used as an appositive.**

She consulted with her **doctor, Linda Montgomery,** about the accident.

I went to see the **executive vice president, F. Ross Byrd**.

Please consult with the **captain, John Blakely,** before making any changes in the boundaries of this precinct.

Such decisions are made solely by the **governor, Paul Whalen**.

Rebecca Dentino inherited the property in Denton, Texas, from her **uncle, Mitchell Marcus**.

c. **In text material, do not capitalize a title that appears after a person's name.**[6]

political title

Tonight at 8 p.m., EST, Bill Clinton, **former president** of the United States, will appear on national television.

Robert Haller, **senator** from Georgia, received an award for outstanding service.

This new bill is awaiting only the signature of Gray Davis, **governor** of California.

military title

Marie Stewart's manuscript deals with the life of Ulysses S. Grant, **commander in chief** of the Union army.

Captain Hogan, the **company commander**, has received new orders from headquarters.

---

[6]The principles presented here are based upon those contained in *The Chicago Manual of Style,* 14th ed. (Chicago: The University of Chicago Press, 1993), 240–44. Some organizations, however, may choose to capitalize the titles of their high-ranking company officals.

business title

You may wish to subpoena Janet Horne, **president** of AMCO Products, to appear in court on May 11.

Carl Irwin, **director of marketing**, wrote the report.

professional title

You will need to address this inquiry to Michael Cornner, **dean of academic affairs**.

If you wish additional information, please contact Laura Jeffreys, **professor of business**, at Simpson Community College.

religious title

Pastor Ellis Jones, **minister** of Ascension Lutheran Church, will deliver the graduation address at Concordia College.

We have invited Dr. David Schultz, **rabbi** of Temple Beth Torah, to give the invocation at the opening banquet of the conference.

d. When a person's title is used in place of his or her name, the title is generally not capitalized. However, in cases of family relationships and direct address, capitalize the title if it *replaces the name*.

Do not capitalize common nouns such as *sir, madam, ladies,* or *gentlemen* used in direct address.

title used in place of name—not capitalized

I was pleased to be able to meet with the **secretary of state** last week.

Please invite the **governor** to attend the conference.

The **auditor** indicated that our books were in order.

After the meeting the **president** directed her **executive assistant** to inform all the department managers that the **director of marketing** had resigned.

family title used in place of name—capitalized

I believe **Grandpa** is eligible for these veteran's benefits.

Do you think **Mother** has a copy of my birth certificate?

family title used as common noun—not capitalized

Both my **mother** and my **father** have personal Web sites on the Internet.

title capitalized in direct address

Did I pass the test, **Professor**?

Yes, **Doctor**, we have your reservation for May 8.

If you wish to change your schedule, **Captain**, please notify me by Friday, May 5.

common noun not capitalized in direct address

I believe, **ladies and gentlemen**, that all our sales personnel will meet their quotas this year.

e. **A person's title is always capitalized in business correspondence when it appears in the inside address, signature line, or envelope address.**

Mrs. Delieu Scopesi, **Director of Human Resources**

Dr. Donald Phelps, **Chancellor**

f. **When the title of an executive officer is used in that organization's formal minutes, bylaws, or rules, it is capitalized. Also capitalize the title of a high-ranking government official when it is used in a formal context (an introduction or acknowledgment).**

The **Treasurer's** report was read and approved.

The **President** will be responsible for the negotiation of all labor contracts.

We gratefully acknowledge the contribution of George L. Bach, **Governor** of Alaska, to promoting research in the conservation of our natural resources.

g. **Descriptive terms such as *ex, elect, late,* and *former* are not capitalized when they are combined with a title.**

ex

Since **ex-**President D. J. Morgan was appointed chairman of the board, our company has prospered.

elect

Councilman-**elect** Norman Rittgers will be sworn in on January 2.

late

The **late** President Eisenhower was an avid golfer.

former

A copy of the report was sent to **former** President Clinton.

3–6 Published and Artistic Works Containing Subdivisions

Capitalize the first letter of the principal words in the title of a published or artistic work. Articles (*a, an, the*), conjunctions (*and, but, or, nor*), and prepositions with three or fewer letters (*of, in, on, to, for, etc.*) are not capitalized unless they appear as the first or last words of the title or as the first word of a subtitle following a colon. The *to* in infinitives (*to write, to exercise, to study*) is also not capitalized unless it appears as the first word in the title or subtitle.

Italicize (or underline, if an italics font is not available) the titles of complete published and artistic works that contain subdivisions. Use italics for the titles of books, magazines, newspapers, booklets, pamphlets, compact disks, plays, musicals, operas, musical albums, Web sites, and other similar works that contain subdivisions such as chapters, articles, columns, acts, episodes, songs, or links. Italicize or underline also the titles of movies and television shows.

book

A copy of *The Random House Dictionary of the English Language* arrived yesterday.

DuPont, the Autobiography of American Enterprise may be purchased at your local bookstore.

Copies of Computers and the Electronic Age will be available next month.

book with subtitle

This question is answered on page 26 of *HOW 9: A Handbook for Office Workers*, 9th edition.

magazine

Use the enclosed coupon to renew your subscription to the *Journal of Higher Education.*

Have you read the latest issue of Better Homes and Gardens?

newspaper

An article in *The Wall Street Journal* yesterday discussed sales trends in our industry.

We will place an advertisement in the Los Angeles Times for nurses and nurses' assistants.

pamphlet or booklet

Distribute copies of *How to Write Effective E-mail Messages* to all members of our administrative staff.

Your Attitude Is Showing is a publication that should be given to all new employees.

Be sure to print at least 500 copies of our new booklet, Employee Programs and Benefits, for distribution to all our employees.

compact disk

For this report I obtained a significant amount of information from Microsoft's *Encarta '99*, an interactive multimedia encyclopedia.

play or musical

Neil Simon's play, *Jake's Women*, was originally performed at the Stevens Center of the North Carolina School of the Arts.

Yesterday we saw the last performance of *Les Miserables*; next month *Phantom of the Opera* will open.

Richard Chamberlain played the leading role in the Los Angeles production of My Fair Lady.

movie title

The latest remake of *Father of the Bride* stars Steve Martin.

Next month local theaters will schedule children's matinees for showings of Disney's *Snow White and the Seven Dwarfs*.

The movie Twelve Angry Men is still considered to be a classic among American films.

television show

Weekly episodes of *Frasier* may currently be viewed on NBC television.

Web site

Have you tried to locate this information through *The Internet Public Library*?

Capitalization 3

3–7 Subdivisions of Published and Artistic Works

a. Capitalize the main words and place in quotation marks the titles of individual chapters, sections, articles, columns, acts, episodes, or songs contained in complete published and artistic works such as books, magazines, booklets, pamphlets, newspapers, compact disks, plays, musicals, operas, television series, and musical albums.

chapter in a book

The last chapter, "Information Processing Systems and Applications," contributed immeasurably to the success of *Contemporary Office Technology and Management*.

section in a pamphlet

Please review the section "Submitting Your Application On-Line" before you apply for a job.

article in a magazine

Did you read "Successful Ideas for the Indoor Gardener" in last month's issue of *Ladies' Home Journal*?

column in a newspaper

Potter's "Financial Outlook" predicted a rising stock market during the next quarter.

section in a compact disk

More detailed information about the big bang theory may be found in "Cosmology" in Microsoft's *Encarta '99.*

act in a play or musical

During the second act, "Homecoming," many people in the audience were tearful.

episode in a television series

"Holiday in London," next week's scheduled broadcast of *Worldwide Travels,* has been postponed.

Rerun marathons of *The Twilight Zone* usually include the popular episode "To Serve Man."

link in a Web site

Just click the "Business Research" link in *CEO Express!* <http://www.ceoexpress.com> to obtain current information on world financial markets.

You may obtain turn-by-turn directions to any address in the city by clicking on "Routes" at *MapsOnUs* <http://www.mapsonus.com>.

b. **In a published work capitalize the first letter of subdivisions such as *preface, contents, glossary, appendix,* and *index* when they refer to a specific work.**

specific work

The rule for punctuating words in a series may be found in the **A**ppendix.

Consult the **I**ndex to find the page on which the explanation of molecular theory begins.

general reference

The **i**ndex generally follows any **a**ppendixes that may be included in a book.

3–8 Published and Artistic Works Without Subdivisions

Capitalize the first letter of the principal words in any title. (See Section 3–6 for an explanation of *principal words.*)

Place in quotation marks the titles of radio programs, poems, songs, paintings, sculptures, and essays—any such published or artistic works that do not contain subdivisions with subtitles.

radio program

Next month we will begin airing our new radio talk show, "Around Cincinnati With Al and Ed."

poem

Her poem "A Mother's Love" has been published in poster format.

song

For his audition Robert Harris chose to sing "Why Can't the English?"

3–9 Unpublished Works

a. **Place the titles of unpublished essays, manuscripts, reports, theses, and dissertations in quotation marks. Capitalize the first letter of the principal words in the title.**

title of a report

Copies of "Report on Progress in Areas of Public Concern" were distributed to the board members last week.

title of a thesis or dissertation

Casey Wong's thesis, "Differences in Accounting Practices of Three Major Accounting Firms As Compared With Accounting Theory Taught in the Three Leading Accounting Textbooks," was approved by the committee last week.

b. **Capitalize the main words and place in quotation marks the titles of lectures and sermons.**

Capitalize the main words and place the subject lines of memorandums and E-mail messages in quotation marks when they are referred to in textual material.

lectures and sermons

Dr. Lipman's dynamic presentation, "Politics and Education," concluded with a challenge the audience could not overlook.

subject line of memorandums or E-mail messages

According to your April 25 E-mail, "Production Schedule Time Line," the Model 483 scanners should be ready for distribution to retail outlets on July 1.

3–10 Headings and Text Headings

a. **In all published or unpublished written works, capitalize the principal words in main headings, secondary headings, centered text headings, and side (or margin) text headings (See Section 3–6 for an explanation of *principal words*.)**

The **A**ge of the **U**niverse
The **S**teady-**S**tate **T**heory
The **B**ig **B**ang **T**heory
Evolution of the **U**niverse

Origins of **C**ommunication
Communication **T**hrough the **A**ges
Communicating at a **D**istance
Developments on the **H**orizon

b. In published and unpublished written works, capitalize only the first word and any proper nouns in paragraph text headings.

Investment in Europe and other foreign markets. During the past year the company has established offices in Frankfurt, London, Paris, Mexico City, and Tokyo. With an overseas staff of 23 and a home office staff of 6 dedicated to enlarging our foreign markets, we expect to . . . .

3–11 Computer Software Program Titles

Capitalize the main words in computer software program titles. Note that in some cases main words are capitalized and written without an intervening space. Follow the format used by the manufacturer. (See Section 3–6 for an explanation of *principal* or *main words*.)

software title written as separate words

Did you use **Microsoft Word** to prepare this manuscript?

Our company has decided to use **Quattro Pro** as its spreadsheet program.

software title written without spaces

What version of **WordPerfect** is your law office presently using?

For high-impact business graphics, you may wish to use **CorelFLOW**.

3–12 Punctuation Format for Literary and Artistic Titles

a. Titles of literary and artistic works are often used in appositive expressions; that is, they are used to rename a previously mentioned noun. In cases where the title is not needed to identify the work, set it off from the rest of the sentence with commas. Where the title is needed for identification, no commas are used.

title unnecessary to determine which article

His latest article, "Marketing Changes in the Automotive Industry," recommended a startling departure from current practices.

title necessary to determine which book

The book *Escape to Riches* should soon make the best-seller list.

b. Periods and commas are *always* placed before the closing quotation mark; semicolons and colons *always* follow the closing quotation mark.

period and comma before closing quotation mark

Hawaii is the location of our new episode, "Mousetrap."

Your last article, "Computerized Accounting Procedures in the Banking Industry," was certainly helpful to me in planning our new system.

semicolon and colon after closing quotation mark

Several hundred readers have requested reprints of your article "Diversifying Your Investment Portfolio"; these reprints will be mailed within the next three weeks.

The following newscasters appear nightly in "Kansas City Reports": Rod Whitcomb, Erika Lovejoy, Steve Markham, and Lisa Darnell.

c. Question or exclamation marks appearing with and at the end of quoted titles are placed before the closing quotation mark. If the question or exclamation mark in a title appears at the end of the sentence, no other form of punctuation is required. However, if the sentence, not the title, is a question or exclamation, place the ending punctuation mark outside the closing quotation mark.

quoted title phrased as question in middle of sentence

The article "Are You Getting the Most for Your Investment Dollars?" will appear next month in our quarterly newsletter to all banking customers.

Have you read the article "Are You Getting the Most for Your Investment Dollars?" that appeared in our last month's newsletter?

statement with quoted title phrased as question at end of sentence

This week's feature article was entitled "What Is Earthquake Readiness?"

question with quoted title phrased as question at end of sentence

Have you read this week's feature article, "What Is Earthquake Readiness?"

quoted title separate from question

What percent of our subscribers read "Talk of the Town"?

3–13 Academic Courses and Subjects

a. The names of numbered courses and specific course titles are capitalized.

names of numbered courses

How many students are enrolled in **Computer Science** 43?

To fulfill your degree requirements, you must complete the following courses: **Psychology** 182, **Anthropology** 1, and **Music** 30.

specific course title

You are scheduled to teach two sections of **Introduction to the Internet** next semester.

Last year Tina took **Speech 125, Introduction to Public Debate**.

b. Capitalize only proper nouns in the names of academic subject areas.

subject area

Please encourage Ms. Harris to take an **accounting** class this spring.

Our college offers over 20 different **history** classes.

subject area containing proper noun

I earned an "A" in my **business English** class.

Perhaps you should take a course in **conversational French** before you leave for Paris.

3–14 Academic Degrees

a. **References to academic degrees are generally not capitalized unless they are used after and in conjunction with the name of an individual.**

general reference

Bill Clark will be awarded a **bachelor of science** degree this June.

She earned her **master's** last summer.

after person's name

Joyce Mooneyhan, **Doctor of Divinity**, will deliver the opening address.

b. **Capitalize abbreviations of academic degrees appearing after a person's name. Remember, though, that the *h* in *Ph.D.* appears in lowercase form.**

Make your check payable to Lawrence W. Erickson, **M.D.**

Marcia McKenzie, **Ph.D.**, will join our clinic in June as a staff psychologist.

James Bennett, **D.D.S., M.D.**, is an excellent oral surgeon.

We have asked Louise Peebles, **D.B.A.**, to be our speaker.

3–15 Organizations

a. **Principal words in the names of all organizations—business, civic, educational, governmental, labor, military, philanthropic, political, professional, religious, and social—are capitalized. Articles (*a, an, the*), conjunctions (*and, but, or, nor*), and prepositions with three or fewer letters (*of, in, on, to, for,* etc.) are not capitalized.**

Boston **C**hamber of **C**ommerce
Los **A**ngeles **B**oard of **E**ducation
Arizona **D**epartment of **M**otor **V**ehicles
Twenty-third **C**ongressional **D**istrict
Foundation for the **J**unior **B**lind
United **S**tates **D**epartment of **D**efense
Young **R**epublicans **C**lub
National **C**ouncil of **C**hurches
Porter **V**alley **C**ountry **C**lub
Tactical **A**ir **C**ommand
American **C**ancer **S**ociety
Illinois **B**ar **A**ssociation
Dream**W**orks
Metro-**G**oldwyn-**M**ayer

b. **When the word *the* precedes the organizational name and is officially part of the name, it must be capitalized.**

We received two letters from **The** Prudential Insurance Company.

c. **When the common noun element of an organization's name is used in place of the full name, it is generally not capitalized. In formal documents and in specific references to national government bodies, however, capitalize the shortened form.**

general communication

All employees of the **company** are allowed ten days' sick leave each year.

The **board of education** convened for a special meeting yesterday to consider the budget crisis.

Two members from our local **chamber** received presidential appointments.

So far only two members of the **city council** have agreed to support our rapid transit proposal.

formal communication

As agent for the **Association**, I am authorized to sign the convention contracts.

On July 15, 2001, the **Company** acquired several additional holdings.

national government bodies

This important bill is now before the **House**. (United States House of Representatives)

Three **Cabinet** members were interviewed by the press. (President's Cabinet)

When will **Congress** reconvene? (United States Congress)

Who is presently majority leader of the **Senate**? (United States Senate)

This issue is now before the **Supreme Court**. (United States Supreme Court)

d. **Government terms such as *federal, government,* and *nation* are often used in place of their respective full names. Because they are used so often and are considered terms of general classification, they are not capitalized.**

federal

Veterans Day is a holiday for all **federal** employees.

government

The **government** is concerned about inflation and its effect on the economy.

Loans such as these are fully guaranteed by the **federal government**.

nation

The **nation** has been able to overcome a number of crises.

e. **Principal words in the official name of a division or department within a business organization are capitalized. When a division or department is referred to by its function because the official or specific name is unknown, do not capitalize this reference.**

Always capitalize main words in a division or department name used in a return address, an inside address, a signature block, or an envelope address.

official or specific name

Please notify the **Department of Human Resources** if you are going to be absent from work.

This contract must be signed by two members of the **Board of Directors**.

A check for this amount must first be approved by the manager of our **Accounting Department**.

We will send a copy of our official findings to your **Department of Research and Development**.

Will you be able to send a member from your **Information Processing Department** to the conference?

official or specific name unknown

The efficiency of your **accounting department** can be increased by using our new computer software.

A member of your **advertising department** may wish to contact one of our account executives to take advantage of this rare opportunity.

return address, inside address, signature block, or envelope address

Mr. Gary Packler, Manager, **C**redit **D**epartment

f. **Capitalize the principal words in the names of departments, bureaus, divisions, offices, and agencies in government organizations.**

We will forward this information to the **Department of Health and Human Services** within the next week.

Have you contacted the **Bureau of Indian Affairs** about this matter?

You may obtain copies of the proposed freeway route from the **Division of Highways**.

This case is under investigation by the **Office of Internal Affairs**.

To work for the **Federal Bureau of Investigation**, you must first receive a security clearance.

g. **Capitalize the main words in the names of specific departments, divisions, and offices within educational institutions. Main words in the names of schools or colleges within universities are also capitalized.**

educational departments, divisions, or offices

Each year the **Music Department** of Banning High School sponsors a spring music festival.

Does Professor Joyce Arntson teach in the **Social Science Division**?

All such budget requests must be submitted to the **Office of Educational Services** by June 30.

Please send your application for admission to the **Admissions Office** by November 1.

university schools or colleges

I am presently taking courses in the **School of Business and Economics** at Kentview State University.

The major in which you are interested is offered in the **College of Letters, Arts, and Sciences**.

3–16 Geographical Locations

a. **The names of places—for example, specific continents, countries, islands, states, cities, streets, mountains, valleys, parks, oceans, lakes, rivers, canals, bays, and harbors—are capitalized. When a geographical term (such as *city, street, bay,* or *island*) appears directly after a place name, it is considered part of the name and is capitalized. Terms used in this way are capitalized in both singular and plural forms.**

A geographical term appearing before the name of a place is generally not capitalized. Capitalize the term only if (1) it is part of the official name or (2) it is used by the governing bodies of that place as part of an official name.

specific place

Our products are distributed throughout **North America**.

Does any airline have a direct flight from **Kansas City** to **New York City**?

Customers in the **Hawaiian Islands** will soon be serviced by their own branch office in **Honolulu**.

The magazine article dealt mainly with camping facilities on the **Colorado River**.

We have a number of tours that take foreign visitors to **Yellowstone National Park**.

Many of our shipments are brought here through the **Panama Canal**.

Property taxes in **Ventura County** have risen steadily during the past five years.

specific places—geographical term in plural form

The excursion will include trips on both the **Mississippi and Missouri Rivers**.

Most of our discoveries have been in the **San Bernardino and San Gorgonio Mountains**.

The new shopping mall is located on the corner of **59th and State Streets**.

geographical term appearing before specific place—not capitalized

Most of our business is conducted within the **state** of Utah.

The **city** of Los Angeles was selected as the site for our next convention.

The estimated 2005 population for the **county** of Ventura is 953,609.

geographical term appearing before specific place—capitalized

Most of our suppliers are located in the **City of Industry**. (Geographical term part of city name.)

The **City of Los Angeles** has approved a new budget plan. (Geographical term used by governing body as part of official name.)

Did the **State of California** adopt a new automobile insurance plan for low-risk drivers? (Geographical term used by governing body as part of official name.)

b. Capitalize nicknames of geographical locations and names of regional areas that have evolved as a result of usage.

geographical nicknames

All our pineapples come directly from the **Aloha State**. (Hawaii)

When were the Olympics held in the **City of Angels**? (Los Angeles)

How many times each year must you go to the **Big Apple**? (New York City)

This year our convention will be held in the **Windy City**. (Chicago)

regional names emerging from usage

Many of our clients are from **Upstate New York**.

Police reports indicate that the **Lower East Side** has the highest crime rate in our city.

Merchants from the **Greater Los Angeles Area** have banded together to support this worthwhile project.

Many residents in the **Bay Area** are concerned about the pollution occurring in San Francisco Bay.

c. **Points of the compass are capitalized when they are used as simple or compound nouns to designate *specific regions*. Points of the compass are not capitalized, however, when they are used to indicate *direction* or *general localities*.**

specific regions

Firms connected with the aerospace industry are heavily concentrated in the **West** and **Southwest**.

Our company has increased its trade to the **Far East**.

The festival was held in **East Los Angeles**.

Sales in our **Southern Region** have increased 25 percent during the past year.

Within the next month we will expand our operations into **East Texas**.

directions

My territory includes all states **east** of the Mississippi River.

The consultant's report recommended that our new plant be located just **northwest** of Baltimore.

To avoid the harsh winter weather, many retirees travel **south** or **west** during the snow season.

By taking the **eastbound** on-ramp, you will get to the center of Madison.

general localities

The **southern** part of our state is suffering a severe drought.

Our delivery service is restricted to the **east** side of Miami.

Customers from the **northwest** section of the city have registered more complaints than customers from any other sector.

Did you survey most of the **western** states?

This new weather stripping is guaranteed to protect you against the severity of **northern** winters.

d. **Words derived from simple or compound nouns representing *specific* regions are capitalized.**

A number of **Midwesterners** have inquired about our franchises.

Southern Californians are known for their casual lifestyle.

This survey includes responses only from **Easterners**.

Atlanta is known for its **Southern** hospitality.

3–17 Dates, Time Periods, and Events

Capitalize days of the week, months of the year, holidays (including religious days), specific special events, and specific historical events or periods.

The names of seasons, decades, and centuries are generally not capitalized. If, however, a season is combined with a year, capitalize the season.

day of week and month

Our committee will meet the first **Monday** in **March**, **June**, **September**, and **December**.

holiday

Will our store be closed on **New Year's Day** this year?

Each year **Veterans Day** is observed on a different date.

specific special event

Our company will celebrate its **Silver Anniversary** next year.

National Secretaries' Week is traditionally observed during the latter part of April.

This year the **Maricopa County Fair** will be held from September 4 through September 27.

How many of your staff members will be attending the **NBEA Convention** this year?

historical event or period

In our **Information Age** the Internet is taking an increasingly important role.

The stock market crash of 1929 brought the **Roaring Twenties** to a dismal end and catapulted our country into the **Great Depression**.

During the **Industrial Revolution** children were often forced to work long hours under intolerable conditions.

season

Our biggest sales item during this **spring** season has been the Model 550 patio set.

None of the **winter** coats we ordered have arrived yet.

If you wish to enroll for the **fall** semester, please submit your application by August 15.

We have received your application for admission for the **Winter 2002** quarter.

decade

During the past year a number of movies portraying life in the **sixties** have been released.

This company was founded in the early **fifties** by Jonathan Hunt.

century

Technological developments during the **twentieth century** have advanced the human race further than all other developments during our previous history.

Many of Mr. Ryan's critics believe that he operates his business on **nineteenth-century** management principles.

3–18 Ethnic and Religious References

a. **Ethnic-related terms (references to a particular language, race, or culture) are capitalized. Generic terms such as *black, white,* and *brown* when used in reference to race are generally not capitalized.**

language

A knowledge of both **German** and **English** is required for the job.

race

The census indicated that many **Asians** are living in this area.

Courses in **African-American** history and culture are taught in many major colleges and universities throughout the United States.

Several **black** leaders have asked to address the city council on this issue.

culture

Cinco de Mayo is observed with many festivities in the **Mexican-American** community.

The predominant native language of **Hispanics** is Spanish, but a significant number claim Portuguese as their native tongue.

b. **Capitalize references to specific religious groups.**

Massive opposition from **Catholic**, **Protestant**, and **Jewish** clergy led to the defeat of this proposed legislation.

A **Mormon** temple will be built on this site in 2004.

3–19 Celestial Bodies

Capitalize the names of celestial bodies—planets, planet satellites, stars, constellations, and asteroids. Do not capitalize the terms *earth, sun,* and *moon,* however, unless they are used as the names of specific bodies in the solar system.

capitalized

We have been studying the orbital paths of **Mars** and **Earth**.

Can you pick out the **North Star** or the **Big Dipper** among the many stars in the sky?

Capitalization 3

When will **Earth** next pass between the **Sun** and the **Moon**?

The background of the scene embraces a darkened sky highlighted only by an array of stars and **Saturn** with its bright rings.

lowercase

Television broadcasts of the first **moon** landing were viewed by millions of Americans.

None of the pieces from the satellite found their way back into the **earth's** atmosphere.

Rays from the **sun** can damage your skin and subsequently cause skin cancer.

Chapter 4

Number Formats and Applications

0.2 / $^{2}/_{10}$ / 20%

Number Formats and Applications Solution Finder

General Format

4–1 General Rules for Numbers

a. A number that begins a sentence *must be* expressed in word form. When the number cannot be written in one or two words, however, change the word order of the sentence so that the number does not begin the sentence. Then write the number in figures. This number rule takes precedence over all others.

number written in words

Twenty-four people responded to our Internet job posting for a senior accountant.

sentence order rearranged for figure form

The questionnaire was returned by **260** individuals who had purchased goods or services on-line. (Not: *Two hundred sixty* [or *260*] individuals . . . returned the questionnaire.)

b. Numbers *one* through *ten* used in a general way are written in words. Write such numbers above *ten* in figures, except those used to begin a sentence (See Section 4–1a). This rule applies only to those numbers not governed by any other number-usage rule.

number ten or below

Would you please ship us **four** additional copies of this software program.

number above ten

We have received **12** letters of complaint about service in our Springfield office during the last month.

Thirty-three of our present employees will not be moving with us to our Santa Maria location.

c. Approximations above *ten* that can be expressed in one or two words may be written in either figures or words. Keep in mind that figures are more emphatic and conform to the rule for the use of general numbers.

approximation written in figures

Nearly **500** people sent letters or faxes to the governor protesting the proposed sales tax increase.

approximation written in words

He expected over **fifty** people to preregister for the conference.

d. Numbers below *100* that are written in word form are hyphenated if they are written as two words; that is, compound numbers *21* through *99* are hyphenated if they are spelled out.

Twenty-seven of the homes in this development were sold last month.

e. **Round numbers in the millions or billions are expressed in a combination of figures and words. Only *one million* used as an approximation is usually written in all word form; otherwise, it is written *1 million*.**

round number

Captain Maez has flown nearly **2 million** miles since he earned his wings.

round number with fraction

Our company manufactured over **3½ billion** pens for worldwide distribution last year.

round number with decimal

Will we exceed our production quota of **1.2 million** automobiles?

one million *as an approximation*

Look to establish additional locations in cities with populations of more than **one million**.

1 million *as an exact figure*

We will recover all development and marketing costs once we have sold **1 million** of these special bolts.

4–2 Related Numbers

a. **Numbers used in a comparable or corresponding manner in the same document are considered related numbers and should be expressed in the same form. Therefore, write numbers *one* through *ten* in figures when they are used with related numbers above *ten*.**

Of the **130** items inspected, only **2** were found to be defective.

Next week we will deliver the **9** reams of laser paper, the **24** boxes of envelopes, and the **2** file trays that were back ordered for you. (Note that items appearing in a series are always considered to be related.)

b. **Round numbers in the millions or billions are expressed in figures when they are used with related numbers below a million or with related numbers that cannot be expressed in a combination of words and figures.**

***combined with number below* 1 million**

Our production of umbrellas rose from **970,000** to **2,000,000** this year.

combined with number over* 1 million *written in figures

During the past two years, our circulation has risen from nearly **3,000,000** copies to **3,875,500** copies.

c. **Unrelated numbers used in the same sentence are considered individually to determine whether they should be expressed in words or figures.**

unrelated numbers in same sentence

Please send each of the **four** vice presidents **15** copies of our monthly report.

For this banquet each of the **14** tables should seat **eight** people.

combination of related and unrelated numbers in same sentence

Our warehouse inventory of **22** dishwashers, **17** refrigerators, and **8** washing machines must be distributed among our **three** stores. (Items in a series are always related.)

These new packing boxes hold **four** cartons that contain **12** bottles each whereas the old boxes held **six** cartons that contained **6** bottles each. (*Cartons* is related to *cartons*; *bottles* is related to *bottles*.)

4–3 Number Format

a. **Numbers expressed as figures are separated by commas into groups of three digits. Exceptions include years, house numbers, telephone numbers, fax numbers, zip codes, serial numbers, page numbers, decimal fractions, and metric measurements. Metric measurements of five or more digits are separated into groups of three with spaces.**

commas in figures with more than three digits

4,782	17,750	385,450	2,865,000	1,567,874,500

no commas in certain figures

2002	Serial No. 14896-AN	1111 Figueroa Street
page 1032	Evansville, IN 47701-1957	(805) 555-6132
0.7534	1000 kilometers	

space in metric measures with five or more digits

Our dairy delivers over **45 000** liters of milk daily to homes in this city.

b. **When two independent figures appear consecutively (one directly after the other) in a sentence, separate the figures with a comma.**

By **2001, 52** homes had been built around the golf course.

Of the **325, 72** questionnaires were not returned.

c. **Two consecutive numbers that act as adjectives modifying the same noun are *not* separated by a comma. Instead, write the first number in words and the second one in figures. If the first number cannot be expressed in *one or two words*, place it in figures also.**

Numbers 4

two numbers modifying a noun, word-figure form

We processed your order for **twelve 48-inch** glass tabletops today.

Each package contains **twenty 3-inch** nails.

Did you order **seventy 50-watt** bulbs?

Each box contains **twelve 6-pack** cartons of Coke.

Our contract calls for **three 25-second** commercials during this broadcast.

The contractor will build **thirty-six 5-bedroom** houses on this land.

two numbers modifying a noun, figure-figure form

Please purchase **150 33-cent** stamps from the post office.

The bank has agreed to finance your purchase of a **1999 30-foot** mobile home.

The prescription was for **175 25-milligram** tablets.

d. **Separate volume numbers from page references with commas. Weights, capacities, and measures that consist of several words are treated as single units and are not separated by commas.**

volume and page number

This information may be found in **Volume IV, page 289**.

weight as a single unit

The Millers' newborn weighed **7 pounds 3 ounces** at birth.

capacity as a single unit

In conventional terms the capacity of the pitcher is **2 quarts 1 cup**.

measure as a single unit

Mr. Knight verified that the room length measured **28 feet 4 inches**.

The flight time has been calculated to be **4 hours 20 minutes**.

e. **The plural of a figure is formed by adding *s*.**

How many **7s** do you see in this serial number?

The **1900s** will be noted for man's first successes in space travel.

Numbers Expressed in Figure Form

4–4 Money

a. **Amounts of money *$1 or more* are expressed in figures. Omit the decimal and zeros in expressing whole dollar amounts, even if they appear with mixed dollar amounts.**

money expressed in figures

We paid **$284.95** for this new Microlite cellular telephone.

omission of decimal and zeros

The list of purchases included items for **$3**, $6.50, $79.45, **$200**, and **$265**.

b. **Amounts of money *less than $1* are expressed in figures combined with the word *cents* unless they are used in conjunction with related amounts of *$1 or more*. Unrelated amounts of money appearing in the same sentence, however, are treated separately.**

amounts less than $1

Last week the basic bus fare was increased from **60 cents** to **75 cents**.

related amounts of money

To mail the three reports, I paid **$.85, $1.40**, and **$2** in postage.

unrelated amounts of money

The tax on this **$8** item was **52 cents**.

c. **Round amounts of money in millions or billions of dollars are expressed in combined figure and word form except when they are used with related dollar figures below a million or related amounts that can be expressed in figures only.**

round amount

The cost of the new building was over **$12½ million**.

Nearly **$3.5 billion** in assets provides the customer confidence that has made Liberty Mutual the largest federal savings bank in the country.

related to amount less than $1 million

We estimate that **$850,000** will be needed to retool the Wilmington plant and **$2,000,000** will be needed for the Van Nuys plant.

related to amount that can be expressed in figures only

Our sales decreased from **$12,458,000** last year to less than **$12,000,000** this year.

d. **Amounts of money in legal documents are expressed in words followed by the figure amount contained in parentheses. The word *and* is used only to introduce cents included in a money amount written in word form.**

round dollar amounts

The Company shall pay up to **One Thousand Dollars ($1,000)** within 90 days upon receipt of a valid release statement.

The amount of indebtedness incurred by the defendant during this period was **Ten Thousand Five Hundred Eighty-three Dollars ($10,583)**.

dollar amount with cents

A check for **Two Thousand Four Hundred Sixty-one Dollars and Forty-eight Cents ($2,461.48)** was received from Westin Industries on May 3.

4–5 Decimals and Percentages

a. **Numbers containing decimals are expressed in figures. To prevent misreading, place a zero before a decimal that does not contain a whole number or begin with a zero.**

decimal with whole number

Our trucks average **12.843** miles per gallon of gasoline.

decimal beginning with 0

This part must be made within **.002** inch of specifications.

decimal not containing whole number or beginning with 0

Only **0.4** percent of all items manufactured this year were rejected because of defective workmanship.

b. **Write percentages in figures followed by the word *percent*. The percent symbol (%) is used only for statistical or technical tables or forms.**

percent used in sentence format

Last month we were able to decrease our energy consumption by only **1 percent**.

This year's travel expenses are up **8 percent** over last year's.

A **12½ percent** pay increase was granted to all office employees.

We expect a **0.5 percent** increase in sales tax this year—from **6 percent** to **6.5 percent**.

% used in statistical tables or forms

32.5%　　80%　　99.9%　　4.3%　　6%　　0.8%

4–6 U.S. Standard Weights and Measures

a. **For quick comprehension express in figures the amount something weighs or measures. Weights and measures (inches, feet, yards, miles, kilometers, ounces, pounds, tons, grams, pints, quarts, gallons, liters, each, dozen, gross, reams, pecks, bushels, degrees, acres, etc.), however, are written out fully in words. Abbreviations or symbols**

representing these units are limited to use in business forms or statistical materials.

general use

This carton is **3 pounds 6 ounces** in excess of the U.S. Postal Service weight limitations.

Over **2 tons** of waste material leave the plant daily.

According to *The Weather Channel* <www.weather.com>, **87 degrees** is the forecasted high for Los Angeles on Tuesday.

Approximately **150 square yards** of carpeting will be needed for this office.

Use **3-inch** screws for this job.

use for forms and statistical materials

4 doz. 12 yd. 84° 9# 9 ft. 85 lb. 12 ea.

b. Standard measures of length may be expressed in mils, inches, feet, yards, rods, furlongs, miles, and leagues. Standard weights may be expressed in grains, drams, ounces, pounds, hundredweights, and tons. Standard capacities may be expressed in teaspoons, tablespoons, ounces, cups, pints, quarts, gallons, pecks, and bushels. The following tables provide equivalents for various standard measures of length, weight, and capacity:

standard measures of length

1 mil	=	0.001 inch
1 inch	=	1,000 mils
12 inches	=	1 foot
3 feet	=	1 yard
16.5 feet	=	1 rod
40 rods	=	1 furlong
8 furlongs or 5,280 feet	=	1 mile
3 miles	=	1 league (land)

standard measures of weight

1 grain	=	0.036 drams
1 dram	=	27.34 grains
16 drams or 437.5 grains	=	1 ounce
16 ounces or 7,000 grains	=	1 pound
100 pounds	=	1 hundredweight
2,000 pounds	=	1 ton

standard measures of capacity

3 teaspoons or 0.5 ounce	=	1 tablespoon
2 tablespoons	=	1 ounce
16 tablespoons or 8 ounces	=	1 cup
2 cups or 16 ounces	=	1 pint
2 pints, 4 cups, or 32 ounces	=	1 quart
4 quarts or 128 ounces	=	1 gallon
8 quarts	=	1 peck
4 pecks	=	1 bushel

4–7 Metric Weights and Measures

a. **The most common metric measurements are based on meters, grams, and liters. Prefixes indicating fractions and multiples of these quantities follow:**

fractions

deci (1/10) centi (1/100) milli (1/1000)

multiples

deka (× 10) hecto (× 100) kilo (× 1000)

b. **Express metric measurements in figures. Use a space to separate numbers of five or more digits into groups of three. No space or comma is used with four-digit figures.**

regular metric measures

We will be using **1.75-liter** bottles for our large-size apple juice.

Our new package of pie crust sticks weighs 11 ounces, which equals **311 grams** or **3.11 hectograms**.

four-digit figures

The distance from Memphis to Boston is over **2000 kilometers**.

The central office ordered **1500 kilograms** of flour and **1200 kilograms** of sugar to be delivered to our bakeries throughout the state.

five-digit figures

His 5 acres is equal to approximately 2 hectares, that is, approximately **20 000 square meters**.

c. **For general correspondence spell out units of measure. Abbreviate units of measure only in technical writing, medical reports, or any kind of forms.**

general correspondence

10 millimeters 4 liters 80 kilometers

technical writing, medical reports, or forms

60 mm 6 mg 25 km 100 cc

d. The following tables show equivalents for metric and standard measures of length, weight, and capacity:

equivalents for measures of length

Metric to Standard	*Standard to Metric*
1 kilometer = 0.6214 (5/8) mile	1 mile = 1.609 kilometers
1 meter = 1.0936 yards	1 yard = 0.9144 meter (exact)
1 meter = 39.37 inches	1 foot = 0.3048 meter (exact)
1 centimeter = 0.3937 (2/5) inch	1 inch = 2.54 centimeters (exact)

equivalents for measures of weight

Metric to Standard	*Standard to Metric*
1 ton (or tonne) = 1.1023 tons	1 ton = 0.90721 ton (or tonne)
1 kilogram = 2.2046 pounds	1 pound = 453.592 grams
1 kilogram = 35 ounces	1 ounce = 28.35 grams
1 gram = 0.035 ounce	

equivalents for measures of capacity

Metric to Standard	*Standard to Metric*
1 hectoliter (hl) = 2.838 bushels	1 bushel = 35.239 liters
1 liter (L) = 0.264 liquid gallon	1 liquid gallon = 3.785 liters
1 liter (L) = 1.057 liquid quarts	1 liquid quart = 0.946 liter
1 liter (L) = 0.908 dry quart	1 dry quart = 1.101 liters
1 milliliter (ml) } = 0.034 fluid ounce	1 fluid ounce = 29.537 milliliters
1 cubic centimeter (cc) } = 0.034 fluid ounce	

e. Two common scales measure temperature: Fahrenheit and Celsius. In Fahrenheit 32 degrees is the point at which water freezes and 212 degrees is the point at which water boils. In Celsius water freezes at 0-degree temperature and boils at 100 degrees.

To convert Celsius temperatures to Fahrenheit, apply the following formula: (Celsius temperature × 1.8) + 32. To convert Fahrenheit temperatures to Celsius, use this formula: (Fahrenheit temperature – 32) ÷ 1.8. The following table illustrates some common conversions:

Fahrenheit to Celsius		*Celsius to Fahrenheit*	
32	0	0	32
40	4	5	41
45	7	10	50
50	10	15	59
55	13	20	68
60	16	25	77
65	18	30	86
70	21	35	95
75	24	40	104
80	27	45	113
85	29	50	122
90	32	100	212
95	35		
100	38		
212	100		

Normal body temperature is **98.6 degrees Fahrenheit** or **37 degrees Celsius**.

The high temperature yesterday in Madrid was **31°C**—or **87°F**.

4–8 Numbers Used With Words, Abbreviations, and Symbols

a. Numbers used directly with words are placed in figures. Page numbers, model numbers, policy numbers, and serial numbers are just a few of the instances in which numerals are used with words. The words preceding the numerals are usually capitalized except for page, paragraph, line, size, and verse references. (See Section 3–4 for capitalization format.)

model number

We ordered your **Model 3** printer for our Information Processing Center.

Our **Model No. 87** magazine rack has been discontinued.

policy and serial numbers

Please return your copy of **Policy 1284691D** to the home office.

Our IBM computer, **Serial No. A32-74603552**, was reported missing from the office.

page number

You will find a picture of this economy unit on **page 21** of our current catalog.

b. Direct reference to the word *number* is the most common instance in which figures are used with an abbreviation. The word *number* is abbreviated in this case except when it appears at the beginning of a sentence.

We expect to replace our camera equipment with your **No. 378** series.

The following checks were returned by your bank: **Nos. 487, 492, and 495**.

Numbers 381, 1209, and 1628 were the winning raffle tickets.

c. The use of symbols is generally avoided in business writing. However, for preparing forms (such as invoices and orders), charts, tables, and other documents where space is limited, symbols are used liberally. Numbers expressed with symbols are written in figures.

2/10, N/30 8% #455

Time

4–9 Dates

a. When the day is written after the month, use cardinal figures (*1, 2, 3,* etc.). Ordinal figures (*1st, 2nd, 3rd,* etc.) are used for expressing days that appear before the month or that stand alone.

month followed by day

March 23, 2003, is the deadline for filing your claim.

Your **October 15** payment is now 30 days past due.

day appearing before month

We expect payment in full by the **10th of April**.

Our new offices should be ready for occupancy by the **3rd of June**.

day used alone

Your reservations for the **9th** and the **24th** have been confirmed.

Please send us your rental payment by the **1st** of each month.

b. Dates used in most domestic business correspondence are expressed in terms of month, day, and year with a comma separating the day and year. In military and international correspondence, dates are generally written day, month, and year without an intervening comma.

domestic business correspondence

November 27, 2002

military or international correspondence

27 November 2002

4–10 Clock Time

a. Figures are used with *a.m., p.m., noon,* or *midnight* to express clock time. Omit the colon and zeros with even times, even if they appear in conjunction with times expressed in hours and minutes.

The terms *noon* and *midnight* may be used with or without the figure *12*. When these terms are used with other clock times containing *a.m.* and/or *p.m.*, however, include the figure *12*. Never use *a.m.* or *p.m.* following *12, noon,* or *midnight*.

a.m., p.m., noon, midnight *with figures*

His plane was scheduled to arrive at **1 p.m.**, but the actual arrival time was **2:27 p.m.**

Our next plant tour will begin at **10:30 a.m.** and conclude by **12 noon**.

The afternoon shift is scheduled from **4 p.m.** until **12 midnight**.

noon *and* midnight *with the figure* 12

She left promptly at **12 noon**.

The new shift starts at **12 midnight**.

This postal station is open Saturdays from **8 a.m.** until **12 noon**.

This Internet site permits access only from **8 a.m.** until **12 midnight**.

noon *and* midnight *without the figure* 12

May we please have your answer before **noon** on July 30.

All envelopes containing tax payments must be postmarked before **midnight**, April 15.

b. Either word or figure form may be used with *o'clock*.

We must leave the office by **eight o'clock** [or **8 o'clock**] if we are to arrive at the airport on time.

c. Phrases such as "in the morning," "in the afternoon," or "at night" may follow clock times expressed with *o'clock* but not with *a.m.* or *p.m.*

Coffee breaks are scheduled at **10 o'clock in the morning** and at **3 o'clock in the afternoon**.

By **two o'clock in the afternoon**, our campus is almost empty; but by **seven o'clock in the evening**, it is filled with students attending night classes.

d. When even clock hours of the day are expressed without *a.m., p.m.,* or *o'clock,* use word form. Either word or figure form may be used, however, when both hours and minutes are expressed.

exact hour

The board meeting is scheduled to begin at **eight** tonight.

hour and minutes

The committee meeting was not adjourned until **6:30** [or **six-thirty**].

The power shut off at **9:05** [or **five after nine**] this morning but resumed operation before **10:30** [or **ten-thirty**].

4–11 Periods of Time

a. Periods of time relating to *days, weeks, months,* or *years* that can be expressed in one or two words are usually written in word form when they are used in a general way. Periods of time that cannot be expressed in one or two words are written in figure form.

General references to clock hours, minutes, or seconds are treated as general numbers: numbers *ten* and below are written in word form and numbers above *ten* are written in figure form.

general time period—days, weeks, months, or years

During the past **sixteen months**, we have shown a slight profit.

We have been in this location for **thirty-two years**.

The auto workers' strike lasted **117 days**.

general references to clock time

Each candidate's speech is limited to **five minutes**.

We offer **24-hour** repair service to all our subscribers.

b. Time-period data related to specific loan lengths, discount rates, interest rates, payment terms, credit terms, or other such information dealing with definite business contracts are expressed in figures.

This loan must be paid in full within **90 days**.

We give a 2 percent discount on all invoices paid within **10 days** of the invoice date.

You have been granted a 9 percent loan for **6 months**.

4–12 Ages and Anniversaries

Ages and anniversaries that can be expressed in one or two words are generally written in word form; those that require more than two words are written in figures. Figures are also used when an age (1) appears directly after a person's name; (2) is used in a legal or technical sense; or (3) is expressed in terms of years, months, and sometimes days. Note that no commas are used to separate the years, months, and days in the expression of ages.

general expression of ages and anniversaries

David will be **twenty-seven** on August 9; his son John will be **three** the same day.

The staff was surprised that Mrs. Wong retired the day after her **fifty-fifth** birthday.

Next month we will celebrate our manager's **twenty-fifth** anniversary with the company.

Our city will celebrate its **150th** anniversary in 2004.

age after name

Ms. Soderstrom, **47**, was promoted to branch manager last week.

age used in technical or legal sense

Employees no longer must retire at the age of **65**.

The legal voting age is **18**.

At **25** you will be eligible for these reduced insurance rates.

age in years, months, and days

According to our records, the insured was **35** years **5** months and **28** days of age upon cancellation of the policy.

Addresses and Telephone Numbers

4–13 Addresses

a. **House numbers are expressed in figures except for the house number *One*. No commas are used to separate digits in house numbers.**

One Alpha Street

One East Broward Boulevard

4 Headquarters Plaza North

18817 Clearview Avenue

b. **Street names that are numbered *ten* or below are expressed in word form with ordinal numbers (*First, Second, Third,* etc.). Street names numbered above *ten* are written in ordinal figures (*st, nd, rd, th*).**

street name ten or below

All visitors to New York City must stroll down **Fifth** Avenue.

Mail your payment to our office at 200 West **Second** Street, Winston-Salem, North Carolina 27101-4036

street name above ten

Please send this order to 1111 **23rd** Street, Denver, Colorado 80205-2145.

His former address is listed as 3624 West **59th** Place.

c. **Apartment numbers, suite numbers, box numbers, and route numbers are expressed in figure form.**

1883 Creek Avenue, Apt. **4**

Post Office Box **1584**

Plaza Medical Building, Suite **102**

Rural Route **2**

d. **Zip codes are expressed in figures (without commas) and typed a single space after the state. Address lines containing zip + 4 are written in the same manner as those containing five-digit zip codes. The only difference is that the four extra digits are separated from the zip code with a hyphen.**

sentence format

Ms. Sherman requested that the refund be sent to her at Pasadena City College, 1570 East Colorado Boulevard, Pasadena, California **91106-2003**.

Redirect this order to Palmer Enterprises, 1586 North Cicero Avenue, Chicago, Illinois **60651-1618.**

inside address or envelope address

Mr. Arthur M. Manuel
7820½ South Eighth Avenue
Inglewood, CA **90305-1004**

Mrs. Janice Harrington
1073 23rd Street, Apt. 2
Moonachie, NJ **07074**

Ms. Eleanor Chu, Vice President
Parke-Dunn Pharmaceutical Company
74 West Michigan Mall, Suite 300
Battle Creek, Michigan **49017-3606**

4–14 Telephone and Facsimile (Fax) Numbers

Telephone and facsimile (fax) numbers are expressed in figures. When the area code is included, place it in parentheses before the number. As an alternate format you may omit the parentheses and separate the area code from the telephone or fax number with a hyphen.

Extension numbers, preceded by the abbreviation *Ext.*, follow telephone numbers. If an extension number concludes a sentence, use a single comma to separate it from the telephone number. However, if an extension number appears in the middle of a sentence, use commas before and after it.

telephone or facsimile (fax) number

You may reach our representative at **728-1694**.

Please ask the doctor to fax the prescription for this prosthesis to **363-6534**.

area code with telephone or facsimile (fax) number

Please fax a copy of this proposal to me at **(714) 555-5235**.

Call our toll-free number, **800-885-3322**, to place your order.

area code, telephone number, extension

You may reach me any weekday at **(617) 555-7139, Ext. 3712**.

We were requested to call **(213) 347-0551, Ext. 244**, within an hour.

Special Forms

4–15 Fractions

a. **Simple fractions that can be expressed in two words are written in word form. Fractions written in word form are not hyphenated unless they are used as compound adjectives.**[1]

[1]"Table of Numbers," footnote 5, *Merriam-Webster's Collegiate Dictionary*, 10th ed. (Springfield, Mass.: Merriam-Webster, Incorporated, 1999), p. 798.

Numbers 4

simple fraction used as a noun

We have already met **three fourths** of our production quota for this year.

Only **one third** of our agents returned the questionnaire.

simple fraction used as a compound adjective

A **two-thirds** majority vote is needed to ratify the contract.

Our investment syndicate wishes to purchase a **one-fourth** interest in the proposed new shopping center.

b. Figures are used to express (1) long and awkward fractions, (2) fractions combined with whole numbers, or (3) fractions used for technical purposes.

long and awkward fraction

The study indicated that **21/200** of a second is needed for the average person to begin reacting in emergency situations.

fraction combined with whole number

Our new plant is located **3½** miles from here.

fraction for technical use

Our department is temporarily out of stock of **⅝**-inch roundhead metal screws.

c. Use the extended character set of your word processing program to key fractions that are written in figures. Those commonly found are ½, ¼, ¾, ⅓, ⅔, ⅛, ⅜, ⅝, and ⅞.

Fractions written in figures that are not found in extended character sets of word processing programs are formed by using the diagonal to separate the two parts. Format the first number for superscript in a smaller font. Format the second number at the normal position on the line in the same smaller size.

In mixed numbers constructed by extended character sets or other font attributes, leave no space between the fraction and any whole number used with the fraction.

On typewriters and with simple word processors, key all fractions in normal type size using the diagonal construction. In mixed numbers leave one space between the whole number and the fraction.

fraction keyed through an extended character set

Our supply of **¾**-inch nails is running low.

mixed number keyed through an extended character set

We shipped **8⅔** tons of beef last week.

Our employees averaged **31½** hours of sick leave last year as compared with **24¼** hours this year.

fraction keyed using a diagonal

These **15/16**-inch screws have been designed especially to assemble the Model 1585A cabinets.

All these parts must be manufactured within **1/100** inch of specifications.

mixed number keyed using a diagonal

Each chair to be recovered in the restaurant will require **3 5/6** yards of fabric.

These panels are exactly **23 11/16** inches wide.

4–16 Ordinals

a. **Ordinal numbers (*first, second, third,* etc.) that can be written in one or two words are generally expressed in word form except those appearing in (1) dates before the month or standing alone and (2) numbered street names above *ten.***

general use

Mr. Cox was elected to represent the **Thirty-fourth** Congressional District.

Mrs. Lang was criticized for managing the company according to **nineteenth**-century practices.

dates

Our next audit is scheduled for the **1st of August**.

Your order will be shipped by the **15th** of this month.

Please submit your report by the **1st** of the year.

numbered streets

Our new store is located at 820 West **Third** Avenue.

I plan to meet Mr. Siegel at noon on the corner of Main and **42nd** Streets.

b. **Ordinals expressed in figure form end in *st, nd, rd,* or *th.***

This note is due the **1st** of March.

May we have your response by the **22nd** of November.

This year marks the **123rd** anniversary of our city.

Our new offices are located at 1560 **12th** Avenue.

4–17 Roman Numerals

a. When typing Roman numerals for chapter or outline divisions, use capital letters to form the numbers. In using word processing programs with an outline feature, adjust the tab settings so that the periods align for Roman numerals as well as for other divisions in the outline.

Use capital letters for expressing years written in Roman numerals.

table of Roman numerals

Arabic Numeral	*Roman Numeral*	*Arabic Numeral*	*Roman Numeral*
1	I	16	XVI
2	II	17	XVII
3	III	18	XVIII
4	IV	19	XIX
5	V	20	XX
6	VI	30	XXX
7	VII	40	XL
8	VIII	50	L
9	IX	60	LX
10	X	70	LXX
11	XI	80	LXXX
12	XII	90	XC
13	XIII	100	C
14	XIV	500	D
15	XV	1,000	M

chapter divisions

Please submit your review of **Chapter IX** by June 1.

divisions in an outline

I. Hardware Requirements
II. Network Capabilities
III. Software Requirements
IV. Training Programs

year expressed in Roman numerals

Chiseled at the top of the archway was the year the old stone church had been built—**MDCLXXXVI**. (1686)

b. The preliminary sections of a report such as the letter of transmittal, the table of contents, and the list of tables are numbered with lowercase Roman numerals. Number the pages consecutively using *i, ii, iii, iv, v,* etc.

Business Calculations

4–18 Rounding Numbers

When answers to arithmetic calculations contain a number of digits after the decimal, they may be rounded for ease of understanding. For example, amounts of money in business calculations are commonly rounded to the nearest cent.

Use the following three-step process to round numbers:

(1) Identify the number of digits needed to the right of the decimal.

(2) Increase the last digit by one if the number to its right is *5* or greater.

(3) Eliminate the extra digits.

figure rounded to three decimal places

\$45.6667 = \$45.666|7 = \$45.667 5.125463% = 5.125|463% = 5.125%

figure rounded to two decimal places

\$45.6667 = \$45.66|67 = \$45.67 5.125463% = 5.12|5463% = 5.13%

figure rounded to one decimal place

\$45.6667 = \$45.6|667 = \$45.7 5.125463% = 5.1|25463% = 5.1%

figure rounded to whole number

\$45.6667 = \$45.|6667 = \$46 5.125463% = 5.|125463% = 5%

4–19 Converting Fractions to Decimals

To convert fractions to decimal form, divide the numerator (top or first number) by the denominator (bottom or second number).

½ = 1÷2 = 0.5 ⅔ = 2÷3 = 0.667 ⅚ = 5÷6 = 0.8333

¾ = 3÷4 = 0.75 ⅞ = 7÷8 = 0.875 11⁄16 = 11÷16 = 0.6875

4–20 Converting Decimals to Percents

To convert decimal numbers to percent form, move the decimal two places to the right and add a percent sign. If an additional digit is needed, add *0*.

0.2 = 20% 0.65 = 65%

0.7152 = 71.52% 1.1582 = 115.82%

4–21 Converting Percents to Decimals

To convert percentages to decimal form, move the decimal two places to the left. Omit any *0*s at the end. For decimal forms without whole numbers, place a *0* before the decimal to avoid misreading.

70% = 0.7 95% = 0.95

32.62% = 0.3262 185.25% = 1.8525

Decimal equivalents and percentages for common fractions are shown in the following table:

Fraction	*Decimal*	*Percent*	*Fraction*	*Decimal*	*Percent*
1/3	.3333	33.33%	1/12	.0833	8.33%
2/3	.6667	66.67%	2/12 (1/6)	.1667	16.67%
1/4	.25	25%	3/12 (1/4)	.25	25%
2/4 (1/2)	.50	50%	4/12 (1/3)	.3333	33.33%
3/4	.75	75%	5/12	.4167	41.67%
1/5	.20	20%	6/12 (1/2)	.50	50%
2/5	.40	40%	7/12	.5833	58.33%
3/5	.60	60%	8/12 (2/3)	.6667	66.67%
4/5	.80	80%	9/12 (3/4)	.75	75%
1/6	.1667	16.67%	10/12 (5/6)	.8333	83.33%
2/6 (1/3)	.3333	33.33%	11/12	.9167	91.67%
3/6 (1/2)	.50	50%	1/16	.0625	6.25%
4/6 (2/3)	.6667	66.67%	3/16	.1875	18.75%
5/6	.8333	83.33%	5/16	.3125	31.25%
1/8	.125	12.5%	7/16	.4375	43.75%
2/8 (1/4)	.25	25%	9/16	.5625	56.25%
3/8	.375	37.5%	11/16	.6875	68.75%
4/8 (1/2)	.50	50%	13/16	.8125	81.25%
5/8	.625	62.5%	15/16	.9375	93.75%
6/8 (3/4)	.75	75%	1/20	.05	5%
7/8	.875	87.5%	1/25	.04	4%

4–22 Determining the Percent of a Total

To determine what percent of a total an amount represents, divide the amount by the total.

Percentage of Department Sales

Dept.	*Sales*	*Calculation*	*Decimal*	*Percent*
A	$42,875	$42,875 ÷ $122,200	0.351	35.1%
B	$22,900	$22,900 ÷ $122,200	0.187	18.7%
C	$56,425	$56,425 ÷ $122,200	0.462	46.2%
Total	$122,200		1.000	100.0%

4–23 Computing Sales Tax

Calculate sales tax by multiplying the purchase amount by the sales tax percentage. Convert the sales tax percentage to a decimal equivalent to perform the calculation.

State and Local Sales Taxes

Amount of Sale	*Sales Tax*	*Calculation*	*Amount of Sales Tax*	*Total Amount*
$72.35	5%	$72.35 × .05	$3.62	$75.97
$145.80	7½%	$145.80 × .075	$10.94	$156.74
$890.50	8¼%	$890.50 × .0825	$73.47	$963.97

4–24 Determining Mileage Expense

Individuals using their vehicles for business purposes are usually reimbursed for the expenses they have incurred. Reimbursement often takes the form of paying the individual a set amount of money for each mile driven on the employer's behalf. This reimbursement is known as *mileage expense.*

Use the following procedures to determine mileage expense:

(1) Subtract the beginning miles from the ending miles on the odometer to obtain the total miles traveled.

(2) Multiply the total miles traveled by the amount of money (usually cents) allowed per mile.

Mileage Expense Calculations

Trip	*Ending Mileage*	*(–)*	*Beginning Mileage*	*(=)*	*Total Miles Traveled*	*(×)*	*Mileage Allowance*	*(=)*	*Total Expense*
A	23,735		23,481		254		$.35		$88.90
B	42,804		41,775		1,029		$.28		$288.12
C	53,777		50,099		3,678		$.22		$809.16

4–25 Calculating Simple Discounts

Simple discounts are often given for quantity purchases and on sale merchandise. These discounts are usually stated as a percentage decrease of a regular price.

Use the following procedures to calculate the dollar amount of the discount and the cost of the purchase:

(1) Convert the percent of discount to its decimal equivalent.

(2) Multiply the regular price by the decimal equivalent of the discount to obtain the discount amount.

(3) Subtract the discount amount from the regular price to find the cost of the purchase.

Simple Discount Calculations

Regular Price	*Discount*	*Caculation (Decimal Equivalent)*	*Amount of Discount*	*Cost of Purchase*
$120.40	30%	$120.40 × .30	$36.12	$84.28
$885.90	45%	$885.90 × .45	$398.66	$487.25
$2,570.50	12%	$2,570.50 × .12	$308.46	$2,262.04

4–26 Determining Percent of Increase or Percent of Markup

Annual sales for a year may be greater than the previous year (the base year). Owners may wish to know by what percent these sales increased over the base year. Business people purchase goods at a certain price (the base price) and sell them at a higher price. These people may wish to know their percent of markup over the base price. Percent of increase and markup are the same; they are calculated identically.

Use the following procedures to calculate percent of increase and percent of markup:

(1) Subtract the base figure (sales, price, etc.) from the more recent or higher figure to obtain the difference.

(2) Divide the difference by the base figure.

(3) Convert the resulting decimal to a percentage.

Percent of Increase

2001 Sales	*2000 Sales (Base Year)*	*Amount of Increase*	*Increase ÷ Base Year*	*Percent of Increase*
$987,695	$765,782	$221,913	0.290	29.0%
$87,843	$76,289	$11,554	0.151	15.1%
$6,841,980	$6,543,902	$298,078	0.046	4.6%

Percent of Markup

Selling Price	*Cost (Base Price)*	*Amount of Markup*	*Markup ÷ Base Price*	*Percent of Markup*
$18.98	$12.43	$6.55	0.527	52.7%
$49.99	$25.70	$24.29	0.945	94.5%
$149.50	$62.00	$87.50	1.411	141.1%

4–27 Determining Percent of Decrease or Percent of Markdown

Annual sales for a year may be less than the previous year (the base year). Owners may wish to know by what percent these sales decreased over the base year. Business people price goods at a certain price (the base price) and then later sell them at a lower price. These people may wish to know their percent of markdown over the base price. Percent of decrease and markdown are the same; they are calculated identically.

Use the following procedures to calculate percent of decrease and percent of markdown:

(1) Subtract from the base figure (sales, price, etc.) the more recent or lower figure to obtain the difference.

(2) Divide the difference by the base figure.

(3) Convert the resulting decimal to a percentage.

Percent of Decrease

2000 Sales (Base Year)	*2001 Sales*	*Amount of Decrease*	*Decrease ÷ Base Year*	*Percent of Decrease*
$764,950	$583,415	$181,535	0.237	23.7%
$53,966	$46,630	$7,366	0.136	13.6%
$2,980,655	$2,743,062	$237,593	0.080	8.0%

Percent of Markdown

Original Price (Base Price)	Discounted Price	Amount of Markdown	Markdown ÷ Base Price	Percent of Markdown
$15.98	$10.50	$5.48	0.343	34.3%
$69.99	$49.99	$20.00	0.286	28.6%
$125.00	$109.00	$16.00	0.128	12.8%

4–28 Finding the Amount of Simple Interest

Simple interest is calculated (1) by multiplying the amount borrowed (principal) (2) by the rate of interest charged (3) by the years (time) for which the principal was borrowed. For loan periods less than a year, time is calculated on either a 365-day year (exact interest) or a 360-day year (ordinary interest).

Simple Interest Calculations

Amount Borrowed	Rate	Time	Calculation (Amount × Rate × Years)	Interest
$4,500	5%	2 years	$4,500 × .05 × 2	$450.00
$12,600	8½%	42 months	$12,600 × .085 × (42/12)	$3,748.50
$20,200	12%	90 days	$20,200 × .12 × (90/365)	$597.70

4–29 Determining Averages

a. **The range in a group of numbers represents the spread between the highest and the lowest number. Determine the *mode* of a range by identifying the most frequently occurring number within the spread.**

range

57 59 63 67 67 68 72 74 74 74 76 76 80 82 86 86 89 90 92 94 96 97

mode

74

b. **The *median* is the middle value in a range of values. Therefore, half the values are greater than the median, and half the values are less than it.**

range

57 59 63 67 67 68 72 74 74 74 76 76 80 82 86 86 89 90 92 94 96 97

median

76

c. **The *mean* is the arithmetic average of a range. Calculate the mean by summing the values in the range and dividing by the number of values in the range. The mean ($\bar{x}$) is the sum (Σ) of the values (x) divided by the number of values (n).**

Mean $(\bar{x}) = \frac{\Sigma x}{n}$

Numbers 4

range

57 59 63 67 67 68 72 74 74 74 76 76 80 82 86 86 89 90 92 94 96 97

mean

Sum of values = 1,719   Number of values = 22   Sum ÷ Number = 78.1

Chapter 5

Grammar and Usage

noun

Grammar and Usage Solution Finder

Grammar and Usage Solution Finder (*continued*)

Sentences

5–1 Complete Sentences

a. **Use complete sentences to express your ideas. A complete sentence (1) contains a verb (a word showing action or describing a condition), (2) has a subject (a noun or pronoun that interacts with the verb), and (3) makes sense (comes to a closure). A complete sentence is an independent clause.**

Verbs appear by themselves or in a verb phrase. The last verb in a verb phrase is considered the main verb.

Subjects are either simple or compound. *Simple subjects* consist of a single noun or pronoun whereas compound subjects contain two or more nouns or pronouns linked by *and, or,* or *nor*.

statements

(simple subject)
Last week several **employees** in our Production Department
(verb)
increased their standard output by 10 percent. (Makes sense)

(compound subject)
Karen and Richard, as a result of their hard work,
(verb phrase)
have been promoted to senior analysts. (Makes sense)

(subject) **(verb)**
This latest **manuscript** by Kym Freeman **is** excellent. (Makes sense)

questions

When **may I expect** your reply? (Simple subject, *I;* verb phrase, *may expect;* makes sense)

How many **members** of your staff **plan** to attend the convention? (Simple subject, *members;* verb, *plan;* makes sense)

requests or commands

Please **return** the questionnaire by March 31. (Simple subject, the word *you* understood; verb, *return;* makes sense)

Do not litter in the parks or on the highways. (Simple subject, the word *you* understood; verb, *do* (not = adverb) *litter;* makes sense)

b. **Simple sentences consist of a single independent clause that contains a subject and a verb or verb phrase. They express only one complete thought.**

The **manager** of our Springfield branch **has been** in our employ for over ten years. (Simple subject, *manager;* verb phrase, *has been;* makes sense)

Partnerships and corporations in this state **are** not eligible for this tax deduction. (Compound subject, *partnerships and corporations;* verb, *are;* makes sense)

c. **Compound sentences contain two independent clauses (each with a subject and a verb or verb phrase) that are usually separated by a coordinating conjunction—*and, but, or,* or *nor.***

Our regional **representative will call** on you next week, **and she will demonstrate** our new line of Creation III cosmetics. (Simple subjects, *representative* and *she;* verb phrases, *will call* and *will demonstrate;* coordinating conjunction, *and*)

Neither of our vice presidents **is** in the office this week, **but** our **general manager** for East Coast operations **will be able** to answer your questions. (Subjects, *neither* and *general manager;* verb and verb phrase, *is* and *will be able;* coordinating conjunction, *but*)

d. **Other compound sentences contain two independent clauses (each with a subject and a verb or verb phrase) that are joined by either (1) a semicolon or (2) a semicolon combined with a transitional expression such as *therefore, however, nevertheless, for example,* or *of course.***

joined by a semicolon

The **loan** on your home **has been transferred** to Certified Home Mortgage Corporation; **you should receive** a new payment booklet from Certified within the next ten days. (Simple subjects, *loan* and *you;* verb phrases, *has been transferred* and *should receive*)

joined by a semicolon and a transitional expression

Professors and administrators at our college **are covered** under the same retirement program; therefore, **administrators** also **are** eligible for retirement at age 55. (Compound and simple subjects, *professors and administrators* and *administrators;* verb phrase and verb, *are covered* and *are;* transitional expression, *therefore*)

e. **Complex sentences include an independent clause and a dependent clause, each of which contains both a subject and a verb or verb phrase. The independent clause can stand alone as a complete sentence because it makes sense, but the dependent clause cannot.**

Dependent clauses begin with (1) relative pronouns such as *who, whom, that,* or *which* or (2) subordinating conjunctions such as *if, when, as, since, because, although, while,* and *whereas.* The dependent clause may begin, interrupt, or conclude the sentence.

complex sentence with a relative pronoun clause

Mr. Johnson asked me **who won the grand prize in our drawing.**

None of the people **whom we interviewed** were willing to accept the position at the salary offered.

The book **that you recommended** is no longer available in our bookstore.

Michael is habitually absent, **which may be the reason for his dismissal**.

complex sentence with a subordinating conjunction

As soon as we receive your check, we will begin processing your application.

In the future you may, **if you wish**, send all your orders directly to our Springfield office.

Our sales have increased substantially **since the new advertising campaign began**.

f. **Compound-complex sentences contain two independent clauses and one dependent clause.**

We are discontinuing our present line of mattresses **because deliveries from the manufacturer have been slow in reaching our customers**, but we expect to replace this line with one of equal or better quality.

We received nearly thirty applications for this opening; but **after I read all the résumés**, I realized that not one of the candidates was qualified for the position.

5–2 Sentence Fragments

a. **Use only sentence fragments that *represent* a complete thought. Such usages should be confined to informal business writing.**

And now to the point.

If only I had known!

What a relief!

b. **For the most part, use concluding punctuation marks (periods, question marks, and exclamation marks) only after complete sentences. Avoid these marks after sentence fragments except in those instances in informal writing where the fragment represents a complete thought (Section 5–2a).**

Not: **In the near future**.

But: **In the near future** we will expand our operations.

Not: **Although the present contract has expired**.

But: **Although the present contract has expired**, both management and union are governed by its provisions until a new contract is negotiated.

Not: **The biggest money-saving event of the year**.

But: We look forward to seeing you at our annual clearance sale, **the biggest money-saving event of the year**.

Nouns

5–3 Nouns[1]

a. **Nouns are words that name something—for example, persons, animals, places, things, objects, time, feelings, qualities, actions, concepts, measures, and states of being.**

person

Please have your **attorney** call me.

Did you refer this **client** to me?

animal

We have been interested in purchasing another **horse**.

This **fish** is too old to eat.

place

The new **park** will be located in our **suburb**.

When will you visit our **city**?

thing

All this **information** is stored on our **network**.

Have the **company** and the **union** reached an **agreement**?

object

Did you find your **purse**?

Place the **computer** on this **table**.

time

Although we signed the contract yesterday, it will not become effective for 30 **days**.

The balloon payment is due next **month**.

feeling

Everyone in the room detected his **anger** as he spoke.

Grammar 5

---

[1]The rules and spellings in this chapter are based on *Merriam Webster's Collegiate Dictionary,* 10th ed. (Springfield, Mass.: Merriam-Webster, Incorporated, 1999). For a complete, up-to-date on-line Internet resource, visit Merriam-Webster at http://www.m-w.com (no fees).

We can certainly sympathize with his **sorrow** and **grief**.

quality

I appreciate your **thoughtfulness** and **generosity**.

Such **irresponsibility** cannot be tolerated.

action

Do you enjoy **swimming**?

Golfing is an individual sport.

concept

Our country was founded on **freedom** of **expression**.

Please report any **progress** you have made.

measure

Our company's assets total nearly **$23 million**.

Three **yards** of fabric will be needed for each chair.

state of being

Her **illness** has not yet been properly diagnosed.

Complacency in this rapidly changing industry could easily lead to **bankruptcy**.

b. **Any noun that names a particular entity is capitalized. These capitalized nouns are known as *proper nouns*. Nouns that do not name specific entities are known as *common nouns*, and they are not capitalized.**

proper nouns

Last month the **Columbus City Council** approved a 4 percent increase in property taxes.

Repairs on the **Golden Gate Bridge** are still in progress.

We must make a decision by **December** 1.

Much of this information is available through the **Internet**.

common nouns

Last month the **city council** approved a 4 percent increase in property taxes.

Repairs on the **bridge** are still in progress.

We must make a decision by the **1st** of next **month**.

Much of this information is available through **on-line network resources**.

c. Although most common nouns consist of single words, many contain two or even three words. These *compound nouns* appear as regular entries in the dictionary and are defined as nouns. Some are hyphenated, but most are separate words without hyphens (*open compounds*).

hyphenated compound nouns

This business is operated by the mayor's **brother-in-law.**

The **vice-chancellor** must approve all faculty appointments.

open compound nouns

Please have the **vice president** sign this purchase order.

Our local **high school** is sponsoring this event.

5–4 Noun Plurals[2]

a. Most nouns form their plurals by adding *s*. However, nouns ending in *s, sh, ch, x,* or *z* form their plurals by adding *es*.

***nouns adding* s**

account	accounts	executive	executives
letter	letters	message	messages

***nouns adding* es**

bus	buses	branch	branches
business	businesses	tax	taxes
wish	wishes	waltz	waltzes

b. Common nouns ending in *y* form the plural in one of two ways. If the letter preceding the *y* is a vowel, just add *s*. However, if the letter preceding the *y* is a consonant, drop the *y* and add *ies*.

y preceded by a vowel

attorney	attorneys	money	moneys
delay	delays	valley	valleys

y preceded by a consonant

company	companies	reply	replies
policy	policies	secretary	secretaries

c. Musical terms ending in *o* form the plural by adding *s*. Other common nouns ending in *o* may form the plural by adding *s* or *es;* the correct plural forms are shown in the dictionary after the singular forms of the words.

[2]Noun plurals, other than those regular ones ending in s or es, are shown in the dictionary immediately after the singular form of the word. For a complete, up-to-date on-line Internet resource, visit Merriam-Webster at http://www.m-w.com (no fees).

musical terms

sopranos	concertos	cellos	solos	pianos

common nouns ending in os

zeros	mementos	dynamos	portfolios	ratios

common nouns ending in oes

cargoes	heroes	potatoes	embargoes	vetoes

d. **Nouns ending in *ff* form the plural by adding *s*. Nouns ending in just *f* or *fe* may add *s*, or they may drop the *f* or *fe* and add *ves*. The plurals of those nouns taking the irregular form by adding *ves* are shown in the dictionary. If the dictionary does not show the plural form, just add *s*.**

plural nouns ending in ffs

bailiff	bailiffs	plaintiff	plaintiffs
cliff	cliffs	sheriff	sheriffs

plural nouns ending in fs or fes

belief	beliefs	roof	roofs
chief	chiefs	safe	safes
proof	proofs	strife	strifes

plural nouns ending in ves

half	halves	shelf	shelves
knife	knives	thief	thieves
self	selves	wife	wives

e. **The plurals of proper nouns are formed by adding *s* or *es*. Those proper nouns ending in *s, sh, ch, x,* or *z* form the plural by adding *es*. All others form the plural by adding *s*.**

proper noun adding es for plural form

Bendix	the Bendixes	Rodriguez	the Rodriguezes
Bush	the Bushes	Ross	the Rosses
Finch	the Finches	Winters	the Winterses

proper noun adding s for plural form

Dixon	the Dixons	Kelly	the Kellys
Griffin	the Griffins	Russo	the Russos
Halby	the Halbys	Wolf	the Wolfs

f. **Many nouns of foreign origin have both an English plural and a foreign plural. Consult your dictionary and use the one that appears first.**

***foreign-derived nouns with preferred English plurals*[3]**

appendix	appendixes	hors d'oeuvre	hors d'oeuvres
auditorium	auditoriums	index	indexes (book)
bureau	bureaus	memorandum	memorandums
formula	formulas	plateau	plateaus
gymnasium	gymnasiums	ultimatum	ultimatums

foreign-derived nouns with preferred foreign-derived plurals

alumna	alumnae	emphasis	emphases
alumnus	alumni	medium	media
analysis	analyses	parenthesis	parentheses
basis	bases	phenomenon	phenomena
crisis	crises	stimulus	stimuli
criterion	criteria	syllabus	syllabi
curriculum	curricula	synopsis	synopses
datum	data	synthesis	syntheses
diagnosis	diagnoses	terminus	termini
ellipsis	ellipses	thesis	theses

g. **Some nouns form their plurals by changing letters within the word or adding letters other than *s* or *es*. These irregular plurals are shown in the dictionary in the same entry with their singular form.**

child	children	mouse	mice
foot	feet	tooth	teeth
man	men	woman	women

h. **Some nouns have the same form in both the singular and the plural. Other nouns are used only with singular verbs while still others are used solely with plural verbs. These unusual constructions are explained in the dictionary in the entry that defines the word.**

nouns with the same singular and plural forms

Chinese	gross	mumps	series
cod	headquarters	odds	sheep
corps	Japanese	politics	species
deer	measles	salmon	vermin
fish	moose	scissors	Vietnamese

nouns always used with singular verbs

aeronautics	genetics	news
economics (course)	mathematics	statistics (course)

[3]Preferences for English and foreign noun plurals are based upon entries shown in *Merriam-Webster's Collegiate Dictionary*, 10th ed. (Springfield, Mass.: Merriam-Webster, Incorporated, 1999). For a complete, up-to-date on-line Internet resource, visit Merriam-Webster at http://www.m-w.com (no fees).

nouns always used with plural verbs

belongings	earnings	premises	thanks
credentials	goods	proceeds	winnings

i. **Hyphenated or open compound nouns containing a main word form their plurals on the main word. Those hyphenated compounds not containing a main word and compound nouns consisting of only one word form the plural at the end.**

plural formed on main word

attorney**s**-at-law	grant**s**-in-aid	notarie**s** public
bill**s** of sale	graphic design**s**	personnel manager**s**
co-owner**s**	leave**s** of absence	sister**s**-in-law
going**s**-over	lieutenant colonel**s**	vice-chancellor**s**

plural formed at end

bookshel**ves**	get-together**s**	stockholder**s**
come-on**s**	go-between**s**	teaspoonful**s**
database**s**	printout**s**	trade-in**s**
follow-up**s**	stand-in**s**	workm**en**

j. **The plurals of numerals, most capital letters, words referred to as words, and abbreviations composed of initials are formed by adding *s* or *es*. For clarity, though, all isolated lowercase letters and the capital letters *A, I, M,* and *U* are made plural by adding an apostrophe before the *s*.**

***plural formed with* s *or* es**

I have difficulty distinguishing between his **1s** and his **7s**.

Can you list the seven **Cs** of good letter writing?

Ms. Smith, our new copy editor, does not use her **whiches** and **thats** correctly.

On the last ballot the **noes** outnumbered the **yeses**.

Mr. Wilson wants this assignment completed without any further **ifs**, **ands**, or **buts**.

Make a list of **dos** and **don'ts** for the care and maintenance of these scanners.

There are two vacancies for **R.N.s** on our team.

How many of your graduates became **CPAs** last year?

All our **c.o.d.s** still need to be sent out.

Type the ***a.m.s*** and ***p.m.s*** in lowercase letters.

***plural formed with an apostrophe and* s**

We were asked to mind our ***p's*** and ***q's*** while the dignitaries were in the building.

To improve your penmanship, be sure to dot your ***i's*** and cross your ***t's***.

Your son received three ***A's*** on his last grade report.

Why are the ***M's*** smudged on this document?

k. **When referring to two or more individuals with the same name and title, make either the name or the title plural, but never both.**

the **Messrs.** Johnson *or* the Mr. **Johnsons**

the **Drs.** Clark *or* the Dr. **Clarks**

the **Mses.** Smith *or* the Ms. **Smiths**

the **Mesdames** Jones *or* the Mrs. **Joneses**

the **Misses** Fry *or* the Miss **Frys**

5–5 Noun Possessives[4]

a. **All nouns *not* ending with a pronounced *s*, whether singular or plural, form the possessive by adding *'s*.**

office of the **attorney**	**attorney's** office
toys belonging to the **children**	**children's** toys
books belonging to **Judy**	**Judy's** books
lounge for **women**	**women's** lounge
state tax of **Illinois**	**Illinois's** state tax
countryside of **Des Moines**	**Des Moines's** countryside
tribal customs of the **Iroquois**	the **Iroquois's** tribal customs
paycheck of **Ms. DuBois**	**Ms. DuBois's** paycheck
restaurant belonging to **Francois**	**Francois's** restaurant

(Note: The final *s* in words such as *Illinois, Des Moines, Iroquois, DuBois,* and *Francois* is not pronounced; therefore, *'s* is used with these possessive forms.)

b. **Nouns ending with a pronounced *s* form the possessive by simply adding an apostrophe unless an additional syllable is pronounced in the possessive form. In the latter case, *'s* is added.**

no extra pronounced syllable

clothing for **girls**	**girls'** clothing
the efforts of two **cities**	two **cities'** efforts
the home belonging to the **Foxes**	the **Foxes'** home
the pen belonging to **Mr. Simons**	**Mr. Simons'** pen

[4]See Section 1–55 for additional examples.

Grammar 5

extra pronounced syllable

grades of the **class**	the **class's** grades
the briefcase belonging to **Mr. Harris**	**Mr. Harris's** briefcase
testimony of the **witness**	the **witness's** testimony

c. In the case of joint ownership, possession is shown only on the last noun. Where individual ownership exists, possession is shown on each noun.

joint ownership

Mary and Alice's office has been newly painted.

The Rodriguezes and the **Martinsons'** store is located on Sixth Avenue.

Mr. Stewart and **Ms. Ross's** partnership agreement was drawn up over two weeks ago.

Clark and **Clark's** handbook is required for this class.

individual ownership

My **mother's** and **father's** clothes were destroyed in the fire.

Bob's and **John's** payroll checks were lost.

Mr. Granados' and **Ms. Stone's** stores are both located on Tampa Avenue in Westfield.

All the **accountants'** and **secretaries'** desks have been moved into the new offices.

d. The possessive form of compound nouns is shown at the end.

investments of my **father-in-law**	my **father-in-law's** investments
the report for **stockholders**	the **stockholders'** report
convention of **attorneys-at-law**	**attorneys-at-law's** convention
report of the **systems manager**	**systems manager's** report

e. Use the possessive form before a gerund.

We would appreciate **Lisa's helping** us with the audit.

There is no record of the **witness's being** subpoenaed.

f. Use an apostrophe with the possessives of nouns that refer to time—minutes, hours, days, weeks, months, and years.

time nouns—singular

peace for a **minute**	a **minute's** peace
work for a **day**	a **day's** work
delay for a **week**	a **week's** delay
notice of a **month**	a **month's** notice
mail from this **morning**	this **morning's** mail
calendar for **tomorrow**	**tomorrow's** calendar

time nouns—plural

work for four **hours**	four **hours'** work
interest for two **weeks**	two **weeks'** interest
trial for three **months**	three **months'** trial
experience for five **years**	five **years'** experience

g. **Use an apostrophe with the possessive of nouns that refer to distance.**

He lives just a **stone's** throw from the office.

The truck missed hitting our car by just an **arm's** length.

h. **Do not use an apostrophe to form possessives for inanimate (non-living) objects, except for time or distance. Instead, use a simple adjective or an *of* phrase.**

Words such as *company, team, organization, association, herd, flock,* and *committee* are not considered inanimate because they are composed of people or other living entities.

adjective

The **armchair** cushion needs repair. (Not: The armchair's cushion needs repair.)

The **computer** monitor was damaged in transit. (Not: The computer's monitor was damaged in transit.)

of phrase

The door **of the supply cabinet** is jammed. (Not: The supply cabinet's door is jammed.)

The stipulations **of the will** were presented by the attorney. (Not: The will's stipulations were presented by the attorney.)

group composed of people or another living entity

Most of the **company's** profits in 2000 were from Internet e-commerce.

The **college's** enrollment has risen significantly during the past five years.

Nearly 50 acres of the **herd's** grazing lands were destroyed by the floods.

i. **In some possessive constructions the item or items owned do not directly follow the ownership word or are not named. The ownership word, however, still shows possession with an apostrophe.**

item owned not directly following the ownership word

The only desk to be refinished is **Mary's.** (Mary's desk)

On Tuesday we will meet at the **Culleys'** to discuss the sale of their property. (The Culleys' property)

item owned not named

Mr. Ardigo left the **attorney's** over an hour ago. (The attorney's office)

Did you leave your briefcase at the **Galloways'**? (The Galloways' home)

Pronouns

5–6 Pronouns

a. **Pronouns are noun substitutes; they take the place of nouns. Business writers use pronouns to add variety and interest to their writing.**

sentence without pronouns

When you see Mr. Lee, please ask Mr. Lee to sign Mr. Lee's time card for this week.

sentence with pronouns

When you see Mr. Lee, please ask **him** to sign **his** time card for this week.

b. **Pronouns perform one of four functions: they may (1) substitute for a person or thing, (2) refer back to a noun used previously in the sentence, (3) substitute for an unspecific person or thing, or (4) act as an adjective by modifying a noun.**

substitute for a person or thing (personal pronoun)

Michael has been ill for three days; **he** should schedule an appointment with a doctor.

Because **Mrs. Scher-Padilla** is in charge of this program, please give the forms to **her**.

The board **members** can only blame **themselves** for this error.

Our **company** has attempted to expand operations to other states. However, **it** still has been unable to increase sales significantly.

reference to a noun named previously in the sentence (relative pronoun)

Please send me the **book that** Tony recommended.

Brian interviewed three **students** from Japan **who** are on an exchange program.

substitute for an unspecific person or thing (indefinite pronoun)

Do you know **someone** who might be interested in this employment opportunity in Buenos Aires?

Neither of these plans is acceptable to the committee.

personal pronoun used as an adjective

His computer needs a new floppy disk drive.

This account is **hers.**

5–7 Personal Pronouns

a. Each personal pronoun may be expressed in three ways; these ways are referred to as *case forms.* The three case forms for personal pronouns are the *subjective,* the *objective,* and the *possessive.*

b. The subjective case[5] personal pronouns follow:

I	she	we	who
he	you	they	it

Use a subjective case pronoun (1) for the subject of a verb, (2) for the complement of a "being" verb (*am, is, are, was, were, be, been*), and (3) after the infinitive "to be" when this verb does not have a subject (a noun or pronoun) directly preceding it.

subject of a verb

She *has applied* for the position.

They *will arrive* at 10 a.m. from Montreal.

Mark, Ellen, and **I** *have been appointed* to the committee.

complement of a being verb

The person who answered the telephone *was* not **I.**

"This *is* **she**," is the appropriate response when a telephone caller asks for you by name.

The visitors could have *been* **they.**

infinitive to be without a subject

Deanna is often thought *to be* **I.**

The doctor on duty during that shift is certain *to be* **he.**

c. The objective case personal pronouns are the following:

me	her	us	whom
him	you	them	it

The objective case is used when the pronoun is (1) the direct or indirect object of a verb (2) the object of a preposition, (3) the subject of any infinitive, (4) the object of the infinitive *to be* when it has a subject, and (5) the object of any other infinitive.

[5]The subjective case is also known as the nominative case.

Grammar 5

direct object of a verb

Mr. Reslaw *will meet* **her** at the airport tomorrow.

You *may ask* **him** for this information.

Ms. Orsini *asked* Ken and **me** to obtain this information by August 1.

indirect object of a verb

Please *mail* **me** *a receipt* as soon as possible.

We *will send* Marie or **him** *these copies* before Friday.

object of a preposition

When was the shipment sent *to* **us**?

Two of the customers asked *for* **her**.

Between **you** and **me**, I do not believe the plan will be approved.

subject of an infinitive

Our department manager expects **her** *to complete* the audit by June 30.

We thought **them** *to be* somewhat overconfident.

object of* to be *with a subject

I wanted the **candidate** *to be* **her**.

Ms. Stapleton thought **them** *to be* **us**.

They expected **Mary** *to be* **me**.

***object of an infinitive other than* to be**

Our office will not be able *to mail* **them** until Monday.

We asked her *to help* **us** with the decorations.

d. **The possessive case personal pronouns are the following:**

my	mine	their	theirs
his, her	his, hers	its	its
your	yours	whose	
our	ours		

All pronoun possessive case forms are written without apostrophes. They should not be confused with contractions.

possessive pronouns—no apostrophes

Its wrapping had been torn.

Is this **your** signature?

The idea was **theirs**.

Whose briefcase was left in the conference room?

contractions—apostrophes

It's (It is) still raining very heavily here on the West Coast.

Let us know if **you're** (you are) going to the convention.

If **there's** (there is) a logical reason for the delay, please inform the passengers.

Who's (Who is) in charge of ordering supplies for our computers?

e. **Use the possessive case immediately before a gerund.**

His leaving the company was quite a surprise.

We would appreciate **your returning** the enclosed card by Friday, March 18.

f. **A pronoun after *than* or *as* may be expressed in either the subjective or objective case, depending on whether the pronoun is the subject or object of the following stated or implied verb.**

subjective case

Are you as concerned about this matter as **I am**? (Stated verb *am*)

He has been with the company two years longer than **I**. (Implied verb *have*)

objective case

Our editor compliments my coauthor more than he compliments **me**. (Stated subject and verb *he compliments*)

She works for Mr. Reece more often than **me**. (Implied subject, verb, and preposition *she works for*, . . . than *she works for* me.)

g. **Pronouns used in apposition take the same case as those nouns or pronouns with which they are in apposition.**

We, Barbara and **I**, will appear in court tomorrow.

Barry told Ms. Larsen to submit her expenses to one of our accounting **supervisors**, John or **me**.

h. **Pronouns followed by an identifying noun (such as *we employees* or *us employees*) are treated as if the noun were not there in determining the proper case form. Therefore, mentally omit the noun in such pronoun-noun combinations (restrictive appositives) to select the correct form.**

subjective case

Within the next week **we ~~employees~~** must decide whether or not we will move with the company to Columbus. (Subject of verb phrase *must decide*)

The victims in this case are **we ~~students~~**. (Complement of being verb *are*)

objective case

The company just gave **us ~~employees~~** the opportunity to purchase company stock at prices below the market value. (Indirect object of verb *gave*)

None of **us ~~students~~** have yet received any enrollment information. (Object of preposition *of*)

i. **Pronouns ending in *self* or *selves* emphasize or reflect a noun or pronoun used previously. They should not be used in place of objective case pronouns.**

emphasizes previous noun or pronoun

Wendy **herself** was not pleased with the results of the advertising campaign.

They themselves could not justify their exorbitant budget requests.

reflects a previous noun or pronoun

Jim addressed the envelope to **himself**.

The **council** voted **themselves** annual salary increases of $4,000.

objective case pronoun used correctly

None of these packages are for **me**. (Not: None of these packages are for *myself.*)

These contracts will be sent directly to **you** after they have been signed by our president. (Not: These contracts will be sent directly to *yourself* after they have been signed by our president.)

j. **The same rules apply to the pronouns *who, whoever, whom, whomever,* and *whose* as apply to the other personal pronouns. *Who* and *whoever* are used for the subjective case; *whom* and *whomever,* for the objective case; and *whose,* for the possessive case.**

To distinguish easily whether to use *who* or *whom,* use the following procedure. See how the model sentence leads to the correct choice. The model sentence for this example is *John is the person [who, whom] I believe Ms. Wilkes will hire.*

(1) Isolate the clause in which the pronoun appears. (*[who, whom] I believe Ms. Wilkes will hire*)

(2) Eliminate any extra clauses. (– *I believe*) (= *[who, whom] Ms. Wilkes will hire*)

(3) Place the clause in subject-verb order if it does not already appear so. (*Ms. Wilkes will hire [who, whom]*)

(4) Apply the rules outlined for the subjective and objective case pronouns in Sections 5–7b and c. Mentally substitute *he* for *who* and *him* for *whom* to help you distinguish between the subjective and objective cases. (*Ms. Wilkes will hire him.* Thus the correct choice for

the example sentence is *whom: John is the person whom I believe Ms. Wilkes will hire.*)

***subjective case*—who or whoever**

Who delivered these contracts to my office? (Subject of verb—*[he]* delivered)

Please give me a listing of **who** called while I was in Amsterdam. (Subject of verb—*[he]* called)

I do not know **who** the caller may have been. (Place clause in subject-verb order.) (Complement of "being" verb *been*—the caller may have been *[he]*)

Please let me know **who** the winner is. (Place clause in subject-verb order.) (Complement of "being" verb *is*—the winner is *[he]*)

Who do you think will be appointed to the board? (Omit extra clause *do you think.*) (Subject of verb phrase—*[he]* will be appointed)

The city council will ratify the appointment of **whoever** is selected. (Subject of verb phrase—*[he]* is selected)

The committee will allow you to select **whoever** you think is qualified. (Omit extra clause *you think.*) (Subject of verb—*[he]* is qualified)

***objective case*—whom or whomever**

Whom did Mr. Williams promote to the position of office manager? (Place clause in subject-verb order.) (Direct object—Mr. Williams did promote *[him]*)

He is a person with **whom** we have done business for over twenty-five years. (Place clause in subject-verb order.) (Object of preposition—we have done business with *[him]*)

Ask Mr. Robbins **whom** he selected to replace Jerome. (Place clause in subject-verb order.) (Direct object—he selected *[him]*)

We do not know **whom** to award the contract. (Place clause in subject-verb order.) (Object of an infinitive—to award *[him]* the contract)

Whom do you think the Savoys will hire as their new manager? (Omit extra clause *do you think.*) (Place clause in subject-verb order.) (Direct object—the Savoys will hire *[him]*)

The committee will allow you to select **whomever** you wish. (Place clause in subject-verb order.) (Direct object—you wish *[him]*)

I'm sure the president will approve **whomever** you choose for the position. (Place clause in subject-verb order.) (Direct object—you choose *[him]*)

possessive case—whose

Whose sales reports have not yet been submitted?

We do not know **whose** recommendations will be adopted to implement our new cost-saving plan.

k. **Pronouns must agree in gender and number with any nouns or other pronouns they represent.**[6]

A **customer** must first register **his** or **her** complaint with an assistant manager.

Both **Ms. Greer** and **Mr. Baty** received **their** orders yesterday.

The **puppy** caught **its** tail in the door.

The **company** will conduct **its** annual inventory next week.

........➤ 5–8 Relative Pronouns

a. **Relative pronouns introduce dependent clauses that refer back (relate) to a noun in the main clause of the sentence. Relative pronoun forms are *who, whom, that,* and *which*.**

b. **Use who and whom to refer to a person or persons. To distinguish between *who* and *whom,* apply the procedures outlined in Section 5–7j.**

subjective case—who

Mr. Vasquez is the *applicant* **who** was selected for the position. (Refers back to *applicant*) (Subject of verb—*[he]* was selected)

The *person* **who** served as the seventh president of our college was Ms. Graham. (Refers back to *person*) (Subject of verb—*[she]* served)

Peter is the *sales representative* **who** I believe will be successful as an editor in the business area. (Refers back to *sales representative*) (Omit extra clause *I believe*.) (Subject of verb—*[he]* will be successful)

Next month our *advertising manager,* **who** has held this position for over twenty years, will retire. (Refers back to *advertising manager*) (Subject of verb—*[he]* has held)

objective case—whom

Mr. Vasquez is the *applicant* **whom** Ms. Jones selected for the position. (Refers back to *applicant*) (Direct object of verb—Ms. Jones selected *[him]*)

Our new *college president,* **whom** the board appointed just yesterday, has already called a meeting of campus administrators. (Refers back to *president*) (Direct object of verb—the board appointed *[him]*)

---

[6]Refer to Section 5–18 for additional information on principles of agreement.

You are a *person* **whom** I know Ms. Ferraro would be pleased to hire. (Refers back to *person*) (Omit extra clause *I know.*) (Object of infinitive—Ms. Ferraro would be pleased to hire *[him]*)

c. Use *that* or *which* to introduce a dependent clause that refers back to a thing or things in the main clause—any noun that does not represent a person or persons. Careful writers use *that* to introduce restrictive dependent clauses and *which* to introduce nonrestrictive dependent clauses.

Restrictive dependent clauses provide essential ideas that refine the information contained in the main clause; that is, they specify *which one. Nonrestrictive dependent clauses* provide extra information that does not alter the substance of the main clause; in other words, the information is not needed to identify *which one.* Nonrestrictive clauses are separated from the main clause with a comma or a pair of commas.

***restrictive dependent clause requiring* that**

Be sure to include on the order form the catalog number of each *item* **that** you order. (Refers back to *item*) (Specifies only items that are ordered)

The *prices* **that** are listed in this catalog are guaranteed until June 30. (Refers back to *prices*) (Specifies which prices)

***nonrestrictive dependent clause requiring* which**

The Catalog No. 8731 lace-embroidered *blouse,* **which** you ordered last week, is no longer available. (Refers back to *blouse*) (Clause not needed to identify which blouse—provides extra idea)

Please credit my account for these *items,* **which** were charged in error to my account. (Refers back to *items*) (Clause not needed to identify which items—provides additional information)

5–9 Indefinite Pronouns

a. *Indefinite pronouns* are pronouns that do not represent a specific person, place, or thing.

b. Simple indefinite pronouns include the following words used as subjects or objects:

each	every
either	neither

c. Compound indefinite pronouns end with *-body, -one,* or *-thing.*

____body	____one	____thing
anybody	anyone	anything
everybody	everyone	everything
nobody	no one	nothing
somebody	someone	something

d. Indefinite pronouns used as subjects require singular verbs.

simple indefinite pronoun as subject

Each of the candidates **has** been given an equal opportunity to address our audience.

Neither of the applicants **is** qualified for the position.

compound indefinite pronoun as subject

Nearly **everybody was** late for the meeting because of the unexpected snowstorm.

Everything in these files **is** outdated.

e. Any other pronouns representing an indefinite pronoun must agree in number and gender with the indefinite pronoun.

Neither of the winners has claimed **his** or **her** prize.

Would **everyone** please return **his** or **her** evaluation form by May 15.

Verbs

5–10 Verbs

a. Verbs are often described as the motor of a sentence—they make a sentence "go." Verbs show action or describe a state of being at a certain point in time. Examples of action verbs are *run, swim, talk,* and *write.* Nonaction verbs, those that describe a state of being, include words such as *seem, feel,* and *smell.* The most commonly used nonaction verbs, however, are derived from the verb *be—am, is, are, was, were,* and *been.*

b. In their infinitive form, verbs are preceded by the preposition *to.*

action verbs	**nonaction verbs**
to go	to be
to demonstrate	to appear
to apply	to taste

c. Verbs appear alone or in phrases with helpers. The last word in a verb phrase is the main verb. Word groups must contain a verb or a verb phrase to be complete sentences.

verb in sentence

David **checks** his E-mail at least twice daily.

Please **send** this order to the customer immediately.

Vista Industries **is** one of our best customers.

verb phrase in sentence

We **have received** several payments from this client.

Our company **has been involved** in two lawsuits during the past year.

Our office **is** presently **processing** your order.

How much money **did** you **spend** on this project?

d. **Verbs require varied forms to signify tenses; that is, points in time. The principal forms or parts of a verb used to construct tenses include the present part, the past part, the past participle, and the present participle.**

5–11 Formation of Parts for Regular Verbs

Most verbs, regular verbs, form their parts in the same way: (1) the present part has the infinitive form without the accompanying *to,* (2) the past part adds *ed* to the present form, (3) the past participle uses the past part with at least one verb helper, and (4) the present participle adds *ing* to the present form and uses at least one verb helper.

infinitive	**present**	**past**
to ask	ask	asked
to collect	collect	collected
to interview	interview	interviewed

past participle	**present participle**
(have, was) asked	(was, has been) asking
(has, had been) collected	(am, have been) collecting
(were, have been) interviewed	(are, will be) interviewing

sentence examples

We need **to collect** more information for this report. (Infinitive)

Jeff **collects** stamps from countries all over the world. (Present part)

The courier **collected** all our mail for overnight delivery about an hour ago. (Past part)

My assistant **has collected** prospectuses from seven major suppliers of health insurance programs. (Past participle with a helping verb)

Our Research Department **is collecting** additional information from consumers. (Present participle with a helping verb)

5–12 Formation of Parts for Irregular Verbs

a. **Many verbs do not form their past part, past participle, and present participle in the usual manner. *All such irregular verb forms are shown in the dictionary; they are listed directly after the present form of the verb.* Any verbs without a listing are regular verbs, and their parts are formed in the regular way described in Section 5–11.**

Grammar 5

b. **A number of irregular verbs form their parts in the same way. Most verbs ending in *e* form their past part and past participle by adding *d*. These same verbs form the present participle by dropping the *e* and adding *ing*.**

Another group of verbs double the final consonant before adding the regular endings to the past part, past participle, and present participle.

***verbs ending in* e**

Infinitive:	to change	to enclose	to complete
Present part:	change	enclose	complete
Past part:	changed	enclosed	completed
Past participle:	(has) changed	(have) enclosed	(have) completed
Present participle:	(is) changing	(are) enclosing	(is) completing

verbs that double the final consonant

Infinitive:	to trim	to stir	to clip
Present part:	trim	stir	clip
Past part:	trimmed	stirred	clipped
Past participle:	(has) trimmed	(has) stirred	(have) clipped
Present participle:	(is) trimming	(are) stirring	(is) clipping

c. **Some irregular verb forms do not follow a particular pattern in forming the past part and the past participle. A list of parts for some such commonly used irregular verbs follows:**

Present Part	*Past Part*	*Past Participle*	*Present Participle*
am	was	been	being
arise	arose	arisen	arising
become	became	become	becoming
begin	began	begun	beginning
bite	bit	bitten	biting
blow	blew	blown	blowing
break	broke	broken	breaking
bring	brought	brought	bringing
burst	burst	burst	bursting
buy	bought	bought	buying
catch	caught	caught	catching
choose	chose	chosen	choosing
come	came	come	coming
dig	dug	dug	digging
do	did	done	doing
draw	drew	drawn	drawing
drink	drank	drunk	drinking
drive	drove	driven	driving
eat	ate	eaten	eating
fall	fell	fallen	falling
fight	fought	fought	fighting

Present Part	*Past Part*	*Past Participle*	*Present Participle*
fly	flew	flown	flying
forget	forgot	forgotten	forgetting
forgive	forgave	forgiven	forgiving
freeze	froze	frozen	freezing
get	got	got	getting
give	gave	given	giving
go	went	gone	going
grow	grew	grown	growing
hang (an object)	hung	hung	hanging
hang (a person)	hanged	hanged	hanging
hide	hid	hidden	hiding
know	knew	known	knowing
lay	laid	laid	laying
lead	led	led	leading
leave	left	left	leaving
lend	lent	lent	lending
lie (to recline)	lay	lain	lying
lie (to tell an untruth)	lied	lied	lying
lose	lost	lost	losing
make	made	made	making
pay	paid	paid	paying
ride	rode	ridden	riding
ring	rang	rung	ringing
rise	rose	risen	rising
run	ran	run	running
see	saw	seen	seeing
set	set	set	setting
shake	shook	shaken	shaking
shrink	shrank	shrunk	shrinking
sing	sang	sung	singing
sink	sank	sunk	sinking
sit	sat	sat	sitting
speak	spoke	spoken	speaking
spring	sprang	sprung	springing
steal	stole	stolen	stealing
strike	struck	struck	striking
swear	swore	sworn	swearing
swim	swam	swum	swimming
take	took	taken	taking
tear	tore	torn	tearing
throw	threw	thrown	throwing
wear	wore	worn	wearing
write	wrote	written	writing

sentence examples

Our holiday sale **begins** this Monday.

We **began** work on this construction project early last June.

Orders from our national television campaign **have begun** flooding our telephone lines.

These stocks **are beginning** to pay substantial dividends.

5–13 Simple Tenses

Verb parts are used to form tenses that place an action or a condition in a time frame. The verb part itself may express tense, or a verb part with helpers (a verb phrase) may be needed to specify the time frame. The most commonly used tenses are the simple tenses—the *present*, the *past*, and the *future*.

a. The present tense is used to indicate an ongoing action or a currently existing condition. Use the present part or a conjugation (changes in spelling to accommodate person) of the present part to form this tense.

Place an *s* at the end of the present part when it is used with any singular subject except *I* and *you*. For verbs ending in *s, sh, ch, x,* and *z,* add *es* instead of *s*.[7]

present tense formations for most verbs

to eat	**to provide**	**to sit**
I eat you eat	I provide you provide	I sit you sit
he eats John eats	he provides John provides	he sits John sits
she eats Mary eats	she provides Mary provides	she sits Mary sits
it eats the cat eats	it provides the company provides	it sits the cat sits
we eat you eat (pl.)	we provide you provide (pl.)	we sit you sit (pl.)
they eat the children eat	they provide the parents provide	they sit the patients sit

***present tense formations for verbs ending in* s, sh, ch, x, *and* z**

to wish	**to teach**	**to relax**
I wish you wish	I teach you teach	I relax you relax

[7]The verbs *do* and *go* add *es* also; i.e., the singular form of do for *he, she,* and *it* is *does.* The corresponding form for *go* is *goes.*

he wishes John wishes	he teaches John teaches	he relaxes John relaxes
she wishes Mary wishes	she teaches Mary teaches	she relaxes Mary relaxes
it wishes the board wishes	it teaches the program teaches	it relaxes the cat relaxes
we wish you wish (pl.)	we teach you teach (pl.)	we relax you relax (pl.)
they wish the children wish	they teach the schools teach	they relax the travelers relax

use of present tense

Our purchasing agent **buys** most of his stock from local sources.

I **recognize** the person in this picture.

Our company **establishes** offices in all countries in which it **conducts** business.

Our cleaning crew **waxes** these floors weekly.

He **goes** to the doctor regularly for checkups.

b. **The *past tense* describes a single past action or event. Simply use the past part of a verb to express the past tense.**

The customer **selected** tan carpeting for his new offices.

I **received** these documents last week.

Our purchasing agent **bought** this equipment from an Internet site.

c. **The *future tense* describes expected or anticipated occurrences. To form the future tense, use the present part with the helping verb *will*.**

I **will call** you within the next few days to confirm your reservation.

The committee **will review** your proposal by March 1, and Mr. Rosen **will notify** you of the committee's decision by March 8.

Our company **will** not **participate** in the bidding for this contract.

5–14 Perfect Tenses

The perfect tenses—the present, past, and future—use the past participle of the verb along with a helping verb formed from *have*.

a. **The *present perfect tense* describes an action or a condition that began in the past and has continued until the present. This tense is formed by using *has* or *have* with the past participle of the verb.**

Mr. Randolf **has worked** in our Accounting Department since July 1990.

The company **has paid** heavy fines during the past three years for environmental-impact violations.

We **have** already **sent** you three reminders about your past-due account.

b. The *past perfect tense* describes a past action that occurred before another past action. Use *had* as a helping verb with the past participle of the main verb to form this tense.

Our client **had signed** this will just three days before he **died**.

We **accepted** this offer only after we **had contacted** three other vendors.

Although we **had paid** for the merchandise, the manufacturer **did** not **ship** it in time for our spring sale.

c. The *future perfect tense* describes an action that will take place before another future action. Use the helping verbs *will have* with the past participle of the main verb to form this tense.

By the time you submit the final manuscript, we **will have spent** over $50,000 in fees to freelance writers.

If allowed to continue, this project at its conclusion **will have cost** United States taxpayers over $3 billion.

5–15 Progressive Tenses

The progressive tenses show action in progress during the present, past, and future. Use the present participle of the verb along with a being verb helper—*am, is, are, was, were,* or *be.*

a. The *present progressive tense* describes an ongoing action during the present time. The being verb helpers *am, is,* and *are* are used with the present participle to form this tense.

I **am taking** several classes in computer applications this semester.

Our company **is sponsoring** a number of youth and adult programs in the community.

Several of our key employees **are relocating** to our main office in Boston.

b. The *past progressive tense* relates an ongoing action that occurred in the past. The being verb helpers *was* and *were* with the present participle of a verb are used to form this tense.

I **was discussing** this problem with the vice president when her administrative assistant interrupted us with an emergency message from the chairman of the board.

Until the end of last year, we **were** still **selling** more copies of the sixth edition than of the seventh edition.

c. The *future progressive tense* forecasts an ongoing future action. To form this tense, use the helping verbs *will* and *be* with the present participle of the verb.

We **will be staffing** this branch office about one month before construction is completed.

Our auditors **will be reviewing** this company's books for at least another two months.

5-16 Passive Voice Constructions

Unlike other verb constructions, the passive voice does not necessarily identify who does what. Instead, the person or thing performing the action may be cloaked in ambiguity.

In business communications the passive voice is often used to soften the impact of a negative idea or to avoid placing blame for an oversight or error. It is also used simply to provide variety in sentence construction. Although grammar checkers (software programs) flag passive voice constructions, they are not grammar errors.

To form a passive voice construction, use the past participle of the verb with one of the following being verb helpers: *is, are, was, were, be,* or *been.*

Each order **is entered** into our computer when it arrives at our factory.

Our products **are sold** only through franchised retailers.

Unfortunately, the shipment **was damaged** in transit.

These eviction notices **were mailed** to the tenants on September 1.

The building **will be restored** within the next year.

All the depositors **have been notified** that the insured deposits of Universal Savings **have been assumed** by First Arizona Savings.

5-17 Use of *Lay* and *Lie*

a. Broadly defined, the verb *lay* means "to place or put" and the verb *lie* means "to recline." Forms of these two verbs are often confused in usage. The principal parts of *lie* and *lay* follow.

Present Part	*Past Part*	*Past Participle*	*Present Participle*
lie	lay	lain	lying
lay	laid	laid	laying

b. Use a form of *lie* when the subject of the verb is performing the action, that is, the subject is what is lying. Otherwise, if the subject of the sentence is not the person or thing doing the lying, use a form of l*ay.*[8]

Always use a form of *lay* when the past participle appears with a "being" verb helper (*is, are, was, were, be, been*).

---

[8]Use of the verb *lay* with three of its parts—*lay, laid,* and (has, have or had) *laid*—is often easily identified by substituting a form of the verb *put.* If *put* or one of its forms makes sense, then the use of *lay* or one of its forms is correct. Otherwise, a form of *lie* is more than likely correct.

***subject is performing the action*—is lying**

The *new shopping center* **lies** at the base of the Flintridge Foothills.

He **lay** unconscious for nearly an hour before the doctor arrived.

Our *mainframe computer* **has lain** idle for nearly six hours.

Your *packages* **are lying** on the bottom shelf of the cupboard.

***subject of verb is not* lying**

We always **lay** all new magazines on the table in the reception area. (*new magazines* are lying on the table—not subject of verb, *We*)

Before leaving the office, she **laid** the contracts on your desk. (*contracts* are lying on the desk—not subject of verb, *she*)

Our shipping clerks **have** always **laid** these booklets horizontally in their packing boxes. (*booklets* are lying in packing boxes—not subject of verb, *shipping clerks*)

Retail stores throughout the country **are laying** plans to capture their share of holiday purchases. (*retail stores*, not *plans* is the subject of the sentence)

always a form of* lay *("being" verb + past participle)

These sandbags have **been laid** here because of impending flood damage.

The carpeting for our new building **was laid** yesterday.

5–18 Principles of Agreement

a. **The verb of a sentence must agree in person and number with the subject. To identify a subject, omit any prepositional phrases that separate the subject and the verb.**

The **legs** of the table **were damaged** in transit. (Omit prepositional phrase *of the table*.)

Our **stock** of cartridges for our Hewlett-Packard and Epson printers **is running** low. (Omit prepositional phrases *of cartridges* and *for our Hewlett-Packard and Epson printers*.)

b. **A pronoun that represents the subject must agree in number and gender with the subject.**

Mr. Charles was asked to prepare **his** report by the end of this week.

Would **every student** please be sure to submit **his** or **her** class schedule by February 5.

Ellen and **Margaret** were asked to resubmit **their** applications for employment.

The **company** filed for bankruptcy because **it** was unable to meet **its** obligations.

c. **Compound subjects joined by *and* generally require the use of a plural verb. When compound subjects are joined by *or* or *nor*, the form of the verb is determined by the part of the subject that is closer to the verb. If one part is plural and the other is singular, place the plural part, where possible, closer to the verb.**

***compound joined by* and**

My **son and daughter-in-law receive** monthly issues of *Business Forecast.*

Outgoing **letters and packages leave** our office on a regularly scheduled basis.

Mr. Lopez and his two assistants were requested to attend the board meeting.

***compound joined by* or *or* nor**

Neither Sharon nor **John was** available for comment to the press.

Either you or **I am** responsible for writing this section of the report.

Ms. Binder or her **assistants are** reviewing the manuscript.

Candy or **flowers are** typically given on this occasion. (Not: Flowers or *candy is* typically given on this occasion.)

d. **Subjects joined by *and* take singular verbs in only two cases: (1) when the parts separated by *and* constitute a single person or thing and (2) when the compound is preceded by *each, every,* or *many a (an).***

single person or thing

Our **accountant and tax attorney has** prepared all the reports for the Internal Revenue Service.

Her **nurse and companion works** six days a week.

Bacon and eggs is served in our restaurant until 11 a.m. each day.

Luckily the **horse and carriage was** stolen after the scene had been shot.

***compound preceded by* each, every, *or* many a (an)**

Each apartment and condominium was inspected by our general manager before it was released for rental.

Every man, woman, and child is responsible for carrying his or her belongings during the tour.

Many a student and instructor has requested additional tickets to our Drama Department's production of *Picnic.*

e. **Indefinite pronouns such as *each, every, everyone, everything, somebody, anybody, either,* and *neither* take singular verbs.**

Each of the books **was** stamped with the company name.

Everyone was pleased with the hotel accommodations.

Grammar 5

Everything in these files **needs** to be transferred to microfiche.

Neither of them **was** present at the meeting.

f. **When the word *there* precedes the verb, select the singular or plural verb form based on the number of the noun that follows. If the noun is singular, then use a singular verb; if it is plural, use a plural verb.**

The same rule applies to those words such as *some, all, none, most, a majority, one fourth,* and *part* that indicate portions. When they function as subjects, the number of the noun that follows governs whether a singular or plural verb is correct.

there *preceding a singular verb form*

There **is** one **person** on the mailing list you may wish to call.

There **appears** to be only one **reason** why we did not receive the contract.

there *preceding a plural verb form*

There **are** three **people** on the reserve list.

There **appear** to be several **reasons** why our bid was not accepted.

portion preceding a singular verb form

Some of the **money has** been invested in U.S. Savings Bonds.

Part of your **order has** been shipped.

One third of our **equipment needs** to be replaced.

portion preceding a plural verb form

All the **materials were** shipped to you yesterday.

Only **one half** of the **packages have** been inspected.

A majority of our **employees receive** extra benefits from our incentive plan.

g. **The words *a number* used as a subject require a plural verb. *The number* used as a subject requires a singular verb. Keep in mind that descriptive adverbs and adjectives may separate the article *a* or *the* from the word *number.***

a number *subject, plural verb*

Under the circumstances, **a number** of our customers **are** requesting a full refund.

A surprisingly small **number** of our students **have** registered late this semester.

the number *subject, singular verb*

We believe that **the number** of employees selecting the DSE insurance option **has** increased.

The large **number** of responses received from our recent advertising campaign **was** far greater than we had anticipated.

h. To express the subjunctive mood (a situation or condition that is untrue or highly unlikely), use *were* instead of *was* after *if, as if, as though,* or *wish.* The verb *was* is used only if the situation after *if, as if,* or *as though* could be true.

***use of* were *instead of* was**

If I **were** you, I would submit another application before the deadline date. (A condition that is untrue—I cannot be you.)

Mr. Greeley took charge **as though** he **were** the owner of the store. (But Mr. Greeley is not the owner of the store.)

I **wish** I **were** able to answer that question for you. (But I cannot answer the question.)

***use of* was**

If Mary **was** here, she did not return the overdue library books. (Mary could have been there.)

The customer acted **as though** he **was** irritated with our credit policies. (The customer may have been irritated.)

i. Avoid splitting an infinitive, that is, placing any words between *to* and the verb form.

Unfortunately, I was unable **to follow logically** the speaker's train of thought. (Not *to logically follow*)

Were you able **to understand fully** the ramifications of this policy change? (Not *to fully understand*)

j. Collective nouns such as *committee, jury, audience, group, team, class, board, crowd,* and *council* may take either singular or plural verbs, depending upon the situation in which the verb is used. If the individual members of the collective noun are operating as a unit, use a singular verb; if the individual members are acting separately, use a plural verb.

In most cases the use of a plural verb with a collective noun results in an awkward-sounding construction. To avoid such situations, restructure the sentence to use a plural-noun subject.

elements of collective noun acting as a unit

When an **audience gives** a speaker a standing ovation, you may be sure that he or she has delivered an exceptional address.

Has the **committee** finished its report?

elements of collective noun acting separately

The **jury were** arguing violently. (Alternative: The jury members were arguing violently.)

The **board have** not yet reached a decision. (Alternative: The board members have not yet reached a decision.)

restructured sentence with plural-noun subject

Unfortunately, the **members** of the council **do** not agree on the purpose of the newly formed committee.

After the game the team **members were** seen arguing with one another on national television.

k. **A relative pronoun clause (a clause commonly beginning with *who* or *that*) must agree in gender and number with the noun or pronoun it modifies.**

Ms. Cohen is a **person** who **is** concerned about maintaining **her** good health.

Our manager is the kind of **man** who **is** always considerate of **his** subordinates.

All the **children** who **attend** this school must maintain **their** grade averages at or above the "*C*" level.

Have you read all the **papers** that **were** placed on your desk?

Our committee **meeting**, which **was** scheduled for next Monday, has been canceled.

l. **Relative pronoun clauses (*who* and *that* clauses) preceded by such phrases as "one of those (or the) doctors," generally agree with the plural noun—in this case, *doctors*. Phrases such as "one of those (or the) executives," "one of those (or the) books," or "one of those (or the) assistants" are in the same category. The entire group is described by the clause; therefore, plural forms must be used.**

In sentences where "one of those (or the) ______" is limited by the word *only*, the relative clause does not refer to the entire group. Singular forms are correct in this instance.

"one of those ______"—plural forms

Mary is one of those business **executives** who **travel** extensively in **their** jobs.

He is one of the **salespersons** who regularly **visit** all **their** customers.

Joshua's Travels is one of those **books** that **have** a tragic ending.

She is one of the **employees** who **work** in Chicago.

"one of those ______" limited by only—singular forms

Mary is the **only one** of the business executives who **travels** extensively in **her** job.

He is the **only one** of those salespersons who regularly **visits** all **his** customers.

Joshua's Travels is the **only one** of those books that **has** a tragic ending.

She is the **only one** of the employees who **works** in Chicago.

Adjectives

5–19 Adjectives Modify Nouns

Adjectives modify nouns or pronouns. They answer such questions as what kind? how many? which one?

what kind?

damaged merchandise	**laser** printers	**stylish** dresses

how many?

three salespersons	**several** years	**two dozen** pencils

which one?

Karen's computer	**those** flight attendants	**your** idea

5–20 Use of the Articles *A* and *An*

Use the article *a* before a word that begins with a consonant sound, a long *u* sound, or an *h* that is pronounced. Use *an* before words that begin with a pronounced vowel sound (except long *u*) or before words that begin with a silent *h*.

***use of* a**

a newspaper	a uniform	a hillside development
a restaurant	a union	a history class

***use of* an**

an answer	an unusual request	an honest person
an opportunity	an upper floor	an hour

5–21 Adjective Comparison

a. Adjectives may be used to compare two or more nouns or pronouns. Use the comparative form (*-er* or *more, less*) for comparing two persons or things and the superlative form (*-est* or *most, least*) for comparing three or more.

b. Most one-syllable adjectives ending in *e* add *r* for the comparative and *st* for the superlative.

Grammar 5

Most one-syllable adjectives ending in consonants add *er* for the comparative and *est* for the superlative, but some double the final consonant before adding *er* or *est*.[9]

***most one-syllable adjectives ending in* e**

He has a **fine** set of golf clubs.

He has a **finer** set of golf clubs than I.

He has the **finest** set of golf clubs I have ever seen.

most one-syllable adjectives ending in a consonant

This is a **short** letter.

This letter is **shorter** than the last one you dictated.

This is the **shortest** letter I have written today.

some one-syllable adjectives ending in a consonant

Do you expect to make a **big** profit on this stock?

Which of these stocks do you think will yield a **bigger** profit?

His **biggest** profit on investments this year came from Internet stocks.

simple	**comparative**	**superlative**
nice	nicer	nicest
tame	tamer	tamest
large	larger	largest
sweet	sweeter	sweetest
mild	milder	mildest
proud	prouder	proudest
sad	sadder	saddest
trim	trimmer	trimmest
drab	drabber	drabbest

c. **Most two-syllable adjectives and all adjectives containing three or more syllables use *more* or *less* and *most* or *least* to construct comparative and superlative forms. Forms for those two-syllable adjectives that do not follow this pattern are shown in the dictionary after their simple form. These words include *costly, friendly, happy, healthy, merry, lovely, pretty*—all ending in *y*.**

***two-syllable adjective with* more, most, less, *or* least**

We interviewed an **outstanding** candidate yesterday.

This candidate is **more outstanding** than the one we interviewed yesterday.

This candidate is the **most outstanding** one we have interviewed so far.

---

[9]Single-syllable adjectives that end in *e* or that double the final consonant before adding *er* (comparative form) or *est* (superlative form) are considered irregular. Therefore, these irregular forms are shown in the dictionary after the positive form.

***three-syllable adjective with* more, most, less, *or* least**

We purchased an **expensive** scanner yesterday.

This phone system is **less expensive** than the one we evaluated yesterday.

This is the **least expensive** grade of carpeting we carry.

***two-syllable adjective using* er *or* est**

We initiated a **costly** program.

The state's highway program is **costlier** than its conservation program.

Our welfare program is the **costliest** one in the nation.

simple	**comparative**	**superlative**
useful	more useful	most useful
	less useful	least useful
suitable	more suitable	most suitable
	less suitable	least suitable
comprehensive	more comprehensive	most comprehensive
	less comprehensive	least comprehensive
practical	more practical	most practical
	less practical	least practical
lonely	lonelier	loneliest
heavy	heavier	heaviest
sloppy	sloppier	sloppiest

d. **Irregular forms for adjective comparison appear in the dictionary. They are listed after the simple forms. A list of commonly used irregular adjective forms follows:**

simple	**comparative**	**superlative**
bad, ill	worse	worst
good, well	better	best
far	farther, further	farthest, furthest
little	littler, less	littlest, least
many, much	more	most

e. **Use *other* or *else* when comparing one person or object with the other members of the group to which it belongs.**

Our London office earns more revenue than any of our **other** foreign branch offices. (Not *any of our foreign branch offices*)

Andrew is more diligent than anyone **else** in the class. (Not *anyone in the class*)

f. **Some adjectives cannot be compared in the regular sense because they are absolute. A partial list of such adjectives follows:**

alive	finished	round
complete	full	straight
dead	perfect	unique

Grammar 5

Absolute adjectives may show comparison by use of the forms "more nearly" or "most nearly."

This water cooler is **full**.

The water cooler in your office is **more nearly full** (not *fuller*) than the one in ours.

The water cooler in the Office of Human Resources is the **most nearly full** (not *fullest*) one on this floor.

The police report is **accurate**.

The *Daily News*' report of this incident was **more nearly accurate** (not *more accurate*) than the one appearing in the *Tribune*.

The *Daily News*' report was the **most nearly accurate** (not *most accurate*) account of this incident that appeared in the media.

5–22 Independent Adjectives[10]

When two or more adjectives appearing before a noun independently modify the noun, separate these adjectives with commas.

His **direct**, **practical** approach to problem solving has created a high degree of respect for him among his staff.

We returned that **boring**, **poorly written** manuscript to its author.

She handled the problem in a **sure**, **calm**, **decisive** manner.

5–23 Adjectives With Linking Verbs

Use adjectives, not adverbs, after linking (no action) verbs. Common linking verbs include *feel, look, smell, sound,* and *taste*.

I **feel bad** that you were not elected. (Not *badly*)

Cakes from Federico's Bakery always **taste delicious**.
(Not *deliciously*)

After the fire the adjoining rooms **smelled terrible**. (Not *terribly*)

5–24 Compound Adjectives[11]

a. **Adjectives containing two or more words that are shown hyphenated in the dictionary are known as *permanent compounds*.[12] These words are always hyphenated when they are used as adjectives.**

---

[10]See Section 1–8 for a detailed explanation of the use of the comma with independent adjectives.

[11]See Section 2–2 for detailed rules regarding the formation of compound adjectives.

[12]All hyphenations for compound adjectives in this reference manual are based on those shown in *Merriam-Webster's Collegiate Dictionary,* 10th ed. (Springfield, Mass.: Merriam-Webster, Incorporated, 1999.) Entries for Merriam-Webster's Collegiate Dictionary may be viewed at http://www.m-w.com.

Your **up-to-date** files have been very helpful in compiling this data.

My present job is only **part-time**, but I will begin looking for a **full-time** job in September.

As one of the oldest players in the league, Steve doesn't seem to know when he is **well-off**.

b. When two or more words appearing before a noun function as a single-thought modifier, place hyphens between the words, even though these words do not appear hyphenated in the dictionary. These compound adjectives are *temporary compounds* and are hyphenated only when they appear before the noun or pronoun they modify.

temporary compound adjective before the modified noun

Upon reading your **well-written** report, the committee members agreed to establish a new community center.

Very little of the **high-priced** merchandise was sold during our clearance sale.

Do not exceed the **65-mile-an-hour** speed limit.

You may advertise this opening as a **$42,000-a-year** position.

temporary compound adjective following the modified noun

Your report is certainly **well written**.

This merchandise is too **high priced** for our store.

The speed limit on this freeway is **65 miles an hour**.

Our manager's salary is at least **$42,000 a year**.

Adverbs

5–25 Functions and Forms of Adverbs

Adverbs modify verbs, adjectives, or other adverbs. They answer such questions as when? where? why? how? to what degree?

a. Most adverbs end in *ly*.

accidentally	daily	finally
carefully	definitely	steadily
cautiously	diligently	usually

b. Some adverbs may either end in *ly* or take the adjective form of the word.[13]

Please drive **slowly** (or **slow**) on this icy road.

---

[13]Both forms of those adverbs that may end in *ly* or just take the adjective form are shown in the dictionary.

Your order will be processed as **quickly** (or **quick**) as possible.

You may call **directly** (or **direct**) to Chicago on this line.

c. Other adverbs do not take an *ly* form. Such adverbs include the following:

again	late	not	there
almost	never	now	very
here	no	soon	well

5–26 Adverb Comparison

a. One-syllable adverbs and some two-syllable adverbs are compared by adding *er* or *est*. For comparisons between two items, use *er*; for comparisons among more than two items, use *est*.[14]

comparison of two

You live **closer** to the library than I.

My assistant left **earlier** than I.

comparison of more than two

Of all the students in the study group, you live **closest** to the library.

Who is scheduled to arrive the **earliest**—Bill, Paula, or Bob?

b. Most adverbs containing two syllables and all adverbs containing more than two syllables form the comparison by adding *more* or *most* (or *less* or *least*) to the positive form. Use *more* (or *less*) in comparing two items and *most* (or *least*) in comparing more than two items.

comparison of two

This conveyer belt travels **more slowly** than the one next to it.

Please pack these items **more carefully** than you have done in the past.

This brand of soap is **less widely** used on the East Coast than in the South.

comparison of more than two

Denver has been mentioned **most often** as the likely site for our next convention.

This conference is the **most unusually** conducted one I have ever attended.

This brand of soap is the **least widely** used of all the major brands.

---

[14]Two-syllable adverbs that show comparison by adding *er* or *est* are considered irregular. Therefore, these forms are shown in the dictionary following the simple form.

5–27 Adverb Placement

a. **Place adverbs as closely as possible to the words they modify. The misplacement of an adverb can change the meaning of a sentence or result in an awkward-sounding sentence.**

changed meaning

Only Beverly and I were invited to attend the seminar on human relations.

Beverly and I were invited to attend **only** the seminar on human relations.

awkward construction

Our costs have **nearly** risen 20 percent this year. (Awkward)

Our costs have risen **nearly** 20 percent this year. (Correct)

b. **Avoid splitting an infinitive with an adverb; place the adverb after the infinitive.**

We will need **to scrutinize carefully** all applicants for this position.

If you wish **to discuss** this situation **further**, please call me.

5–28 Adverbs vs. Adjectives

Use an adverb after a verb that shows action; use an adjective, however, after a nonaction (or linking) verb.

Verbs relating to the senses (*feel, look, smell*) may function as nonaction verbs. In some cases you may test such occurrences by substituting a form of *to be* (*am, is, are, was, were*). If the sentence reads smoothly, use the adjective form for any descriptive word that modifies the verb.

action verb

You **did well** on your six-month evaluation.

The pedestrian **crossed** the street **cautiously**.

Most of the committee **opposed bitterly** the controversial measure.

The professional soccer team **was beaten badly** in yesterday's game.

nonaction or linking verb

If we do not brew fresh coffee every two hours, it begins to **taste bitter**. (. . . is bitter.)

The employees' lounge **smells terrible**. (. . . is terrible.)

John **looked angry** when he received the news. (. . . was angry . . . .)

I **feel bad** about Mr. Johnson's predicament.

The entrée at the Sunday evening banquet **was delicious**.

5–29 Double Negatives

Use only one negative word or limiting adverb to express a single idea.

Do **not** release this information to **anybody**. (Not *nobody*)

I did **not** receive **anything** from our insurance agent. (Not *nothing*)

I **can** (not *can't* or *cannot*) **scarcely** believe that our president would make such a foolish statement.

We **were** (not *weren't* or *were not*) **hardly** in the office when Ms. Kawamura gave us the disappointing news.

He **had** (not *hadn't* or *had not*) **barely** finished computing the results when the Board of Directors requested him to report his findings.

Prepositions

5–30 Prepositions as Connectors

a. Prepositions link descriptive words to other words or ideas in a sentence. The most commonly used prepositions are *of* and *for*. Occasionally used ones are *about, during, except,* and *but* (meaning *except*). Other commonly used prepositions, those listed below, can easily be identified by picturing what an airplane can do in relation to clouds: the airplane can fly ______ the clouds.

above	down	over
after	from	through
alongside	in	to
among	inside	toward
around	into	under
at	near	up
before	off	upon
behind	on	with
below	opposite	within
between	outside	without

b. Prepositions begin a phrase that ends with a noun or pronoun. This phrase is related to another word in the sentence—it describes, limits, or modifies the word in some way by clarifying who, what, when, where, how, why, or to what degree.

Our staff **of accountants** is available to assist you at any time. (*Of accountants* is related to *staff*—specifies what.)

You may park your car **behind the building**. (*Behind the building* is related to *park*—specifies where.)

5–31 Prepositional Phrases

In determining subject-verb agreement, generally ignore any prepositional phrases that separate the subject and the verb. (See Section 5–18l for subject-verb agreement principles related to prepositional phrases appearing before relative pronoun clauses [clauses beginning with *who* or *that*]).

One of your brothers **is** waiting in your office. (Omit *of your brothers* to match "One . . . is.")

A large **quantity** of goods **has** been ordered for the sale. (Omit *of goods* to match "quantity . . . has.")

Last Monday our **supply** of paper goods and kitchen utensils **was** destroyed. (Omit *of paper goods and kitchen utensils* to match "supply . . . was.")

5–32 *In, Between,* or *Among?*

When a preposition has a single object, use *in*. For two separate objects, use *between;* for three or more objects, use *among*.

in

There are several discrepancies **in** the auditor's report.

The prosecution noted several discrepancies **in** the witness's testimony.

between

Between you and me, I believe this Internet stock will split within the next month.

There were several discrepancies **between** the two witnesses' reports.

among

Please distribute these supplies **among** the various branch offices.

Among themselves the Board of Directors had consented previously to withdraw their bid to acquire this software company.

5–33 Prepositions Used With Certain Words

Certain words require particular prepositions, depending upon the meaning to be conveyed. Other words often acquire prepositions incorrectly. A list of commonly used correct combinations follows:

Agree **on** or **upon** (mutual ideas or considerations—to reach an understanding)
Agree **to** (undertake an action)
Agree **with** (a person or his or her idea)

All **of** (Use *of* when followed by a pronoun; omit *of* when followed by a noun. *All of us . . . . All the people . . . .*)

Angry **about** (a situation or condition)
Angry **at** (things)
Angry **with** (a person or a group of persons)

Both **of** (Use *of* when followed by a pronoun; omit *of* when followed by a noun. *Both of them . . . . Both the managers . . . .*)

Buy **from** (Not *off* or *off of*)

Compare **to** (show a likeness)
Compare **with** (look for differences as well as similarities)

Comply or compliance **with** (Not *to*)

Conform **to** (to act in accordance with prevailing standards)
Conform **with** (to be similar or in agreement)

Convenient **to** (a location)
Convenient **for** (a person)

Correspond **with** (a person—by writing)
Correspond **to** (a thing)

Discrepancy **in** (one thing)
Discrepancy **between** (two things)
Discrepancy **among** (three or more things)

Different **from** (Not *than*)

From (a person) (Not *off* a person)

Help (doing something) (Not *help from.* He could not *help* laughing at . . . .)

Identical **with** (Not *to*)

Inside (Not *inside of*)

Off (a thing) (Not *off of*)

Opposite (Not *opposite to* or *opposite of*)

Outside (Not *outside of*)

Plan **to** (Not *plan on*)

Retroactive **to** (Not *retroactive from*)

Take **off** (a thing)
Take **from** (a person)

Conjunctions

Conjunctions join words or groups of words within a sentence. While some conjunctions join equal ideas, others join contrasting ideas or introduce dependent clauses.

5–34 Coordinating Conjunctions

a. The most commonly occurring coordinating conjunctions—*and, but, or,* and *nor*—are used to join like or equal ideas within a sentence. These ideas may be words, phrases, or clauses.

words

Please place copies of the **proposal** and **contract** in each client's file.

You may obtain additional information from **Mr. Parr**, **Ms. Dow**, or **me**.

phrases

Please post these notices **on all campus bulletin boards** and **in student gathering places throughout the campus**.

Ms. Ross has agreed to **edit the manuscript** and **follow it through all the production stages**.

clauses

If you accept our offer, **we will sign a guarantee of completion by May 1** and **you will be protected against any losses beyond this date**.

Our advertising funds for this year have been depleted, but **we are interested in considering your proposal for our next year's budget**.

b. Because coordinating conjunctions join equal ideas, the ideas they join must be expressed in the same way; that is, they must have *parallel structure.* Parallel structure requires that the connected ideas have the same format. For example, if the first idea begins with a noun or pronoun, so must any others. If the first idea begins with an infinitive, then all others must begin with an infinitive. Be sure to match each idea—gerund with gerund, verb with verb, prepositional phrase with prepositional phrase, and so forth.

parallel structure with gerunds

You may obtain your free trial subscription by **calling** or **writing** our main office.

We would appreciate your **paying** this bill as soon as possible and **sending** us a copy of the receipt issued at the time of payment.

parallel structure with verb phrases (past participles)

The contractor has already **leveled** the construction site and **poured** the foundation.

As you requested, we have **notified** our delinquent customers of their status, **requested** immediate payment of all overdue amounts, and **halted** any charge orders in progress.

parallel structure with clauses (subject and verb)

As soon as we receive your credit application, **we will check** your credit rating and our **Credit Department will contact** you.

Our local **chamber of commerce has endorsed** this proposal, but other **chambers of commerce** in the county **are opposed** to it.

5–35 Conjunctions Used in Pairs

a. Use *either . . . or* for positive statements; use *neither . . . nor* for negative statements. The same grammatical construction should be used after each part.

***positive statements,* either . . . or**

Either Ms. Saunders **or** Mr. Ramirez will inspect the property.

You may specify **either** black **or** brown on your order.

***negative statements,* neither . . . nor**

Neither an Explorer **nor** a Suburban is available for rental this week.

I could not believe that **neither** Larry **nor** Debbie would accept the assignment.

b. Use the same grammatical construction after each part of the conjunctive pair *not only . . . but also.*

Our company manufactures **not only** furniture **but also** major appliances. (Not: Our company *not only* manufactures furniture *but also* major appliances.)

Our company **not only** manufactures and services major appliances **but also** services small appliances.

c. In comparisons use *as . . . as* for positive ideas and *so . . . as* for negative ideas.

***positive ideas,* as . . . as**

Our Model 874 cellular phone has become **as** popular **as** our Model 923.

I believe that her understudy is **as** talented **as** Ms. Saito.

***negative ideas,* so . . . as**

Our Model 874 cellular phone is not **so** popular **as** our Model 923.

Avocados are not **so** expensive **as** they were last year.

5–36 Subordinating Conjunctions

Words such as *if, when, as, since,* and *because* (subordinating conjunctions) may be used to introduce word groups (dependent clauses). A partial listing of subordinating conjunctions follows:

if	because	while
as	since	before
when	although	after

a. When a subordinating conjunction with its corresponding clause introduces a sentence, place a comma after the introductory clause.

If you wish any additional information, Mr. Johnson will be pleased to supply it.

Before you sign these contracts, you should speak with some of this company's former clients.

b. When a subordinating conjunction with its corresponding clause follows a main clause, separate the two clauses with a comma only if the subordinating conjunction introduces an additional or nonessential (nonrestrictive) idea.

no comma separating clauses—essential (restrictive) idea

We will ship your merchandise **when we receive your authorization.**

You may wish to verify this information **before you purchase these bonds**.

comma separating clauses—additional (nonrestrictive) idea

Mr. Johnson would be pleased to supply you with any additional information**, if you need it**.

My clients have agreed to settle this matter out of court**, although I advised them against doing so**.

Grammar 5

5–37 As vs. Like

As is a conjunction and is used when the following construction is a clause (a word group containing a subject and a verb). *Like* is a preposition and is used when the construction results in a prepositional phrase (a phrase ending with a noun or pronoun).

as ***introducing a clause***

They did not package the order **as** (not *like*) **he expected they would.**

As (not *like*) **you indicated in your E-mail**, we cannot expect to make a profit during our first year of operation.

like ***introducing a prepositional phrase***

We need more qualified agents **like you**.

Please order another desk **like the one** you have in your office.

Interjections

5–38 Use of Interjections

Interjections impart sudden emotion or strong feeling, but they do not contribute substantially to the meaning of the sentence. When used alone, interjections are followed by an exclamation mark. When they are used within a sentence, the sentence is generally concluded with an exclamation mark. Examples of interjections used alone follow:

Absolutely not!	Never!	Well!
Ah!	No!	Whew!
Great!	Oh!	Wow!
Indeed not!	Terrific!	Yes!

interjections used alone

Whew! I'm certainly glad the work for this tax period is behind us.

Absolutely not! Only employees with security clearances are permitted in this area.

interjections in sentences

Oh, you can't expect us to have these photographs developed by tomorrow!

No, we cannot make any exceptions to this company policy!

Chapter 6

Abbreviations and Symbols

c.o.d.

Abbreviations and Symbols Solution Finder

Abbreviations

6–1 Use of Abbreviations

a. Use abbreviations only when you are confident the reader understands their meaning. Confine your primary use of abbreviations to (1) business forms; (2) suitable technical documents; and (3) tables, charts, graphs, and other such visual aids.

b. Limit your use of abbreviations in running copy. If used, spell out the words and place the abbreviation in parentheses the first time the words are used.

Before taking this deduction, you may wish to check with the **Internal Revenue Service (IRS)** on its legitimacy. Several recent **IRS** rulings in this area may affect your ability to use these losses as a deduction.

c. Use consistently throughout your document the same form for an abbreviated word or sequence of words.

Application deadlines for admittance to **California State University, Northridge (CSUN)** are due by March 1. Housing requests for **CSUN** and other state universities are due by June 1. (Not: *Cal State Northridge*)

6–2 Titles

a. The abbreviations *Mr., Ms., Mrs.,* and *Dr.* are used for courtesy titles.

Mr. Peter Miller
Ms. Frances Cates
Mrs. Carole Eustice
Dr. James Korkosz

b. Write out a civil, educational, military, or religious title used before and in conjunction with a person's full name or last name only. Lengthy titles (those containing more than one word) may be abbreviated, however, when they appear before a person's *full* name and brevity is required.

title written out—with full name

I believe **Professor** Sharlene Pollyea is in charge of the project.

title written out—with last name only

Dear **Governor** Reece:

Address the letter to the attention of **Lieutenant Governor** Miller.

title abbreviated—with full name

Please invite **Lt. Col.** Donald Curry to the meeting. (Lieutenant Colonel)

c. Abbreviate and capitalize personal titles (*Jr., Sr., Esq.,* etc.), professional designations (*CPA, CLU, R.N., R.P.T.,* etc.), or academic degrees (*M.D.,*

Ph.D., Ed.D., LL.B., M.L.S., etc.) that follow a person's name. A comma is used before and after an abbreviation appearing within a sentence and before an abbreviation appearing at the end of a sentence. The personal titles *Jr.* and *Sr.* may appear with or without commas, depending on the individual's preference.

Abbreviations of academic degrees and professional designations are separated by periods except for the designations *CPA* (Certified Public Accountant), *CPS* (Certified Professional Secretary), *PLS* (Professional Legal Secretary), and *CLU* (Chartered Life Underwriter).

personal title

John A. Wrigley **Jr.** was elected to the Lynwood City Council.

The airline reservation is for Robert J. Brown, **Sr.**

Please send a copy of the report to Robert Lucio, **Esq.**, by March 1.

professional designation

Cynthia Armstrong, **CPA**, was present at the meeting.

The charge nurse during that shift is Eric Blake, **R.N.**

academic degree

Our new college president, David Wolf, **Ph.D.**, met with the Board of Trustees yesterday.

First fill the prescriptions written by Dorothy Salazar, **M.D.**

6–3 Organizations

a. The names of well-known business, educational, governmental, professional, military, labor, philanthropic, and other organizations or agencies may be abbreviated. No periods or spaces are used to separate the individual letters.

business organizations

ALCOA	Aluminum Co. of America
ARCO	Atlantic Richfield Co.
BA	BankAmerica Corp.
GE	General Electric Co.
GMC	General Motors Corp.
IBM	International Business Machines Corp.
ITP	International Thomson Publishing
AA	American Airlines

educational organizations

ERIC	Educational Resources Information Center
NYU	New York University
PCC	Pasadena City College
UCLA	University of California, Los Angeles

government organizations

CIA	Central Intelligence Agency
FBI	Federal Bureau of Investigation
FCC	Federal Communications Commission
FDA	Food and Drug Administration
FTC	Federal Trade Commission
HUD	Department of Housing and Urban Development
ICC	Interstate Commerce Commission
OSHA	Occupational Safety and Health Administration
SSA	Social Security Administration
SEC	Securities and Exchange Commission
UNESCO	United Nations Educational, Scientific, and Cultural Organization
USDA	U.S. Department of Agriculture
USPS	U.S. Postal Service
VA	Veterans Administration

professional organizations

ABA	American Bankers Association; American Bar Association
ABC	Association for Business Communication
AIA	American Institute of Architects
AIB	American Institute of Banking
AMA	American Medical Association
ARMA	Association of Record Managers and Administrators
NBEA	National Business Education Association
IAAP	International Association of Administrative Professionals

other organizations

AAA	American Automobile Association
AFL-CIO	American Federation of Labor and Congress of Industrial Organizations
BBB	Better Business Bureau
NAACP	National Association for the Advancement of Colored People
NOW	National Organization for Women
YMCA	Young Men's Christian Association
YWCA	Young Women's Christian Association

b. **Television and radio station call letters are written in all capital letters without periods or spaces.**

ABC CBS CNN KFI KNXT PBS NBC

c. **In the names of business firms, abbreviations such as *Co., Corp., Inc., Ltd.,* and *Mfg.* are used only if they are part of the official organizational name.**

We ordered the parts from Corway **Mfg.** Co.

Johnson Products **Inc.** will receive the contract.

6–4 Dates and Time

a. **Spell out days of the week and months of the year. Abbreviate them only in lists, tables, graphs, charts, illustrations, or other such visual presentations where space is limited.**

days and months spelled out in text

Our next committee meeting will be held on **Monday, January 18**.

Next **Tuesday, October 8**, will mark the company's fifth anniversary.

days of the week abbreviated in graphics

Sun.	Mon.	Tues. (Tue.)	Wed.	Thurs. (Thu.)	Fri.	Sat.
Su	M	Tu	W	Th	F	Sa

months of the year abbreviated in graphics

Jan.	Feb.	Mar.	Apr.	May	June (Jun.)
July (Jul.)	Aug.	Sept. (Sep.)	Oct.	Nov.	Dec.

b. **The abbreviations *a.m.* (ante meridiem) and *p.m.* (post meridiem) are used for expressing clock time. They are placed in lowercase letters followed by periods. No space follows the first period.**

Would you prefer to take the flight at 8:45 **a.m.** or the one at 2 **p.m.**?

He arrived at 3:30 **p.m.**

c. **United States time zones—*EST* (Eastern Standard Time), *CST* (Central Standard Time), *MST* (Mountain Standard Time), *PST* (Pacific Standard Time), *AST* (Alaska Standard Time), and *HST* (Hawaii Standard Time)—are usually abbreviated. Time zones for daylight saving time are abbreviated *EDT, CDT, MDT, PDT,* and *ADT*. Hawaii does not go on daylight saving time.**

Our operators are available to take your orders from 8 a.m. to 9 p.m., **EST**.

According to the latest report, his plane will arrive in Denver at 6:05 p.m., **MDT**.

d. **The abbreviations *B.C.* (before Christ) and *A.D.* (anno Domini) are sometimes used in expressing dates. Both follow the year and are shown in capital letters with periods. In formal writing, however, *A.D.* appears before the year.**

B.C.

Professor Farhood claims that the statue dates back to 400 **B.C.**

***A.D.* after the year**

Ms. Lopez's thesis deals with the rise of Christianity from 200 to 350 **A.D.**

***A.D.* before the year**

The Spanish legions, under the leadership of Galba, conquered Rome in **A.D.** 68.

6–5 Standard Units of Measure

Common units of measure such as distance, length, temperature, volume, and weight are usually spelled out in business documents. Abbreviations, however, may be used on invoices, packing slips, and other business forms where space is limited. In abbreviating units of measure, place periods after one-word abbreviations and use the singular form. Omit the periods in abbreviations representing more than one word.

general business documents

All perishable goods shipped over **100 miles** should be kept below **40 degrees** Fahrenheit.

business forms, one-word abbreviations

12 **ft.** 2 **in.** (12 feet 2 inches)	3 **lb.** 2 **oz.** (3 pounds 2 ounces)
75°**F** (75 degrees Fahrenheit)	3 **doz.** pens (3 dozen pens)

business forms, multiple-word abbreviations

100 **wpm** (100 words per minute)   65 **mph** (65 miles per hour)

6–6 Metric Units of Measure

a. **In regular business documents metric units of measurement are generally written out. However, in business forms and tables and in scientific and technical writing, they are often abbreviated. These abbreviations are written without periods, and the singular and plural forms are the same. Common abbreviations for measurements related to distance, weight, and volume follow:**

prefixes

deka	**da**	(× 10)	deci	**d**	(1/10)
hecto	**h**	(× 100)	centi	**c**	(1/100)
kilo	**k**	(× 1000)	milli	**m**	(1/1000)
mega	**m**	(× 1 000 000)			
giga	**g**	(× 1 000 000 000)			

common units of measure

meter	**m**	centimeter	**cm**	kilometer	**km**
gram	**g**	kilogram	**kg**	milligram	**mg**
liter	**L**	milliliter	**ml**		

cubic centimeter **cc** square meter **sq m**

kilobyte **KB** megabyte **MB** gigabyte **GB**

b. **The abbreviation for *liter* is a capital *L* because the lowercase letter "l" and the numeral "1" (one) for many fonts look the same. Therefore, to avoid confusion, the capital *L* is used instead.**

1 **L** milk *but* 1 **ml** vaccine (abbreviation is clear)

c. **Temperatures in the metric system are expressed on the Celsius scale. This term is abbreviated *C*.**

37°**C** 25°**C**

d. **Express abbreviations relating to kilometers per hour with a diagonal.**

The maximum speed permitted on this highway is **105 km/h** (65 mph).

Slow down to **40 km/h** (25 mph) in the school crossing zone.

6–7 Business and General Terms

a. **When the word *number* is not followed by a numeral, spell it out. The abbreviation *No.*, however, is used when a numeral directly follows the term unless the term begins the sentence.**

The stock **number** of the item you requested is **4-862**.

We plan to discontinue stocking these **No. 1370** metal plates.

Please ship us three **Model No. 17A** electric motors.

Number 18-A replacement shelves are no longer stocked in our warehouse.

b. **Most commonly abbreviated business and computer terms are typed in all capital letters with no spaces or periods separating the letters. A few business terms, when used in business correspondence, however, are written in lowercase letters separated by periods. See Section 6–11 for an additional listing of business and computer terms.**

capitalized abbreviation of business term

TQM (total quality management)
PERT (program evaluation and review technique)
LIFO (last in, first out)
FIFO (first in, first out)
SOP (standard operating procedures)

capitalized abbreviation of computer term

RAM	(random-access memory)
CPU	(central processing unit)
CRT	(cathode-ray tube)
EDP	(electronic data processing)
OCR	(optical character recognition)

lowercase letters for abbreviation in correspondence

c.o.d.	(collect on delivery)
f.o.b.	(free on board)

c. **Capitalize and abbreviate the word *extension* (*Ext.*) when it appears in conjunction with telephone numbers.**

You may reach me at 987-9281, **Ext.** 1201, any weekday between 9 and 11 a.m.

Please call me by Friday at (714) 555-3827, **Ext.** 248.

d. **Some commonly abbreviated terms are derived from Latin expressions. They are generally typed in lowercase letters and are followed by a period at the close of each abbreviated word.**

abbreviations from Latin expressions

e.g.	(for example)
et al.	(and others)
i.e.	(that is)
etc.	(and so forth)
cf.	(compare)
pro tem.	(temporarily)
id.	(the same)
P.S.	(postscript)
ad hoc	(for a specific purpose)
N.B.	(note well)
viz.	(namely)
ibid.	(in the same place)
loc. cit.	(in the place cited)
op. cit.	(in the work cited)
a.m.	(after midnight until noon)
p.m.	(after noon until midnight)
B.C.	(year before Christ)
A.D.	(year after Christ)
ca.	(approximately; around)

6–8 Plurals

Apostrophes are not used to form the plurals of abbreviations; most plural abbreviations are formed by adding only *s* to the singular form. Some words, however, use the same abbreviation for the singular and plural forms.

plural formed by adding s

hr., **hrs.**
mgr., **mgrs.**
c.o.d., **c.o.d.s**
IOU, **IOUs**
CPA, **CPAs**
R.N., **R.N.s**

singular and plural forms identical

deg., **deg.** ft., **ft.** in., **in.**

6–9 Addresses and Geographical Expressions

a. For addresses in business correspondence, street designations such as *Boulevard, Street, Avenue, Lane, Place,* and *Road* are spelled out. *Boulevard,* however, may be abbreviated (*Blvd.*) if space is limited for expressing long street names.

street designation spelled out

Ms. Lila Green
462 Olive **Avenue**
Iowa City, IA 52240

Woodcutt Escrow Company
5700 Jefferson **Boulevard**
Columbus, OH 43266-0309

Boulevard *abbreviated with long street name*

Mr. James F. Campenelli
1873 San Fernando Mission **Blvd.**
San Francisco, CA 94127

b. Terms indicating direction (*North, South, East, West*) that precede a street name are spelled out. Compound directions such as *N.W. (Northwest),* however, are abbreviated when they are used before or after the street name.

simple direction before street name

851 **East** Lake Street

compound direction with street name

7059 Capitol Avenue, **N.E.**

4411 **S.W.** 34th Street

c. The U.S. Postal Service recommends that the names of states be abbreviated on all mailings by using the official state designations. (They are typed in capital letters with no periods or spaces.) These two-letter state designations are shown in Section 6–12 and on the page opposite the inside back cover.

However, since modern optical scanning equipment no longer requires the use of the two-letter designations, either the full state name or the two-letter state designation may be used, depending on which form more nearly balances with the other lines of the address. If both forms provide balance, use the two-letter state designation.

two-letter state designation

Mrs. Marjory Clark, PLS
Los Angeles Pierce College
6201 Winnetka Avenue
Woodland Hills, **CA** 91371

state spelled out fully

Fielder Publishing Company
9836 West Seventh Avenue
Ridgewood, **New Jersey** 07541

d. Since 1974 the U.S. Postal Service has recommended a format for addressing envelopes that uses all capital letters, abbreviations, and no internal punctuation marks. As yet, this format has not been widely accepted for individually typed correspondence or even computer-generated form correspondence; its use has been mainly with standard bulk mailings.

e. A period is placed after each abbreviated word in geographical abbreviations. Only with the two-letter state designations recommended by the U.S. Postal Service are the periods omitted.

capital letters

U.S.A. (United States of America) U.K. (United Kingdom)
G.B. (Great Britain) R.O.C. (Republic of China)

capital and lowercase letters

So. Nev. (Southern Nevada) Ire. (Ireland)

postal service designation

MT (Montana) IA (Iowa)

6–10 Abbreviation Format

a. The capitalization of abbreviations is generally governed by the format of the original word or words. Proper nouns are always capitalized while common nouns generally appear in lowercase letters. Some common noun abbreviations, however, are capitalized.

capital letters for proper noun

His father is a member of the **AFL-CIO**.

lowercase letters for common noun

Please send the order **c.o.d.**

capital letters for some common nouns

How many **VCRs** did our sales staff sell during the holiday season?

Be sure to ask the **TV** repair service to send the bill to our home office.

b. Abbreviations that appear in all capital letters are generally typed without periods or spaces. Exceptions are (1) geographical expressions, most professional designations, and academic degrees, which are typed with periods but no spaces and (2) initials in a person's name

and most abbreviations containing capital and lowercase letters, which are typed with both periods and spaces.

general rule—no periods and no spaces

We heard the news from an **NBC** reporter.

Be sure to turn your dial to **KBIG** for beautiful music.

geographical expressions—periods with no spaces

Their travel agency in Bonn, Germany, sponsored several tours of the **U.S.A.** last summer.

Please submit these completed forms to the **U.S.** Department of Agriculture.

Our new store location is 800 Tufts Avenue, **S.W.**

professional designations—periods with no spaces

Jodi Myers, **R.P.T.**, is the physical therapist who is handling this case.

Will Robert Soto, **R.N.**, be the new director of our nursing program?

academic degrees—periods with no spaces

Mr. Fujimoto earned an **M.A.** in music last June.

Sharon Lund O'Neil, **Ph.D.**, was offered the position.

initials—periods and spaces

Please deliver this report to Ms. **J. T.** Kelley.

Only Gerald **H.** Monroe applied for the position.

abbreviations with capital and lowercase letters—periods and spaces

So. Calif. (Southern California) **N. Mex.** (New Mexico)

c. **In abbreviations beginning with lowercase letters, a period is generally placed after each letter or group of letters representing a word. No space appears between periods and letters in compound abbreviations. Periods are not used, however, in abbreviations of metric measurements and compound abbreviations representing "measures per time."**

general rule—periods

c.o.d.	(collect on delivery)	**mgr.**	(manager)
a.m.	(ante meridiem)	**qt.**	(quart)
ft.	(foot or feet)	**amt.**	(amount)

metric measurements—no periods

mm	millimeter	**ml**	milliliter
cm	centimeter	**kg**	kilogram
cc	cubic centimeter		

time measurements—no periods

rpm	revolutions per minute	**wam**	words a minute
wpm	words per minute	**mph**	miles per hour

d. **If an abbreviation containing a period falls at the end of a sentence that requires a period, use only a single period. In a question or an exclamation, place a closing question or exclamation mark directly after the period appearing in the abbreviation.**

period

The hotel clerk awakened Mr. Sykiski at **8 a.m.**

question mark

Did you send the order **c.o.d.?**

exclamation mark

The plane was three hours late arriving in the **U.S.A.!**

6–11 Abbreviations of Terms Commonly Used in Business

Abbreviation	*Term*
A.A.	associate in arts (degree)
acct.	account
A.D.	anno Domini (in the year of our Lord)
ad, advt.	advertisement
addl., add'l	additional
Adm.	admiral (military title)
adm., admin.	administration, administrative
ADT	Alaska Daylight Time
afft.	affidavit
agcy.	agency
agt.	agent
AI	artificial intelligence
a.k.a., AKA	also known as
a.m.	ante meridiem (before noon)
amt.	amount
ans.	answer
AP	accounts payable
approx.	approximately
APR	annual percentage rate (of interest)
Apr.	April
AR	accounts receivable
ARM	adjustable rate mortgage
A.S.	associate in science (degree)
ASAP	as soon as possible
ASCII	American Standard Code for Information Interchange
assoc., Assoc.	associate, associates

Abbreviation	*Term*
assn., Assn., assoc., Assoc.	association
asst., ass't.	assistant
AST	Alaska Standard Time
ATM	automated teller machine
att.	attachment
attn.	attention
atty.	attorney
Aug.	August
AV	audiovisual
av., avg.	average
ave.	avenue
B.A., A.B.	bachelor of arts (degree)
bal.	balance
B.B.A.	bachelor of business administration (degree)
bbl.	barrel, barrels
B.C.	before Christ
BIOS	basic input-output system
bit	binary digit
bl.	bale, bales
B/L, BL	bill of lading
bldg.	building
BO	back order
bps	bits per second
Brig.	brigadier (military title)
bros., Bros.	brothers
B.S.	bachelor of science (degree)
B/S, BS	bill of sale
bu.	bushel, bushels
c	copy
C	Celsius
CAD/CAM	computer-aided drafting/computer-aided manufacturing
CAI	computer-aided instruction
cap.	capital
Capt.	captain
CAT	computer-aided transcription
cc	cubic centimeter
cc, CC	carbon copy, courtesy copy
CD	certificate of deposit, compact disk
CD-ROM	compact disk read-only memory
CDT	Central Daylight Time
CEO	chief executive officer
CFO	chief financial officer
cg	centigram
CGA	color graphics adapter
chg.	charge
c.i.f., CIF	cost, insurance, and freight

Abbreviation	*Term*
CLU	Certified Life Underwriter
cm	centimeter
c/o	care of
co., Co.	company
COBOL	Common Business Oriented Language
c.o.d., COD	collect on delivery
Col.	colonel (military title)
COLA	cost-of-living adjustment
COM	computer output microfilm
comm.	commission
cont.	continued
COO	chief operating officer
corp., Corp.	corporation
CPA	Certified Public Accountant
cpi	characters per inch
cps	characters per second
CPS	Certified Professional Secretary
CPU	central processing unit
cr.	credit
CRT	cathode-ray tube
CST	Central Standard Time
ctn.	carton
cu.	cubic
cwt.	hundredweight
D.A.	doctor of arts (degree)
D.B.A.	doctor of business administration (degree)
d.b.a., DBA	doing business as
DBMS	data base management system
D.D.	doctor of divinity (degree)
D.D.S.	doctor of dental surgery (degree)
Dec.	December
depr.	depreciation
dept.	department
disc., dis.	discount
dist.	district
distr.	distributed, distribution, distributor
div.	dividend; division
DJIA	Dow Jones Industrial Average
DOS	disk operating system
doz., dz.	dozen
DP	data processing
dpi	dots per inch
dr.	debit
dr.	dram, drams
Dr., Drs.	doctor, doctors
DSS	decision support system
DST	daylight saving time
dstn.	destination

Abbreviation	*Term*
dtd.	dated
DTP	desktop publishing
dup.	duplicate
D.V.M.	doctor of veterinary medicine (degree)
ea.	each
ed.	editor
Ed.D.	doctor of education (degree)
EDP	electronic data processing
EDT	Eastern Daylight Time
e.g.	for example
EGA	enhanced graphics adapter
E-mail	electronic mail
enc., encl.	enclosure
EOF	end of file
e.o.m., EOM	end of month
Esq.	Esquire
EST	Eastern Standard Time
ETA	estimated time of arrival
exp.	expense
ext., Ext.	extension
F	Fahrenheit
f.a.s., FAS	free alongside ship
FAQ, FAQs	frequently asked question(s)
fax	facsimile
f.b.o., FBO	for the benefit of
Feb.	February
FIFO	first in, first out (inventory)
f.o.b., FOB	free on board
FORTRAN	FORmula TRANslator
Fri.	Friday
frt.	freight
ft.	foot, feet
FTP	File Transfer Protocol (Internet)
ft-tn	foot-ton, foot-tons
fwd.	forward
FY	fiscal year
FYI	for your information
g	gram
gal.	gallon, gallons
GB	gigabyte (billion bytes)
GDP	gross domestic product
gen.	general
Gen.	general (military title)
GIGO	garbage in, garbage out
GM	general manager
gr.	gross
GUI	graphical user interface
hdlg.	handling

Abbreviation	*Term*
HMO	health maintenance organization
HP, hp	horsepower
HQ, hdqrs.	headquarters
HR	Human Resources (department)
hr., hrs.	hour, hours
HST	Hawaii Standard Time
HTML	Hypertext Markup Language
ID	identification data
i.e.	id est (that is)
in.	inch, inches
inc., Inc.	incorporated
incl.	includes, including
info	information
ins.	insurance
int.	interest
intl., intnl.	international
inv.	invoice
invt.	inventory
I/O	input/output
IOU	I owe you
ips	inches per second
IQ	intelligence quotient
IRA	individual retirement account
ISP	Internet Service Provider
Jan.	January
J.D.	doctor of jurisprudence, doctor of law (degrees)
K	thousand (in reference to computer disk or memory)
K, KB	kilobyte, kilobytes (thousand bytes)
kg	kilogram, kilograms
km	kilometer, kilometers
km/h	kilometers per hour
L	liter
l., ll.	line, lines
LAN	local area network
laser	light amplification stimulated emission radiation
lb.	pound, pounds
L/C	Letter of Credit
l.c.l., LCL	less-than-carload lot
LIFO	last in, first out (inventory)
LL.B.	bachelor of laws (degree)
lpm	lines per minute
Lt.	lieutenant
ltd., Ltd.	limited
m	meter
M.A.	master of arts (degree)
Maj.	major (military rank)
Mar.	March

Abbreviation	*Term*
max.	maximum
MB, M	megabyte, megabytes (million bytes)
M.B.A.	master of business administration (degree)
MC (represents *emcee*)	master of ceremonies, mistress of ceremonies
M.D.	doctor of medicine (degree)
mdse.	merchandise
MDT	Mountain Daylight Time
memo	memorandum
Messrs.	Misters
mfg., Mfg.	manufacturing
mfr., mfrs.	manufacturer, manufacturers
mg	milligram, milligrams
mgmt.	management
mgr.	manager
MHz	megahertz
mi.	mile, miles
min.	minute, minutes; minimum
MIS	management information system
misc.	miscellaneous
ml	milliliter, milliliters
mm	millimeter, millimeters
MO	mail order
MO	money order
mo., mos.	month, months
modem	modulator/demodulator
Mon.	Monday
M.P.A.	master of public administration (degree)
mpg	miles per gallon
M.P.H.	master of public health (degree)
mph	miles per hour
Mr.	Mister
Mrs.	Mistress
M.S.	master of science (degree)
MSP	moved, seconded, and passed
MST	Mountain Standard Time
M.S.W.	master of social work (degree)
n/30	net in 30 days
NA	not applicable; not available
ND	no date
No., Nos.	number, numbers
Nov.	November
NSF	not sufficient funds
nt. wt.	net weight
OC	overcharge
OCR	optical character recognition
Oct.	October
o.d., OD	overdraft
OAG	*Official Airline Guide*

Abbreviation	Term
OK	okay
opt.	optional
org.	organization
orig.	original
O/S	out of stock
OS	operating system (computer)
OTC	over-the-counter
oz.	ounce, ounces
p., pp.	page, pages
PC	personal computer
pd.	paid
PDT	Pacific Daylight Time
PERT	program evaluation and review technique
p and h, P/H	postage and handling
Ph.D.	doctor of philosophy (degree)
phone	telephone
photo	photograph
PIN	personal identification number
pkg.	package
P & L, P/L	profit and loss
p.m.	post meridiem (after noon)
P.O.	post office
P.O., PO	purchase order
p.o.e., POE	port of entry
ppd.	postpaid, prepaid
PR	public relations
pr., prs.	pair, pairs
pres.	president
PROM	programmable read-only memory
P.S., PS	postscript
PST	Pacific Standard Time
pt.	part; pint, pints
pt., pts.	point, points
qr.	quire, quires
qt.	quart, quarts
qtr.	quarter, quarterly
qty.	quantity
RAM	random-access memory
R & D	research and development
recd.	received
reg.	registered; regular
req.	requisition
ret.	retail
ret.	retired
retd.	returned
rev.	revised, revision
RFD	rural free delivery
rm.	ream, reams

Abbreviation	Term
ROM	read-only memory
rpm, RPM	revolutions per minute
R.S.V.P., RSVP	respond, if you please
rwy., ry.	railway
/S/	signed by
SASE	self-addressed, stamped envelope
Sat.	Saturday
scuba	self-contained underwater breathing apparatus
sec.	second, seconds
sec., secy., sec'y	secretary
sect.	section
Sept., Sep.	September
Sgt.	sergeant
shpt.	shipment
shtg.	shortage
S.O., SO	shipping order
SOP	standard operating procedure
sq.	square
std.	standard
stge.	storage
stmt.	statement
Sun.	Sunday
Thurs., Thu.	Thursday
TQM	total quality management
treas.	treasurer
Tues., Tue.	Tuesday
TV	television
TWX	Western Union Teleprinter Exchange Service
UPC	Universal Product Code
URL	Uniform Resource Locator (Web site address)
VAT	value-added tax
VCR	video cassette recorder
VDT	video display terminal
VGA	video graphics array
VIP	very important person
vol.	volume
V.P.	vice president
vs., v.	versus
wam	words a minute
WAN	wide area network
WATS	Wide Area Telephone Service
Wed.	Wednesday
whsle.	wholesale
wk., wks.	week, weeks
w/o	without
wp	word processing
wpm	words per minute
wt.	weight

Abbreviation	*Term*
WWW	World Wide Web
WYSIWYG	What you see is what you get.
Y2K	year 2000
yd.	yard, yards
yr., yrs.	year, years
zip, ZIP	Zone Improvement Plan

6–12 Abbreviations of States and Territories

State or Territory	*Two-Letter Postal Designation*	*Standard Abbreviation*
Alabama	AL	Ala.
Alaska	AK	—
Arizona	AZ	Ariz.
Arkansas	AR	Ark.
California	CA	Calif., Cal.
Colorado	CO	Colo., Col.
Connecticut	CT	Conn.
Delaware	DE	Del.
District of Columbia	DC	D.C.
Florida	FL	Fla.
Georgia	GA	Ga.
Guam	GU	—
Hawaii	HI	—
Idaho	ID	—
Illinois	IL	Ill.
Indiana	IN	Ind.
Iowa	IA	—
Kansas	KS	Kans., Kan.
Kentucky	KY	Ky.
Louisiana	LA	La.
Maine	ME	—
Maryland	MD	Md.
Massachusetts	MA	Mass.
Michigan	MI	Mich.
Minnesota	MN	Minn.
Mississippi	MS	Miss.
Missouri	MO	Mo.
Montana	MT	Mont.
Nebraska	NE	Nebr., Neb.
Nevada	NV	Nev.
New Hampshire	NH	N.H.
New Jersey	NJ	N.J.
New Mexico	NM	N. Mex.
New York	NY	N.Y.
North Carolina	NC	N.C.
North Dakota	ND	N. Dak.
Ohio	OH	—

State or Territory	*Two-Letter Postal Designation*	*Standard Abbreviation*
Oklahoma	OK	Okla.
Oregon	OR	Oreg., Ore.
Pennsylvania	PA	Pa., Penn., Penna.
Puerto Rico	PR	P.R.
Rhode Island	RI	R.I.
South Carolina	SC	S.C.
South Dakota	SD	S. Dak.
Tennessee	TN	Tenn.
Texas	TX	Tex.
Utah	UT	—
Vermont	VT	Vt.
Virgin Islands	VI	V.I.
Virginia	VA	Va.
Washington	WA	Wash.
West Virginia	WV	W. Va.
Wisconsin	WI	Wis., Wisc.
Wyoming	WY	Wyo.

6–13 Two-Letter Postal Designations for Canadian Provinces and Territories

Province or Territory	*Designation*
Alberta	AB
British Columbia	BC
Labrador	LB
Manitoba	MB
New Brunswick	NB
Newfoundland	NF
Northwest Territories	NT
Nova Scotia	NS
Nunavut	NT
Ontario	ON
Prince Edward Island	PE
Quebec	QC
Saskatchewan	SK
Yukon Territory	YT

Contractions

6–14 Contractions

a. Contractions are similar to abbreviations in that they are shortened forms. Unlike most abbreviations, however, contractions always contain an apostrophe to indicate where letters have been omitted. The use of single-word contractions is generally limited to business forms and tables. Some common single-word contractions follow:

ack'd	(acknowledged)	rec't	(receipt)
ass't	(assistant)	sec'y	(secretary)
gov't	(government)	cont'd	(continued)
nat'l	(national)	'99	(1999)

b. A second kind of contraction occurs with verb forms. By using an apostrophe to indicate where letters have been omitted, two words may be combined into one. The use of verb contractions is generally limited to informal business writing. A sampling of commonly used verb contractions follows:

aren't	(are not)	weren't	(were not)
shouldn't	(should not)	I'll	(I will)
can't	(cannot)	what's	(what is)
should've	(should have)	I'm	(I am)
couldn't	(could not)	where's	(where is)
that's	(that is)	isn't	(is not)
didn't	(did not)	who's	(who is)
there's	(there is)	it's	(it is)
doesn't	(does not)	won't	(will not)
they're	(they are)	I've	(I have)
don't	(do not)	wouldn't	(would not)
wasn't	(was not)	let's	(let us)
hasn't	(has not)	you'd	(you would)
we'll	(we will)	she's	(she is)
haven't	(have not)	you're	(you are)
we're	(we are)	you've	(you have)
he's	(he is)		

Symbols

6–15 Symbols on the Standard Computer Keyboard

a. Except for the dollar sign ($) in amounts of money, the asterisk (*) in unnumbered footnotes, and the ampersand (&) in company names, avoid using symbols in running copy. Limit the use of symbols to business forms, statistical material, tables, charts, graphs, and other documents or visuals where space is limited.

dollar sign, asterisk, and ampersand in running copy

Unauthorized charges of **$247.56**, **$153.29**, and **$73.20** appeared on our last month's credit card statement.

Use **ASCII*** characters to prepare your résumé for this on-line career center.

We have retained **Leavitt, Kahn & Moss** to handle this legal matter for our firm.

symbols in forms, statistical materials, and visuals

3 @ $6.80 #507 23# 82% 5'2" tall 3:1

b. Use standard keys on the computer keyboard for the following commonly used symbols:

Symbol	*Description*	*Examples*
/	abbreviated word separator	c/o, w/o
&	and (ampersand)	Johnson & Sons, Inc., AT&T
@	at, each at (Internet domain)	50 @ $39.95 ClarksHOW@aol.com
×	by	4 × 6 inches
"	ditto, same as (quotation marks)	30 unformatted floppy disks 40 IBM formatted " "
/	divided by (diagonal)	May Sales/Annual Sales, $4,500/3
$	dollar, dollars	$1,593.62
=	equals	Price + Tax = Cost
'	foot/feet (apostrophe)	12' × 15' room, 5' 9" tall
/	fraction separator (diagonal)	1/2, 2/3, 3/4
>	greater than	100 > 90
"	inch/inches (quotation marks)	8 1/2" × 11" paper
<	less than	90 < 100
'	minute, minutes (apostrophe)	60' sessions
–	minus	Price – Discount, 75 – 50
×	multiplied by	12 × 12 = 144
*	multiplied by (asterisk)	12 * 12 = 144
#	number	#678452, #3 pencil
%	percent	43.5%
+	plus	Principal + Interest, 8 + 4
#	pound, pounds	24# paper
:	ratio (colon)	3:1 ratio
"	second, seconds (quotation marks)	5" intervals
*	unnumbered footnote (asterisk)	. . . for diacritical marks.*
/	word separator (diagonal)	and/or

6–16 Symbols Not on the Standard Computer Keyboard

Many commonly used symbols do not appear on the standard computer keyboard. Contemporary word processing programs, though, have extended character sets and provide access to many of these symbols. With just a few keystrokes or mouse movements, you can access the following symbols:

Symbol	*Description*	*Examples*
¢	cents	85¢
©	copyright	Copyright © 2000 by South-Western College Publishing
°	degree, degrees	72°
÷	divided by	144 ÷ 12 = 12
–	en dash	pages 41–47, March 11–14
—	em dash	We have three colors in this style—red, blue, and black.
1/2	fractions	1/2, 1/4, 3/4, 2 1/3, 25 3/8
≥	greater than or equal to	$x \geq 10$
≤	less than or equal to	$x \leq 12$
é	letter with diacritical mark	résumé, La Cañada, Fraülein
∓	minus or plus	∓4
¶	paragraph, paragraphs	¶23, ¶¶123–132
||	parallel to	Main Street || Hill Street
±	plus or minus	±$2
®	registered	Kinko's®, Pentium®
§	section, sections	§12, §§56–59
SM	service mark	The new way to office.SM
√	square root	$\sqrt{4} = 2$
Σ	sum	$\Sigma n = 286$
TM	trademark	The Computer Inside.TM

Abbreviations 6

Chapter 7

Words Often Confused and Misused

a/an

Words Often Confused and Misused Solution Finder

All entries in this chapter appear in alphabetical order.

A/An

A (ARTICLE; used before a word beginning with a consonant sound or a long $\bar{u}$ sound)—Please call ***a t***echnician to service the network. ***A u***nion representative met with us yesterday.
An (ARTICLE; used before a word beginning with a vowel sound other than long $\bar{u}$) — Please make ***an a***ppointment for me to meet with Señor Lopez while I am in Puerto Rico.

A lot/Allot/Alot

A lot (ARTICLE + NOUN; combination meaning "many" or "much")—***A lot*** of our customers from Switzerland will be attending our user conference. We have spent ***a lot*** of time investigating your proposal.
Allot (VERB; to allocate, assign)—How much money will we ***allot*** for Internet advertising next year?
Alot (misspelling of *a lot*)

A while/Awhile

A while (ARTICLE + NOUN; combination meaning "a short time")—He will be here in ***a while***.
Awhile (ADVERB; meaning "*for* a short time")—Exercise ***awhile*** each day to maintain your good health.

Accede/Exceed

Accede (VERB; to agree or consent)—I will ***accede*** to this request only if the tenants sign a one-year lease.
Exceed (VERB; to surpass a limit)—Many accidents occur when drivers ***exceed*** the posted speed limit.

Accelerate/Exhilarate

Accelerate (VERB; to speed up)—We must ***accelerate*** our progress in improving our voice-recognition software if we expect to stay ahead of all our competition.
Exhilarate (VERB; to make cheerful; to refresh or stimulate)—The entire staff was ***exhilarated*** by the news that our office was No. 1 in sales. All of us attending the retreat at Blue Pines were ***exhilarated*** by the crisp, fresh air.

Accept/Except

Accept (VERB; to take or receive)—We do not ***accept*** checks written on out-of-state banks.
Except (conjunction; with the exclusion of, but)—No one outside the company ***except*** you knows about the proposed merger.

Access/Excess

Access (NOUN; admittance or approachability)—Everyone in the office should have ***access*** to these files.

Excess (ADJECTIVE; beyond ordinary limits; a surplus)—You may return all ***excess*** flooring materials for full credit within 60 days of purchase.

Ad/Add

Ad (NOUN; abbreviated form of *advertisement*)—We sold the entire lot of these municipal bonds by running an ***ad*** in Sunday's edition of the *Los Angeles Times*.
Add (VERB; to increase by uniting or joining)—These new computers will ***add*** to the productivity of our office staff.

Adapt/Adept/Adopt

Adapt (VERB; to adjust or modify)—We must readily ***adapt*** ourselves to new situations in this rapidly changing market.
Adept (ADJECTIVE; skilled)—The person hired for this position must be ***adept*** at dealing with customer complaints.
Adopt (VERB; to take and follow as one's own)—We will ***adopt*** Mrs. Williams' proposal to computerize our accounting system.

Add: see Ad.

Addict/Edict

Addict (NOUN; one who is habitually or obsessively dependent; devotee)—Our clinic has noted success with the rehabilitation of drug ***addicts***. Many of today's teenagers are rock music ***addicts***.
Edict (NOUN; order or command)—When did our manager issue this ***edict***?

Addition/Edition

Addition (NOUN; the process of uniting or joining; an added part)—The increased production quotas require the ***addition*** of factory floor space in all our facilities.
Edition (NOUN; a particular version of printed material)—Only the second ***edition*** of this book is now available.

Adept: see Adapt.

Adherence/Adherents

Adherence (NOUN; a steady attachment or loyalty)—A strict ***adherence*** to all safety procedures is required of all personnel.
Adherents (NOUN; loyal supporters or followers)—The many ***adherents*** to the space program believe in its importance to the human race.

Adopt: see Adapt.

Adverse/Averse

Adverse (ADJECTIVE; opposing; antagonistic)—Rising interest rates have had an ***adverse*** effect on real estate sales and new home developments.
Averse (ADJECTIVE; unwilling; reluctant)—One of Carol's many attributes is that she is not ***averse*** to working long hours to meet specific production schedules.

Advice/Advise

Advice (NOUN; a suggestion, an opinion, or a recommendation)—He would have avoided the problem if he had followed his attorney's ***advice***.

Advise (VERB; to counsel or recommend)—We had to ***advise*** her not to sign the contract in its present form.

Affect/Effect

Affect (VERB; to influence)—Large pay increases throughout the country will ***affect*** the rate of inflation. Increased costs will ***affect*** our pricing policies on all merchandise.
Effect (VERB; to bring about or cause to happen; to create)—Our government plans to ***effect*** a change in the rate of inflation by tightening bank credits. Rising costs of raw materials will ***effect*** large price increases in May.
Effect (NOUN; a result or consequence)—Inflation usually has a negative ***effect*** on our economy. The new vacation policy had no apparent ***effect*** on company morale.

Aggravate/Irritate

Aggravate (VERB; to exacerbate; to make something worse)—To bring in legal counsel at this time would only ***aggravate*** the situation further. By scratching the infected area, you will only ***aggravate*** the itching and puffiness.
Irritate (VERB; to create an annoying condition)—If you do not refund the full purchase price, you will surely ***irritate*** the customer.

Aid/Aide

Aid (VERB, to help or assist; NOUN, assistance)—The United States ***aids*** many foreign countries. Your application for financial ***aid*** is currently being processed.
Aide (NOUN; a person who assists another)—Please ask your ***aide*** to deliver these papers to Dr. Powell's office by Friday afternoon.

Aisle/Isle

Aisle (NOUN; a passageway for inside traffic)—After the show the ***aisles*** of the theater were littered with empty popcorn containers and candy wrappers.
Isle (NOUN; a piece of land surrounded by water; island)—This script centers around two teenagers marooned on a tropical ***isle***.

All ready/Already

All ready (ADJECTIVE; prepared)—We are ***all ready*** to offer distance learning courses as soon as the programs arrive from the publisher.
Already (ADVERB; by or before this time)—Orders for our August sale have ***already*** been placed with the suppliers.

All right/Alright

All right (ADJECTIVE; satisfactory or agreeable)—Changing your vacation dates from June to July seems to be ***all right*** with our supervisor.
Alright (An informal spelling of ***all right*** that is not appropriate for business writing.)

All together/Altogether

All together (ADVERB + ADVERB; wholly as a group; counted or summed up)— We must work ***all together*** if the company is to survive this crisis. ***All together***, 87 families signed up for the company picnic.

Altogether (ADVERB; entirely or completely; in all; on the whole)—This problem is ***altogether*** different from the one we faced last year. We believe he has embezzled over $200,000 ***altogether***. Although we did not reach our goal of $3 million in sales, our results may ***altogether*** be considered successful.

All ways/Always

All ways (ADJECTIVE + NOUN; by all methods)—We must try ***all ways*** possible to increase Internet access for our rapidly expanding list of on-line subscribers.
Always (ADVERB; at all times; continually)—Our agency is ***always*** looking for qualified office personnel with experience in Word, Excel, and PowerPoint.

Allot: see A lot.

Allowed/Aloud

Allowed (VERB; permitted)—We are ***allowed*** to sell our products only through contracted retail outlets.
Aloud (ADVERB; audibly)—The president's resignation was read ***aloud*** to all board members present.

Allude/Elude

Allude (VERB; to mention or refer to)—As proof of Americans' lack of concern for economy, I ***allude*** to the increased popularity of SUVs during recent years.
Elude (VERB; to evade or escape)—The senator has been able to ***elude*** severe criticisms of his program by anticipating and counteracting objections.

Allusion/Delusion/Illusion

Allusion (NOUN; an indirect reference)—Several ***allusions*** were made to Mr. Reed's apparent laziness.
Delusion (NOUN; a false belief instilled through purposeful deception)—Many people invested heavily in these oil stocks because they operated under the ***delusion*** that the company's wells were active producers.
Illusion (NOUN; a misconception or misapprehension)—Many of our employees originally had the ***illusion*** that this new electronic system would reduce our staff by one half, but they were pleased to learn that it would only increase their productivity.

Almost/Most

Almost (ADVERB; nearly)—By the end of the third quarter, this company had sold ***almost*** 600,000 copies of its low-end voice-recognition software through on-line sources.
Most (ADJECTIVE; the greatest in amount or number)—Patricia Lynn received the ***most*** votes in the election for faculty senate treasurer.

Alot: see A lot.

Aloud: see Allowed.

Already: see All ready.

Alright: see All right.

Altar/Alter

Altar (NOUN; a structure used for worship)—The wedding flowers are to be placed on the ***altar*** by 6 p.m.
Alter (VERB; to change)—Please ***alter*** your schedule so that you will be able to attend the monthly committee meetings.

Alternate/Alternative

Alternate (VERB ['ȯl-tər-ˌnāt], to change from one to another repeatedly; NOUN ['ȯl-tər-nət], one that substitutes for another; ADJECTIVE ['ȯl-tər-nət], separate and distinct)—Our conferences ***alternate*** between the northern and southern parts of the state. Jack Smith has agreed to serve as my ***alternate*** on the budget committee. For the next few months, motorists will be required to use an ***alternate*** route to the downtown area.
Alternative (NOUN; a choice between two or among several)—We were left with only two ***alternatives***—either accept the lease conditions or find another location. None of the ***alternatives*** presented by the committee were acceptable to the Board of Directors.

Altogether: see All together.

Always: see All ways.

Among/Between

Among (PREPOSITION; refers to more than two persons or things)—Distribute the supplies equally ***among*** the three departments.
Between (PREPOSITION; refers to two persons or things)—The final selection for the position is ***between*** Ms. Claffey and Mr. Thompson.

Amount/Number

Amount (NOUN; used with singular NOUNs and mass items that cannot be counted)— Only a small ***amount*** of the cake was eaten. The store manager has not yet determined the ***amount*** of money that was stolen. Because of the power failure, a significant ***amount*** of the frozen food had deteriorated and was discarded.
Number (NOUN; used with plural NOUNs and items that can be counted)—Only a small ***number*** of spaces have been allotted for visitor parking. This year the ***number*** of children in each classroom has been reduced by three.

An: see A.

Anecdote/Antidote

Anecdote (NOUN ['a-nik-ˌdōt]; a story or a brief account of an event)—We all had to laugh at Tom's ***anecdote*** about the customer who insisted upon returning a product our store doesn't even sell.
Antidote (NOUN ['an-ti-ˌdōt]; a remedy that counteracts a harmful substance or circumstance)—Dr. Martin has consented to write an article about the new ***antidote*** he developed to counteract five different household poisons.

Annual/Annul

Annual (ADJECTIVE; yearly)—The company's ***annual*** report will be mailed to all stockholders of record next week.

Annul (VERB; to void or abolish)—We had to ***annul*** the contract because of unexpected legal complications.

Antidote: see Anecdote.

Anxious/Eager

Anxious (ADJECTIVE; worried or apprehensive)—Donna is ***anxious*** about taking the upcoming real estate brokers' examination.
Eager (ADJECTIVE; anticipating with enthusiasm)—Mr. Adams is ***eager*** to begin his new job with Girard Enterprises next week.

Any one/Anyone

Any one (ADJECTIVE + PRONOUN; any one person or thing in a group [always followed by *of*])—You may assign me to assist ***any one*** of the new employees in our department.
Anyone (PRONOUN; any person at all)—If you know of ***anyone*** who has these qualifications, please have that person e-mail our manager of human resources.

Any time/Anytime

Any time (ADJECTIVE + NOUN; an unspecified *point* in time; an amount of time)—Please let us know ***any time*** you have questions about our products or services. ***Any time*** we can be of service, just call our toll-free number and a telephone representative will assist you. We do not have ***any time*** to review this case.
Anytime (ADVERB; at any time *whatsoever*)—Drop by our offices ***anytime***. In an emergency you may call Dr. Mulcahy ***anytime***, day or night. During the last quarter of the year, you may take your vacation ***anytime***.

Any way/Anyway

Any way (ADJECTIVE + NOUN; any method)—Is there ***any way*** we can step up production to advance our July 1 release date?
Anyway (ADVERB; in any case)—Considering the low bids of our competitors, I don't believe we would have received the contract ***anyway***.
Anyways (An informal form of *anyway* that is not appropriate for business writing.)

Appraise/Apprise

Appraise (VERB; to estimate the value or nature)—Before we can liquidate this company, we must hire an outside firm to ***appraise*** its assets.
Apprise (VERB; to inform or notify)—Please ***apprise*** all employees immediately of this change in policy.

As/Like

As (CONJUNCTION; used at the beginning of a clause)—I will get the material to you by Friday, ***as*** (not *like*) I promised. Our manager always acts ***as if*** (not *like*) he knows more than anyone else.
Like (PREPOSITION; used when the sentence requires a preposition meaning "similar to" [followed by a noun or pronoun and its modifiers])—This new adhesive feels ***like*** wet cement. I have never met anyone else ***like*** him. These cookies taste ***like*** the chocolate chip cookies my mother used to make.

Ascent/Assent

Ascent (NOUN; rising or going up)—The recent ***ascent*** of stock market prices has encouraged more small investors to enter the market.
Assent (VERB; to agree or consent)—Everyone at the meeting will surely ***assent*** to the plan you have outlined in this report.

Assistance/Assistants

Assistance (NOUN; help or aid)—The project could not have been completed on time without your ***assistance***. If you need financial ***assistance***, please fill out these forms.
Assistants (NOUN; people who aid or help a superior)—The consultant's staffing report indicates that our general manager should have three ***assistants***.

Assume/Presume

Assume (VERB; to take for granted as true; to take on)—I ***assumed*** these sales figures had been corrected before they were submitted to the general manager. Who will be assigned to ***assume*** these extra duties?
Presume (VERB; to anticipate with confidence)—After this episode we can no longer ***presume*** that this vendor will stand behind its products or fulfill the conditions of its warranties. In our justice system defendants are ***presumed*** innocent until proven guilty.

Assure/Ensure/Insure

Assure (VERB; to promise; to make a positive declaration)—I ***assure*** you that the loan will be repaid according to the terms specified in the note. Please ***assure*** the patient that this procedure is not painful.
Ensure (VERB; to make certain)—To ***ensure*** the timely completion of this project, please hire additional qualified personnel.
Insure (VERB; to protect against financial loss)—We ***insure*** all our facilities against earthquake damage.

Attendance/Attendants

Attendance (NOUN; being present or attending)—At least two thirds of the members of this committee must be in ***attendance*** before the meeting can be called to order.
Attendants (NOUN; those who attend with or to others)—The ***attendants*** had difficulty parking all the cars for such a large crowd.

Averse: see Adverse.

Awhile: see A while.

Bad/Badly

Bad (ADJECTIVE; an adjective or subject complement used after such intransitive or nonaction verbs as *is*, *was*, *feel*, *look*, or *smell*)—I feel ***bad*** that your transfer request was denied. Profits for the first quarter of this year look ***bad*** in view of the additional expenses incurred by our sales staff. The air in this office smells ***bad***.
Badly (ADVERB; used with transitive or action VERBS)—We ***badly*** need the advice of a tax attorney before we invest further in this project. The defeated candidate behaved ***badly*** before thousands of television viewers.

Bail/Bale

Bail (NOUN; guarantee of money necessary to set a person free from jail until the trial)—***Bail*** in your client's case has been set at $25,000.
Bale (NOUN; a large bundle)—One ***bale*** of used clothing was lost in transit.

Bare/Bear

Bare (ADJECTIVE; uncovered, empty, plain, or mere)—The paint had chipped and peeled so badly that the ***bare*** wood was showing. After the break-in the two outer offices were ***bare*** of furniture and equipment. Every year our work group retreats for three days to a ***bare*** wooden cabin in the mountains. I had time to cover only the ***bare*** facts involved in this issue.
Bear (VERB; to support, carry, or bring forth)—Unfortunately, he had to ***bear*** the brunt of the losses. Our travel agency will secure for you guides who have donkeys to ***bear*** the luggage and provisions. As a result of the surgery, the patient was able to ***bear*** children.

Base/Bass

Base (NOUN; bottom part of something; foundation)—When did the ***base*** of this marble column crack?
Bass (ADJECTIVE; a low-pitched sound; musical instrument having a low range)—We could use his ***bass*** voice in our quartet. Do you play the ***bass*** violin?

Bazaar/Bizarre

Bazaar (NOUN; a fair for the sale of articles)—Our Lady of Lourdes Church will hold its annual ***bazaar*** during the Memorial Day weekend.
Bizarre (ADJECTIVE; strikingly out of the ordinary)—Floyd's Fashions has often been described as carrying ***bizarre*** clothing lines and accessories.

Bear: see Bare.

Berth/Birth

Berth (VERB, to bring into a berth; NOUN, the place where a ship lies at anchor; place to sit or sleep on a ship or vehicle)—When will the Song of Norway next ***berth*** in Puerto Rico? How many ***berths*** does your port have for ships from major cruise lines? The only sleeping accommodations not yet reserved are upper ***berths***.
Birth (NOUN; the emergence of a new individual from the body of its parent)—Hospital policy permits only the father and one other family member to be present during the ***birth*** of a child.

Beside/Besides

Beside (PREPOSITION; by the side of)—Please place the new scanner on the table ***beside*** Ms. Capron's computer.
Besides (PREPOSITION; in addition to)—What other Internet Service Providers ***besides*** America Online have you contacted?

Between: see Among.

Bi-/Semi-

Bi- (prefix; two)—Our newsletter is published ***bi***monthly: January, March, May, July, September, and November.
Semi- (prefix; half)—Bulletins to the staff are issued ***semi***monthly, on the 1st and 15th of each month.

Biannual/Biennial

Biannual (ADJECTIVE; occurring twice a year)—The stockholders' ***biannual*** meetings are held in January and July.
Biennial (ADJECTIVE; occurring once every two years)—According to our society's constitution, the ***biennial*** election of officers should be held in November.

Bibliography/Biography

Bibliography (NOUN; a list of works consulted by an author for a production)—Be sure to include in the ***bibliography*** all the sources—books, magazines, newspapers, compact disks, Internet resources, etc.—you used for this report.
Biography (NOUN; history of a person's life written by someone else)—This ***biography*** of Henry Ford is exceptionally well written.

Billed/Build

Billed (VERB; charged for goods or services)—You will be ***billed*** on the 10th of each month.
Build (VERB; to construct)—We plan to ***build*** a new plant in Korea.

Biography: see Bibliography.

Birth: see Berth.

Bizarre: see Bazaar.

Boarder/Border

Boarder (NOUN; one who is provided with regular meals and lodging)—Owners of homes in residential areas are limited in the number of ***boarders*** they may solicit for commercial purposes.
Border (NOUN; an outer part or edge; boundary)—Which ***border*** did you select for the cover page of the report? If you plan to cross the ***border*** into Mexico, be sure to take your passport with you.

Bolder/Boulder

Bolder (ADJECTIVE; more fearless or daring)—Perhaps we need a ***bolder*** person as president of the university.
Boulder (NOUN; a large rock)—Damage to the insured's left-front tire was apparently caused by a ***boulder*** in the road.

Born/Borne

Born (ADJECTIVE; brought forth by birth; originated)—This patient was ***born*** on February 14, 1946. One can hardly believe that this multibillion-dollar industry was ***born*** in a garage fewer than three decades ago.
Borne (VERB; past participle of *bear*)—Mrs. Talbert has already ***borne*** six children, and she is currently expecting her seventh. Our school district has ***borne*** these financial burdens for over six years.

Bouillon/Bullion

Bouillon (NOUN ['bü(l)-,yän]; a clear soup)—For the first course I have ordered beef ***bouillon***.
Bullion (NOUN ['bul-yən]; uncoined gold or silver in bars or ingots)—Mr. Reece had hidden in his home nearly $45,000 in gold ***bullion***.

Boulder: see Bolder.

Breach/Breech

Breach (NOUN; a violation of a law or agreement; a hole, gap, or break)—The judge ruled that a ***breach*** of contract transpired when the building was not finished by the date agreed upon. If contract negotiations are to continue, we must narrow the ***breach*** between union and management negotiators.
Breech (NOUN; part of a firearm or cannon that is located behind the barrel)—They had difficulty firing the old cannon because the ***breech*** would not work properly.

Bring/Take

Bring (VERB; to carry toward [a place])—Please ***bring*** (not *take*) all your receipts when you meet with our accountant.
Take (VERB; to carry away; to carry from one place to another)—You may ***take*** any one of these samples. Please ***take*** these brochures to our Springfield office.

Build: see Billed.

Bullion: see Bouillon.

Calendar/Colander

Calendar (NOUN; a schedule of days and months for a period of time)—Please order a supply of desk ***calendars*** for the new year.
Colander (NOUN; a strainer)—Use a ***colander*** to drain the pasta before placing it in the sauce.

Callous/Callus

Callous (ADJECTIVE; insensitive; without feeling)—Everyone on the committee agreed that Mr. Bush's ***callous*** remark concerning Ms. Wright's attire was in poor taste.
Callus (NOUN; hard, thick skin)—Pointed-toe shoes can cause permanent ***calluses*** on your feet.

Can/May

Can (VERB; to have the ability to do something)—You ***can*** develop a Web site without knowing hypertext markup language (HTML).
May (VERB; to express permission or possibility)—Yes, you ***may*** take a day's vacation tomorrow. ***May*** we have these files translated into ASCII files by next Wednesday?

Canvas/Canvass

Canvas (NOUN; a firm, closely woven cloth)—Use these ***canvas*** coverings to protect the new cars as they arrive.
Canvass (VERB; to survey or solicit in an area)—Do you have a volunteer who will ***canvass*** the residences on Jersey Street?

Capital/Capitol

Capital (NOUN; a city in which the official seat of government is located; the wealth of an individual or firm)—The ***capital*** of Wisconsin is Madison. Much of our ***capital*** is tied up in equipment.
Capital (ADJECTIVE; punishable by death; foremost in importance)—Treason is a ***capital*** crime in many countries. The forthcoming election is ***capital*** in the minds of the school board members.
Capitol (NOUN; a building used by the U.S. Congress [always capitalized])—Senator Cano must be in the ***Capitol*** by 9 a.m. for the hearings. The United States ***Capitol*** is a major tourist attraction in Washington, D.C.
Capitol (NOUN; a building in which a state legislature convenes [capitalized only when used in full name of building])—The ***capitol*** was surrounded by angry pickets waving placards. Is this office located in the California State ***Capitol***?

Carat/Caret/Carrot/Karat

Carat (NOUN; a unit of weight for gems)—The total diamond weight in this ring is 2.17 ***carats***.
Caret (NOUN; a proofreading symbol similar to an inverted *v* that is placed at the bottom of a line to show insertions in edited copy)—Our editor placed a ***caret*** between the two words where the company name is to be inserted.
Carrot (NOUN; a vegetable)—A ***carrot*** can be just as delicious raw as it is cooked.
Karat (NOUN, GENERALLY USED AS ADJECTIVE; a unit of weight for gold)—This Italian chain is made of 18-***karat*** gold.

Cease/Seize

Cease (VERB; to come to an end or stop)—Please ***cease*** shipment of any further orders to the Hogan Company until its current balance has been paid.
Seize (VERB; to take possession of; to take)—Will the Internal Revenue Service ***seize*** all the company's assets for the payment of back taxes? You may wish to ***seize*** this opportunity to ask Mr. Rodriguez for a salary increase.

Ceiling/Sealing

Ceiling (NOUN; overhead inside lining of a room; upper limit)—Have you checked all the acoustical ***ceilings*** in this apartment complex to ensure they are free from asbestos? ***Ceilings*** on rent increases are controlled by the city council.
Sealing (NOUN; closing with a coating to make secure)—These glue sticks are used mostly for ***sealing*** envelopes.

Censor/Censure

Censor (VERB, to examine materials and delete objectionable matter; NOUN, one who censors)—We will need to ***censor*** scenes from this movie for television viewing. When will the ***censor*** finish reviewing the script?
Censure (VERB, to criticize or condemn; NOUN, condemnation)—The city council ***censured*** the mayor for awarding the contract to his brother-in-law's firm. After the facts were disclosed, Senator Dillon was subjected to public ***censure***.

Census/Senses

Census (NOUN; an official count of population within a specified geographical area)—The United States conducts an official ***census*** every ten years.
Senses (NOUN; the specialized functions of sight, hearing, smell, taste, and touch)—Our client's ***senses*** of hearing and touch were impaired as a result of the accident.

Cent/Scent/Sent

Cent (NOUN; a coin known as a *penny*)—Your tallies always balance to the last ***cent***.
Scent (NOUN; a distinctive smell or odor)—Because Webby Bakery is located in our industrial complex, the ***scent*** of freshly baked bread permeates the area each morning.
Sent (VERB; the past tense and past participle of *send*)—Your order was ***sent*** by United Parcel Service yesterday.

Cereal/Serial

Cereal (NOUN; a breakfast food made from grain)—Your diet calls for a daily serving of wheat ***cereal***.
Serial (ADJECTIVE; arranged in a series)—The ***serial*** numbers of all our equipment should be on file in your office.

Choose/Chose

Choose (VERB; to select or make a choice)—We do not know whom he will ***choose*** for his executive assistant.
Chose (VERB; past tense of *choose*)—The new president ***chose*** Ms. Randall to be his executive assistant.

Cite/Sight/Site

Cite (VERB; to quote or mention; to summon to a court appearance)—Dr. Rosenthal can ***cite*** many authorities who have studied the problem of pollution in major United States cities. Did the police officer ***cite*** you for speeding while you were in a company vehicle?
Sight (VERB, to see; NOUN, a view or spectacle)—Unfortunately, the salesperson did not ***sight*** Ms. Brown leaving the office. The Statue of Liberty is a frequently visited tourist ***sight*** in New York City.
Site (NOUN; a location)—This 20-acre land parcel is a perfect ***site*** for the proposed housing project.

Close/Clothes/Cloths

Close (VERB; to shut; to stop or end)—We ***close*** the safe at 5 p.m. every afternoon. Our accountant ***closes*** our books at the end of each month.
Clothes (NOUN; wearing apparel)—The previous tenant still needs to remove his ***clothes*** from the apartment.
Cloths (NOUN; pieces of fabric)—Use these ***cloths*** to clean the glass showcases.

Coarse/Course

Coarse (ADJECTIVE; rough texture)—This material is too ***coarse*** for our use.

Course (NOUN; a particular direction or route; part of a meal; a unit of learning)—We are now committed to a ***course*** of action that we hope will increase our sales volume. Which menu item have you selected for the main ***course***? You need only three more ***courses*** to graduate.

Colander: see Calendar.

Collision/Collusion

Collision (NOUN; a crash)—Fortunately, no one was hurt in the ***collision***.
Collusion (NOUN; an agreement to defraud)—No one suspected the seller, broker, and escrow officer of ***collusion*** in the sale of this unstable hillside property.

Command/Commend

Command (VERB, to order or direct; NOUN, an order)—The sergeant ***commanded*** his troops to return to base by 0600. This dog has been trained to obey only its owner's ***commands***.
Commend (VERB; to praise or compliment)—Please ***commend*** the staff for the fine job it did in promoting our line at the San Francisco convention.

Complement/Compliment

Complement (VERB; to complete or make perfect)—The paintings you have selected for the reception area will ***complement*** the office decor. You may wish to select one of our fine wines to ***complement*** your meal.
Compliment (VERB; to praise or flatter)—Mr. Rose did ***compliment*** me on the fine job I had done.

Complementary/Complimentary

Complementary (ADJECTIVE; serving mutually to blend, fill out, or complete)—Both these wall coverings are ***complementary*** to the carpeting you have selected.
Complimentary (ADJECTIVE; favorable; given free)—We appreciate receiving your ***complimentary*** letter about the service you received in our Fifth Avenue store. To receive your ***complimentary*** copy of this textbook, merely fill out and return the enclosed postcard.

Confidant/Confident

Confidant (NOUN; a trusted friend)—He has been his closest ***confidant*** for years.
Confident (ADJECTIVE; sure of oneself)—Mrs. Allen was ***confident*** she would get the position.

Conscience/Conscious

Conscience (NOUN; the faculty of knowing right from wrong)—In the last analysis, his ***conscience*** required him to release the funds.
Conscious (ADJECTIVE; aware or mentally awake)—Yes, we are ***conscious*** of the new global marketing opportunities available to our firm. Most of our patients are ***conscious*** during this type of surgery.

Console/Consul

Console (NOUN; a cabinet)—The popularity of our Model 4750 stereo may be attributed to its attractive ***console***.

Consul (NOUN; an official representing a foreign country)—Travel information can often be obtained by contacting the ***consul*** of the country one wishes to visit.

Continual/Continuous

Continual (ADJECTIVE; a regular or frequent occurrence)—The ***continual*** complaints from customers in the Vancouver area warrant inquiry into the activities of our Seattle office.

Continuous (ADJECTIVE; without interruption or cessation)—The ***continuous*** humming of the new air-conditioning system is disturbing everyone in the office.

Convince/Persuade

Convince (VERB; to bring a person to your point of view)—Do you think you will ***convince*** the board that these proposed policies will increase our profits?

Persuade (VERB; to induce a person to do something)—An effective banner on a popular Internet site will ***persuade*** visitors to that site to purchase your products.

Cooperation/Corporation

Cooperation (NOUN; working together)—The full ***cooperation*** of all employees is needed to reduce our high rate of absenteeism.

Corporation (NOUN; one type of business organization)—We are looking into the possibility of forming a ***corporation***.

Corespondent/Correspondence/Correspondents

Corespondent (NOUN; person named as guilty of adultery with the defendant in a divorce suit)—Who was named as ***corespondent*** in this divorce case?

Correspondence (NOUN; letters or other written communications)—When did we receive the last E-mail ***correspondence*** from Mr. Flores?

Correspondents (NOUN; message writers or news reporters)—Be sure to have one of our ***correspondents*** answer these customers' letters within the next three days. African ***correspondents*** have reported that several countries are now suffering severe food shortages.

Corporation: see Cooperation.

Corps/Corpse

Corps (NOUN ['kōr]; a body of persons having a common activity or occupation)—A ***corps*** of students have been soliciting funds for the stadium lights. Representatives from the Marine ***Corps*** will visit our campus next week.

Corpse (NOUN ['kȯrps]; a dead body)—The identity of the ***corpse*** is still unknown.

Correspondence: see Corespondent.

Correspondent: see Corespondent.

Council/Counsel

Council (NOUN; a governing body)—We will present the proposal to the city ***council*** in the morning.

Counsel (VERB, to give advice; NOUN, advice)—Our staff ***counsels*** at least eighty students each day. In this situation the president received good ***counsel*** from his advisors.

Course: see Coarse.

Credible/Creditable

Credible (ADJECTIVE; believable)—The excuses offered by Ms. Day for her many absences are hardly ***credible***.

Creditable (ADJECTIVE; good enough for praise or esteem; reliable)—Ms. Kawakami's perfect attendance record is certainly ***creditable***. Keep in mind that not all Internet resources are ***creditable***.

Deceased/Diseased

Deceased (ADJECTIVE; dead)—Two of the company founders are already ***deceased***.

Diseased (ADJECTIVE; sick)—Be sure to spray all these ***diseased*** rose bushes with insecticide.

Decent/Descent/Dissent

Decent (ADJECTIVE; in good taste; proper)—The ***decent*** solution to the problem would have been for the salesperson to apologize for his rude behavior.

Descent (NOUN; moving downward; ancestry)—The view of the city from the sky was breathtaking as the plane began its ***descent*** into the Denver airport. Mr. Sirakides is of Greek ***descent***.

Dissent (NOUN; differences or disagreement)—There was no ***dissent*** among the council members concerning the resolution to expand our city's parking facilities.

Defer/Differ

Defer (VERB; to put off or delay)—Our company has decided to ***defer*** this project until next spring.

Differ (VERB; to vary or disagree)—Doctors ***differ*** in their views about the best treatment for this particular virus.

Deference/Difference

Deference (NOUN; yielding to someone else's wishes)—In ***deference*** to many shoppers' requests, the store remained open until 9 p.m. during the summer months.

Difference (NOUN; state of being different; dissimilarity)—There is very little ***difference*** between these two product brands.

Delusion: see Allusion.

Deprecate/Depreciate

Deprecate (VERB; to disapprove or downgrade)—His speech did nothing but ***deprecate*** the present zoning system.

Depreciate (VERB; to lessen the value)—The tax code allows us to ***depreciate*** this new equipment over a five-year period.

Descent: see Decent.

Desert/Dessert

Desert (NOUN; an arid, barren land area)—Palm Springs was once a ***desert*** area occupied only by Agua Caliente Indians.

Dessert (NOUN; a sweet course served at the end of a meal)—Apple pie and ice cream is a traditional American ***dessert***.

Device/Devise

Device (NOUN; an invention or mechanism)—The ***device*** worked perfectly during the demonstration.

Devise (VERB; to think out or plan)—Were you able to ***devise*** an overtime plan that would be equitable to all employees?

Dew/Do/Due

Dew (NOUN; drops of moisture)—The heavy ***dew*** forecast for this morning was instead a heavy layer of fog, which caused the airport officials to delay all flights.

Do (VERB; to perform or bring about)—We must ***do*** everything possible to ship the order by June 17.

Due (ADJECTIVE; immediately payable)—Your payments are ***due*** by the 10th of each month.

Die/Dye

Die (VERB; to pass from physical life)—During the summer months water your grass twice daily so that it will not ***die***.

Dye (VERB; to change a color with a coloring substance)—We can custom ***dye*** this carpeting to your color choice.

Differ: see Defer.

Difference: see Deference.

Disapprove/Disprove

Disapprove (VERB; to withhold approval)—Our manager will ***disapprove*** any plan that is not properly justified.

Disprove (VERB; to prove false)—We must ***disprove*** the rumor that we are cutting back production next month.

Disburse/Disperse

Disburse (VERB; to pay out; to distribute methodically)—A new system has been devised to ***disburse*** commissions more rapidly. The property will be ***disbursed*** according to the provisions set forth in Mr. Williams' will.

Disperse (VERB; to scatter; to cause to become spread widely)—The crowd ***dispersed*** rapidly after the ball game. Those factories that ***disperse*** pollutants into the environment will continue to be subject to heavy fines. Please ***disperse*** this information to consumers nationwide.

Discreet/Discrete

Discreet (ADJECTIVE; showing good judgment in conduct and speech)—Ms. Harris is ***discreet*** in discussing patients' cases with other hospital personnel.
Discrete (ADJECTIVE; separate)—There are several ***discrete*** possibilities for distributing our products in Europe and parts of Asia.

Diseased: see Deceased.

Disinterested/Uninterested

Disinterested (ADJECTIVE; impartial)—All the judges for this competition have been certified to be ***disinterested*** parties.
Uninterested (ADJECTIVE; indifferent)—Those employees who are ***uninterested*** in the success of the company are certainly not candidates for promotion.

Disprove: see Disapprove.

Dissent: see Decent.

Do: see Dew.

Done/Dun

Done (VERB; past participle of *do*)—Our company has not ***done*** any further research in this area.
Dun (VERB, to make persistent demands for payment; NOUN OFTEN USED AS ADJECTIVE, a variable drab color, usually a neutral brownish gray)—Ms. Green's main responsibility is to ***dun*** slow-paying customers. One of our tasks is to repaint these ***dun***-colored walls to achieve a more cheerful atmosphere.

Due: see Dew.

Dun: see Done.

Dye: see Die.

Edict: see Addict.

Edition: see Addition.

Effect: see Affect.

E.g./I.e.

E.g. (PREPOSITION + NOUN; Latin abbreviation meaning *for example*)—Our company specializes in office furniture; ***e.g.***, desks, cabinets, bookcases, chairs, and reception area furniture.
I.e. (PRONOUN + VERB; Latin abbreviation meaning *that is*)—You may telephone your order to us at any time; ***i.e.***, we have operators on duty 24 hours a day every day.

Elicit/Illicit

Elicit (VERB; to draw out or bring forth)—Was the speaker able to ***elicit*** questions from the audience?
Illicit (ADJECTIVE; unlawful)—One of our agents was cited for ***illicit*** business practices.

Eligible/Illegible

Eligible (ADJECTIVE; qualified to be chosen)—To be ***eligible*** for these employment opportunities, applicants must be at least 21 years of age.

Illegible (ADJECTIVE; unreadable)—The handwriting on this student's paper is ***illegible***.

Elude: see Allude.

Emigrate/Immigrate

Emigrate (VERB; to move from a country)—The Johnsons ***emigrated*** from Norway in 1990.

Immigrate (VERB; to enter a country)—How many Canadians were permitted to ***immigrate*** to the United States last year?

Eminent/Imminent

Eminent (ADJECTIVE; prominent, distinguished)—Mr. Mendez is an ***eminent*** authority on labor relations.

Imminent (ADJECTIVE; impending, likely to occur)—There is ***imminent*** danger of equipment breakdown unless periodic service checks are made.

Ensure: see Assure.

Envelop/Envelope

Envelop (VERB; to wrap, surround, or conceal)—Each tamale is ***enveloped*** in a corn husk before it is boiled. The chief said his fire fighters would ***envelop*** the fire by morning. Each day a layer of early morning fog ***envelops*** the city.

Envelope (NOUN; a container for a written message)—Please send me your answer in the return ***envelope*** provided for your convenience.

Every day/Everyday

Every day (ADJECTIVE + NOUN; each day)—I will e-mail you ***every day*** and give you a status report on the new project.

Everyday (ADJECTIVE; ordinary)—Sales meetings seem to be an ***everyday*** occurrence in this office.

Every one/Everyone

Every one (ADJECTIVE + PRONOUN; each person or thing in a group [always followed by *of*])—***Every one*** of our staff is proficient in the use of our word processing, spreadsheet, and presentation software.

Everyone (PRONOUN; all people in a group)—***Everyone*** on the executive staff is expected to be present for the stockholders' meeting.

Example/Sample

Example (NOUN; something serving as a pattern to be imitated)—Please illustrate each of these principles with a meaningful ***example***.

Sample (NOUN; a representative part or a single item from a larger whole)—When purchasing See's candy, each customer is offered a ***sample***. How large of a ***sample*** population do you need to validate the results of the proposed study?

Exceed: see Accede.

Except: see Accept.

Excess: see Access.

Executioner/Executor

Executioner (NOUN; one who puts others [usually criminals] to death)—The ***executioner***-style murders still remain unsolved.
Executor (NOUN; person appointed to carry out the provisions of a will)— Whom have you named as ***executor*** of your will?

Exhilarate: see Accelerate.

Expand/Expend

Expand (VERB; to enlarge)—The plan to ***expand*** our storage facilities was approved.
Expend (VERB; to use up or pay out)—Ms. Smith ***expends*** too much time dealing with insignificant matters. If you do not ***expend*** these moneys by June 30, they will revert to the general fund.

Expansive/Expensive

Expansive (ADJECTIVE; capable of expanding; extensive)—An ***expansive*** commercial development is planned for this area.
Expensive (ADJECTIVE; costly)—The consultant's recommendations were too ***expensive*** to implement.

Expend: see Expand.

Expensive: see Expansive.

Explicit/Implicit

Explicit (ADJECTIVE; expressed clearly)—The accompanying booklet gives ***explicit*** instructions for assembling this piece of equipment.
Implicit (ADJECTIVE; implied)—By reading between the lines, one can discern an ***implicit*** appeal for additional funds.

Extant/Extent

Extant (ADJECTIVE; currently or actually existing)—Please provide me with a three-year budget for all ***extant*** and projected programs.
Extent (NOUN; range, scope, or magnitude)—Unfortunately, we will be unable to assess the ***extent*** of the damage until next week.

Facetious/Factious

Facetious (ADJECTIVE; humorous or witty, often in an inappropriate manner)—His seemingly ***facetious*** remark contained a kernel of truth.
Factious (ADJECTIVE; creating a faction or dissension)—A series of ***factious*** disputes eventually led to the dissolution of the partnership.

Factitious/Fictitious

Factitious (ADJECTIVE; artificial)—One manufacturer created a ***factitious*** demand for copper alloy by spreading rumors of shortages.
Fictitious (ADJECTIVE; nonexistent; imaginary; false)—Many people believe that the reported UFO sightings are ***fictitious***. This suspect has been known to operate under a number of ***fictitious*** names.

Fair/Fare

Fair (NOUN, an exhibition; ADJECTIVE, marked by impartiality and honesty; mediocre)—Our annual county ***fair*** is usually held during the first week of September. Further legislation was passed recently to enforce ***fair*** employment practices. He did a ***fair*** job.

Fare (VERB, to get along or succeed; NOUN, price charged to transport a person)—Our company did not ***fare*** well in its last bidding competition. How much is the first-class airline ***fare*** from Chicago to New York?

Farther/Further

Farther (ADJECTIVE; a greater distance [always a measurable amount of space])—The distance from the warehouse to the plant is ***farther*** than I thought.

Further (VERB, to help move forward; ADVERB, to a greater degree or extent; ADJECTIVE, additional)—The Truesdale Foundation has contributed $5 million to ***further*** research in spinal cord injuries. Stock market prices declined even ***further*** after the president's announcement. Refer to my July 8 memo for ***further*** details.

Feasible/Possible

Feasible (ADJECTIVE; capable of being done or carried out)—Installing tape backup systems in all our computers is certainly ***feasible***, but budget restraints prohibit our doing so at this time.

Possible (ADJECTIVE; being within the limits of realization)—Although networking all our computers would increase productivity, such a plan will not be ***possible*** until next year.

Feat/Fete

Feat (NOUN ['fēt]; an act of skill, endurance, or ingenuity)—Human beings under stress have been known to perform ***feats*** beyond their normal capabilities.

Fete (VERB ['fāt], to honor or commemorate; NOUN, a large elaborate party)—A banquet is being planned to ***fete*** our company president upon his retirement in September. The ***fete*** to honor our company president will be held on August 19.

Fever/Temperature

Fever (NOUN; a rise of body temperature above the normal)—When the child was brought into the emergency room, he had a ***fever***.

Temperature (NOUN; degree of hotness or coldness measured on a definite scale)—Normal body ***temperature*** is 98.6 degrees. Be sure to record patients' ***temperatures*** on their charts.

Fewer/Less

Fewer (ADJECTIVE; used with items that can be counted and plural nouns)—We had ***fewer*** sales this month. Reserve this checkout for customers with ten or ***fewer*** items. ***Fewer*** than half the employees elected to purchase stock options.

Less (ADJECTIVE; used with mass items that cannot be counted and singular nouns)—You will get by with ***less*** work if you follow my suggestions. ***Less*** than half the cake had been eaten.

Fictitious: see Factitious.

Finally/Finely

Finally (ADVERB; in the end)—The missing part was ***finally*** delivered.

Finely (ADVERB; elegantly or delicately; in small parts)—We all admired the ***finely*** embroidered tapestry. This engine has been ***finely*** tuned by our expert mechanics. You may purchase these ***finely*** chopped nuts in 8- and 16-ounce packages.

Fiscal/Physical

Fiscal (ADJECTIVE; relating to financial matters)—The ***fiscal*** year for our school district begins on July 1 and ends on June 30.

Physical (ADJECTIVE; concerned with the body and its needs)—Every individual should do a minimum amount of ***physical*** exercise daily.

Flagrant/Fragrant

Flagrant (ADJECTIVE; glaring, scandalous)—His behavior was a ***flagrant*** violation of company policy.

Fragrant (ADJECTIVE; sweet smelling)—She received a ***fragrant*** bouquet of flowers from the staff.

Flair/Flare

Flair (NOUN; a natural talent or aptitude)—Ms. Strehike has a ***flair*** for making people feel at ease when they enter her office.

Flare (VERB, to blaze up or spread out; NOUN, a signal light)—The gusty winds could easily cause the fire to ***flare*** out of control. ***Flares*** in the road guided motorists around the accident.

Flaunt/Flout

Flaunt (VERB; to make a gaudy or defiant display)—Although Mrs. Paige is recognized as one of the most affluent Hartford residents, she does not ***flaunt*** her wealth.

Flout (VERB; to mock or show contempt for; to defy)—As a new driver, the young man continued to ***flout*** the posted speed limit.

Flew/Flu/Flue

Flew (VERB; past tense of *fly*)—Our plane ***flew*** to the West Coast in record time.

Flu (NOUN; abbreviated form of *influenza*)—Nearly 30 percent of our employees are absent because of the ***flu***.

Flue (NOUN; a duct in a chimney)—If the ***flue*** is closed, smoke from a burning fire cannot escape through the chimney.

Flout: see Flaunt.

Flu: see Flew.

Flue: see Flew.

Foreword/Forward

Foreword (NOUN; prefatory comments, as for a book)—Thomas S. Healy, president of the New York Public Library, wrote the ***foreword*** for the 1992 publication of *The New York Public Library Book of Twentieth-Century American Quotations*.

Forward (ADVERB; to or toward what is ahead)—Since its beginnings our company has moved ***forward*** in research and development at a rapid pace.

Formally/Formerly

Formally (ADVERB; in a formal manner)—At our next meeting you will be ***formally*** initiated into the organization.
Formerly (ADVERB; in the past)—Marie Martin was ***formerly*** the president of a large metropolitan area community college.

Former/Latter

Former (ADJECTIVE; first of two things or belonging to an earlier time)—Your ***former*** suggestion appears to be the better one. As a ***former*** employee, Lois Oliver is always invited to all the company social functions.
Latter (ADJECTIVE; second of two things or nearer to the end)—Of the two proposals the ***latter*** one seems to be more economical. Mail deliveries in your area are scheduled for the ***latter*** part of the day.

Forth/Fourth

Forth (ADVERB; forward)—The president requested that any objections to his plan be brought ***forth*** at this time.
Fourth (a numeric term; the ordinal form of *four*)—The ***fourth*** member of our group never arrived.

Fortunate/Fortuitous

Fortunate (ADJECTIVE; having good luck)—We were ***fortunate*** to obtain the contract to rebuild the Northridge Mall after the earthquake.
Fortuitous (ADJECTIVE; accidental; happening by chance)—Only through ***fortuitous*** circumstances were we able to purchase these airline tickets at such a reduced price.

Forward: see Foreword.

Fourth: see Forth.

Fragrant: see Flagrant.

Further: see Farther.

Good/Well

Good (ADJECTIVE; meaning *of favorable quality* in describing a noun or pronoun; meaning *fit, wholesome* in describing a person's well-being)—Mr. Collins writes ***good*** letters. I always feel ***good*** after finishing my exercises at the gym.
Well (ADVERB; meaning *properly, skillfully* in describing an action; ADJECTIVE, meaning *fit, healthy* in describing a person's health)—The majority of our nursing graduates do ***well*** on their state board examinations. My assistant did not look ***well*** today.

Grate/Great

Grate (VERB, to reduce to small particles by rubbing on something rough; to cause irritation; NOUN, a frame of parallel or crossed bars blocking a passage)—In the future please use a food processor to ***grate*** the cheese for our pizzas. His continual talking could ***grate*** on anyone's nerves. Be sure to place a ***grate*** over this excavation when you have finished removing the dirt.

Great (ADJECTIVE; large in size; numerous; eminent or distinguished)—From the cruise ship we often sight a ***great*** white shark. A ***great*** many people have expressed an interest in purchasing our Model No. 47A videocassette recorder. Many ***great*** performers from stage and screen will be present at our annual benefit.

Guarantee/Guaranty

Guarantee (VERB, to assure the fulfillment of a condition; NOUN, assurance of the quality or length of service of a product)—I ***guarantee*** that your children will enjoy immensely the adventures Disneyland has to offer. All our cars have a one-year or 50,000-mile ***guarantee***.

Guaranty (VERB, to agree to pay the debt of another in case of default; NOUN, an assurance to pay the debt of another in case of default)—The federal government will ***guaranty*** all loans made under this new first-time home buyer program. John Fletcher's car loan will be approved as soon as we receive his parents' signed ***guaranty***.

Hail/Hale

Hail (VERB, to greet or summon; NOUN, rain that falls in the form of small ice balls)—On rainy afternoons you may find it difficult to ***hail*** a taxi in New York City. Unfortunately, the unexpected ***hail*** this season has damaged our strawberry crops.

Hale (ADJECTIVE; healthy)—Let's hope you will return from this adventuresome vacation ***hale*** and hearty.

He/Him/Himself

He (PRONOUN; the subject of a clause or a complement pronoun)—***He*** is the person I interviewed for the job. The person in our group with the best singing voice has always been ***he***.

Him (PRONOUN; a direct object, an indirect object, or an object of a preposition)—The president asked ***him*** to head the project. Doris Waters gave ***him*** the results of the study yesterday. The choice is between you and ***him***.

Himself (PRONOUN; a reflexive PRONOUN used to emphasize or refer back to the subject)—He ***himself*** had to solve the problem. Rick Bogart addressed the envelope to ***himself***.

Healthful/Healthy

Healthful (ADJECTIVE; beneficial to health of body or mind; promotes one's well-being or good health)—Millions of Americans consider vitamin supplements to be ***healthful***. Mary tries to eat only ***healthful*** foods. Many doctors recommend daily exercise as a ***healthful*** activity.

Healthy (ADJECTIVE; being well or fit; enjoying health and vigor of body, mind, or spirit)—Be sure to keep only ***healthy*** plants in our nursery section. Most of our clients have selected the one-year membership program to remain ***healthy*** and maintain their physical fitness.

Hear/Here

Hear (VERB; to perceive by the ear)—Yes, I can ***hear*** you clearly.

Here (ADVERB; in this place or at this point)—Install the telephone line ***here***.

Her/Herself/She

Her (PRONOUN; a direct object, an indirect object, or an object of a preposition)—When Paulette arrived, Mr. Schultz asked ***her*** for the information. Barbara offered ***her*** a chair. The check is for ***her***.

Herself (PRONOUN; a reflexive pronoun used to emphasize or refer back to the subject)—Wendy ***herself*** wrote and dictated the entire audit report using voice-recognition software. Kristen often talks to ***herself***.

She (PRONOUN; the subject of a clause or a complement pronoun)—***She*** went to lunch about 15 minutes ago. The person who designed this spreadsheet was ***she***.

Here: see Hear.

Herself: see Her.

Hew/Hue

Hew (VERB; to cut with blows of a heavy cutting instrument)—Which famous faces have been ***hewed*** on Mount Rushmore?

Hue (NOUN; color or gradation of color; aspect)—The ***hues*** of the rainbow glistened in the sunlight. Persons from every political ***hue*** criticized the president for not informing the American public of his actions.

Him: see He.

Himself: see He.

Hoard/Horde

Hoard (VERB; to store or accumulate for future use)—Please do not ***hoard*** stationery and other supplies.

Horde (NOUN; a multitude)—A ***horde*** of people were waiting for the doors to open.

Hoarse/Horse

Hoarse (ADJECTIVE; low, husky sound)—Your voice is too ***hoarse*** to make these telephone calls today.

Horse (NOUN; a large animal)—For this commercial we will need at least eight ***horses***.

Hole/Whole

Hole (NOUN; an opening or open place)—Burglars had entered the jewelry store by cutting a ***hole*** through the outer wall.

Whole (ADJECTIVE; complete, entire)—Too many inexperienced managers make decisions before knowing the ***whole*** story.

Holy/Wholly

Holy (ADJECTIVE; sacred)—Visitors continually flock to Jerusalem's ***holy*** shrines.

Wholly (ADVERB; completely)—Do you agree ***wholly*** with the committee's plan to invest additional funds in the proposed shopping center?

Horde: see Hoard.

Hue: see Hew.

Human/Humane

Human (ADJECTIVE; characteristic of people)—Please remember that all of us are guilty of possessing ***human*** frailties.
Humane (ADJECTIVE; marked by compassion, sympathy, or consideration)—The treatment of elderly people in this convalescent facility is certainly less than ***humane***.

Hypercritical/Hypocritical

Hypercritical (ADJECTIVE; excessively critical)—Many of his coworkers believe Mr. Reed to be ***hypercritical*** of new employees.
Hypocritical (ADJECTIVE [ˌhi-pə-ˈkri-ti-kəl]; falsely pretending)—Because Jodi pretended to be friendly to other staff members and then gossiped about their shortcomings, she was eventually fired for her ***hypocritical*** behavior.

I/Me/Myself

I (PRONOUN; a subject of a clause or a complement pronoun)—***I*** finished the sales report last night. If you were ***I***, what would you do under these circumstances?
Me (PRONOUN; a direct object, an indirect object, or an object of a preposition)—Jolene Mack telephoned ***me*** this morning. Pat gave ***me*** the sales report last week. None of this material is for ***me***.
Myself (PRONOUN; a reflexive pronoun used to emphasize or refer back to the subject)—I wrote the entire report ***myself***. I can blame only ***myself*** for losing this sale.

Ideal/Idle/Idol

Ideal (ADJECTIVE; perfect, model)—Your proposal outlines an ***ideal*** solution to the problem.
Idle (ADJECTIVE; doing nothing)—The production line was ***idle*** for almost a week.
Idol (NOUN; an object for religious worship; a revered person or thing)—One of the church ***idols*** had been vandalized. Money is often the ***idol*** of ambitious, greedy people.

I.e.: see E.g.

Illegible: see Eligible.

Illicit: see Elicit.

Illusion: see Allusion.

Immigrate: see Emigrate.

Imminent: see Eminent.

Implicit: see Explicit.

Imply/Infer

Imply (VERB; to suggest without stating)—Does that statement ***imply*** that I have made a mistake?
Infer (VERB; to reach a conclusion)—From the results of this independent survey, we can only ***infer*** that our advertising campaign in the Pittsburgh area was ineffective.

In behalf of/On behalf of

In behalf of (PREPOSITION + NOUN + PREPOSITION; speak for or represent; in the interest or benefit of)—Because Ms. Shields was scheduled to be out of town, she requested Mary Ann to present the award ***in behalf of*** the company.

On behalf of (PREPOSITION + NOUN + PREPOSITION; plead a person's case; in support or defense of)—Dr. Phillips spoke ***on behalf of*** Ms. Jones at the hearing.

Incidence/Incidents

Incidence (NOUN; occurrence; rate of occurrence)—There has yet to be an ***incidence*** of theft within the company. The low ***incidence*** of traffic accidents over this holiday weekend may be attributed to our television safety campaign.

Incidents (NOUN; events or episodes)—Several ***incidents*** have occurred recently that require us to review our safety policies and practices.

Incite/Insight

Incite (VERB; to urge on or provoke action)—The speaker attempted to ***incite*** the audience to take action. Poverty, depression, and starvation ***incited*** riots throughout the country.

Insight (NOUN; keen understanding)—Bob's ***insight*** and patience prevented the situation from developing into a major problem.

Indigenous/Indigent/Indignant

Indigenous (ADJECTIVE; native of a particular region)—I believe that this tree is ***indigenous*** only to the Northwest.

Indigent (ADJECTIVE; poor, needy)—He began as an ***indigent*** refugee from war-torn Europe.

Indignant (ADJECTIVE; insulting, angry)—Successful store managers must know how to deal with ***indignant*** customers.

Infer: see Imply.

Ingenious/Ingenuous

Ingenious (ADJECTIVE; marked by originality, resourcefulness, and cleverness)—This ***ingenious*** plan could save our company thousands of dollars annually.

Ingenuous (ADJECTIVE; showing innocent or childlike simplicity; natural)—Mr. Warren's ***ingenuous*** smile and warm personality have contributed immeasurably to his successful political career.

Insight: see Incite.

Insure: see Assure.

Interstate/Intrastate

Interstate (ADJECTIVE; between states)—Since expanding operations to New Jersey, we must abide by all laws governing ***interstate*** commerce.

Intrastate (ADJECTIVE; within a state)—This firm, an Illinois corporation, is primarily concerned with ***intrastate*** product sales.

Irregardless/Regardless

Irregardless (an incorrect usage for ***regardless*** that is not acceptable for speaking or writing).

Regardless (ADVERB; despite everything)—We must vacate these premises by July 31, ***regardless***!
Regardless of (PREPOSITION; without taking into account; in spite of)—***Regardless of*** price, which one of these models has the best performance record? We have opened an account for Ritter's Clothing Store ***regardless of*** its slow-pay payment record.

Irritate: see Aggravate.

Isle: see Aisle.

It's/Its

It's (PRONOUN + VERB; contraction of *it is*)—Although this model microwave oven has become very popular, ***it's*** not our best-seller.
Its (PRONOUN USED AS ADJECTIVE; possessive form of *it*)—The company had ***its*** stockholders' meeting in Atlanta last week.

Karat: see Carat.

Later/Latter

Later (ADVERB; after the proper time)—The shipment arrived ***later*** than we had expected.
Latter (ADJECTIVE; the second thing of two things mentioned)—Your ***latter*** suggestion is more likely to be adopted. *See also* **Former**.

Lay/Lie

Lay (VERB; to put or place; a transitive verb that needs an object to complete its meaning; *lay, laid, laid,* and *laying* are the principal parts of this VERB)—Please ***lay*** the message on my desk. I ***laid*** the message on your desk. I have ***laid*** several messages on your desk from Fred Obermiller. We are ***laying*** the foundation for the new building today.
Lie (VERB; to recline; an intransitive VERB that does not have an object; *lie, lay, lain,* and *lying* are the principal parts of this VERB)—May I ***lie*** down? He ***lay*** in the hospital waiting room for over three hours before a doctor saw him. These papers have ***lain*** on your desk since Monday. Mrs. Hartman is ***lying*** down.

Lead/Led

Lead (NOUN USED AS ADJECTIVE ['led]; a metallic element)—How many feet of ***lead*** pipe did the contractor order for this apartment house complex?
Led (VERB; past tense of *lead* ['lēd], meaning *to provide direction*)—Before his retirement Mr. Andrews ***led*** this company from a $3 million deficit to a $6 million annual profit.

Lean/Lien

Lean (VERB, to rest against; to be inclined toward; ADJECTIVE, not fat)—Do not ***lean*** against these railings. I believe that most of our employees ***lean*** toward accepting increased medical benefits rather than greater salaries. We use only first-quality ***lean*** ground beef in our hamburgers.
Lien (NOUN; a legal right or claim to property)—If he refuses to pay, we will be forced to place a ***lien*** against his property.

Leased/Least

Leased (VERB; property rented for a specified time period)—This suite of offices has been ***leased*** by our company for the past eight years.
Least (ADJECTIVE; smallest, slightest, lowest)—This year we showed the ***least*** profit since our company was founded in 1972.

Led: see Lead.

Lend/Loan

Lend (VERB; to give for temporary use with the understanding that the same or equivalent will be returned)—Has the bank agreed to ***lend*** us additional funds for expansion?
Loan (NOUN; something given for a borrower's temporary use)—Your $3,000 ***loan*** will be fully paid with your October 1 payment.

Less: see Fewer.

Lessee/Lesser/Lessor

Lessee (NOUN; one to whom a lease is given)—As specified in the lease agreement, the ***lessee*** must pay a monthly rent of $750 to the landlord.
Lesser (ADJECTIVE; smaller or less important)—Although the judge ruled in favor of the defendant, he awarded a ***lesser*** amount than we had expected.
Lessor (NOUN; one who grants a lease)—The ***lessor*** for all our company cars is Allied Car Rental Service.

Lessen/Lesson

Lessen (VERB; to make smaller)—Chris Timmins recommended that we ***lessen*** our efforts in the manufacturing area.
Lesson (NOUN; a unit of study; something from which one learns)—The experience was a good ***lesson*** in how miscommunication can cause problems.

Lesser: see Lessee.

Lessor: see Lessee.

Levee/Levy

Levee (NOUN; the bank of a river or a boat landing)—The river overflowed the ***levee***.
Levy (NOUN; an order for payment)—To pay for the flood damage, the governor ordered a 1 percent ***levy*** on gasoline sales.

Liable/Libel/Likely

Liable (ADJECTIVE; legally responsible, obligated)—The court ruled that the company was ***liable*** for all damages resulting from the accident.
Libel (NOUN; a false or damaging written statement about another)—Don refused to include the statement in his article because he feared he would be sued for ***libel***.
Likely (ADJECTIVE, probable; ADVERB, probably)—He is a ***likely*** candidate for the position. If you break a law, you are ***likely*** (not *liable*) to be arrested.

Lie: see Lay.

Lien: see Lean.

Lightening/Lightning

Lightening (VERB [GERUND]; illuminating or brightening; lessening or alleviating)—Please select colors that will result in ***lightening*** the reception area. Only by ***lightening*** her workload can we expect to retain Ms. Burton.
Lightning (NOUN; the flashing of light produced by atmospheric electricity)—During the storm flashes of ***lightning*** streaked across the sky.

Like: see As.

Likely: see Liable.

Loan: see Lend.

Local/Locale

Local (ADJECTIVE; limited to a particular district)—Only persons living in the ***local*** area were interviewed.
Locale (NOUN [lō'kal]; a particular location)—This parcel of land is an ideal ***locale*** for a shopping center.

Loose/Lose

Loose (ADJECTIVE; not fastened, not tight or shut up)—A ***loose*** connection was the probable cause of the power failure on the fifth floor of the Fisher Building.
Lose (VERB; to fail to keep; to mislay)—We do not want to ***lose*** any of our accounts in the Philippines. If you ***lose*** your keys, please call Mr. Drew in Plant Facilities.

Magnate/Magnet

Magnate (NOUN; a powerful or influential person)—As the first ***magnate*** of the automobile industry, Henry Ford changed the lifestyle of people throughout the world.
Magnet (NOUN or ADJECTIVE; something that has the ability to attract)—Picking up the spilled paper clips with a ***magnet*** was an easy task. This ***magnet*** school has many talented musicians.

Main/Mane

Main (ADJECTIVE; principal or most important part)—Our ***main*** selling feature is still customer service.
Mane (NOUN; the heavy hair on the neck of a horse or lion)—The horse's ***mane*** had become entangled in the wire fence.

Manner/Manor

Manner (NOUN; method; a customary or particular way)—Unless the company changes its ***manner*** of doing business, it will lose many more customers. Chancellor Phelps' congenial ***manner*** has endeared him to both faculty and students alike.
Manor (NOUN; a main house or mansion)—Although the decor of the ***manor*** dates back to the early years of the twentieth century, it is still well maintained and elegant.

Marital/Marshal/Martial

Marital (ADJECTIVE; pertaining to marriage)—Use "***marital*** bliss" as the primary appeal in your advertising copy for this client.

Marshal (NOUN; a military or law enforcement rank; the head of a ceremony)—If you wish to have a ***marshal*** serve these papers, there is an additional $40 fee. Jack Williams was asked to act as honorary ***marshal*** of the parade.

Martial (ADJECTIVE; warlike, military)—Several bands played ***martial*** music at the Veterans Day commemoration.

May: see Can.

May be/Maybe

May be (VERB; a verb phrase [a helping verb and a main verb] derived from the infinitive *to be*)—This ***may be*** the last year we will be able to lease these facilities.

Maybe (ADVERB; perhaps)—***Maybe*** you could ask the sales representatives to e-mail this information to you as they call upon their various accounts.

Me: see I.

Medal/Meddle

Medal (NOUN; a metal disk; an award in the form of a metal disk)—This gold religious ***medal*** was found lying on the sidewalk outside the church. He should receive a ***medal*** for his heroic efforts.

Meddle (VERB; to interfere)—This argument was one in which she dared not ***meddle***.

Miner/Minor

Miner (NOUN; a person who works in a mine)—He listed his last job as that of coal ***miner***.

Minor (NOUN, a person under legal age; ADJECTIVE, a lesser thing)—Please post a sign that reads "No ***minors*** allowed." Your forgetting to fax the proposal yesterday proved to be only a ***minor*** error.

Mode/Mood

Mode (NOUN; style or preferred method)—What ***mode*** of transportation will you use to reach the airport?

Mood (NOUN; feeling or disposition)—Before you ask Mr. Smith for a salary increase, be sure he is in a good ***mood***.

Moral/Morale

Moral (ADJECTIVE; pertaining to right and wrong; ethical)—She made the decision on a ***moral*** basis rather than on a practical basis.

Morale (NOUN; a mental condition)—Announcement of an across-the-board 7 percent pay increase instantly boosted employee ***morale***.

Morning/Mourning

Morning (NOUN; the time from sunrise to noon)—Would you be able to schedule an appointment for me to see Dr. Rose on Friday ***morning***?

Mourning (NOUN; showing signs of grief)—Please allow the family to observe this period of ***mourning*** without any interruptions concerning business matters.

Most: see Almost.

Mourning: see Morning.

Myself: see I.

Naval/Navel

Naval (ADJECTIVE; relating to a navy)—Last week Mr. Marsh's son accepted an assignment with ***naval*** intelligence.
Navel (NOUN; a depression in the middle of the abdomen)—According to Dr. Chin, the incision will leave a small scar directly below the ***navel***.

Number: see Amount.

On behalf of: see In behalf of.

Ordinance/Ordnance

Ordinance (NOUN; a local regulation)—The city has an ***ordinance*** banning excessive noise after 10 p.m.
Ordnance (NOUN; military weapons)—We should know by the end of the month whether we will receive the army ***ordnance*** contract.

Overdo/Overdue

Overdo (VERB; to exaggerate; to do in excess)—Exercise is healthful if one does not ***overdo*** it.
Overdue (ADJECTIVE; late)—Your payment is 15 days ***overdue***.

Pair/Pare/Pear

Pair (NOUN; two of a kind; made of two corresponding parts)—The ***pair*** of shoes the customer attempted to return showed signs of considerable wear.
Pare (VERB; to reduce in size or trim; to peel)—I hope you can ***pare*** this budget at least 15 percent.
Pear (NOUN; a fruit)—Our market carries three brands of canned ***pears***.

Partition/Petition

Partition (NOUN; something that divides)—Office efficiency increased substantially after each workstation was separated by a ***partition***.
Petition (NOUN; a formal written request)—Have you signed the ***petition*** to create curb cutouts at major intersections in the downtown business district?

Passed/Past

Passed (VERB; past tense or past participle of *pass*, meaning *to go by* or *circulate*)—Once you have ***passed*** the intersection, look for our store on the right side of the street. Lisa ***passed*** out copies of the job announcement to all eligible employees in the company.
Past (NOUN or ADJECTIVE; time gone by or ended)—Our weak profit picture is all in the ***past***. From ***past*** experience we have learned not to extend credit to this company.

Patience/Patients

Patience (NOUN; calm perseverance)—Your ***patience*** in working with these handicapped children is certainly to be admired. Accessing the Internet with an older, slower modem requires considerable ***patience***.

Patients (NOUN; people undergoing medical treatment)—George Allison is one of Dr. Hedge's ***patients***.

Peace/Piece

Peace (NOUN; truce; tranquillity)—As long as the hostilities exist, there can be no ***peace*** among these nations. Since Ms. Seraydarian began the project, she has not had a moment's ***peace***.

Piece (NOUN; a part of a defined quantity)—Each of the three beneficiaries inherited a ***piece*** of the prime property.

Peak/Peek

Peak (ADJECTIVE or NOUN; highest point; top)—Our ***peak*** sales period is from September through November. KLAC's transmitter is located at the ***peak*** of Mount Baldy.

Peek (VERB; to glance)—Some of the buyers have already had a ***peek*** at the new fall fashions by major designers.

Peal/Peel

Peal (VERB; to give out a loud sound or succession of sounds)—The bells ***pealed*** from the church tower.

Peel (VERB, to remove by stripping; NOUN, skin or rind)—Ask the customer to ***peel*** off the mailing label and affix it to the enclosed postcard. Do any of these recipes require the use of lemon ***peel***?

Pear: see Pair.

Peek: see Peak.

Peel: see Peal.

Peer/Pier

Peer (VERB, to gaze; NOUN, one belonging to the same social group)—Do customers often ***peer*** into the bakery shop window before entering the store? Most teenagers imitate the behavior of their ***peers***.

Pier (NOUN; a structure extending into navigable waters)—No fishing is allowed from this ***pier***.

Persecute/Prosecute

Persecute (VERB; to harass persistently)—If your supervisor continues to ***persecute*** you, please contact your union representative at Ext. 3543.

Prosecute (VERB; to conduct legal proceedings against someone)—We are not sure whether the district attorney will ***prosecute*** the case.

Personal/Personnel

Personal (ADJECTIVE; private; individual)—Be careful to whom you disclose ***personal*** information, especially over the Internet. Each full-time employee has been assigned a ***personal*** parking place.

Personnel (NOUN, employees; ADJECTIVE, relating to employment)—All ***personnel*** are requested to work overtime until the inventory has been completed. Your annual performance evaluation will be placed in your ***personnel*** file.

Perspective/Prospective

Perspective (NOUN; a mental picture or outlook)—His ***perspective*** is distorted by greed.
Prospective (ADJECTIVE; likely, expected)—Last week we interviewed several ***prospective*** candidates for our Accounting Department.

Persuade: see Convince.

Peruse/Pursue

Peruse (VERB; to read hastily or casually)—Each morning at breakfast I ***peruse*** the newspaper for any items of interest to our industry.
Pursue (VERB; to follow; to proceed with a course of action)—May I suggest you ***pursue*** this sales lead further.

Petition: see Partition.

Physical: see Fiscal.

Piece: see Peace.

Pier: see Peer.

Plaintiff/Plaintive

Plaintiff (NOUN; one who initiates a lawsuit to obtain a remedy for injury to his or her rights)—Who is the attorney for the ***plaintiff***?
Plaintive (ADJECTIVE; expressive of suffering or woe)—In a ***plaintive*** voice the witness described how the gunmen carried out the robbery.

Pole/Poll

Pole (NOUN; a long, slender object that is usually cylindrical)—The teachers will need a ***pole*** to open the top row of windows in these classrooms.
Poll (NOUN; counting of opinions or votes cast; place where votes are cast [usually *polls*])—Our latest ***poll*** shows that consumers prefer Revel toothpaste over any other. Be sure to urge all registered voters to go to the ***polls*** next Tuesday.

Populace/Populous

Populace (NOUN; the masses; population of a place)—The winning candidate must have the support of the ***populace***. During the flood the ***populace*** of Evansville was evacuated.
Populous (ADJECTIVE; densely populated)—At present we have restaurants only in ***populous*** areas.

Pore/Pour

Pore (VERB, to read studiously or attentively; NOUN, a small opening in a membrane)—How long did the auditors ***pore*** over these books? Hot water will open the ***pores*** of your skin, and cold water will close them.
Pour (VERB; to dispense from a container; to move with a continuous flow)—Please ask the servers to ***pour*** the water before the guests are seated. Even before the game ended, spectators began to ***pour*** out of the stadium.

Possible: see Feasible.

Practicable/Practical

Practicable (ADJECTIVE; describes an idea or plan that in theory seems to be feasible or usable; capable of being put into practice)—The plan to build cars that run on electricity seems to be ***practicable***.

Practical (ADJECTIVE; describes an idea or plan that is feasible or usable because it has been successfully tried or proved by past experience; fit for actual practice)—Because gasoline prices in Europe are very high, many people find small cars to be the ***practical*** solution to controlling transportation costs.

Pray/Prey

Pray (VERB; to make a request in a humble manner; to address a god)—I ***pray*** that these bureaucrats will listen to my request. Children may not be required to ***pray*** in public schools.

Prey (VERB, to have an injurious or destructive effect; NOUN, victim)—Ms. Rice should not let this experience constantly ***prey*** on her thoughts. Do not become ***prey*** to the quick-rich schemes of such con artists.

Precede/Proceed

Precede (VERB [pri-'sēd]; to go before)—Mrs. Andrews' presentation will directly ***precede*** the convention's first general session.

Proceed (VERB [prō-'sēd]; to go forward or continue)—Please ***proceed*** with your analysis of the financial statements.

Precedence/Precedents

Precedence (NOUN ['pre-cə-dən(t)s]; priority)—Please give ***precedence*** to training our sales and middle management personnel in the use of voice-recognition software.

Precedents (NOUN ['pre-cə-dənts]; things done or said that can be used as an example)—There are no legal ***precedents*** in our state for this particular case.

Presence/Presents

Presence (NOUN; condition of being present; stately or distinguished bearing of a person)—Please ensure the ***presence*** of all supervisors and managers at this meeting. Everyone was impressed by the confidence and ***presence*** with which the new president addressed the faculty.

Presents (NOUN; gifts or things given)—Company employees donated a record number of ***presents*** to needy children this year.

Presume: see Assume.

Prey: see Pray.

Principal/Principle

Principal (NOUN; a capital sum; head of a school)—Both the ***principal*** and the interest paid are shown on your loan statement each month. As ***principal*** of Lindberg High School, Mrs. Brereton was proud that so many seniors attended college upon graduation.

Principal (ADJECTIVE; highest in importance)—The ***principal*** reason for changing our promotion procedures was to encourage all employees within the company to upgrade their skills.

Principle (NOUN; an accepted rule of action; a basic truth or belief)—Her knowledge of accounting ***principles*** is questionable. Our country was founded on the ***principle*** that all persons are created equal.

Proceed: see Precede.

Propose/Purpose

Propose (VERB; to suggest)—I ***propose*** that we borrow sufficient funds to purchase all the new equipment at once.
Purpose (NOUN; a desired result)—The ***purpose*** of this meeting is to discuss ways of increasing our sales through e-commerce.

Prosecute: see Persecute.

Prospective: see Perspective.

Purpose: see Propose.

Pursue: see Peruse.

Quiet/Quite

Quiet (ADJECTIVE; peaceful; free from noise)—Our client wishes to purchase a home in a ***quiet*** residential neighborhood. The ***quiet*** operation of this printer is one of its main sales features.
Quite (ADVERB; completely or actually)—Our salespeople seem to be ***quite*** satisfied with the new commission plan.

Raise/Raze/Rise

Raise (VERB; to lift something up, increase in amount, gather together, or bring into existence; a transitive verb that needs an object to complete its meaning; *raise, raised, raised,* and *raising* are the principal parts of this verb)—Please do not ***raise*** your voice. The company ***raised*** our sales quota 30 percent last month. We have ***raised*** $200 for Mrs. Morgan's retirement gift. A number of our stockholders are ***raising*** questions about the proposed merger.
Raze (VERB; to tear down to the ground)—When does your company plan to ***raze*** this old warehouse?
Rise (VERB; to go up or to increase in value; an intransitive verb that does not have an object; *rise, rose, risen,* and *rising* are the principal parts of this verb)—Our sales should ***rise*** beyond the $1 million mark this quarter. The rocket ***rose*** 30,000 feet before it exploded. Our sales have ***risen*** for the third month in a row. Production has been ***rising*** steadily since the new equipment was installed.

Real/Really

Real (ADJECTIVE; actual, true; genuine)—The new accounting software is a ***real*** help in getting out our monthly statements on time.
Really (ADVERB; very, certainly)—Susan was ***really*** disappointed that Robert did not accept the position.

Reality/Realty

Reality (NOUN; that which is real, that which exists)—Our problems began when the general plant manager would not face ***reality*** in negotiating with the employees' representatives.

Realty (NOUN or ADJECTIVE; real estate)—The last ***realty*** company that tried to sell my property could not find a qualified buyer.

Receipt/Recipe

Receipt (NOUN; a written acknowledgment of receiving goods or money)—No refunds can be made without a ***receipt***.

Recipe (NOUN; a set of instructions)—Mama Lucia's has always kept secret the ***recipe*** for its delicious spaghetti sauce.

Regardless: See Irregardless.

Residence/Residents

Residence (NOUN; place where one lives)—This house has been Mrs. Scott's ***residence*** for the past twenty years.

Residents (NOUN; people who live in a place)—One of the retirement home ***residents*** reported that the heater in her room emits only cold air. The ***residents*** of Nashville have elected a new mayor.

Respectably/Respectfully/Respectively

Respectably (ADJECTIVE; in a correct or decent manner)—The vagrant was dressed ***respectably*** for his court appearance.

Respectfully (ADVERB; a manner denoting high regard; word used in the body or complimentary close of a letter to show high regard or respect for the addressee)—Please remember to treat all our customers ***respectfully***. Letter closing: ***Respectfully*** yours.

Respectively (ADVERB; each in turn or in order)—Janice Jackson, John Zelinsky, and Al Turnbull were first-, second-, and third-prize winners, ***respectively***.

Ring/Wring

Ring (VERB; to give out a resounding sound)—Remind all patients to ***ring*** their bells if they need any assistance.

Wring (VERB; to squeeze or twist)—For each of these garments, make sure that the care instructions caution consumers to "Hand wash only. Do not ***wring*** dry; blot dry with towel."

Rise: see Raise.

Role/Roll

Role (NOUN; proper function of a person or thing; a part or character assumed)—Mr. Hayworth is very successful in his ***role*** as mediator for grievances within the company. What ***role*** will you play in this theater production?

Roll (VERB, to move by turning or rotating; NOUN, something wound around a core; a list of names)—Be sure to ***roll*** back the bathroom carpeting before attempting any plumbing repairs. Please order 3 dozen ***rolls*** of transparent packaging tape from Hillsdale Stationers. How many students are on your ***roll***?

Rote/Wrote

Rote (NOUN; mechanical or repetitious procedure)—All fourth-grade children are expected to learn the multiplication tables *one* through *ten* by ***rote***.
Wrote (VERB; past tense of *write*)—We ***wrote*** to all our clients last week informing them of our merger with American Financial Corporation.

Rout/Route

Rout (NOUN ['raůt—sounds like *out*]; a disorderly assembly or disastrous defeat)—The game turned into a ***rout*** after the opposing team scored 30 points during the first quarter.
Route (NOUN ['rüt]; a course taken in traveling from one point to another)—Most of our city delivery ***routes*** were changed based upon the consultant's recommendations.

Sample: see Example.

Scene/Seen

Scene (NOUN; place of an occurrence; an exhibition of anger)—The police arrived at the ***scene*** of the robbery shortly after the security guard telephoned them. How would you handle a hostile customer who was creating a ***scene***?
Seen (VERB; past participle of *to see*)—I have not ***seen*** our sales manager for three days.

Scent: see Cent.

Sealing: see Ceiling.

Seize: see Cease.

Semi-: see Bi-.

Senses: see Census.

Sent: see Cent.

Serial: see Cereal.

Set/Sit

Set (VERB; to place, position, or arrange; a transitive VERB that generally needs an object to complete its meaning; *set*, *set*, *set*, and *setting* are the principal parts of this VERB)—Please ***set*** the calculator on my desk. He ***set*** the clocks ahead one hour for daylight saving time. I have ***set*** the times for all your medical appointments this week. We are ***setting*** higher quotas for all our sales personnel this year.
Sit (VERB; to be seated or occupy a seat; an intransitive verb that does not have an object; *sit*, *sat*, *sat*, and *sitting* are the principal parts of this verb)—***Sit*** here, Ms. Brown. I ***sat*** for over an hour awaiting his return. He has ***sat*** in that chair all day watching television. If Mr. Weaver calls, tell him I am ***sitting*** in on a meeting of the department heads.

Sew/So/Sow

Sew (VERB; to fasten by stitches with thread)—Please have someone in the Alterations Department ***sew*** a button on this coat.
So (ADVERB, to that degree; CONJUNCTION, in a way indicated; in order that; therefore)—We are ***so*** interested in entering the Brazilian market that we have set up an office in Rio. ***So*** that we may update our files, please complete the enclosed form and mail it to us in the return envelope. Our company is moving its offices to Columbus, Ohio; ***so*** now we are in the process of recruiting new personnel in this city.
Sow (VERB; to scatter seed)—This machine can ***sow*** more seed in a day than any 15 farmhands.

Shall/Will

Shall (HELPING VERB; denotes future time in the first person in formal writing)—I ***shall*** give your request the utmost consideration. We ***shall*** initiate legal proceedings on November 1.
Will (helping VERB; used with all three persons in business style)—I (or We) ***will*** call you tomorrow. You ***will*** receive your refund when you return the merchandise. He (or She or They) ***will*** finish the project according to schedule unless he (or she or they) encounter(s) bad weather conditions.

She: see Her.

Shear/Sheer

Shear (VERB; to cut, strip, or remove)—We had to ***shear*** off the bolts before we could remove the wheel.
Sheer (ADJECTIVE; transparently thin; utterly; steep)—None of the ***sheer*** fabrics are suitable for the kind of draperies we have in mind. This conference was a ***sheer*** waste of time. Did any of the prisoners attempt to scale the ***sheer*** cliffs?

Shone/Shown

Shone (VERB; past tense and past participle of *shine*)—If flashing red lights had been ***shone*** through the dense fog, the accident might have been avoided.
Shown (VERB; past participle of *show*)—The PowerPoint slide presentation describing our new products has been ***shown*** to all our salespeople and is available for their use in sales presentations.

Should/Would

Should (HELPING VERB; denotes future time in the first person in formal writing)—We ***should*** appreciate your returning the signed contracts by Friday, March 23.
Would (HELPING VERB; used with all three persons in business style)—I (or We) ***would*** appreciate receiving a copy of that report. She (or He or They) said that she (or he or they) ***would*** be willing to work overtime if the report isn't finished by 5 p.m. Did you say that you ***would*** be interested in having a demonstration of our new Model 1100 fax machine?

Shown: see Shone.

Sight: see Cite.

Sit: see Set.

Site: see Cite.

So: see Sew.

Soar/Sore

Soar (VERB; to fly aloft or about; to rise or increase dramatically)—These miniature aircraft are built to ***soar*** through the sky without motor or battery power. News of the merger will cause the price of our stock to ***soar***.
Sore (ADJECTIVE; painfully sensitive)—If you overdo an exercise program, your muscles will become ***sore***. Last year's financial losses have become a ***sore*** point for our company president.

Sole/Soul

Sole (NOUN, the undersurface of a foot; ADJECTIVE, being the only one)—Distribute your weight evenly between the ***sole*** and the heel of your foot. John is the ***sole*** heir to his father's fortune.
Soul (NOUN; the immaterial essence of an individual; living example of moral principle)—Most contemporary religions believe that the ***soul*** of an individual continues on after his or her physical death. Mr. Perry is the ***soul*** of honesty and integrity.

Some/Somewhat

Some (ADJECTIVE; an indefinite amount)—The report revealed that we will have to make ***some*** structural changes when we move into our new offices.
Somewhat (ADVERB; to some degree)—Most members of our sales force feel that your sales projections for next year are ***somewhat*** optimistic.

Some time/Sometime/Sometimes

Some time (ADJECTIVE + NOUN; a period of time)—Our staff will need ***some time*** to review your proposal before we can make a decision.
Sometime (ADVERB; an indefinite time; anytime)—Your order should be delivered ***sometime*** during the early part of next week.
Sometimes (ADVERB; occasionally)—We are ***sometimes*** forced to hire personnel from temporary agencies.

Somewhat: see Some.

Sore: see Soar.

Soul: see Sole.

Sow: see Sew.

Staid/Stayed

Staid (ADJECTIVE; sedate, composed)—A more ***staid*** individual is needed to fill this position.
Stayed (VERB; past tense and past participle of *stay*)—She ***stayed*** long after regular hours to finish the report.

Stationary/Stationery

Stationary (ADJECTIVE; not movable)—Only two of the interior walls in this suite are ***stationary***.

Stationery (NOUN OR ADJECTIVE; writing material)—Mr. Troy wants this letter prepared on his personal ***stationery***. Our order for additional ***stationery*** supplies was placed last week.

Statue/Stature/Statute

Statue (NOUN; a carved or molded image of someone or something)—Meet me in front of the ***statue*** of Lincoln at 2 p.m.
Stature (NOUN; the height of an object or a body; status gained by attainment)—The ***stature*** alone of the pyramids is overwhelming. Dr. Sunayama is a person of great ***stature*** within the community.
Statute (NOUN; law enacted by a legislature)—There is a ***statute*** in this state that prohibits gambling in any form.

Stayed: see Staid.

Straight/Strait

Straight (ADJECTIVE, free of bends, curves, or angles; ADVERB, in a direct manner)—Use a ruler with a ***straight*** edge to draw these lines. Ms. Torti always seems to be able to go ***straight*** to the source of the problem.
Strait (NOUN; a narrow space or passage connecting two bodies of water)—The ship and its cargo were damaged while going through the ***strait***.

Suit/Suite

Suit (NOUN ['süt]; an action filed in court; a set of garments)—A & Z Computer Corporation has already filed ***suit*** against Compco for patent infringements. Be sure to wear a dark-colored business ***suit*** for the interview.
Suite (NOUN ['swēt]; a group of things forming a unit; a set)—Were you able to reserve a ***suite*** for the week of March 25 at the Americana Hotel? (refers to a group of rooms) How many pieces are featured in this bedroom ***suite***? (refers to pieces of furniture in a set)

Sure/Surely

Sure (ADJECTIVE; an adjective or subject complement meaning *certain* or *positive*)—Nancy was ***sure*** she had made the right decision.
Surely (ADVERB; certainly or undoubtedly)—The employees believed that they would ***surely*** get a raise this year.

Take: see Bring.

Tare/Tear/Tier

Tare (NOUN ['tar—sounds like *care*]; a deduction from the gross weight of goods and their container made to allow for the weight of the container)—The ***tare*** on this shipment is 210 pounds.
Tear (NOUN ['tir]; a saline fluid that flows from the eye, usually signifying distress or extreme joy)—A ***tear*** flowed down the child's face as she viewed her brother in the hospital bed.
Tear (VERB ['tar], to pull apart or rip; NOUN ['tar], a rip)—When you open the envelope, be careful not to ***tear*** the contents. The customer complained about a ***tear*** in the sweater she had purchased yesterday.
Tier (NOUN ['tir]; placed one above or behind the other)—Our company's season tickets are on the first ***tier*** of the stadium.

Temperature: see Fever.

Than/Then

Than (CONJUNCTION; used to show comparison)—Ms. Espinoza has more experience ***than*** I in writing contract proposals.
Then (ADVERB; at that time)—Once all the data has been gathered, you may ***then*** begin organizing the report.

That/Which

That (PRONOUN; refers to animals or things; introduces a restrictive or essential subordinate clause)—We have in stock, Mr. Harrington, all the merchandise ***that*** you requested. All dogs ***that*** are found wandering in the streets will be impounded. This is the telephone ***that*** has been out of order since this morning.
Which (PRONOUN; refers to animals or things; introduces a nonrestrictive or nonessential subordinate clause)—The security staff recommended that we acquire a watchdog, ***which*** would be kept inside the plant at night. Our new credit system, ***which*** will be installed next week, will cost over $50,000.

Their/There/They're

Their (PRONOUN USED AS ADJECTIVE; the possessive form of *they*)—As a result of ***their*** recommendation, we installed an Apex Security System in our main warehouse.
There (ADVERB; at that place or at that point)—Please be ***there*** promptly at ten o'clock in the morning.
They're (PRONOUN + VERB; contraction of *they are*)—Although the union representatives rejected our first offer, ***they're*** willing to consider our second proposal.

Theirs/There's

Theirs (PRONOUN; possessive form of *they*)—This copy of the contract is ***theirs***.
There's (PRONOUN + VERB; contraction of *there is* or *there has*)—***There's*** still much to be done before we can open our new store. ***There's*** been too much time lost in attempting to install this new operating system on our network.

Them/They

Them (PRONOUN; a direct object, an indirect object, or an object of a preposition)—I asked ***them*** to please wait outside. I sent ***them*** a bill last week. I waited for ***them*** all morning.
They (PRONOUN; subject of a clause or a complement pronoun)—***They*** are meeting with the Board of Directors this afternoon. The two persons who cochaired the committee were ***they***.

Then: see Than.

There: see Their.

There's: see Theirs.

They: see Them.

They're: see Their.

Threw/Through/Thru

Threw (VERB; past tense of *throw*)—Mr. Samuels accidentally ***threw*** away the report on equipment purchases for the current year.
Through (PREPOSITION; in one end and out the other; movement within a large expanse; during the period of; as a consequence of)—May I give you a tour ***through*** our plant? The messenger pigeons flew gracefully ***through*** the air. This sale will be in progress ***through*** June. You may order this software at a 15 percent discount from June 15 ***through*** June 30. We have retained this account ***through*** your diligent efforts.
Thru (A variation of *through* that is not acceptable for business writing.)

Tier: see Tare.

To/Too/Two

To (PREPOSITION, function word to indicate direction toward; THE SIGN OF AN INFINITIVE, for example, *to go*)—Please return these materials ***to*** me when you have finished reviewing them. She wanted ***to*** see for herself the condition of the plant cafeteria.
Too (ADVERB; also; to an excessive extent)—I was there ***too***. Because the office was ***too*** noisy, I had difficulty hearing you on the telephone.
Two (NOUN; the number between *one* and *three*)—There was just too much work for the ***two*** of us to finish by five o'clock.

Tortuous/Torturous

Tortuous (ADJECTIVE; winding, twisting)—The ***tortuous*** road leading to Hana Bay has been the scene of many automobile accidents.
Torturous (ADJECTIVE; causing pain)—Filling out all these reports is a ***torturous*** task.

Toward/Towards

Toward (PREPOSITION; in the direction of)—Set up these workstations so that all the screens on the computer monitors face ***toward*** the west wall.
Towards (Secondary form of *toward*; use *toward* instead of *towards* in business writing.)

Uninterested: see Disinterested.

Us/We

Us (PRONOUN; a direct object, an indirect object, or an object of a preposition)—The vice president took ***us*** on a tour of the plant. The manager gave ***us*** a copy of the report. The reception was planned for ***us***.
We (PRONOUN; the subject of a clause or a complement pronoun)—***We*** must decide upon a definite course of action by 3 p.m. The singers selected to perform for this special broadcast were ***we***.

Vain/Van/Vane/Vein

Vain (ADJECTIVE; unduly proud or conceited)—Tom would be more popular with his fellow workers if he were not so ***vain***.
Van (NOUN; a covered truck)—Our hospital ***van*** is used primarily for transporting patients.

Vane (NOUN; a thin object used to show wind direction)—The weather ***vane*** indicated that the wind was coming from a westward direction.
Vein (NOUN; a tubular vessel that carries blood to the heart; mode or style)—The laboratory technician had difficulty finding a ***vein*** from which to obtain a blood sample. Although Mr. Bates had been warned about his unfriendly attitude toward other employees, he continued to behave in that ***vein***.

Vary/Very

Vary (VERB; to change)—The new advertising manager said that for the time being he would not request us to ***vary*** any procedures.
Very (ADVERB; extremely)—These figures are ***very*** difficult to verify from the information available.

Vein: see Vain.

Vice/Vise

Vice (NOUN; immoral habit; personal fault)—Drug abuse by America's populace is a ***vice*** that must be curtailed. Cigar smoking is his only ***vice***.
Vise (NOUN, a clamp; ADJECTIVE, strong hold or squeeze)—Please order a ***vise*** for our new carpenter. He shook my hand with a ***vise***-like grip.

Waive/Wave

Waive (VERB; to relinquish; to refrain from enforcing)—Do you ***waive*** your right to a jury trial? You must petition the dean of academic affairs to ***waive*** this requirement.
Wave (VERB; to swing something back and forth or up and down)—The angry customer was determined to ***wave*** his bill in everyone's face.

Waiver/Waver

Waiver (NOUN; the relinquishment of a claim)—Please sign the enclosed ***waiver*** to release our company from any further responsibility for your injury.
Waver (VERB; to shake or fluctuate)—I believe he is beginning to ***waver*** concerning my request for an early vacation.

Wave: see Waive.

Waver: see Waiver.

We: see Us.

Weather/Whether

Weather (VERB, to bear up against; NOUN, the state of the atmosphere)—We are glad to learn that you were able to ***weather*** the high rate of employee turnover during the summer months. Today's ***weather*** forecast was for a cold, rainy day.
Whether (CONJUNCTION; an introduction of alternatives)—We will not know until next week ***whether*** our company or Artistry in Motion will be awarded the contracts.

Well: see Good.

Whether: see Weather.

Which: see That.

Who/Whom

Who (PRONOUN; the subject of a subordinate clause or a complement pronoun)—I was the one ***who*** asked you to attend. I cannot tell you ***who*** the person at the door was.
Whom (PRONOUN; a direct object or an object of a preposition)—***Whom*** have you hired as my assistant? Here is the address of the person with ***whom*** we met for legal assistance. (See Section 5–7j for a further explanation of how to use *who* and *whom*.)

Whole: see Hole.

Wholly: see Holy.

Whom: see Who.

Who's/Whose

Who's (PRONOUN + VERB; a contraction of *who is*)—Please let me know ***who's*** taking over for you during August.
Whose (PRONOUN USED AS ADJECTIVE; possessive form of *who*)—He is the fellow ***whose*** position was abolished.

Will: see Shall.

Would: see Should.

Wring: see Ring.

Wrote: see Rote.

Your/You're

Your (PRONOUN USED AS ADJECTIVE; possessive form of *you*)—***Your*** assistant told me that you had invited the mayor to the reception.
You're (PRONOUN + VERB; contraction of *you are*)—If ***you're*** still interested in the position, please e-mail me at ClarksHOW@aol.com.

Chapter 8

Proofreading and Editing

Proofreading and Editing Solution Finder

Editing

Proofreading

Spelling

Spelling

Proofreading and editing have taken on new roles as spell checkers and grammar checkers have become integral parts of word processing programs. In many ways the burden of proofreading and editing has been lightened, but only to add different approaches and tasks.

The process of producing documents with correct spellings has been automated to a great extent. However, standard dictionaries and other resources still play a major role in proofreading and/or editing documents for spelling errors.

The increasing popularity of voice-recognition software has added yet another dimension to the proofreading and editing process. Although all dictated words are spelled correctly, the words dictated may not always match the words printed on the screen. Words that sound alike but are spelled differently (to, too, two) require correction—as do words that are misunderstood entirely.

8–1 Use of the Dictionary to Locate Correct Spellings

a. Use a recognized up-to-date collegiate, desk, or unabridged dictionary to locate any spellings of words you do not know or about which you are unsure. The dictionary used for all spellings in this manual is the 1999 printing of *Merriam-Webster's Collegiate Dictionary,* tenth edition, published by Merriam-Webster, Incorporated.

b. When the dictionary offers two spellings for a word in the same entry, use the first spelling.

judgment not: *judgement* ***canceled*** not: *cancelled*

c. When verifying the spelling of words, match the word with its correct counterpart in the dictionary. For example, if the word is used as a noun in the sentence, then compare it with the noun spelling of this word in the dictionary. As an illustration of differences in spellings, note that *under way* used as an adverb is two words but *underway* as an adjective is one. Similar situations occur with many other words.

mark up (verb)	markup (noun)
break down (verb)	breakdown (noun)
set up (verb)	setup (noun)
double-space (verb)	double space (noun)

d. The spellings of irregular plural nouns and irregular verb forms appear in the dictionary directly after the root word in the entry. Therefore, when in doubt about the formation of these words, consult your dictionary for their spellings. (See Sections 5–4 and 5–12 for additional information and examples relating to irregular plural nouns and verb forms.)

irregular plural nouns

secretary	secretaries	tomato	tomatoes
half	halves	child	children
analysis	analyses	alumnus	alumni

irregular verb forms

bring	brought	brought
sing	sang	sung
run	ran	run
lie	lay	lain
see	saw	seen

e. **The spellings of irregular adjective and adverb comparisons appear in the dictionary directly after the root word in the entry. Check your dictionary to verify these spellings. (See Sections 5–21 and 5–26 for rules and additional examples on adjective and adverb comparisons.)**

irregular adjective comparisons

costly	costlier	costliest
good	better	best

irregular adverb comparisons

early	earlier	earliest
far	farther	farthest

f. **To locate easily the spellings of unfamiliar words in the dictionary, acquaint yourself with the various letter combinations that represent sounds in the written English language. Both consonants and vowels may have different letter combinations that represent the same sound. The chart below presents just a few of the sounds and combinations with which you should become familiar.**

Sound	*Letter Combinations to Represent the Sound*
ā	***a***lienate, ***ai***de, g***au***ge, st***ea***k, f***ei***gn, w***eigh***t
ak	***ac***tual, ***acc***olade, ***ack***nowledgment, ***acq***uiesce, ***aq***ueduct
ar	***aer***osol, ***air***borne, ***ar***eas, ***arr***ogant
as	***as***piration, ***asc***ending, ***ass***ertive
aw	f***a***ther, ***au***dacity, t***augh***t, ***aw***esome, ***o***stracize, ***ough***t
ē	***e***dict, ***ea***sement, d***ee***m, rec***ei***pt, p***eo***ple, f***i***asco, p***ie***ce
er	simil***ar***, ***er***adicate, ***ear***nings, ***err***oneous, f***ir***mly, w***orr***isome, t***our***nament, ***ur***banization
f	***f***elony, e***ff***icient, ***ph***onetic, rou***gh***age
g	***g***rimace, ***gh***astly, ***gu***ardian
h	***h***azardous, ***wh***olly
ī	***ai***sle, h***eigh***t, ***i***dentify, t***ie***d, th***igh***, h***y***draulic
j	ju***dg***ment, ***g***ermane, exa***gg***eration, ***j***eopardize
k	***c***oincide, a***cc***ountant, ***ch***emistry, ***k***ilometer, ***q***uandary
m	***m***iraculous, pa***lm***istry
n	***gn***aw, ***kn***otty, ***mn***emonic, ***n***arrative, ***pn***eumonia

Sound	*Letter Combinations to Represent the Sound*
ō	b***eau***, ***o***dor, fl***oa***t, d***oe***skin, p***ou***ltry, d***ough***nut, sn***ow***
oi, oy	sp***oi***l, ann***oy***ance
oo	n***eu***tral, fl***ew***, ad***ieu***, t***o***mb, l***oo***se, l***ou***ver, thr***ough***, n***u***trition, tr***ue***, s***ui***t
ow	ann***ou***nce, fl***ow***er
r	***r***etrieve, ***rh***ythm, ***wr***est
s	***c***ertainty, ***s***alable, ***ps***ychologist, ***sc***intillate
sh	ma***ch***inery, espe***ci***ally, ***s***urely, con***sc***ience, ***sch***nauzer, nau***se***ous, ***sh***rewd, preci***si***on, substan***ti***al
t	***pt***omaine, ***t***ranslate
ū	b***eau***tiful, f***eu***d, sk***ew***ed, ***u***niform, f***ue***l, ***yu***letide
w	ch***o***ir, q***u***arterly, ***w***asteful, ***wh***imsical

8–2 Use of Word Processing Spell Checkers

a. **Use the spell check feature of your word processing program to check the spelling of any document you have created. All words in the dictionaries of your word processor will be used to correct the words you have keyboarded. Any word not in the dictionary of your word processor will be flagged and must be verified through a standard dictionary, a reputable on-line reference site,[1] or other sources. Spellings of names of individuals and many other proper nouns fall into this category.**

Frequently used technical terms or proper nouns not appearing in the main dictionary of a word processor may be added to a supplemental dictionary. By clicking the Add option during a spell check, the word is added to your supplemental dictionary. Right-clicking on the word and then selecting the Add option from the drop-down menu also adds the word to your supplemental dictionary. Be careful, though, not to add misspellings to your dictionary.

b. **Most word processors provide a "spell-as-you-go" feature. A wavy red line under a word signals the keyboarder when he or she enters a word that is not spelled correctly according to the dictionaries of the word processor. For standard words the person keyboarding may right click on the word to obtain a list of choices to correct the spelling of the underlined word.**

Word processors also provide a "correct-as-you-go" feature. A limited number of misspellings along with their correct spellings are stored in a listing. When the keyboarder enters the misspelling exactly as shown in the listing, it is corrected automatically. Misspellings and corrections may be added to the list. This feature is useful if a keyboarder often misspells a certain word or wishes to have a word, number, or symbol formatted in a particular way.

[1] Merriam-Webster maintains a free-access dictionary and thesaurus Internet Web site at <http://www.m-w.com>.

8–3 Use of On-Line Resources

a. For up-to-date spellings of emerging terminology or words with spellings that appear to be in transition, such as Internet terms, consult a reputable on-line dictionary reference. Merriam-Webster provides a Web site at which you may obtain the latest dictionary and thesaurus entries free of charge. The Internet address is <http://www.m-w.com>.

b. At the Merriam-Webster Web site, you may also e-mail questions to the editors requesting assistance with the appropriate spellings for words and expressions that appear to be in transition.

Proofreading

Proofreading is the process of checking one document against another to ensure that it conforms with the original in all respects. Proofreaders are responsible for checking a prepared document to correct only spelling errors, typographical errors, and any additions or omissions that do not conform to the document with which it is being compared. The proofreader does not make changes in wording or content.

8–4 Proofreading On-Screen Documents

a. Use the spell check features of your word processing program before beginning the proofreading process. Follow these guidelines to spell check the document:

(1) Enable the "check spelling as you type" feature of your word processing program. As you type, any words not in the dictionaries of your word processor will appear with a wavy red underline.

(2) Correct a word with a wavy red underline by right-clicking on it. Select the correct spelling from the drop-down list that appears. If the word is not listed, check your original copy or an up-to-date dictionary for the correct spelling.

(3) You may wish to correct all spelling or typographical errors after completing the document instead of correcting each word separately. In this case, run a spell check once you have completed the document. Correct proper nouns and technical vocabulary by checking their spellings with the original copy. Spellings of other words not in the dictionary of the word processor should be verified with the dictionary.

b. Check for consistency of style throughout the document before actually beginning to read the text.

(1) Assess the appropriateness of margins (top, bottom, left, and right).

(2) Check the line spacing between paragraphs, before and after main or text headings, within letter closing lines, etc.

(3) Inspect to ensure that the document contains no widow or orphan

lines (single lines of a paragraph at the top or bottom of a page). To avoid such occurrences within a multiple-page document, activate the widow-orphan protection feature of your word processing program.

widow line—last line of a paragraph at top of page or column

4

as listed on page 3 of our summer catalog.

A number of items we featured in our summer catalog were sold out early in the season. Our buyers evidently did not foresee the great

orphan line—first line of a paragraph left at bottom of page or column

Committee. Members need to select one person from their region who is willing to review the applications. The proposed turn-around time on the review of applications will be from three to four weeks.

The person selected from each region will remain anonymous so

(4) Inspect to ensure that no isolated text headings appear at the end of a page. At least two lines of text from the following paragraph must accompany any heading that appears within the document. Use the block-protect feature of your word processing program to force any isolated headings to the next page.

(5) Evaluate the general appearance of the document through the page preview feature of your word processing program. Check headers, footers, and page numbering carefully.

c. **Read the text for accuracy. Check it carefully against the original copy. Place the original copy on a copy stand next to your screen. Read a group of words in the original copy; then compare these words with those corresponding ones on the screen. Continue this process until you have proofread the entire document. Use the following criteria in evaluating the keyboarded document:**

(1) Are any letters transposed or omitted? Are all words spelled correctly? The spell check feature of your word processing program will have located most spelling errors, but it will not have detected such errors as using *form* for *from*, *an* for *and*, or *effect* for *affect*.

(2) Have any letters, words, sentences, or paragraphs been omitted? Pay close attention to ensure that no *s*'s have been dropped from plural

nouns or *ed*'s from the past tense or the past participle of verb forms. Ensure that no words, sentences, or paragraphs have been skipped.

(3) Have any words, phrases, or sentences been repeated? Repeated words are flagged by your word processing spell checker, but repeated phrases or sentences are not detected electronically.

(4) Are all names and unfamiliar words spelled correctly? When proofreading names and unfamiliar words or terminology, check each spelling meticulously—letter by letter.

(5) Have all figures been typed correctly? Are all calculations correct? Double-check all figures carefully with the original source. For long numbers verify the number of digits and then compare the digits in groups of three. If the numbers are in a column with a total, the easiest method of proofreading is to use a calculator to check the total in the original document and then check the same total in the document being proofread.

d. Print the document only when you are satisfied that it has been proofread properly and all aspects are correct.

8–5 Proofreading Printed Copy

a. Check for consistency of style throughout the document before actually beginning to read the text.

(1) Assess the appropriateness of margins (top, bottom, left, and right).

(2) Check the line spacing between paragraphs, before and after main or text headings, within letter closing lines, etc.

(3) Inspect to ensure that the document contains no widow or orphan lines (single lines of a paragraph at the top or bottom of a page). See Section 8–4b for illustrations of widow and orphan lines.

(4) Inspect to ensure that no isolated text headings appear at the end of a page. At least two lines of text from the following paragraph must accompany any heading that appears within the document.

(5) Evaluate the general appearance of the document. Check headers, footers, and page numbering carefully.

b. Proofread the printed document for accuracy. Read the document carefully and ask yourself the following questions to correct any keyboarding errors:

(1) Are any letters transposed or omitted? Are all words spelled correctly? The spell check feature of the word processing program will have located most spelling errors, but it will not have detected such errors as using *form* for *from*, *an* for *and*, or *effect* for *affect*.

(2) Have any letters, words, sentences, or paragraphs been omitted? Pay close attention to ensure that no *s*'s have been dropped from plural nouns or *ed*'s from the past tense or the past participle of verb forms. Ensure that no words, sentences, or paragraphs have been skipped.

(3) Have any words, phases, or sentences been repeated?

(4) Are all names and unfamiliar words spelled correctly? When proofreading names and unfamiliar words or terminology, check each spelling meticulously—letter by letter.

(5) Have all figures been typed correctly? Are all calculations correct? Double-check all figures carefully with the original source. For long numbers verify the number of digits and then compare the digits in groups of three. If the numbers are in a column with a total, the easiest method of proofreading is to use a calculator to check the total in the original document and then check the same total in the document being proofread.

e. **When proofreading hard copy, use the pen-and-forefinger technique to maintain attention and keep the eyes focused on the line being proofread. To use this technique, hold the pen in the hand with which you will be making corrections and place the copy to be proofread on that side. Place the original on the opposite side and use the forefinger of that hand to follow along as you compare the two copies.**

f. **When proofreading hard copy, use the standardized proofreaders' marks shown in Section 8–6 and also on the inside back cover of this manual to show your corrections.**

8–6 Standardized Proofreaders' Marks to Show Corrections

a. **Standardized proofreaders' marks are used to show corrections in handwritten, typewritten, computer-generated, or printed copy. These symbols are used so that anyone who reads the document will interpret the corrections in the same way. Use the following marks and symbols to make changes in words or word groups:**

Instruction	*Mark or Symbol*	*Example*	*Marginal Note*
Boldface word(s).	~~~	received by November 1	(bf)
Capitalize letter.	≡	to the Retailers association	(cap)
Capitalize letters.	═══	from Unesco	(caps)
Change word(s).	——	Because In view of the fact that you have	
Close up space.	⁀	You can, never the less, receive	
Delete letter.	/	occassion	
Delete stroke.	⁄ with delete loop	policy, and send us	
Delete word(s).	—— with delete loop	a postal money order for $50	

Instruction	Mark or Symbol	Example	Marginal Note
Hyphenate word(s).	=	up=to=date records	
Insert a space.	#	In addition, you will be	
Insert apostrophe.	’	its a good deal	
Insert colon.	(:)	follows pen, ink, and paper.	
Insert comma.	^,	On Tuesday, May 23 we	
Insert em dash.	M	comments--all are welcome!	
Insert en dash.	N	January 14-16	
Insert here (caret).	^	Insert at this place.	
Insert parentheses.	( )	end of this month April 30.	
Insert period.	(.)	by 10 am tomorrow	
Insert question mark.	(?)	Do you agree.	
Insert quotation marks.	“ ”	article, Access on the Web, that	
Insert semicolon.	^;	now, therefore, you	
Insert word(s).	^	your latest income tax form	
Italicize word(s).	____	The Wall Street Journal	ital
Join to word.	⁀	in our micro computer laboratory	
Lowercase letter.	/	of the Association	lc
Lowercase letters.	/‾‾	the UNITED STATES OF AMERICA	lc
Restore word(s).	......	our furniture warehouse in Toledo	stet
Roman type.	____	book titles in *italic* type	rom
Small capital letters.	═══	our red tag sale on	sm caps
Spell out word or number.	◯	3 stores on Fifth Ave.	sp
Transpose letters.	∽	all thier profits.	tr
Transpose words.	⊔⊓	to legibly print your name	tr
Underscore word(s).	____	We cannot overemphasize	u'score

b. **Use the following symbols to move words or word groups:**

Instruction	*Mark or Symbol*	*Example*	*Marginal Note*
Align horizontally.	═	In the past two years	
Align vertically.	‖	‖(1) New courses (2) New curriculum	
Center.	] [	]PROOFREADERS' MARKS[	
Combine paragraphs.	no ¶	no ¶You may also wish to	
Double-space copy.		As a result of this investigation, we have decided to reduce expenses.	ds
Indent 0.5 inch.	.5"	.5" During the last month	
Insert line space.	>	COMPUTER SALES SUMMARY February 2001	+1ℓ#
Move as shown.		for the next year	
Move to next line.		give the contract to Mr.	
Move to the left.	[	[You may wish to	
Move to the right.	]	You]may wish to	
New paragraph.	¶	¶Many customers do not	
Single-space copy.		As a result of this investigation, we have decided to reduce expenses.	ss

Editing

The proofreading process involves the comparison of one document with another to assess the correctness of the prepared copy. Editing is a more challenging process because editors do not have "correct" copies upon which they may rely to determine if the copy they are reading has been prepared properly. Editors themselves are responsible for determining the accuracy and appropriateness of all language and format applications.

8–7 Preparing to Edit

a. **If possible, use the document word processing file to spell check the document electronically. If you are the document originator or preparer, use the spell-as-you-go feature of your word processor to flag potential**

spelling errors. These potential spelling errors are shown with a wavy red underline. You may correct common errors from a drop-down menu by right-clicking on the underlined word.

b. If possible, use the document word processing file and the grammar checker of your word processor to flag any potential grammar errors. Follow these guidelines in using an electronic grammar checker:

(1) Keep in mind that you will need to make judgments when using a grammar checker. All flagged items are not errors, and often the suggested corrections are incorrect.

(2) Use a reliable reference to verify any grammatical constructions about which you are unsure. Although electronic grammar checkers can be helpful to the expert grammarian, they can be a hindrance to the novice because of their high incidence of error.

(3) Use the correct-grammar-as-you-go feature if you are the document originator or preparer. A wavy blue or green line under a word or sequence of words signifies a potential grammar error. Right-clicking on the potential error produces a drop-down menu that provides an opportunity to correct the error or investigate further the reason the grammar checker has flagged the error.

c. Edit documents from printed copy. If you are the document originator or the person who has prepared the document, print it for editing.

d. Assemble all the materials you will need to edit a document:

(1) An up-to-date (printed within the last three years) collegiate, desk, or unabridged dictionary, e.g., *Merriam-Webster's Collegiate Dictionary,* tenth edition[2]

(2) An up-to-date (published within the last three years) reference manual, e.g., *HOW 9: A Handbook for Office Workers,* ninth edition

(3) An up-to-date (published within the last five years) thesaurus, e.g., *Roget's II: The New Thesaurus*[3]

(4) Reference sources from which the document was created; e.g., rough drafts, authorization letters, file copies, meeting notes, etc.

(5) Any other published references that may relate to the document; e.g., mailing lists, telephone directories, zip code directories, maps, encyclopedias, books, magazines, newspapers, etc.

(6) Addresses (URLs) of any Internet references or resources that may be needed.

8–8 Editing the Document

a. Work from printed copy to edit a document. Because the editor does not just "check" a document against another source, you will probably

---

[2]Merriam-Webster provides free on-line Internet access to entries in this dictionary at its Web site: <http://www.m-w.com>.

[3]Merriam-Webster provides free access to its thesaurus at its Internet Web site: <http://www.m-w.com>.

need to read the material several times. As an editor you must evaluate the overall effectiveness of a document in terms of its attaining the goal for which it was written. Therefore, you will wish to read the material critically with several criteria in mind:

(1) Are there any omissions in ideas or content? All important ideas should be included in the document as well as any information to substantiate the ideas. Check to make sure the document is complete in every respect.

(2) Is the document well organized so that the reader can easily follow the ideas as they are presented? Coherent writing results in clarity and allows the reader to understand easily the purpose and contents of the document. The editor needs to make sure that ideas are placed in logical order and that each sentence flows smoothly and lucidly from the previous sentence.

(3) Is the document correct in every way—content, format, grammar, spelling, punctuation, capitalization, and number expression? Be sure to check the accuracy of all the data. In addition, make sure that all the conventions of correct language usage have been observed and that the document has been formatted appropriately.

(4) Is the content easily understood? Examine the document to ensure that the ideas are presented vividly and with ample illustrations so that the reader can picture concretely what the writer had in mind.

(5) Have all the ideas been expressed in as few words as possible? Look at each sentence to make sure that it does not contain extra wording. Evaluate sentences and paragraphs to see if they contribute to achieving the overall purpose of the document. Any excess words, sentences, or paragraphs should be deleted.

(6) Are all abbreviations, number expressions, and other format considerations handled in the same way? Check for inconsistencies in these areas and in the contents of the document.

(7) Are the tone and language appropriate for accomplishing the purpose of the document? Check to make sure that letters are written in a friendly and courteous manner. Reports, in contrast, should have a more formal tone. Match the formality of tone and language with the purpose of the document.

b. **Use proofreaders' marks and symbols to indicate changes made during the editing process. These marks and symbols are explained and illustrated in Section 8–6 and on the inside back cover of this manual.**

c. **Consider double-spacing rough drafts of documents that are to be edited. Double spacing not only makes the document easier to read but also makes changes easier to interpret.**

8–9 Editing Documents Created With Voice-Recognition Software

a. **Voice-recognition software enables document originators to enter text into word processing programs, E-mail templates, and calendaring**

programs by dictating directly to the screen. With continuous voice dictation you no longer need the keyboard to enter text; you can watch the words appear on the computer screen as you speak.

Voice-recognition software not only permits continuous voice dictation for text entry but also enables the document originator to issue voice commands to edit, navigate, and format documents, depending upon the program in which the software is used.

Major developers of voice-recognition software include Dragon Systems, IBM, Lernout & Hauspie, and Philips Electronics. Prices range from moderate to high, with the more expensive versions containing additional features and enhancements. Requirements for using as well as features and enhancements of voice-recognition software are listed here:

(1) Minimum hardware requirements include a 300 MHz Pentium processor with Windows 95 or higher, at least 64K of RAM, a high-quality microphone, speakers, a CD-ROM drive to install the program, and sufficient hard disk space to accommodate the size of the program. Naturally, the faster the processor and the greater the amount of random access memory, the more satisfactorily the software will perform.

(2) Low-end voice-recognition programs provide a CD-ROM that contains the software needed to use the program, a headset-microphone recommended for use with the software, and a booklet of instructions. These programs are capable of producing text from continuous speech and implementing voice program commands.

Words are spelled correctly based on the large dictionary of the software. In addition, most low-end programs permit users to expand the vocabulary of the program.

Low-end programs are capable of transferring voice to text in a limited number of programs. Developers boast of 95 percent to 98 percent accuracy in transferring the spoken word to text.

(3) Medium-priced voice-recognition programs include all the features of the low-end programs. They may provide a higher quality microphone. Additionally, they provide audio playback for the text dictated and usually have larger built-in dictionaries. Often, too, they permit direct dictation into a larger selection of programs.

(4) High-end voice-recognition programs add a new dimension to this software—a remote voice-to-text system. These packages include a battery-operated, pocket-size digital voice recorder. Documents may be dictated anywhere at anytime. Upon plugging in the mobile recorder to your desktop computer and transferring the voice files to your voice-recognition program, the software will transcribe your document into any one of a wide selection of text-based programs—where you can review, edit, and format it.

b. All voice-recognition programs require a training time for each user. Training times vary, depending upon the software package and the voice of the user—anywhere from ten minutes to two hours. As each user continues to dictate into the program and follows the recommended procedures for correcting transcription errors, the transcription accuracy of the program improves. Most software developers claim 95 percent to 98 percent transcription accuracy for their programs.

c. Voice-recognition software plays a major role in originating documents in medical, legal, business, and government offices. Documents created with this software must be edited using the same criteria as those created using a keyboard. However, because the software often substitutes other words for those dictated, exchanges singular and plural forms, and does not always recognize past and past participle forms, additional attention must be given to editing documents created with voice-recognition software. Follow these guidelines in the editing process:

(1) Read the text carefully for meaning. Because voice-recognition software is generally perceived to attain between 95 and 98 percent accuracy, undetected word-recognition errors may result in nonsense-sounding sentences.

(2) Pay close attention to word endings. Voice-recognition software often adds or omits the "s" at the end of nouns and verb forms. Similarly, the software often adds or omits the "ed" at the end of a verb form. Only by reading the text slowly and carefully for meaning can such errors be detected.

(3) Check carefully for errors in number recognition and format. These kinds of errors can easily occur and go unnoticed. Use the same strategies recommended for proofreading numbers in Section 8–5b.

(4) Double-check the spelling of proper nouns. Although voice-recognition software "learns" the spelling of unusual proper nouns and differentiates among the various spellings of other proper nouns, it may occasionally substitute an incorrect spelling.

(5) Do not rely on the Read Back feature of your voice-recognition software to assist you with the proofreading or editing process. The Read Back feature merely reads back the words exactly as they appear on the screen—errors and all. The copy is not read as it was dictated.

(6) Use any available voice files to assist you with the proofreading or editing process. If the document was created on a mobile digital voice recorder, replay the voice recording of the document as you edit it. This recording will assist you in recognizing words misinterpreted by the voice-recognition software.

Chapter 9

Using the Internet

http://

Using the Internet Solution Finder

Using the Internet

Connecting to the Internet

Accessing the World Wide Web

The Internet, an extensive system of connected computers, comprises a vast number of networks that are made up of millions of host computers. Web servers alone number more than 7 million.[1] This on-line global network, which is accessible in over 170 countries and has nearly 160 million users worldwide,[2] has promoted information exchange between almost every segment of our society.

From major universities and giant corporations to the single user at a home computer, all may access the wealth of information that the Internet provides. In the United States alone, approximately 37 percent of personal computer users regularly connect to the Internet.[3]

Business people often need to consult reference material to gather information for general operations, decision making, and document preparation. Major sources were previously limited to printed reference materials. With advances in technology, however, other forms of information exchange—on-line resources—provide access to the information needed by today's fast-paced business environment.

E-commercing, the sale of goods and services through Web sites, has had a major impact on the purchasing patterns of both consumers and businesses. Fledgling enterprises and long-established business organizations have flocked to the Internet to capture a part of this burgeoning consumer marketplace. Sales through e-commercing are growing rapidly.

9–1 Using the Internet

a. Although business people may wish to use the Internet to visit famous museums, plan a vacation, or join a newsgroup, such personal applications are separate from accessing information that relates directly to business operations. Major interest today lies in accessing the Internet's World Wide Web and its exploding abundance of resources.

The Internet and other on-line resources provide the following kinds of information often needed for research, planning, and implementation:

(1) General references such as directories of reference materials, dictionaries, encyclopedias, thesauri, atlases, telephone white and yellow pages (nationally), currency exchange rates, world time-zone charts, and measurement conversions

(2) Stock and bond market quotations, company profiles, and other business and financial resources

(3) Travel reservations and resources—airline schedules and reservations, hotel reservations, rental cars, restaurants, attractions and events, and mapped driving routes

---

[1]"The Netcraft Web Server Survey," *Netcraft Secure Server Survey,* August 1999, <http://www.netcraft.co.uk/Survey/> (12 September 1999).

[2]"Part 1: The Size of the Internet," *Tutorial: Guide to Effective Searching of the Internet,* Mata Hari,® May 6, 1999, <http://www.thewebtools.com/tutorial/part1.htm> (16 September 1999).

[3]AC Market Intelligence, "IP Services Home," *AT&T IP Services,* <http://www.ipservices.att.com/index.html> (14 September 1999).

(4) Current news and weather—locally, nationally, and internationally
(5) Articles published in major newspapers and magazines worldwide
(6) Services and rates of domestic and international mail service providers such as the United States Postal Service, United Parcel Service, FedEx, and other private carriers
(7) Products and services provided by companies throughout the world
(8) Career services and company profiles
(9) Government information and services

b. Individuals, small businesses, and major corporations are increasingly using the Internet to market their products and services. By creating Web sites and advertising their addresses (Uniform Resource Locators—URLs), they are soliciting sales through e-commercing, the trading of goods and services through the Internet.

9–2 Connecting to the Internet

The Internet is a collection of millions of computers all linked together on a vast network, which permits all its component computers to communicate with one another. An individual or home computer is usually linked to the Internet using a modem and a normal phone line that connects to an Internet service provider (ISP). A computer in a business or university has a network interface card (NIC) that connects it directly to a local area network (LAN) inside the organization. The LAN is then connected to an ISP using a high-speed phone line (a T line).

ISPs connect to larger ISPs, and the largest ISPs maintain fiber-optic "backbones" for a nation or a region, as shown by the following diagram.[4] Backbones around the world are connected through fiber-optic lines, undersea cables, or satellite links. In this way, every computer on the Internet is connected to every other.

Individual Computer Connectivity to Internet Backbones

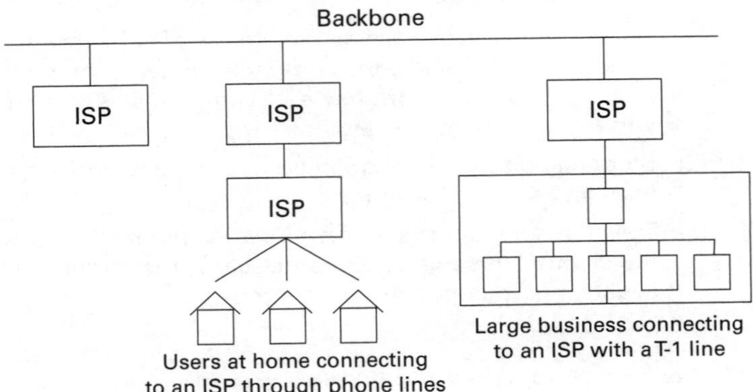

[4]Marshall Brain, "How the Internet Works," *How Stuff Works*, <http://www.howstuffworks.com/web-server.htm> (12 September 1999).

a. **For individuals or small businesses, computer connections to the Internet may be achieved in a number of ways. The most common access requires a computer, a modem, a telephone line, communications software, an on-line service provider, and a browser.**

Most modern computers provide as standard features a built-in modem with preloaded communications software. Users need only to plug in to a regular telephone jack, and they are ready to be connected to an on-line service.

Telephone line connections to on-line services may be achieved in one of the following ways:

(1) *Through an Internet service provider with a local telephone number.* Internet service providers (ISPs) supply E-mail capabilities and access to the Internet. Some providers furnish software for accessing (browsing) the Internet's World Wide Web (WWW); others require members to purchase their own browsers. Two popular Web browsers are Netscape Navigator and Microsoft Internet Explorer.

To locate an Internet service provider in your local area, consult your *Yellow Pages* under "Internet Access" or "Internet Access Providers." Internet service providers may also be located through an Internet connection at <http://www.thelist.com>.

(2) *Through a commercial on-line service provider such as America Online, AT&T WorldNet, MSN, CompuServe, or Prodigy Internet.* In addition to providing E-mail capabilities, Internet access, and a World Wide Web browser, commercial on-line services often provide features such as these:

News and weather
Stock reports and other financial news
Sports scores, headlines, and news
Magazine and newspaper articles
Reference (dictionaries and encyclopedias) and education sources
Computing support
Professional forums
Travel information
Entertainment options
Shopping opportunities
Home and leisure activities
Web page postings
Chat rooms

b. **Recent advances in technology have brought faster Internet access to individual and small business computer users. One such advance, Digital Subscriber Lines (DSL), refers to several new digital technologies for fast two-way data connections over ordinary telephone lines. DSL connections are currently available in major United States cities and are continually being made available in other cities through AT&T and local telephone companies. Features of DSL include the following:**

(1) *Increased access speed.* You may access audio, video, and enhanced graphics over the Internet with download speeds that are from 25 to 100 times faster than a 56 KBPS (kilobytes per second) modem.

(2) *Instantaneous Internet access.* With DSL technology there is no waiting-to-receive mode because there is no need to dial in—the connection is always on.

(3) *E-mail capability.* DSL services provide from one to five E-mail accounts, depending upon the level of service selected.

(4) *Flat monthly fee.* Digital Subscriber Lines are available at a flat monthly fee for unlimited Internet connection time. Providers offer several subscription levels.

DSL connections generally require a DSL modem, a network interface card (NIC), and a splitter (interface between the DSL modem and the copper telephone lines at your location). For availability in your location, requirements, and cost, visit AT&T's DSL Web site at <http://www.ipservices.att.com/ipaccess/dsl/> or the Web site of your local telephone company.

c. Recent technological advances in high-speed Internet access have resulted in the development of a cable modem. A cable modem works with signals from television cables, which use fiber optics for distant connections and coaxial cable locally to the individual computer or office network. Cable modems are capable of much higher speeds than conventional modems. There is enough capacity (bandwidth) in these cables to carry television signals as well as multiple Internet connections. Some features of cable modem connections follow:

(1) *Increased access speed.* You may access audio, video, and enhanced graphics over the Internet with download speeds from 10 to 27 megabytes per second, depending upon the path the data travels.

(2) *Instantaneous Internet access.* The connection to the cable service is always active. By pressing a button, you will have split-second access to the Internet and its resources.

(3) *Connectivity as an Internet service provider or a commercial on-line service provider.* With cable modem access, subscribers may continue to use their commercial services such as America Online, CompuServe, and others. These commercial services provide other features besides Internet access. However, to use an internet service provider that provides only Internet access would be financially unwise since this connectivity is provided by the cable television company in its basic fee. Some cable television companies are also acting as commercial providers by providing on-line content services.

(4) *E-mail capability.* Providers of cable modem on-line access allow customers to send and receive E-mail. Subscribers may have between one and five accounts, depending upon the cable company and level of service selected.

(5) *Independent from television viewing.* Although local cable television companies are the providers of cable modem access from computers, television viewing does not interfere with computer on-line

access. Cable modems use a group of cable frequencies that are not used for television signals at this time.

(6) *Flat monthly fee.* Cable modem services are available at a flat monthly fee for unlimited Internet connection time.

Cable modem on-line computer connections are available through the local cable television company that services your area. Such connections generally require a cable modem, an Ethernet card, and a cable line. For availability in your location, requirements, and cost, visit the Web site of your local cable television company.

Another technology provides Internet access through your television and its remote control without the use of a computer. Visit <http://www.webtv.com> for information on this access mode.

d. **Large corporations, universities, colleges, and government agencies obtain Internet access through Internet providers (IPs) such as AT&T, MCI, and Sprint. These organizations lease special high-bandwidth telephone lines (T lines) that can support a large number of users simultaneously, such as those in a local area network (LAN) for a whole company.**

(1) *T-1 Line:* A high-bandwidth telephone line that provides an Internet connection and transmits data at 1.5 megabytes per second.

(2) *T-3 Line:* A high-bandwidth telephone line that provides an Internet connection and transmits data at 45 megabytes per second.

Large corporations, universities, colleges, and government agencies furnish Internet access free of charge to their employees and students. On-site computers are available for easy access. In many cases users at remote sites (home computers) may dial in to the host computer at the university, college, or agency site and gain Internet access from there.

9–3 Accessing the World Wide Web

a. **The World Wide Web, the Internet's most popular source, provides an interactive, graphical presentation of information that connects similar data at different locations. On-line documents known as Web pages contain hypertext, highlighted words that link you to other areas containing related information. With just a mouse click, hypertext will enable you to do the following:**

(1) Migrate easily to documents, graphics, or other Web pages

(2) Connect to other kinds of Internet resources such as newsgroups and ftp (file transfer protocol) files

(3) Download graphics, photos, sounds, music, and movies to a computer

b. **Using the World Wide Web requires a Web browser in addition to the standard communications software that usually comes preloaded on today's computers. Commercial on-line service providers supply their subscribers with a browser; many local Internet service providers make Web browsers available to their members at no cost or for a nominal fee. Two popular commercial browsers, Netscape Navigator and Microsoft Internet Explorer, are available for free download or at a low cost.**

c. Locating information through your Web browser is accomplished in several ways:

(1) *Through an Internet address.* Any Internet site may be reached through its address (Uniform Resource Locator [URL]). Each Web site has a specific address, and by typing the correct address in the appropriate box shown on your Web browser screen, you will be transported to that site. (See Chapter 15 for business-related sites.)

All World Wide Web addresses begin with *http://* (Hypertext Transfer Protocol); the succeeding letters, spaces, and symbols must be entered exactly as shown in order to access the site. In most cases you need not key the *http://*. By keying the remaining letters in the address box, you can access the site. For example, *http://www.usps.gov* may be accessed by keying *www.usps.gov* instead of the full address.

In this reference manual, all Internet addresses are shown in angle brackets (< >) to avoid confusion with any sentence punctuation marks. Enter only the information within the angle brackets. For example, the U.S. Postal Service's Web site may be reached by entering the following address: <http://www.usps.gov> or <www.usps.gov>.

(2) *Through a search site.* All Web browsers have at least one search site readily available, or search sites may be accessed through their own Web sites. Search sites permit you to locate information by entering key words.

If you were trying to find job listings on the Internet using a search site, you might enter *employment resources jobs resumes career*. This search string will give you the information you need; it relies on a series of synonyms to capture the various employment-related information that is available. From the listing produced by this search, you can connect directly to any of the sites listed.

(3) *Through a link in a Web site.* Hypertext permits Web sites to link to other Web sites. By clicking on an icon, underlined text, or highlighted text, you can be transported from one information source to another. Related information is frequently linked through hypertext, so often you can locate needed information through a link.

d. Search sites provide access to locating information on the Internet. Specific search sites may be accessed by entering their addresses (URLs) in the address box of your browser. These resources use various means for classifying sites and produce results based upon search strings entered in a search box. Different search sites using the same search string commonly produce different results. That is why persons researching a topic often rely on two or three search sites to gather information. Popular and reliable search sites, along with their Internet addresses, include the following:

(1) AltaVista <http://www.altavista.com/>

(2) Excite <http://www.excite.com/>

(3) HotBot <http://www.hotbot.com/>

(4) InfoHiway <http://www.infohiway.com/>

(5) Infoseek <http:/infoseek.go.com/>

(6) LookSmart <http://www.looksmart.com/>

(7) Lycos <http://www.lycos.com/>

(8) Metacrawler <http://www.go2net.com/search.html>

(9) Northern Light <http://www.nlsearch.com/>

(10) WebCrawler <http://www.webcrawler.com/>

(11) Yahoo! <http://www.yahoo.com/>

e. **Search strings composed of isolated keywords often produce thousands of results, many of which are not related to the search question. Any document containing any of the key words is included in the results. Consequently, to refine search results, many people use Boolean operators in their search strings.**

Boolean operators are not recognized by every search site, but they produce better results with the major search sites: AltaVista (Advanced Search), Excite, HotBot, Lycos, Northern Light, and Yahoo! The search results obtained may be reduced or expanded by using Boolean operators.

Just a few concepts are needed to use Boolean operators effectively: *AND* and *OR,* the value *NOT,* the limiter *NEAR,* and grouping operators (parentheses and quotation marks). Key Boolean operators in all capital letters.

(1) *Basic Boolean operators AND and OR.* The operator *AND* retrieves items containing all terms connected by *AND. Stocks AND bonds* retrieves all items containing both "stocks" and "bonds." Some search engines permit the use of a plus sign to replace the *AND* operator. In this case the plus sign is keyed directly before the linked word without an intervening space. Thus *stocks AND bonds* would appear as *stocks +bonds.* Several items may be linked with the *AND* operator, and each linked word refines the search further.

The operator *OR* retrieves items containing either term. *Stocks OR bonds* retrieves all items containing either "stocks" or "bonds." *OR* is useful for synonyms (e.g., "cars" OR "automobiles") and when different terms (e.g., "colleges" OR "universities") will retrieve what you want. While the operator *AND* will refine your search, the operator *OR* will produce more search results.

(2) *Basic Boolean operator NOT. NOT* excludes terms that would otherwise clutter retrieval. Any items that contain the word or phrase following the *NOT* operator are not included in the search results. Therefore, *jaguar NOT car* will eliminate any item with the word "car."

Be careful in using the *NOT* operator; you may exclude items that contain important information and have only an incidental reference to the word you are excluding. The reference *DSL NOT modem* would exclude any items with the word "modem," even if it was used only to compare DSL transmission speeds with modem speeds. Use this operator only with a search that is returning too many results or with a word or phrase that is often associated with your topic but unrelated to it.

For the *NOT* operator, some search engines use *AND NOT*; others use the minus sign. The minus sign is placed directly before the word or phrase to be excluded without an intervening space. To exclude tigers from your search on information about cats, you would key *cats NOT tigers* (or *cats –tigers*) in your search string.

(3) *Advanced operator NEAR. NEAR* is an *AND* search in which the terms must appear within a specified word count of one another to be included in the results. Generally, most search engines that support the *NEAR* operator have a set value of ten words as a maximum distance. Consequently, the search string *2002 NEAR calendar NEAR holidays* would have a better chance of locating a calendar of holidays for the year 2002 than would the search string *2002 AND calendar AND holidays. NEAR* increases the chance that the terms are actually related to each other in the item.

A few search sites allow you to specify how many words may be between terms before they are included in the results. Use the following syntax for this refinement: term NEAR# term (Greek NEAR15 restaurant). Other search sites permit the tilde (~) to substitute for the word *NEAR.* The tilde is keyed directly before the following word or phrase without an intervening space: *2002 ~calendar ~holidays.*

(4) *Grouping operators.* Grouping operators determine the order in which Boolean operators are applied or signify words that should be treated as a single unit.

Place parentheses around the words and Boolean operators that are to be evaluated together. Just as in mathematical equations, the parentheses signify that the items within parentheses are to be treated as a unit. The parentheses say, "Do this first." For example, if you entered *brokerages AND Internet OR Web* and then entered *brokerages AND (Internet OR Web),* you would get quite different results. The first string would give you all items containing both the words "brokerages" and "Internet" and all items containing the word "Web." The second string would give you all items containing "brokerages" and "Internet" and all items containing "brokerages" and "Web."

Use quotation marks (double quotes) around words that should be considered as a single unit. Examples are *"Internet service provider"* and *"Mona Lisa"* and *"money market"* and *"municipal bonds."* Only those items containing the exact words shown in quotation marks will be retrieved.

(5) *Wild cards.* The asterisk may be used in AltaVista as a wild card to represent any combination of letters. Its most common use is with truncated words like *educat** to retrieve all forms of the word (educate, educates, educated, educating, education, etc.).

(6) *Case-sensitive searches.* Most search sites are not case sensitive; that is, if you enter the word *"web,"* the search will return items with *"web"* and *"Web."* If, however, you capitalize the word in the search string, you are likely to receive only items in which the word is capitalized.

Chapter 10

Electronic Messaging

Electronic Messaging Solution Finder

E-mail Messaging

Facsimile (Fax) Transmittals

Networks

Networks

Computer communication is a key factor in information exchange. Computers that are linked together can communicate with one another and are part of a network. Electronic messages are transmitted through networks.

10-1 Local Area Networks

Local area networks use telephone wires, radio waves, coaxial cable, or fiber optics to link computers that are geographically close; that is, computers within a building, several adjacent buildings, or the same geographical area. Data can be transmitted within seconds from one location to another. The receiving station may store or print the information for further use.

10-2 Wide Area Networks

Local networks can be linked to larger networks that enable individuals and companies to send and receive information throughout the United States and worldwide. These wide area networks or global networks use combinations of telephone lines, underground cables, fiber optics, and satellites to transmit information within minutes.

Facsimile (Fax) Transmissions

10-3 Fax Machine-to-Fax Machine Messaging

a. Facsimile transmission of computer-generated, typewritten, and handwritten documents; charts, graphs, and diagrams; photographs; and other kinds of hard copy has become an everyday occurrence. It is one of the most popular methods of electronic document transmission used by modern businesses today.

(1) Businesses, individuals, or other kinds of stations using facsimiles (faxes) require a telephone line to which they connect their fax machine. The fax machine scans any hard copy, and a built-in modem converts the scanned images to analog signals that are transmitted over telephone lines to a receiving fax machine. Here the signals are reconverted to images and a replica of the hard copy is produced at the receiving station, often thousands of miles from the sending source. Fax machines are capable of both sending and receiving documents to and from locations locally or around the world.

(2) Costs include the purchase of a facsimile, paper to reproduce the transmitted replicas, installation and monthly service charges for a telephone line, and regular local and long-distance telephone rates for on-line transmission. Simple documents are sent and received in just a matter of minutes.

(3) Fax machine transmissions require a cover sheet. Standard cover sheets may be purchased from office supply stores, or individualized cover sheets may be created from word processing templates. Individualized cover sheets may also be created on a word processor without the aid of a template.

Fax machine cover sheets generally contain the following information or provisions:

- Name of the addressee
- Company name, if any
- Destination fax number
- Destination city (include state or country also if lesser-known city)
- Name, complete address, fax number, telephone number, and E-mail address of originator
- Date (and time, optional)
- Subject line
- Space for any message
- Number of pages transmitted
- Request to telephone if transmission is unsuccessful

An example of a fax cover sheet is shown on page 285.

b. **Use of fax transmission is not restricted to those individuals and businesses that have stations on-site. This high-speed, low-cost method of document transmission is also available to the general public through the U.S. Postal Service, private mail receiving and forwarding services, stationery stores, and various other businesses in major cities throughout the United States.**

10–4 Computer Fax-to-Computer Fax, Computer Fax-to-Fax Machine, and Fax Machine-to-Computer Fax Messaging

Most computers purchased in today's market are equipped with built-in fax software, a modem, and a fax management system. These features enable fax transmissions to occur between computers and between computers and fax machines.

(1) Businesses, individuals, or other kinds of stations using computer faxes require a telephone line to which they connect their modem. On-screen documents or computer files are transmitted by the fax software and modem to their destination. The modem converts the data to analog signals that are transmitted over telephone lines to a receiving computer or fax machine. Here the signals are reconverted to their former images and a replica of the original file is produced at the receiving station—in file form at a computer station and in hard-copy form at a fax machine station.

(2) Computers are capable of sending and receiving documents to and from locations locally or around the world. To receive fax messages, the computer must be turned on and the "fax manager" must be resident. Messages received in computer files may be printed if a printer is attached to the computer.

(3) Costs include the purchase of a computer (with fax software and a modem), installation and monthly service charges for a telephone

fax machine cover sheet

James and Lyn Clark

17225 Superior Street, Northridge, CA 91325
(818) 701-9770
Fax: (818) 772-8108
E-mail: ClarksHOW@aol.com

Fax Transmittal and Cover Letter

Date: *

Please deliver the following pages to

Name: *

Firm: *

City: *

Fax No.: *

From: *

Subject: *

Message: *

We are transmitting * page(s) (including this cover letter). If you do not receive all the pages, please call us as soon as possible.

line, and regular local and long-distance telephone rates for on-line transmission. Simple documents are sent and received in just a matter of minutes.

(4) The fax management system of a computer generally provides a fax cover sheet that may be sent with each transmission. These cover sheets make provisions for entering some or all of the following information:

- Name of the addressee
- Company name of addressee, if any
- Destination fax number
- Destination telephone number

- Destination address or city name
- Standardized and personalized sender information—name, company (if any), complete address, fax number, and telephone number of originator
- Date and time
- Subject of fax
- Space for any message

An example of a computer fax management system cover sheet template is shown below.[1]

computer fax cover sheet template

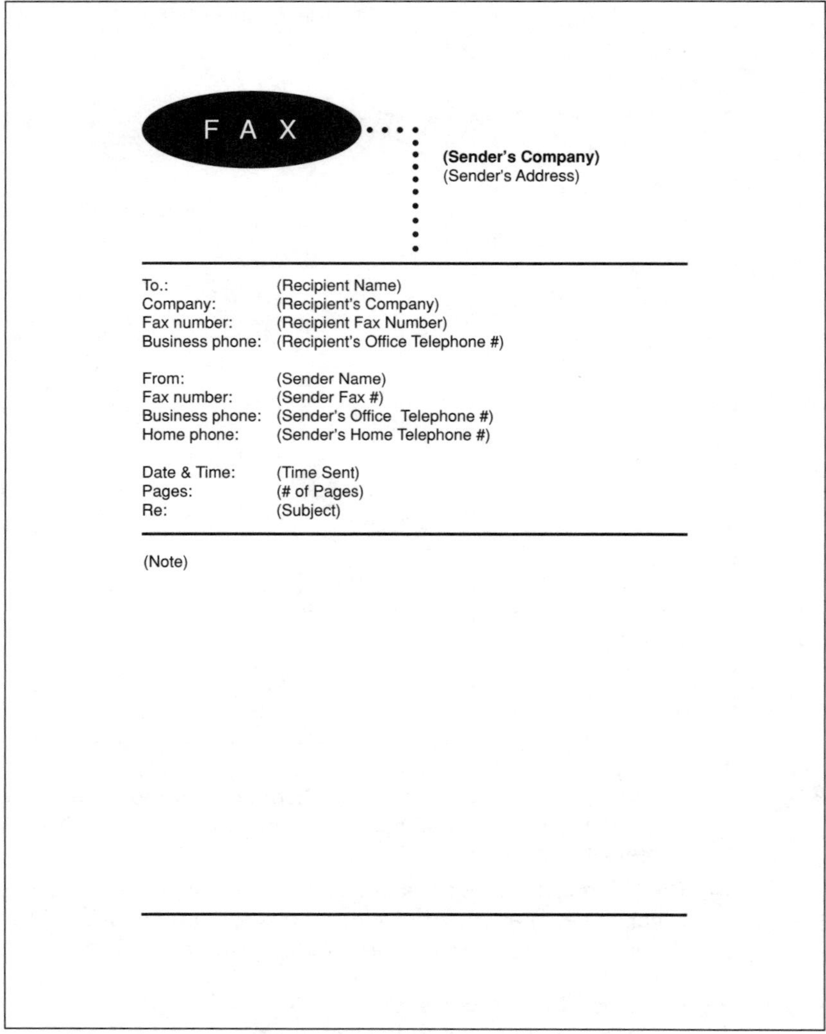

FAX

(Sender's Company)
(Sender's Address)

To.: (Recipient Name)
Company: (Recipient's Company)
Fax number: (Recipient Fax Number)
Business phone: (Recipient's Office Telephone #)

From: (Sender Name)
Fax number: (Sender Fax #)
Business phone: (Sender's Office Telephone #)
Home phone: (Sender's Home Telephone #)

Date & Time: (Time Sent)
Pages: (# of Pages)
Re: (Subject)

(Note)

[1]This computer fax cover sheet template is the *generic* cover sheet template contained in Microsoft Exchange, a computer message management system.

E-Mail Messages

E-mail (electronic mail) is a system by which people communicate with one another through computers and networks. Individuals each have an electronic "mailbox" in their computers and an "address" to which communiqués are directed. Messages sent to the mailbox by other E-mail participants are stored until the recipients open their "mailboxes." After reading the messages, recipients may print them, store them on the computer, or delete them.

In 1995 an average day in the United States had E-mail traffic of 300 million messages. By 1999 this number had risen to 3.5 billion. Forecasts for 2002 project 8 billion messages on an average day for the United States alone.[2]

The rate of information exchange through E-mail messages conveyed on the Internet is rising faster than any other method of message transmission. Advances in accessing the Internet have brought E-mail messaging to the "fingertips" of anyone who has a computer.

10–5 Purpose and Function

E-mail messages are not substitutes for business letters or memorandums. They are used to convey short messages, request information, respond to inquiries, acknowledge receipt of merchandise or mail, or act as cover documents for attached files.

(1) The purpose of E-mail is to convey ***short*** messages quickly and easily without encountering the expense of long-distance telephone charges or mail carrier express charges. Not only are E-mail messages economical and easily created but also they are convenient—they may be received in a matter of minutes (sometimes even seconds) and read at the recipient's discretion.

(2) The E-mail message originator composes a message and "sends" it on its way. Intraorganizational messages are directed to the recipient's computer mailbox via the organization's network. Messages directed outside an organizational network must be transmitted through the Internet.

(3) An E-mail message sent through the Internet leaves the originator's computer and first arrives at the host computer of the originator's on-line access source. Here the message is routed from computer to computer until it reaches the host of the recipient's on-line access source. Once at this destination, the message is in residence until the recipient opens his or her mailbox and retrieves the message from the host computer.

(4) E-mail messages do not replace letters or memorandums that are lengthy, need paper copies, require confidentiality, or discuss significant information or issues. Messages of this nature that are for immediate delivery should be prepared on company letterhead or a

---

[2]International Data Corp. as cited in "Like It or Not, You've Got E-Mail," *BusinessWeek,* 4 October 1999, 184.

memorandum form and sent by fax machine to the recipient's fax machine. Also, the U.S. Postal Service and private mail carriers offer overnight delivery to most cities in the continental United States.

(5) Keep in mind that electronic mail is not protected or private. Because network security is not infallible, you must assume that anyone with a computer has the potential to read your message. Be careful not to include any information in E- mail messages that you would not want disclosed publicly or that would cause you embarrassment. Also, remember that with a click of the mouse, you can inadvertently send your message to the wrong person.

10–6 E-mail Features

On-line access providers and Web browsers supply forms or templates from which you can create E-mail messages. These forms contain a series of boxes into which you can enter information and a series of buttons that permit you to activate E-mail options. Although these forms vary from provider to provider and from browser to browser, each furnishes a variety of the following features, some of which are illustrated in the compose template on page 290.

(1) *An E-mail address book.* In the E-mail address book, you may store the E-mail addresses of those persons to whom you write on a regular basis. Most address books provide options for recording the addresses of individuals as well as recording individual addresses in a group file. Group files permit you to send the same message to all members in the group simultaneously.

(2) *The address box with the guide word **To:**.* Clicking on an address (or a group address) in the address book will enter the recipient's E-mail address in the address box. You may also type in the recipient's address. Do so carefully since one wrong character or space will prevent your message from being delivered—at least to its intended destination.

(3) *The courtesy copy box with the guide abbreviation **cc:**.* If you want others to receive copies of your message, enter their E-mail addresses in the courtesy copy box—either from your address book or by typing them in.

(4) *The blind courtesy copy box with the guide abbreviation **bcc:**.* Most forms provide for sending blind courtesy copies. In this case courtesy copies are sent to the E-mail addresses listed, but the recipient specified in the address box is not shown that the message was also sent to these addresses. This box is useful when the message is sent to a large group of individuals. It prevents showing a long list of E-mail addresses before the actual message appears.

(5) *The subject line box with the guide word **Subject:**.* Type in the subject line box a brief and descriptive phrase that summarizes the topic of your E-mail message. Use initial capital letters for each principal or main word[3] in the subject line.

---

[3]See the opening paragraph of Section 3–6 for an explanation of words to be capitalized. Follow the same formats that are used for published and artistic works.

(6) *The message composition window.* Type a message in the message composition window. If possible, limit your message to a screenful or two of data. Use attachments for transmitting lengthy messages and other pertinent data.

(7) *The attachments window or button.* Use the attachments window or button to select (browse) the path and the name of any file or image you wish to send with your E-mail message or to designate a Web site you wish to attach to your message. You may attach files to be downloaded by the recipient. The recipient must have the application program in which the file was created to open the file.

(8) *The out box and the in box.* E-mail messages should be composed off-line by accessing the mail feature of your Internet browser or Internet service provider's software. Messages are saved in the out box until you connect to your Internet access provider and send them. Once connected to your Internet access provider, you may also "get mail" and retrieve it from your in box.

(9) *A Draft or Send Later button.* The Draft or Send Later option permits you to interrupt composing an E-mail message and store it for editing at another time. This feature is useful if you need to collect additional data or verify information before sending the message.

(10) *A spell feature, a dictionary, and a thesaurus.* Most E-mail programs provide a spell check feature by which you can electronically correct any spelling errors. They also contain a thesaurus that may be accessed to locate synonyms for words used in your E-mail messages. A few programs also provide dictionaries that permit you to look up word meanings as you are composing your message.

(11) *The send button.* The send button sends the message and any attachments.

(12) *The print feature.* Through the *File-Print* menu in your E-mail program, you may print incoming and outgoing messages.

(13) *The reply and the reply all buttons.* The reply and reply all features simplify your providing responses to incoming messages. By clicking the reply button within an incoming E-mail message, you will obtain a fresh "compose" template. The address of the sender is inserted automatically in the address box, and the subject preceded by *Re:* appears in the subject line. All that is needed before you click *Send* is your reply in the message composition window. By using the reply all feature, you send your response to the E-mail message originator as well as to all those who received courtesy copies of the original message.

(14) *The forward message feature.* By using the forward message feature, you may direct a message in your inbox to another person. This feature may be used when another person should see the message contents or should take responsibility for answering the message because it has been directed to the wrong person.

(15) *An E-mail filing cabinet.* E-mail programs provide systems for saving, deleting, and organizing both incoming and outgoing messages.

(16) *Other features.* Depending upon your E-mail software, you may be able to create signature files, mark messages as "unread" (to be read

later), use various fonts and font attributes, use E-mail stationery, paste pictures within messages, attach Web pages, send your messages as greeting cards, automatically file messages, or schedule sending messages.

E-mail compose template

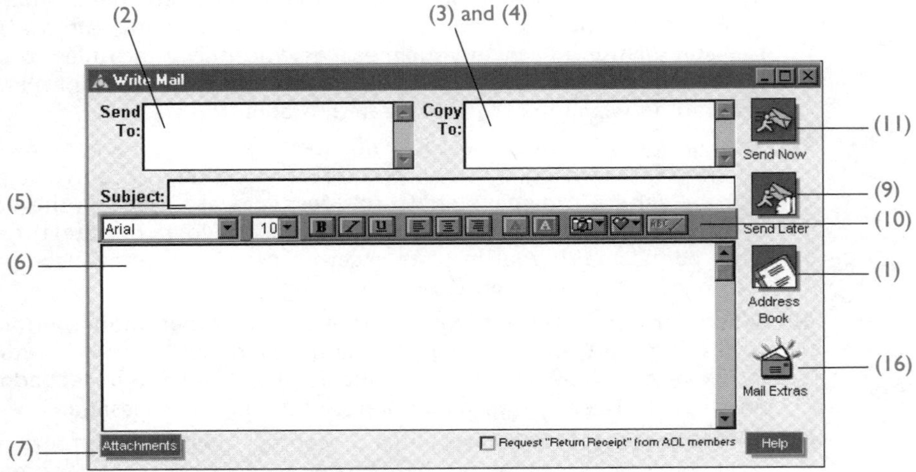

See pages 288–90 for complete descriptions of corresponding numbered items.

10–7 E-Mail Systems

a. Large organizations—commercial enterprises, educational institutions, government entities, and other such organizations—provide E-mail capabilities for their employees or employees and students.

(1) E-mail messages within organizations are commonly sent through a computer network established to serve the organization. Stations are connected by either coaxial cable (within a building) or by phone lines (between buildings or sites). Messages are transmitted from station to station by cable or phone lines. E-mail messages sent outside an organizational network are transmitted through the Internet, a world-wide global network.

(2) Each member of the organization is given a mailbox that may be accessed through a unique user name and password. The E-mail message originator composes a message and "sends" it on its way. Intraorganizational messages are directed to the recipient's computer mailbox via the organization's network. Messages directed outside an organizational network must be transmitted from the organization's network to an Internet backbone computer, where it is routed through the Internet.

---

(3) Access to the E-mail mailbox is generally obtained from a computer located within the organization. Increasingly, however, organizations are furnishing employees with telephone numbers to provide dial-up access to their organizational E-mail mailboxes from home computers or other computers outside the organization.

b. Internet service providers (ISPs) provide E-mail services to their clients as part of their subscription fee for Internet access.

(1) Individual users or small businesses may obtain access to E-mail messaging through their Internet service provider (ISP). Those services that furnish Internet access also provide subscribers from one to five E-mail accounts.

(2) Users of subscription electronic mail must have the following:
- A computer, monitor, and keyboard
- A modem and connection to a telephone line
- A subscription to an Internet service provider (ISP)

(3) Internet service providers supply the connection to the Internet. Commonly known Internet service providers are America Online, Earthlink, CompuServe, and MSN. Thousands of others are scattered in cities throughout the United States and may be easily located through a city's *Yellow Pages* under "Internet access" or on-line at <http://www.thelist.com>. Internet service providers usually furnish the communications software needed for E-mail and other Internet access. See Section 9–2 for additional information.

(4) Internet service providers supply each subscriber with a screen name (a user I.D.) that is unique for that subscriber. The screen name followed by the at sign (@) and the Internet name of the Internet service provider comprise the subscriber's E-mail address. Examples of E-mail addresses are *ClarksHOW@aol.com, lrclark@telis.org,* and *jlclark214@pacificnet.net.* An explanation of extensions following the Internet name of the E-mail provider follows:

Identifier	*Definition*
com	commercial organization
edu	educational site
gov	government organization
mil	military
net	organization administering a network
org	miscellaneous organization

(5) Messages are sent from one E-mail address to another through the Internet service providers. An originator's message is sent to the computer of his or her provider, where it is directed along the Internet to the computer of the recipient's Internet service provider. Here it is stored until the recipient logs on to his or her provider's computer and retrieves the message.

(6) Subscribers have access to their E-mail only when they are logged on through their particular Internet service provider. They may not access their E-mail from a company E-mail mailbox or from an E-mail account with another E-mail service provider.

(7) On-line service providers furnish an on-screen form to compose and send messages. The E-mail message illustrated below was written on the template provided by AmericaOnline.

on-screen E-mail message

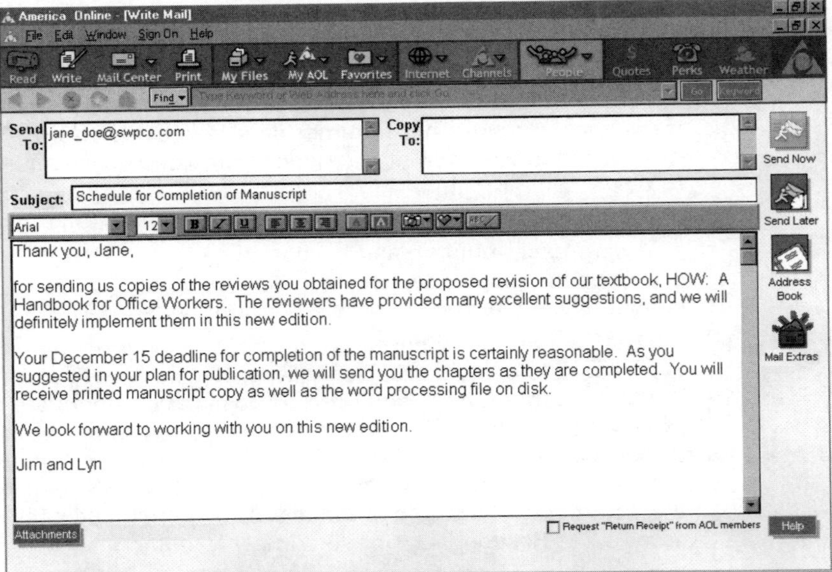

America Online - [Write Mail]

File Edit Window Sign On Help

Read Write Mail Center Print My Files My AOL Favorites Internet Channels People Quotes Perks Weather

Send To: jane_doe@swpco.com

Copy To:

Subject: Schedule for Completion of Manuscript

Thank you, Jane,

for sending us copies of the reviews you obtained for the proposed revision of our textbook, HOW: A Handbook for Office Workers. The reviewers have provided many excellent suggestions, and we will definitely implement them in this new edition.

Your December 15 deadline for completion of the manuscript is certainly reasonable. As you suggested in your plan for publication, we will send you the chapters as they are completed. You will receive printed manuscript copy as well as the word processing file on disk.

We look forward to working with you on this new edition.

Jim and Lyn

Send Now · Send Later · Address Book · Mail Extras

Attachments · Request "Return Receipt" from AOL members · Help

c. An increasing number of Internet sites provide free Internet E-mail accounts to anyone on-line who requests them.

(1) Internet E-mail accounts are unique. Not only are they usually free to anyone worldwide who has any Internet connection but also they may be accessed *anywhere* at *anytime* from *any* computer that is connected to the Internet. Individuals, then, may communicate with friends, relatives, business associates, colleagues, classmates, and all other persons worldwide—from any connected computer.

(2) Many major sites provide free Internet E-mail accounts. Among the most popular are MSN Hotmail <http://www.hotmail.com>, Netscape Webmail <http://webmail.netscape.com>, Yahoo! Mail <http://mail.yahoo.com>, and Lycos MailCity <http://www.mailcity.com/>. Messages are stored on a computer owned by the host (for those sites mentioned—Microsoft, Netscape, Yahoo! and Lycos), not on the restricted computer of an Internet service provider, the message originator, or the message recipient. Consequently, messages may be retrieved, stored, reread, and deleted from any computer as long as it is connected to the Internet.

(3) Messages from an Internet E-mail account may be sent to the mailbox of any E-mail address, regardless of the source of its Internet

access. Conversely, messages from any E-mail address with access to the Internet may be sent to the mailbox of any Internet E-mail account.

(4) Internet E-mail accounts provide templates that usually have these E-mail features for their users:
- An in box and an out box
- An address line
- A subject line
- A courtesy copy line and a blind courtesy copy line
- A message box
- The send button
- A draft button (finish or send later)
- An address file (for individuals and groups)
- An attachment button
- A spell feature, a dictionary, and a thesaurus
- An add signature button
- A save button
- A print option
- A filing cabinet with file folders (capacity to add additional folders)
- A forward button
- A reply button and a reply all button
- A next button, a previous button, a delete button, and a move button.

(5) Internet E-mail messaging has advanced from sending simple messages to including graphics, attaching documents, and adding text

compose template for Internet E-mail (Hotmail)

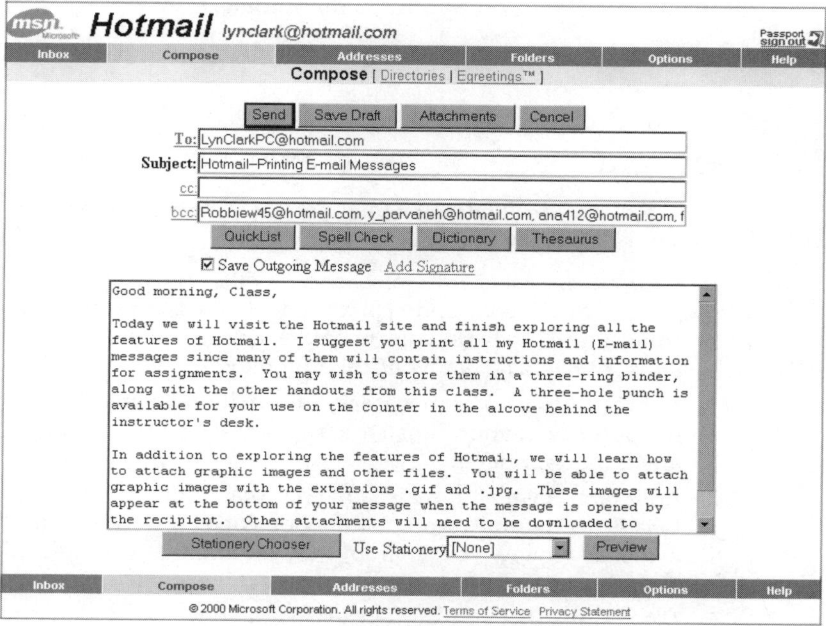

enhancements. Photographs and other images with the extensions .jpg or .gif may be attached to a message. They will either appear at the end of the message or be shown as a link for download. Clicking on the link will display the image. The image may then be saved with the message, deleted, copied, or saved to disk in a separate file. Internet E-mail accounts also permit the transfer of word processing, spreadsheet, and database documents. For example, documents prepared in Microsoft Word, WordPerfect, PowerPoint, and Microsoft Excel arrive in the recipient's mailbox ready to be downloaded in the format they were sent. Attachments sent to the recipients can easily be read once they are downloaded (from anywhere) and brought up in the program in which they were created. Files may be stored on disk or printed for reference.

(6) Most Internet E-mail sites can filter unwanted E-mail and block junk E-mail. These sites permit each user to store from 2000 KB to 5000 KB of messages and attachments for each log-in name. Many, however, do not support file attributes such as different font styles, bolding, italics, or underlining. Attachments, also, have varying size limitations.

10–8 Message Preparation

a. **Just as business letters and memorandums are forms of one-way communication, so are E-mail messages. Since an E-mail message will not be accompanied by facial expressions or voice inflections, it will be taken at face value. No opportunities exist for the receiver to ask questions, clarify statements, or obtain feedback. Therefore, writers of E-mail messages must plan and write their messages as carefully as they would any other form of written communication.**

b. **Begin your E-mail message with a friendly greeting. Examples of such greetings follow:**

Hi, Bob,	Thank you, Paula,	Dear John Morrow,
Hello, Anna,	Greetings, Don,	Dear Sandra,

c. **Use the following guidelines to construct your messages. Review them to ensure that they are**

(1) *Courteous.* Make your message "smile" by using words such as *please, thank you, appreciate,* and *gladly.* Select positive words to convey your ideas; avoid negative words, innuendos, and accusations. Above all, keep your tone friendly.

(2) *Complete.* Has all the necessary information been included to achieve the purpose of your E-mail message? Make sure you have not left out any important data.

(3) *Coherent.* Have all the ideas been placed in logical order so that one idea flows naturally from the previous one? Make sure that the reader can easily follow your train of thought and that you finish discussing one idea before moving on to the next.

(4) *Clear.* Construct your sentences so that they are worded clearly. Make sure that "who does what" and "what is what" leaves no question in

the reader's mind. Avoid long, complicated sentences. Place modifiers as closely as possible to the words they modify, and do not use ambiguous pronouns.

(5) *Concrete.* Write in terms of specifics, and use concrete nouns instead of generalities. Dates and times should be expressed explicitly. Likewise, assignments and expectations need to be described in precise terms that are understood similarly by both the writer and the reader.

(6) *Concise.* Use as few words as possible to construct your message, but make sure you have included all the necessary information. Avoid including extra words and extraneous ideas. Remember to keep your E-mail messages as short as possible.

(7) *Correct.* Use the spell checker of your E-mail software. If your software does not have a spelling checker, keep a dictionary handy as you compose your messages. Proofread your messages carefully for typographical errors, repeated words, omitted words, words used incorrectly, spelling errors, and grammar errors. E-mail messages represent you as much as any other kind of written communication.

d. Conclude your E-mail message with a "signature," even if it is only your first name. Some people prefer also to sign off with a cordial farewell remark such as Best wishes, especially in informal messages to people whom they know.

Signature lines vary in content. Some people may use only their name. Others will include their name, title, organization, and telephone number. Whatever you choose to use, place the information in no more than four lines.

10–9 E-mail Emoticons (Smileys)

Some writers of E-mail messages use emoticons (smileys) to express emotion in their messages. Because E-mail messages are one-way communications, the "Internet community" has developed a series of symbols to express emotion—emoticons, often called "smileys." Emoticons should be used only in personal E-mail messages or in E-mail messages to business associates with whom you have a close working relationship. Commonly used emoticons are these:

(1) :-) This basic smiley is used to show approval or indicate that a statement is made jokingly.

(2) ;-) The wink smiley is flirtatious; it means that what I have just said is a joke.

(3) :-(The frowning smiley is used to show disappointment with a situation.

(4) :-I The indifferent smiley is used to show that the outcome of a situation makes no difference to the writer.

Many more E-mail emoticons are popular in the Internet community. One site that illustrates and explains E-mail emoticons is *The Unofficial Smiley Dictionary* <http://paul.merton.ox.ac.uk/ascii/smileys.html>.

10–10 E-Mail Netiquette

Netiquette (net etiquette) is a set of behaviors that should be adhered to when using the Internet. Excluding conduct prohibited by federal laws, the Internet community itself has devised etiquette standards for Internet use. Those applying to E-mail follow:

(1) Construct your E-mail messages off-line, where possible, so you do not unnecessarily tie up the network.

(2) Use E-mail to accomplish a specific purpose. Do not tie up the network with E-mail messages that are needless or unnecessary. At the same time, send courtesy copies only to people who will benefit from or who need the information contained in your E-mail message.

(3) When replying to E-mail messages on-line, make your reply as succinct as possible. If courtesy copies were routed to others, evaluate whether these individuals need your response before sending your reply. Avoid cluttering the network with unnecessary replies.

(4) Be courteous in your E-mail messages. Sending rude messages is known as "flaming" and is frowned upon by the Internet community.

(5) Avoid using a series of all capital letters in the body of your letter. Besides hindering readability, all capital letters are considered the E-mail equivalent of shouting and may be construed as rude.

(6) If your E-mail software does not support font attributes (boldface, italics, underlining), use the following substitutions. Enclosing a word or phrase in asterisks indicates a mild emphasis and may be equated with using italics. Placing an underline before and after a published work may be construed as a continuous underline, thus distinguishing it as a title.

asterisks for italics

Please mark the package *Fragile*.

Megatone Utilities checks for boot sector viruses, often called *system sector viruses*, as well as for file viruses.

single underlines for a continuous underline

On page 23 of the July 28 issue of _BusinessWeek_, you will find an analysis of profits in the telecommunications industry for the last three years.

Please send me three copies of _Learning the Internet for Personal and Business Applications_.

(7) Keep your E-mail messages short, generally no more than one or two screenfuls of data. If you send a long message, tell the recipient at the beginning so he or she has the option to download it for later reading.

(8) Do not send chain letters over the Internet. Many Internet service providers prohibit chain letters and sending them may result in a revocation of Internet privileges.

Chapter 11

Address Format and Forms of Address

Mrs./Ms.

Address Format and Forms of Address Solution Finder

General Address Format

11–1 General Address Format

a. Use combinations of the following to address general business correspondence: full name of person with appropriate courtesy title, professional title, company name, street address, city, state, and zip code (5 digits or 9 digits, depending upon the availability of the 9-digit code).

Coordinate the person's name, title, and company name so that line endings in the inside address are as nearly even as possible. Use the two-letter postal state designation or spell out the state name to achieve further a balanced appearance. (See Section 6–9c.)

Use the same format for both the inside address of the letter and the envelope used to mail it.

addressed to individual

Ms. Marie La Grasta
8730 Beach Boulevard, Apt. 2
San Clemente, CA 92672-2036

Dear Ms. La Grasta:

Mr. Anthony L. Caruana
2231 Washington Avenue
Des Moines, Iowa 50310

Dear Mr. Caruana:

addressed to individual within company

Mr. Jay V. Berger, Manager
Policy Issue Department
General Insurance Company of America
600 Prospect Avenue, Suite 600
Hartford, Connecticut 06105-2920

Dear Mr. Berger:

Mrs. Brenda Ingram-Cotton
Vice President of Operations
Nation's Bank
5420 Bayshore Boulevard
Tampa, Florida 33611-4122

Dear Mrs. Ingram-Cotton:

addressed to company

F. M. Tarbell Company
2740 S.W. Troy Street
Portland, OR 97219-2553

Ladies and Gentlemen:

Cinamerica
Post Office Box 20077
Encino, CA 91416-0077

Ladies and Gentlemen:

b. An address may have a maximum of six lines and a minimum of two lines.

maximum six-line address

Ms. Stephanie R. Whitaker
Chief Operations Manager
Quality Control Department
Neware Aluminum Accessories
3600 Chelwood Park Blvd., N.E.
Albuquerque, NM 87111-5416

minimum two-line address

Phillips Foods, Inc.
Morristown, NJ 07960-3305

Names and Titles

11–2 Courtesy Titles

a. **Abbreviate the courtesy titles *Mr.* and *Mrs.* when they are used with the names of individuals. The courtesy title *Ms.* ends with a period, although it is not an abbreviation. Always spell out the courtesy title *Miss*; do not conclude it with a period.**

In the salutations of business letters, use the courtesy title with the last name only.

courtesy title with full name

Mr. Stanley Hutchinson

Mrs. Sharlene Pollyea

Ms. Frances Cates

Miss Natalia Granados

courtesy title in salutation

Dear **Mr.** Hutchinson:

Dear **Mrs.** Pollyea:

Dear **Ms.** Cates:

Dear **Miss** Granados:

b. **When the name of an individual does not signify whether the person is a man or a woman, omit the courtesy title. Use the same format for the salutation in a business letter.**

name does not signify gender

Lynn Sebastian

Casey R. Elliott

Cory Williams

Cary Antonovich

Chris V. Stauber

Jaime Bennett

T. R. Najjar

B. Kelly Clemens

Duong Nguyen

salutation for name that does not signify gender

Dear T. R. Najjar:

Dear Cory Williams:

Dear Chris V. Stauber:

Dear B. Kelly Clemens:

c. **When addressing a woman, use the courtesy title *Ms.* unless *Mrs.* or *Miss* is specified by the addressee. Use the courtesy title *Miss* for young girls under the age of thirteen.**

woman does not indicate a title preference

Ms. Laura Rankin

Ms. Ellen Togo

girl under age thirteen

Miss Kristen Fielding

Miss Claudia Martinez

d. **The courtesy title *Master* is used for addressing young boys, usually below the age of thirteen.**

Master William J. Clark　　**Master** Charles Bentley

e. **The abbreviated courtesy title *Esq.* (*Esquire*) is sometimes used after the surname of a lawyer. In such cases no courtesy title precedes the name.**

Murray T. Silverstein, **Esq.**　　Lorraine H. Clark, **Esq.**

f. **Female correspondents who have a courtesy title preference other than *Ms.* should indicate this preference in the signature lines of their correspondence by enclosing the preferred title in parentheses before their names. Correspondents who have names that do not indicate gender may also wish to indicate a courtesy title preference by enclosing it in parentheses before their names in a signature line.**

female with courtesy title preference other than Ms.

(Mrs.) Susan Willett　　(Dr.) Karen L. Butler

male or female whose name does not indicate gender

(Ms.) J. T. Robinson　　(Ms.) Lonnie Abrams

(Mrs.) Chris Dobrian　　(Mrs.) Lee Haberman

(Mr.) Dana Andrews　　(Mr.) Leslie Mitchell

11–3 Professional Titles

a. **Except for *Dr.* and long professional titles consisting of more than one or two words, write out and capitalize all professional titles when they precede the names of individuals. *Professor, Dean, The Reverend, Governor, Senator, Colonel, Lieutenant,* and *The Honorable* are examples of titles that are capitalized and written in full.**

Doctor abbreviated

Dr. Allen Wiedmeyer　　**Dr.** Shannon T. Goar

professional title written out

Professor Marly Bergerud　　**The Honorable** Victor S. Ryan

long professional title abbreviated

Lt. Col. Ret. Maurice P. Wiener (Lieutenant Colonel Retired)

b. **In addressing business correspondence or completing signature lines, capitalize and write out professional titles that follow an individual's name.**

single-line address format

Mr. David Johnson, **Dean**　　Ms. Patricia A. Wilson, **Vice President**

two-line address format

Ms. Margaret M. Fielding
Plant Superintendent

Mr. Michael T. Livingston Jr.
Assistant Vice President

single-line signature format

(Dr.) Jennifer Loucks, **Dean**

William A. Murillo, **Manager**

(Mrs.) Joyce Moore, **President**

Rebecca L. Roberts, **Supervisor**

two-line signature format

John S. Minasian
Plant Superintendent

(Ms.) Orolyn L. Ruenz-Clark
Vice President of Operations

(Mrs.) Brenda Browning
Collections Manager

Thomas C. Johnson
Customer Service Representative

c. **Capitalize professional titles *not* appearing in address format or signature lines only when they precede and are used directly with an individual's name in place of a courtesy title. Do not capitalize titles following an individual's name.**

title preceding name

President Lloyd W. Bartholome will deliver the main address.

One of the senators from Wyoming, **Senator** Alan K. Simpson, will be the luncheon speaker.

title following name

Lloyd W. Bartholome, **president** of A & P Enterprises, will deliver the main address.

The Honorable Scot Ober, **senator** from Michigan, has agreed to deliver the main address.

d. **Only one courtesy or professional title with the same meaning should appear with a single name. Use *Dr.* or *M.D.*, but not both titles, with the same name.**

titles with the same meaning

Dr. James V. Glaser *or* James V. Glaser, **M.D.**

Dr. Cheng Wong *or* Cheng Wong, **D.D.S.**

titles with different meanings

Dr. Sue Rigby, **Professor**

e. **Do not capitalize professional titles that substitute for individuals' names.**

The **general** scheduled a staff meeting for Thursday afternoon.

Did the **governor** appear for the press conference?

11-4 Company Names

Spell out company names in full unless the company itself uses abbreviations in its official name.[1] *Inc.* and *Ltd.* usually appear in abbreviated form, but some companies write these words in full.

company name written in full

Pacific Mutual Life Insurance Company
Merriam-Webster, Incorporated
Richter and Sons
Watson Corporation

company name containing abbreviation

Consolidated Factors, **Ltd.**
International Computer **Corp.**
McKnight, Fisher **&** Donovan
Lyons Investment Group **Inc.**

Places

11-5 Buildings and Units

Capitalize the names of buildings and the names of any units therein. Place the unit, suite, or apartment location after the building name, but separate the two with a comma.

If an address contains a unit location without a building name, place it after the street address. Separate the street address and the unit location with a comma.

Use numerals for all unit numbers.

building name with unit location

California State Capitol, **Office 243F**
Medical Arts Center, **Suites 680–681**
Tishman Building, **Suite 103**
Greenwich Apartments, **Unit 3**

unit location without building name

140 Willow Street, **Suite 103**
9830 Grand Oaks Avenue, **Unit 22**
18564 Clark Street, **Apt. 4**
5426 S.W. 43rd Street, **#105**

11-6 Street Addresses

a. Use numerals to express house or building numbers. Only the house or building number *one* is written in word form.

***house or building number* one**

One Lakeview Terrace
One Riverwalk Place

---

[1]The official name of a company may be determined from its printed letterhead or from any of its contracts. Official company names are also listed in the directories referenced in Chapter 15, copies of which may be found in most public libraries.

house or building number in numerals

8 Burbank Lane

210 Third Avenue, Apt. 303

17225 Lassen Street

10239-3 White Oak Avenue

b. Spell out simple compass directions (*North, South, East,* and *West*) that appear in a street address. Compound compass points (*Northeast, Northwest, Southeast,* and *Southwest*) in an address are abbreviated. Any compound compass directions following the street address are preceded by a comma.

simple compass point in street address

1864 **East** 37th Street

2160 Century Park **East**

1040 **North** Brand Boulevard

240 Manchester Street **West**

compound compass point within street address

2830 **N.E.** 17th Street

121 **S.W.** Morrison Street

compass point following street address

1301 K Street, **N.W.**

4210 Broxten Street, **S.E.**, Apt. 23

c. All street number names *ten* and below are written in words using ordinal numbers—*first, second, third,* etc. Street number names above *ten,* however, are written in numerals. Use ordinal numbers (*11th, 12th, 13th,* etc.) when expressing these street names.

street number name ten or below

1183 **Fifth** Avenue

983 West **First** Street

street number name above ten

980 North **21st** Street

3624 West **59th** Place

2036 **42nd** Street

1843 **123rd** Street

d. Spell out street designations such as *Boulevard, Avenue, Street, Place, Drive,* and *Lane.* Only the street designation *Boulevard* may be abbreviated (*Blvd.*) with exceptionally long street names.

street designation spelled out

18394 Lankershim **Boulevard**

street designation abbreviated

9263 North Coldwater Canyon **Blvd.**

e. Spell out where possible mailing designations such as *Rural Route* or *Post Office Box* that are used in the place of street addresses. Abbreviate the mailing designation only with long addresses.

postal designation spelled out

Post Office Box 207

Rural Route 2, Box 1620

postal designation abbreviated

P.O. Box 1269, Terminal Annex

f. Apartment, suite, and unit numbers are expressed in numerals and are generally included on the same line as the building name. In addresses without building names, these numbers appear on the same line with the street address. The term Apartment may be abbreviated when it appears on the same line as the street address.

With long street addresses, apartment numbers may be placed on the following line. The term Apartment in these cases is spelled out.

apartment, suite, or unit number with building

Richmond Medical Plaza, **Suite 540**

unit number with street address

6176 Arroyo Road, **Unit 2**

apartment number with street address

3964 West 81st Street, **Apt. 3**

no specific designation with street address

16932 Wilshire Boulevard, **C-110**

apartment number on line following street address

8564 Kensington Street, S.W.
Apartment 230

11–7 City, State, and Zip Code

a. Spell out in full the names of cities.

Saint Louis New York Fort Worth Los Angeles

b. Use the two-letter post office designation for state names or spell out in full the state name. Select either style based upon (1) the degree of formality of the correspondence or (2) the one that provides better balance for setting up the entire address. Should both be equally suitable, use the two-letter postal designation. Use the same form for both the inside address and the envelope used to mail the correspondence.

state two-letter zip code designation

Ms. Jessica Morton
108 Academy Avenue
Weymouth, MA 02188-4204

Mr. Richard A. Chui
9540 Barr Drive, Apt. 204
Indianapolis, IN 46229-1214

state name written in full

Mr. William R. Stephenson
257 American Legion Highway
Revere, Massachusetts 02151

Mrs. Shirley Schnair-Goldman
1124 Jefferson Boulevard
Flint, Michigan 48507-4201

c. **Zip codes are keyed a single space after the state.**

Atlanta, GA 30331-8732 *or* Atlanta, Georgia 30331

Address Format for Foreign Correspondence

11–8 Address Format for Foreign Correspondence

a. **Addresses for foreign correspondence contain combinations of the following: (1) full name of addressee with appropriate courtesy title, (2) professional title of addressee, (3) company name, (4) street address, (5) city and any city numbering codes or section name, (6) state or region, if applicable, and (7) destination country.**

b. **The sequencing of the address components varies among countries. Some countries place the name of the addressee first but place the city information before the street address. Some place the house number after the street name or the postal code before the city name. Others follow the familiar street address, city, state, and postal code format used in the United States. Where possible, follow the conventions of the destination country. For mail posted from the United States, however, always place the name of the destination country in all capital letters as the last line of the mailing address.**

Mr. Atsushi Ishiki
1-6-302 Wutsukusigaoka
1 Chome–C1Z Midoriku
Yokohama
JAPAN

Alexandria
Stanly
237 Zaky Badway Mohamed St.
Mrs. Iman Gaber El-Desoky
EGYPT

c. **If possible, use courtesy titles that reflect the language of the country. *Herrn, Frau,* and *Fraülein* (German); *Señor, Señora,* and *Señorita* (Spanish); and *Monsieur, Madame,* and *Mademoiselle* (French) are just a few examples of foreign courtesy titles that represent the English *Mr., Mrs.,* and *Miss.***

In most foreign countries a comparable term for *Miss* is used for young women. Adult women are addressed with the courtesy title comparable to the English *Mrs.,* regardless of their marital status.

Use English courtesy titles in those cases where the comparable title is unknown or impractical to reproduce on English-based keyboards. However, use the extended character sets of your word processor to form those characters that are supported by the software.

Le Lien
c/o Mr. Lucien Aubert
14, rue Roger-Radisson
69322 Lyon
FRANCE

Srta. Kristina Chagas Tavares
Rua 706, nº=152/178
Balneario Camboriú, SC
CEP 88330
BRAZIL

d. When addressing foreign correspondence, use the English version of a country name (*GERMANY,* not *DEUTSCHLAND*) to ensure the correspondence is routed to the correct country from the United States. For city names, however, select the foreign spelling to hasten delivery within the country (*Köln,* not *Cologne; Wien,* not *Vienna; Venezia,* not *Venice; Ogasawara Islands,* not *Bonin Islands*). If possible, use all the appropriate letters and diacritical marks in spelling names, streets, cities, and other parts of the address. Consult the geographical reference section of your dictionary for assistance in selecting the correct name and its spelling.[2]

Herrn Paul-Erich Rünz
Diplomat-Kaufman
Gemarkenstraße 290
5000 Köln 80—Dellbrück
GERMANY

On-Line Address Formats

The Internet,[3] which is accessible to over 160 million users worldwide, has promoted information exchange between virtually any segment of our society. From individuals in major universities and giant corporations to the single user at a home computer, all may access the wealth of information Internet access provides and all may communicate with each other through E-mail.

11–9 Internet Addresses

Internet popularity has soared since the introduction of the World Wide Web (WWW) and its first browser, Netscape Navigator, in 1992. Companies, government offices, educational institutions, organizations, and individuals have established Web sites—computer "pages" on which they provide information, sell products or services, and/or recruit employees. Each page has an address so it can be reached easily by merely typing in the address. An Internet address is known as a *Uniform Resource Locator—URL,* pronounced "you are el." A description of URL parts follows:

(1) A typical Internet address (URL) might appear as **http://www.odci.gov/cia/publications/factbook/index.html** in a listing.

(2) The first part, **http://**, indicates the type of protocol needed to retrieve the information at the site. In this case **http** represents *hypertext transfer protocol.* World Wide Web sites are accessed by Web

[2]The spellings shown here are based on those in Merriam-Webster's *Collegiate Dictionary,* 10th Ed. (Springfield, Mass.: Merriam-Webster, Incorporated, 1999). Note that in this dictionary the foreign spelling is shown after the English spelling in the primary reference and also listed separately in a secondary reference.

[3]See Chapter 9 for additional information on accessing and using the Internet. See Chapter 15 for useful Internet site addresses.

browsers using this protocol. Other protocols include **gopher://**, which identifies a gopher resource, and **ftp://**, which identifies a file transfer protocol resource. Both of these are older protocols used for text files.

(3) The **www** following the protocol type symbolizes World Wide Web. The name of the host computer, **odci** (Office of the Director of Central Intelligence), is followed by its identifier, **gov**, which distinguishes the Web site as a government entity. Note the common URL identifier extensions in the following table:

Identifier	*Definition*
com	commercial organization
edu	educational site
gov	government organization
mil	military
net	organization administering a network
org	miscellaneous organization

(4) The link **cia** from the host computer moves to the Web site of The Central Intelligence Agency where **publications**, **factbook**, and **index.html** are accessed.

(5) Keying in **http://www.odci.gov/cia/publications/factbook/index.html**, therefore, will take you directly to the contents for *The World Factbook 1999* or an updated version. The **html** extension after **index** represents "HyperText Markup Language." Clicking on any item in the contents will access the text in the current world fact book.

11–10 E-Mail Addresses

Just as everyone has an address for mail delivery by the U.S. Postal Service and private mail carriers, anyone who wishes to send and receive mail through the Internet must have an Internet E-mail (electronic mail) address.

(1) An E-mail address is divided into two basic parts: the user name and the user domain. The user name is the combination of letters and/or numbers assigned to a specific user when the user signs up with an on-line service or other E-mail provider; formats for the user name are governed by the E-mail provider. The user domain identifies the location of the computer that receives the user's mail—the on-line service or other E-mail provider.

(2) The user name and the user domain are separated by @ (an "at" sign). Examples of E-mail addresses follow:

E-mail Address	*Definition*
ClarksHOW@aol.com[4]	The user name is *ClarksHOW;* the on-line service provider is America Online, an on-line service provider that is classified as a commercial organization.

[4]See Section 11–9 for an explanation of extensions *com, edu, gov, mil, net,* and *org.*

E-mail Address	Definition
jdoe@swcollege.com	The user name is *jdoe* (J. Doe); the E-mail provider is South-Western College Publishing, a commercial organization.
allison.jones@sdsu.edu	The user name is allison.jones (Allison Jones); the E-mail provider is San Diego State University, an educational site.
bsmith@csupomona.edu	The user name is *bsmith* (B. Smith); the E-mail provider is California State Polytechnic University, Pomona, an educational site.
JLConnor87@earthlink.net	The user name is *JLConnor87;* the on-line service provider is Earthlink, an on-line service provider that is classified as an organization administering a network.
lthamilton@pacbell.net	The user name is *lthamilton* (L. T. Hamilton; the E-mail/Internet access service is an organization administering a network.
az876@lafn.org	The user name is *az876;* the E-mail/Internet service provider is Los Angeles Free Net, a miscellaneous organization.
rljones@rain.org	The user name is *rljones* (R. L. Jones); the E-mail/Internet service provider is Regional Area Information Network, a miscellaneous organization.

Forms of Address

11–11 Personal and General Professional Titles

The following table lists the proper forms of address, salutation, and complimentary close for correspondence addressed to a general individual, two or more general individuals, certain professionals, and a company:

Addressee	Address on Letter and Envelope	Salutation and Complimentary Close
Man	Mr. (full name) (local address)	Dear Mr. (last name): Sincerely,
Married woman	Mrs. (husband's first name, last name) (local address)	Dear Mrs. (last name): Sincerely,
	Mrs. or Ms. (wife's first name, last name)[5] (local address)	Dear Mrs. or Ms. (last name): Sincerely,

[5]This form is also used for a woman who is separated or divorced from her husband.

Addressee	*Address on Letter*	*Salutation and Complimentary Close*
Single woman	Ms. or Miss (full name) (local address)	Dear Ms. or Miss (last name): Sincerely,
Woman, marital status unknown	Ms. (full name) (local address)	Dear Ms. (last name): Sincerely,
Widow	Mrs. (husband's first name, last name) (local address)	Dear Mrs. (last name): Sincerely,
	Mrs. or Ms. (wife's first name, last name) (local address)	Dear Mrs. or Ms. (last name): Sincerely,
Two or more men	Mr. (full name) Mr. (full name) (local address)	Dear Mr. (last name) and Mr. (last name): *or* Dear Messrs. (last name) and (last name): *or* Gentlemen: Sincerely,
Two or more women	Mrs. (full name) Mrs. (full name) (local address)	Dear Mrs. (last name) and Mrs. (last name): *or* Dear Mesdames (last name) and (last name): *or* Mesdames: Sincerely,
	Mrs. (full name) Ms. (full name) (local address)	Dear Mrs. (last name) and Ms. (last name): Sincerely,
	Ms. (full name) Ms. (full name) (local address)	Dear Ms. (last name) and Ms. (last name): *or* Dear Mses. (last name) and (last name): Sincerely,
One woman and One man	Ms. (full name) Mr. (full name) (local address)	Dear Ms. (last name) and Mr. (last name): Sincerely,
Married couple	Mr. and Mrs. (husband's full name) (local address)	Dear Mr. and Mrs. (last name): Sincerely,
Married couple with different last names	(title) (full name of husband) (title) (full name of wife) (local address)	Dear (title) (husband's last name) and (title) (wife's last name): Sincerely,
Professional married couple with same title and same last name	(title in plural form) (husband's first name) and (wife's first name) (last name) (local address)	Dear (title in plural form) (last name): Sincerely,

Addressee	Address on Letter and Envelope	Salutation and Complimentary Close
Professional married couple with different titles and same last name	(title) (full name of husband) (title) (full name of wife) (local address)	Dear (title) and (title) (last name): Sincerely,
President of a college or university (Doctor)	Dr. (full name), President (name of institution) (local address)	Dear Dr. (last name): Sincerely,
Dean of a school or college	Dean (full name) School of (name) (name of institution) (local address)	Dear Dean (last name): Sincerely,
	Dr. or (Mr./Mrs./Ms.) (full name) Dean of (title) (name of institution) (local address)	Dear Dr. or (Mr./Mrs./Ms.) (last name): Sincerely,
Professor	Professor (full name) (name of department) (name of institution) (local address)	Dear Professor (last name): Sincerely,
	Dr. (full name), Professor (name of department) (name of institution) (local address)	Dear Dr. (last name): Sincerely,
	Dr. or (Mr./Mrs./Ms.) (full name) Assistant (or Associate) Professor (name of department) (name of institution) (local address)	Dear Dr. or (Mr./Mrs./Ms.) (last name): Sincerely,
Physician	(full name), M.D. (local address) *or* Dr. (full name) (local address)	Dear Dr. (last name): Sincerely,
Lawyer	(Mr./Mrs./Ms.) (full name) Attorney-at-Law (local address) *or* (full name), Esq. (local address)	Dear (Mr./Mrs./Ms.) (last name): Sincerely,
Service personnel	(full rank, full name, and abbreviation of service designation) (*Retired* is added to rank if applicable.) (unit assignment) (local address) Example: Brigadier General Retired, United States Marine Corps Brig. Gen. Ret. Casey Rhodes, USMC (local address)	Dear (rank) (last name): Sincerely, Dear General Rhodes: Sincerely,

Addressee	Address on Letter and Envelope	Salutation and Complimentary Close
Service personnel (*continued*)	Example: Lieutenant Colonel, United States Air Force Lieutenant Colonel Cory Adams, USAF Headquarters Squadron, 22nd Bomb Group March Air Force Base Riverside, California 92506	Dear Colonel Adams: Sincerely,
Company or corporation, men	(full name of organization) (local address)	Gentlemen: Sincerely,
Company or corporation, men and women	(full name of organization) (local address)	Ladies and Gentlemen: Sincerely,
Company or corporation, women	(full name of organization) (local address)	Ladies: Sincerely,

11–12 Government Officials

The following table shows the proper forms of address, salutation, and complimentary close for specific government officials:

Addressee	Address on Letter	Salutation and Complimentary Close
President of the United States	(Mr./Mrs./Ms.) (full name), President The White House 1600 Pennsylvania Avenue, N.W. Washington, DC 20500	Dear (Mr./Madam) President: Respectfully,
Former president[6]	Honorable (full name) Former President of the United States (local address)	Dear (Mr./Mrs./Ms.) (last name): Sincerely,
President-elect	Honorable (full name) President-elect of the United States (local address)	Dear (Mr./Mrs./Ms.) (last name): Sincerely,
Wife of the president	Mrs. (full name) The White House Washington, DC 20500	Dear Mrs. (last name): Sincerely,
Assistant to the president	Honorable (full name) Assistant to the President The White House Washington, DC 20500	Dear (Mr./Mrs./Ms.) (last name): Sincerely,
Vice president of the United States	The Vice President United States Senate Washington, DC 20510 *or* The Honorable (full name) Vice President of the United States United States Senate Washington, DC 20510	Dear (Mr./Madam) Vice President: Sincerely,

[6]This form of address may be adapted to address other former high-ranking government officials.

Addressee	Address on Letter and Envelope	Salutation and Complimentary Close
Chief Justice of the United States	The Chief Justice of the United States The Supreme Court of the United States Washington, DC 20543	Dear (Mr./Madam) Chief Justice: Sincerely,
Associate Justice	(Mr./Madam) Justice (last name) The Supreme Court of the United States Washington, DC 20543	Dear (Mr./Madam) Justice: Sincerely,
United States senator	Honorable (full name) United States Senate Washington, DC 20510 *or* Honorable (full name) United States Senator (local address)	Dear Senator (last name): Sincerely,
United States senator-elect	(Mr./Mrs./Ms.) (full name) Senator-Elect, United States Senate (local address)	Dear (Mr./Mrs./Ms.) (last name): Sincerely,
United States representative	Honorable (full name) House of Representatives Washington, DC 20515 *or* Honorable (full name), Member United States House of Representatives (local address)	Dear (Mr./Mrs./Ms.) (last name): Sincerely,
Cabinet Member	Honorable (full name) Secretary of (name of department) Washington, DC 00000	Dear (Mr./Madam) Secretary: Sincerely,
	Honorable (full name) Postmaster General Washington, DC 20260	Dear (Mr./Madam) Postmaster General: Sincerely,
	Honorable (full name) Attorney General Washington, DC 20503	Dear (Mr./Madam) Attorney General: Sincerely,
Deputy secretary, assistant, or undersecretary	Honorable (full name) Deputy Secretary of (name of department) Washington, DC 00000 Honorable (full name) Assistant Secretary of (name of department) Washington, DC 00000 Honorable (full name) Undersecretary of (name of department) Washington, DC 00000	Dear (Mr./Mrs./Ms.) (last name): Sincerely,
Head of independent office or agency	Honorable (full name) Comptroller General of the United States General Accounting Office Washington, DC 20548	Dear (Mr./Mrs./Ms.) (last name): Sincerely,

Addressee	Address on Letter and Envelope	Salutation and Complimentary Close
Head of indepen-dent office or agency (*continued*)	Honorable (full name) Chairman, (name of commission) Washington, DC 00000	Dear (Mr./Madam) Chairman: Sincerely,
	Honorable (full name) Director, Bureau of the Budget Washington, DC 20503	Dear (Mr./Mrs./Ms.) (last name): Sincerely,
American ambassador	Honorable (full name) American Ambassador (address and city) (country)	Sir: or Madam: (formal) Very truly yours, *or* Dear (Mr./Madam) Ambassador: (informal) Sincerely,
American consul general or American consul	(Mr./Mrs./Ms.) (full name) American Consul General (or American Consul) (address and city) (country)	Dear (Mr./Mrs./Ms.) (last name): Sincerely,
Foreign ambassa-dor in the United States	His Excellency (full name) Ambassador of (country) (local address)	Excellency: (formal) Very truly yours, *or* Dear (Mr./Madam) Ambassador: (informal) Sincerely,
Governor of state	Honorable (full name) Governor of (name of state) (address) (city), (state) 00000	Dear Governor (last name): Sincerely,
Lieutenant governor	Honorable (full name) Lieutenant Governor of (name of state) (address) (city), (state) 00000	Dear (Mr./Mrs./Ms.) (last name): Sincerely,
State senator	Honorable (full name) (name of state) State Senate (address) (city), (state) 00000	Dear Senator (last name): Sincerely,
State representa-tive, assembly-person, or delegate	Honorable (full name) (name of state) House of Representa-tives (or State Assembly or House of Delegates) (address) (city), (state) 00000	Dear (Mr./Mrs./Ms.) (last name): Sincerely,
Mayor	Honorable (full name) Mayor of (name of city) (address) (city), (state) 00000	Dear Mayor (last name): Sincerely,
President of a board of commissioners	Honorable (full name), President Board of Commissioners of (name of city) (address) (city), (state) 00000	Dear (Mr./Mrs./Ms.) (last name): Sincerely,

Addressee	Address on Letter and Envelope	Salutation and Complimentary Close
Judge	Honorable (full name) (name of court) (local address)	Dear Judge (last name): Sincerely,

11–13 Religious Dignitaries

The following table shows the proper forms of address, salutation, and complimentary close for specific religious dignitaries:

Addressee	Address on Letter and Envelope	Salutation and Complimentary Close
Catholic clergy		
Cardinal	His Eminence (given name) Cardinal (last name) Archbishop of (diocese) (local address)	Your Eminence: (formal) *or* Dear Cardinal (last name): (informal) Sincerely,
Archbishop	The Most Reverend (full name) Archbishop of (diocese) (local address)	Your Excellency: (formal) *or* Dear Archbishop (last name): (informal) Sincerely,
Bishop	The Most Reverend (full name) Bishop of (city) (local address)	Your Excellency: (formal) *or* Dear Bishop (last name): (informal) Sincerely,
Monsignor	The Right Reverend Monsignor (full name) (local address)	Right Reverend Monsignor: (formal) *or* Dear Monsignor (last name): (informal) Sincerely,
	or	
	The Very Reverend Monsignor (full name) (local address)	Very Reverend Monsignor: (formal) *or* Dear Monsignor (last name): (informal) Sincerely,
Priest	The Reverend (full name), (add initials of order, if any) (local address)	Reverend Sir: (formal) Dear Father (last name): (informal) Sincerely,
Mother superior	Mother (full name), (initials of order, if used) Superior, (name of convent) (local address)	Dear Mother (full name): Sincerely,
Nun	Sister (full name), (initials of order, if used) (name of convent) (local address)	Dear Sister (full name): Sincerely,

Addressee	Address on Letter and Envelope	Salutation and Complimentary Close
Monk	Brother (full name), (initials of order, if used) (local address)	Dear Brother (full name): Sincerely,
Jewish clergy	Rabbi (full name) (local address)	Dear Rabbi (last name): Sincerely,
Protestant clergy		
Bishop	The Right Reverend (full name) Bishop of (name) (local address)	Right Reverend Sir: (formal) *or* Dear Bishop (last name): (informal) Sincerely,
	or The Reverend (full name) Bishop of (name) (local address)	Reverend Sir: (formal) *or* Dear Bishop (last name): (informal) Sincerely,
Dean	The Very Reverend (full name) Dean of (name of church) (local address)	Very Reverend Sir: (formal) *or* Dear Dean (last name): (informal) Sincerely,
Minister	The Reverend (full name) (title, if any) (name of church) (local address)	Dear Reverend (last name): *or* Dear (Dr./Mr./Mrs./Ms.) (last name): Sincerely,
Chaplain	Chaplain (full name) (full rank, service designation) (post office address of organization and station) (local address)	Dear Chaplain (last name): Sincerely,
Lay clergy	Deacon (full name) (name of church) (local address)	Dear Deacon (last name): Sincerely,
	(Brother/Sister) (full name) (name of church) (local address)	Dear (Brother/Sister)(last name): Sincerely,

11–14 Undetermined Individual or Group

Although addressing correspondence to an undefined or undetermined individual or group should generally be avoided, circumstances sometimes provide no other alternative. In these cases the letter contains no inside address. The phrase *To Whom It May Concern:* replaces the standard salutation, and the complimentary close is either *Sincerely yours,* or *Yours very truly,*.

Chapter 12

Business Letters and Memorandums

Enc.

Business Letters and Memorandums Solution Finder

Letter Styles

12–1 Full Block

Business letters may be formatted in several styles.[1] The full block is the most streamlined letter style because all parts and all lines begin at the left margin.

full block letter

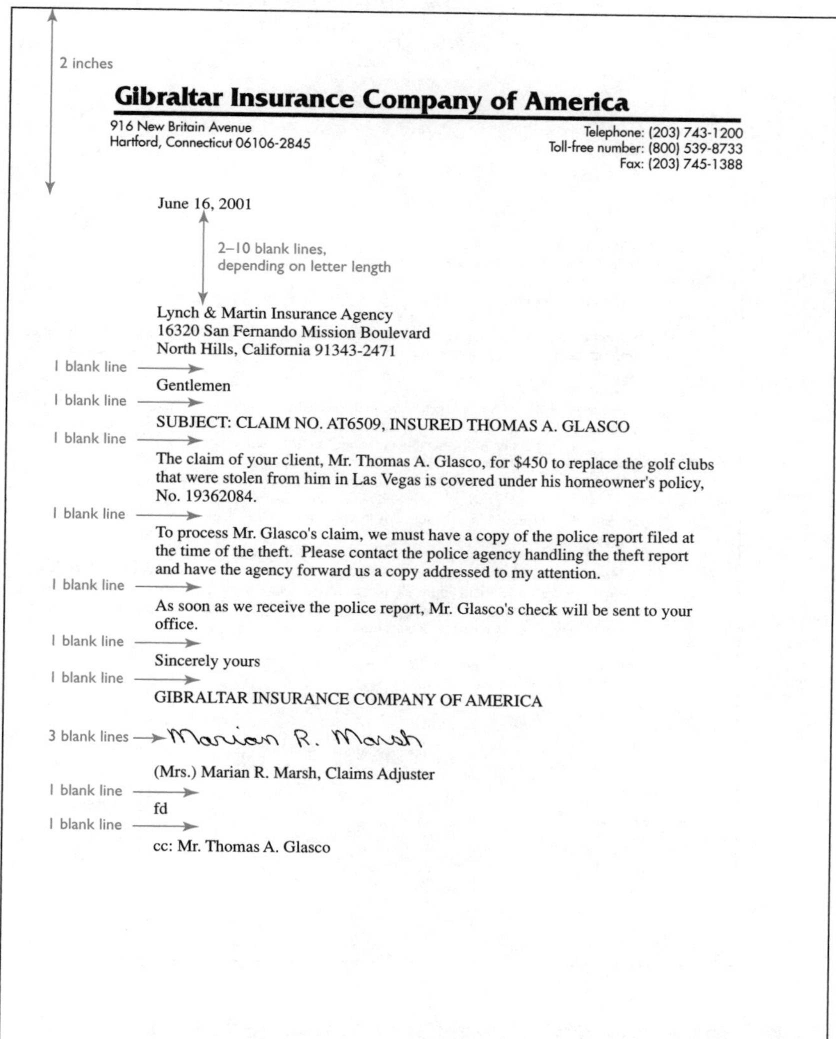
2 inches

Gibraltar Insurance Company of America
916 New Britain Avenue
Hartford, Connecticut 06106-2845
Telephone: (203) 743-1200
Toll-free number: (800) 539-8733
Fax: (203) 745-1388

June 16, 2001

2–10 blank lines, depending on letter length

Lynch & Martin Insurance Agency
16320 San Fernando Mission Boulevard
North Hills, California 91343-2471

1 blank line

Gentlemen

1 blank line

SUBJECT: CLAIM NO. AT6509, INSURED THOMAS A. GLASCO

1 blank line

The claim of your client, Mr. Thomas A. Glasco, for $450 to replace the golf clubs that were stolen from him in Las Vegas is covered under his homeowner's policy, No. 19362084.

1 blank line

To process Mr. Glasco's claim, we must have a copy of the police report filed at the time of the theft. Please contact the police agency handling the theft report and have the agency forward us a copy addressed to my attention.

1 blank line

As soon as we receive the police report, Mr. Glasco's check will be sent to your office.

1 blank line

Sincerely yours

1 blank line

GIBRALTAR INSURANCE COMPANY OF AMERICA

3 blank lines

Marian R. Marsh

(Mrs.) Marian R. Marsh, Claims Adjuster

1 blank line

fd

1 blank line

cc: Mr. Thomas A. Glasco

[1]All letters appearing in this chapter have been designed by the authors for illustrative purposes. They are not reproductions of actual letters.

12–2 Modified Block

a. **The modified block letter style with blocked paragraphs is the most popular letter style used in business. All lines except the return address (if used), the date, and the closing lines begin at the left margin.**

modified block letter with blocked paragraphs

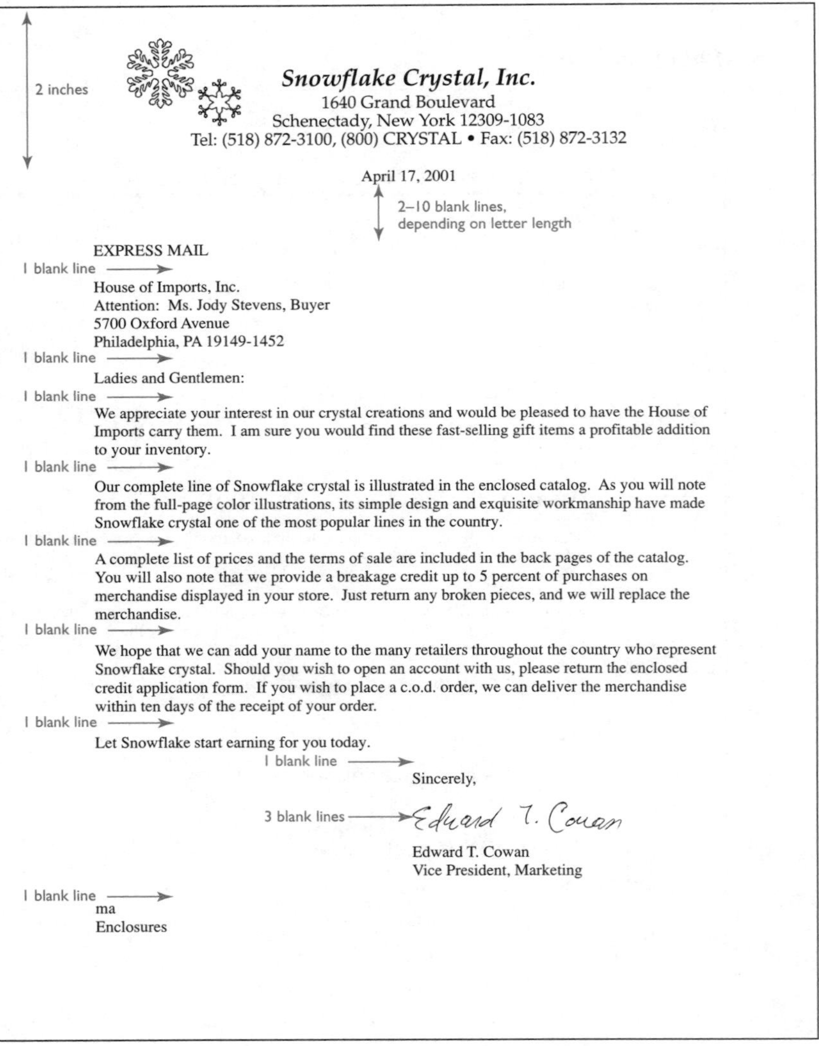

2 inches

Snowflake Crystal, Inc.
1640 Grand Boulevard
Schenectady, New York 12309-1083
Tel: (518) 872-3100, (800) CRYSTAL • Fax: (518) 872-3132

April 17, 2001

2–10 blank lines, depending on letter length

EXPRESS MAIL

1 blank line →

House of Imports, Inc.
Attention: Ms. Jody Stevens, Buyer
5700 Oxford Avenue
Philadelphia, PA 19149-1452

1 blank line →

Ladies and Gentlemen:

1 blank line →

We appreciate your interest in our crystal creations and would be pleased to have the House of Imports carry them. I am sure you would find these fast-selling gift items a profitable addition to your inventory.

1 blank line →

Our complete line of Snowflake crystal is illustrated in the enclosed catalog. As you will note from the full-page color illustrations, its simple design and exquisite workmanship have made Snowflake crystal one of the most popular lines in the country.

1 blank line →

A complete list of prices and the terms of sale are included in the back pages of the catalog. You will also note that we provide a breakage credit up to 5 percent of purchases on merchandise displayed in your store. Just return any broken pieces, and we will replace the merchandise.

1 blank line →

We hope that we can add your name to the many retailers throughout the country who represent Snowflake crystal. Should you wish to open an account with us, please return the enclosed credit application form. If you wish to place a c.o.d. order, we can deliver the merchandise within ten days of the receipt of your order.

1 blank line →

Let Snowflake start earning for you today.

1 blank line →

Sincerely,

3 blank lines → Edward T. Cowan

Edward T. Cowan
Vice President, Marketing

1 blank line →

ma
Enclosures

b. **The modified block letter style with indented paragraphs is also used frequently. All lines except the first line of each paragraph, the return address (if used), the date, and the closing lines begin at the left margin.**

modified block letter with indented paragraphs

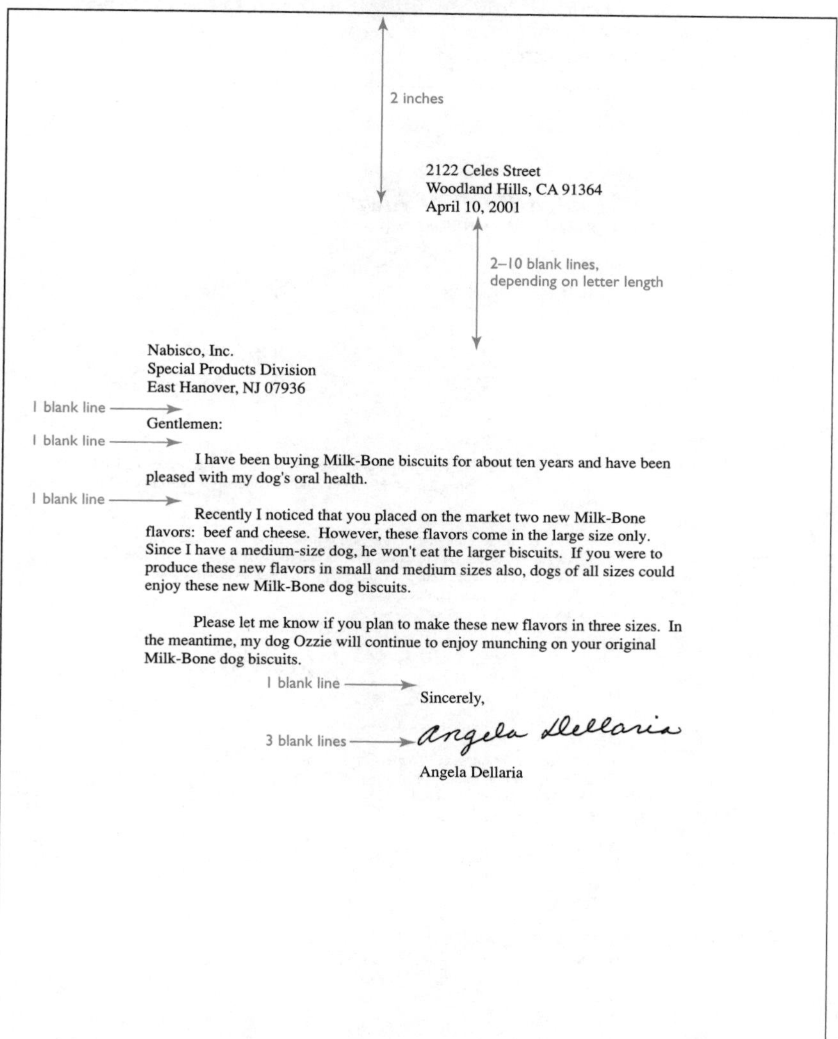

2122 Celes Street
Woodland Hills, CA 91364
April 10, 2001

Nabisco, Inc.
Special Products Division
East Hanover, NJ 07936

Gentlemen:

I have been buying Milk-Bone biscuits for about ten years and have been pleased with my dog's oral health.

Recently I noticed that you placed on the market two new Milk-Bone flavors: beef and cheese. However, these flavors come in the large size only. Since I have a medium-size dog, he won't eat the larger biscuits. If you were to produce these new flavors in small and medium sizes also, dogs of all sizes could enjoy these new Milk-Bone dog biscuits.

Please let me know if you plan to make these new flavors in three sizes. In the meantime, my dog Ozzie will continue to enjoy munching on your original Milk-Bone dog biscuits.

Sincerely,

Angela Dellaria

Angela Dellaria

12–3 Social Business

The social business letter style is used for social business correspondence. In this informal format the inside address is placed after the closing lines. The salutation may be followed by a comma instead of a colon, and the typed signature line is optional. Paragraphs are either indented or blocked.

No subject or attention lines are used in the social business letter style. Reference initials, enclosure notations, and copy notations are usually omitted on the original, but these parts may be included below the inside address on the file copy or on the copies for distribution. Leave

a double space after the inside address, and single-space on all copies except the original any notations that are to be included.

social business letter

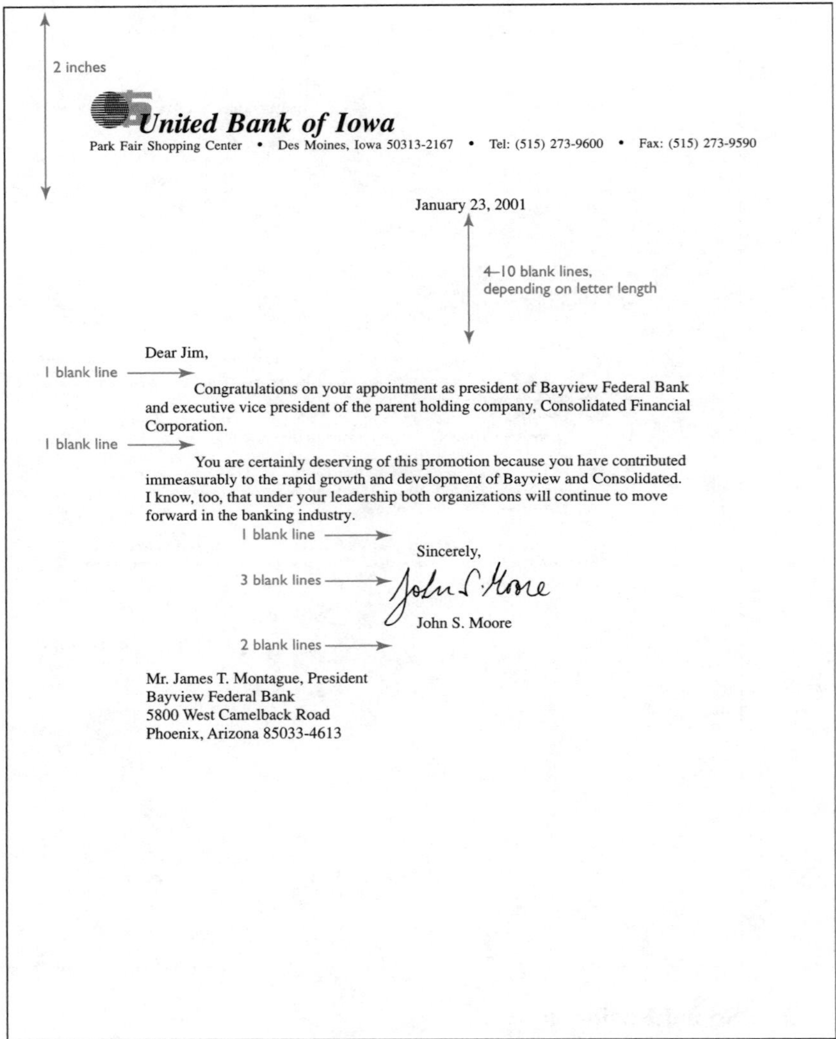

2 inches
United Bank of Iowa
Park Fair Shopping Center • Des Moines, Iowa 50313-2167 • Tel: (515) 273-9600 • Fax: (515) 273-9590
January 23, 2001
4–10 blank lines, depending on letter length
Dear Jim,
1 blank line
Congratulations on your appointment as president of Bayview Federal Bank and executive vice president of the parent holding company, Consolidated Financial Corporation.
1 blank line
You are certainly deserving of this promotion because you have contributed immeasurably to the rapid growth and development of Bayview and Consolidated. I know, too, that under your leadership both organizations will continue to move forward in the banking industry.
1 blank line
Sincerely,
3 blank lines
John S. Moore
2 blank lines
Mr. James T. Montague, President
Bayview Federal Bank
5800 West Camelback Road
Phoenix, Arizona 85033-4613

12–4 Simplified

In the simplified style all parts of the letter begin at the left margin. A subject line keyed in all capital letters replaces the salutation. Two blank lines are left before and after the subject line. No complimentary close is used in the simplified letter style. Instead, the signature line is keyed on the fifth line (leave four blank lines) below the last line of the message. Use all capital letters and a single line for the signature line.

simplified letter

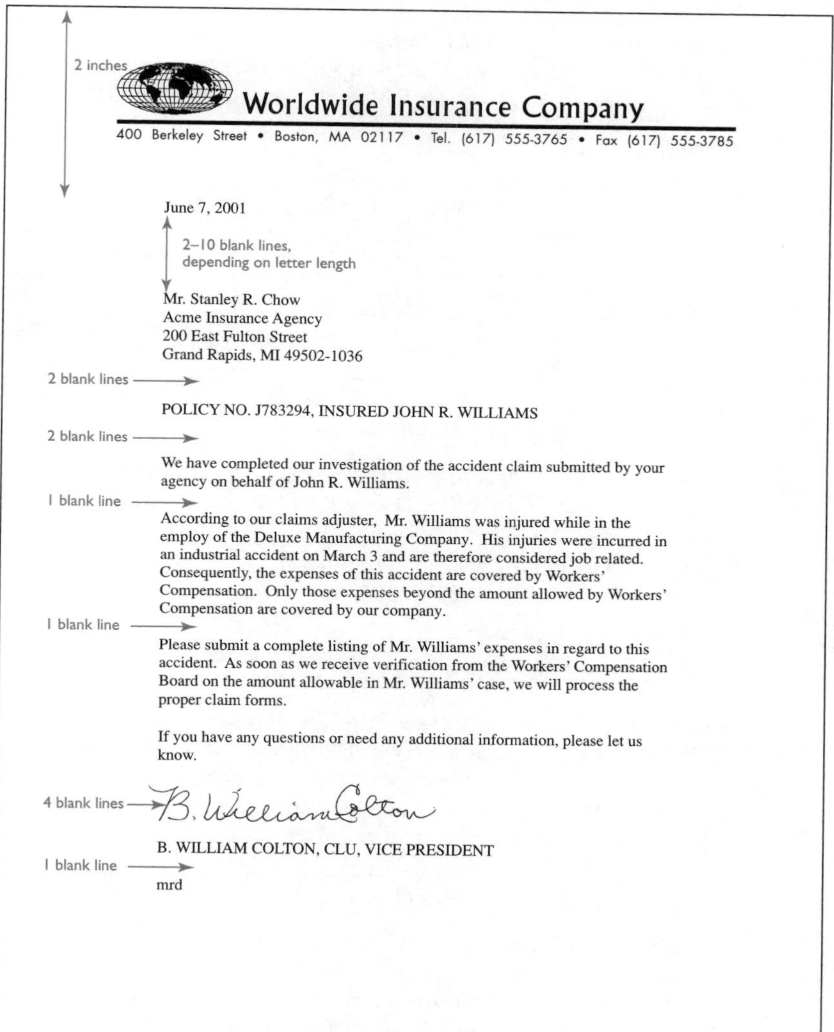
2 inches

Worldwide Insurance Company
400 Berkeley Street • Boston, MA 02117 • Tel. (617) 555-3765 • Fax (617) 555-3785

June 7, 2001

Mr. Stanley R. Chow
Acme Insurance Agency
200 East Fulton Street
Grand Rapids, MI 49502-1036

POLICY NO. J783294, INSURED JOHN R. WILLIAMS

We have completed our investigation of the accident claim submitted by your agency on behalf of John R. Williams.

According to our claims adjuster, Mr. Williams was injured while in the employ of the Deluxe Manufacturing Company. His injuries were incurred in an industrial accident on March 3 and are therefore considered job related. Consequently, the expenses of this accident are covered by Workers' Compensation. Only those expenses beyond the amount allowed by Workers' Compensation are covered by our company.

Please submit a complete listing of Mr. Williams' expenses in regard to this accident. As soon as we receive verification from the Workers' Compensation Board on the amount allowable in Mr. Williams' case, we will process the proper claim forms.

If you have any questions or need any additional information, please let us know.

B. William Colton

B. WILLIAM COLTON, CLU, VICE PRESIDENT

mrd

Letter Format and Placement of Major Parts

12–5 Margins and Vertical Placement With Word Processing Software

a. **Use a 2-inch top margin for the first page of a business letter printed on letterhead stationery. Any second and succeeding pages of a business letter have 1-inch top margins. Use left justification.**

Select the side margins according to the number of words in the letter and the size of the font used to prepare the letter. Set the margins *after*

keying the letter and using the word count feature of your word processing program.

The following tables may be used as guidelines for preparing standard and long letters. The first table applies to 12-point fonts;[2] the second table applies to 11-point and 10-point fonts.[3]

12-point fonts

Margin Settings for Business Letters Printed in 12-Point Fonts

Letter Length	*Number of Words*	*Margin Settings*		*Line Length*
		Left	*Right*	
Standard	Up to 200	1.5"	1.5"	5.5 inches
Long	200+	1"	1"	6.5 inches

11-point and 10-point fonts

Margin Settings for Business Letters Printed in 11-Point and 10-Point Fonts

Letter Length	*Number of Words*	*Margin Settings*		*Line Length*
		Left	*Right*	
Standard	Up to 200	1.75"	1.75"	5 inches
Long	200+	1.25"	1.25"	6 inches

b. Leave 2 or 3 blank lines between the date and inside address in letters with two or more pages. Balance single-page letters vertically by regulating the number of lines between the date and the inside address. Use the following procedures on your word processing program to achieve this balance *after* the margins have been set:

(1) Count the number of blank lines between the date and the inside address. (Example: 3 blank lines)

(2) Directly after the *last* line of the letter (usually reference initials or an enclosure notation), press the *Enter* key until the page break is reached. Count the number of blank lines from the last line of the letter until the page break. (Example: 6 blank lines)

(3) Total the two line counts. (Example: 6 + 3 = 9) Divide this total by two. (Example: 9 ÷ 2 = 4.5) Disregard any fractional part. (Example: 4 blank lines)

(4) Insert or delete blank lines, if necessary, to ensure that the number of blank lines between the *date and the inside address* EQUALS the result obtained in Step (3) above. Do not, however, leave fewer than two or more than ten blank lines between the date and the inside

---

[2]This table may also be used for fonts measuring 10 characters per inch. Other names used to describe this font size are 10 cpi, 10 pitch, and pica.

[3]This table may also be used for fonts measuring 12 characters per inch. Other names used to describe this font size are 12 cpi, 12 pitch, and elite.

address. (Example: Insert 1 additional blank line between the date and the inside address.)

(5) Delete any extra blank lines at the bottom of the page.

examples for balancing a letter vertically on the page

Blank Lines Between Date and Inside Address	*Blank Lines Between Letter End and Page Break*	*Sum of Blank Lines*	*Blank Lines ÷ 2 / Remainder Dropped*	*Revised Number of Blank Lines Needed Between Date and Inside Address*	*Number of Blank Lines to be Inserted or Deleted*
4	2	4+2=6	6÷2=3	3	–1
3	7	3+7=10	10÷2=5	5	+2
4	1	4+1=5	5÷2=2.5=2	2	–2
3	8	3+8=11	11÷2=5.5=5	5	+2
4	–1	4–1=3	3÷2=1.5=1	At least 2	–2

12–6 Margins and Vertical Placement With Typewriters

a. **Use a 2-inch top margin for the first page of a business letter prepared on printed letterhead stationery. Any second and succeeding pages of a business letter have 1-inch top margins.**

b. **For letters prepared on standard or electronic typewriters, use the following table to determine the side margins and the number of blank lines to be left between the date and the inside address.**

The table takes into consideration ordinary business letters—those without delivery notations, addressee notations, attention lines, subject lines, tables, and postscripts. Letters containing supplementary parts should be adjusted (in margin settings and/or number of lines between the date and the inside address) to accommodate these parts.

Letter Formatting Guide

Number of Words in Letter	*Left and Right Margin Settings:* *12 Point or 10 Pitch*	*Left and Right Margin Settings:* *10 or 11 Point or 12 Pitch*	*Blank Lines Between Date and Inside Address*
Under 200	1.5"	1.75"	4–10
Over 200	1"	1.25"	2–3

12–7 Return Address

a. **No return address is needed for business letters prepared on paper containing a complete company letterhead. Similarly, business letters prepared on word processing programs with a letter template do not require a return address.**

printed company letterhead

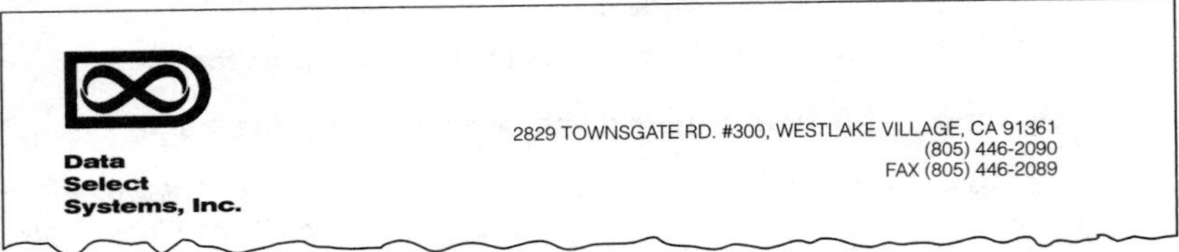

letterhead produced from a word processing template

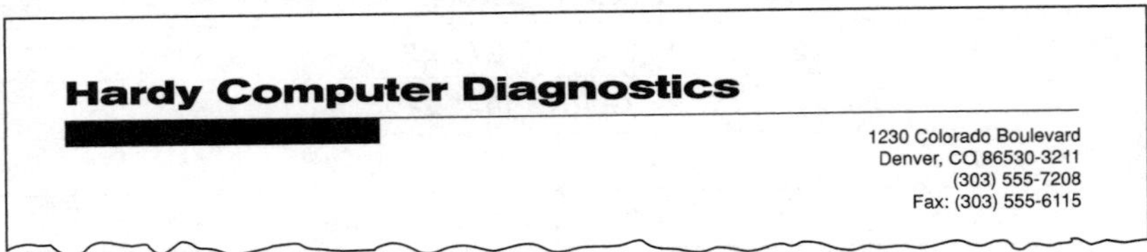

b. When plain bond paper or letterhead paper without a mailing address is used, a return address must be included.

On plain bond paper begin the return address so that the date is 2 inches from the top edge of the paper. Although the date appears directly below the last line of the return address, it is not considered part of the return address.

On letterhead paper without a mailing address, begin the return address a double space below the last line in the letterhead or end it so the date is 2 inches below the top edge of the paper. Select the option that places the return address in the lower position.

c. *Modified block or social business letter styles.* In the modified block or social business styles, each line of the return address may be centered. Lines in the return address may also (1) begin at the center of the page, (2) begin 0.5 inch to the left of the page center, or (3) align at the right margin. The return address in a modified block letter style is illustrated in Section 12–2b, page 321.

Full block or simplified letter styles. In the full block and simplified letter styles, all lines begin at the left margin.

return address in modified block or social business letter style without letterhead

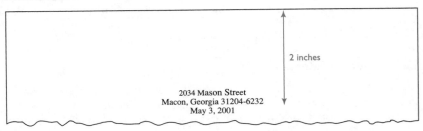

return address in full block or simplified letter style without letterhead

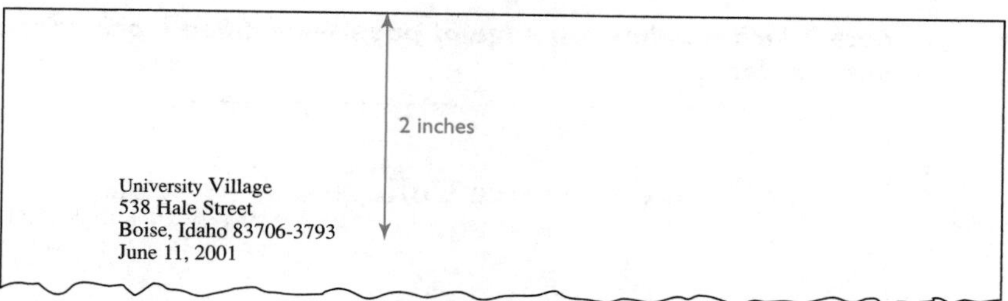

letterhead with return address ending 2 inches from top edge of paper—modified block or social business letter

Continental Floors
A Subsidary of Meredith Corporation

2 inches

1728 North King Street
Honolulu, HI 96819-5912
March 10, 2001

letterhead with return address begun a double space below letterhead—full block or simplified letter

Committee for the Reelection of the Governor
A Nonprofit Organization

Endorsed by:

1 blank line →

9978 Access Road
Minneapolis, MN 55431-3642
September 27, 2001

12–8 Date

a. On letterhead paper with a mailing address, place the date a double space below the last line in the letterhead or allocate a 2-inch margin from the top edge of the paper. Select the procedure that places the date in the lower position.

Modified block and social business letter styles. In modified block and social business letters, the date may be (1) centered, (2) begun at the center of the page, or (3) aligned with the right margin.

Full block and simplified letter styles. In full block or simplified letters, place the date at the left margin.

date 2 inches below top edge of paper—modified block or social business letter

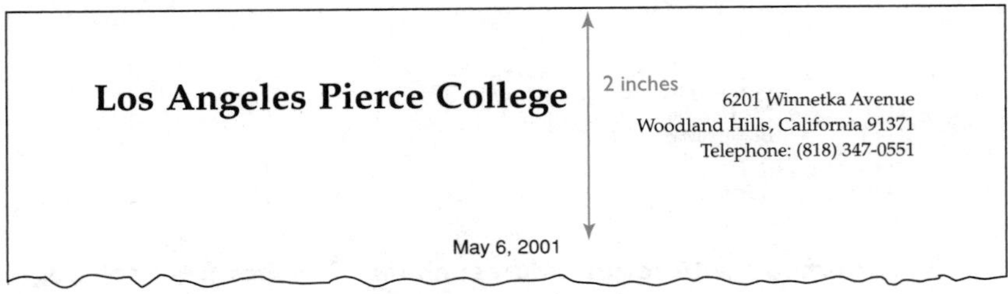
Los Angeles Pierce College

6201 Winnetka Avenue
Woodland Hills, California 91371
Telephone: (818) 347-0551

May 6, 2001

date placed a double space below letterhead—full block letter

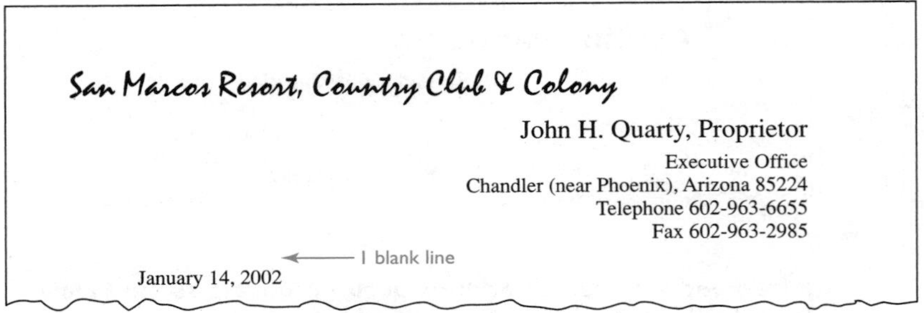
San Marcos Resort, Country Club & Colony

John H. Quarty, Proprietor

Executive Office
Chandler (near Phoenix), Arizona 85224
Telephone 602-963-6655
Fax 602-963-2985

January 14, 2002

b. In letters requiring return addresses, place the date on the line directly below the last line of the return address. A date used with the return address in a complete letter is illustrated in Section 12–2b, p. 321.

date with return address

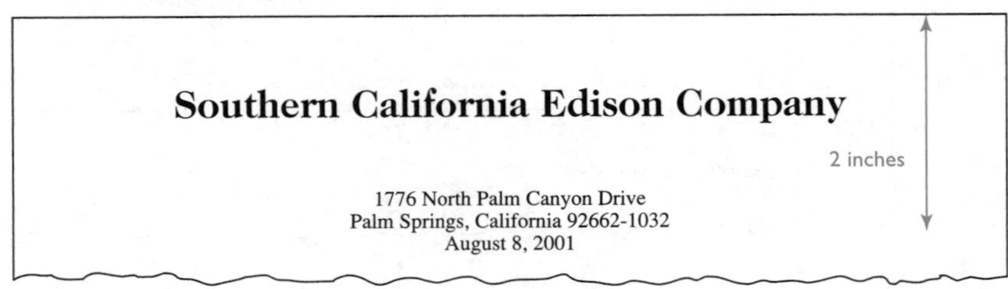
Southern California Edison Company

1776 North Palm Canyon Drive
Palm Springs, California 92662-1032
August 8, 2001

12–9 Addressee and Delivery Notations

a. Addressee notations such as *Personal* and *Confidential* are entered in all capital letters a double space above the inside address.

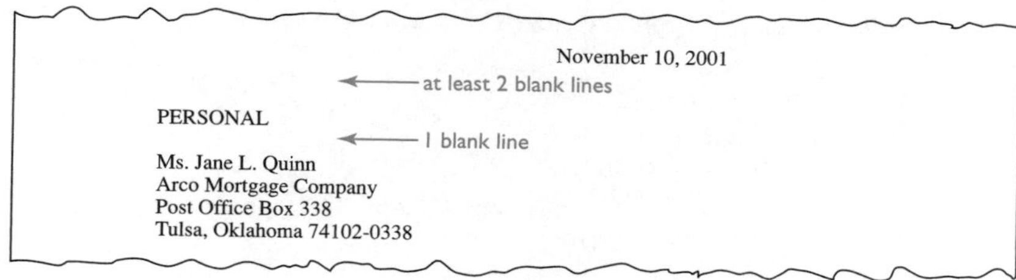
November 10, 2001

PERSONAL

Ms. Jane L. Quinn
Arco Mortgage Company
Post Office Box 338
Tulsa, Oklahoma 74102-0338

b. **Delivery notations such as *Certified Mail, Express Mail, Federal Express, Air Mail, Registered Mail, Fax Transmittal,* and *Messenger Delivery* are entered in all capital letters either (1) a double space above the inside address or (2) a single or double space below the reference initials or enclosure notation, whichever appears last. A delivery notation is illustrated in a complete letter in Section 12–2a, p. 320.**

delivery notations a double space above inside address

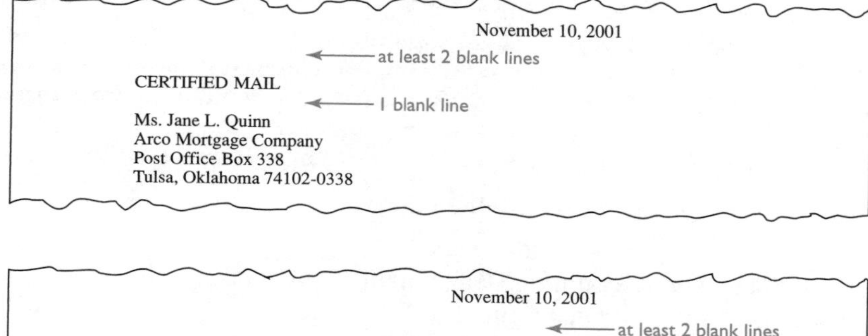
November 10, 2001

CERTIFIED MAIL

Ms. Jane L. Quinn
Arco Mortgage Company
Post Office Box 338
Tulsa, Oklahoma 74102-0338

November 10, 2001

FAX TRANSMITTAL

Ms. Jane L. Quinn
Arco Mortgage Company
Post Office Box 338
Tulsa, Oklahoma 74102-0338

delivery notation after reference initials or enclosure notation

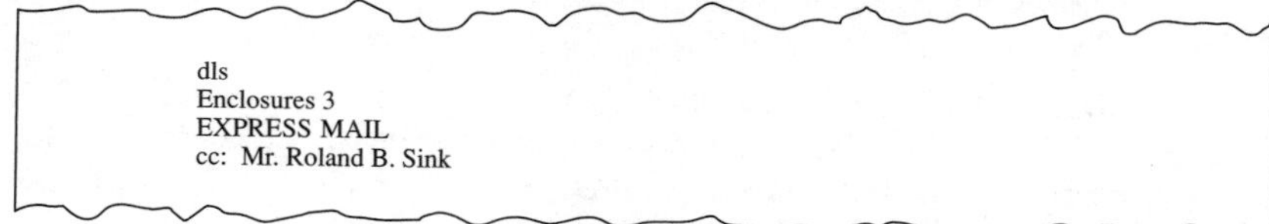
dls
Enclosures 3
EXPRESS MAIL
cc: Mr. Roland B. Sink

c. **If an addressee and a delivery notation appear in the same letter, place the addressee notation on the third line above the inside address and the delivery notation on the line directly below. Use all capital letters for both notations. Leave *at least* two blank lines between the date and the addressee notation.**

Business Letters 12

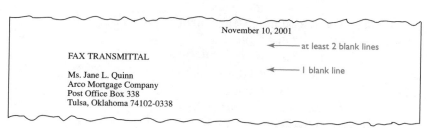

addressee and delivery notations in same letter

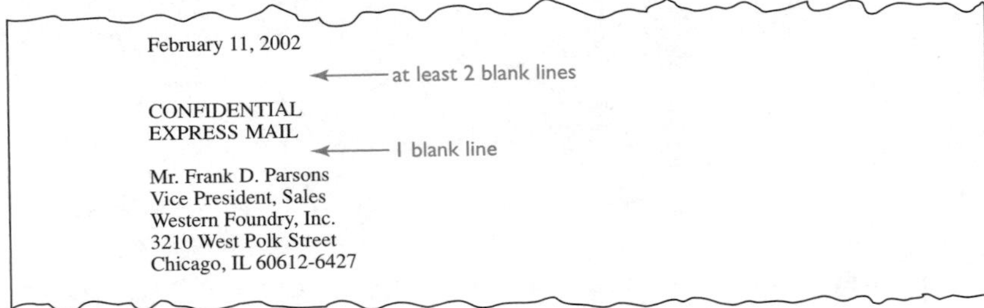
February 11, 2002

CONFIDENTIAL
EXPRESS MAIL

Mr. Frank D. Parsons
Vice President, Sales
Western Foundry, Inc.
3210 West Polk Street
Chicago, IL 60612-6427

12–10 Inside Address

a. **The inside address follows the date and any delivery or addressee notations. It contains some or all of the following: courtesy title, full name, professional title, department name, company name, street or mailing address, city, state, and zip code. Single-space and begin at the left margin those parts necessary to direct the letter to the addressee.**

Place the courtesy title and full name on the first line. The professional title and department name have no specific line designations; they should be positioned to balance with the remaining parts of the inside address. The street or mailing address appears on a separate line. Arrange the city, state, and zip code together on another separate line.

arrangement of an inside address

Ms. Margaret A. Williamson
Manager, Accounting Department
General Insurance Company
6750 East Independence Boulevard
Charlotte, North Carolina 28212-7610

Mr. Jeffrey Davis, Manager
Department of Human Resources
Eastern Federal Bank
3452 West Sixth Street
Charlotte, NC 28212-4310

b. **Abbreviate only the courtesy titles *Mr., Mrs.,* and *Dr.* The courtesy title *Ms.* is not an abbreviation; its only form is *Ms.***

Spell out all street designations such as *Street, Avenue,* and *Boulevard. Boulevard* may be abbreviated, however, with exceptionally long street names. Spell out the state name or use the two-letter post office abbreviation, whichever form achieves balance with the remaining lines.

An inside address may contain from a minimum of two lines to a maximum of six lines.

two-line inside address

Holiday Inn
Cedar Rapids, IA 52406

six-line inside address

Mr. M. J. Fujimoto
Airline Training Specialist
Division of Personnel Instruction
TransAmerica-Continental Airlines
12700 East Funston Street
Wichita, Kansas 67207-3402

c. ***Modified block, full block, and simplified letter styles.*** **In the modified block, full block, and simplified letter styles, the inside address usually follows the date. The number of blank lines between the date and the inside address is determined by the length of the letter.**

For letters prepared with word processing software, refer to Section 12–5 for detailed instructions on setting margins and determining the number of blank lines to leave between the date and inside address. Section 12–6 provides the same information for letters prepared on electronic or regular typewriters.

inside address in modified block letter

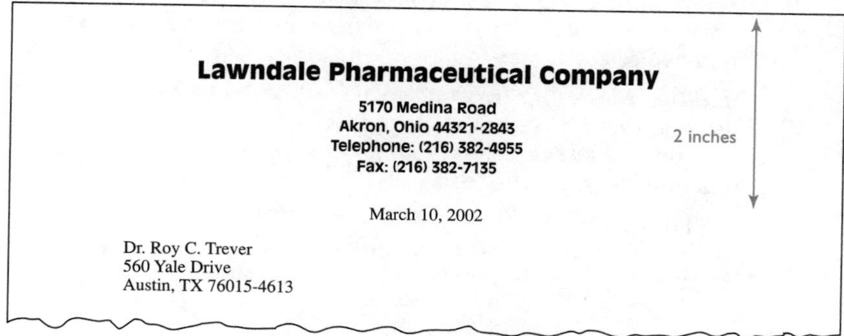

Lawndale Pharmaceutical Company
5170 Medina Road
Akron, Ohio 44321-2843
Telephone: (216) 382-4955
Fax: (216) 382-7135

March 10, 2002

Dr. Roy C. Trever
560 Yale Drive
Austin, TX 76015-4613

d. ***The social business letter style.*** **In the social business letter, the inside address is placed after the closing lines. If the typed signature line is omitted, leave five or six blank lines after the complimentary close before beginning the inside address. If a typed signature line is included, leave two blank lines after the typed signature before beginning the inside address.**

social business letter without typed signature

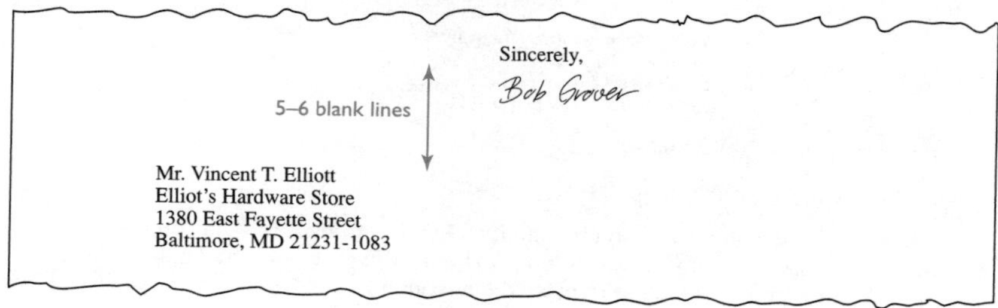

Sincerely,

Bob Grover

Mr. Vincent T. Elliott
Elliot's Hardware Store
1380 East Fayette Street
Baltimore, MD 21231-1083

social business letter with typed signature

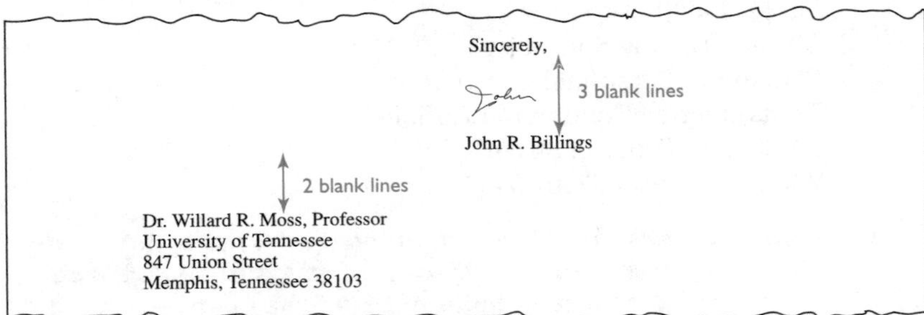
Sincerely,

3 blank lines

John R. Billings

2 blank lines

Dr. Willard R. Moss, Professor
University of Tennessee
847 Union Street
Memphis, Tennessee 38103

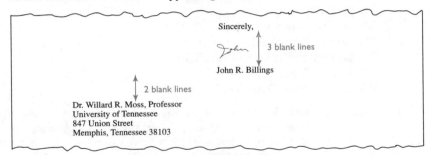

12–11 Attention Line

a. The attention line is used for directing correspondence to an individual or department within a company while still officially addressing the letter to the organization. It is also useful for directing correspondence to a person whose name is unknown.

b. The modern trend is to place the attention line in the inside address on the line directly below the company name and use the same format for the envelope address.[4]

Modified block and full block letter styles. As an alternate to including the attention line in the inside address, it may be placed at the left margin a double space below the last line of the inside address in the modified and full block styles.

Use (1) a combination of initial capital letters and lowercase letters or (2) all capital letters. Using a colon after the word *Attention* is optional. An attention line is illustrated in a complete letter in Section 12–2a, page 320.

Simplified letter style. In the simplified letter style, the attention line is included in the inside address and placed directly below the organization's name. The attention line is treated as any other line in the inside address. The word *Attention* may or may not be followed by a colon.

Social business letter style. The attention line is not used in the social business style.

attention line included in inside address

Valley Manufacturing Company
Attention: General Manager
18600 Sierra Bonita Boulevard
San Bernardino, CA 91763-5201

[4]Correspondence using an attention line is addressed to the company, not an individual. Therefore, the name of the company should appear before the attention line. The U.S. Postal Service recommendation to place the attention line before the company name does not follow this protocol.

attention line at left margin below inside address

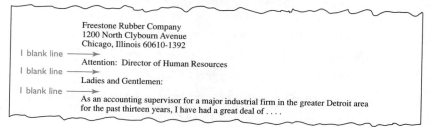

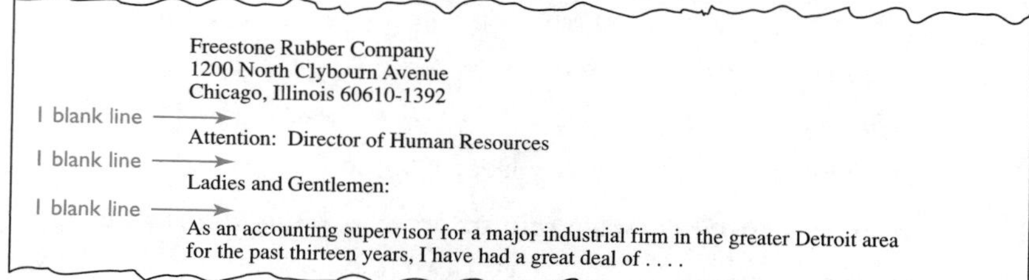
Freestone Rubber Company
1200 North Clybourn Avenue
Chicago, Illinois 60610-1392
1 blank line →
Attention: Director of Human Resources
1 blank line →
Ladies and Gentlemen:
1 blank line →
As an accounting supervisor for a major industrial firm in the greater Detroit area for the past thirteen years, I have had a great deal of . . . .

12–12 Salutation

a. The content of the salutation depends upon to whom the letter is addressed in the inside address and the degree of familiarity between the addressee and the writer.[5] See Section 12-12b-f for selecting standard salutations.

Modified block and full block letter styles. Begin the salutation at the left margin and place it a double space below the last line of the inside address or the attention line, if used. Conclude the salutation with a colon for the mixed punctuation format; use no ending punctuation mark for the open punctuation format.

Simplified letter style. Omit the salutation in the simplified letter style.

Social business letter style. In the social business style, position the salutation at the left margin after the date. Use the mixed punctuation format; place a colon or a comma after the salutation.

salutation in a modified block or full block letter

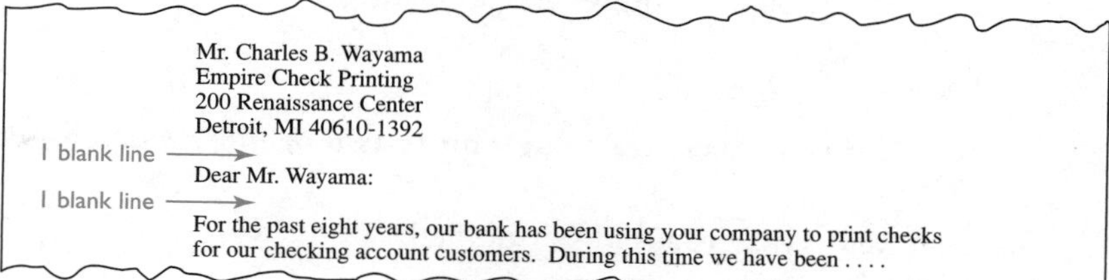
Mr. Charles B. Wayama
Empire Check Printing
200 Renaissance Center
Detroit, MI 40610-1392
1 blank line →
Dear Mr. Wayama:
1 blank line →
For the past eight years, our bank has been using your company to print checks for our checking account customers. During this time we have been . . . .

salutation in a social business letter

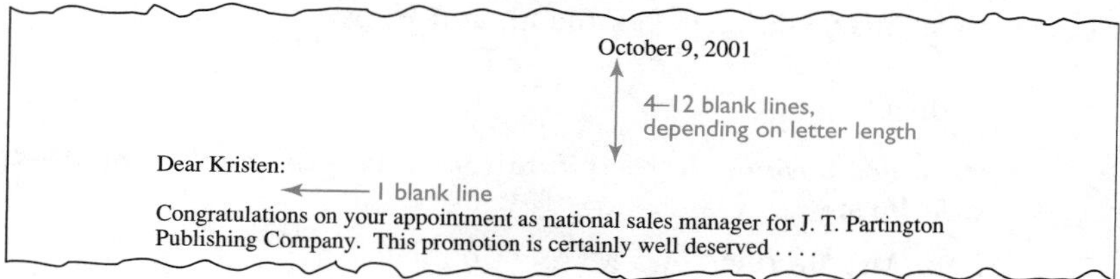
October 9, 2001
4–12 blank lines, depending on letter length
Dear Kristen:
← 1 blank line
Congratulations on your appointment as national sales manager for J. T. Partington Publishing Company. This promotion is certainly well deserved . . . .

[5]See Sections 11–11 through 11–14 for additional information on the proper use of formal titles, salutations, and complimentary closes.

b. In letters addressed to individuals, use one of the following salutations, depending upon the degree of formality desired. Use a colon after the salutation if mixed punctuation is used; use no punctuation mark if open punctuation is used.

informal salutation

Dear Fred: Dear Connie:

standard business letter salutation to a single addressee

Dear Mr. Hampton: Dear Miss Baker:

Dear Ms. Harris: Dear Mrs. Chin:

standard business letter salutation to two or more men

Dear Mr. Andrews and Mr. Cranston:

or

Dear Mr. Andrews, Mr. Cranston, and Mr. Phillips:

or

Dear Messrs. Andrews, Cranston, and Phillips:

or

Gentlemen:

***standard business letter salutation to two or more women—courtesy title* Ms.**

Dear Ms. Bailey and Ms. Johnson:

or

Dear Ms. Bailey, Ms. Horike, and Ms. Johnson:

or

Dear Mses. Bailey, Horike, and Johnson:

or

Ladies:

***standard business letter salutation to two or more women—courtesy title* Miss**

Dear Miss Frazier and Miss Goodlad:

or

Dear Miss Frazier, Miss Goodlad, and Miss Hoover:

or

Dear Misses Frazier, Goodland, and Hoover:

or

Ladies:

***standard business letter salutation to two or more women—courtesy title* Mrs.**

Dear Mrs. Koonce and Mrs. O'Donnell:

or

Dear Mrs. Bedrosian, Mrs. Koonce, and Mrs. O'Donnell:

or

Dear Mesdames Bedrosian, Koonce, and O'Donnell:

or

Mesdames: *or* Ladies:

standard business letter salutation to two or more persons with different courtesy titles

Dear Ms. Knott and Mr. Wade:

Dear Ms. Gallagher, Ms. Lee, and Mrs. Moreno:

Dear Mrs. Andrino, Ms. Hopi, Mr. Lopez, and Ms. Mullens-King:

Ladies: (women only)

Gentlemen: (men only)

Ladies and Gentlemen:

Dear Colleagues: (or other appropriate general reference designation)

standard salutations to persons with professional titles

Dear Dr. Parsons:

Dear Professor Bredow:

Dear Colonel Jones:

formal salutations for certain government officials and religious dignitaries

Sir:

Excellency:

Reverend Sir:

Your Eminence:

c. **If the gender of an addressee is unknown, use the full name of the person without a courtesy title. Use the courtesy title *Ms.* for a woman unless another title is specified by the addressee.**

full name without courtesy title

Orolyn Ruenz (Dear Orolyn Ruenz:)

Chris Meister (Dear Chris Meister:)

J. T. Weyenberg (Dear J. T. Weyenberg:)

courtesy title for a woman

Ms. Sharon Reember (Dear Ms. Reember:)

Ms. Laura Nguyen (Dear Ms. Nguyen:)

d. **In correspondence addressed to companies, associations, or other groups, use one of the following salutations:**

salutations for groups composed of men and women

Ladies and Gentlemen: Gentlemen and Ladies:

salutation for groups composed entirely of men

Gentlemen:

salutations for groups composed entirely of women

Mesdames: Ladies:

e. **Letters addressed to a firm but directed to the attention of an individual within the company receive the salutation used to open a letter to a group: *Gentlemen, Ladies and Gentlemen, Gentlemen and Ladies, Mesdames,* or *Ladies*.**

Arroyo Textile Manufacturing Company
Attention Accounts Receivable Manager
2850 Central Avenue, N.W.
Albuquerque, New Mexico 87105-1742
← 1 blank line
Ladies and Gentlemen:
← 1 blank line
On September 10 we purchased from your company twelve 50-yard bolts of Royal Luster velvet upholstery fabric (Invoice No. GY-14953). Payment for . . . .

f. **Letters to an undetermined individual or group of individuals should generally be avoided. When used, such letters contain no inside address and use *To Whom It May Concern:* as the salutation.**

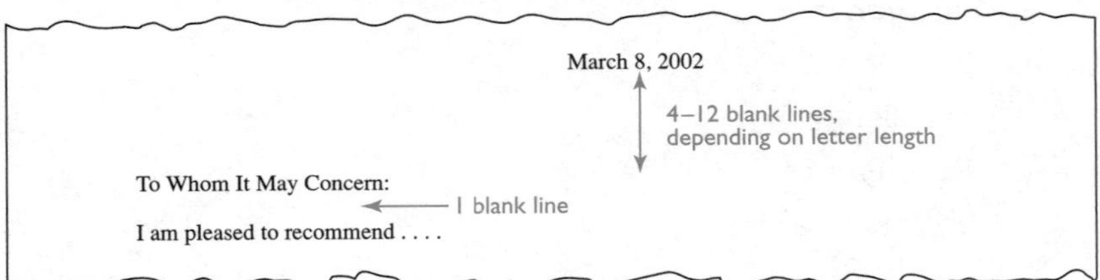
March 8, 2002
4–12 blank lines, depending on letter length
To Whom It May Concern:
← 1 blank line
I am pleased to recommend . . . .

12–13 Subject Line

a. **The subject line briefly describes the contents of the letter.**

Modified block and full block letter styles. **For modified and full block letters, begin the subject line at the left margin a double space below the salutation. Double-space after the subject line.**

Use (1) initial capital letters for the main words[6] or (2) all capital letters. The word *Subject* followed by a colon usually introduces the line. The subject line is illustrated in a full block letter in Section 12-1, p. 319.

If an attention line appears in the same letter a double-space below the inside address, use the same format for both the attention and the subject lines.

[6]Main words are (1) the first and last words; (2) all words except the articles a, an, the; (3) the conjunctions *and, but, or, nor;* (4) the word *to* used with an infinitive; and (5) prepositions containing two or three letters (*of, for, on,* etc.).

subject line at left margin

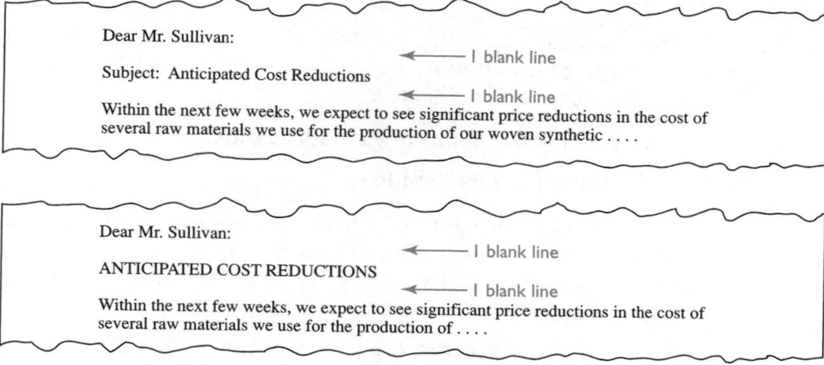

Dear Mr. Sullivan:

← 1 blank line

Subject: Anticipated Cost Reductions

← 1 blank line

Within the next few weeks, we expect to see significant price reductions in the cost of several raw materials we use for the production of our woven synthetic . . . .

Dear Mr. Sullivan:

← 1 blank line

ANTICIPATED COST REDUCTIONS

← 1 blank line

Within the next few weeks, we expect to see significant price reductions in the cost of several raw materials we use for the production of . . . .

two-line subject with book title

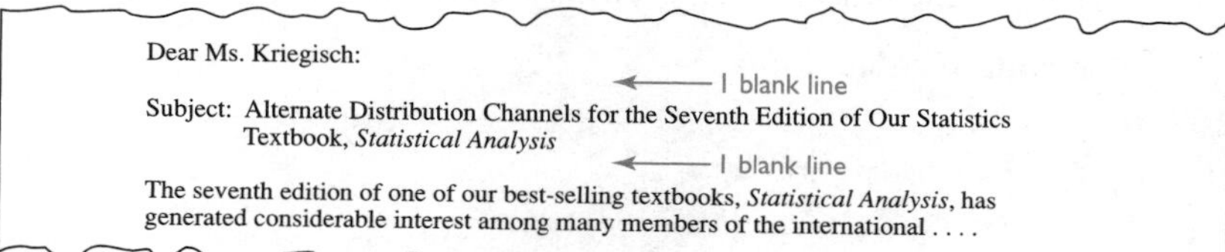

Dear Ms. Kriegisch:

← 1 blank line

Subject: Alternate Distribution Channels for the Seventh Edition of Our Statistics Textbook, *Statistical Analysis*

← 1 blank line

The seventh edition of one of our best-selling textbooks, *Statistical Analysis*, has generated considerable interest among many members of the international . . . .

attention and subject lines in the same letter

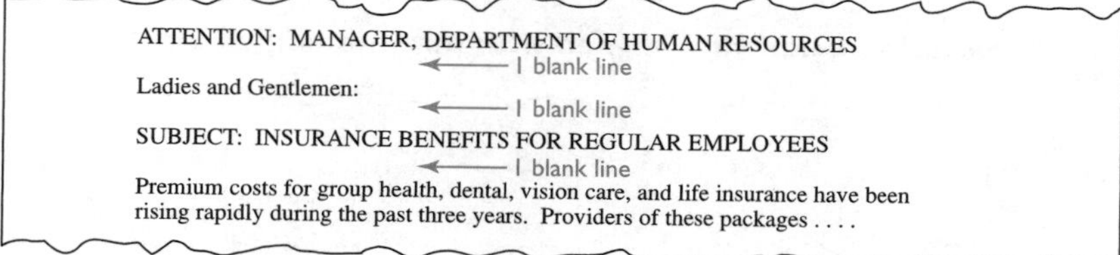

ATTENTION: MANAGER, DEPARTMENT OF HUMAN RESOURCES

← 1 blank line

Ladies and Gentlemen:

← 1 blank line

SUBJECT: INSURANCE BENEFITS FOR REGULAR EMPLOYEES

← 1 blank line

Premium costs for group health, dental, vision care, and life insurance have been rising rapidly during the past three years. Providers of these packages . . . .

Simplified letter style. **The subject line replaces the salutation in the simplified style. Begin the subject line at the left margin a triple space below the inside address. Type it in all capital letters without the term *Subject:*. Triple-space between the subject line and the first line of the body of the letter.**

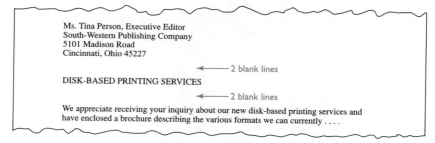

Ms. Tina Person, Executive Editor
South-Western Publishing Company
5101 Madison Road
Cincinnati, Ohio 45227

← 2 blank lines

DISK-BASED PRINTING SERVICES

← 2 blank lines

We appreciate receiving your inquiry about our new disk-based printing services and have enclosed a brochure describing the various formats we can currently . . . .

Social business letter style. A subject line is not used in the social business letter style.

b. Insurance and financial institutions, attorneys, and government offices often use the abbreviation *Re:* or *In re:* in place of the word *Subject:* at the beginning of the subject line.

Re: Policy 489-6342, Insured Michael T. Block

IN RE: TOLBERT VS. FEINBERG

c. When initiating or replying to correspondence that has a special policy number, order number, account number, or other such reference, include this information in a subject line or in a specific reference below and aligned with the date.

If guide words are not printed on the letterhead, supply labels such as *When replying, refer to:, File No.:, In reply to:, Re:, Your reference:, Refer to:,* etc. These notations are typed in initial capital and lowercase letters; they are placed a double space below the date.

standard subject line

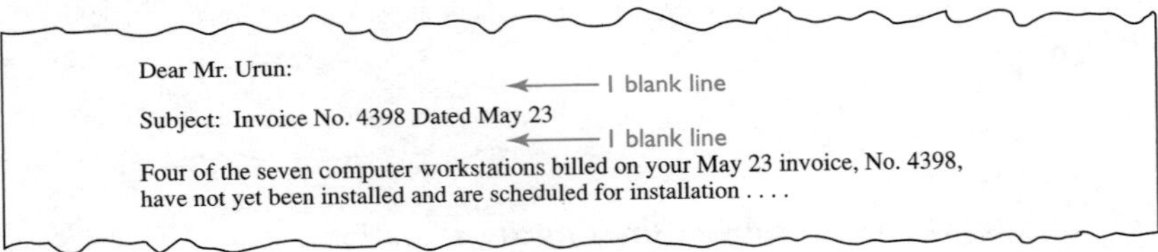

notation below and aligned with date—modified block letter

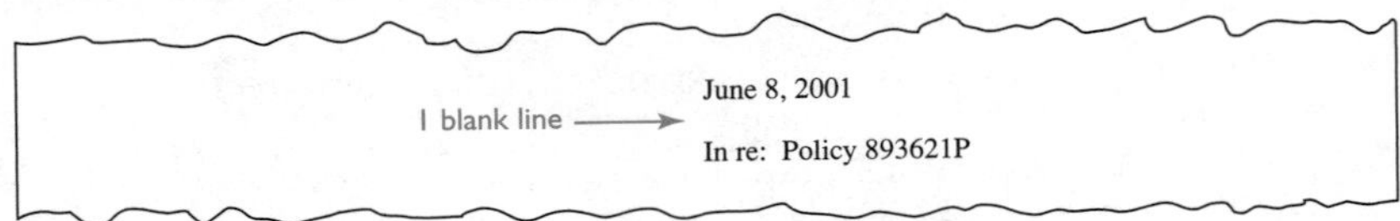

d. Some companies prefer to place the subject line above the salutation. In such cases begin the subject line a double space below the inside address. If an attention line follows the inside address, then begin the subject line a double space below the attention line.

Use (1) initial capital letters with lowercase letters or (2) all capital letters. The caption *Subject, Re,* or *In re* precedes the content and is followed by a colon. If an attention line appears in the same letter, use the same format for both lines.

Double-space after the subject line to begin the salutation.

subject line above salutation

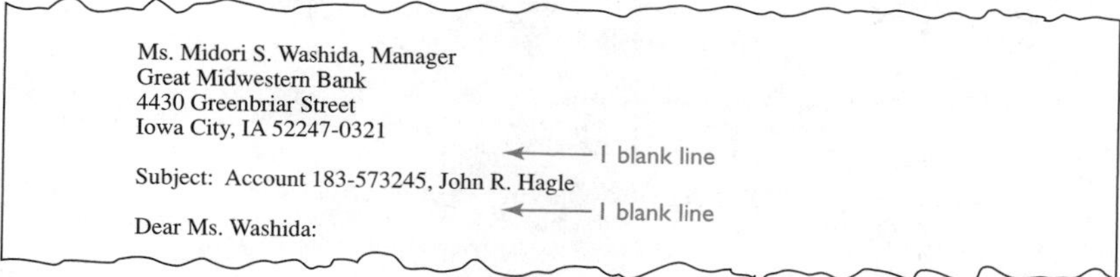

Ms. Midori S. Washida, Manager
Great Midwestern Bank
4430 Greenbriar Street
Iowa City, IA 52247-0321

Subject: Account 183-573245, John R. Hagle

Dear Ms. Washida:

subject and attention lines above salutation

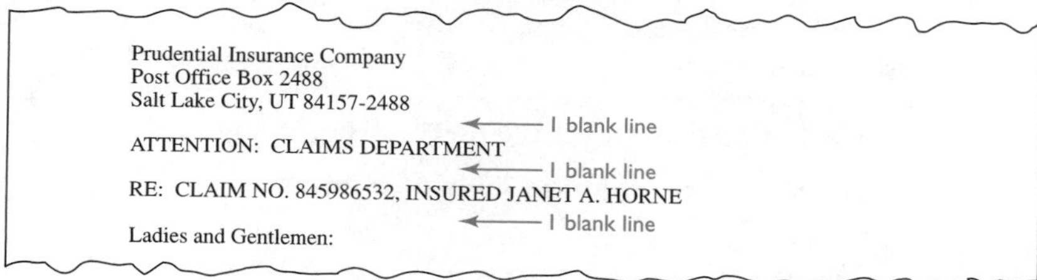

Prudential Insurance Company
Post Office Box 2488
Salt Lake City, UT 84157-2488

ATTENTION: CLAIMS DEPARTMENT

RE: CLAIM NO. 845986532, INSURED JANET A. HORNE

Ladies and Gentlemen:

12–14 Body of the Letter

a. The body of the letter contains the message. It begins a double space below the salutation or the subject line, if used. Single-space paragraphs within the body of the letter and double-space between each paragraph.

Modified block and social business letter styles. **The first line of paragraphs in the modified block or social business letter styles may be either blocked or indented 0.5 inch.**

Full block and simplified letter styles. **Always block the first line of paragraphs in the full block and simplified letter styles.**

body of letter with blocked paragraphs

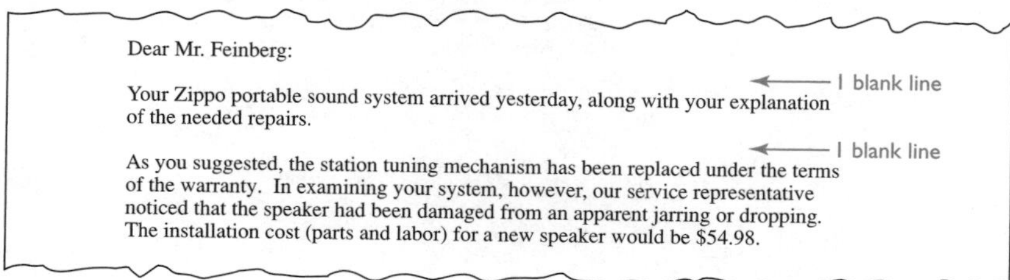

Dear Mr. Feinberg:

Your Zippo portable sound system arrived yesterday, along with your explanation of the needed repairs.

As you suggested, the station tuning mechanism has been replaced under the terms of the warranty. In examining your system, however, our service representative noticed that the speaker had been damaged from an apparent jarring or dropping. The installation cost (parts and labor) for a new speaker would be $54.98.

body of letter with indented paragraphs

Dear Mrs. Russell:

← 1 blank line

We learned a great deal from your interesting presentation on the dynamics of color that you gave to Dr. Sullivan's business management class last Saturday. Thank you for sharing your valuable ideas with us.

← 1 blank line

The class especially appreciated the material you gave us on the Wilson color wheel. Everyone agreed that this information will certainly be helpful in making color selections for the employee work environment and ensuring comfortable working conditions.

b. **Quoted materials, listings, tables, and graphics are often included within the body of a letter. All these visual enhancements are placed within the left and right margins. See Section 1-25 for instructions on formatting long quotations, Section 13-9 for preparing horizontal and vertical listings, and Section 13-11 for preparing tables and charts.**

quoted material within the body of a letter

recommendations have been based on an economic forecast published in one of our leading trade magazines. This forecast appeared in an article on pages 101–103 of the September issue of *Bankers' Financial World*:

← 1 blank line

> Although interest rates for the next quarter will remain at the same low rate, building of new homes and commercial buildings will continue to decline. The large number of bank foreclosures on real property during the last year has driven values down so low that builders are ceasing to develop new projects.

↔ 0.5" ↔ 0.5"

← 1 blank line

The article, "Foreclosures and Their Rippling Effect on the Banking Industry," was written by Joseph L. Langham, a prominent economist and professor at Stanford University. Dr. Langham is noted for his success in predicting trends and . . . .

listing within the body of a letter

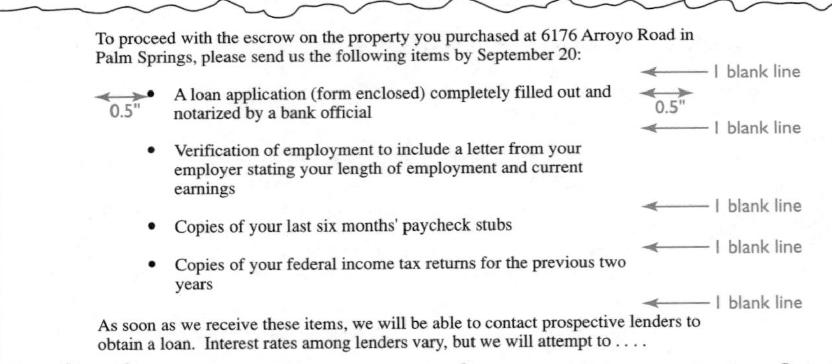

To proceed with the escrow on the property you purchased at 6176 Arroyo Road in Palm Springs, please send us the following items by September 20:

← 1 blank line

- A loan application (form enclosed) completely filled out and notarized by a bank official

↔ 0.5" ↔ 0.5"

← 1 blank line

- Verification of employment to include a letter from your employer stating your length of employment and current earnings

← 1 blank line

- Copies of your last six months' paycheck stubs

← 1 blank line

- Copies of your federal income tax returns for the previous two years

← 1 blank line

As soon as we receive these items, we will be able to contact prospective lenders to obtain a loan. Interest rates among lenders vary, but we will attempt to . . . .

table within the body of a letter

We certainly appreciate your interest in purchasing a catalog that illustrates our fine Foster porcelain figurines. The following catalogs are presently available for purchase:

← 1–2 blank lines

2001/02 Foster Catalog Set		
Current Retail Pricing		
Catalog or Supplement	**Price for Members**	**Price for Nonmembers**
Foster Core Catalog	$16.25	$32.50
Foster Limited Edition Catalog	8.75	17.50
Gres Supplement	2.50	5.00
Elite Catalog	10.00	20.00
Limited Edition Gres Catalog	7.50	15.00
Gres Catalog	5.00	10.00
Complete Catalog Set With Price List	$50.00	$100.00

← 1–2 blank lines

Both the *Foster Core Catalog* and the *Foster Limited Edition Catalog* contain color photographs of the figurines currently available. All other catalogs contain black-and-white photographs. As a member of the Foster Collectors' Society, you are eligible for the members' price. Shipping and handling . . . .

12–15 Complimentary Close

a. **The complimentary close begins the closing lines of a letter. The closing selected to conclude a business letter must conform to the formality of the salutation. Sample salutations as well as suitable complimentary closes are listed here.**

formal correspondence

Salutation	*Complimentary Close*
Dear Mr. President	Respectfully Very truly yours Sincerely yours
Excellency	Respectfully Very truly yours Sincerely yours
Dear Senator Monroe	Respectfully Very truly yours Sincerely yours

general business correspondence

Salutation	*Complimentary Close*
Dear Mr. Siebert	Sincerely yours Sincerely
Dear Ms. Mendoza	Sincerely yours Sincerely
Dear Dr. Wilson	Sincerely yours Sincerely

Salutation	*Complimentary Close*
Ladies and Gentlemen	Sincerely yours Sincerely

informal business correspondence

Salutation	*Complimentary Close*
Dear Bill	Sincerely yours Sincerely Cordially yours Cordially
Dear Karen	Sincerely yours Sincerely Cordially yours Cordially

b. **Place the complimentary close a double space below the last line of the message. Capitalize only the first word. Conclude the complimentary close with a comma for the mixed punctuation format; use no ending punctuation mark for the open punctuation format.**

Modified block and social business letter styles. **For the modified block and social business letter styles, begin the closing lines at the center of the page.**

Full block letter style. **Begin the closing lines at the left margin when using the full block letter style.**

Simplified letter style. **The complimentary close is omitted in the simplified letter style.**

complimentary close begun at page center

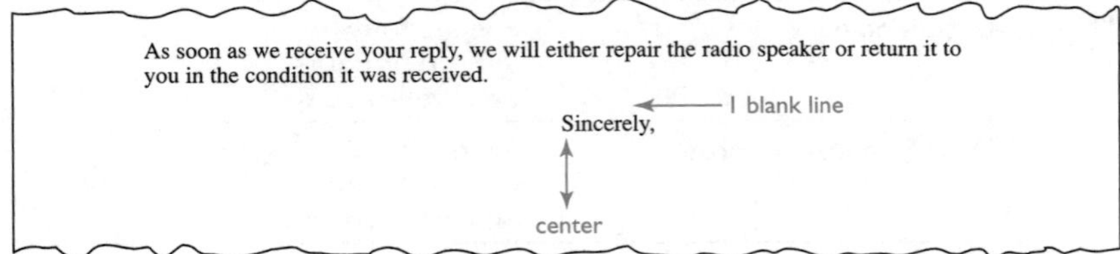
As soon as we receive your reply, we will either repair the radio speaker or return it to you in the condition it was received.
1 blank line
Sincerely,
center

complimentary close begun at left margin

May I please have an opportunity to review my qualifications with you? Just call me at 349-8211, and I will be pleased to come to your office for an interview.

1 blank line

Sincerely yours,

12–16 Signature Block

a. The signature block identifies the writer of the letter by name. In most cases the writer's professional title is also included.

Modified and full block letter styles. Some business firms include the name of the company in the closing lines. In such cases the name of the company is placed in all capital letters a double space below and aligned with the complimentary close.

Company signature lines are used only in the modified block and full block letter styles. Use of the company name in the closing lines is illustrated in a full block letter in Section 12–1, p. 319.

modified block letter

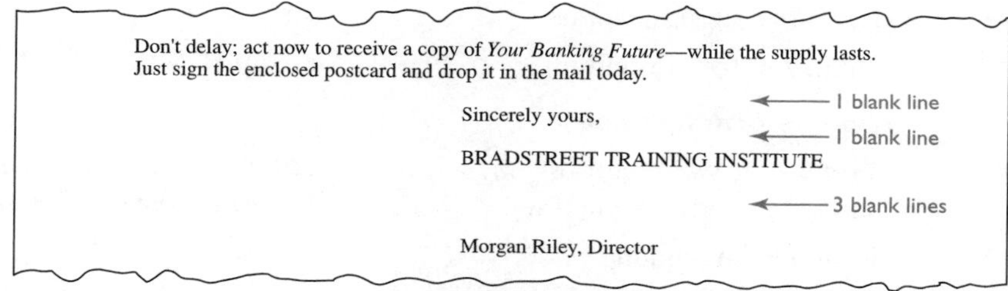

Don't delay; act now to receive a copy of *Your Banking Future*—while the supply lasts.
Just sign the enclosed postcard and drop it in the mail today.

Sincerely yours,

BRADSTREET TRAINING INSTITUTE

Morgan Riley, Director

full block letter

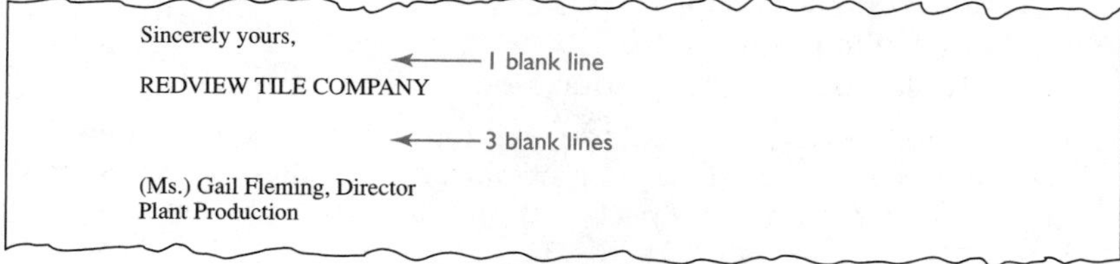

Sincerely yours,

REDVIEW TILE COMPANY

(Ms.) Gail Fleming, Director
Plant Production

Place the writer's signature line or lines on the fourth line below the previous line, which will be either the complimentary close or the company name. Align the first letter of the individual's name with the first letter of the complimentary close and/or the company name.

modified block letter

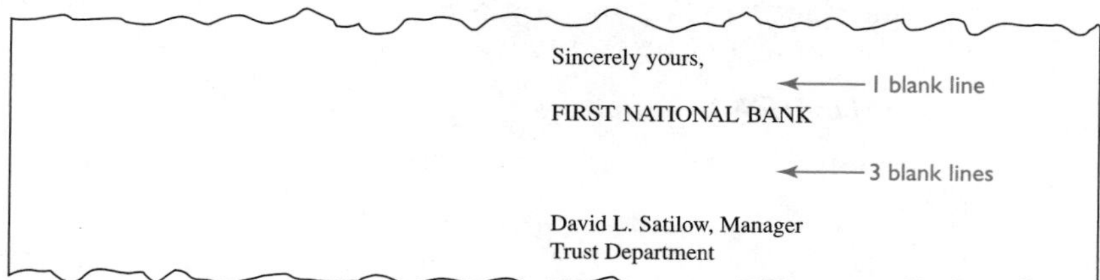

Sincerely yours,

FIRST NATIONAL BANK

David L. Satilow, Manager
Trust Department

full block letter

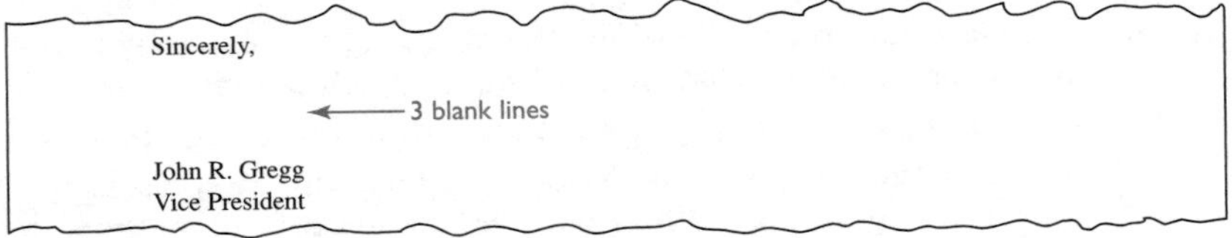
Sincerely,

← 3 blank lines

John R. Gregg
Vice President

Place combinations of names, titles, and organizational sectors so that the contents of the signature lines appear balanced. The name and title may appear on the same line or on separate lines, depending upon the length of each item. Use commas to separate categories within the same line, but do not use commas to conclude any of the signature lines.

single-line signature line

Phillip Ashton, President

Susan R. Mayfield, M.D.

two-line signature line

Margaret T. Washington
Manager, Credit Department

John S. Ross, Supervisor
Data Processing Department

Horace F. Tavelman
Accounts and Sales Representative

three-line signature line

Roberta Casselman, Ed.D.
Curriculum Consultant
Division of Secondary Education

Simplified letter style. **In the simplified letter style, the entire signature line is typed in all capital letters on a single line. It begins at the left margin on the fifth line below the last line of the message.**

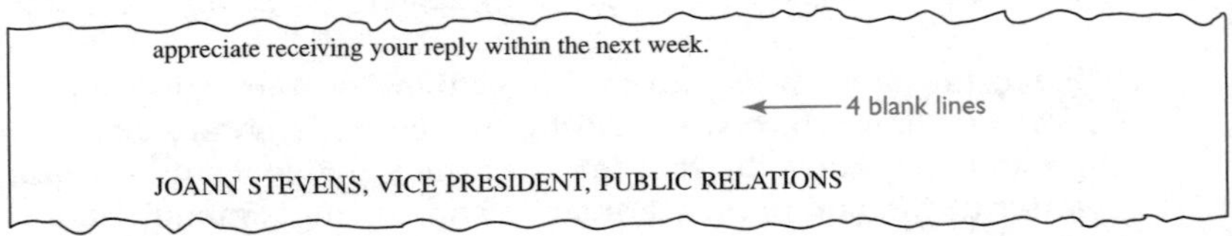
appreciate receiving your reply within the next week.

← 4 blank lines

JOANN STEVENS, VICE PRESIDENT, PUBLIC RELATIONS

Social business letter style. **In the social business letter style, the printed signature line may be omitted. If it is included, only the individual's name, not title, is written.**

typed signature line omitted

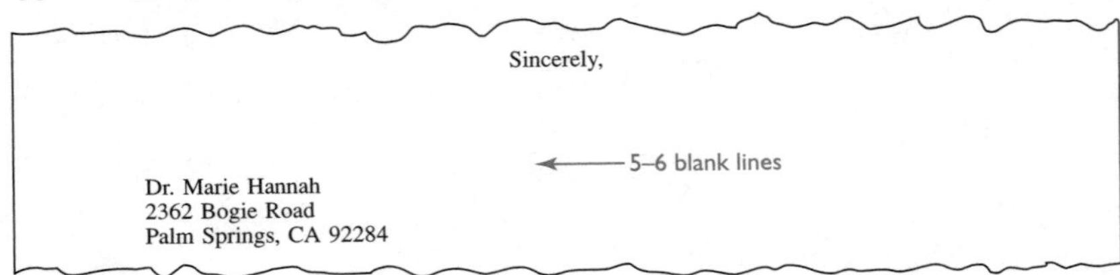
Sincerely,

← 5–6 blank lines

Dr. Marie Hannah
2362 Bogie Road
Palm Springs, CA 92284

typed signature line included

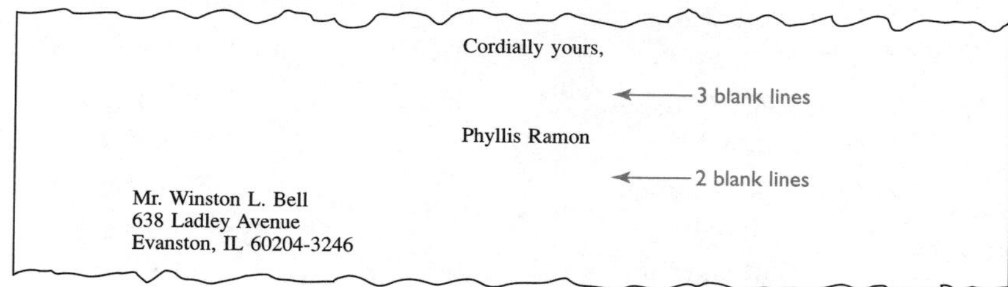
Cordially yours,

← 3 blank lines

Phyllis Ramon

← 2 blank lines

Mr. Winston L. Bell
638 Ladley Avenue
Evanston, IL 60204-3246

b. **Signature lines containing the names of men are generally not preceded by the courtesy title *Mr.* Only with initials, international names, and gender-equal names should a man use *Mr.* if the addressee does not know him. *Mr.* may be written with or without parentheses.**

If a man has the title *Dr.,* either (1) place the abbreviation of the degree after the name of the individual or (2) place the title *Dr.*—with or without parentheses—before the name of the individual.

***signature lines containing name of man to be addressed as* Mr.**

George R. Bezowski
Regional Manager

(Mr.) Huy Cao Nguyen
Assistant Vice President

Mr. R. L. Rothstein
Realtor Associate

(Mr.) Leslie Neible
Customer Service Representative

***signature lines containing name of man to be addressed as* Dr.**

Cory V. Stephenson, Ph.D.
Professor of Economics

Vahi Urun, D.D.S.

(Dr.) Donald C. Cook
Occupational Coordinator

Dr. Donald C. Cook
Occupational Coordinator

c. **Signature lines containing the names of women should be preceded by a courtesy title if the writer prefers to be addressed as *Mrs.* instead of the standard *Ms.* in any return correspondence. Courtesy titles (*Ms.* or *Mrs.*) should also be used before female names that are not readily distinguishable as male or female, names containing only initials, and international names. The title is usually placed in parentheses, but it may appear without them.**

If a woman has the title *Dr.,* either (1) place the abbreviation of the degree after the name of the individual or (2) place the title *Dr.*—with or without parentheses—before the name of the individual.

signature lines containing name of woman

Sally Abramowitz, Manager
Production Department

Alice H. Duffy, Coordinator
Training and Development

signature lines distinguishing courtesy title of woman

(Mrs.) Miho Tabata Administrative Assitant	*or*	Mrs. Miho Tabata Administrative Assistant
(Mrs.) Kelly Krusee Sales Associate	*or*	Mrs. Kelly Crusee Sales Associate
(Ms.) M. R. Stevens General Manager	*or*	Ms. M. R. Stevens General Manager
(Ms.) Tran Huynh Vice President	*or*	Ms. Tran Huynh Vice President

***signature lines containing name of woman addressed as* Dr.**

Ermonia C. Gevorkian, D.B.A. Associate Professor	Lynn V. Stauber, M.D.
(Dr.) Alecia Morley, Dean Academic Affairs	Dr. Alecia Morley, Dean Academic Affairs

d. **Correspondence that is signed by a person other than the one whose name appears in the signature line usually shows the initials of the person signing the letter.**

Sincerely yours,

Wallace C. Murietta (lc)

Wallace C. Murietta
Chairman of the Board

e. **Sometimes more than one signature is required in a business letter. Arrange the signature lines in order of rank within the organization. If ranking is unimportant, arrange the signature lines in alphabetical order.**

Modified block letter style. **In the modified block letter, align multiple signatures vertically beginning at the horizontal center of the page. Leave three blank lines between each signature block.**

Full block letter style. **In a full block letter, arrange multiple signatures (1) side by side or (2) aligned vertically at the left margin with three blank lines separating each typed signature block.**

multiple signature lines in modified block letter

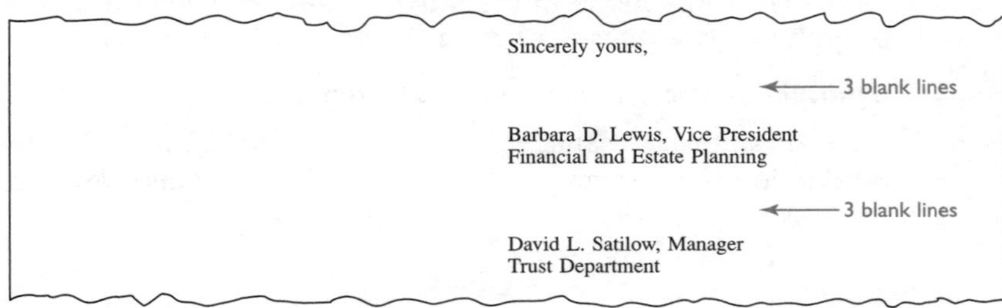
Sincerely yours,

Barbara D. Lewis, Vice President
Financial and Estate Planning

David L. Satilow, Manager
Trust Department

side-by-side signature lines in full block letter

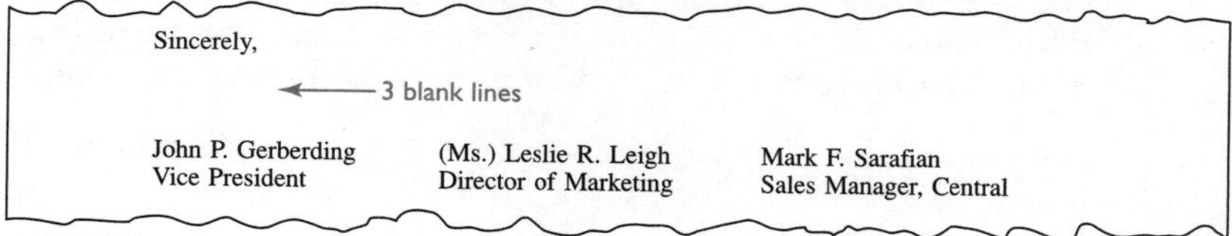
Sincerely,

3 blank lines

John P. Gerberding
Vice President

(Ms.) Leslie R. Leigh
Director of Marketing

Mark F. Sarafian
Sales Manager, Central

vertically aligned signature lines in full block letter

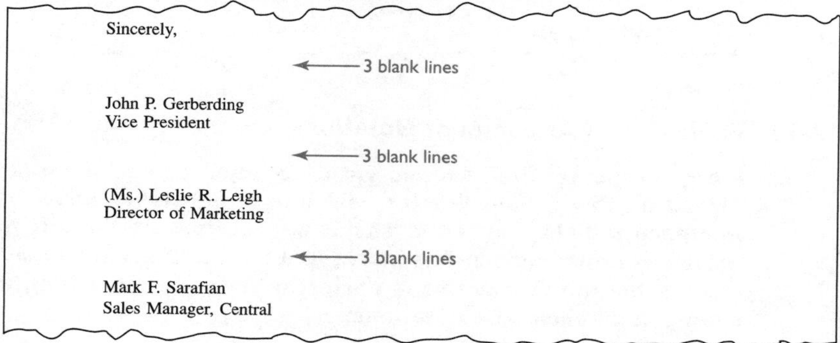
Sincerely,

3 blank lines

John P. Gerberding
Vice President

3 blank lines

(Ms.) Leslie R. Leigh
Director of Marketing

3 blank lines

Mark F. Sarafian
Sales Manager, Central

12–17 Reference Initials

a. Reference initials are used to show who keyed and formatted the letter. In all letter styles except the social business style, the preparer's initials are placed in lowercase letters at the left margin a double space below the last line in the signature block.

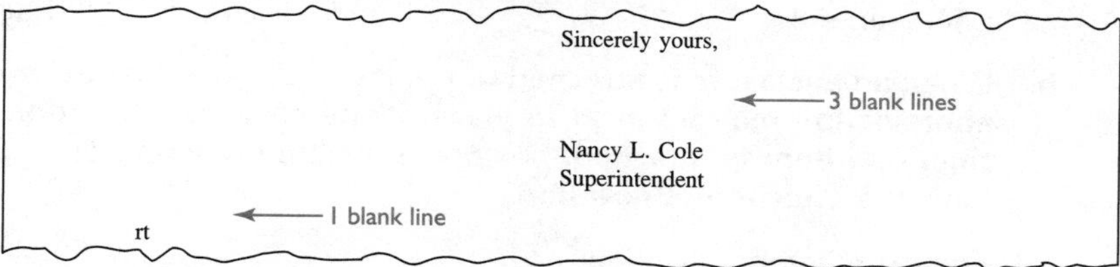
Sincerely yours,

3 blank lines

Nancy L. Cole
Superintendent

1 blank line

rt

b. The initials of both the writer and the preparer *may* be included in the reference notation. When the person whose name appears in the signature lines is the one who wrote the letter, his or her initials appear in capital letters before the preparer's initials. The initials are separated by a colon or a diagonal line.

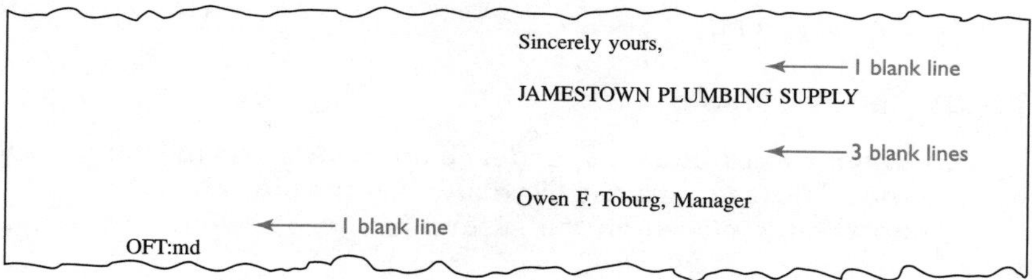
Sincerely yours,

1 blank line

JAMESTOWN PLUMBING SUPPLY

3 blank lines

Owen F. Toburg, Manager

1 blank line

OFT:md

c. **When correspondence is written by a person other than the one whose name appears in the signature lines, the writer's name or capitalized initials precede the initials of the preparer. Separate the name or initials of the writer from the preparer's initials by a colon or a diagonal line.**

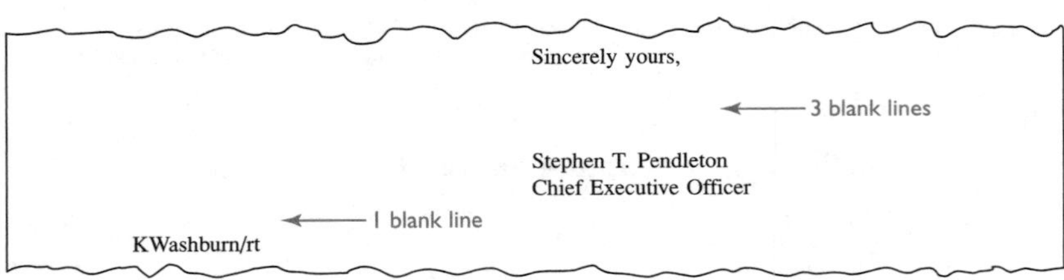

Sincerely yours,
3 blank lines
Stephen T. Pendleton
Chief Executive Officer
1 blank line
KWashburn/rt

12–18 Enclosure or Attachment Notations

a. **If any enclosures are included with the letter, an enclosure notation is placed on the second line (or next line to conserve space) below the reference initials. Begin the enclosure notation at the left margin. If more than one enclosure is included, be sure to list the enclosures or include the number with the enclosure notation. Following are some examples of enclosure notations:**

one enclosure

Enclosure   Enc.   Check enclosed   Enclosure: Wilson Contract

more than one enclosure

Enclosures: Check for $200
Copy of Invoice 1362   2 Enc.   Enc. 2

Enclosures 2   Enclosures (2)   2 Enclosures

b. **When an enclosure is attached to the letter, the word *Attachment* or its abbreviation may be used in place of the enclosure notation. If more than one item is attached, be sure to include a listing or the number with the attachment notation.**

one attachment

Attachment   Attachment: Survey results   Att.

more than one attachment

Attachments: Application for admission
Student information form   Attachments 2

2 Attachments   Att. 2

12–19 Copy Notations

a. **When copies of correspondence are directed to individuals other than the addressee, note the distribution at the bottom of the letter. The copy notation is placed on the second line (or next line to conserve space)**

following the enclosure notation, if used. Otherwise, it appears a single or double space below the reference initials. However, if a delivery notation follows the reference initials or enclosure notation, the copy notation is placed below it.

copy notation following reference initials

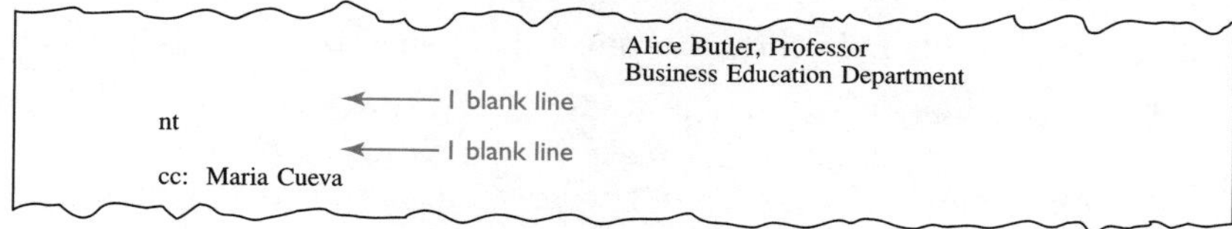

copy notation with additional notations

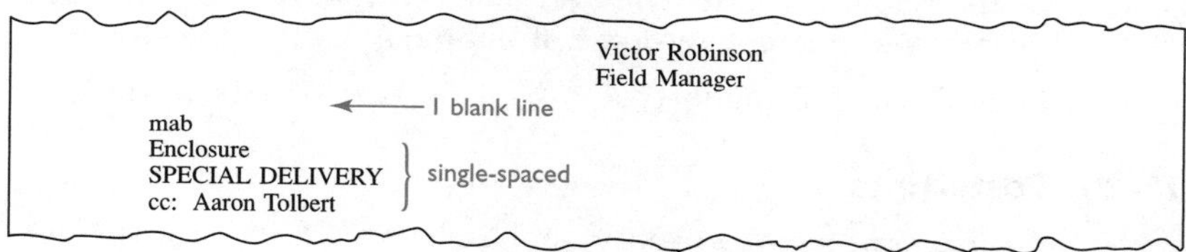

b. Copies of correspondence are prepared with a photocopier, a printer, or—in rare cases—carbon paper. The traditional *cc* notation represents the terms *courtesy copy* or *carbon copy,* so this notation is appropriate for copies produced by any method. Some writers use only *c* for *copy.*

Copy notations may include a combination of the courtesy title, name, position, department, company, and complete address of an individual. Following are some examples of appropriate copy notations:

cc: Mr. John R. Robinson
1865 Rinaldi Street
Oklahoma City, OK 73103

c: Francis P. Olsen, President, Wilson Corporation

cc Alice Morley, Credit Clerk

c Vahi Urun

Some companies prefer to note copies made on a photocopier in the following ways:

copy: Ms. Janice Welch

copies: Bill Acevedo
Donna Mellert

c: Sales Department Staff

C: Mrs. Phuong Nguyen

copy to Mr. Bill Hughes, Manager, Hillsdale Paper Corporation

c. If copies are directed to more than one individual, list the individuals according to rank. If the individuals are equal in rank or ranking is unimportant, alphabetize the list. The list may be prepared either vertically or horizontally.

ranked list

cc: R. F. Gillham, President
T. L. McMillan, Vice President
F. S. Brotherton, General Manager

alphabetized list

cc Marcus L. Brendero, Anne S. Langville, David M. Silverman

d. **If sending a copy of the letter to other individuals is unnecessary or inappropriate for an addressee to know, use a blind copy notation. The blind copy notation appears only on copies of the letter, not on the original.**

The blind copy notation may be placed (1) one inch from the top edge of the page at the left margin or (2) where the regular copy notation normally appears. Examples of blind copy notations follow:

bcc: David P. Dougherty   bcc Ms. Marty Hayes

12–20 Postscripts

A postscript may be used to emphasize an idea or add an idea that was unintentionally omitted from the body of the letter. The postscript is placed in last position; it may be keyed or handwritten with or without the abbreviation *P.S.* or *PS*.

Treat the postscript as any other paragraph in the letter. If the first line is blocked, then block the first line and all succeeding lines. If the first line is indented, then indent the first line and begin the remaining lines at the left margin.

***with abbreviation* P.S. *or* PS**

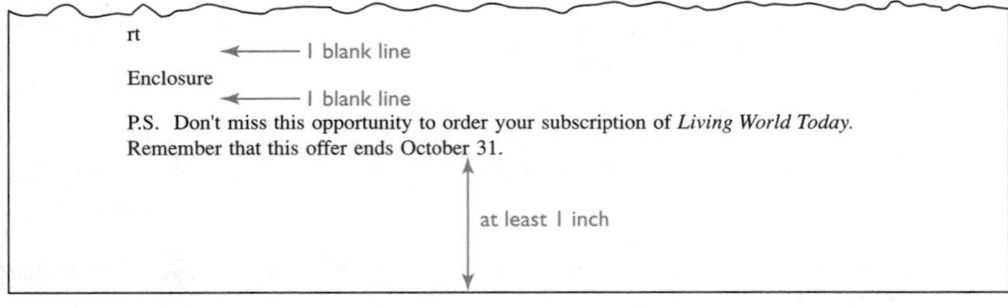

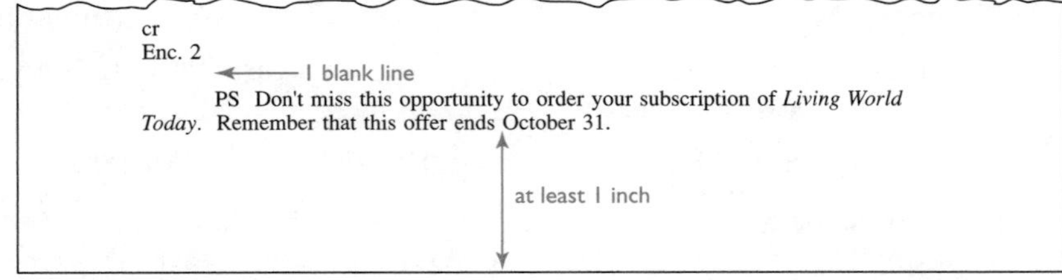

without abbreviation P.S. or PS

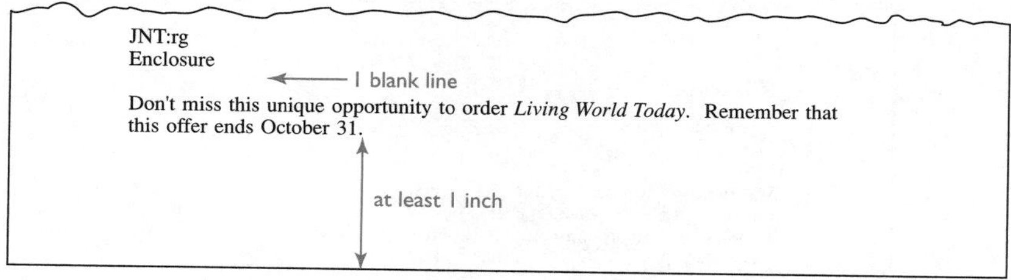

JNT:rg
Enclosure

Don't miss this unique opportunity to order *Living World Today*. Remember that this offer ends October 31.

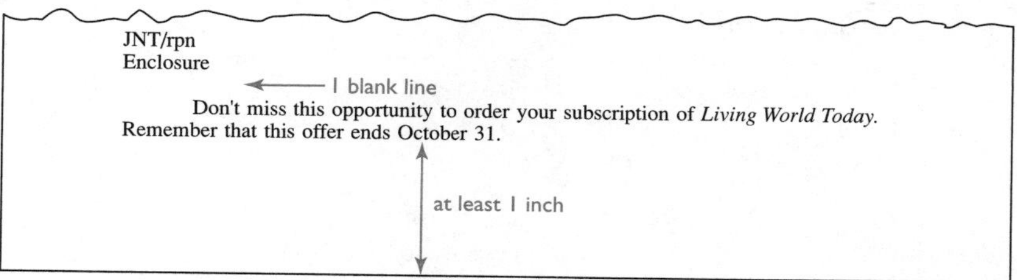

JNT/rpn
Enclosure

Don't miss this opportunity to order your subscription of *Living World Today*. Remember that this offer ends October 31.

12–21 Computer File Notations

Some companies prefer to place within the document the path and file name of letters produced on word processors. Since these notations are file references, they should appear only on file copies—not on copies sent to the addressee or other recipients. Place computer file notations a single space below the last keyed line of the letter on the file copy only.

Marie La Grasta, Manager
Western Regional Sales

jr

cc: Robert Levy
c:\dayton\corres\ackerman.doc

12–22 Second-Page Headings

a. **Prepare headings for second and succeeding pages on plain paper. Allow a 1-inch top margin, and use the same side margins that appear on the first page. These continuation-page headings include the name of the addressee, the page number, and the date. Either a horizontal or a vertical format may be used.**

b. **Before resuming the message, space down three lines from the last line of the heading. Two blank lines should separate the heading and the continuation of the message.**

horizontal format

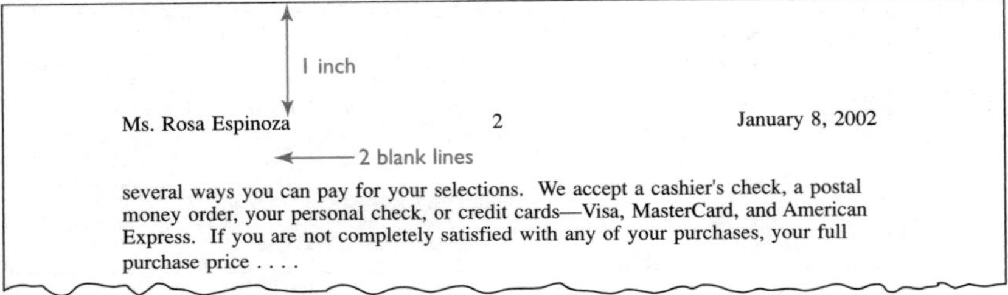

Ms. Rosa Espinoza 2 January 8, 2002

several ways you can pay for your selections. We accept a cashier's check, a postal money order, your personal check, or credit cards—Visa, MasterCard, and American Express. If you are not completely satisfied with any of your purchases, your full purchase price . . . .

vertical format

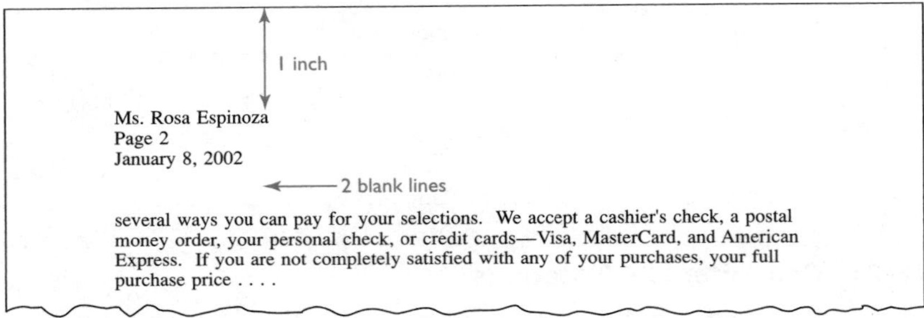

Ms. Rosa Espinoza
Page 2
January 8, 2002

several ways you can pay for your selections. We accept a cashier's check, a postal money order, your personal check, or credit cards—Visa, MasterCard, and American Express. If you are not completely satisfied with any of your purchases, your full purchase price . . . .

c. If a page does not end at the conclusion of a paragraph, include *at least* the first two lines of any new paragraph begun at the bottom of the page. Do not divide the last word on the page. Likewise, carry forward to the next page *at least* the last two lines from a paragraph begun on the previous page. Use the widow/orphan line protection feature of your word processing program to prevent isolated lines from a paragraph appearing at the top or the bottom of a page.

Leave at least 1 inch, but no more than 1.5 inches, at the bottom of each page—except, of course, the last one.

d. The closing lines of a business letter should not be isolated on a continuation page. At least two lines of the message must precede the complimentary close or signature lines (when no complimentary close is used).

Punctuation Style

12–23 Mixed Punctuation

The most popular punctuation style for business letters is mixed punctuation. In this format a colon follows the salutation and a comma appears after the complimentary close. No other closing punctuation marks are used except those concluding an abbreviation or ones appearing within the body of the letter.

business letter with mixed punctuation

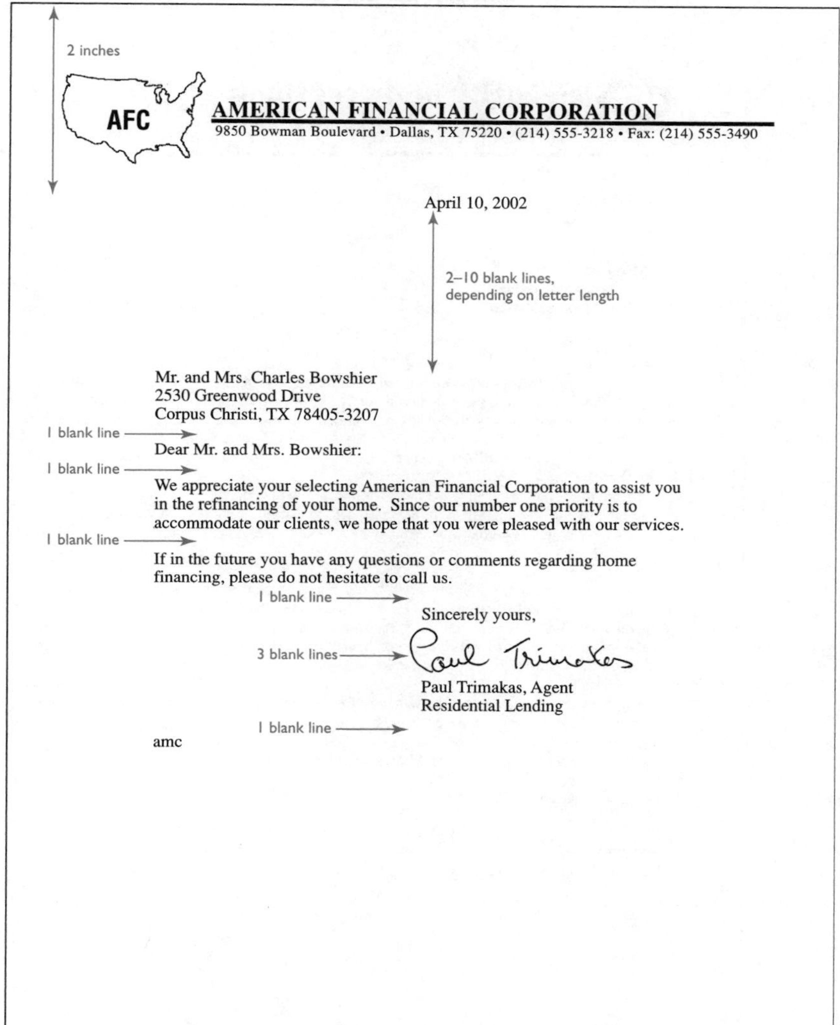

2 inches

AFC

AMERICAN FINANCIAL CORPORATION

9850 Bowman Boulevard • Dallas, TX 75220 • (214) 555-3218 • Fax: (214) 555-3490

April 10, 2002

2–10 blank lines, depending on letter length

Mr. and Mrs. Charles Bowshier
2530 Greenwood Drive
Corpus Christi, TX 78405-3207

1 blank line

Dear Mr. and Mrs. Bowshier:

1 blank line

We appreciate your selecting American Financial Corporation to assist you in the refinancing of your home. Since our number one priority is to accommodate our clients, we hope that you were pleased with our services.

1 blank line

If in the future you have any questions or comments regarding home financing, please do not hesitate to call us.

1 blank line

Sincerely yours,

3 blank lines

Paul Trimakas

Paul Trimakas, Agent
Residential Lending

1 blank line

amc

12–24 Open Punctuation

Writers of business letters sometimes use open punctuation. No closing punctuation marks except those concluding an abbreviation appear after the letter parts. The only other ending punctuation marks are ones used within the body of the letter.

business letter with open punctuation

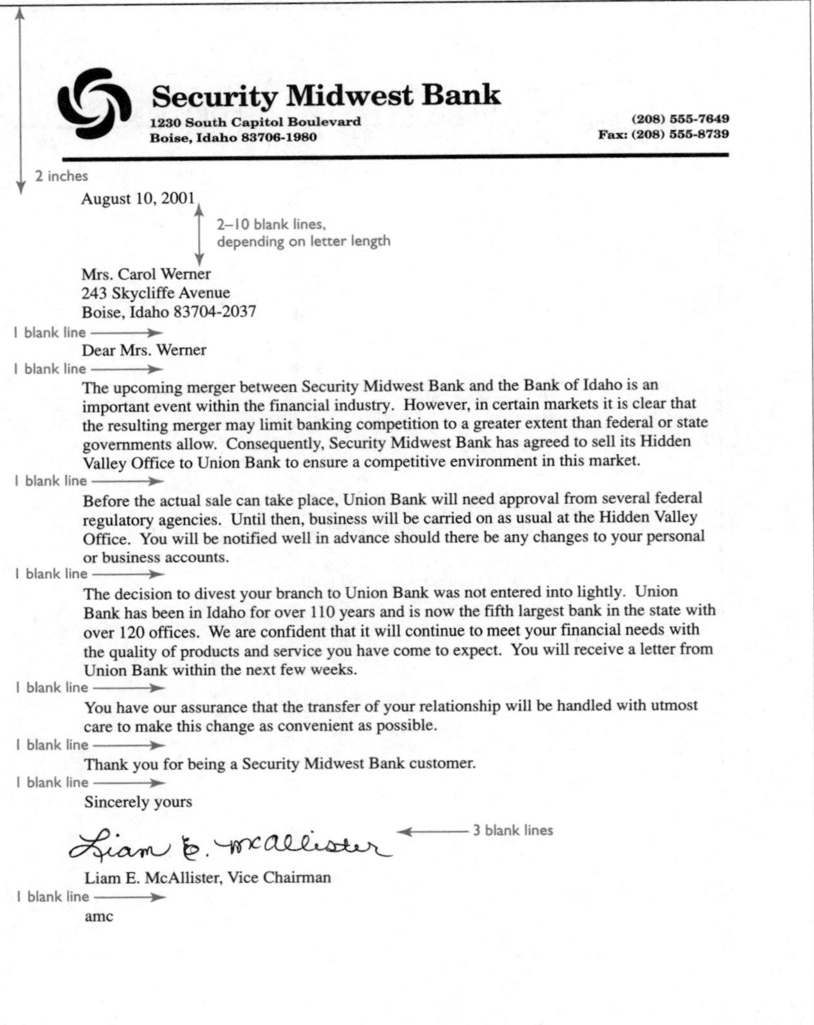

Security Midwest Bank
1230 South Capitol Boulevard
Boise, Idaho 83706-1980
(208) 555-7649
Fax: (208) 555-8739

August 10, 2001

Mrs. Carol Werner
243 Skycliffe Avenue
Boise, Idaho 83704-2037

Dear Mrs. Werner

The upcoming merger between Security Midwest Bank and the Bank of Idaho is an important event within the financial industry. However, in certain markets it is clear that the resulting merger may limit banking competition to a greater extent than federal or state governments allow. Consequently, Security Midwest Bank has agreed to sell its Hidden Valley Office to Union Bank to ensure a competitive environment in this market.

Before the actual sale can take place, Union Bank will need approval from several federal regulatory agencies. Until then, business will be carried on as usual at the Hidden Valley Office. You will be notified well in advance should there be any changes to your personal or business accounts.

The decision to divest your branch to Union Bank was not entered into lightly. Union Bank has been in Idaho for over 110 years and is now the fifth largest bank in the state with over 120 offices. We are confident that it will continue to meet your financial needs with the quality of products and service you have come to expect. You will receive a letter from Union Bank within the next few weeks.

You have our assurance that the transfer of your relationship will be handled with utmost care to make this change as convenient as possible.

Thank you for being a Security Midwest Bank customer.

Sincerely yours

Liam E. McAllister, Vice Chairman

amc

Addressing Envelopes

12–25 Automated Envelope Addressing

Use the envelope feature of your word processing program to prepare envelopes for your correspondence and other mailings. Adapt the default settings to correspond to your needs by following these guidelines:

(1) Select the envelope size from the menu of types provided by your software. If the correct envelope size is not available, create and select it. Be sure that your printer will support the envelope size selected.

(2) Adjust the left and top margin settings of your return address placement to accommodate any lines to be added to a printed return address or to accommodate a keyed return address. See Section 12–26b.

(3) Adjust the left and top margin settings of your mailing address placement to accommodate the envelope size selected. See Section 12–27 for the margin settings to be used for No. 10 (legal-size), No. 6¾ (letter-size), No. 7 (monarch), and No. 5⅜ (baronial) envelopes.

(4) Use the option to insert a bar code, if desired. Before using this option, make sure your printer supports it.

envelope printed with envelope feature of a word processing program

Continental Insurance Company
460 North Ashley Drive
Tampa, Florida 33601-1469

CONFIDENTIAL

CERTIFIED MAIL

Mr. Thomas R. Paige, Manager
Allied Insurance Agency
6200 Beachwood Boulevard
Tampa, Florida 33609-2147

12–26 Return Address

a. **The return address is usually printed in the upper left corner of the envelope. In large companies the writer's or sender's initials or name and location are typed above the company name and return address. This practice facilitates routing the letter to the sender in case of nondelivery by the post office.**

Jeffrey Edwards, Trust Department
United Bank of Iowa
1640 Medina Road
Des Moines, Iowa 50313-2167

b. **On an envelope without a printed return address, place the return address in the upper left corner. Single-space the lines and include (1) the name of the individual; (2) the title of the individual, if applicable; (3) the company name, if applicable; (4) the mailing address; and (5) the city, state, and zip code. Begin the return address 0.3 inch from the top and 0.4 inch from the left edge of the envelope.**

0.3"
John R. Stevens
460 Old Dorsett Road
Hazelwood, MO 63043-2367
0.4"

12–27 Mailing Address

a. **Single-space the mailing address, using at least two lines. The last line of the address should contain the city, state, and zip code. If the envelope is used to mail correspondence, key the address exactly as it appears in the inside address.**

b. **On legal-size envelopes, No. 10 envelopes (9.5 by 4.13 inches), allow a 2-inch top margin. Begin the address 4.25 inches from the left edge of the envelope.**

No. 10 envelope

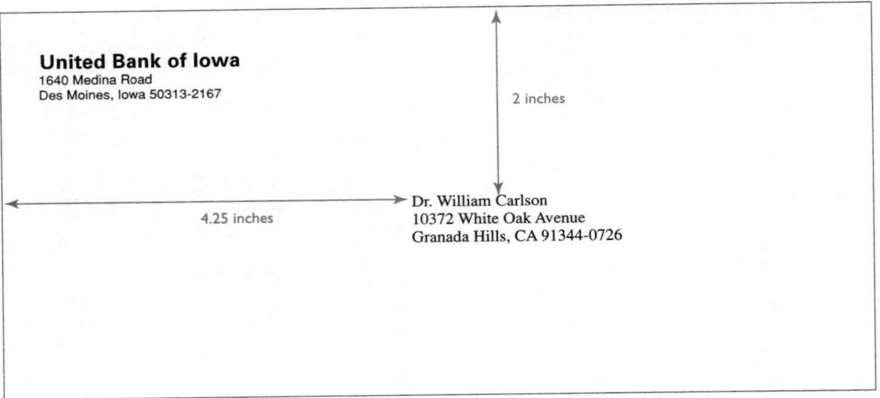

c. **On letter-size envelopes, No. 6¾ envelopes (6.5 by 3.63 inches), allow a 1.75-inch top margin. Begin the mailing address 2.5 inches from the left edge of the envelope.**

No. 6¾ envelope

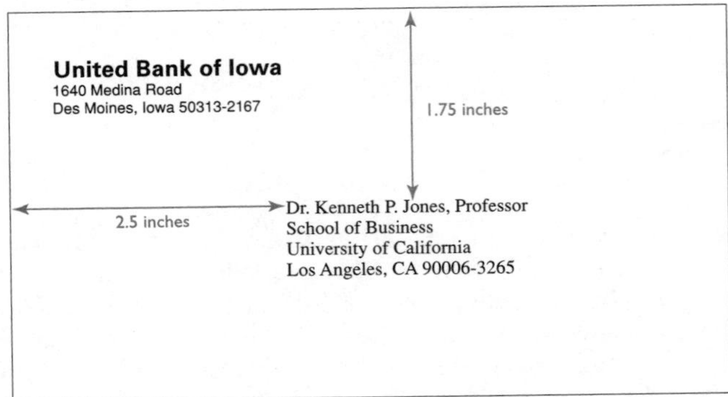

d. **No. 7 (7.5 by 3.88 inches) and No. 5⅜ (5.94 by 4.63 inches) envelopes are used less frequently than the standard No. 10 and No. 6¾ envelopes. On No. 7 envelopes allow a 1.75-inch top margin; on No. 5⅜ envelopes allow a 2-inch top margin. Begin typing the mailing address 0.5 to 1 inch left of the envelope center, depending upon the length of the address lines.**

No. 7 envelope

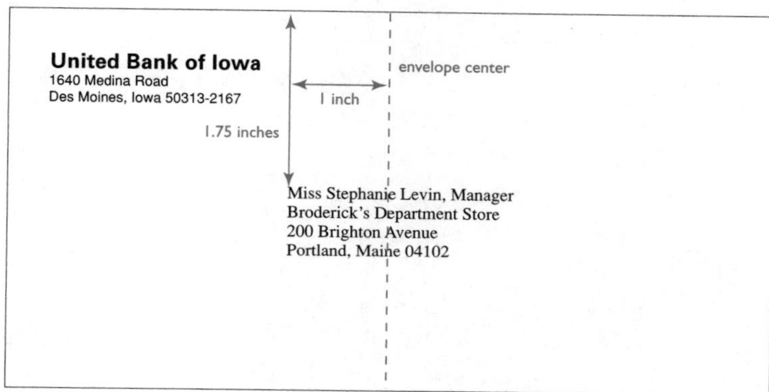

No. 5⅜ envelope

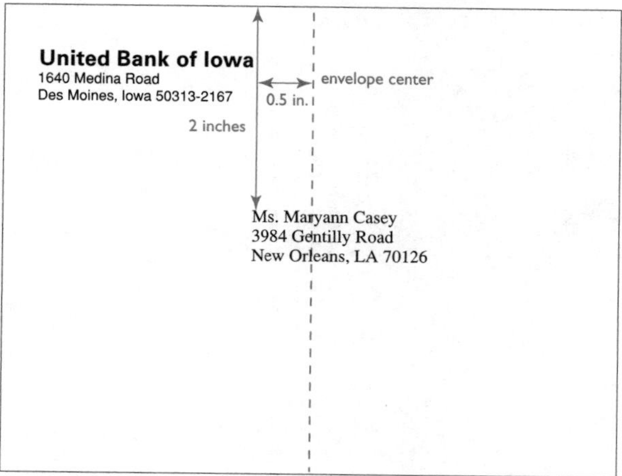

e. **Letter-size manila envelopes (9 by 12 inches or 10 by 12 inches) may have the address keyed directly on the envelope or have a label with the address affixed to the envelope. In either case, position the envelope so that the flap and opening are on the right side. Place the first line of the mailing address 4.5 inches (for 9- by 12-inch envelopes) or 5 inches (for 10- by 12-inch envelopes) from the top edge and 4.5 to 5 inches from the left edge, depending upon the length of the address lines.**

Business Letters 12

letter-size manila envelope

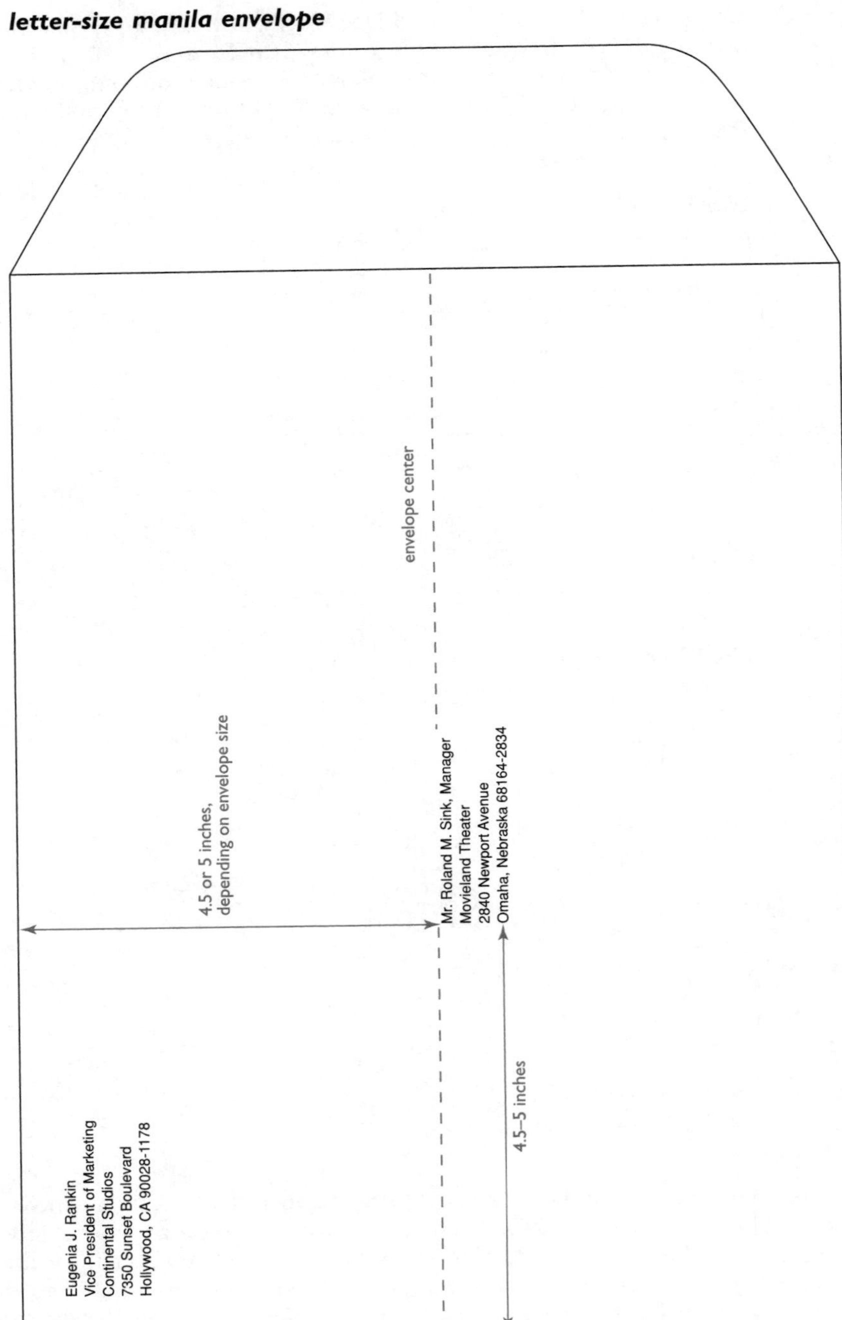

envelope center
4.5 or 5 inches,
depending on envelope size
Mr. Roland M. Sink, Manager
Movieland Theater
2840 Newport Avenue
Omaha, Nebraska 68164-2834
4.5–5 inches
Eugenia J. Rankin
Vice President of Marketing
Continental Studios
7350 Sunset Boulevard
Hollywood, CA 90028-1178

12–28 Addressee Notations

If an attention line appears in the inside address of a letter, include it within the envelope address. If an attention line is placed below the inside address in the letter, treat it the same as you would any other addressee notation.

Type an attention line or an addressee notation such as *Personal, Confidential, Please Forward,* or *Hold for Arrival* a double space below the last line of the return address or 1.5 inches from the top edge of the envelope, whichever position is lower. Begin typing 0.5 inch from the left edge of the envelope, and use all capital letters.

attention line included with address

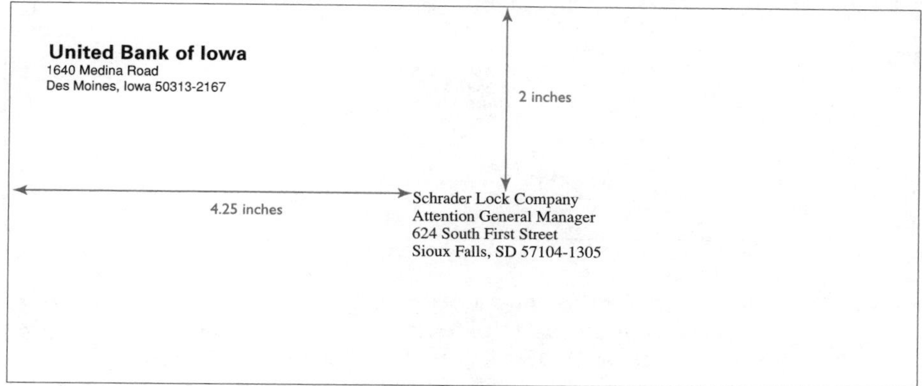

addressee notation below return address

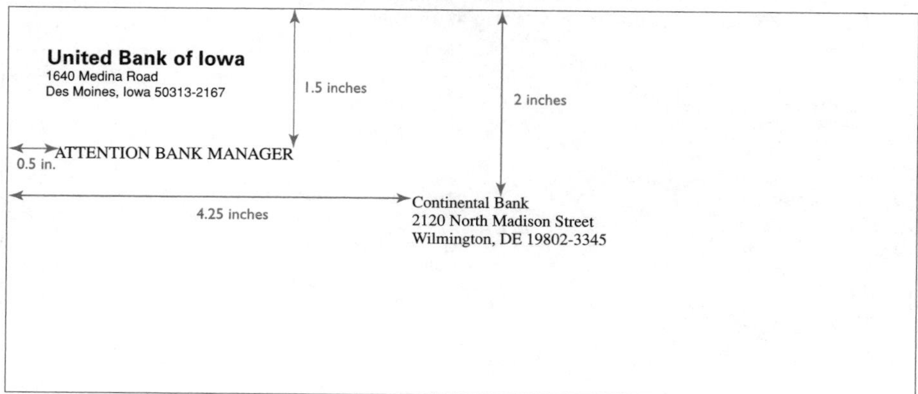

12–29 Delivery Notations

a. Place delivery notations such as *Air Mail* (for foreign destinations), *Certified Mail,* or *Registered Mail* in all capital letters below the stamp, 1.5 inches from the top edge of the envelope. End the notation 0.5 inch from the right edge of the envelope.

Envelope delivery notations are of lesser significance than they were previously, except for *Air Mail,* which is used exclusively for international mailings. *Express Mail* and other fast-delivery options provided by private courier services have their own supplier-provided envelopes. *Registered Mail* must be presented at the post office for mailing, where it is marked and routed appropriately. *Certified Mail,* too, is usually taken to the post office and marked accordingly.

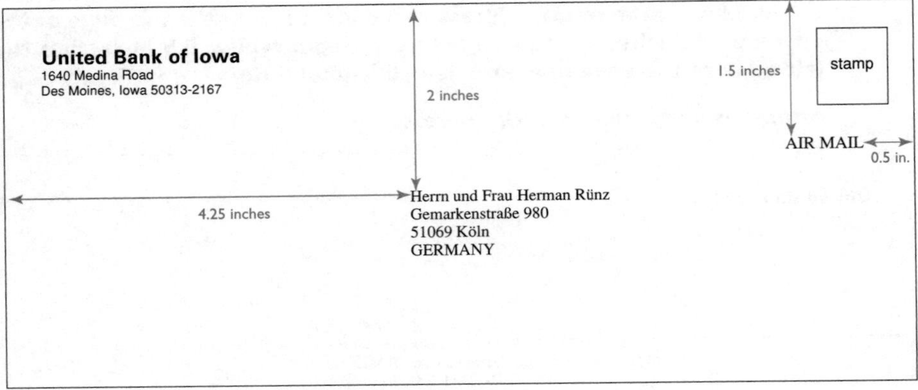

b. If an addressee notation and a delivery notation are on the same envelope, type both in all capital letters. The addressee notation appears a double space below the last line of the return address or 1.5 inches from the top edge of the envelope, whichever position is lower. Begin this notation 0.5 inch from the left envelope edge. Delivery notations are placed below the stamp, 1.5 inches from the top edge of the envelope. They end 0.5 inch from the right edge.

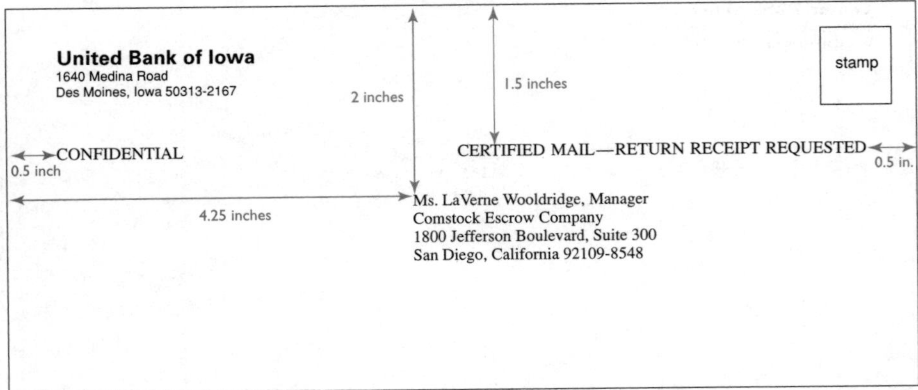

12–30 Computer-Generated Address Labels

Word processing programs as well as database programs can easily generate mailing labels from a database merge file or a database file. Addresses are compiled and formatted for printing on predefined label forms prepared commercially by companies such as Avery or 3M. The following example was prepared on a word processor using an Avery 5162 address label form for a laser printer.

Mr. George R. Simms, Vice President
Great Western Bank
19300 Devonshire Street
Chatsworth, CA 93471-1046

Ms. Elizabeth Candiotti, President
Woodland Hills Chamber of Commerce
20220 Ventura Boulevard, Suite 130
Woodland Hills, CA 91365-3281

Ms. Veronica Richmond, Director
Human Resources Department
Harman International
6200 Balboa Boulevard
Northridge, CA 91324-1954

Dr. Sandra L. Washington, President
California State University, Northridge
18600 Nordhoff Street
Northridge, CA 91327

Mr. Charles E. Buchanan, Manager
Coldwell Banker Realty
8750 Arroyo Parkway
Camarillo, CA 92374-3209

Mr. Anthony Murillo, Vice President
International Operations
Amgen Corporation
30375 Victory Boulevard
Thousand Oaks, CA 94509-1001

12–31 Zip + 4

a. **To process mail faster and more economically, the U.S. Postal Service has assigned four additional digits to the zip codes of mailing addresses that do not have their own separate zip codes. This series of four digits is separated from the zip code with a hyphen.**

Northridge, CA 91325-**6213** Boise, Idaho 83702-**4819**

Jackson, MS 39203-**1073** Reno, Nevada 89503-**2103**

b. **The use of Zip + 4 is recommended by the U.S. Postal Service. Reduced rates for the use of Zip + 4 can be obtained by bulk mailers.**

c. **Zip + 4 codes may be located through various media available for purchase from the U.S. Postal Service[7] and from various private software companies. Zip + 4 codes for specific addresses may be retrieved free of charge at the U.S. Postal Service Web site <www.usps.gov>.**

[7]For information about Zip + 4 products, telephone the National Customer Support Center, U.S. Postal Service, (800) 238-3150.

Folding and Inserting Correspondence

12–32 No. 10 and No. 7 Envelopes

a. **Fold up one third of the page.**

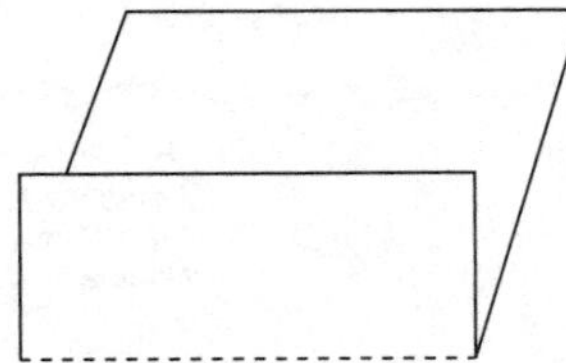

b. **Fold down the upper third of the page so that the top edge is approximately ⅓ inch above the first fold.**

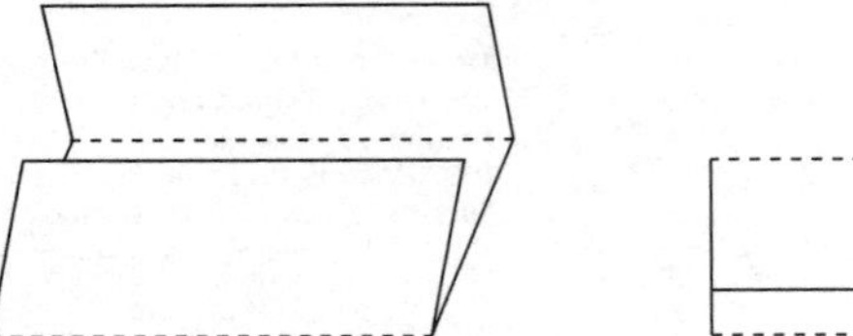

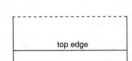

c. **Insert the page so that the top edge is near the top edge of the envelope.**

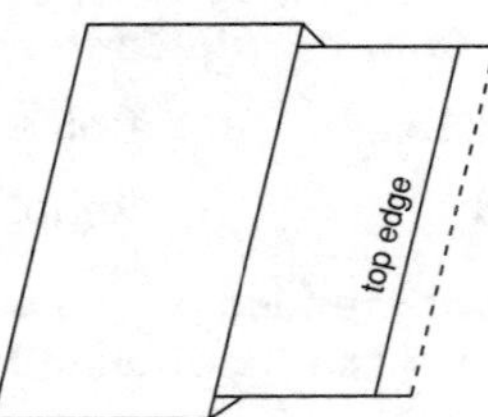

12–33 No. 6¾ Envelopes

a. **Fold up one half of the page so that the bottom edge is approximately ⅓ inch below the top edge.**

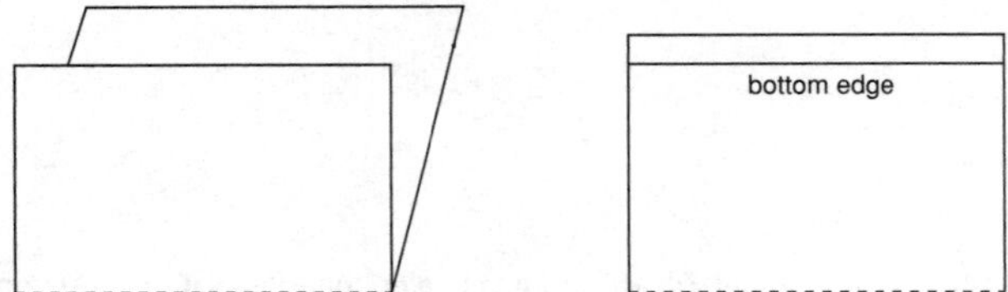

b. From the right side fold over one third of the page.

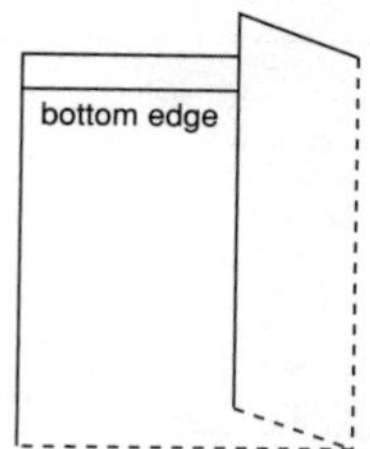

c. Fold over the second third of the page so that the left edge is approximately ⅓ inch from the right fold.

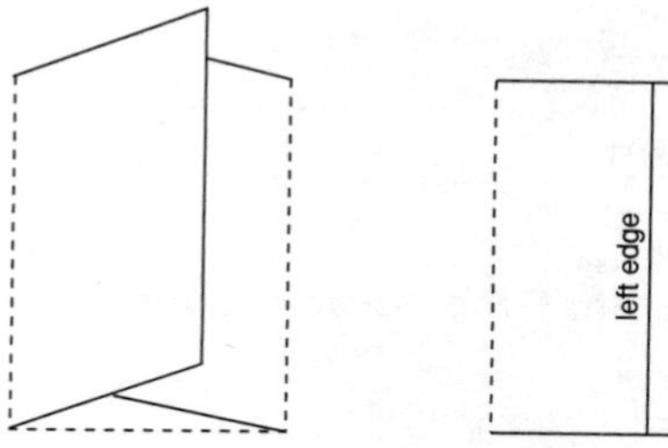

d. Insert the page so that the left edge is near the top edge of the envelope.

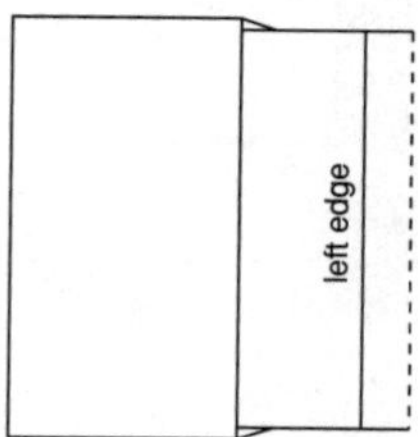

12–34 Window Envelopes

a. Fold up one third of the letter.

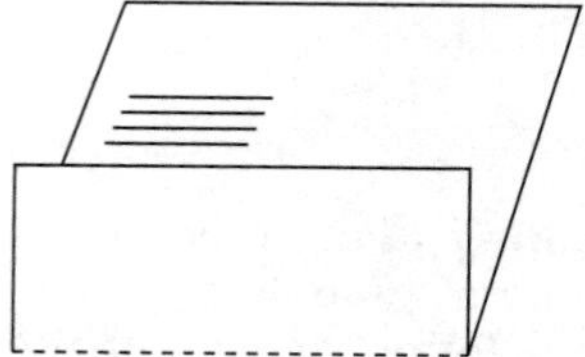

b. Turn the folded letter face down.

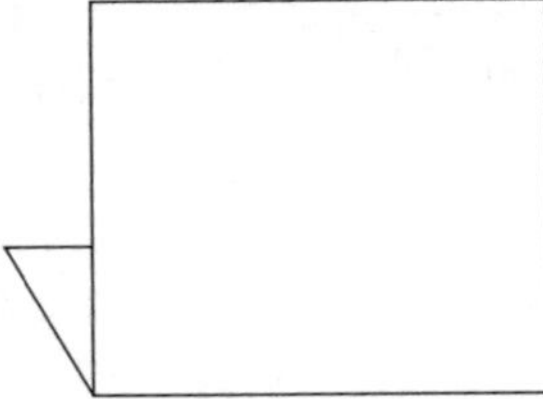

c. Fold down the upper third of the letter so that the top edge meets the first fold.

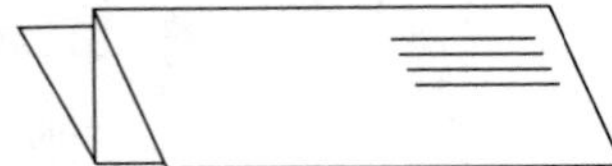

d. Insert the letter so that the address appears in the window of the envelope.

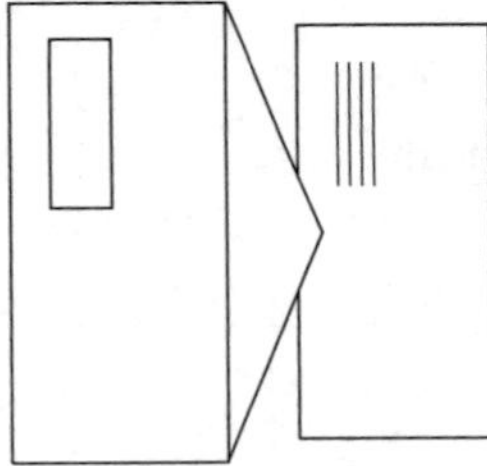

Memorandums

12–35 Usage

While letters generally involve the transmission of written messages sent outside an organization, memorandums are used for internal written communication. Once the major form of internal written communication, memorandums have declined in use since the advent of E-mail messaging.

12–36 Preparation

a. Procedures for preparing memorandums vary widely from office to office, but a few general guidelines exist. Most organizations have printed memorandum forms or custom word processing templates. These forms or templates contain guide words for directing the message to an addressee, specifying the name of the writer, providing the date written, and identifying the subject content. Although the arrangement and design may vary, these basic elements are found in most printed memorandum forms.

printed memorandum forms or custom templates

Northridge Manufacturing Company
Interoffice Memorandum

To:
From:
Date:
Subject:

MATTEL **Mattel Toys Memo** MAT-3497-8

TO: DATE:

FROM: REFERENCE:

SUBJECT:

GENERAL MOTORS ACCEPTANCE CORPORATION
INTRAORGANIZATION LETTERS ONLY

TO: ADDRESS:
FROM: ADDRESS:
SUBJECT: DATE:

b. Memorandums may be prepared on preprinted memorandum forms using word processing software. For standard 8½- by 11-inch printed memorandum forms, create a form document to assist you with completing the preliminary lines: *Date:, To:, From:, Subject:,* etc. Each time you are required to use this printed form, you can use the form document to assist you with the proper placement of information after each guide word.

(1) Use 1-inch top and bottom margins and 1.25-inch left and right margins.

(2) Use a ruler to measure the horizontal and vertical position of the first letter to be keyed after each guide word in the memorandum form.

(3) Move your cursor to the horizontal and vertical position (as shown in the status line of your program) of the first letter to be keyed after the first guide word; key an asterisk (*). Follow the same procedure for each guide word in the printed form. If any preliminary parts will be completed with standard information, key in this standard information instead of an asterisk.

(4) Triple-space after the asterisk marking the beginning of the last guide word, usually the one that introduces the subject line.

(5) Save the form document as a separate file.

When a memorandum needs to be prepared, open the form document and save it with a new name. Use the search feature of your program to locate the asterisks and substitute the variable information needed for the current memorandum.

c. Companies that do not have standardized forms for preparing memorandums use company letterhead, custom templates with plain paper, word processing templates with plain paper, or plain paper. In these cases apply the following procedures:

(1) A memorandum is usually prepared on 8½- by 11-inch paper. For short memorandums, however, a half sheet (8½ by 5½ inches) may be used, although this size is usually avoided because of handling and filing difficulties.

(2) On 8½- by 11-inch paper, begin the preliminary lines 2 inches from the top edge of the paper. For memorandums prepared on half sheets, begin the preliminary lines 1 inch from the top edge of the paper.

(3) Use 1.25-inch left and right margins for memorandums prepared on 8½- by 11-inch paper and 1-inch margins for memorandums prepared on half sheets.

(4) Key in all capital letters and double-space the guide words *DATE:*, *TO:*, *FROM:*, and *SUBJECT:* at the left margin. Align the information following the guide words after the colon in the *SUBJECT:* heading. Any other guide words the company may wish to use should be placed on the same lines as the *DATE:*, *TO:*, or *FROM:* headings and begin after the information for those guide words.

(5) Triple-space after *SUBJECT:*, and begin typing the body of the memorandum at the left margin. Single-space the message, but double-space between paragraphs.

(6) If you regularly prepare memorandums on plain paper or letterhead stationery, create a form document or macro for the preliminary lines of the memorandum.

d. Reference initials are used to show who keyed and formatted the memorandum. The preparer's initials are placed in lowercase letters at the left margin a double space below the last line of text.

When a memorandum is written by a person other than the one whose name appears after the *FROM:* guide word, the writer's name or capitalized initials precede the initials of the preparer. Separate the name or initials of the writer from the preparer's initials by a colon or a diagonal line.

e. **If any enclosures or attachments are included with the memorandum, an enclosure or attachment notation is placed on the second line (or next line to conserve space) below the reference initials. Begin the notation at the left margin. If more than one enclosure or attachment is included, be sure to list the items or include the number with the notation. Following are examples of enclosure and attachment notations:**

Enclosure Enc. Directory Enclosure: Mason Contract

Enclosures: Receipt from agent
Copy of application 2 Enc. Enc.

Enclosures 2 Enclosures (2) 2 Enclosures

Attachment Attachment: Survey results Att.

Attachments: Application for admission
Student information form Attachments 2

2 Attachments Att. 2

f. **When copies of memorandums are directed to individuals other than the addressee, note the distribution at the bottom of the memorandum. The copy notation is placed on the second line (or next line to conserve space) following the enclosure notation, if used. Otherwise, it appears a single or double space below the reference initials. For copy notations in memorandums, use the same formats and procedures as shown for business letters in Section 12–19.**

cc: John R. Robinson, Agent
1865 Rinaldi Street
Oklahoma City, OK 73103

c: Donna Huberman cc Cory Pallini, Supervisor

c Vahi Urun, Vice President, Operations

copy: Ms. Jennell Warren c: Sales Department Staff

copies: Bill Acevedo
Kristen Mellert C: Mrs. Phuong Nguyen

copy to Mr. John Harrington, Manager, Kelly Paper Corporation

cc: R. F. Gillham, President
T. L. McMillan, Vice President
F. S. Brotherton, General Manager

cc Marcus L. Brendero, Anne S. Langville, David M. Silverman

memorandum prepared on company letterhead

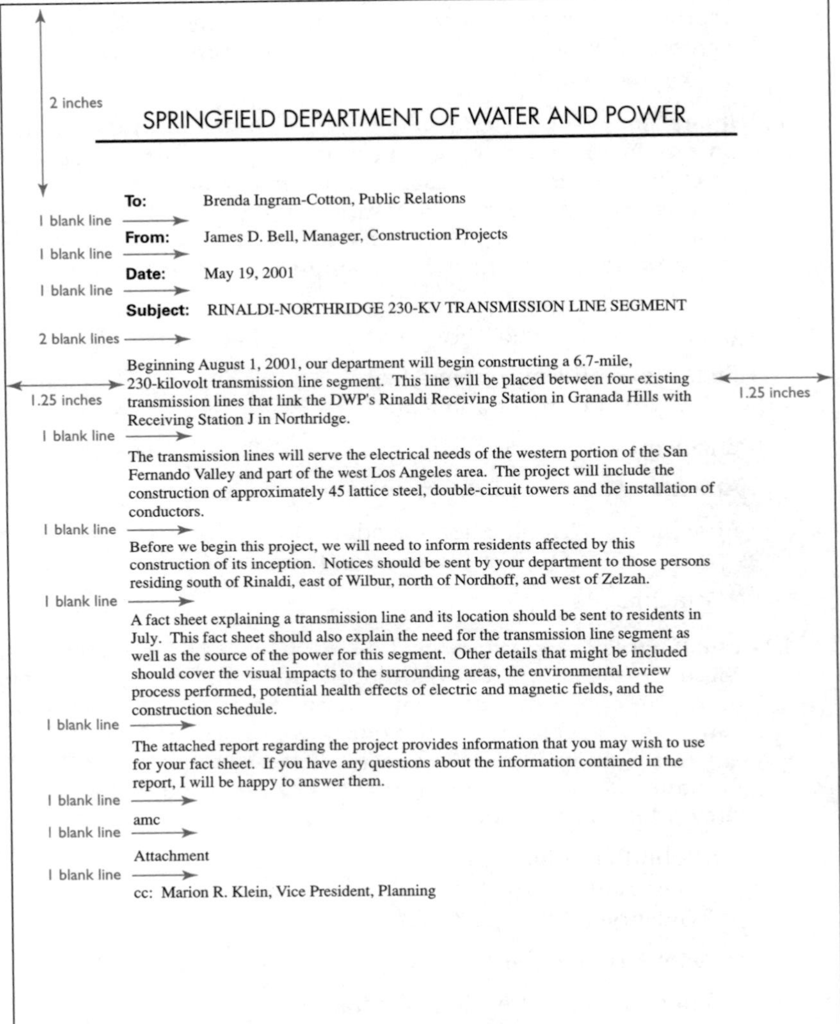

SPRINGFIELD DEPARTMENT OF WATER AND POWER

To: Brenda Ingram-Cotton, Public Relations

From: James D. Bell, Manager, Construction Projects

Date: May 19, 2001

Subject: RINALDI-NORTHRIDGE 230-KV TRANSMISSION LINE SEGMENT

Beginning August 1, 2001, our department will begin constructing a 6.7-mile, 230-kilovolt transmission line segment. This line will be placed between four existing transmission lines that link the DWP's Rinaldi Receiving Station in Granada Hills with Receiving Station J in Northridge.

The transmission lines will serve the electrical needs of the western portion of the San Fernando Valley and part of the west Los Angeles area. The project will include the construction of approximately 45 lattice steel, double-circuit towers and the installation of conductors.

Before we begin this project, we will need to inform residents affected by this construction of its inception. Notices should be sent by your department to those persons residing south of Rinaldi, east of Wilbur, north of Nordhoff, and west of Zelzah.

A fact sheet explaining a transmission line and its location should be sent to residents in July. This fact sheet should also explain the need for the transmission line segment as well as the source of the power for this segment. Other details that might be included should cover the visual impacts to the surrounding areas, the environmental review process performed, potential health effects of electric and magnetic fields, and the construction schedule.

The attached report regarding the project provides information that you may wish to use for your fact sheet. If you have any questions about the information contained in the report, I will be happy to answer them.

amc

Attachment

cc: Marion R. Klein, Vice President, Planning

memorandum prepared using a word processing template

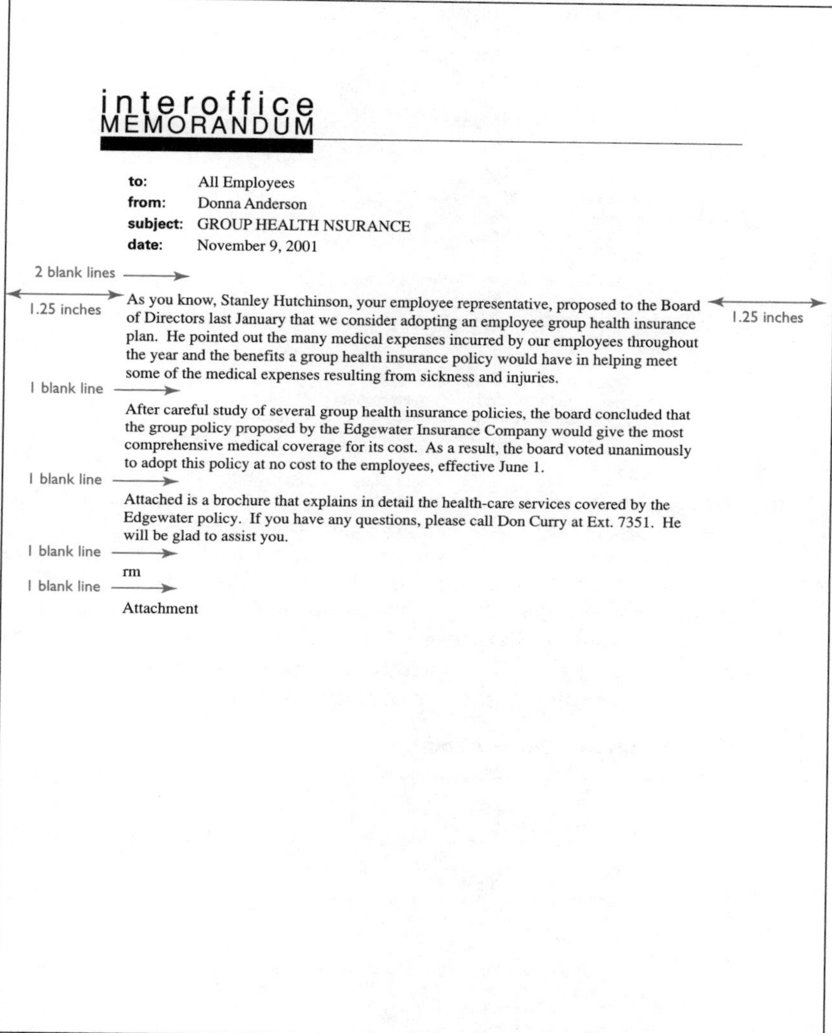

interoffice
MEMORANDUM

to: All Employees
from: Donna Anderson
subject: GROUP HEALTH NSURANCE
date: November 9, 2001

As you know, Stanley Hutchinson, your employee representative, proposed to the Board of Directors last January that we consider adopting an employee group health insurance plan. He pointed out the many medical expenses incurred by our employees throughout the year and the benefits a group health insurance policy would have in helping meet some of the medical expenses resulting from sickness and injuries.

After careful study of several group health insurance policies, the board concluded that the group policy proposed by the Edgewater Insurance Company would give the most comprehensive medical coverage for its cost. As a result, the board voted unanimously to adopt this policy at no cost to the employees, effective June 1.

Attached is a brochure that explains in detail the health-care services covered by the Edgewater policy. If you have any questions, please call Don Curry at Ext. 7351. He will be glad to assist you.

rm

Attachment

memorandum prepared on blank paper

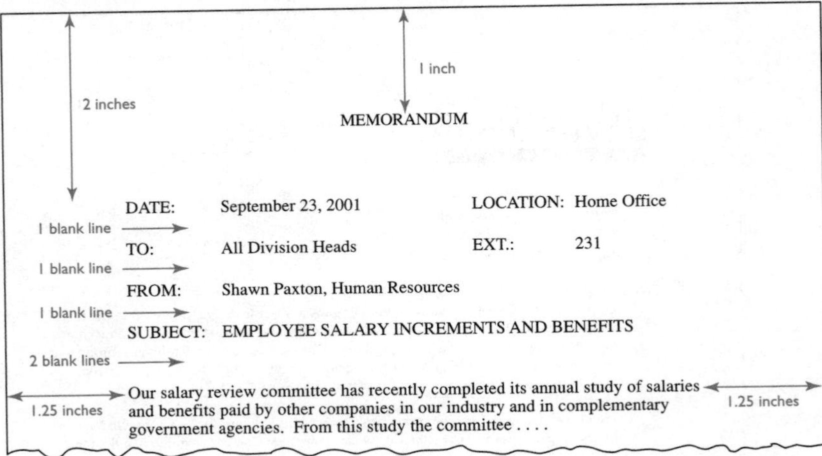
MEMORANDUM

DATE:	September 23, 2001	LOCATION:	Home Office
TO:	All Division Heads	EXT.:	231
FROM:	Shawn Paxton, Human Resources		
SUBJECT:	EMPLOYEE SALARY INCREMENTS AND BENEFITS		

Our salary review committee has recently completed its annual study of salaries and benefits paid by other companies in our industry and in complementary government agencies. From this study the committee . . . .

g. When a memorandum contains more than one page, the heading for the second and succeeding pages should have a 1-inch top margin. Show the name of the person or group to whom the memorandum is addressed, the page number, and the date. This information may be arranged vertically at the left margin or be placed on a single line with the name beginning at the left margin, the page number centered, and the date aligned with the right margin. Triple-space after the heading before continuing the body of the memorandum.

vertical second-page heading

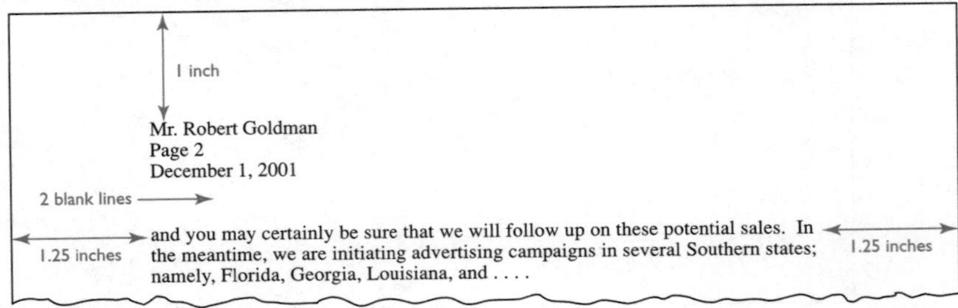
Mr. Robert Goldman
Page 2
December 1, 2001

and you may certainly be sure that we will follow up on these potential sales. In the meantime, we are initiating advertising campaigns in several Southern states; namely, Florida, Georgia, Louisiana, and . . . .

horizontal second-page heading

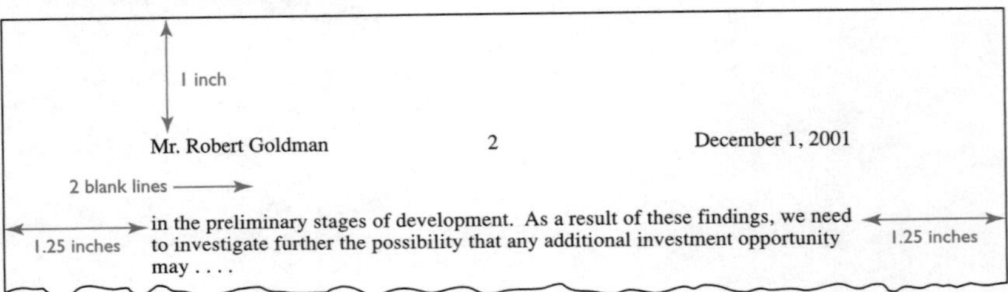
Mr. Robert Goldman   2   December 1, 2001

in the preliminary stages of development. As a result of these findings, we need to investigate further the possibility that any additional investment opportunity may . . . .

Chapter 13

Reports and Other Business Documents

Ibid.

Reports and Other Business Documents Solution Finder

General Formats for Reports and Manuscripts

13–1 Purpose, Content, and General Style

Reports are used in business mainly to convey information, analyze data, or support proposals. Those reports written for public distribution, such as reports to stockholders, are printed and usually appear in booklet form. Other reports, those for internal use or limited distribution, are generated internally using word processing software. Regardless of their final form—printed, desktop published, keyed and printed from word processing software, or typewritten—the report formats recommended here should be used for the preparation and editing process. Except for printed and desktop published reports, these formats also represent the final product.

All reports and manuscripts contain a title page and the body of the report. Other parts may be added, depending upon the length, complexity, and formality of the document. The parts of a report or manuscript may include the following:

Title page
Letter of transmittal
Summary (or Executive summary)
Table of contents
List of tables (and/or List of illustrations)
Contents of the report
Endnotes (if applicable)
Bibliography
Appendix (or Appendixes)

a. Reports and manuscripts may be prepared with either 1.25-inch left and right margins or 1-inch left and right margins, depending upon the preference of the originator. If the report or manuscript is to be bound on the left, allow an additional 0.25 inch for the left margin.

b. The first page of major parts (title page, table of contents, bibliography, etc.) and the opening page of sections or chapters require a 2-inch top margin, 2.25 inches for top-bound documents.

section opener with 2-inch top margin

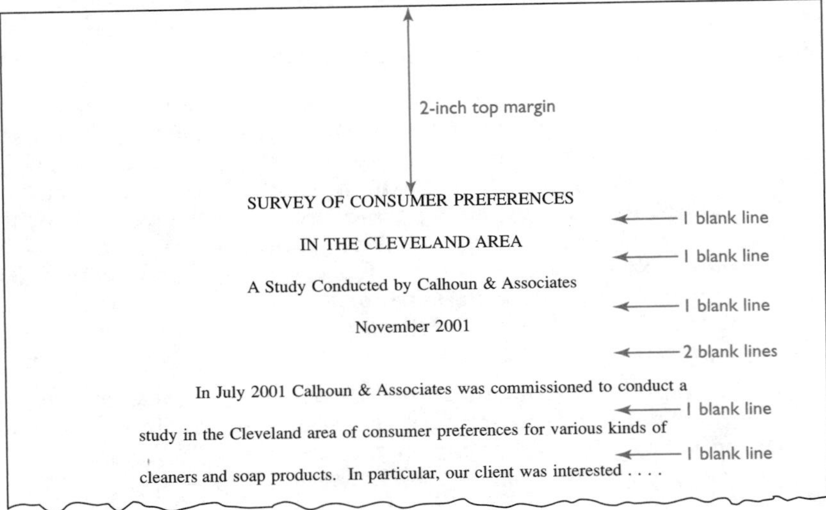

The opening pages of major sections are included in the page count, but the page number is usually not printed on the page.

section opener without page number

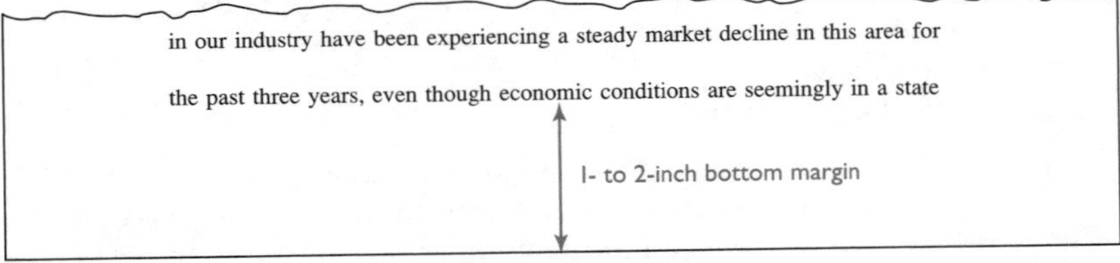

If a page number is to be included on the section opener, select one of the following formats:

(1) **Page number 1 inch from bottom edge of page.** Center the page number on a line 1 inch from the bottom edge of the paper. Leave at least one blank line separating the page number from the last line of text.

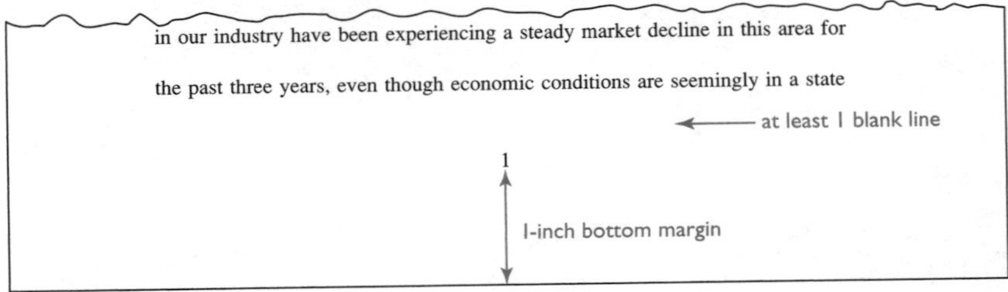

(2) **Page number 0.5 inch from bottom edge of page.** Center the page number on a line 0.5 inch from the bottom edge of the paper. Leave at least two blank lines separating the page number from the last line of text.

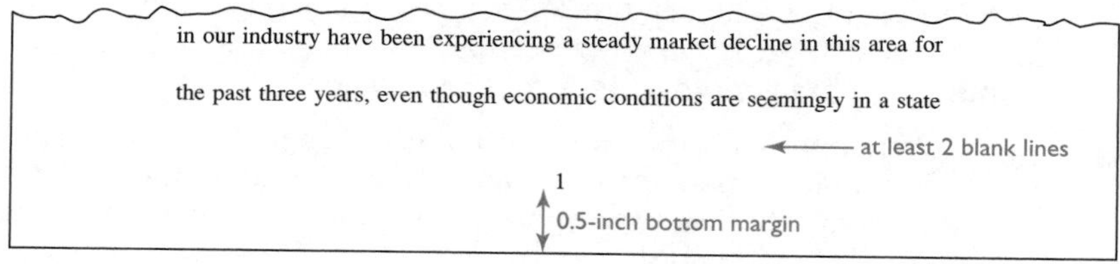

c. Number preliminary pages (those preceding the contents of the report) consecutively in lowercase Roman numerals (*i, ii, iii, iv, v,* etc.). Count the title page as page *i* even though no number is shown on that page; number the letter of transmittal *ii,* if used.

Create a footer or use the page numbering feature of your word processing program to number any preliminary pages. Suppress the footer or page numbering on the title page. Use one of the following two formats:

(1) **Page number 1 inch from bottom edge of page.** Center the page number on a line 1 inch from the bottom edge of the paper. Leave at least one blank line separating the page number from the last line of text.

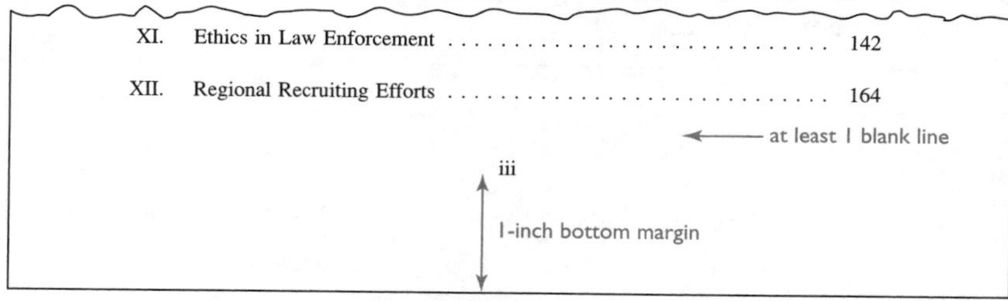

(2) **Page number 0.5 inch from bottom edge of page.** Center the page number on a line 0.5 inch from the bottom edge of the paper. Leave at least two blank lines separating the page number from the last line of text.

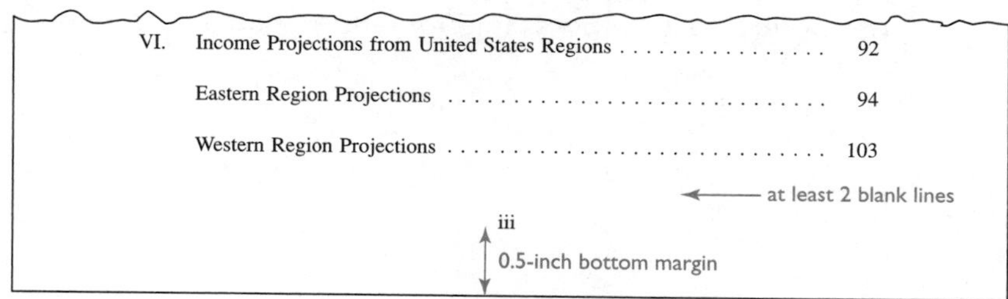

Discontinue the footer or this mode of pagination at the conclusion of the preliminary parts.

d. **Use a 1-inch top margin (1.25 inches for top-bound documents) for all pages except those with main headings. The page number begins the page.**

Create a header or use the page numbering feature of your program to number pages. Select one of the following page-numbering formats; use consistent formats for numbering the preliminary pages and the remaining pages of the report or manuscript.

(1) **Page number 1 inch from top edge of page.** Place the page number in Arabic numerals 1 inch below the top edge of the paper. Align the page number with the right margin, and leave one or two blank lines before beginning the text.

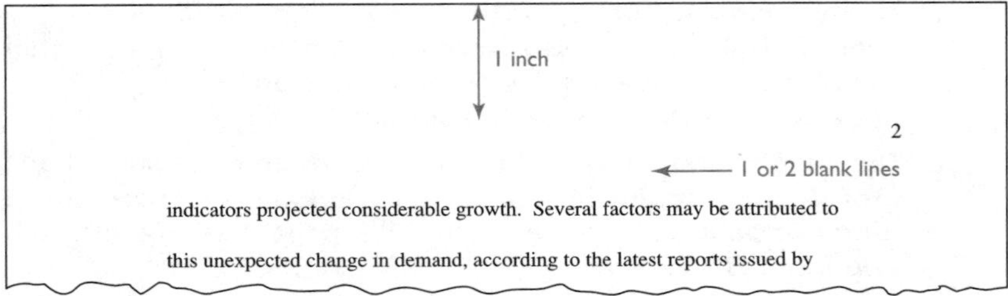

(2) **Page number 0.5 inch from top edge of page.** Place the page number in Arabic numerals 0.5 inch below the top edge of the paper and 0.5 inch from the right edge of the paper. Leave two blank lines before beginning the text.

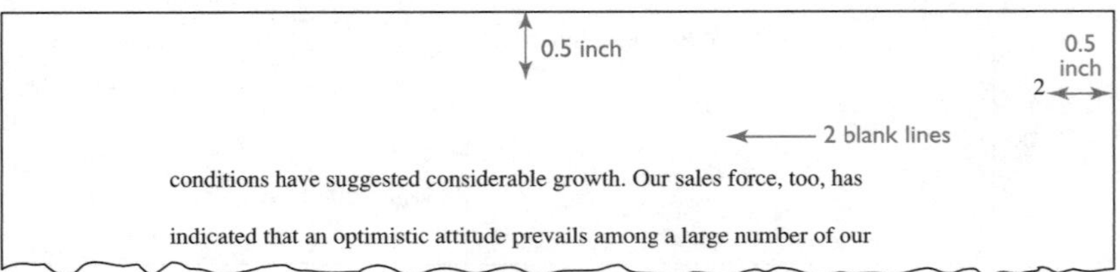

e. **In the body of the report, indent the first line of paragraphs 0.5 inch. Indent long quotations and vertical listings 0.5 inch from both the left and right margins.**

Use a tab to indent each paragraph and the "left-right indent" feature of your word processing program to indent long quotations and vertical listings.

0.5 inch
←→Besides providing local advertising, screening prospective tenants, and collecting rents for your rental property, we provide you with an annual statement for your income tax records. In addition, we have available at cost to each of our clients the following services:

- Appliance, electrical, or plumbing repairs by a reputable, licensed service center

0.5 inch ←→ 0.5 inch

- Daily, weekly, or monthly cleaning service to include linen change, kitchen and bathroom maintenance, dusting and vacuuming, and window cleaning ←→

- Painting and general maintenance or repairs

0.5 inch
←→As you can see, we are a full-service rental agency. We have been serving the Coachella Valley for over . . . .

f. **A single line that belongs to a paragraph may not be isolated at the top or bottom of a different page. In addition, an isolated text heading may not be the last line on a page. Conclude the report or manuscript text 1 to 2 inches from the bottom edge of the page, ensuring that *at least* two lines of a paragraph appear at the bottom of a page. A minimum of two lines (one full line and at least one word on a second line) must appear at the top of a page for any paragraphs carried over from a previous page.**

Use the widow/orphan protection feature of your word processing program to prevent single lines of a paragraph from appearing on a separate page. For any text headings appearing as the last line on the page, use the page-break control feature to keep lines together and force the heading to the next page.

concluding lines of page

We have been advertising this product line for the past six months in the Dallas area. Television, radio, and newspaper campaigns have focused on all

continuation of paragraph on next page

> 6
>
> hair-care products in our Lustre Plus line. Billboard advertising has been confined to featuring only our shampoo and conditioner.
>
> Preliminary results from this advertising campaign show between a 25 and 30 percent increase in sales for . . . .

g. In your word processing program, create macros, create styles, or use system shortcuts to change line spacing instantly (single spacing, double spacing, triple spacing). Use these macros, styles, and/or shortcuts to produce the following results in formatting the report or manuscript:[1]

(1) Double-space and center main headings (all capital letters) and any secondary headings (uppercase and lowercase letters); triple-space before beginning the first line of text. Always triple-space after a main heading if no secondary heading is used.

(2) Double-space the textual material in the body of the report; indent the first line of each paragraph 0.5 inch.

(3) Triple-space before and double-space after first- and second-degree text headings. Third-degree headings are considered part of the paragraph they introduce and are spaced like regular text.

(4) Single-space and indent 0.5 inch from the left and right margins any long quotations; omit the quotation marks. Long quotations are those consisting of more than three lines or more than two sentences. Double-space before and after the long quotation.[2]

(5) Vertical listings consisting of single-line items may be single or double spaced. For listings with items containing more than one line, single-space the items and leave one blank line between items. Double-space before and after the vertical listing.

(6) Tables and illustrations should be centered between the left and right margins. Either double- or triple-space before and after any tables and illustrations interrupting the text narrative. Be consistent in your choice of spacing before and after all visual displays within the text material.

h. Use the spell check feature of your word processing program to correct any spelling or typographical errors.

i. If you must frequently prepare manuscripts or reports, use the styles feature of your word processing program to format your reports.

---

[1]See the following sections in this chapter for specific instructions and examples for the preparation of report and manuscript parts, main headings, secondary headings, text headings, vertical listings, report or manuscript text (body), tables, and illustrations.

[2]See Chapter 1, Punctuation, Section 1-48, for further information on using and formatting long quotations in manuscripts and reports.

report pages with text headings, a table, and a chart

for inventories valued at LIFO, inventories at December 31 would have been $66.5 million and $66.4 million higher than reported for 2000 and 2001, respectively. The FIFO cost of inventories at these dates approximated replacement cost or net realizable value.

Inventories at December 31 consisted of the following:

Table 4 INVENTORIES 2000–2001		
Type	2000 (in millions)	2001 (in millions)
Finished goods	$ 187.5	$ 175.0
Work-in-process	96.4	115.1
Raw materials	70.0	69.5
Inventories	$ 353.9	$ 359.6

Dispositions and Restructuring

In 1999 the company's Board of Directors approved plans to offer for sale the businesses that comprised the Industrial Products and Technetics Divisions of the company's Technical segment except for Technetics' golf shaft operation, which was transferred to the Marsh-Barnhardt Division on January 1, 1997. The disposition of these businesses was completed in 1997. A pretax gain on the dispositions of $84.2 million ($46.7 million after taxes) was recorded in 1998. Net proceeds from the sale of assets of

***report pages with text headings, a table, and a chart* (continued)**

35

$213.1 million, primarily from the sales of these businesses, were used to pay off privately placed commercial paper borrowings.

Results of Operations—2001 vs. 2000

Differences in net sales, interest and other items, and income taxes showed a general decline from the beginning of fiscal year 1999 through fiscal year 2001.

Net Sales. As shown in Figure 4, the company's consolidated net sales declined 12.5 percent in 2000. Decreases in the Marine and Technical segments were responsible for the consolidated decline.

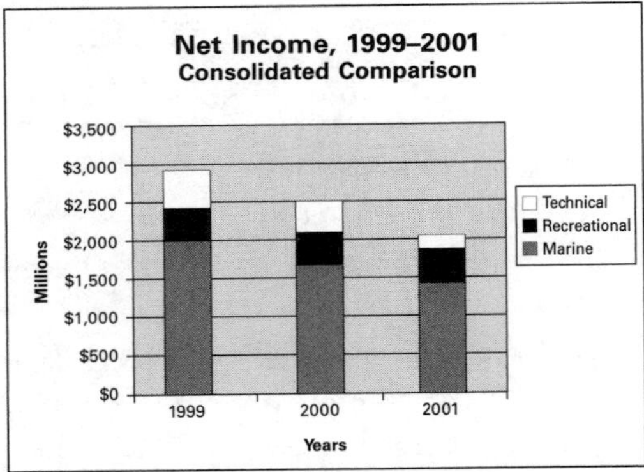

Figure 1. Consolidated Net Income Comparison, 1999–2001

Parts of a Report or Manuscript

13–2 Title Page

a. **The title page generally contains the following information, but its contents are not restricted to these items:**

(1) The name or title of the report or manuscript

(2) The name and title of the person and/or the name of the group or organization for whom it was written

(3) The name and title of the person and/or the name of the group who wrote it

(4) The date it was submitted

b. **Use the following guidelines to prepare a title page. To prepare the title page easily, access the center-page feature of your word processing program.**

(1) Allow 2-inch top and bottom margins.

(2) Center all lines horizontally.

(3) Type the title of the report or manuscript in all capital letters. Single-space any titles containing more than one line.

(4) Space equally between the top and bottom margins all other parts following the title.

(5) Count the title page in the pagination, but do not number the page.

An illustration of a title page appears on page 382.

13–3 Letter of Transmittal

a. **The letter of transmittal, if used, introduces the reader to the report or manuscript. Although the content of the transmittal letter will depend upon the complexity and scope of the report or manuscript, it should basically tell the reader the following:**

(1) What the topic is

(2) Why the report was written

(3) How the report was compiled (method of research)

(4) Who worked on it or helped with its development

(5) What major findings or conclusions resulted (if a synopsis or summary page is not included)

b. **The letter of transmittal should be friendly and concise, usually concluding with the writer expressing appreciation for the opportunity to produce the report or manuscript. Use the following guidelines to prepare the transmittal letter:**

(1) Use any acceptable business letter style.

(2) Place the letter of transmittal after the title page.

(3) Number the page with a lowercase Roman numeral centered at the bottom of the page. Place the page number 1 inch or 0.5 inch from the bottom edge of the page, depending upon the page-numbering format selected for the document. See Section 13–1c for further information on the page-numbering formats.

An illustration of a letter of transmittal appears on page 383.

title page

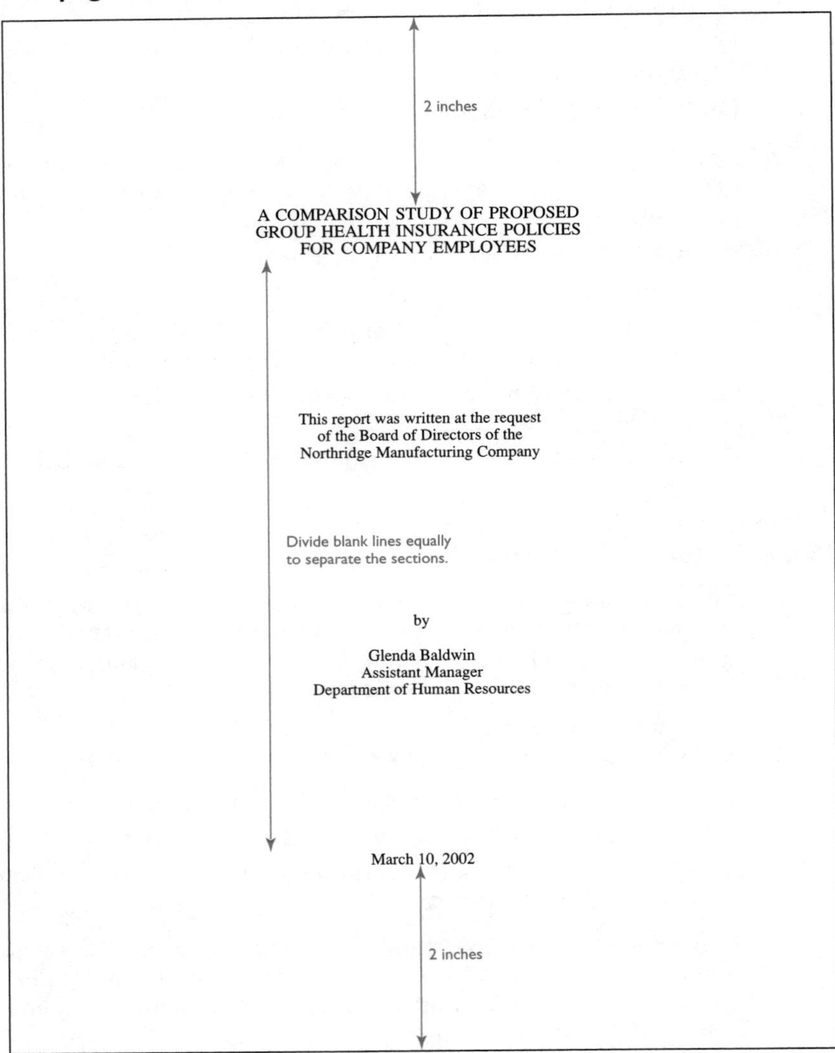

A COMPARISON STUDY OF PROPOSED
GROUP HEALTH INSURANCE POLICIES
FOR COMPANY EMPLOYEES

This report was written at the request
of the Board of Directors of the
Northridge Manufacturing Company

by

Glenda Baldwin
Assistant Manager
Department of Human Resources

March 10, 2002

letter of transmittal

Northridge Manufacturing Company

170 East Parkland Avenue
Dallas, Texas 75214

(214) 383-5757
Fax: (214) 383-5783

March 10, 2001

Mr. Don Washington, President
Northridge Manufacturing Company
170 East Parkland Avenue
Dallas, Texas 75214

Dear Mr. Washington:

As requested by our Board of Directors, I have prepared a report comparing the employee group health insurance policies that were submitted by eight companies.

The policies were compared in the following ways:

1. Company cost per employee
2. Cost to employees
3. Kinds of illnesses and/or injuries covered
4. Hospital, out-patient, and home-visit coverage
5. Total annual health benefits allowed
6. Miscellaneous coverages such as medicines, X rays, physical therapy, private nursing, etc.
7. Family members covered

As shown by the summary table on page 19, the Edgewater policy is superior in all categories except one–company cost per employee. I recommend we select the Edgewater proposal. The additional $3.16 annual cost per employee is relatively small considering the substantial benefits over any one of the other less expensive policies.

Thank you for the opportunity to conduct this study. I appreciate the help and cooperation I received from the employees' representative and from the representatives of the insurance companies.

If you have any questions or if I can be of further help, please let me know.

Sincerely,

Glenda Baldwin

Glenda Baldwin, Assistant Manager
Department of Human Resources

ba

ii

0.5 in.

13–4 Summary of the Report

Long reports—especially those not including a letter of transmittal or those including a letter of transmittal without a synopsis—usually require a summary, sometimes referred to as an *executive summary.* Use the following guidelines to prepare the summary:

(1) Allow a 2-inch top margin. Center the main heading *SUMMARY* or *EXECUTIVE SUMMARY* in all capital letters on the line directly following the top margin. Triple-space after the main heading.

(2) Double-space the text of the summary; indent each paragraph 0.5 inch. Begin by stating the purpose of the report. Briefly describe the procedures used in preparing the report, and end with a concise presentation of the conclusions and recommendations.

(3) Number the summary page or pages with lowercase Roman numerals centered at the bottom of the page. Place the page number 1 inch or 0.5 inch from the bottom edge of the page, depending upon the page-numbering format selected for the document. See Section 13–1c for further information on the page-numbering formats.

13–5 Table of Contents

The content and format of a table of contents vary with the length and complexity of the report or manuscript, but the following guidelines may be used for its preparation:

(1) Allow a 2-inch top margin. Center the main heading *TABLE OF CONTENTS or CONTENTS* in all capital letters on the line directly following the top margin.

(2) Place the word *Page* a triple space below the *TABLE OF CONTENTS* heading; align it with the right margin.

(3) Use all capital letters and double-space the listing for the preliminary sections of the report (e.g., letter of transmittal, summary, list of tables, or list of illustrations). Begin a double space below Page and at the left margin. Although it is counted and paginated with a lowercase Roman numeral, the table of contents is not included in this listing.

(4) Begin the major division heading of the report (e.g., *Chapter, Section, Unit,* or *Topic*) at the left margin. The major division heading may either appear on the same line as *Page* or be placed a double space below the preliminary parts.

(5) Number major sections of the report, if desired, by using uppercase Roman numerals. Align the longest numeral with the left margin, and indent the shorter numerals so the periods following the numerals are aligned. Use a decimal tab in your word processing program to achieve this alignment.

(6) Use all capital letters for listing major sections of the report. Those sections of lesser degree should be indented, placed in capital and lowercase letters, and arranged in the same sequence as they appear in the report.

(7) Use leaders (a line of alternating periods and spaces) to assist the reader in locating the page number of a particular section, and align vertically the leaders for each section or subsection of the report. Although all major headings must have corresponding page numbers, the assignment of page numbers to subheadings appearing in the table of contents is optional. To obtain leaders in your word processing program, set a right decimal with dot leaders adjacent to the right margin.

(8) Number the table of contents with lowercase Roman numerals centered at the bottom of the page. Place the page number 1 inch or 0.5 inch from the bottom edge of the page, depending upon the page-numbering format selected for the document. See Section 13–1c for further information on the page-numbering formats.

table of contents

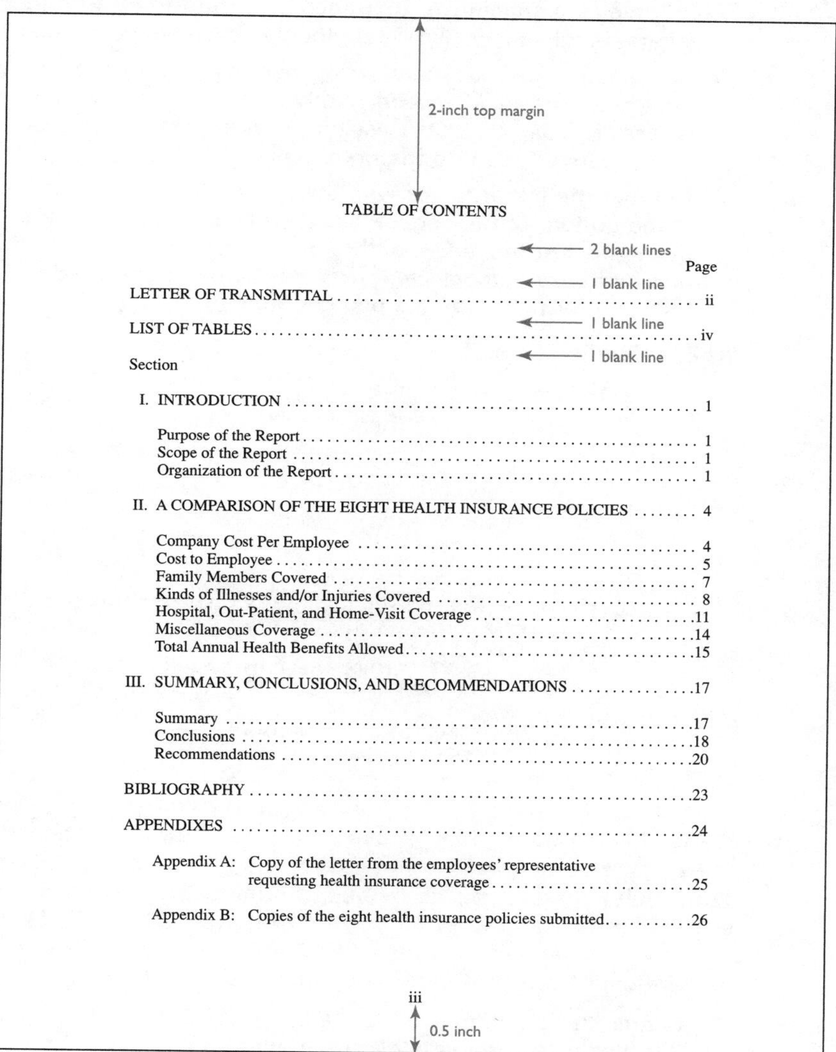

13–6 List of Tables or List of Illustrations

a. **When a report or manuscript contains several tables, include as a helpful reference to the reader a list of tables after the table of contents. Guidelines for formatting the list of tables follow:**

(1) Center the heading *LIST OF TABLES* in all capital letters 2 inches from the top edge of the page.

(2) Triple-space after the *LIST OF TABLES* heading. Place the word *Table* at the left margin, and align the last letter of the word *Page* with the right margin.

(3) Indent 0.25 inch from the left margin. Key the number of each table followed by spacing of 0.25 inch and the table title in all capital letters. Single-space each title; double-space between titles.

(4) Use leaders (a line of alternating periods and spaces) to assist the reader in locating the page number of a particular table. To obtain leaders in your word processing program, set a right decimal with dot leaders adjacent to the right margin.

(5) Number the list of tables with lowercase Roman numerals centered at the bottom of the page. Place the page number 1 inch or 0.5 inch from the bottom edge of the page, depending upon the page-numbering format selected for the document. See Section 13–1c for further information on the page-numbering formats.

list of tables

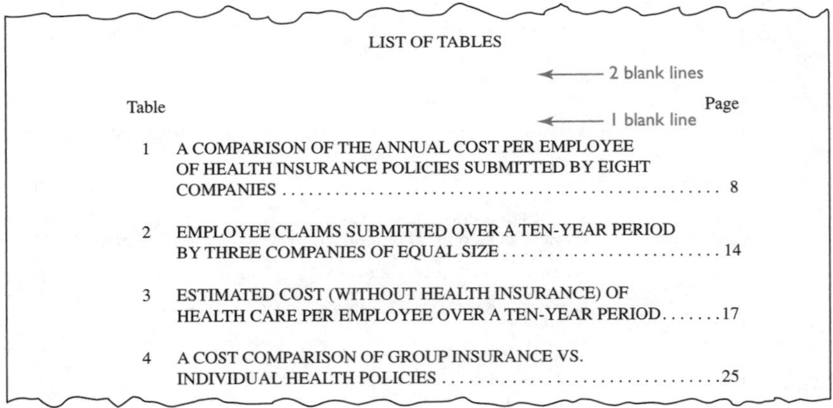

LIST OF TABLES

← 2 blank lines

Table | Page

← 1 blank line

1 A COMPARISON OF THE ANNUAL COST PER EMPLOYEE OF HEALTH INSURANCE POLICIES SUBMITTED BY EIGHT COMPANIES 8

2 EMPLOYEE CLAIMS SUBMITTED OVER A TEN-YEAR PERIOD BY THREE COMPANIES OF EQUAL SIZE 14

3 ESTIMATED COST (WITHOUT HEALTH INSURANCE) OF HEALTH CARE PER EMPLOYEE OVER A TEN-YEAR PERIOD. 17

4 A COST COMPARISON OF GROUP INSURANCE VS. INDIVIDUAL HEALTH POLICIES 25

b. **A list of illustrations may be used for a report or manuscript that contains figures or a combination of tables and figures. For one that contains only figures, use the same format described in the previous section for a list of tables. Change the title to *LIST OF ILLUSTRATIONS* and the word *Table* to *Figure*. Use the following guidelines to format a list of illustrations that contains both tables and figures:**

(1) Center the heading *LIST OF ILLUSTRATIONS* in all capital letters 2 inches from the top edge of the page.

(2) Triple-space after the *LIST OF ILLUSTRATIONS* heading, and center the subheading *A. Tables* in capital and lowercase letters. Double-space after the subheading. Place *Table* at the left margin, and align the last letter of the word *Page* with the right margin. Double-space before beginning the listing.

(3) Indent 0.25 inch from the left margin. Key the number of each table followed by spacing of 0.25 inch and the table title in all capital letters. Single-space each title; double-space between titles. Use leaders (a line of alternating periods and spaces) to assist the reader in locating the page number. To obtain leaders in your word processing program, set a right decimal tab with dot leaders adjacent to the right margin. Triple-space after the last title.

(4) Center the subheading *B. Figures* in capital and lowercase letters. Double-space after the subheading; place *Figure* at the left margin and align the last letter of the word *Page* with the right margin. Double-space before beginning the listing.

(5) Indent 0.25 inch from the left margin. Key the number of each figure followed by spacing of 0.25 inch and the figure title in all capital letters. Use leaders to assist the reader in locating the page number. Single-space each title; double-space between titles.

(6) Number the list of illustrations with lowercase Roman numerals centered at the bottom of the page. Place the page number 1 inch or 0.5 inch from the bottom edge of the page, depending upon the page-numbering format selected for the document. See Section 13–1c for further information on the page-numbering formats.

list of illustrations

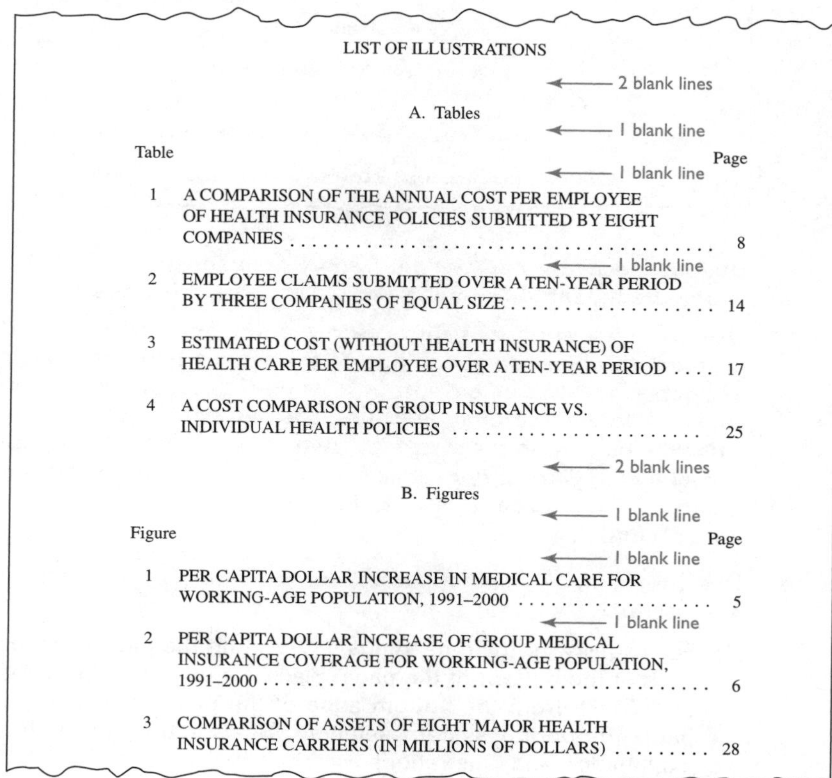

LIST OF ILLUSTRATIONS

← 2 blank lines

A. Tables

← 1 blank line

Table . . . Page

← 1 blank line

1 A COMPARISON OF THE ANNUAL COST PER EMPLOYEE OF HEALTH INSURANCE POLICIES SUBMITTED BY EIGHT COMPANIES 8

← 1 blank line

2 EMPLOYEE CLAIMS SUBMITTED OVER A TEN-YEAR PERIOD BY THREE COMPANIES OF EQUAL SIZE 14

3 ESTIMATED COST (WITHOUT HEALTH INSURANCE) OF HEALTH CARE PER EMPLOYEE OVER A TEN-YEAR PERIOD 17

4 A COST COMPARISON OF GROUP INSURANCE VS. INDIVIDUAL HEALTH POLICIES 25

← 2 blank lines

B. Figures

← 1 blank line

Figure . . . Page

← 1 blank line

1 PER CAPITA DOLLAR INCREASE IN MEDICAL CARE FOR WORKING-AGE POPULATION, 1991–2000 5

← 1 blank line

2 PER CAPITA DOLLAR INCREASE OF GROUP MEDICAL INSURANCE COVERAGE FOR WORKING-AGE POPULATION, 1991–2000 6

3 COMPARISON OF ASSETS OF EIGHT MAJOR HEALTH INSURANCE CARRIERS (IN MILLIONS OF DOLLARS) 28

13–7 Preparing the Body of the Report or Manuscript

a. Allow a 2-inch top margin on pages that begin the body of the report or manuscript or major sections of the body. Center the heading in all capital letters; double-space multiple-line main headings. Triple-space after the main heading if it is not followed by a secondary heading.

b. Secondary headings are often used to explain or elaborate on a main heading. These headings begin a double space below the main heading and appear in capital and lowercase letters. All lines are centered, and multiple lines are double spaced. Triple-space after the secondary heading.

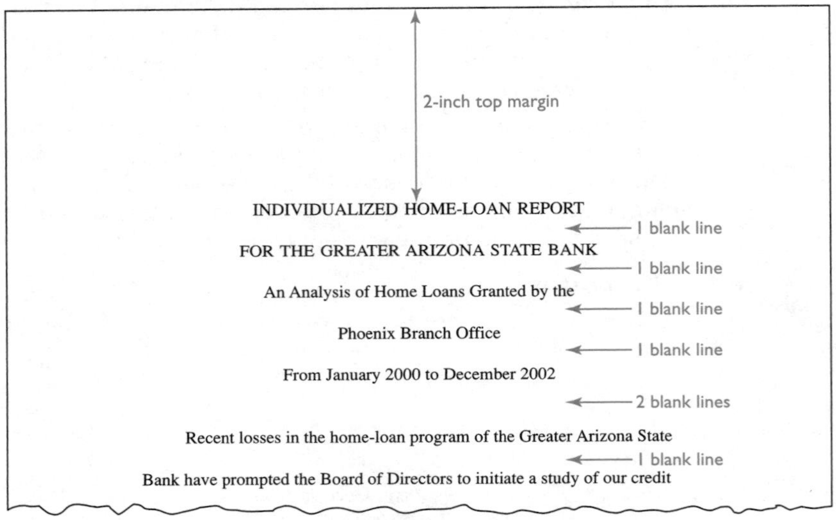

c. Double-space the body of the report or manuscript. Each paragraph should be indented 0.5 inch to offset it clearly from the previous one.

Use the widow/orphan protection feature of your word processing program to adjust page endings so that single lines from a paragraph are not at the top or bottom of a page. (These single lines are often called *widow and orphan lines.*) If page and paragraph endings do not coincide, be sure to place at least two lines of a new paragraph at the end of a page and carry over at least two lines from the previous paragraph to a new page (one complete line and a minimum of one word on a second line).

d. Use the following guidelines to number the pages of the report or manuscript:

(1) For pages with main headings, either omit the page number or center it at the bottom of the page. Place the page number either 1 inch or 0.5 inch from the bottom edge of the page, depending upon the page-numbering system selected. See Section 13–1b for further explanation and illustrations.

(2) For pages without main headings, place the page number either 1 inch or 0.5 inch from the top edge of the page, depending upon the page-numbering system selected. See Section 13-1d for further explanation and illustrations.

body of report

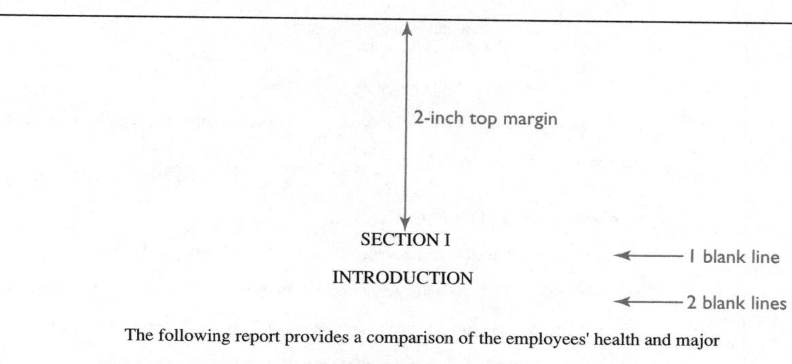

SECTION I

INTRODUCTION

The following report provides a comparison of the employees' health and major medical insurance programs submitted by eight major insurance companies.

Purpose of the Report

Last January Norman Rittgers, one of the employee representatives of our company, requested that company-sponsored health insurance be considered by the Board of Directors as a supplement to our wage and salary schedule. As a result, the board directed the Department of Human Resources to (1) contact insurance companies to determine what health insurance coverages were available and (2) compare the coverages to determine which policy would most cost effectively meet our employees' health insurance needs.

Scope of the Report

The scope of this investigation was limited to an analysis of the written proposals and copies of policies submitted by the participating insurance companies. Of the 28 insurance companies contacted, the majority provided only verbal explanations as to what the estimated coverage and cost of a group health and major medical insurance program would be for our employees. Only eight of these companies submitted written documents for our consideration. Proposals and policies from these companies were evaluated according to the following criteria:

***body of report* (continued)**

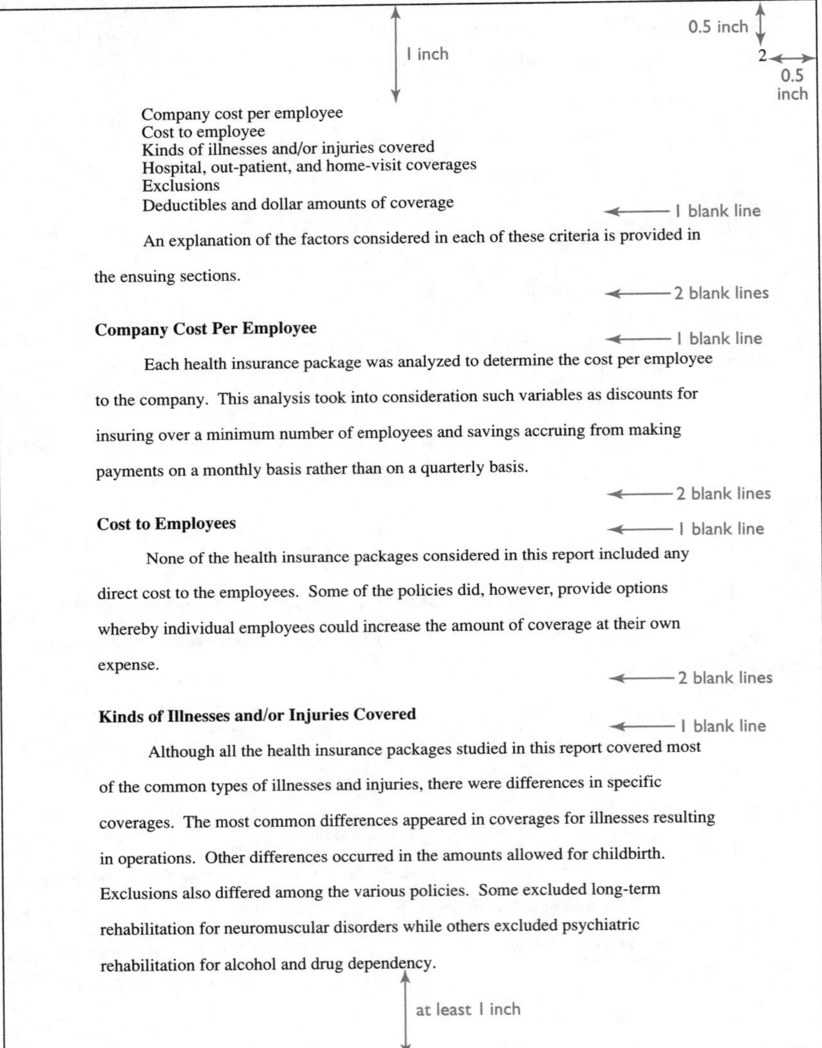

0.5 inch
1 inch
2
0.5 inch
Company cost per employee
Cost to employee
Kinds of illnesses and/or injuries covered
Hospital, out-patient, and home-visit coverages
Exclusions
Deductibles and dollar amounts of coverage
1 blank line
An explanation of the factors considered in each of these criteria is provided in the ensuing sections.
2 blank lines
Company Cost Per Employee
1 blank line
Each health insurance package was analyzed to determine the cost per employee to the company. This analysis took into consideration such variables as discounts for insuring over a minimum number of employees and savings accruing from making payments on a monthly basis rather than on a quarterly basis.
2 blank lines
Cost to Employees
1 blank line
None of the health insurance packages considered in this report included any direct cost to the employees. Some of the policies did, however, provide options whereby individual employees could increase the amount of coverage at their own expense.
2 blank lines
Kinds of Illnesses and/or Injuries Covered
1 blank line
Although all the health insurance packages studied in this report covered most of the common types of illnesses and injuries, there were differences in specific coverages. The most common differences appeared in coverages for illnesses resulting in operations. Other differences occurred in the amounts allowed for childbirth. Exclusions also differed among the various policies. Some excluded long-term rehabilitation for neuromuscular disorders while others excluded psychiatric rehabilitation for alcohol and drug dependency.
at least 1 inch

13–8 Text Headings

a. **Text headings of different degrees signal content in a report or manuscript and contribute to its readability. A common classification of text headings includes first-, second-, and third-degree headings. Text headings are usually boldfaced, but they may have a larger font size with or without bolding. Guidelines for formatting each text heading follow and are repeated in the context of its corresponding illustration.**

(1) **First-degree text headings.** Center a first-degree text heading, and capitalize the first letter of each main word. The heading may be boldfaced and/or keyed in a larger font size than the report or manuscript text. Triple-space before a first-degree text heading, and double-space after it.

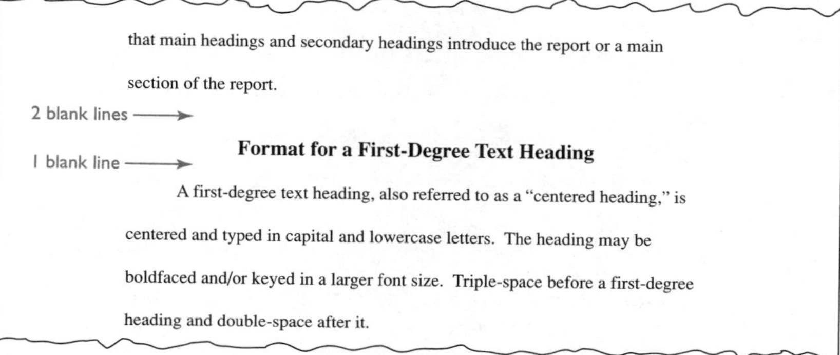

that main headings and secondary headings introduce the report or a main section of the report.

2 blank lines →

Format for a First-Degree Text Heading

1 blank line →

A first-degree text heading, also referred to as a "centered heading," is centered and typed in capital and lowercase letters. The heading may be boldfaced and/or keyed in a larger font size. Triple-space before a first-degree heading and double-space after it.

(2) **Second-degree text headings.** Begin the second-degree text heading at the left margin. Capitalize the first letter of each main word. Boldface the heading, or use a larger font size with or without bolding. If changed, the font size must be smaller than that used for first-degree text headings and larger than that used for the report or manuscript text. Triple-space before a second-degree text heading, and double-space after it.

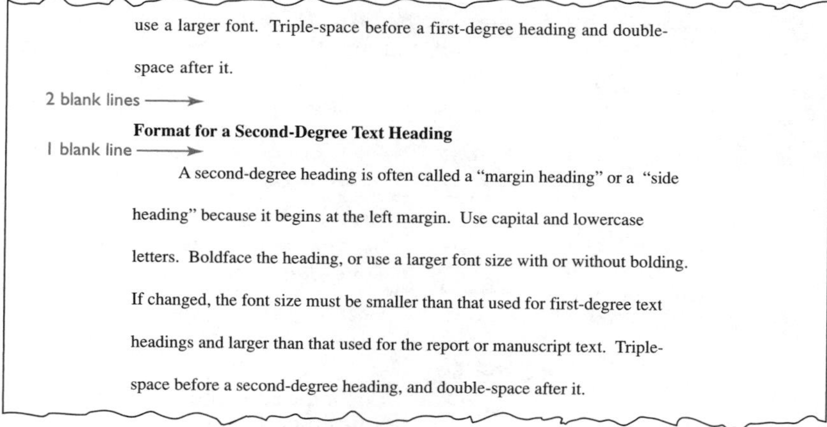

use a larger font. Triple-space before a first-degree heading and double-space after it.

2 blank lines →

Format for a Second-Degree Text Heading

1 blank line →

A second-degree heading is often called a "margin heading" or a "side heading" because it begins at the left margin. Use capital and lowercase letters. Boldface the heading, or use a larger font size with or without bolding. If changed, the font size must be smaller than that used for first-degree text headings and larger than that used for the report or manuscript text. Triple-space before a second-degree heading, and double-space after it.

(3) **Third-degree text headings.** The third-degree text heading begins a paragraph, so it is indented from the left margin the same amount of space as any other paragraph—usually 0.5 inch. Capitalize only the first word and any proper nouns. Boldface the heading and conclude it with a period. Use the same font size as the report or manuscript text. Double-space before a third-degree text heading, and begin keying the paragraph text two spaces after the period that concludes the heading.

used for the report or manuscript text. Triple-space before a second-degree text heading and double-space after it.

1 blank line →

Format for a third-degree text heading. Because the third-degree heading is part of the paragraph that follows, it is also referred to as a "paragraph heading." Only the first word and proper nouns in the heading are capitalized.

The third-degree heading is boldfaced (in the same typeface and size as the report or manuscript text) and followed by a period. Double-space before a third-degree heading, and begin keying the paragraph on the same line directly after the heading.

b. **Text headings indicate divisions of a topic or subtopic; therefore, if a first-, second-, or third-degree heading is used, it must be followed by at least one or more matching headings. For example, if you use one first-degree heading in the report or manuscript, you must use at least one other first-degree heading in the same document.**

c. **All text headings should be separated by at least two lines of text, regardless of their place in the heading hierarchy. In other words, a lesser-degree text heading may not follow another heading without any intervening text.**

d. **Text headings must be used in ascending order of degree from first degree to third degree, *but* the first-degree heading may be omitted if only one or two levels of headings are required in a report. The following table illustrates what heading levels may be used based upon the number of levels or divisions required:**

Number of Text Headings Required	*Levels of Text Headings to Be Used*
3	First-degree heading, Second-degree heading, and Third-degree heading
2	First-degree heading and Second-degree heading *or* Second-degree heading and Third-degree heading
1	First-degree heading *or* Second-degree heading

13–9 Listings

a. **Both vertical and horizontal listings are often used in letters, memorandums, reports, and manuscripts. Whether to use a horizontal listing**

or a vertical listing depends upon (1) the number of items in the listing, (2) the number of words contained in each item, and (3) the degree of emphasis the writer wishes to assign to the listing.

Vertical listings are more emphatic than horizontal listings. They may be numbered, unnumbered, or bulleted. Lengthy and complex listings are more readily understood in the vertical format.

Horizontal listings are less emphatic. They are generally used with short listings that are few in number. Each item in a horizontal listing is preceded by an Arabic numeral or a lowercase letter enclosed in parentheses.

b. *Numbered vertical listings* are numbered in consecutive order with Arabic numerals. In all business letters, memorandums, reports, and manuscripts, use the following guidelines for listing numbered items vertically:

(1) Introduce a vertical listing with a complete sentence.

(2) Indent the listing 0.5 inch from both the left and right margins. Use the left/right indent feature of your word processing program. In business letters and memorandums, vertical listings may assume the left and right margins of the main text.

(3) Number each item; use the left indent feature of your word processing program to align the text after the period in the number. (Any second and succeeding lines should begin directly under the first word, not the number, of the item.) Single-space items that are more than one line.

(4) Use parallel construction; that is, use all complete sentences, all the same kind of phrases, or all single words that begin with the same part of speech and have the same form. Place a period after each item *only* in listings that contain complete sentences.

(5) Capitalize the first word in each listed item.

(6) Double-space before the first item, between items, and after the last item in the listing.

numbered vertical listing—complete sentences

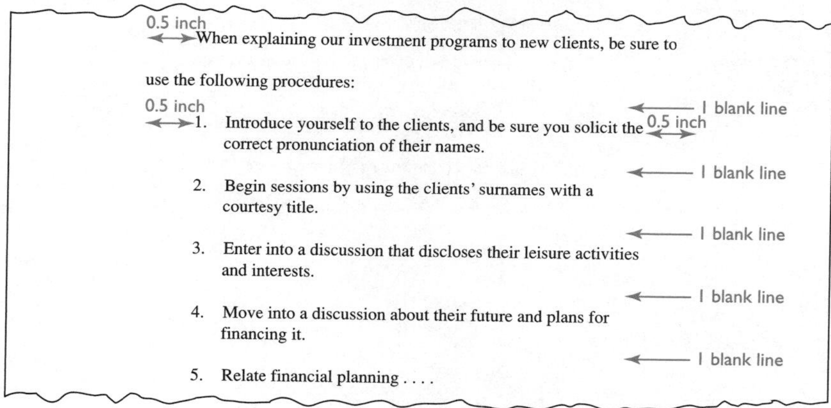
When explaining our investment programs to new clients, be sure to

use the following procedures:

1. Introduce yourself to the clients, and be sure you solicit the correct pronunciation of their names.

2. Begin sessions by using the clients' surnames with a courtesy title.

3. Enter into a discussion that discloses their leisure activities and interests.

4. Move into a discussion about their future and plans for financing it.

5. Relate financial planning . . . .

Reports 13

c. ***Unnumbered vertical listings*** **are similar in most respects to numbered vertical listings. Use the following guidelines for listing unnumbered items vertically:**

(1) Introduce a vertical listing with a complete sentence.

(2) Indent the listing 0.5 inch from both the left and right margins. Use the left/right indent feature of your word processing program.

(3) Use parallel construction; that is, use all complete sentences, all the same kind of phrases, or all single words that begin with the same part of speech and have the same form. Place a period after each item *only* in listings containing complete sentences.

(4) Capitalize the first word in each listed item.

(5) Double-space before the first item, between items, and after the last item in the listing. Single-space items that are more than one line.

unnumbered vertical listing—complete sentences

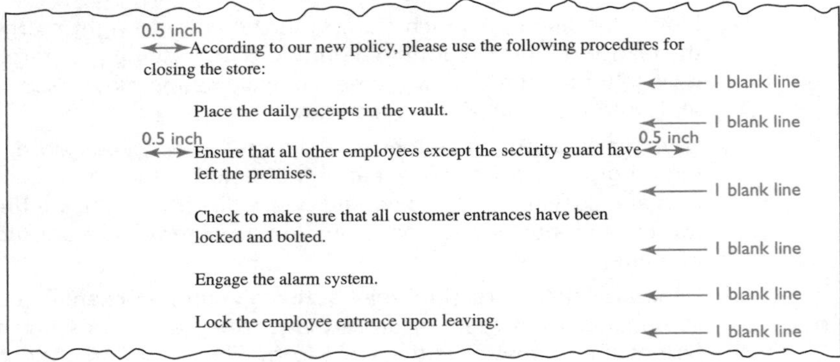

unnumbered vertical listing—words or phrases

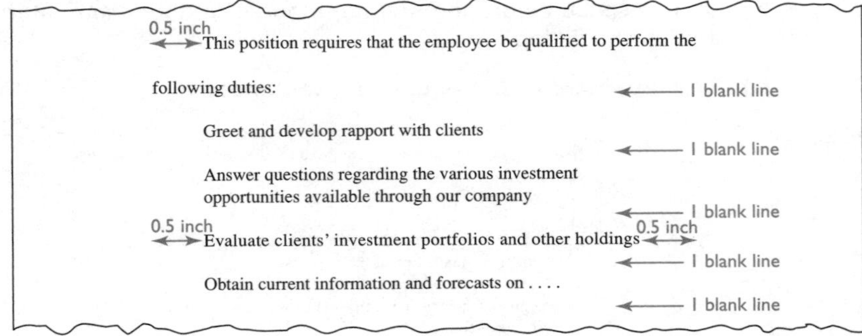

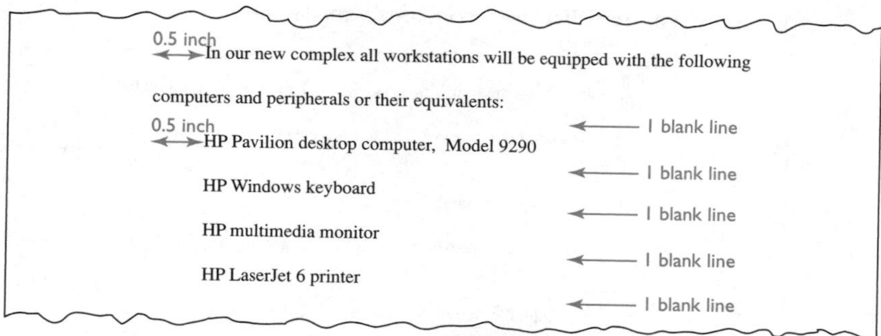

Unnumbered vertical listings consisting of words or phrases that are keyed on single lines *may* be single-spaced, although a double space still appears before and after the listing. Such a listing is shown below.

unnumbered vertical listing—words or phrases single-spaced

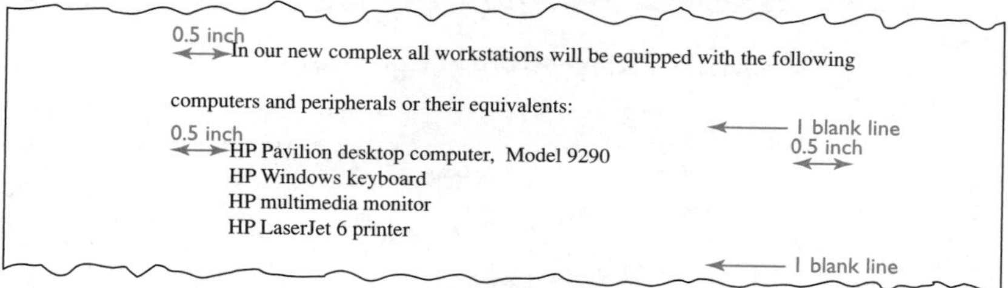

d. ***Bulleted listings*** **are similar to numbered listings. Typographic symbols (small solid circles, hollow circles, solid squares, hollow squares, check marks, etc.) replace the number. These symbols may be accessed through the extended character set feature of a word processing program. In all business letters, memorandums, reports, and manuscripts, use the following guidelines for listing bulleted items vertically:**

(1) Introduce a vertical listing with a complete sentence.

(2) Indent the listing 0.5 inch from both the left and right margins. Use the left/right indent feature of your word processing program. In business letters and memorandums, vertical listings *may* assume the left and right margins of the main text.

(3) Insert the typographic symbol; use the left indent feature of your word processing program to align the text after the typographic symbol. (Any second and succeeding lines should begin directly under the first word, not the symbol, of the item.) Single-space items that are more than one line.

(4) Use parallel construction; that is, use all complete sentences, all the same kind of phrases, or all single words that begin with the same part of speech and have the same form. Place a period after each item *only* in listings containing complete sentences.

(5) Capitalize the first word in each listed item.

(6) Double-space before the first item, between items, and after the last item in the listing.

bulleted vertical listing—complete sentences

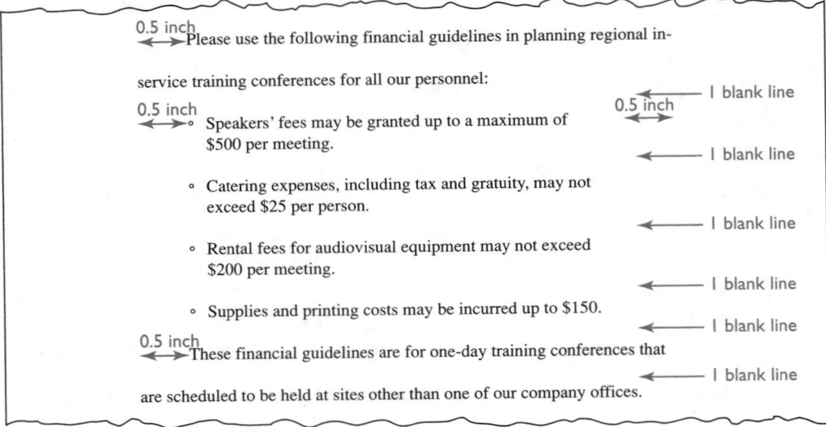
0.5 inch Please use the following financial guidelines in planning regional in-

service training conferences for all our personnel:

- Speakers' fees may be granted up to a maximum of $500 per meeting.
- Catering expenses, including tax and gratuity, may not exceed $25 per person.
- Rental fees for audiovisual equipment may not exceed $200 per meeting.
- Supplies and printing costs may be incurred up to $150.

These financial guidelines are for one-day training conferences that

are scheduled to be held at sites other than one of our company offices.

bulleted vertical listing—words or phrases

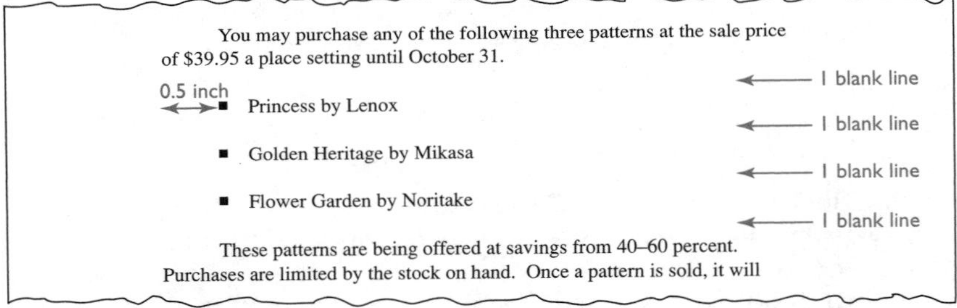
You may purchase any of the following three patterns at the sale price of $39.95 a place setting until October 31.

- Princess by Lenox
- Golden Heritage by Mikasa
- Flower Garden by Noritake

These patterns are being offered at savings from 40–60 percent. Purchases are limited by the stock on hand. Once a pattern is sold, it will

e. Horizontal listings may be part of a sentence, or they may be introduced by a complete thought followed by a colon. Whenever a horizontal listing contains three or more items, the items are separated by commas or semicolons. Use commas to separate words or phrases; use semicolons to separate complete thoughts or items that contain internal commas. Use the following guidelines for listing items horizontally:

(1) Use a colon to introduce the list *only when it is preceded by a complete thought.*

(2) Capitalize the first word of each item *only if it is a proper noun.*

(3) Identify the listed items by enclosing either lowercase letters or numbers in parentheses before each item. Do not conclude a line with only a letter or number enclosed in parentheses; at least one word of the item must appear after the letter or numeral. Use the non-breaking space feature of your word processing program to wrap an isolated number or letter to the next line.

horizontal listing—items separated by commas

as requested. Each team will consist of (a) an administrator, (b) a scientist, (c) two engineers, (d) an administrative assistant, and (e) a secretary. The team will function under the supervision of our project coordinator, who will

horizontal listing—items separated by semicolons

on Tuesday, June 10. While I am in New York, would you please take care of the following items: (1) complete the negotiations with AAA Computer System Services for an additional one-year contract; (2) respond to and follow through on the inquiry from Medco Financial Services regarding our medical software line; and (3) contact dental offices to review, test, and evaluate our newly developed line of software. If you are unable to complete any of these items,

13–10 Methods of Citing Sources

When either direct quotations or other information needs to be cited in a report or manuscript, any one of a number of methods may be used. The most common ones include footnotes, bibliographical notes, endnotes, the MLA (Modern Language Association) style of notation, and the APA (American Psychological Association) style of notation.

The MLA style of notation is generally used in literary writings while the APA style of notation is predominantly used by writers in the social sciences. Business writers, on the other hand, usually employ a conventional footnote or endnote style because it is easier to associate the cited information with its source and authenticate its contents. Therefore, the following styles shown for footnotes and endnotes are recommended for use in business reports.[3]

a. **Use the *footnote* feature of your word processing program to ensure that notations and corresponding documentation appear consistently on the same page. Guidelines for preparing footnotes for off-line sources are listed below:**

---

[3]The formats suggested here for footnotes and endnotes for published and unpublished works (except for noted deviations) are *based* on the traditional format alternatives contained in the following sources:

The Chicago Manual of Style, 14th ed. (Chicago and London: The University of Chicago Press, 1993), 487–635.

Kate L. Turabian, *A Manual for Writers of Term Papers, Theses, and Dissertations,* 6th ed., revised by John Grossman and Alice Bennett (Chicago and London: The University of Chicago Press, 1996), 116–164.

The AMA Style Guide for Business Writing (New York: American Management Association, 1996), 44, 81–84.

(1) Indicate the presence of a footnote by typing a superior (slightly raised) figure after the material to be documented. Place the footnote itself at the bottom of the page on which the reference notation appears. By accessing the footnote feature of a word processing program, these procedures will be performed automatically.

(2) Set off the footnotes from the rest of the page with a 1.5- or 2-inch line at the left margin, at least a single space after the last line of text on the page. Double-space after this line. By accessing the footnote feature of a word processing program, these procedures will be performed automatically.

(3) Indent 0.5 inch, and number each footnote consecutively with a superior (slightly raised) figure at the beginning of the footnote. By accessing the footnote feature of a word processing program, these procedures will be performed automatically.

(4) Single-space each footnote, but double-space between footnotes.

(5) Begin the footnote by typing the name of the author, if any, in a first-name, last-name sequence.

(6) Provide the complete title of the cited reference. Place the titles of magazine articles, sections of books, newspaper columns, and other such section or segment titles in quotation marks. Italicize (or underline) the titles of books, pamphlets, magazines, newspapers, and other complete works with subdivisions.

(7) Include next, where applicable, the publishing information. Enclose in parentheses the geographical location of the publisher followed by a colon, the name of the publisher, and the date of publication. Eliminate the state name from the geographical location when the city is commonly known; otherwise, use the standard state abbreviation with the city name.

(8) Follow the complete title of magazines and newspapers with the date of publication.

(9) Conclude footnotes with the page location of the cited material.

(10) Separate the parts of a footnote with commas.

book, one author

---

[1]Susan A. McAllister, *An Introduction to Microcomputers: Basic Concepts*, 3rd ed. (Cincinnati: South-Western Publishing Company, 2000), 87–91.

book, two authors

---

[2]E. Bryant Phillips and Andrea Kessler, *Principles of Small Business Management*, 4th ed. (New York: John Wiley & Sons, Inc., 1997), 108.

book, more than two authors

[3]Patricia Whitman, David Kane, James E. Wellington, and Ida Mason, *Fundamentals of Finance and Banking* (New York: McGraw-Hill, Inc., 2000), 208–14.

book, editor(s) only

[4]John M. Sakasian and Carol L. Jones, eds., *Readings in Management Theory* (Belmont, Calif.: Wadsworth Publishing Co., 2000), 307–9.

CD-ROM

[5]"Securities and Exchange Commission," *Microsoft Bookshelf '99* (CD-ROM: Microsoft Corporation, 1999).

company memorandum

[6]Meredith Garcia, "Medical Insurance Programs Available to Employees" (Boston: Interstop Corporation memorandum, 8 June 2000).

company report—published

[7]Shel Holtz, "A Partnership in Japan," *Insights* (Irvine, Calif.: Allergan, Inc., published report, May 2001), 2.

company report—unpublished (internal)

[8]Terry Thomsen, "An Analysis of Current Manufacturing Facilities" (Detroit: General Motors, Chevrolet Division, unpublished report, March 2001), 32–37.

correspondence

[9]George Bush (as vice president of the United States), response letter to author, 17 October 1986.

encyclopedia article—signed

[10]Robert D. Patton, "Management," *The World Book Encyclopedia* (Chicago: Field Enterprises Educational Corporation, 1998), 13:97.

encyclopedia article—unsigned

[11]"Adams, John," *The Encyclopaedia Britannica,* 18th ed. (Chicago: Encyclopaedia Britannica, Inc., 2000), 1:83–84.

film, videocassette, or audiocassette

[12]*Barriers to Effective Global Communication,* videocassette (Chicago: Visual Education Corporation, 2000).

government publication

[13]*Statistical Abstract of the United States,* U.S. Bureau of the Census (Washington, D.C.: U.S. Government Printing Office, 1990), 256.

interview

[14]James Montgomery (CEO, Great Western Federal Bank), interview by author, Woodland Hills, Calif., 24 July 1998.

magazine article with author

[15]A. T. Stadthaus, "The Common Market With a Reunified Germany," *BusinessWeek,* 20 August 2000, 32–33, 57.

magazine article without author

[16]"The Declining Dollar in Our International Economy," *Changing Times,* December 2000, 40–42.

newspaper article with author

[17]Richard A. Donnelly, "Commodities Corner," *Los Angeles Times,* 10 November 2000, San Fernando Valley edition, sec. D, p. 6, cols. 3–4.

paperback book

[18]Mark T. Mathews, *Managerial Psychology in a Global Economy* (Chicago: University of Chicago Press, 2000), 105.

professional journal article (with volume number)

[19]Joel P. Bowman and Inge Klopping, "Bandstands, Bandwidth, and Business Communication: Technology and Sanctity of Writing," *Business Communication Quarterly* 62:1 (March 1999): 82–90.

radio or television broadcast

[20]"Work Camps in China," *60 Minutes* (Los Angeles: Repeat KCBS telecast, 26 July 1999).

secondary source citation

[21]Stuart Williams and Peter Conway, *Internationally Known* (New York: Penguin Books USA Inc., 1990), 79, as cited in Michael Doran, *Succeeding in the Global Marketplace* (New York: Random House, Inc., 1992), 109.

table, source in

[22]Lennie Copeland and Lewis Griggs, table "U.S. Merchandise Trade by Area," *Going International* (New York: Plume of Penguin Books USA Inc., 1988), xviii.

unpublished book or booklet

[23]John Wooden, "John Wooden Basketball Fundamentals Camp, Player's Notebook" (unpublished and undated booklet), 9.

unpublished book or booklet without author, section

[24]"History of Bruin Basketball," The UCLA Alumni Association, Occasional Paper #9 (unpublished booklet, 1975), 2.

Once a reference has been cited, a shortened form may be used when the same reference is shown again. These shortened forms—*Ibid., loc. cit., and op. cit.*—are explained and illustrated in the following discussion.

Ibid. **is used when the reference cited is identical to the one in the preceding footnote. If the reference source is the same but the page numbers differ, use *Ibid.* with appended page numbers.**

Ibid.—identical reference

[3]Patricia Whitman, David Kane, James E. Wellington, and Ida Mason, *Fundamentals of Finance and Banking* (New York: McGraw-Hill, Inc., 2000), 208–14.

[4]Ibid.

Ibid.—same reference but different page number(s)

[5]Mark T. Mathews, *Managerial Psychology in a Global Economy* (Chicago: The University of Chicago Press, 2000), 105.

[6]Ibid., 134.

The notation *loc. cit.* means "in the place cited." It is used when the reference and the same page numbers have been previously cited but intervening citations have occurred. Begin the citation with the last name of the author. For two authors separate the last names with and; for more than two authors, just add *et al.* after the last name of the first author. Conclude the citation with *loc. cit.*[4]

loc. cit.

[3]Patricia Whitman, David Kane, James E. Wellington, and Ida Mason, *Fundamentals of Finance and Banking* (New York: McGraw-Hill, Inc., 2000), 208–14.

[4]Ibid.

[5]Mark T. Mathews, *Managerial Psychology in a Global Economy* (Chicago: The University of Chicago Press, 2000), 105.

[6]Ibid., 134.

[7]Whitman et al., loc. cit.

---

[4]*The Chicago Manual of Style* recommends the use of the short-title form in place of the term *loc. cit.* (pp. 582–83).

The notation *op. cit.* (meaning "in the work cited") also refers to a previously cited reference, but different page numbers are being referenced and intervening references have occurred.[5] Begin the citation with the last name of the author. For two authors separate the last names with *and*; for more than two authors, merely add *et al.* after the last name of the first author. Conclude the citation with *op. cit.* and the new page number(s).

op. cit.

---

[5]Mark T. Mathews, *Managerial Psychology in a Global Economy* (Chicago: The University of Chicago Press, 2000), 105.

[6]Ibid., 134.

[7]E. Bryant Phillips and Andrea Kessler, *Principles of Management,* 2nd ed. (New York: John Wiley & Sons, Inc., 1997), 108.

[8]Mathews, op. cit., 147.

Formats for citing on-line Internet sources (World Wide Web [WWW] sites, FTP [file transfer protocol] sites, E-mail messages, Web discussion forum postings, Telnet sites, gopher sites, listserv messages, newsgroup messages, and linkage data) have emerged only within the past several years. Use the following guidelines for citing World Wide Web sites:[6]

(1) Use the footnote feature of your word processing program to achieve the formats used for other types of sources.

(2) Begin with the author's full name, if known. Continue with the full title of the document in quotation marks, the title of the complete work (if applicable) in italics, the name of a sponsoring body or government organization (if applicable), and the date of publication or last revision (if available; otherwise, use *n.d.*). Separate each item with a comma.

(3) Enclose within angle brackets (< >) the complete address (URL).

(4) Enclose in parentheses the date (day, month, year) the site was visited.

(5) Conclude the citation with a period.

Reports 13

---

[5]*The Chicago Manual of Style* recommends the use of the short-title form in place of the term *op. cit.* (pp. 582–83).

[6]The formats suggested here are adaptations based on *The Chicago Manual of Style* as contained in the following sources:

Andrew Harnack and Eugene Kleppinger, "Using Chicago Style to Cite and Document Sources," *Online! A Reference Guide to Using Internet Sources* (New York: St. Martin's Press, 1998), 109–21.

Andrew Harnack and Eugene Kleppinger, "Using Chicago Style to Cite and Document Sources," *Online! Citation Styles,* 1998, <http://www.bedfordstmartins.com/online/citex.html> (11 February 2000).

personal Web site

[1]Richard J. Follett, *Professor Richard J. Follett's Web Site,* n.d., <http://www.lapc.cc.ca.us/usr/FollettR/index.html> (11 February 2000).

general Web site

[2]*How to Conduct an Effective Job Search,* n.d., <http://www2.jobtrak.com/help_manuals/jobmanual/> (11 February 2000).

on-line book

[3]Andrew Harnack and Eugene Kleppinger, *Online! Citation Styles,* 1998, <http://www.bedfordstmartins.com/online/> (21 February 2000).

on-line article in a magazine

[4]Mark L. Clifford and Pete Engardio, "Rebuilding Asia," *BusinessWeek* (int'l edition), 29 November 1999, <http://www.businessweek.com/premium/99_48/b3657024.htm> (26 January 2000).

on-line government publication

[5]*Y2K Success!* U.S. Postal Service, 2000, <http://www.usps.gov/year2000/> (11 February 2000).

[6]Graham R. Mitchell, Kelly H. Carnes, Esq., and Cheryl Mendonsa, *America's New Deficit: The Shortage of Information Technology Workers,* Office of Technology Policy, Department of Commerce, n.d., <http://www.ta.doc.gov/reports/itsw/itsw.pdf> (11 February 2000).

Use the following guidelines for citing E-mail messages:

(1) Use the footnote feature of your word processing program to achieve the formats used for other types of sources.

(2) Begin with the author's full name, if known. Enclose within angle brackets (< >) the author's E-mail address. Place in quotation marks the subject line of the message. Furnish the date the message was sent.

(3) Designate the type of message (personal E-mail, distribution list, office communication).

(4) Enclose in parentheses the date (day, month, year) of access.

(5) Separate items with a comma; conclude the citation with a period.

---

[7]Karen L. Savage, <ClarksHOW@aol.com>, "CBEA 2000 Breakout Session Speakers," 9 December 1999, distribution list, (5 January 2000).

b. ***Bibliographical notes,*** **references to the bibliography, may be used as alternatives to formal footnotes. The reference to the bibliography is shown in parentheses at the end of the cited material by referring first to the number of the reference in the bibliography followed by a colon and the page number(s) of the source. The complete source appears in the bibliography following the body of the paper (see Section 13–12).**

bibliographical note

. . . income has risen 16 percent during the last fiscal period. To offset this increased income, however, expenses have risen 21 percent over the same period. (6:10–11)

c. **Another alternative to footnotes or bibliographical notes is *endnotes.* Indicate the presence of an endnote by typing a superior (slightly raised) figure after the reference material to be documented. Endnotes are placed on a separate page at the end of the body of the report or at the end of each chapter in a long report. Use the endnotes feature of your word processing program and the following guidelines to prepare endnotes:**

(1) Allow a 2-inch top margin. Center the heading *NOTES* or *ENDNOTES* in all capital letters.

(2) Triple-space after the heading. Single-space each note, but double-space between notes.

(3) Number the notes consecutively using Arabic numerals followed by a 0.3-inch left indent.

(4) Use the same content and sequence for endnotes as shown for footnotes in Section 13–10a. Use a footer to number the page at the bottom, or omit (but count) the page number—select whichever style was used for the beginning pages of other major sections in the body of the report.

(5) Use a 0.5- or 1-inch top margin for any second and succeeding pages, depending upon the page numbering format selected. Be sure to follow the same format used for the body of the report.

endnotes page

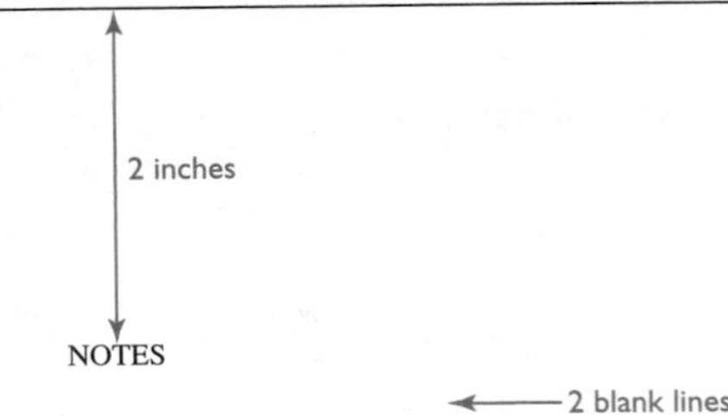

NOTES

← 2 blank lines

1. Michael J. Hendrix, R. Louise Preston, and Ornorio Torti, *Effective Management Principles* (Eden Prairie, Minn.: EMC/Paradigm Publishing International, 2001), 118–22.

2. Maria L. Cueva and Richard C. Follett, *Employee Motivation in the International Workplace*, 2nd ed. (New York: McGraw-Hill, Inc., 2001), 206.

3. Ibid., 212.

4. Barbara S. Kawakami, *Union and Employee Relations*, 4th ed. (Upper Saddle River, N.J.: Prentice Hall, Inc., 2000), 49–51.

5. E. Bryant Phillips and Andrea Kessler, *Principles of Management*, 2nd ed. (New York: John Wiley & Sons, Inc., 1997), 108.

6. Hendrix et al., op. cit., 139–41.

7. Mark T. Mathews, *Managerial Psychology in a Global Economy* (Chicago: The University of Chicago Press, 2000), 105.

8. Phillips and Kessler, loc. cit.

d. The *MLA (Modern Language Association) referencing style,*[7] used predominantly in the humanities, is another method for citing sources. In this style a short description of the source and the pertinent page number(s) appear in parentheses after the information to be cited. The main purpose of the parenthetical reference is to point the reader to a specific work in the Works Cited, the MLA version of a bibliography.

Use the following guidelines to cite sources according to the MLA referencing style:

(1) Begin with the last name of the author or authors. If the work has more than three authors, use only the first author's last name

[7]For a complete discussion of the preparation of reports and manuscripts according to the MLA style, consult Joseph Gibaldi, *MLA Handbook for Writers of Research Papers,* 5th ed. (New York: The Modern Language Association of America, 1999).

For a concise interpretation of citing on-line sources according to the MLA style, consult Andrew Harnack and Eugene Kleppinger, "Using MLA Style to Cite and Document Sources," *Online! A Reference Guide to Using Internet Sources* (New York: St. Martin's Press, 1998), 75–81, OR Andrew Harnack and Eugene Kleppinger, "Using MLA Style to Cite and Document Sources," *Online! Citation Styles,* 1998, <http://www.bedfordstmartins.com/online/citex.html> (11 February 2000).

followed by *et al.* with no intervening punctuation, e.g., Greenburg et al.

(2) Begin the citation with the title of the work or a shortened version of the title, e.g., *Employment Trends in Manufacturing* or *Employment Trends,* if a work has no author listed.

(3) Follow the author or title reference with the relevant page number(s), but do not use any intervening punctuation.

(4) Place the citation in parentheses directly after the referenced material. Examples of such references would be (Greenburg et al. 113) and (*Employment Trends in Manufacturing* 65–67).

(5) Include only the page number(s) in the citation if the author(s) or source is named in the context of the text.

(6) Provide a full description of all cited sources in the Works Cited.[8]

MLA referencing style

According to recent surveys, investment in desktop and laptop computers continues to be a major investment item for United States corporations. Advances in technology have forced corporations to update continually with hopes of obtaining a competitive edge (McAllister and Doyle 32). Between now and the year 2005, corporations will spend between $20 billion and $25 billion on individual workstations and their peripherals (*U.S. News and International Report* 114).

MLA page reference only

According to McAllister and Doyle (32), investment in desktop and laptop computers continues to be a major investment item for United States corporations. Advances in technology have forced corporations to update continually with hopes of obtaining a competitive edge. Between now and the year 2005, as reported in *U.S. News and International Report,* corporations will spend between $20 billion and $25 billion on individual workstations and their peripherals (114).

[8]Refer to Section 13–12c of this manual for information on preparing the Works Cited, the MLA version of a bibliography.

e. Another method for citing sources is the *APA (American Psychological Association) style,*[9] which is used predominantly by writers in the sciences.

To cite a specific part of a source or a direct quotation in this style, place in parentheses a short description of the source, the year of publication, and the pertinent page number(s) after the information to be cited. To cite a complete source, place in parentheses a short description and the year of publication. Each item is separated by a comma.

The main purpose of the parenthetical reference is to point the reader to a specific work in the reference list—the bibliography. Use the following guidelines to cite sources according to the APA referencing style:[10]

(1) Begin the citation with the last name of the author. If a source has two authors, cite both authors' last names each time the source is referenced. For sources with three to six authors, cite each author's last name in the first reference; additional references require only the first author's last name followed by *et al.*

(2) Join the names in a multiple-author citation with an ampersand (&) instead of the word and when they appear in parentheses or in the reference list, e.g., (Hendrix, Preston & Torti, 2000).

(3) Begin the citation with the first two or three words of the entry in the reference list—usually the title of the work—if a work has no author listed. Use quotation marks around titles of articles or chapters; underline the names of books or magazines. Capitalize the main words, e.g., (Employment Trends, 2000).

(4) Follow the author or title reference with the date of publication. For direct quotations or specific material, include any relevant page number(s) preceded by p. or pp. Additional examples of such references are (Hendrix et al., 2000) and ("Marketing Aspects," 2001, pp. 87–88).

(5) Include only the date of publication (and any applicable page numbers for direct quotations or specific material) in the citation if the author(s) or source is named in the context of the text. Omit the parenthetical reference for an entire work if both the source and date appear in the text.

---

[9]For a complete discussion of the preparation of reports and manuscripts according to the APA style, consult *Publication Manual of the American Psychological Association,* 4th ed. (Washington, D.C.: American Psychological Association, 1994).

For a concise interpretation of citing on-line sources according to the APA style, consult Andrew Harnack and Eugene Kleppinger, "Using APA Style to Cite and Document Sources," *Online! A Reference Guide to Using Internet Sources* (New York: St. Martin's Press, 1998), 93–98, OR Andrew Harnack and Eugene Kleppinger, "Using APA Style to Cite and Document Sources," *Online! Citation Styles,* 1998, <http://www.bedfordstmartins.com/online/citex.html> (11 February 2000).

[10]For an on-line abstract of the APA referencing style, consult *Documenting Your Sources: APA Style,* n.d., <http://www.ucalgary.ca/UofC/eduweb/grammar/guide/apastyle.htm> (11 February 2000).

(6) Provide a full description of cited sources in the reference list, the APA version of a bibliography.[11] However, personal letters, telephone calls, and other material that cannot be retrieved are not listed in *References*; they are cited only in the text, e.g., "Brenda Baity (E-mail message, November 5, 2000) confirmed that . . . ."

APA referencing style

According to several recent surveys, investment in desktop and laptop computers continues to be a major investment item for United States corporations. Advances in technology have forced most corporations to update continually with hopes of obtaining a competitive edge. (McAllister & Doyle, 2000). "Between now and the year 2000, corporations will spend between $20 billion and $25 billion on individual workstations and their peripherals" (U.S. News, 2001, p. 134).

APA year and page reference only

According to McAllister and Doyle (2000), investment in desktop and laptop computers continues to be a major investment item for United States corporations. Advances in technology have forced most corporations to update continually with hopes of obtaining a competitive edge. "Between now and the year 2005, as reported in *U.S. News and International Report,* corporations will spend between $20 billion and $25 billion on individual workstations and their peripherals" (2001, p. 114).

f. Business writers may use a reference style that suits their purpose. In citing sources, though, use a style that meets the following criteria:

(1) The citation can be easily located from its point of reference within the report.

(2) The citation contains sufficient information so that the reader can readily locate the source and authenticate the information cited.

(3) All citations, regardless of media, are complete and expressed in a similar and consistent format.

Reports 13

[11]Refer to Section 13–12d of this manual for information on how to prepare a reference list, the APA version of a bibliography.

13–11 Illustrations

Visuals in the form of tables, pie charts, bar charts (column charts), or line charts may be used to illustrate data in a report or manuscript. Where possible, a table or chart should appear on the same page as the narrative describing it. If there is insufficient space on the same page for the table or chart and its explanation, then the illustration should be placed on the following page. A statement such as "As shown in Table 3 on page 9, ..." must be used in the narrative to direct the reader to the illustration. The type of illustration used will vary according to the kind of data presented; guidelines for preparing each type of illustration follow:

a. *Tables* arrange data in an orderly fashion by employing a system of headings and columns to present information. Either open tables or ruled tables may be used in business documents.

Although the length, style, and number of table columns will vary according to the type of data presented, use the following general procedures to set up tables:

(1) Use the Tables feature of your word processing program to create tables. For open tables eliminate the lines and condense the row height. For ruled tables select the line enhancements or one of the preformatted table formats provided by your word processing program.

(2) Leave two blank lines before and after a table if it does not appear on a separate page. (Some authorities prefer three blank lines before and after the table; be consistent in the use of whichever of the two formats you choose.)

(3) Number each table consecutively with Arabic numerals if more than one table appears in the report. *Center Table* and its corresponding number over the proposed position of the table. (If only one table appears in a report, begin the table with its title.)

(4) Double-space, and then center under the table number the title of the table; use all capital letters. If a subtitle is needed, center and use capital and lowercase letters. Place the subtitle a double space below the main title. Triple-space after the last line of either the main title or the subtitle.

(5) Center the entire table between the left and right margins of the report or manuscript. Allow a sufficient amount of space for each column, keeping in mind that the column heading is part of the column.

(6) Use capital and lowercase letters for column headings. Boldface and center each column heading.

(7) Center both horizontally and vertically a table appearing on a separate page.

an open table

Table 1

I blank line →

A COMPARISON OF THE MONTHLY COST PER EMPLOYEE OF HEALTH INSURANCE POLICIES SUBMITTED BY EIGHT COMPANIES

I blank line →

March 3, 2002

2 blank lines →

Company	Plan A[1]	Plan B[2]	Plan C[3]
Chicago General	$375.00	$492.50	$545.00
Concord	325.00	450.00	520.00
D & D Life	385.50	485.50	585.50
Edgewater	312.50	443.50	511.50
Lincoln	415.00	500.00	635.00
Morgan	309.34	440.25	524.15
New Jersey	350.00	475.00	530.00
Western	405.60	585.00	620.30

[1]$500,000 maximum coverage
[2]$1,000,000 maximum coverage
[3]$1,500,000 maximum coverage

simple ruled table

Table 1

I blank line →

A COMPARISON OF THE MONTHLY COST PER EMPLOYEE OF HEALTH INSURANCE POLICIES SUBMITTED BY EIGHT COMPANIES

I blank line →

March 3, 2002

2 blank lines →

Company	Plan A[1]	Plan B[2]	Plan C[3]
Chicago General	$375.00	$492.50	$545.00
Concord	325.00	450.00	520.00
D & D Life	385.50	485.50	585.50
Edgewater	312.50	443.50	511.50
Lincoln	415.00	500.00	635.00
Morgan	309.34	440.25	524.15
New Jersey	350.00	475.00	530.00
Western	405.60	585.00	620.30

[1]$500,000 maximum coverage
[2]$1,000,000 maximum coverage
[3]$1,500,000 maximum coverage

enhanced ruled table

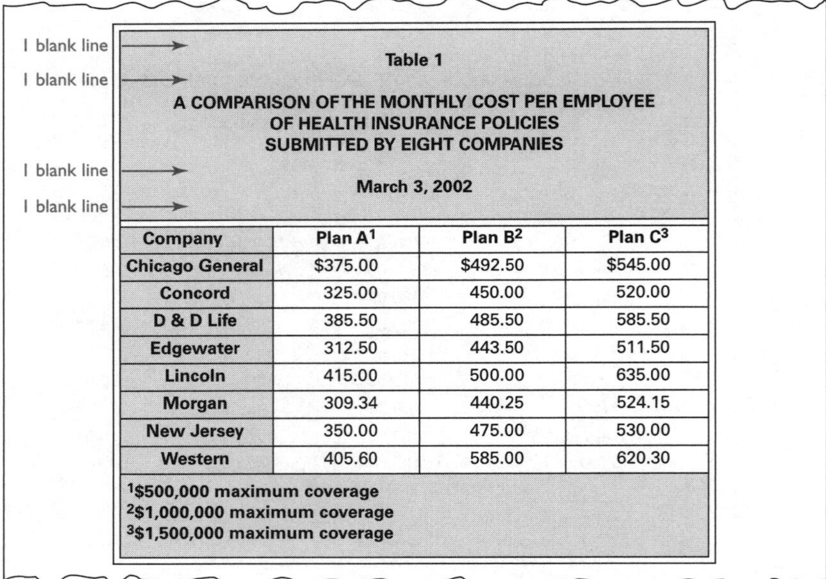

Table 1

A COMPARISON OF THE MONTHLY COST PER EMPLOYEE OF HEALTH INSURANCE POLICIES SUBMITTED BY EIGHT COMPANIES

March 3, 2002

Company	Plan A[1]	Plan B[2]	Plan C[3]
Chicago General	$375.00	$492.50	$545.00
Concord	325.00	450.00	520.00
D & D Life	385.50	485.50	585.50
Edgewater	312.50	443.50	511.50
Lincoln	415.00	500.00	635.00
Morgan	309.34	440.25	524.15
New Jersey	350.00	475.00	530.00
Western	405.60	585.00	620.30

[1]$500,000 maximum coverage
[2]$1,000,000 maximum coverage
[3]$1,500,000 maximum coverage

b. ***Pie charts*** **are used to illustrate the parts of a whole when that whole represents 100 percent of something. To achieve maximum clarity in this type of visual, do not exceed seven or eight segments in the illustration.**

simple pie chart

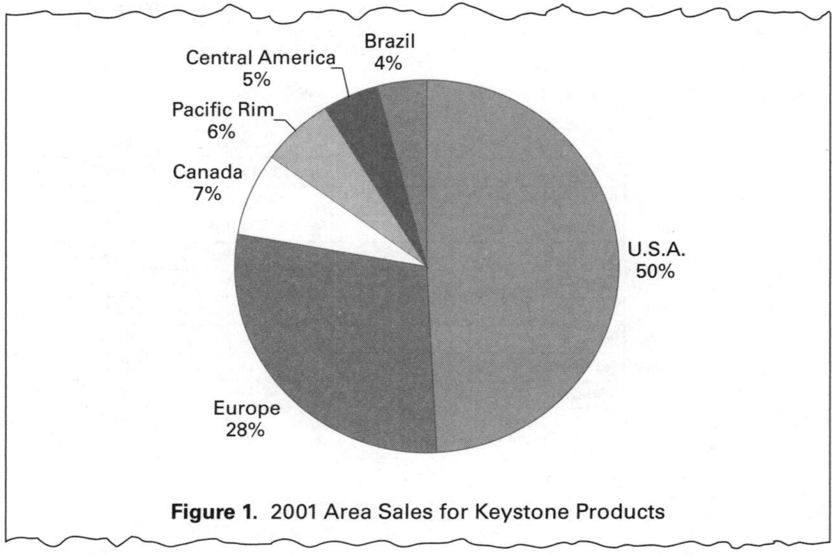

Figure 1. 2001 Area Sales for Keystone Products

simple pie chart with exploded segment

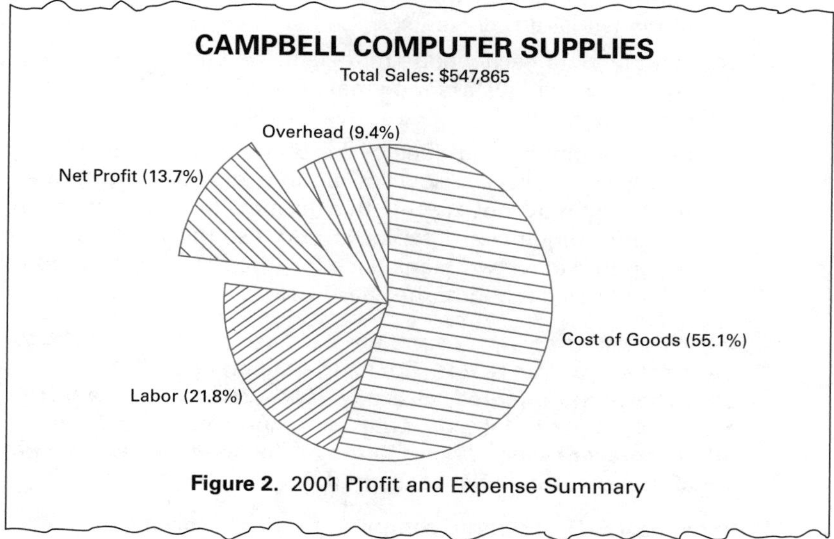

Figure 2. 2001 Profit and Expense Summary

3-D pie chart

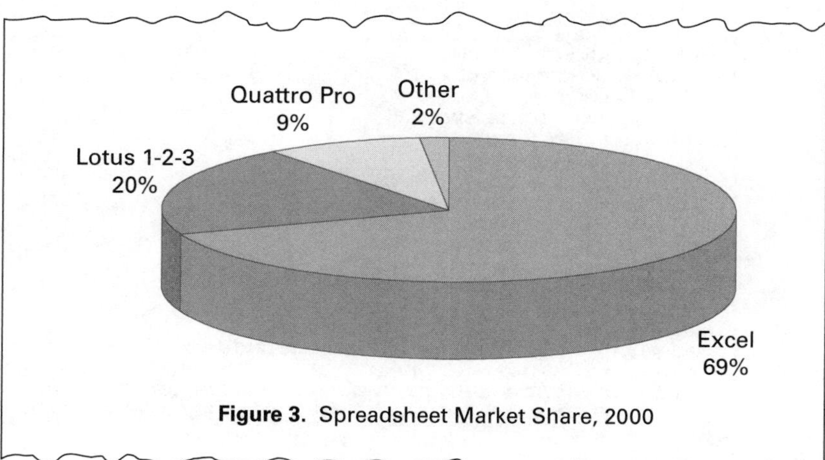

Figure 3. Spreadsheet Market Share, 2000

If possible, use the graphics feature of your spreadsheet program to create and import charts into your word processing program. Follow these guidelines to create pie charts:

(1) Begin the illustration two blank lines (some authorities prefer three) below the last line of text.

(2) Slice the pie in appropriate wedges, showing the largest wedge first. Start at the 12 o'clock position of the circle and move clockwise. The

remaining wedges may or may not be in descending order of size, but the size of each wedge should be proportional to the percentage of the whole it represents.

(3) Identify what each wedge represents and its corresponding percentage. If the wedges are too small, use a legend to identify what each wedge represents.

(4) Center numbers and titles of pie charts in capital and lowercase letters a triple space below the bottom of the chart. Some software, however, may not permit this format. In those cases where the program requires a different format, use the format dictated by the program. Leave two blank lines (or three, depending upon the number of lines left before the chart) before resuming the narrative.

c. ***Bar charts* and *column charts* are used to compare quantities within a class or over a time period. Bar charts are oriented horizontally, and column charts are oriented vertically. These charts require both a vertical axis and a horizontal axis. One axis represents the quantity and the other represents the varying items in the class or the time period over which the quantities are measured.**

horizontal 3-D bar chart comparing a single variable

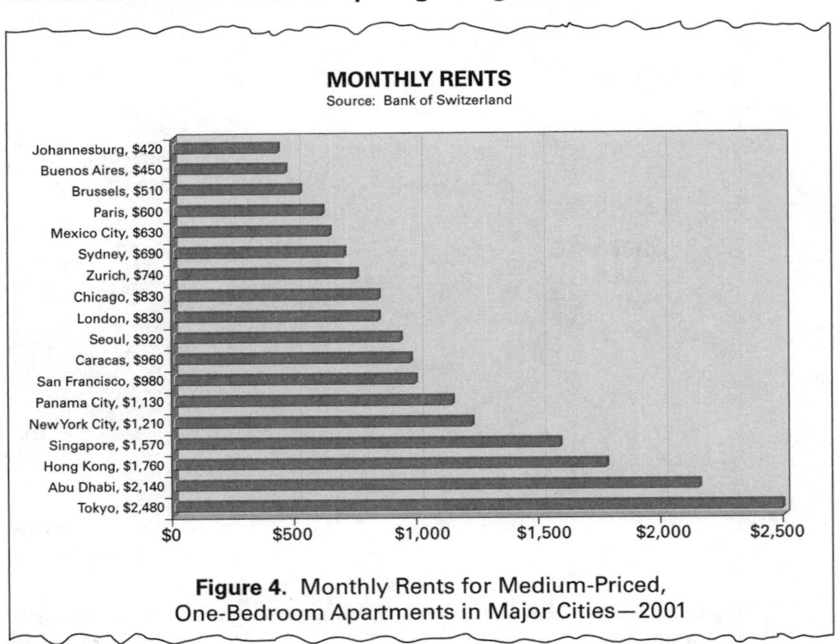

Figure 4. Monthly Rents for Medium-Priced, One-Bedroom Apartments in Major Cities—2001

column chart comparing a single variable

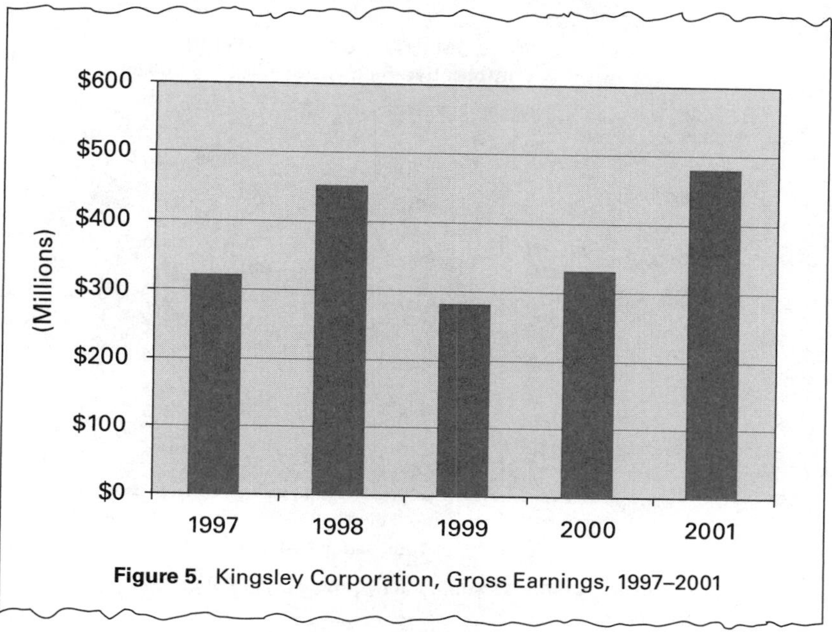

Figure 5. Kingsley Corporation, Gross Earnings, 1997–2001

column chart comparing multiple variables

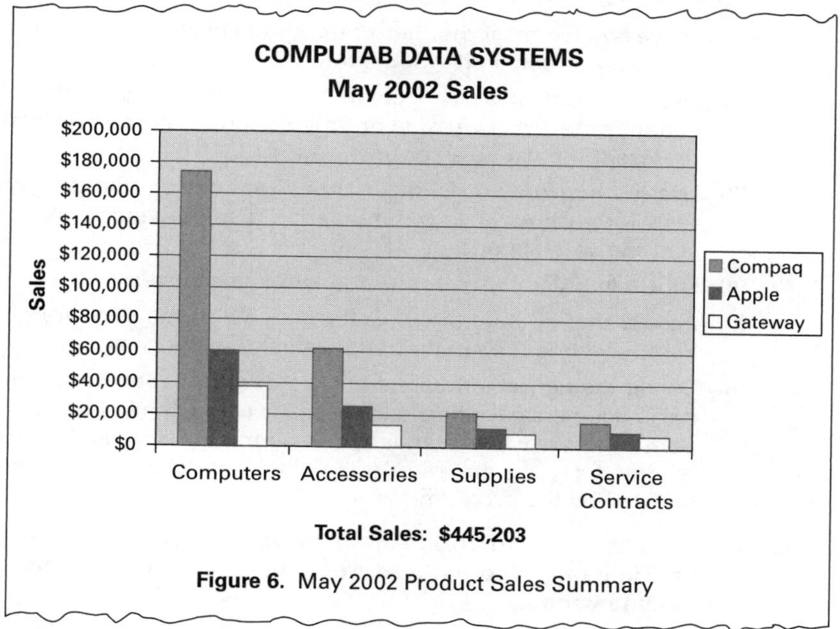

Figure 6. May 2002 Product Sales Summary

Reports 13

3-D stacked column chart

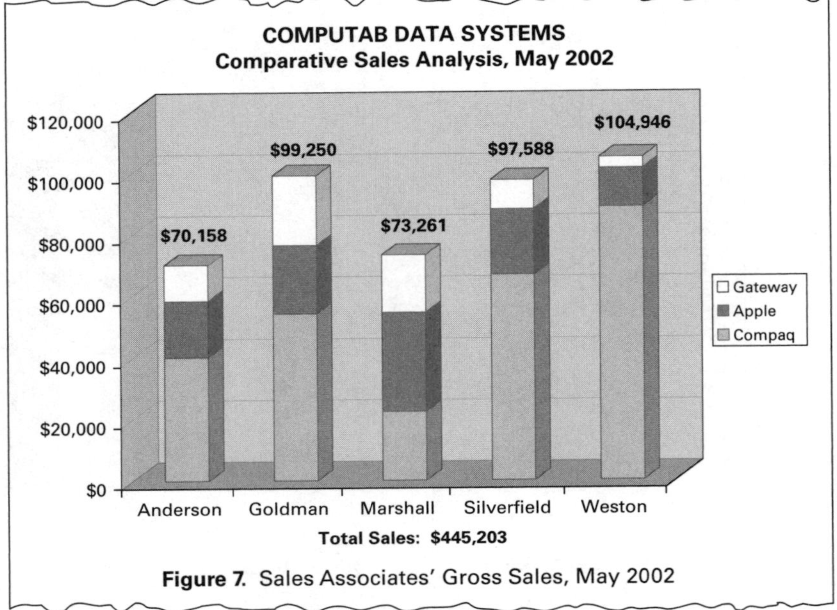

Figure 7. Sales Associates' Gross Sales, May 2002

Use your spreadsheet program and the following guidelines for constructing column or bar charts:

(1) Leave two (some authorities prefer three) blank lines before and after a column or bar chart when it interrupts the narrative.

(2) Use the vertical axis in column charts to represent the different quantities for each variable or time period; use the horizontal axis to represent the variables or time periods.

(3) Use the horizontal axis in bar charts to represent the different quantities for each variable or time period; use the vertical axis to represent the variable or time period.

(4) Label clearly both the horizontal and vertical axes.

(5) Ensure that all bars are of uniform width. If the bars are not touching, they should be placed equidistantly in the chart.

(6) Center the figure numbers and titles of column and bar charts in capital and lowercase letters a triple space below the bottom of the chart. Some software, however, may not permit this format. In those cases where the program requires a different format, use the format dictated by the program.

c. ***Line charts* are used to illustrate movement or trends over a time period. They may also be used to compare two or more sets of data over a time period.**

line chart plotting a single variable

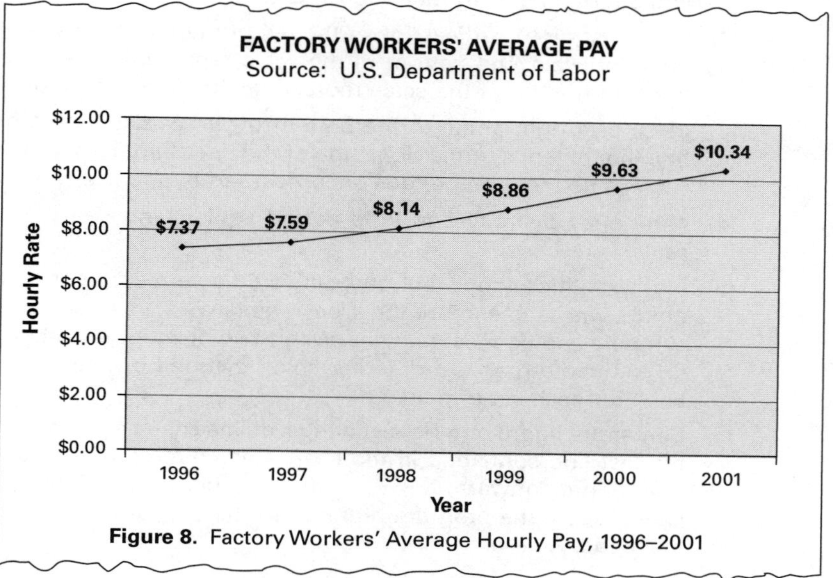

Figure 8. Factory Workers' Average Hourly Pay, 1996–2001

line chart plotting multiple variables

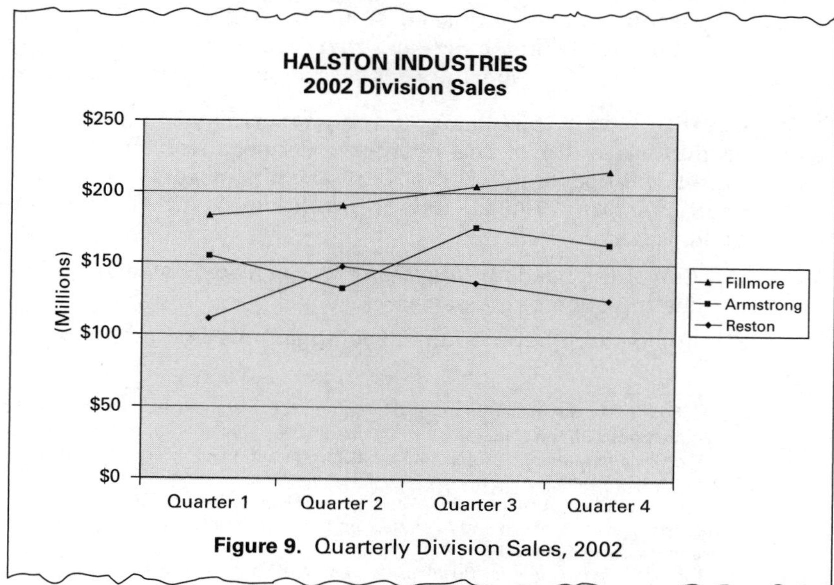

Figure 9. Quarterly Division Sales, 2002

Use your spreadsheet program and the following guidelines to construct line charts that plot both single and multiple variables:

(1) Leave two (some authorities recommend three) blank lines before and after a line chart that interrupts text.

(2) Place a straight vertical line at the left of the line chart to portray the quantity scale. The bottom of the scale represents the lowest quantity, and the top of the scale represents the largest quantity.

(3) Place at a right angle to the bottom of the vertical line a horizontal line that extends to the right side of the line chart. This horizontal line represents the time periods encompassed by the chart.

(4) Mark each quantity and time period equidistantly on its respective scale.

(5) Plot quantities above their respective time periods. Connect the cross points with a line, mark the cross points with a symbol, or use both symbols and connecting lines. When two or more factors are plotted on the same graph, a different color, symbol, or line style must be used for each set of data.

(6) Center the figure numbers and titles of line charts a triple space below the last line contained in the chart. Capitalize all main words in the title. Some software, however, may not permit this format. In those cases where the program requires a different format, use the format dictated by the program.

13–12 Bibliography

a. **The bibliography[12] follows immediately after the body of the report or manuscript and contains all sources cited in the text. Any source material that is not cited but that has contributed directly to the development of a report or manuscript should also be included.**

b. **List the items in the bibliography alphabetically by authors' last names or the first entry of the reference. Consecutively number each item in the bibliography if the bibliographical form of footnoting is used (Section 13–10b). Use the following guidelines to prepare a bibliography:**

(1) Center the heading *BIBLIOGRAPHY* in all capital letters 2 inches from the top edge of the page.

(2) Triple-space between the heading and the first reference.

---

[12]The formats suggested here for bibliographical references (except for noted deviations) are based on the traditional format alternatives contained in the following sources:

The Chicago Manual of Style, 14th ed. (Chicago and London: The University of Chicago Press, 1993), 487–635.

Kate L. Turabian, *A Manual for Writers of Term Papers, Theses, and Dissertations,* 6th ed., revised by John Grossman and Alice Bennett (Chicago and London: The University of Chicago Press, 1996), 165–230.

The AMA Style Guide for Business Writing (New York: American Management Association, 1996), 41–44, 221.

Andrew Harnack and Eugene Kleppinger, *Online! A Reference Guide to Using Internet Sources* (New York: St. Martin's Press, 1998), 121–22, AND Andrew Harnack and Eugene Kleppinger, "Using Chicago Style to Cite and Document Sources," *Online! Citation Styles,* 1998, <http://www.bedfordstmartins.com/online/citex.html> (11 February 2000).

(3) Single-space each reference and double-space between references. If a reference requires more than one line, use the hanging indent feature of your word processing program to indent the second and succeeding lines 0.5 inch.

(4) Type a 0.5-inch underline followed by a period in place of an author's name if he or she has more than one reference listed. Begin this procedure with the second reference for that author.

(5) Alphabetize the reference by title when the author is unknown.

(6) End the citations for magazines, journals, or other such source articles with page references.

(7) Enclose within angle brackets (< >) the complete Uniform Resource Locator (URL) for Internet sites.

unsigned encyclopedia article

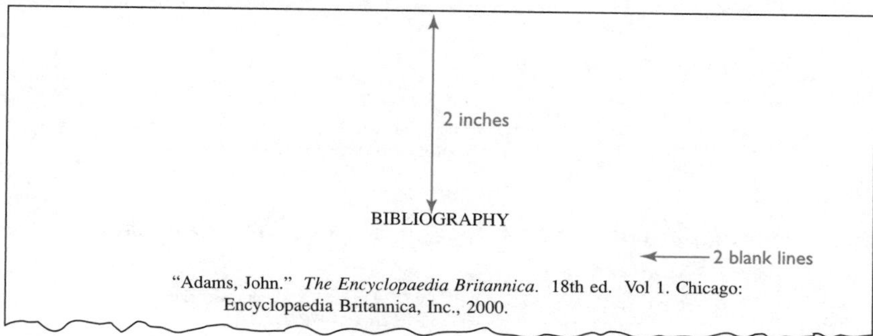

BIBLIOGRAPHY

"Adams, John." *The Encyclopaedia Britannica.* 18th ed. Vol 1. Chicago: Encyclopaedia Britannica, Inc., 2000.

film, videocassette, or audiocassette

Barriers to Effective Global Communication. Videocassette. Chicago: Visual Education Corporation, 2000.

article in a professional journal with volume number

Bowman, Joel P., and Inge Klopping. "Bandstands, Bandwidth, and Business Communication: Technology and Sanctity of Writing." *Business Communication Quarterly* 62:1 (March 1999): 82–90

business correspondence

Bush, George (as vice president of the United States). Response letter to author, 17 October 1986.

source in table

Copeland, Lennie, and Lewis Griggs. Table "U.S. Merchandise Trade by Area." *Going International.* New York: Plume of Penguin Books USA Inc., 1988, xviii.

newspaper column with author

Doran, Lawrence J. "Computer File." *Los Angeles Times,* 19 November 2001.

magazine article with author

Drew, Richard. "Multinational Corporations in the International Marketplace." *BusinessWeek*, 17 August 2001, 19–20.

magazine article without author

"Electronic Games Still the No. 1 Toy." *Consumer Reports*, March 2001, 47–51.

company memorandum

Garcia, Meredith. "Medical Insurance Programs Available to Employees." Boston: Interstop Corporation memorandum, 8 June 2000.

section in unpublished book or booklet without author

"A History of Bruin Basketball." The UCLA Alumni Association, Occasional Paper #9. Unpublished booklet, 1975, 1–4.

published company report

Holtz, Shel. "A Partnership in Japan." *Insights*. Irvine, Calif.: Allergan, Inc., published report, May 2001, 2–3.

signed encyclopedia article

Karlen, Delmar. "Criminal Justice: 1. Criminal Justice in England and the U.S." *The Encyclopedia Americana*. International ed. Vol. 8. Danbury, Conn.: Grolier Incorporated, 1999.

paperback book

Larson, Harold G., and Charlene L. Morimoto. *Principles of Small Business Management*. 6th ed. Chicago: The University of Chicago Press, 2001.

interview

Montgomery, James (CEO, Great Western Federal Bank). Interview by author, Woodland Hills, Calif., 24 July 1999.

book, one author

Morrison, Alice T. *Microcomputers: Introductory Concepts and Applications.* 2nd ed. Cincinnati: South-Western College Publishing, 2002.

book, same author

———. *Microcomputers: Business and Accounting Spreadsheet Applications.* Cincinnati: South-Western College Publishing, 2001.

book, two authors

Patterson, L. David, and Kathy Lim. *Principles of Real Estate.* 3rd ed. New York: John Wiley & Sons, Inc., 2001.

book, three or more authors

Rodriguez, Rose P., Charles T. Bove, and Saad Najjar. *Fundamentals of Accounting.* 2nd ed. Pittsfield, Mass.: The Financial Press, 1997.

book, editor(s) only

Sakasian, John M., and Carol L. Jones, eds. *Readings in Management Theory.* Belmont, Calif.: Wadsworth Publishing Company, 2000.

CD-ROM

"Securities and Exchange Commission." *Microsoft Bookshelf '99.* CD-ROM. Microsoft Corporation, 1999.

government publication

Statistical Abstract of the United States. U.S. Bureau of the Census. Washington, D.C.: U.S. Government Printing Office, 1990.

internal unpublished company report

Thomsen, Terry. "An Analysis of Current Manufacturing Facilities." Detroit: General Motors, Chevrolet Division, unpublished report, March 2001.

Internet, World Wide Web (WWW)

Walker, Janice R. "MLA-Style Citations of Electronic Sources." *The Columbia Guide to Online Style*. January 1999. <http://www.cas.usf.edu/english/walker/mla.html> (11 February 2000).

secondary source citation

Williams, Stuart, and Peter Conway. *Internationally Known*. New York: Penguin Books USA Inc., 1990. As cited in Michael Doran. *Succeeding in the Global Marketplace*. New York: Random House, Inc., 1992.

unpublished book or booklet

Wooden, John. "John Wooden Basketball Fundamentals Camp, Player's Notebook." Unpublished and undated booklet.

radio or television broadcast

"Work Camps in China." *60 Minutes*. Los Angeles: Repeat KCBS telecast, 26 July 1999.

c. **Reports prepared according to the MLA (Modern Language Association) style title the bibliography *Works Cited.*[13] References are listed alphabetically as in any other bibliography. Guidelines for formatting the Works Cited follow:**

(1) Place the title *Works Cited* 1 inch from the top edge of the page; number the page in the upper right corner, 0.5 inch from the top edge and aligned with the right margin.

(2) Double-space after the heading, and double-space within and between the entries. Begin each entry at the left margin, but use the hanging indent feature of your word processor to indent any subsequent lines 0.5 inch from the left margin.

---

[13]For a complete discussion of arrangements and formats for the Works Cited according to the MLA style, consult Joseph Gibaldi, *MLA Handbook for Writers of Research Papers,* 5th ed. (New York: The Modern Language Association of America, 1999), 114–202.

For a concise interpretation of documenting on-line sources according to the MLA style, consult Andrew Harnack and Eugene Kleppinger, "Using MLA Style to Cite and Document Sources," *Online! A Reference Guide to Using Internet Sources* (New York: St. Martin's Press, 1998), 81–91, OR Andrew Harnack and Eugene Kleppinger, "Using MLA Style to Cite and Document Sources," *Online! Citation Styles,* 1998, <http://www.bedfordstmartins.com/online/citex.html> (11 February 2000).

Works Cited—MLA bibliographical style

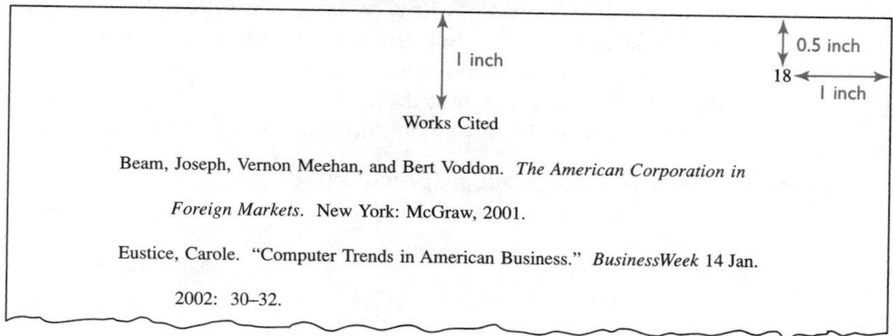

Works Cited

Beam, Joseph, Vernon Meehan, and Bert Voddon. *The American Corporation in Foreign Markets.* New York: McGraw, 2001.

Eustice, Carole. "Computer Trends in American Business." *BusinessWeek* 14 Jan. 2002: 30–32.

d. Reports prepared according to the APA (American Psychological Association) style refer to the bibliography as a *reference list.*[14]

References are listed alphabetically as in any other bibliography. Guidelines for formatting the reference list follow:

(1) Begin the reference list on a new page, and place the title *References* 1 inch from the top edge of the page (use 1-inch bottom, left, and right margins).

(2) Number all pages in the upper right corner. Align numbers with the right margin between the top edge of the page and the first line of text. Place a shortened version of the report or manuscript title on the same line, separating the title and page number by approximately 0.5 inch.

(3) Double-space after the heading, and double-space within and between the entries.

(4) Begin the reference at the left margin. Use the hanging indent feature of your word processing program to indent the second and succeeding lines the same amount of space used for paragraphs within the body of the report or manuscript (usually 0.5 inch).

(5) Provide authors' last names and first initials in inverted order for book entries. Use an ampersand (&) instead of the word *and* to link multiple names. Follow the authors' names with the date of publication enclosed in parentheses.

(6) Capitalize only the first word and any proper nouns in the title or subtitle of a work. Underline the name of the work.

(7) Provide next the facts of publication, listing the city first. Give the two-letter U.S. Postal Service state designation for little-known cities. The location is followed by a colon and the name of the publisher.

---

[14]For a complete discussion of arrangements and formats for the reference list according to the APA style, consult *Publication Manual of the American Psychological Association,* 4th ed. (Washington, D.C.: American Psychological Association, 1994), 174–234.

For a concise interpretation of documenting on-line sources according to the APA style, consult Andrew Harnack and Eugene Kleppinger, "Using APA Style to Cite and Document Sources," *Online! A Reference Guide to Using Internet Sources* (New York: St. Martin's Press, 1998), 98–107, OR Andrew Harnack and Eugene Kleppinger, "Using APA Style to Cite and Document Sources," *Online! Citation Styles,* 1998, <http://www.bedfordstmartins.com/online/citex.html> (11 February 2000).

(8) List the names of magazine article authors in the same format used for authors of books. Follow with the publication date enclosed in parentheses. Do not place quotation marks around magazine article titles, and capitalize only the first word or proper nouns. Capitalize all main words and underline the titles of periodicals; include the volume or issue number (if any). Conclude the reference with page numbers.

reference list—APA bibliographical style

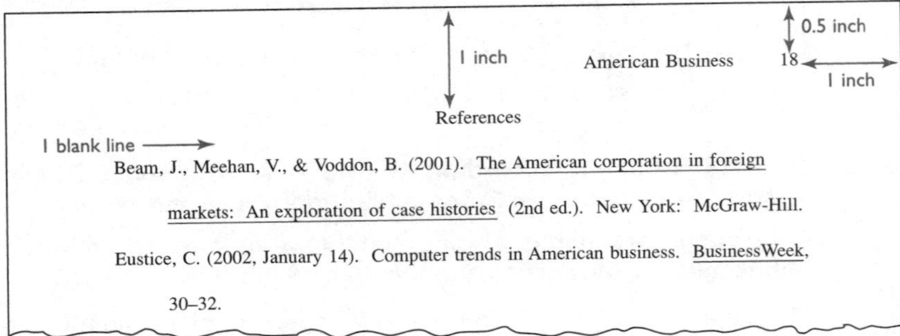

0.5 inch
1 inch
American Business 18
1 inch
References
1 blank line
Beam, J., Meehan, V., & Voddon, B. (2001). The American corporation in foreign markets: An exploration of case histories (2nd ed.). New York: McGraw-Hill.
Eustice, C. (2002, January 14). Computer trends in American business. BusinessWeek, 30–32.

13–13 Appendix

a. The appendix follows the bibliography and contains supportive material. This material may include such items as letters, copies of questionnaires, maps, contracts, lists, tables, and other documents not shown elsewhere.

b. The appendix may be preceded by a page entitled *APPENDIX* or *APPENDIXES* (keyed in all capital letters and centered both horizontally and vertically). The introductory page may also include a list of the items contained in the appendix. In this case (1) both the title and the listing are centered vertically or (2) the title is placed 2 inches from the top edge of the page with the listing beginning a triple space thereafter. The material should be numbered with alphabetic letters if more than one item appears in the appendix.

introductory appendix page

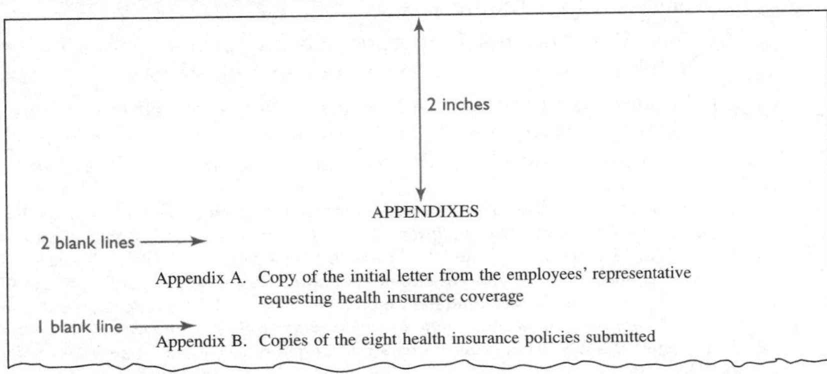

2 inches
APPENDIXES
2 blank lines
Appendix A. Copy of the initial letter from the employees' representative requesting health insurance coverage
1 blank line
Appendix B. Copies of the eight health insurance policies submitted

13–14 Word Processing Templates

Word processing programs—Microsoft Word and WordPerfect, specifically—provide templates to simplify the process of preparing and formatting reports.[15]

report template—Microsoft Word

SECTION I INTRODUCTION

The following report provides a comparison of the employees' health and major medical insurance programs submitted by eight major insurance companies.

Purpose of the Report

Last January Norman Rittgers, one of the employee representatives of our company, requested that company-sponsored health insurance be considered by the Board of Directors as a supplement to our wage and salary schedule. As a result, the board directed the Department of Human Resources to (1) contact insurance companies to determine what health insurance coverages were available and (2) compare the coverages to determine which policy would most cost effectively meet our employees' health insurance needs.

Scope of the Report

The scope of this investigation was limited to an analysis of the written proposals and copies of policies submitted by the participating insurance companies. Of the 28 insurance companies contacted, the majority provided only verbal explanations as to what the estimated coverage and cost of a group health and major medical insurance program would be for our employees. Only eight of these companies submitted written documents for our consideration. Proposals and policies from these companies were evaluated according to the following criteria:

[15]Microsoft at its Web site <http://officeupdate.microsoft.com/> (31 January 2000) provides access to free downloads for additional Microsoft Word business-form templates.

Meeting Minutes

13–15 Purpose and Contents

Minutes are compiled to provide a written record of announcements, reports, significant discussions, and decisions that have taken place during a meeting. Although the degree of formality and extent of coverage may vary, the specific information contained in meeting minutes usually includes the following:

(1) Name of group and meeting

(2) Date, place, time meeting called to order, and time of adjournment

(3) Names of persons present (if applicable, names of persons absent)

(4) Disposition of any previous minutes

(5) Announcements

(6) Summaries of reports

(7) Motions presented and actions taken on motions

(8) Summaries of significant discussions

(9) Name and signature of person compiling minutes

13–16 Organization and Format of Formal Minutes

a. Use 8½- by 11-inch white bond paper, and set 1.25-inch left and right margins. Count the first page in the pagination, but do not number it. Begin page numbering on the second page, and place the number 0.5 inch from the top and right edge of the page.

Center the name of the group and/or meeting in all capital letters 2 inches from the top edge of the page. Double-space down; then center in capital and lowercase letters the date and scheduled time of the meeting. The place where the meeting was held appears another double space below the time and date. This information, too, is centered in capital and lowercase letters. See page 428 for an illustration of the heading format for meeting minutes.

b. A listing of those persons attending the meeting follows the preliminary information. This listing is placed a triple space below the meeting place. Begin the listing with a phrase such as *Members Present:*, *Managers Present:*, or *Persons Present:*. Then list horizontally or vertically the names of the individuals present at the meeting in the order of their importance or in alphabetical order.

In addition to showing the members or persons in attendance, those regular members absent from a meeting may be noted. In this case a separate listing appears a double space below the listing of members present. It is usually preceded by *Members Absent:*, *Persons Absent:*, or another such designation. Examples of vertical attendance listings appear on page 428.

c. The initial paragraph of the meeting minutes appears a triple space below the attendance listing or listings. It generally begins with a statement giving the exact time the meeting was called to order and by whom. This statement is usually followed by one giving the dispensation of any previous minutes.

d. If there were any announcements, these are listed after the opening paragraph. Use a side heading to introduce the announcements, allowing two blank lines above the heading and one blank line below it. Then number and list each announcement made. If only one announcement occurred, show it in paragraph form without a number.

e. Many meeting agendas are organized according to old business and new business. These two categories may be used for topic headings (use side headings) in presenting the motions and discussions that have taken place during short meetings. For lengthy meetings, however, readers can more easily locate information in the minutes if the topic headings describe concretely the subject matter discussed, reported, or voted upon.

f. Reports presented at a meeting should be noted and in some cases summarized. The amount of information provided in the minutes will depend upon their purpose, formality, and use. Include with the reference to the report contents the name of the person giving the report as well as its disposition.

g. The exact wording of motions must be given in the meeting minutes. Persons making and seconding the motions may be named in the motion statement. Include a brief summary of the discussion for each motion. Finally, indicate whether the motion was passed, defeated, or tabled. The number of yeses, noes, and abstentions for each motion should be recorded.

h. If the meeting is not concluded with a motion for adjournment, the person preparing the minutes should indicate the time the meeting was adjourned and by whom. This information is placed in the concluding paragraph of the meeting minutes.

i. The printed or typed signature of the person preparing the minutes usually appears on the fourth line below the concluding paragraph. It may be placed at the left margin or begun at the page center. The preparer's signature is placed directly above the printed signature line.

The complimentary closing *Respectfully submitted* may precede the signature line. In this case the entire signature block simulates the signature block of a business letter. Place *Respectfully submitted* a double space below the concluding paragraph, and leave three blank lines for the written signature before displaying the preparer's name. This style of signature block may also begin at the left margin or page center.

The major components of formal meeting minutes are illustrated in the following example on pages 428–29.

formal meeting minutes

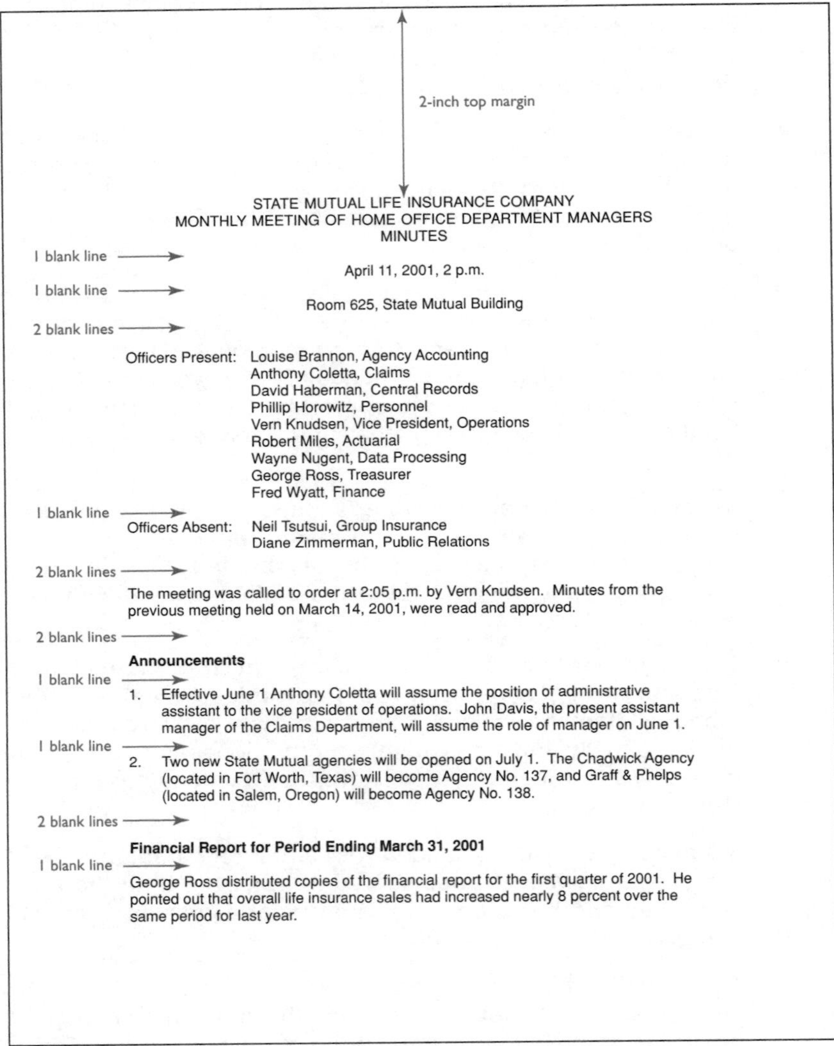

STATE MUTUAL LIFE INSURANCE COMPANY
MONTHLY MEETING OF HOME OFFICE DEPARTMENT MANAGERS
MINUTES

April 11, 2001, 2 p.m.

Room 625, State Mutual Building

Officers Present: Louise Brannon, Agency Accounting
Anthony Coletta, Claims
David Haberman, Central Records
Phillip Horowitz, Personnel
Vern Knudsen, Vice President, Operations
Robert Miles, Actuarial
Wayne Nugent, Data Processing
George Ross, Treasurer
Fred Wyatt, Finance

Officers Absent: Neil Tsutsui, Group Insurance
Diane Zimmerman, Public Relations

The meeting was called to order at 2:05 p.m. by Vern Knudsen. Minutes from the previous meeting held on March 14, 2001, were read and approved.

Announcements

1. Effective June 1 Anthony Coletta will assume the position of administrative assistant to the vice president of operations. John Davis, the present assistant manager of the Claims Department, will assume the role of manager on June 1.

2. Two new State Mutual agencies will be opened on July 1. The Chadwick Agency (located in Fort Worth, Texas) will become Agency No. 137, and Graff & Phelps (located in Salem, Oregon) will become Agency No. 138.

Financial Report for Period Ending March 31, 2001

George Ross distributed copies of the financial report for the first quarter of 2001. He pointed out that overall life insurance sales had increased nearly 8 percent over the same period for last year.

formal meeting minutes (continued)

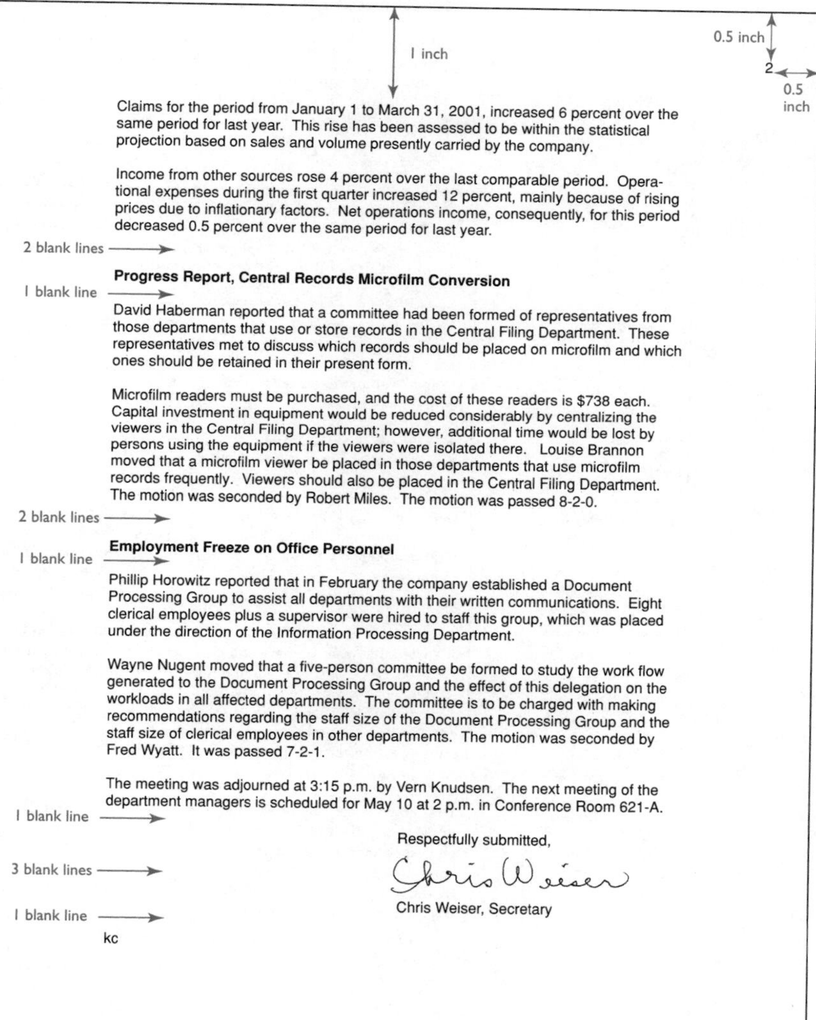

Claims for the period from January 1 to March 31, 2001, increased 6 percent over the same period for last year. This rise has been assessed to be within the statistical projection based on sales and volume presently carried by the company.

Income from other sources rose 4 percent over the last comparable period. Operational expenses during the first quarter increased 12 percent, mainly because of rising prices due to inflationary factors. Net operations income, consequently, for this period decreased 0.5 percent over the same period for last year.

Progress Report, Central Records Microfilm Conversion

David Haberman reported that a committee had been formed of representatives from those departments that use or store records in the Central Filing Department. These representatives met to discuss which records should be placed on microfilm and which ones should be retained in their present form.

Microfilm readers must be purchased, and the cost of these readers is $738 each. Capital investment in equipment would be reduced considerably by centralizing the viewers in the Central Filing Department; however, additional time would be lost by persons using the equipment if the viewers were isolated there. Louise Brannon moved that a microfilm viewer be placed in those departments that use microfilm records frequently. Viewers should also be placed in the Central Filing Department. The motion was seconded by Robert Miles. The motion was passed 8-2-0.

Employment Freeze on Office Personnel

Phillip Horowitz reported that in February the company established a Document Processing Group to assist all departments with their written communications. Eight clerical employees plus a supervisor were hired to staff this group, which was placed under the direction of the Information Processing Department.

Wayne Nugent moved that a five-person committee be formed to study the work flow generated to the Document Processing Group and the effect of this delegation on the workloads in all affected departments. The committee is to be charged with making recommendations regarding the staff size of the Document Processing Group and the staff size of clerical employees in other departments. The motion was seconded by Fred Wyatt. It was passed 7-2-1.

The meeting was adjourned at 3:15 p.m. by Vern Knudsen. The next meeting of the department managers is scheduled for May 10 at 2 p.m. in Conference Room 621-A.

Respectfully submitted,

Chris Weiser

Chris Weiser, Secretary

kc

13–17 Organization and Format of Informal Minutes

The organization and format of informal minutes may vary. The only requisite is that the minutes provide an adequate record of the information needed by the group or organization and that this information be presented in an easy-to-understand fashion. Use the tables feature of your word processing program to simplify the formatting of informal minutes.

informal meeting minutes

COMPUTER APPLICATIONS ADVISORY COMMITTEE
PIERCE COMMUNITY COLLEGE
TUESDAY, APRIL 4, 2001, 2–4 P.M.
BUSINESS 3216

MINUTES

Activity/Discussion	Issues/Relative Information	Resolution
Survey of Classrooms and Laboratories	The faculty familiarized the committee with the equipment presently used for classroom instruction.	Information only.
Language Skills	The faculty described the five departmental courses that meet the requirements for its certificate programs. Two additional courses are required for students completing a degree program in business. The committee emphasized the importance of language skills and how these skills relate to the productive use of a computer.	Information only.
Equipment Training: Hardware Issues	The committee discussed the specifications the department should use in ordering replacement computers, printers, and other peripheral components.	**MSP** to purchase computer replacements with the following: 700 Mhz, 128 RAM, 20 GB hard drive.
	A discussion about printer usage in business indicated that laser printers and color printers are used predominantly. Although dot-matrix printers are appropriate for rough-draft copies, all final work is produced on laser printers. In addition, laser printers are required to produce output formatted with desktop publishing software.	**MSP** to replace present dot matrix printers with laser printers and acquire four-color printers.
	The committee felt that students should understand the use of modems, facsimiles, and other telecommunicating equipment. Telecommunications and the Internet play a paramount role in business and industry today. Students should be well trained in these areas.	**MSP** that the department network be connected to the college network to obtain Internet connectivity. **MSP** that a course in telecommunications and the Internet be implemented.
Equipment Training: Software Issues	A discussion was held concerning the philosophy of upgrading software versions in the business community.	Recommendaton: Upgrade software as soon as possible.

informal meeting minutes (continued)

Computer Applications Advisory Committee
MINUTES—April 4, 2001
Page 2

Activity/Discussion	Issues/Relative Information	Resolution
	Knowing more than one software program enhances a student's job opportunities. For example, the student has an advantage if he or she has been trained in at least one word processing program as well as in a spreadsheet, presentations, and database program.	Recommendation: Students should be familiar with desktop publishing and graphics software as well.
Job-Related Issues:	Entry-level salaries vary from location to location and from specialization to specialization. Students should be trained to be flexible in their expectations and to study the overall package that an employer offers. In our geographical area entry-level salaries range from $1,800 to $2,300 a month.	Information only.
	Language skills and a knowledge of accounting continue to be requisite skills for entry-level positions and for promotional opportunities. All employers ask for human relations skills at all levels.	Information only.
Recommendations for Future Meetings	Survey technology, software, and business trends by circulating a questionnaire to all advisory committee members prior to the meeting date.	Information only.

Submitted by: Barbara Jacobson, Professor
Computer Applications and Administrative Support Department

Format developed by and used with permission of K. Basil and Associates.

13–18 Meeting Agendas

a. Meeting agendas forecast the items to be considered at a scheduled meeting. Basic information that appears on an agenda includes the following:

(1) Name of committee, name of group, or purpose of meeting

(2) Date, time, and location of meeting

(3) Kind of document—*Meeting Agenda* or *Agenda*

(4) List of items to be considered, along with the names of any persons designated to present the item.

b. Use the agenda template of your word processing program or the following guidelines to create an agenda:

(1) Use a 2-inch top margin and the default left and right margins of your word processing program.

(2) Center and place in all capital letters the name of the committee, the name of the group, or the purpose of the meeting. Double-space.

(3) Center and place in capital and lowercase letters *Meeting Agenda* or *Agenda*. Double-space.

(4) Center and place in capital and lowercase letters the date, time, and location of the meeting. Triple-space.

(5) Number with Arabic numerals the items to be considered at the meeting. Follow the topic with the name of the presenter, if any. Single-space the items and double-space between them.

agenda

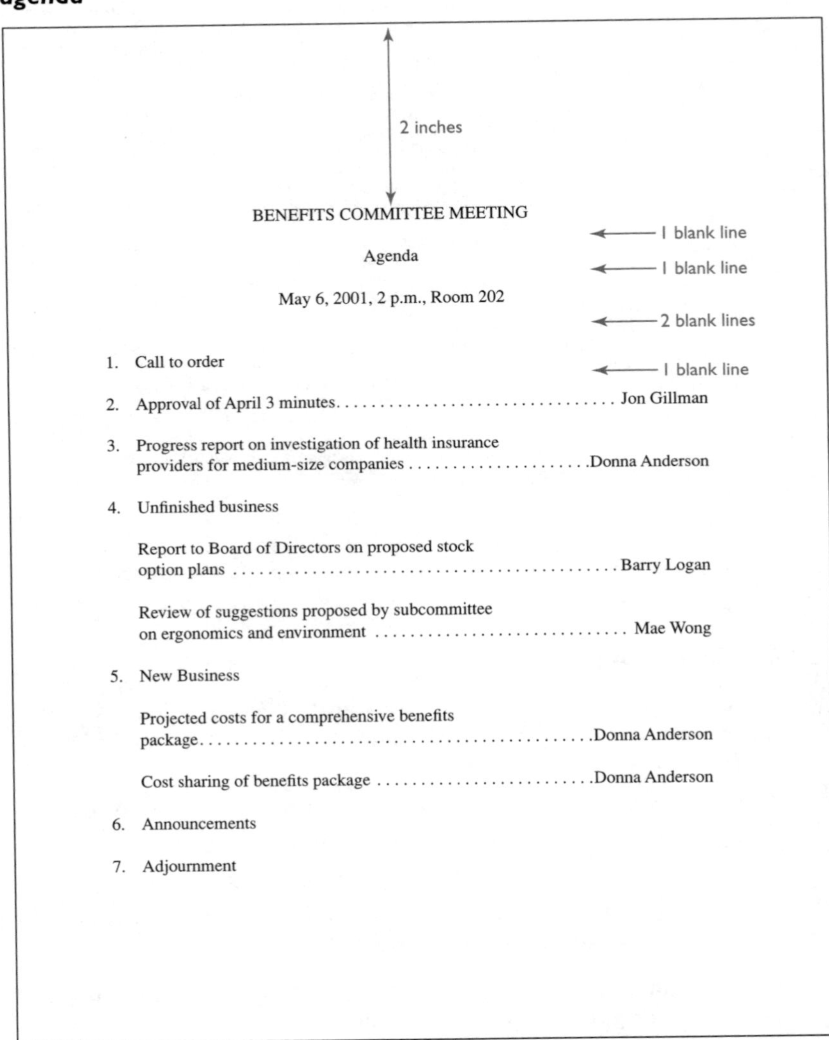

agenda prepared with a word processing template—Microsoft Word

Agenda	**Weekly Sales Meeting** **7/21/01** **2:00 PM to 3:35 PM** **Conference Room 2**	
Meeting called by:	Bill Armstrong	
Type of meeting:	Weekly Sales Meeting	
Facilitator:	Bill Armstrong	
Note taker:	Janice Morris	
Timekeeper:	Jerry Phillips	
Attendees:	Bill Armstrong Barbara Berkowitz Anita Gonzalez Daniel Ho Janice Morris Jerry Phillips Laura Sullivan Mark Turbian	
Please read:	The attached article	
Please bring:	Copy of national sales report	
	Agenda topics	
2:00-2:10 PM	Minutes from July 21 meeting	Janice Morris
2:10-2:20 PM	Weekly sales summary and report	Bill Armstrong
2:20-2:35 PM	New sales promotions	Anita Gonzalez
2:35-2:45 PM	Discontinued products	Daniel Ho
2:45-3:05 PM	Introduction of new products	Daniel Ho
3:05-3:25 PM	Discussion of problem areas	Bill Armstrong
3:25-3:35 PM	Adjournment	
Observers:	Andrea Schwartz, Intern, Cromwell University	
Resource persons:	Robert Goldman, National Sales Manager	
Special notes:	Note that our usual meeting place has been changed.	

13–19 Itineraries

Itineraries plot out events in a travel plan. Use the tables feature of your word processing program and the following guidelines to prepare an itinerary:

(1) Begin the itinerary with a heading that describes the purpose of travel, the name of the person traveling, and the dates of travel.

(2) Use a table or column format with three columns. Set up *Date, Time,* and *Activity* as columnar headings.

(3) Specify all airline flights, hotel reservations, car rental reservations, business appointments, and meal reservations. Include addresses, telephone numbers, and confirmation numbers.

itinerary

MEETING WITH NationsBank REPRESENTATIVES Itinerary for Kym Freeman March 23–26, 2002		
Date	**Time**	**Activity**
Monday, March 23	7:11 a.m.	Depart Burbank airport, American Airlines Flight 1502, light breakfast, Seat 23D, check-in at gate required
	12:13 p.m.	Arrive Dallas-Fort Worth airport
	2:25 p.m.	Depart Dallas-Fort Worth airport, American Airlines Flight 1564, beverage service only, Seat 19D, check-in at gate required
	5:46 p.m.	Arrive Tampa airport
		Reservations at the Marriott Airport Hotel; hotel located on airport premises; Tel: (813) 879-5151; Confirmation No. 987T385R
Tuesday, March 24	8:00 a.m.	Obtain rental car at Hertz airport booth, Confirmation No. ZBT4314
	10:00 a.m.	Meet with Robin Fielding and Chris Perez, NationsBank downtown offices, 400 North Ashley Drive, Room 450, (813) 555-2236
	12 noon	Lunch with Robin Fielding, Chris Perez, and Michael Morris at the Tampa Club, Barnett Bank Building, 22nd Floor, 437 North Commonwealth Street, (813) 555-8732
	2:30 p.m.– 4:30 p.m.	Conduct orientation session of DLDS computerized loan tracking system for all members of the Loan Department at NationsBank downtown office
	7:30 p.m.	Dinner with Jeff and Janet Spiegel at the Outrigger Steak House, 814 Bayview Drive, (813) 555-7892
Wednesday, March 25	8:30 a.m.– 11:30 a.m.	Conduct training sessions on DLDS computerized loan tracking system for all members of the Loan Department
	1:00 p.m.– 4:00 p.m.	Conduct training sessions on DLDS computerized loan tracking system for all members of the Loan Department
	6:00 p.m.	Dinner with Robin Fielding and Chris Perez at the University Club, 1120 University Avenue, (813) 555-0930
Thursday, March 26	6:57 a.m.	Depart Tampa airport, American Airlines Flight 1573, light breakfast, Seat 20B, check-in at gate required
	8:42 a.m.	Arrive Dallas-Fort Worth airport
	9:22 a.m.	Depart Dallas-Fort Worth airport, American Airlines Flight 1465, beverage service only, Seat 20B, check-in at gate required
	10:43 a.m.	Arrive Burbank airport

13–20 Press Releases

Press releases contribute to an organization's visibility and goodwill within the community. Important events and occurrences within an organization should be described on a press release and sent to the news media in the area.

Use the press release template of your word processing program and/or the following guidelines to prepare a press release on your word processor:

(1) Label the document in large bold letters *Press Release* or *News Release.*

(2) Specify the date for release or the words *For immediate release.*

(3) Include the name, address, telephone number, and fax number of the contact person.

(4) Provide a headline (centered and in all capital letters) that summarizes the content of the press release.

(5) Begin the opening paragraph with the city, state, and date. State immediately the essence of your news—who, what, when, where, and why. Follow with the details in subsequent paragraphs.

(6) Prepare the press release on letterhead or 8½- by 11-inch white bond paper. Use a 2-inch top margin and the default left and right margins of your word processor. Triple-space before and after the headline and double-space the text.

(7) Number multiple-page press releases with Arabic numbers in the upper right corner beginning with page 2. Center the word —more— at the bottom of the first page and all other pages except the last.

(8) Conclude the press release by centering a double space below the last line one of the following: *-30-, -# # #-, or -end-.*

press release prepared on company letterhead

2 inches

Northridge Manufacturing Company

170 East Parkland Avenue
Dallas, Texas 75214

(214) 383-5757
Fax: (214) 383-5783

Press Release

For Immediate Release

From Donna Anderson
Phone: (214) 363-5757
Fax: (214) 363-5788

BYRON R. TEAGUE NEW PRESIDENT OF NORTHRIDGE MANUFACTURING

Dallas, Texas, March 10. The Board of Directors of Northridge Manufacturing Company announced yesterday the appointment of Byron R. Teague as its new president, effective June 30.

Mr. Teague, 47, has been with Northridge Manufacturing for nine years. He is presently serving as vice president of operations, a position he has held for the past three years. During this time the company has increased its sales 32 percent and expanded operations into New Mexico, Oklahoma, and Louisiana. Mr. Teague resides with his wife and two children in Dallas.

Mr. Teague will replace William R. Byrd, who will retire on May 30. Mr. Byrd has served as president of Northridge Manufacturing for the past sixteen years.

-30-

press release prepared on word processing template—Microsoft Word

Northridge Manufacturing Company News Release

For Details, Contact:
Donna Anderson
Northridge Manufacturing Company
Phone
(214) 363-5757

Northridge Manufacturing Company
170 East Parkland Avenue
Dallas, Texas 75214-5693
Phone (214) 363-5757
Fax (214) 363-5783

Byron R. Teague Appointed New President of Northridge Manufacturing Company

For Immediate Release

Dallas, Texas, March 10. The Board of Directors of Northridge Manufacturing Company announced yesterday the appointment of Byron R. Teague as its new president, effective June 30.

Mr. Teague, 47, has been with Northridge Manufacturing for nine years. He is presently serving as vice president of operations, a position he has held for the past three years. During this time the company has increased its sales 32 percent and expanded operations into New Mexico, Oklahoma, and Louisiana. Mr. Teague resides with his wife and two children in Dallas.

Mr. Teague will replace William R. Byrd, who will retire on May 30. Mr. Byrd has served as president of Northridge Manufacturing for the past sixteen years.

-30-

April 5, 2001

Chapter 14

Employment Application Documents

Employment Application Documents Solution Finder

During the employment process, candidates seeking positions are usually faced with preparing several kinds of documents: a résumé, a letter of application, an application form, reference request letters, and follow-up letters. Candidates may be required to prepare each of these documents or just one or two before obtaining the position they wish. Guidelines for formulating these kinds of job-seeking instruments are presented here.

The initial document, and probably the most crucial document, is the résumé. A résumé provides the prospective employer with a capsulized visual of an applicant's qualifications. Its chart-like features summarize for the busy executive the attributes a candidate will bring to the position.

Résumés may have various formats and be organized in different ways. The commonly recognized résumé styles are chronological, functional, and a combination of these two. In addition, candidates must take into consideration the possibility that their résumé will be subjected to a computer scan before it is ever read by human eyes. Increasingly, too, many companies are requiring candidates to submit résumés on-line and providing them with form documents to do so.

Today's job seekers need to prepare their résumés in two formats—one in a traditional format and another suitable for on-line transmission and assessment by an automated applicant tracking system.

The Chronological Résumé

14-1 Information to Include in the Chronological Résumé

The résumé is often the only document an employer will use to screen individuals for an interview; therefore, it must succinctly describe your abilities and present you in a favorable light. The résumé style favored by most employers is the *chronological résumé* because it is easy to follow and assess. Guidelines for preparing this résumé style follow:

(1) Select carefully the information you include in your résumé so that the information can be presented on a single page. Only in those situations where an applicant has considerable experience or other qualifications related specifically to a position should the résumé exceed one page.

(2) Incorporate facts about your education, employment background, abilities, achievements, and awards. Besides the usual name, address, and telephone number, information in a résumé should also designate an employment or career objective. Optional categories include college extracurricular activities, professional memberships, willingness to relocate, and references. Personal statistics (age, height, weight, gender), marital status, race, religion, ethnicity, birthplace, high school grades and activities, church responsibilities,

hobbies, and interests should not be included in the résumé—unless they relate specifically to the job for which you are applying.

(3) Begin your résumé with a main heading (name, address, telephone number, fax number [if applicable], and E-mail address [if applicable]) followed by your career objective. Whether you begin the presentation of your credentials with a profile of your educational history and performance, special skills and aptitudes, or work experience depends upon where your greatest strengths lie. Launch the display of your abilities with the category that is most likely to get you the job. Follow up with other categories in the order of their importance to the career objective stated initially. Use text headings such as the following for the categories in your résumé:

Objective or Career Objective

Education, Educational Background, Academic Preparation, or Professional Training

Employment, Experience, or *Employment Experience*

Skills and Abilities

Activities; Honors and Awards; or *Honors, Awards, and Activities*

References

14–2 Main Heading

The main heading opens the résumé and displays your name, address, and telephone number. If you have a fax number and/or an E-mail address, include these also. Follow these guidelines for the main heading:

(1) Set up the main heading so that a prospective employer can easily spot your name and where to reach you for an interview.

(2) Include the addresses and telephone numbers for your *temporary* and *permanent* residences if you have both a college and home residence. If you know an ending date for your temporary residence, indicate it in the heading also.

main heading showing single residence

Jeffrey D. Schultz
2430 Brockton Drive
Upper Marlboro, Maryland 20772
(301) 555-4374

main heading showing temporary and permanent residences

Brian R. Garvey

Temporary Residence:	Permanent Residence:
830 Willow Street, Apt. 6	5460 Roundtree Circle
Columbia, South Carolina 29207	Atlanta, Georgia 30315
(803) 555-7863	(404) 555-9066

14–3 Career or Employment Objective

a. Include in your résumé a career or employment objective so that prospective employers know the kind of position you are seeking. Prepare an objective related to a specific job or one that would make you employable in a number of job categories, depending upon your qualifications and interests.

specific employment objective

Objective: To obtain a position as a legal office trainee in a medium-size legal office

general employment objective

Career Objective

To begin a career in marketing with exposure to retail sales, customer relations, market research, and advertising. Long-range goal is to become a department manager in a large metropolitan area department store.

b. Prepare separate résumés if you have more than one employment area in which you wish to apply. Write the career objective to pertain to each of the positions in which you are interested, and tailor the other sections to emphasize the position stated in your objective.

14–4 Educational History and Performance

Résumés furnish the opportunity to provide prospective employers with information substantiating an applicant's academic preparation to perform the job for which he or she is applying. Use these guidelines to present your academic qualifications in the chronological résumé:

(1) Begin this section with the college, university, or other postsecondary institution you attended most recently. Include the name and location of the institution, school or department within the institution, major and minor fields of study, degrees or diplomas received, and dates

of attendance. If you expect to earn a degree, list the degree and include the expected date or a statement such as *to be granted June 2003.*

(2) Provide your grade-point average within this section, but only if it reflects favorably upon you. You may wish to provide your overall grade-point average and/or a grade-point average in your major courses of study. Include the scale on which the grade-point average is based—e.g., 3.65/4.00.

(3) Avoid listings of courses completed. Furnish only those course names and other educational experiences that are directly related to performing successfully in the desired position.

(4) List all collegiate or other postsecondary institutions attended. Include your high school education only if your postsecondary education has not resulted in a degree, an anticipated degree, a diploma, or a certificate.

example of educational background entry in a résumé

Education

- University of Southern California, Los Angeles, Graduate School of Business Administration, Master of Science Degree in Management of Human Resources to be awarded May 2003, 3.9/4.0 grade-point average

  Courses in management of human resources, management-union relations, contract negotiations, and international resource development

- University of Montana, Missoula, Montana, College of Engineering, Bachelor of Science in Mechanical Engineering, June 1999, 3.2/4.0 grade-point average

14–5 Work Experience

Reportings of successful work experiences tell prospective employers that applicants have been productive in the work environment. This section gives you an opportunity to show that you respond positively to supervision, have good work habits, and work well with others.

a. **If your work experience is limited, include all the positions you have held—even though they do not relate to the position for which you are applying. They indicate to the employer that you are familiar with the work world and have performed successfully in its environment.**

b. **If your work experience is vast and varied, include only those positions that are most recent and/or are related to the job for which you are applying.**

c. **In the chronological résumé list your work experience in reverse chronological order, that is, your most recent employment first. Include the following information for each position listed:**

(1) *Employer's or company name and address.* Include only the city and state for the address.

(2) *Dates of employment.* State the month and year you began work and the month and year you terminated. You need not state a reason for leaving the position or provide salary information.

(3) *Job title.* Supply only the title of the most important or the last position held before leaving the employer.

(4) *Significant duties, activities, accomplishments, and promotions.* Use parallel construction and action verbs to describe succinctly and concretely the activities involved in your employment. Use action verbs such as *composed, conducted, created, designed, initiated, maintained, organized, prepared,* and *upgraded.* For previous employment activities, use the past tense; for ongoing employment activities, use the present tense. As much as possible select those responsibilities and accomplishments that feature your attributes for the position you are seeking.

d. **In cases of part-time employment, indicate the part-time status in parentheses after the dates of employment. No notation is necessary for positions held as a full-time employee.**

example of work experience entry in a résumé

Work Experience

Freestone Industries, Inc., Portland, Oregon, *Payroll Accountant,* July 2000–present
Enter and maintain payroll records using a computerized payroll system
Issue weekly and monthly payroll checks
Complete payroll and tax reports for local, state, and federal agencies
Submit withholding and other payroll taxes

Ritter's Clothing Emporium, Eugene, Oregon, *Bookkeeper-Accountant,*
September 1998–March 2000 (part-time)
Entered daily sales receipts and expense disbursements
Prepared checks for signature
Maintained payroll records

Barton-Hagan Ice Cream Parlor, Eugene, Oregon, *Service Representative,*
September 1997–August 1998 (part-time)
Served and packed ice cream
Cashiered customer purchases

14–6 Skills and Abilities

a. **Your educational background and work experience may not show all the traits and abilities that relate to the job you are seeking. Qualities that fall into the skills and abilities category include knowledge of specific computer programs or the ability to speak a foreign language. In some cases extensive travel in another country or knowledge pertaining to another culture might prove of value. Include in this category only those skills and abilities that pertain to your job objective. Omit this section in your chronological résumé if the information can be incorporated into another part.**

b. **Follow these guidelines to list your skills and abilities:**

(1) Begin, if possible, each item in the listing with an action verb stated in the present tense.

(2) Use parallel construction to list your special abilities.

example of skills and abilities entry in a résumé

Skills and Abilities

Use proficiently the following computer application programs: Microsoft Word, Excel, PowerPoint, Access, Outlook, and WordPerfect

Access and navigate the Internet to retrieve needed information

Speak and write Spanish fluently

14–7 Awards, Honors, and Activities

a. **If you have a number of awards and honors (at least three) and also a number of collegiate extracurricular activities (at least three), you may wish to show these items in two categories (*Honors and Awards* and *Activities*) instead of just one.**

b. **If your career experiences are more important than your education in obtaining the desired position, this category may well be replaced by a listing of your activities in professional and community organizations.**

c. **Use these guidelines to present any activities, honors, or awards in the chronological résumé:**

(1) Begin with the most recent occurrence.

(2) List the names of the honors and awards and the dates they were earned or received.

(3) List the name of the organization, any offices held, and the dates of participation for each activity.

example of honors, awards, and activities entry in a résumé

Honors, Awards, and Activities

Awarded *The Wall Street Journal* scholarship for academic excellence, February 2001

Dean's Honor Roll, September 2000–Present

Fenton College Student Council, Associated Student Body Representative, Business Department, Spring 2000 and Fall 2000 semesters

Alpha Gamma Sigma, honor society, February 1999–Present

Phi Beta Lambda, business fraternity, September 1999–Present
- Treasurer, Spring 2000 semester
- Vice President, Fall 2000 semester
- President, Spring 2001 semester

chronological résumé

LORRAINE V. HOOVER

Temporary Address:
3460 S.W. 16th Street, #12
Gainesville, FL 32608
(904) 555-3250

Permanent Address:
7520 Beachway Drive
Tampa, FL 33609
(813) 555-2840

Objective To begin a career in accounting with immediate objective to gain experience for certification as a Certified Public Accountant

Education

Master of Accounting (3/2 program) — **May 2000**
Bachelor of Science in Accounting — **May 1999**
Fisher School of Accounting
University of Florida, Gainesville, Florida
GPA 3.53/4.0 (accounting), 3.68/4.0 (overall)

Honors

Beta Alpha Psi	Spring 1998
Becker CPA Review Scholarship	Spring 1998
Golden Key Honor Society	Spring 1998
Dean's List	Summer 1997–present
President's Honor Roll	Spring 1997

Activities

Beta Alpha Psi	
Reporting Secretary	Spring 1998–present
Fisher School of Accounting Council	
Vice President	Spring 1998—Spring 1999
Audit Team	Spring 1998
Student Representative to Programs Board	Spring 1998
Class Representative	Fall 1997–Spring 1998
Becker CPA Review	
Student Representative	May 1998–present
Florida Accounting Association	Fall 1998–present
American Marketing Association	
Promotion Cochair	Fall 1997

Work Experience

Alpert, Josey and Grilli, P.A., Tampa, Florida — Summer 1996
Assistant Bookkeeper
- Reconciled monthly bank statements and daily deposits
- Recorded and updated billable time for legal fees
- Prepared clients' monthly bills
- Revised clients' financial files

Zudar's Cafe, Server, Tampa, Florida — Summer 1995
Tampa Eye Clinic, Tampa, Florida — August 1994–May 1995
Doctor's Assistant
- Updated patients' files
- Prepared patients for examination

Computer Knowledge Excel, Lotus 1-2-3, Access, Microsoft Word, WordPerfect

References

Peter Grilli
Alpert, Josey and Grilli, P.A.
100 Ashley Drive South
Tampa, Florida 33601
(813) 555-4131

Dr. Lewis Lauring
Tampa Eye Clinic
3000 Dr. Martin Luther King Jr. West
Tampa, Florida 33601
(813) 555-2020

Employment 14

14–8 References

a. The inclusion of references in the chronological résumé is optional. The statement *References furnished upon request* is not necessary if you decide not to furnish names, addresses, and telephone numbers on the résumé itself. Prospective employers assume that at the point of interview you will be able to furnish them from three to five former professors and/or employers who will be able to provide firsthand information about you.

b. Select your references carefully. A bad reference is worse than no reference at all. Before giving the name of a reference, check with that person to ensure that he or she is agreeable to giving you a recommendation. Give each reference a copy of your résumé.

c. Use the following guidelines for including references in your résumé:

(1) Limit the number of references to two or three. Space is better allocated to presenting your qualifications for the job you are seeking.

(2) Provide the name and title of the individual; the company or institution name; the street address; the city, state, and zip code; and the telephone number for each reference cited.

Examples of references are shown in the chronological résumé on page 445.

chronological résumé

DANIEL HO

6201 Rathburn Avenue • Northridge, California 91325 • (818) 555-9770

Objective

To obtain a responsible and challenging position as an administrative assistant where my education and work experience will be of value

Education

Los Angeles Pierce College Woodland Hills, California	
Certificate in Office Administration, General Administrative	May 2001
Associate in Arts degree, Quality Control Engineering	June 1998
Associate in Arts degree, Landscape Maintenance	June 1996

Work Experience

Los Angeles Pierce College Woodland Hills, California Computer Laboratory Assistant Assist students with computer assignments Provide instructional support during evening classes Maintain equipment in working order	August 1998– Present (part-time)
Nordskog Industries, Inc. Van Nuys, California CNC Operator Assembled and operated CNC (Computerized Numerical Control) machine Checked and modified CNC program Assembled and bonded parts for commercial airplane galleys	July 1994– September 1998

Computer Skills

Training in the following computer programs emphasizing the production of documents typically found in business and office applications:

- Microsoft Word for Windows
- WordPerfect
- Excel
- Lotus 1-2-3
- Access

Ability to type 50 wpm

The Functional Résumé

14–9 Preparation of the Functional Résumé

The functional résumé, shown on page 448, focuses on an applicant's skills, abilities, and accomplishments. Rather than beginning with an education or employment history, the functional résumé presents competencies and accomplishments in special categories.

a. You may wish to use a functional résumé if you have changed jobs frequently or if there are gaps in your employment history. Applicants with little employment experience also find this form of résumé appealing.

b. Although the functional résumé emphasizes abilities, it should also include information about a candidate's education; previous employment; and any pertinent honors, activities, and affiliations. Use the following guidelines to prepare a functional résumé:

(1) Begin with a main heading that displays your name, address, and telephone number. If you have a fax number and/or an E-mail address, include these also. Follow the main heading with your employment objective.

(2) Continue the functional résumé with a listing of your significant abilities, skills, activities, and accomplishments. As much as possible select items that feature your attributes for the position you are seeking. Group the items into meaningful categories, and use a descriptive heading for each category.

(3) Use parallel construction and action verbs to describe succinctly and concretely the items in your listing. Use action verbs such as *assisted, compiled, coordinated, developed, edited, established, managed, planned,* and *translated.* For previous accomplishments, use the past tense; for present skills and abilities, use the present tense.

(4) Include in the functional résumé a history of your academic preparation (see Section 14–4) and a brief account of your previous employment (see Section 14–5).

(5) Conclude the functional résumé with a listing of any awards, extracurricular activities, or professional affiliations (see Section 14–7).

functional résumé

Claudia Martinez

3221 Nordhoff Street · Northridge, California 91326 · (818) 555-6497

OBJECTIVE

Obtain a secretarial or an administrative assistant position with opportunity for advancement

SKILLS AND ABILITIES

- *Operate proficiently the following software programs:* Microsoft Word for Windows, WordPerfect for Windows, Excel, Lotus 1-2-3, Access, FileMaker Pro, PowerPoint, Windows 98 and 2000
- Transcribe and proofread business documents accurately
- Compose and prepare routine correspondence
- Perform computerized accounting functions using QuickBooks
- Speak and write English and Spanish fluently
- Type 55 words a minute

ACCOMPLISHMENTS

- Trained and supervised student workers
- Performed database entries using FileMaker Pro on a Macintosh computer and Microsoft Access on a personal computer
- Reorganized instructional media for easier access and availability to faculty
- Maintained audio and video equipment
- Filed invoices and catalogs
- Answered telephone inquiries and took reservations for equipment loans
- Duplicated audiocassettes for students

EDUCATION

Los Angeles Pierce College, Woodland Hills, California. Associate in Arts degree, May 2000, Office Administration–General Administrative. Overall GPA 3.9/4.0.

EXPERIENCE

Instructional Media Center, Los Angeles Pierce College, Woodland Hills, California. August 1998 to present (part-time).

HONORS AND AWARDS

- Certificate of Recognition from Alpha Gamma Sigma, the scholastic honor society, for "Outstanding Scholarship and Placement" on the Dean's List each semester
- Frances M. Heinze Memorial Scholarship for outstanding scholastic achievement, May 1999
- Teresa A. Caruana Memorial Award for overall outstanding achievement, May 2000
- Office Administration Department, Highest GPA Award, May 2000

The Combination Résumé

14–10 Preparation of the Combination Résumé

The combination résumé, shown on page 450, blends the strongest qualities of the chronological and functional résumés.

a. **For candidates who are recent graduates but have some full-time experience, the combination résumé offers the opportunity to highlight both their competencies and their experience.**

b. **The combination résumé continues to focus on an applicant's abilities, skills, activities, and accomplishments. It differs from the functional résumé in that the combination résumé provides a complete employment history. Use the following guidelines to prepare a combination résumé:**

(1) Begin with a main heading that displays your name, address, and telephone number. If you have a fax number and/or an E-mail address, include these also. Follow the main heading with your employment objective.

(2) Continue the combination résumé with a listing of your significant abilities, skills, activities, and accomplishments. As much as possible select items that feature your attributes for the position you are seeking. Group the items into meaningful categories, and use a descriptive heading for each category.

(3) Use parallel construction and action verbs to describe succinctly and concretely the items in your listing. Use action verbs such as *assisted, compiled, coordinated, developed, edited, established, managed, planned,* and *translated.* For previous accomplishments, use the past tense; for present skills and abilities, use the present tense.

(4) Include in the combination résumé a history of your academic preparation (see Section 14–4) and your previous employment (see Section 14–5). Place first the category that is more likely to qualify you for the job for which you are applying.

(5) Conclude the combination résumé with a listing of any awards, extracurricular activities, or professional affiliations (see Section 14–7).

combination résumé

MARLENE CAPPETTO

6240 Winnetka Avenue ◆ Encino, CA 91371 ◆ (818) 555-4210 ◆ mcappetto213@aol.com

EMPLOYMENT OBJECTIVE To obtain a paralegal position offering challenge, responsibility, and personal growth

CAPABILITIES AND SKILLS
- Draft complaints/answers
- Compose interrogatories/answers
- Prepare motions
- Conduct legal research
- Access and use WESTLAW
- Compose and prepare business correspondence
- Operate proficiently WordPerfect, Microsoft Word for Windows, Lotus 1-2-3, Quicken, and Access
- Type 70 words per minute
- Operate the numeric 10-key pad proficiently
- Speak and write English and Spanish fluently

EDUCATION

University of California, Los Angeles, Extension, Attorney Assistant Training Program, Certificate in Litigation, November 1998
This program is offered in cooperation with the UCLA School of Law and is approved by the American Bar Association.

Los Angeles Pierce College, Woodland Hills, Associate in Arts degree, Office Administration—Word Processing, May 1998

EXPERIENCE

July 1998–Present — **Litigation Assistant, O'Melveny & Myers, Los Angeles**
Perform automated document management on multiple projects
Review documents and prepare information for discovery
Investigate facts and case law

February 1998–July 1998 (part-time) — **Legal Secretary, Law Offices of Duane Lübbe, Encino**
Composed and prepared business correspondence using WordPerfect
Managed documents for personal injury cases
Transcribed dictation
Maintained business calendars

HONORS

Dean's Honor List, 1995–1998
The National Dean's List Award, 1997–98
Teresa A. Caruana Memorial Award, May 1998
2,000 Notable American Women Award

AFFILIATIONS

Phi Theta Kappa International Honor Society
UCLA Extension Attorney Assistant Alumni Association
Los Angeles Paralegal Association
National Association for Female Executives
National Association of Legal Assistants

Conventional Résumé Formats

14–11 Formats for the Résumé

The appearance of your résumé creates a first impression, the first impression a prospective employer forms of you. If the résumé is well designed and well written, it is more likely to be read and to lead to an interview. Use the following guidelines to prepare your résumé:

(1) Use 20- or 24-pound high-quality white bond paper to prepare your résumé. Ensure that the print quality is high density, equal to that of a laser printer.

(2) Strive for optimal top, bottom, left, and right margins—1 inch. Use no less than 0.75 inch for each of these margins.

(3) Select a font or typeface that is easy to read. Use no smaller than an 11-point font, and do not condense the line spacing so that the copy becomes difficult to read.

(4) Use headings for each of your major categories. Differentiate through size and/or attribute (bold or italic) these text headings from the regular text. Use regular second-degree text headings as shown in Section 13–8a and the example résumé on page 446 or parallel headings as shown in the example résumés on pages 445, 448, and 450.

(5) Use font attributes (bold, italic, all capital letters) to make your résumé more attractive and easily comprehensible. Be careful, though, not to overuse these attributes and to apply them consistently for the same features.

(6) Single-space the items listed within each section, but double-space between the items. Use parallel construction for all entries within a section, and place a period only at the end of complete sentences. Use no punctuation mark to conclude incomplete word groups unless they are followed by complete sentences or another word group.

Automated Applicant Tracking Systems

14–12 Preparation for Computerized Résumé Searches

a. **Large companies are increasingly relying on automated applicant tracking systems to screen candidates. These computers are not programmed to assess personal skills, initiative, motivation, drive, attitude, disposition, or other such attributes. Instead, they look for the marketable skills possessed by a candidate. Automated applicant tracking systems generally operate in the following way:**

(1) On-line résumés are loaded directly into the tracking system. A paper résumé is scanned, and its scanned image is sent to a computer equipped with optical character recognition (OCR) software. Here the computer "reads," classifies, and stores each résumé quickly.

(2) When a job opening occurs, the employer tells the tracking system the keywords for the position. The computer looks for keywords (nouns that match the candidates' education, experience, skills, abilities, and knowledge with the job requirements).

(3) Applicants' résumés are selected and ranked according to the number of keywords appearing in the résumé. Only applicants whose résumés contain the keywords are candidates for the interview. These résumés are then subjected to human scrutiny for a decision as to whether the applicant will be invited for an interview.

(4) Automated applicant tracking systems generate response letters to prospective job candidates—interview offers, acknowledgments, and rejections. Most résumés are stored for a stipulated time before they are purged from the system.

b. Keywords are the core of automated applicant tracking systems. Computers assess what a person can *do*. They look for substantiated facts, definitive quantities, and concrete nouns that describe specific, identifiable skills and accomplishments.

Keywords *differ* for each job title and each industry. Some companies will use keywords for the specific job opening and other keywords to assess familiarity with terms in the industry. Consider the following examples:

(1) If a company were looking for a tax accountant with at least two years' experience with a Big 5 accounting firm, keywords for this position might be as follows:

B.A. in Accounting	public accounting experience
B.S. in Accounting	Excel
Masters of Accounting	computer skills
Masters of Tax Law	communication skills
CPA	Arthur Andersen
auditing	Coopers & Lybrand
tax accounting	Deloitte & Touche
tax law	Ernst & Young
corporate tax	KPMG Peat Marwick
tax return preparation	Price Waterhouse

(2) A major pharmaceutical company posted the following job opening for an "Admin Coordinator II" at its Web site, informing applicants that their résumés would be processed using an "electronic résumé database system."

Duties: provide administrative support for two associate directors including traveling and meeting coordination; agenda and minutes preparation; development and preparation of spreadsheets and databases; administrative support for extramural studies; preparation of routine and nonroutine correspondence; assist in preparing monitoring of research agreements through computer tracking; other duties as required.

Education: high school or equivalent.

Experience: typically, three years of general secretarial experience is expected for this position.

Skills required: Excel, MS Word, E-mail; good organizational skills; familiarity with financial and administrative process requirements of a large firm; ability to exercise judgment and support a team-oriented environment.

Based on the job description provided, an applicant might assume that the employer would suggest the following keywords for the automated applicant tracking system:

Excel	travel coordination
MS Word	meeting coordination
E-mail	correspondence preparation
organizational skills	spreadsheet
team-oriented	database
high school diploma	administrative support
general secretarial experience	meeting agendas
computer tracking	meeting minutes

Additional industry-specific keywords this employer may look for include these:

biology	health industry
medical terminology	research
chemistry	pharmaceutical
life science	anatomy

c. **Check with prospective employers to see if your résumé will be evaluated by an automated applicant tracking system. If so, devise a list of keywords from your qualifications that you think may be used by the employer to select people for the position in which you are interested.**

After the personal information (name, address, and telephone number) in your résumé, begin your listing of qualifications with a keyword summary. Use the following guidelines to prepare this section of your résumé:

(1) Label the section *Keyword Summary*, *Keywords*, or *Keyword Profile*. Use no font attributes such as boldface, italics, or underlining.

(2) Use nouns to feature what you can do or what you have accomplished. Follow each keyword with a period, and list the keywords horizontally across the page.

(3) Begin the listing with the most important qualifications, and follow these keywords with those of lesser significance.

(4) Use variants of the keywords in the main text of your résumé to increase your chances of matching the keyword images of the optical character reading (OCR) software; for example, substitute Associate in Arts for A.A., spreadsheet for Excel, or administrative assistant for secretary.

Keyword Profile

Microsoft Word. WordPerfect. Excel. Lotus 1-2-3. Access. PowerPoint. E-mail. 3 years' general secretarial experience. Office Administration. Administrative support. A.A. Help Desk. Typing. Filing. Agendas. Meeting minutes. Itineraries. Phones. Scheduling. Mail. Correspondence. Well organized. Good written and oral communication skills. Team-oriented.

d. Paper résumés submitted to automated applicant tracking systems are scanned and forwarded to optical character recognition equipment (OCR) for reading. An example of a résumé prepared for scanning is shown on page 455. So that your résumé is read correctly, you need to ensure it meets the following criteria:

(1) Use black print equal to the quality of a laser or an inkjet printer on 24-pound, 8½- by 11-inch smooth-surfaced white bond paper.

(2) Use standard fonts (10 to 14 points in size) in which none of the characters touch each other (Arial, Univers, Helvetica, New Century Schoolbook), and avoid attributes such as underscores, italics, or shadows that are hard for optical scanning equipment to read. Use boldface and/or all capital letters for section headings and emphasis, as long as letters don't touch each other.

(3) Keep your résumé free from graphics, boxed text, and shading; you may use solid bullets or asterisks for a listing, as long as you leave a space after them. Confine your résumé to a single-column format; multiple columns often run together in translations by OCR software.

(4) Place your name on the first line of the résumé. Following lines should include your complete address and telephone number. Include also your fax number and E-mail address, if applicable.

(5) Begin your description of qualifications with a keyword summary (nouns used by the computer to match candidates' traits with job requirements).

(6) Continue to employ keywords to describe specifically what you can do in relation to the job for which you are applying. Examples are (1) perform bookkeeping and accounting functions such as payroll, accounts receivable, and accounts payable; (2) use computer programs such as Microsoft Word, WordPerfect, Lotus, Excel, and Access; (3) work in retail sales and customer relations; and (4) prepare, edit, and proofread reports.

(7) Avoid using abbreviations; use them only if they are common to your profession or after you have spelled them out in full.

(8) Send the résumé in a large envelope, and be sure to include a cover letter. Do not fold or staple the pages; fasten them with a paper clip.

résumé prepared for an automated applicant tracking system

Corey T. Roberts
2380 Vista Avenue
Thousand Oaks, California 95609
(805) 553-2196

Keyword Profile

Microsoft Word. WordPerfect. Excel. Lotus 1-2-3. Access. PowerPoint. E-mail. 4 years' general secretarial experience. A.A. Office Administration. Administrative assistant. Help Desk. Typing. Filing. Agendas. Meeting minutes. Itineraries. Phones. Scheduling. Mail. Correspondence. Well organized. Good written and oral communication skills.

Objective

Administrative support position in a large pharmaceutical corporation

Experience

1997 to Present, ABCO Resource and Consulting Services, Administrative Assistant to the General Manager, Woodland Hills Office

- Handle phones and incoming calls on Help Desk
- Schedule meetings, prepare agendas, take minutes, and prepare meeting minutes for distribution
- Make travel arrangements and prepare itineraries
- Use word processing equipment to prepare all written documents and answer routine incoming correspondence
- Use spreadsheet software for budget and expense reports
- Use presentation software to assist staff in developing sales presentations
- Maintain a database of current and potential contract employees
- Maintain a filing system
- Process incoming mail

1996 to 1997, Salvation Corps, Administrative Clerk

- Handled all incoming phone calls and greeted visitors
- Scheduled pickup of nonmonetary donations
- Used spreadsheet software to track monetary donations, prepare budgets, and record expenses
- Used a Macintosh to prepare fliers
- Processed all incoming mail and handled the filing system

1994 to 1996, Secretary to Professor Linda Atkinson (part-time)

- Used a personal computer to prepare manuscript for publication
- Proofread page proofs

Education

Associate in Arts, Office Administration, Office Automation option, Brookview Community College, 1996. Additional courses taken include biology, anatomy, and medical terminology.

High school diploma, Wilson High School, 1993.

On-line Career Resources

The Internet is increasingly playing a more dominant role in the job-seeking process. On-line career centers (1) post job openings in organizations throughout the United States, (2) allow applicants to apply for openings on-line, and (3) permit job-seeking candidates to post résumés. Many of these career sites also offer suggestions for preparing résumés and provide general career advice.

Most major corporations that maintain Web sites have established career centers within their sites. Here they list job openings within their organizations and provide opportunities for interested candidates to submit their résumés on-line.

14–13 Locating Career Centers on the Internet

The Internet furnishes access to a large variety of career centers and services. Career centers usually provide information about employers, post employment opportunities, assist candidates in placing their résumés on-line, and grant employers access to candidates' résumés. Many of these career centers are free of charge to the prospective employee and employer, but others charge the employer or both the employer and employee. Follow these guidelines to locate various career centers on the Internet:

(1) Use a search engine (AltaVista, Excite, etc.) to locate a listing of career centers and services for your area of interest and expertise—business, health services, law, entertainment, computing, etc.

(2) Explore a number of the career centers and services your search produces to determine the one or ones suitable for you. Consider job classifications, location of opportunities, kinds of applicants targeted, kinds of employers, scope of coverage, and cost (if any). You may also wish to visit the following Web site that contains links to a large number of career centers and services on the Internet:

Yahoo! Business and Economy:Employment:Jobs. <http://dir.yahoo.com/Business/Employment/jobs/>. This site provides a listing, brief description, and link to a large number of career resources on the Internet.

(3) Visit well-known, popular career centers that post job openings and candidates' résumés. Some of these are listed here:

America's Job Bank. <http://www.ajb.dni.us>. America's Job Bank is a partnership between the U.S. Department of Labor and the state-operated public Employment Service, which provides labor exchange service to employers and job seekers through a network of 1,800 offices throughout the United States. America's Job Bank lists over 1.4 million jobs and posts résumés. No fee; registration required for résumé posting.

Career Magazine. <http://www.careermag.com>. This Web site is an on-line career magazine with information on job openings, employers, résumé banks, job fairs, and various articles on current topics such as diversity in the workplace. No fee; registration required for résumé posting.

CareerMosaic. <http://www.careermosaic.com>. This Web site is popular with college students since it has a job database, a "usenet" to perform searches of jobs listed in regional and occupational newsgroups, an on-line job fair, a career resource center, and an international gateway to link to CareerMosaic sites around the world. This Web site strives to be a valuable source to both the employer and the job seeker. See pages 460–61 to view its template for on-line résumé posting. No fee; no registration required.

CareerPath.com. <http://www.careerpath.com>. Career Path lists approximately 250,000 jobs. You may also access classified ads from over 90 major newspapers—e.g., the *Boston Globe, New York Times, Los Angeles Times, Chicago Tribune, Washington Post,* and *San Jose Mercury News.* No fee; registration required for résumé posting.

JobDirect.com. <http://www.jobdirect.com>. JobDirect connects entry-level job seekers with employers who want qualified applicants. This Web site is designed to help students and recent college graduates find internships, part-time jobs, or career positions. No fee; registration required.

JOBTRAK.COM. <http://www.jobtrak.com/>. Jobtrak has job listings for full-time jobs, part-time jobs, temporary jobs, and internships. This site provides an on-line career fair, job search tips, career forums, and a career contact network. Students and alumni from more than 900 colleges and universities may view job listings posted and/or post résumés by obtaining a password from their college or university.

Monster.com. <http://www.monster.com>. This is one of the most popular Web sites for job seekers. The site offers a variety of hypertext links to job-search resources and connections to job listings. No fee; registration required.

Monster.com health industry site. <http://www.medsearch.com>. This site, formerly *MedSearch America,* lists job openings and posts résumés for all classifications of positions in the health industry.

USA TODAY Career Center. <http://findjob.usatoday.com/search.html>. Provides job listings accessible by location and career objective. No fee; no registration required.

Yahoo! Classifieds. <http://classifieds.yahoo.com/employment.html>. This site provides a nationwide listing of job openings. Categories are refined by state, major city (includes surrounding area), general field, and keywords. No fee; registration required.

14–14 Accessing Corporate On-line Career Centers

a. **Major corporations generally include career centers in their Web sites. Here they describe career opportunities and post job openings in their organization. If you are interested in employment with a particular organization, visit its Web site, view its advertised positions, and submit your résumé.**

b. **Most company Web sites may be accessed by entering *www.(companyname).com* in the address box of your browser. Specific examples are *www.dole.com* and *www.amgen.com.* If this strategy does not produce the desired result, use one of the two following procedures:**

(1) Use a search engine (AltaVista, Excite, etc.) to locate the company Web site you wish to access or to locate an up-to-date directory of company Web sites.

(2) Access the two company Web site directories listed here. Both these directories provide links to major United States corporations.

1999 Fortune 5 Hundred. <http://www.fortune.com/fortune500/500list.html>. This site provides links to capsulized descriptions of Fortune 500 companies; these links contain links to the respective company's Web sites.

Websense, "Company Locator." <http://www.websense.com/locator.htm>. You may use this page to search for a company's Web site. This page uses the Internic's list of registered domain names as the underlying database and the InterNIC database of registered companies. Results will produce primarily United States companies

c. **Some companies accept résumés only for the positions that are advertised. Others accept all résumés and store them for a specified time. Should an opening occur that requires the qualifications of an applicant on file, the applicant may then be considered for the position.**

Résumés submitted on-line are routed into an automated applicant tracking system. Follow the procedures described in Section 14–12 to prepare your résumé; keywords will be used to determine your qualifications for openings in the organization. In addition, follow the procedures outlined in Section 14–15 to prepare your résumé in text format for transmission over the Internet.

14–15 Preparing and Posting an On-line Résumé

a. **Select one or more career centers on which to post your résumé. Use the chronological style résumé described in Section 14–1, and prepare a version of your résumé in ASCII format. Cut and paste from this version to accommodate the templates required by the career centers. A résumé prepared in ASCII format is shown on page 459.**

You may also use your prepared résumé as a guide to complete the fill-in blanks of a résumé builder provided by a career center or company career site. An example résumé builder appears on pages 460–61.

b. **Use the following guidelines to prepare your résumé for posting at an Internet career center or for on-line transmission to a company career site:**

(1) Prepare your résumé in ASCII text. To create an ASCII résumé, key your résumé in a word processing program and save it as a text-only document (sometimes called Rich Text Format or RTF). This should be an option under your "Save As" command. You may also use a simple text program to compose your résumé.

(2) Align all text at the left margin. Do not use the tab key; use the space bar for any indentations.

(3) Use hard returns for line breaks; do not rely on the word wrap feature of your word processing program.

(4) Avoid special characters and font attributes such as italics, underlining, and bolding. Fonts will become whatever a computer uses as its default typeface and size.

(5) Spell check and carefully proofread your résumé before you save it as an ASCII file.

résumé prepared in ASCII format

JORDAN W. J. SAVAGE
6683 Kreag Road
Pittsford, NY 14536
(716) 555-8438
jwjsavage@telis.org

OBJECTIVE
To obtain a position that allows me to use my skills as a Web site designer and HTML programmer.

EMPLOYMENT HISTORY
February 1999 - Present, Webmaster, Moran Food Corporation, Albany, New York
**Design all pages for Web site of Moran Food Corpration, domestic and international
**HTML code all Web pages for Moran Food Corporation
**Maintain all Web sites for Moran Food Corporation

June 1998 - January 1999, Graphic Designer, Moran Food Corporation, Albany, New York
**Created magazine ads for national magazines
**Created multimedia presentations for the marketing staff
**Created designs for recipe booklets and other promotional materials
**Provided integration assistance between the art and information processing departments

August 1997 - May 1998, Assistant Graphic Designer, Wilmont College, Boston, Massachusetts (part-time)
**Assisted in the development of advertising materials including a Macromedia Director presentation
**Designed flyers for promotional events
**Assisted in producing mechanicals

EDUCATION
B.S. in Computer Science, major in computer science and minor in graphic design, Wilmont College, Boston, Massachusetts, 1998
GPA: 3.7/4.0

ADDITIONAL SKILLS
**Programming/Scripting Languates: C++, COBOL, and HTML
**Operating Systems: MacOS, Windows 2000, Unix
**Software: PowerPoint, Aldus PageMaker, Adobe Photoshop, Excel, Access, Microsoft Word, Quark Xpress

career center template for on-line résumé posting—CareerMosaic

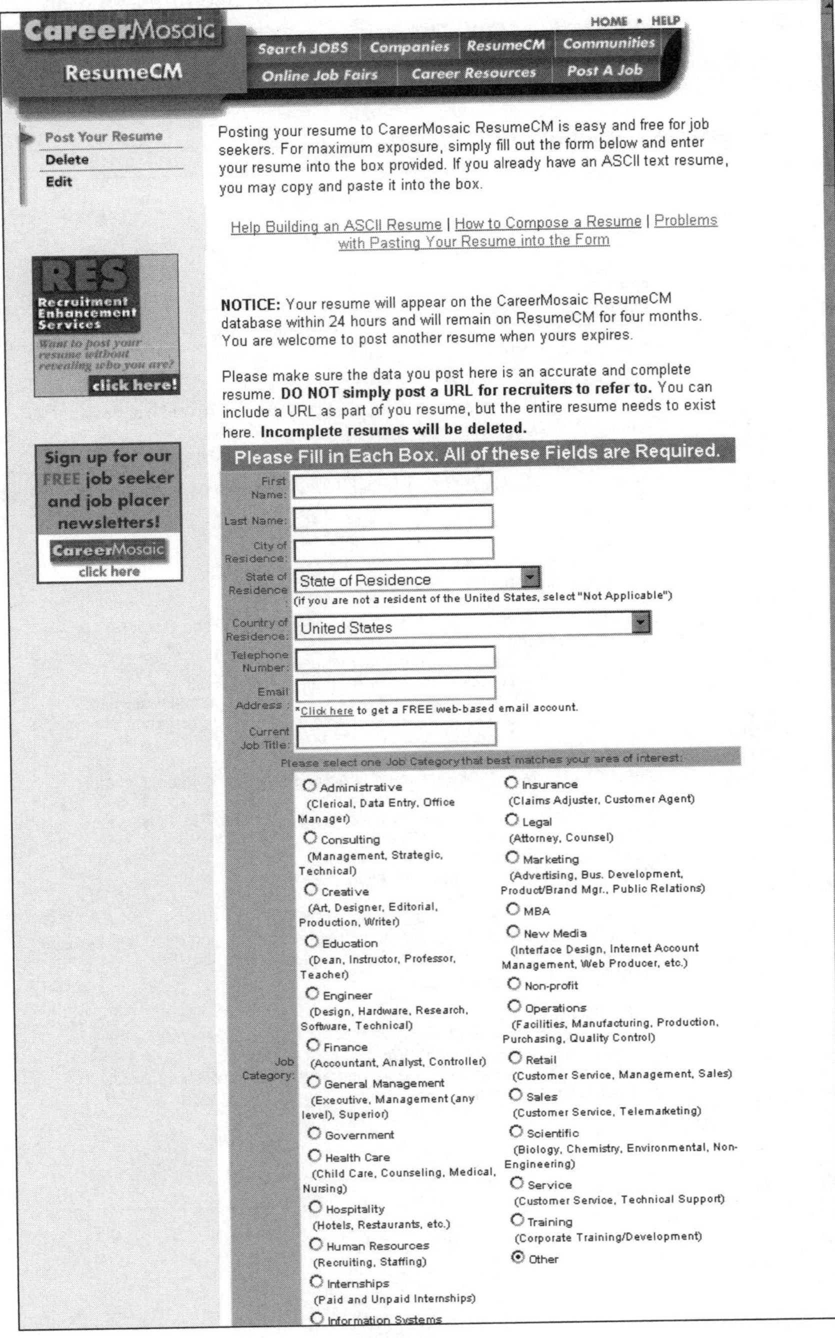

CareerMosaic

ResumeCM

HOME • HELP

Search JOBS | Companies | ResumeCM | Communities

Online Job Fairs | Career Resources | Post A Job

Post Your Resume

Delete

Edit

Posting your resume to CareerMosaic ResumeCM is easy and free for job seekers. For maximum exposure, simply fill out the form below and enter your resume into the box provided. If you already have an ASCII text resume, you may copy and paste it into the box.

Help Building an ASCII Resume | How to Compose a Resume | Problems with Pasting Your Resume into the Form

RES Recruitment Enhancement Services

Want to post your resume without revealing who you are?

click here!

NOTICE: Your resume will appear on the CareerMosaic ResumeCM database within 24 hours and will remain on ResumeCM for four months. You are welcome to post another resume when yours expires.

Please make sure the data you post here is an accurate and complete resume. **DO NOT simply post a URL for recruiters to refer to.** You can include a URL as part of you resume, but the entire resume needs to exist here. **Incomplete resumes will be deleted.**

Sign up for our FREE job seeker and job placer newsletters!

CareerMosaic

click here

Please Fill in Each Box. All of these Fields are Required.

First Name:

Last Name:

City of Residence:

State of Residence: State of Residence

(if you are not a resident of the United States, select "Not Applicable")

Country of Residence: United States

Telephone Number:

Email Address: *Click here to get a FREE web-based email account.

Current Job Title:

Please select one Job Category that best matches your area of interest:

Job Category:

- Administrative (Clerical, Data Entry, Office Manager)
- Consulting (Management, Strategic, Technical)
- Creative (Art, Designer, Editorial, Production, Writer)
- Education (Dean, Instructor, Professor, Teacher)
- Engineer (Design, Hardware, Research, Software, Technical)
- Finance (Accountant, Analyst, Controller)
- General Management (Executive, Management (any level), Superior)
- Government
- Health Care (Child Care, Counseling, Medical, Nursing)
- Hospitality (Hotels, Restaurants, etc.)
- Human Resources (Recruiting, Staffing)
- Internships (Paid and Unpaid Internships)
- Information Systems
- Insurance (Claims Adjuster, Customer Agent)
- Legal (Attorney, Counsel)
- Marketing (Advertising, Bus. Development, Product/Brand Mgr., Public Relations)
- MBA
- New Media (Interface Design, Internet Account Management, Web Producer, etc.)
- Non-profit
- Operations (Facilities, Manufacturing, Production, Purchasing, Quality Control)
- Retail (Customer Service, Management, Sales)
- Sales (Customer Service, Telemarketing)
- Scientific (Biology, Chemistry, Environmental, Non-Engineering)
- Service (Customer Service, Technical Support)
- Training (Corporate Training/Development)
- Other

career center template for on-line résumé posting—CareerMosaic

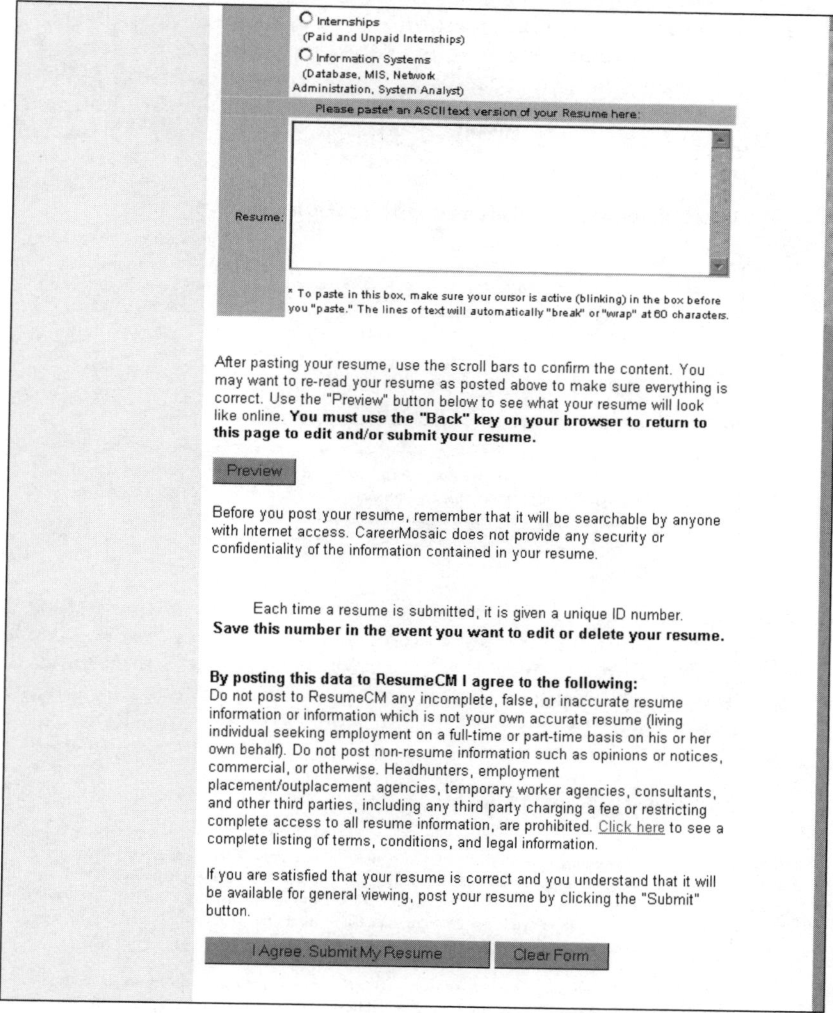

○ Internships
(Paid and Unpaid Internships)

○ Information Systems
(Database, MIS, Network Administration, System Analyst)

Please paste* an ASCII text version of your Resume here:

Resume:

* To paste in this box, make sure your cursor is active (blinking) in the box before you "paste." The lines of text will automatically "break" or "wrap" at 60 characters.

After pasting your resume, use the scroll bars to confirm the content. You may want to re-read your resume as posted above to make sure everything is correct. Use the "Preview" button below to see what your resume will look like online. **You must use the "Back" key on your browser to return to this page to edit and/or submit your resume.**

Preview

Before you post your resume, remember that it will be searchable by anyone with Internet access. CareerMosaic does not provide any security or confidentiality of the information contained in your resume.

Each time a resume is submitted, it is given a unique ID number.
Save this number in the event you want to edit or delete your resume.

By posting this data to ResumeCM I agree to the following:
Do not post to ResumeCM any incomplete, false, or inaccurate resume information or information which is not your own accurate resume (living individual seeking employment on a full-time or part-time basis on his or her own behalf). Do not post non-resume information such as opinions or notices, commercial, or otherwise. Headhunters, employment placement/outplacement agencies, temporary worker agencies, consultants, and other third parties, including any third party charging a fee or restricting complete access to all resume information, are prohibited. Click here to see a complete listing of terms, conditions, and legal information.

If you are satisfied that your resume is correct and you understand that it will be available for general viewing, post your resume by clicking the "Submit" button.

I Agree. Submit My Resume | Clear Form

The Application Letter

Although the letter of application functions as a cover letter in the transmittal of your résumé, its importance must not be minimized. This document is your initial introduction to the employer, so care must be taken to make a good first impression. This letter represents you. If it is prepared poorly, there is a good chance that your résumé will not be read.

14–16 Contents of the Application Letter

a. Begin the letter of application with a statement that attracts the interest of the reader and is related to the purpose of the letter. If an opening has been announced and applications are being solicited, use a direct approach. If, on the other hand, you are investigating whether an opening may exist, use a different strategy by approaching your purpose indirectly.

direct opening for solicited application

> The opening for an administrative assistant in your Publications Department that you filed with the Loma Vista College Career Center appears to be interesting and challenging. As you can see by the enclosed résumé, my specialty in the office administration area has been desktop publishing.

indirect opening for unsolicited application

> My high regard for Allerman Corporation and its products has prompted me to inquire whether you could use the services of a knowledgeable administrative assistant who has specialized in desktop publishing.

b. Continue the letter of application with information that explains the purpose of your letter and convinces the reader to consider your qualifications further. Do not summarize your résumé; instead, amplify and briefly explain one or two of your strongest qualifications and relate them to the job for which you are applying. Refer the reader to the enclosed résumé.

body of application letter

> My formal study of computer application programs—word processing, desktop publishing, spreadsheet, and database—at Loma Vista College culminated with an internship program at Data Select. Here I was able to use my word processing and desktop publishing skills to produce an instructional manual for one of the company's new software programs.
>
> In addition to my course work and experience in applications software, courses in business English, transcription, and business communication have enabled me to develop the proofreading, editing, and writing skills needed to produce error-free business documents. Information regarding my other qualifications is included in the enclosed resumé.

c. A request for action closes the letter of application. Usually the action requested is an invitation for an interview. It may, however, merely be that the reader mail an employment application or refer your letter and résumé to a local office or representative. Whatever the request may be, preface it with *please* or another such appreciative expression.

In requesting an interview, make it easy for the reader to reply by furnishing your telephone number and the times you may be reached at that number. Serious job seekers, however, invest in answering machines, beepers, and even portable cellular phones so they are readily reachable when opportunities arise.

Applicants should also furnish E-mail addresses through which they may be contacted, should the prospective employer prefer this method of responding to the letter of application. If you furnish an E-mail address, be sure to check your in box frequently.

closing for application letter

> May I have an opportunity to discuss my qualifications with you further? To arrange an interview, please call me at (212) 555-5865. I can be reached personally before 10 a.m. and after 3 p.m., and my answering machine picks up messages between 10 a.m. and 3 p.m. I can arrange to meet with you at any time convenient for your schedule.

14–17 Preparation of the Application Letter

Like the résumé, the application letter represents you and forms a first impression. To form a favorable first impression, follow these guidelines:

(1) Use 20- or 24-pound high-quality white bond paper to prepare your application letter. Ensure that the print quality is high density, equal to that of a laser printer. Select a typeface and font size that complement the ones used in your résumé.

(2) Use one of the three following business letter formats: full block, modified block with blocked paragraphs, or modified block with indented paragraphs. Detailed instructions for preparing letters in these formats are contained in Sections 12–1 and 12–2. An example application letter is shown on page 464.

(3) Limit your application letter to one page. Keep in mind that it is a transmittal letter for your résumé and, in most cases, a request for an interview. Highlight and expand only one or two of your major qualifications. Letters that are too long are less likely to be read. Similarly, letters prepared in fonts smaller than 11 points will receive less attention.

(4) Be sure to begin the application letter with a return address. Although your address and telephone number are prominently displayed in the résumé, your address must also appear on the application letter.

(5) Other parts of a business letter to be used include an inside address, a salutation, the letter body, a complimentary close, a signature line, and an enclosure notation. Specific instructions for the placement and format of these letter parts are contained in Sections 12–7 through 12–18.

letter of application

1116 East 59th Street, Apt. 301
Chicago, IL 60615-3022
March 1, 2001

Ms. Denise R. Cueva, Vice President
Human Resources and Development
First National Bank of Arizona
10370 Camelback Road
Phoenix, Arizona 85030-1900

Dear Ms. Cueva:

As a growing bank in the Phoenix area, does First National have a need for a qualified representative in its trust and estate planning area?

In June I will earn a bachelor of science degree in business finance from Chicago State University. Besides fulfilling all the requirements for the regular curriculum in finance, I have completed additional course work in estate planning, trust initiation and management, tax law for trusts, and ethics in trust management.

As you can see by the enclosed résumé, for the past year the knowledge gained in my course work has been applied in a part-time position at Illinois Federal Bank. Here I met with new customers and assisted in setting up trusts to meet their individual needs. I also worked closely with trust officers in establishing and maintaining present clients' trusts.

May I have an opportunity to discuss with you how my education and experience can be put to work for First Federal? I plan to be in Phoenix from April 12 to 16 and would appreciate your scheduling an interview during that time. You may reach me by mail at the above address, by E-mail at rgferreira1531@msn.com, or by telephone at (312) 555-8732. I look forward to hearing from you.

Sincerely,

Robert Ferreira

Robert Ferreira

Enclosure

The Application Form

Many organizations require candidates to complete formal application forms even though they have submitted résumés. Application forms permit employers to obtain and organize standardized information about applicants—and those whom they hire as employees.

14–18 Procedures for Completing Application Forms

Use the following guidelines to assist you in completing application forms efficiently and completely:

(1) Carry with you a copy of your résumé when visiting prospective employers' offices. Much of the information contained in your résumé will be needed to complete the application form.

(2) Write on the reverse side of your résumé copy any information that may be needed for the application form but is not included on your résumé. Such information may include the following:

Social security number

Driver's license number

Beginning and ending dates of *all* employment

Salary history

Name, title, complete address, and telephone number of all former supervisors

Name, title, complete address, and telephone number of all references

(3) Read over all the questions before you begin to answer them. Write neatly and legibly. If you have poor handwriting, print your responses.

(4) Answer all questions on the application form. If a question is not applicable to your situation, respond with a statement such as *Not applicable*.

(5) Write *Negotiable* or *Open* on application forms that contain questions regarding the salary you expect to earn. This strategy is best used when you are uncertain what others in comparable positions are earning.

Reference Request Letters

14–19 Reference Request Letters

a. **Prospective employers will undoubtedly ask you to furnish two or three references, persons who can verify your abilities and/or former employment. Provide the names of former professors or employers who will present you in a favorable light. Do not provide "character" references from family friends, personal friends, or relatives.**

b. **Request permission from potential references to use their names; select people who you feel will enthusiastically endorse you. Remember that a poor recommendation is worse than no recommendation at all.**

c. **Solicit the recommendation endorsement in person or by telephone, and follow up a "yes" response with an acknowledgment letter. Use the following guidelines for writing this letter:**

(1) Express appreciation for the person's willingness to provide you with a recommendation should a prospective employer contact him or her.

(2) Provide a description of the job for which you are applying. If appropriate, relate one of your accomplishments or skills (that the person has observed personally) to the qualifications for the job.

(3) Include and refer to a copy of your résumé.

(4) Invite the reference to contact you if he or she has any questions.

reference request letter

Dear Professor Simons:

I appreciate your willingness to provide me with a reference for a position as a legal assistant should you be contacted by a prospective employer.

My immediate objective is to obtain a position in a large legal firm where I will have an opportunity for advancement. The courses I took from you—word processing, legal office procedures, and legal transcription—have certainly prepared me well to begin my career in a legal office.

After graduating from Pierce College, I continued my education in the area of legal assisting. As you can see by the enclosed résumé, I enrolled in the Attorney Assistant Training Program at the University of California, Los Angeles, Extension. Here I earned a Certificate in Litigation.

Thank you for your support. If you have any questions or wish any additional information, please let me know.

Follow-up Letters

Follow-up letters may be written when no response is received to an application letter or form. They are also written after an interview. The follow-up letter reminds the prospective employer that you are interested in a position with that employer or company.

14–20 Application Follow-Up Letter

If you have not received a response to an application letter or an application form within a reasonable period of time, you may wish to send an application follow-up letter. Such a letter shows serious interest and reminds the personnel officer of your qualifications.

(1) Begin the application follow-up letter with a statement reaffirming your interest in the job for which you formerly applied. Remind the addressee of your letter or application and mention one of your qualifications—or provide any new information that may enhance your likelihood of obtaining the position. Close with a statement expressing the hope that your application will be kept active.

(2) Use one of the following three business letter formats: full block, modified block with blocked paragraphs, or modified block with indented paragraphs. Detailed instructions for preparing letters in

these formats are contained in Sections 12–1 and 12–2. An example application follow-up letter is shown below.

(3) Be sure to begin the application follow-up letter with a return address. Other parts of a business letter to be used include an inside address, a salutation, the letter body, a complimentary close, and a signature line. Specific instructions for the placement and format of these letter parts are contained in Sections 12–7 through 12–18.

application follow-up letter

1116 East 59th Street, Apt. 301
Chicago, IL 60615-3022
March 25, 2001

Ms. Denise R. Cueva, Vice President
Human Resources and Development
First National Bank of Arizona
10370 Camelback Road
Phoenix, Arizona 85030-1900

Dear Ms. Cueva:

I am still very interested in becoming a representative in the Estate Planning and Trust Department of First National Bank of Arizona.

As I mentioned in my March 1 letter, I will be in Phoenix from April 12 through April 16 and would be available for an interview anytime that week. If these dates are not convenient for you, please write me at the above address, e-mail me at rgferreira1531@msn.com, or call me at (312) 555-8732 to set up an appointment to meet with you another time.

If you do not have an opening at the present time, please let me know. I would appreciate, however, your keeping my application in your active file and notifying me when an opportunity with First National arises.

Sincerely,

Robert Ferreira

Robert Ferreira

14–21 Interview Follow-Up Letter

After you have been interviewed, send a brief letter of appreciation to the interviewer. Not only will this courtesy thank the interviewer for his or her time but also it will remind that person of your meeting. Sending a follow-up letter will reaffirm your interest in the position and at the same time distinguish you from the other candidates. More than likely, others will not take this extra step.

(1) Write and send the interview follow-up letter immediately after the interview. A delay will impair its effectiveness. In addition to expressing appreciation and thanks, remind the interviewer of a topic discussed during your conversation and conclude with a positive statement indicating your interest in the position.

(2) Use one of the following three business letter formats: full block, modified block with blocked paragraphs, or modified block with indented paragraphs. Detailed instructions for preparing letters in these formats are contained in Sections 12–1 and 12–2. An example interview follow-up letter is shown on page 469.

(3) Be sure to begin the interview follow-up letter with a return address. Other parts of a business letter to be used include an inside address, a salutation, the letter body, a complimentary close, and a signature line. Specific instructions for the placement and format of these letter parts are contained in Sections 12–7 through 12–18.

interview follow-up letter

1116 East 59th Street, Apt. 301
Chicago, IL 60615-3022
April 19, 2001

Ms. Denise R. Cueva, Vice President
Human Resources and Development
First National Bank of Arizona
10370 Camelback Road
Phoenix, Arizona 85030-1900

Dear Ms. Cueva:

Thank you for meeting with me in Phoenix last week. My interview with you and Mr. Sabian has convinced me even more that I would like to become part of the First National Bank of Arizona staff.

Since there are no openings in your Estate Planning and Trust Department at the present time, I appreciate your suggesting the management training program in the interim. Please consider me for an opening in this program.

Because of my experience at Illinois Federal Bank, I could be a productive member of your staff. I look forward to hearing your decision about my entering the management training program at First National.

Sincerely,

Robert Ferreira

Robert Ferreira

Chapter 15

Information Sources

Information Sources Solution Finder

Business people often need to consult reference material to gather information for general operations, decision making, and document preparation. Major sources were previously confined to printed reference materials. With advances in technology, however, other forms of information exchange—electronic media and on-line resources—provide access to the information needed by today's fast-paced business environment.

Reference materials are abundant. Numerous kinds and extensive listings are available in libraries, in bookstores, from software vendors, and on the Internet. Some are valuable tools for the business person; others are not. The intent of this chapter is to provide a selective listing of printed materials, electronic media, and on-line resources that will be most valuable for a business person. The sources listed may be (1) purchased at reasonable prices from bookstores or software vendors, (2) located at local public or university libraries, or (3) accessed on the Internet.

Published Materials

15–1 Dictionaries

a. **Although word processing programs provide a spell checker, this feature has its limitations. It does not differentiate between words that sound alike but are spelled differently, flag words that are used incorrectly, or assess whether a term should be spelled as one or two words (e.g., *mark down* or *markdown*). Dictionaries provide spellings, syllabication, pronunciation guides, definitions, irregular verb and adjective forms, and synonyms in their entries—all useful information in preparing business documents.**

b. **Dictionaries are generally published in paperback-pocket format, collegiate editions, or complete unabridged versions. Collegiate editions—because of their compact, comprehensive nature and annual update printings—are considered the best source for office use. Update your office dictionary every three years, and select an authoritative one such as those listed below:**

Abate, Frank, ed. *The Oxford American Dictionary of Current English.* New York: Oxford University Press, Incorporated, 1999.

Abate, Frank, ed. *The Oxford American Dictionary and Language Guide.* New York: Oxford University Press, Incorporated, 1999.

Merriam-Webster's Collegiate Dictionary. 10th ed. Springfield, Mass.: Merriam-Webster, Incorporated, 1999. (Updated annually)

Pearsall, Judy, ed. *Concise Oxford Dictionary.* New York: Oxford University Press, Incorporated, 1999.

Random House Webster's College Dictionary. New York: Random House, Inc., 1998.

Random House Webster's Unabridged Dictionary. New York: Random House, Inc., 1999.

Webster's New World College Dictionary. 4th ed. New York: Macmillan, Inc., 1999.

Webster's Third New International Dictionary, Unabridged. Springfield, Mass.: Merriam-Webster, Incorporated, 1993.

c. **Consider whether specialized dictionaries are needed in your office. Besides the regular array of foreign language-English dictionaries, investigate the usefulness of dictionaries that define business terms, computer terms, legal terms, medical terms, and foreign expressions.**

The American Heritage Stedman's Medical Dictionary. Boston: Houghton Mifflin Company, 1995.

Ammer, Christine. *The American Heritage Dictionary of Idioms.* Boston: Houghton Mifflin Company, 1997 .

Black, Henry Campbell. Bryan A. Garner, ed. *Black's Law Dictionary.* 7th ed. St. Paul, Minn.: West Publishing Company, 1999.

DeVries, Mary A. *Encyclopedic Dictionary of Business Terms.* New York: Berkley Publishing Group, 1997.

Dictionary of Business, Oxford Paperback Reference Series. 2nd ed. New York: Oxford University Press, Incorporated, 1997.

Gifis, Steven H. *Law Dictionary.* Hauppauge, N.Y.: Barron's Educational Series, Inc., 1996.

The Houghton Mifflin American Heritage Dictionary of Geography: Places and Peoples of the World. Boston: Houghton Mifflin Company, 1997.

Merriam-Webster's Geographical Dictionary. 3rd ed. Springfield, Mass.: Merriam-Webster, Incorporated, 1998.

Microsoft Press Computer Dictionary. 3rd ed. Redmond, Wash.: Microsoft Press, 1997.

Oxford Essential Dictionary of Foreign Terms in English: The World's Most Trusted Dictionaries. New York: Berkley Publishing Group, 1999.

Thomas, Clayton L., ed. *Taber's Cyclopedic Medical Dictionary.* 18th ed. Philadelphia: F. A. Davis Company, 1997.

Webster's New World Dictionary of Computer Terms. 7th ed. New York: Macmillan, 1999.

15–2 Thesauri

Use a thesaurus to add variety to your writing style. Locate words with the same meaning to substitute for those words you tend to overuse. A partial listing of thesauri follows:

Bartlett's Roget's Thesaurus. Boston: Little, Brown and Company Inc., 1996.

Chapman, Robert L., ed. *Roget's International Thesaurus.* 5th ed. New York: HarperCollins Publishers, 1992.

Roget's II, The New Thesaurus. 3rd ed. Boston: Houghton Mifflin Company, 1995.

15–3 Encyclopedias and Almanacs

Encyclopedias and almanacs provide answers for questions that might arise concerning events and trends.

Almanacs, published annually, describe significant events of the past year; provide information about government officials, states, the United States, and other nations; and supply facts on weather and other topics.

For people involved in international communication, encyclopedias furnish background information about countries' political systems, history, customs, and other relevant information. In addition, encyclopedias provide a concise synopsis on virtually thousands of topics.

The following sources may prove valuable in collecting facts and information:

The Encyclopaedia Britannica (32 volumes). Chicago: Encyclopaedia Britannica, Inc.

The Encyclopedia Americana. Danbury, Conn.: Grolier Publishing.

Hale, Judson. *The Old Farmer's Almanac*. Dublin, N.H.: Yankee Publishing, Incorporated. (Published annually)

Time Almanac 2000. Boston: Little, Brown and Company Inc., 1999. (Published annually)

The World Almanac and Book of Facts. Mahwah, N.J.: World Almanac Books. (Published annually)

Wright, John W. *New York Times Almanac 2000*. New York: Viking Penguin, 1999. (Published annually)

15-4 Atlases

Atlases provide maps of cities, states, countries, continents, and the world. Accompanying a wide variety of maps is often information about population, weather, terrain, agricultural production, and economic orientation. Consult atlases such as the following:

America. Skokie, Ill.: Rand McNally and Company, 2000.

Hammond Atlas of the World. Maplewood, N.J.: Hammond Incorporated, 1999.

Millennium World Atlas (with CD-ROM). Skokie, Ill.: Rand McNally and Company, 1999.

Muster, Bill, and Rand McNally Facts Books Staff. *World Facts & Maps, 2000 Edition*. Skokie, Ill.: Rand McNally and Company, 1999. (Published annually)

Oxford Concise Atlas of the World. 5th ed. New York: Oxford University Press, Inc., 1999.

Premier World Atlas. Skokie, Ill.: Rand McNally and Company, 1999.

15-5 Style Manuals

Style manuals govern the presentation style of reports and manuscripts. Three styles dominate the preparation of reports and manuscripts: (1) the Modern Language Association (MLA) style is endorsed by those writing in the fields of language and arts; (2) the American Psychological Association (APA) style is endorsed by those writing in the social sciences; and (3) *The Chicago Manual of Style* prescribes a traditional style usable for business, researchers, and students.

The following listing gives the latest authoritative published sources for preparing manuscripts or reports according to the MLA style, the APA style, or the Chicago Style Manual style. Three other sources—popular among students and business people—have also been included.

The AMA Style Guide for Business Writing. New York: American Management Association, 1996.

The Chicago Manual of Style. 14th ed. Chicago: The University of Chicago Press, 1993.

Gibaldi, Joseph. *MLA Handbook for Writers of Research Papers.* 5th Ed. New York: The Modern Language Association of America, 1999.

Harnack, Andrew, and Eugene Kleppinger. *Online! A Reference Guide to Using Internet Sources.* New York: St. Martin's Press, 1998.

Publication Manual of the American Psychological Association. 4th Ed. Washington, D.C.: American Psychological Association, 1994.

Turabian, Kate L., John Grossman, and Alice Bennett. *A Manual for Writers of Term Papers, Theses, and Dissertations (Chicago Guides to Writing, Editing, and Publishing).* 6th ed. Chicago: The University of Chicago Press, 1996.

15–6 Quotations

Books of famous quotations are often useful in preparing speeches, written presentations, or marketing brochures. Collections of famous quotations are organized according to topic so suitable selections can be made easily. Several books of quotations are listed below:

Bartlett, John. Justin Kaplan, ed. *Bartlett's Familiar Quotations.* 16th ed. Boston: Little, Brown and Company, Inc., 1992.

Frank, Leonard Roy, ed. *Random House Webster's Quotationary.* New York: Random House, 1999.

Caruth, Gorton, ed. *American Quotations.* New York: Random House Value Publishing, Incorporated, 1999.

Peter, Laurence J. *Peter's Quotations: Ideas for Our Time.* New York: HarperTrade, 1993.

15–7 Etiquette Standards

Business etiquette and general etiquette standards are important in establishing and maintaining business relationships. Etiquette standards and customs differ throughout the world so the international business person should be well acquainted with not only American standards but also standards of other cultures. The following books address a variety of domestic situations and international customs:

Axtell, Roger E. *The Do's and Taboos of International Trade.* New York: John Wiley & Sons, Inc., 1993.

Axtell, Roger E. *Gestures: The Do's and Taboos of Body Language Around the World.* New York: John Wiley & Sons, Inc., 1998.

Axtell, Roger E., Tami Briggs, and Margaret Corcoran. *Do's & Taboos Around the World for Women in Business.* 2nd ed. New York: John Wiley & Sons, Inc., 2000.

Moore, June H. *The Etiquette Advantage: Rules for the Business Professional, Life at Work Series.* Nashville, Tenn.: Broadman & Holman Publishers, 1998.

Morrison, Terri, Wayne A. Conaway, and George A. Borden. *Kiss, Bow, or Shake Hands: How to Do Business in Sixty Countries.* Holbrook, Mass.: Adams Media Corporation, 1995.

Morrison, Terri, Wayne A. Conaway, and Joseph J. Douress. *Dun & Bradstreet's Guide to Doing Business Around the World.* Upper Saddle River, N.J.: Prentice Hall, 1997.

Post, Peggy (Introduction). *Emily Post's Etiquette.* 16th ed. New York: HarperCollins, 1997.

Post, Peggy, and Peter Post. *Emily Post's The Etiquette Advantage in Business: Personal Skills for Professional Success.* New York: HarperResource, 1999.

Tuckerman, Nancy, and Nancy Dunnan. *The Amy Vanderbilt Complete Book of Etiquette.* Garden City, N.Y.: Doubleday & Company, Inc., 1995.

15-8 Business Information Sources

The following publications contain information that may be used for job seeking, meetings, research, mailings, writing style, or general information:

Adams Electronic Job Search Almanac 2000. Holbrook, Mass.: Adams Media Corporation, 1999.

Books in Print 1999–2000. 52nd ed. New Providence, N.J.: R. R. Bowker, 1999.

Directories in Print. 18th ed. New York: Gale Research Inc., 1999. (Published annually)

Hahn, Harley. *Harley Hahn's Internet and Web Yellow Pages, Millennium Edition.* New York: Osborne, 1999.

Rozakis, Laurie. *Merriam-Webster's Rules of Order.* Springfield, Mass.: Merriam-Webster, Inc., 1997.

Robert, Henry M., and William J. Evans, eds. *Robert's Rules of Order.* 9th ed. New York: HarperCollins Publishers, 1997.

Smith, Rebecca. *Electronic Resumes & Online Networking: How to Use the Internet to Do a Better Job Search, Including a Complete, Up-to-Date Resource Guide.* Franklin Lakes, N.J.: Career Press, Incorporated, 1999.

Strunk, William Jr., and E. B. White. *The Elements of Style.* 4th ed. Boston: Allyn and Bacon, 2000.

Turner, Marcia Layton. *Official World Wide Web Yellow Pages.* 9th ed. Indianapolis, Ind.: Que Corporation, 1999.

Electronic Media

15-9 Basic Resource Materials

CD-ROM and DVD-ROM drives on computers permit access to volumes of data previouly accessible only through printed material. CD-ROMs

and DVD-ROMs contain volumes of information that can be read and/or captured while working on a Windows program.

The following listing focuses on dictionaries, thesauri, encyclopedias, atlases, and other such general reference material. Some are single-source references; other packages contain multiple volumes. CD-ROM and DVD-ROM publishers generally maintain Web sites on the Internet for users to obtain product information and updates. Internet addresses are shown in angle brackets (< >).

Bookshelf 2000. CD-ROM. Redmond, Wash.: Microsoft, 1999. <http://www.microsoft.com/encarta/bookshelf/bookshelf.htm>.
- The American Heritage Dictionary of the English Language, Third Edition
- The Original Roget's Thesaurus of English Words and Phrases
- The Columbia Dictionary of Quotations
- Encarta Manual of Style and Usage
- Microsoft Press Computer and Internet Dictionary
- Encarta Desk Encyclopedia
- Encarta Desk World Atlas
- The Encarta 2000 New World Almanac
- The Encarta 2000 New World Timeline

Britannica DVD 2000. DVD-ROM. Chicago: Encyclopaedia Britannica, Inc., 1999. <http://www.britannica.com>.

Compton's Encyclopedia 2000. CD-ROM. Novato, Calif.: Mindscape, 1999. <http://www.shopmattel.com>.

Compton's Interactive World Atlas. CD-ROM. Novato, Calif.: Mindscape, n.d. <http://www.shopmattel.com>.

Encarta Encyclopedia Deluxe 2000. CD-ROM. Redmond, Wash.: Microsoft Corporation, 1999. <http://www.microsoft.com/encarta/>.

Encarta Interactive World Atlas 2000. CD-ROM. Redmond, Wash.: Microsoft Corporation, 1999. <http://www.microsoft.com/encarta/>.

Encarta Reference Suite 2000. CD-ROM. Redmond, Wash.: Microsoft Corporation, 1999. <http://www.microsoft.com/encarta/>.
- Encarta Encyclopedia Deluxe 2000
- Encarta Interactive World Atlas 2000
- Encarta World English Dictionary
- Encarta Online Deluxe

Encarta World English Dictionary. CD-ROM. Redmond, Wash.: Microsoft Corporation, 1999. <http://www.microsoft.com/encarta/>.

Encyclopaedia Britannica 99, Multimedia Edition. CD-ROM (2). Novato, Calif.: Mindscape, 1999. <http://www.shopmattel.com>.

Encyclopedia Britannica CD 2000 Deluxe. CD-ROM. Novato, Calif.: Mindscape, 1999.

Merriam-Webster's Collegiate Dictionary, Deluxe Audio Edition (with complete text of *Merriam-Webster's Collegiate Thesaurus*). 10th ed. CD-ROM. Springfield, Mass.: Merriam-Webster, Incorporated, 1997. <http://www.m-w.com>.

Merriam-Webster's Collegiate Dictionary and Thesaurus, Electronic Edition. 10th ed. v. 1.5. CD-ROM. Springfield, Mass.: Merriam-Webster, Incorporated, 1999. <http://www.m-w.com>.

Merriam-Webster's Medical Audio Dictionary. CD-ROM. Springfield, Mass.: Merriam-Webster, Incorporated, 1997. <http://www.m-w.com>.

Simon & Schuster New Millennium Encyclopedia, Deluxe Edition. CD-ROM. New York: Simon & Schuster Interactive, 1999.

Webster's Encyclopedia 2000: The Century. CD-ROM (10). Countertop Video, 1999.

Webster's Gold Encyclopedia 2000, Deluxe Edition. CD-ROM (5). Countertop Video, 1999.

World Book 2000, Premiere Edition. CD-ROM. IBM Multimedia, 1999.

Year 2000 Grolier Multimedia Encyclopedia Deluxe. CD-ROM. Danbury, Conn.: Grolier Interactive, 1999. <http://www.grolier.com>.

15–10 Directories and Other Locators

Businesses often wish to locate names of individuals and other businesses, addresses, phone numbers, fax numbers, zip codes, Web sites, and other such kinds of information on a nationwide basis. Printed volumes are costly and cumbersome. Inexpensive and easy access to these nationwide lists is now possible through CD-ROMs. Following are several kinds of directories and locators presently available:

9-Digit Zip Code Directory, 2000 Edition. CD-ROM. Omaha, Neb.: CDUSA, Annual subscription. (800) 555-5666.

104 Million Businesses & Households, 2000 Edition. CD-ROM and DVD-ROM. Omaha, Neb.: CDUSA, Annual subscription with updates. <http://www.infoUSA.com>.

250 Million Mega Listings, 2000 Edition. CD-ROM and DVD-ROM. Omaha, Neb.: CDUSA, Annual subscription. <http://www.infoUSA.com>.

Business Credit Ratings USA. CD-ROM. Omaha, Neb.: CDUSA, Annual subscription. (800) 992-3766.

Door to Door 2000 Deluxe. CD-ROM. TravRoute, 1999.

Expedia Streets & Trips 2000. CD-ROM. Redmond, Wash.: Microsoft Corporation, 1999.

MapPoint 2000. CD-ROM. Redmond, Wash.: Microsoft Corporation, 1999.

Phone Search USA. v. 5.0. CD-ROM. Yarmouth, Maine: DeLorme. n.d. <http://www.delorme.com>.

Rand McNally StreetFinder. CD-ROM. Skokie, Ill.: Rand McNally, 1999.

Rand McNally TripMaker. CD-ROM. Skokie, Ill.: Rand McNally, 1999.

SelectPhone: 100 Million U.S. Businesses and Residential Listings on 9 CD-ROMs, 2000 Edition. CD-ROM and DVD-ROM. ProCD, Annual subscription with updates. <http://www.infoUSA.com>.

Street Atlas USA. v. 7.0. CD-ROM. Yarmouth, Maine: DeLorme. <http://www.delorme.com>.

Streets USA 2000. CD-ROM and DVD-ROM. Omaha, Neb.: CDUSA, 1999. <http://www.infoUSA.com>.

Streets USA Deluxe Business Edition. CD-ROM. ABI, 1999.

The Thomas Guide on CD-ROM for [Local Area]. CD-ROM. Irvine, Calif.: Thomas Brothers Maps.

Topo USA. v. 2.0. CD-ROM and DVD-ROM. Yarmouth, Maine: DeLorme. <http://www.delorme.com>.

Xmap Business. CD-ROM. Yarmouth, Maine: DeLorme. <http://www.delorme.com>.

On-Line Resources

The wealth of information available on the Internet is overwhelming.[1] Not all of it is valid or reliable—and not all of it is obtainable free of charge. The Internet user must use good judgment and discretion in selecting sources. Also, the Internet user must decide if subscription membership fees to access certain kinds of information are worth their costs. The sites recommended here are just a sampling of the vast resources available on the World Wide Web.

15–11 References

Reference sources such as dictionaries, thesauri, encyclopedias, almanacs, and atlases are available for access on the Internet. A number of such sites follow. The dates in parentheses show when these sites were last visited.[2]

Acronym Finder. Mountain Data Systems, 2000. <http://www.acronymfinder.com/> (24 January 2000). A search site that locates the meaning of acronyms or locates the acronyms for terms.

Beard, Robert. *A Web of On-line Dictionaries.* 2000. <http://www.facstaff.bucknell.edu/rbeard/diction.html> (24 January 2000). An index of on-line dictionaries and other language reference sources.

Dictionary.com. Lexico LLC, 2000. <http://www.dictionary.com/dictionary/> (24 January 2000). A listing of dictionaries and other references on the Internet.

Encyclopaedia Britannica Online. Encyclopaedia Britannica, n.d. <http://www.eb.com/> (24 January 2000). A subscription Web-based encyclopedia.

Encyclopedia.com. Electric Library, Infonautics Corporation, 1999. <http://www.encyclopedia.com> (24 January 2000). A free on-line encyclopedia with over 14,000 articles.

FindLaw. 2000. <http://www.findlaw.com> (24 January 2000). Links to numerous legal resources including a dictionary of legal terms.

Howe, Denis, ed. *FOLDOC: Free On-line Dictionary of Computing*, 1999. <http://wombat.doc.ic.ac.uk/foldoc/index.html> or <http://foldoc.doc.ic.ac.uk/> (24 January 2000). A dictionary of computer terms with over 12,000 entries.

The Internet Public Library Reference Center. Ann Arbor, Mich.: University of Michigan, School of Information, 1998. <http://www.ipl.org/ref> and <http://www.ipl.org/ref/RR/static/ref0000.html> (24 January 2000). Links to almanacs, biographies, census data, dictionaries, encyclopedias, news, quotations, style guides, telephone directories, and other references on the Internet.

---

[1]See Chapter 9 for complete information on connecting to the Internet and accessing World Wide Web sites.

[2]Additional sources may be located through search sites. See Section 9–3d–e.

James, Vincent, and Erin Jansen. *NetLingo.* NetLingo Inc., 2000. <http://www.netlingo.com> (24 January 2000). An extensive glossary of Internet terms.

Martindale, Jim. *Martindale's "The Reference Desk."* 2000. <http://www-sci.lib.uci.edu/~martindale/Ref.html> (24 January 2000). Links to a vast number of reference resources—from dictionaries to geoscience.

Merriam-Webster Online. Springfield, Mass.: Merriam-Webster, Incorporated, 2000. <http://www.m-w.com> (24 January 2000). The on-line version of *Merriam-Webster's Collegiate Dictionary,* 10th ed., and *Merriam-Webster's Collegiate Thesaurus.*

Moody, H. *Online Resources for Writers.* Professional Training Company, 1999. <http://www.protrainco.com/info/links/gramlink.htm#top> (24 January 2000). Links to dictionaries, thesauri, and other language resources on the Internet.

OneLook Dictionaries. Rocky Mountain Internet, n.d. <http://www.onelook.com/> (24 January 2000). A dictionary search site that accesses more than 500 sources to locate words.

Refdesk.com. Refdesk.com, Inc., 2000. <http://www.refdesk.com/main.html> (13 February 2000). Links to all kinds of reference sources, e.g., dictionaries, encyclopedias, atlases, calendars, currency calculations, newspapers, magazines, columns, movies, etc.

Thesaurus.com. Lexico LLC, 2000. <http://www.thesaurus.com> (24 January 2000). An on-line thesaurus based on *Roget's Thesaurus.*

Webmath. n.d. <http://www.webmath.com> (24 January 2000). A site that leads visitors step-by-step through a variety of math applications from simple arithmetic to calculus.

The World Factbook 1999. Washington, D.C.: Central Intelligence Agency, 1999. <http://www.odci.gov> or <http://www.odci.gov/cia/publications/factbook/index.html> (24 January 2000). Links to current information on countries throughout the world.

15–12 News and Weather Sources

News and weather sources—news channels, weather channels, newspapers, and magazines—are available on-line. Several sites are listed here:

BusinessWeek Online. <http://www.businessweek.com/> (24 January 2000).

CNN.com. <http://www.cnn.com/> (21 March 2000).

Discovery Channel Online. <http://www.discovery.com/> (24 January 2000).

E & P Media Links Online Media Directory. Editor & Publisher and BPI Communications, 2000. <http://emedia1.mediainfo.com/emedia/> (13 February 2000). Links to media throughout the world.

Intellicast: Weather for Active Lives. WSI Corporation, n.d. <http://www.intellicast.com/> (24 January 2000).

National Geographic.com. <http://www.nationalgeographic.com/> (24 January 2000).

The New York Times on the Web. <http://www.nytimes.com/> (24 January 2000).

Information 15

Snap. <http://www.snap.com> (24 January 2000).

Sorensen, Soran Isak. *Electronic Newsstand.* iSyndicate, Inc., 1999. <http://home.worldonline.dk/~knud-sor/en/> (13 February 2000). International site that links to newspapers, weather, sports, multimedia, e-zines, cartoons, film and music, and computer information.

TIME.com. <http://www.pathfinder.com> (24 January 2000).

USA TODAY. <http://www.usatoday.com/> (24 January 2000).

U.S. News Online. <http://www.usnews.com/> (24 January 2000).

The Wall Street Journal Interactive Edition. <http://www.wsj.com/> (24 January 2000).

The Weather Channel. <http://www.weather.com> (24 January 2000).

weatherOnline! weatherOnline!, 1999. <http://www.weatheronline.com/> (24 January 2000).

15–13 Government Sites

Government offices provide information through the Internet. Mailing, tax, and census information may be obtained at the following sites:

1999 Statistical Abstract of the United States. Washington, D.C.: U.S. Census Bureau, 1999. <http://www.census.gov/statab/www/> (24 January 2000).

The Electronic Embassy. TeleDiplomacy, Inc., 2000. <http://www.embassy.org/> (24 January 2000). A site that provides information about foreign embassies in Washington, D.C.

FedWorld Information Network. Springfield, Va.: United States Department of Commerce, National Technical Information Service, n.d. <http://www.fedworld.gov/> (24 January 2000).

Forms and Publications—IRS. Washington, D.C.: United States Treasury Department, Internal Revenue Service, 2000 (Updated continually). <http://www.irs.ustreas.gov/prod/forms_pubs/index.html> (24 January 2000).

THOMAS: Legislative Information on the Internet. Washington, D.C.: United States Library of Congress, n.d. (Updated continually). <http://thomas.loc.gov/> (13 February 2000).

United States Postal Service Home Page. Washington, D.C.: U.S. Postal Service, n.d. <http://www.usps.gov/> (24 January 2000).

U.S. Census Bureau Home Page. Washington, D.C.: U.S. Census Bureau, n.d. <http://www.census.gov/> (24 January 2000).

USPS ZIP+4 Code Look-up. Washington, D.C.: U.S. Postal Service, n.d. <http://www.usps.gov/ncsc/lookups/lookup_zip+4.html> (24 January 2000).

15–14 Private Delivery Services

Private delivery services maintain Web sites that allow package tracking and provide information about their services. Web site addresses for several such providers are listed below:

Airborne Express Home Page. Airborne Express, n.d. <http://www.airborne-express.com/> (24 January 2000).

DHL Worldwide Express Home Page. DHL International Ltd., 2000. <http://www.dhl.com/> (24 January 2000).

FedEx Home Page. Federal Express Corporation, 1999. <http://www.fedex.com/> (24 January 2000).

UPS Home Page. United Parcel Service of America, Inc., 2000. <http://www.ups.com/> (24 January 2000).

15–15 On-Line Directories

On-line directories provide addresses, telephone numbers, fax numbers, E-mail addresses, Web site addresses (URLs—Uniform Resource Locators), and other similar types of information for individuals, businesses, organizations, and government agencies. A select list of on-line locators follows:

Airline Toll-Free Numbers and Web Sites. Princeton University, 2000. <http://www.princeton.edu/Main/air800.html> (25 January 2000).

The Electronic Embassy. TeleDiplomacy, 2000. <http://www.embassy.org/embassies/index.html> (25 January 2000). Links to location and contact information for all embassies in Washington, D.C.

EmbassyWeb.com. infoCatch, 1998. <http://www.embassyweb.com/> (25 January 2000). Listings for diplomatic posts worldwide.

Infobel.com. Kapitol S.A., 1999. <http://www.infobel.com/> (25 January 2000). An international telephone directory.

InfoSpace.com. InfoSpace.com, Inc., 2000. <http://www.infospace.com/> (25 January 2000). Links to white pages, yellow pages, and general information.

InfoSpace.com.Government. InfoSpace.com, Inc., 2000. <http://pic1.infospace.com/_1_8337641_yp.ad/index_gov.htm> (13 February 2000). Links to a U.S. government Web directory; federal, state, county, and local government information; addresses of government officials; and contact information for embassies in Washington, D.C.

Maps On Us. Etak, Inc, 2000. <http://www.mapsonus.com/> (23 March 2000). A site that provides mapping and turn-by-turn directions from one location to another throughout the United States.

MapQuest. MapQuest.com, Inc., 2000. <http://www.mapquest.com> (23 March 2000). A site that provides mapping and turn-by-turn directions from one location to another.

Switchboard.com. Switchboard Incorporated, 2000. <http://www.switchboard.com/> (25 January 2000). A national telephone directory.

WhoWhere? People Finder. WhoWhere? Inc., a Lycos Network site, 2000. <http://www.whowhere.lycos.com/> (13 February 2000). An address, a telephone number, and an E-mail address locator.

WorldPages.com. Web YP, Inc., 2000. <http://www.worldpages.com/> (25 January 2000). A locator for addresses, telephone numbers, E-mail addresses, Web site connections, and mapping.

"Zip2.com." *AltaVista Connections.* Zip2 Corp., 1999. <http://www.zip2.com> (25 January 2000). A site that provides mapping and turn-by-turn directions from one location to another throughout the United States.

15–16 Writing Style Manuals

Adaptations of writing style manuals are available on the Internet:

A Guide for Writing Research Papers Based on Modern Language Association (MLA) Documentation. Hartford, Conn.: Humanities Department and the Arthur C. Banks, Jr., Library, Capital Community College, 10 January 2000. <http://webster.commnet.edu/mla.htm> (13 February 2000).

Citing Electronic Resources, Modern Language Association. The University Library, University of California, Davis, 1999. <http://www.lib.ucdavis.edu/citing/MLA.html> (25 January 2000). Listing (and links) of resources on the Internet.

Dewey, Russell A. *APA Style Resources.* 18 August 1999. <http://www.psychwww.com/resource/apacrib.htm> (13 February 2000). Links to on-line interpretations of APA style.

Shimek, Gary, and David Tietyen. *Documentation and Style Guide.* 1999. <http://www.msoe.edu/gen_st/style/stylguid.html> (25 January 2000). A summary of *The Chicago Manual of Style* documentation and styles of presentation.

Walker, Janice R., and Todd Taylor. *The Columbia Guide to Online Style.* New York: Columbia University Press, 1998. <http://www.columbia.edu/cu/cup/cgos/idx_basic.html (25 January 2000).

15–17 Career Centers

Job searches are no longer dominated by the traditional résumé and letter of application. Most major companies today maintain career centers on their Web sites and accept résumés on-line. In addition, the Internet hosts a large number of career centers that post job openings, post résumés, permit on-line application for job postings, and offer career advice. The following sites are among the most popular ones on the Internet:

America's Job Bank. <http://www.ajb.dni.us> (14 February 2000). America's Job Bank is a partnership between the U.S. Department of Labor and the state-operated public Employment Service, which provides labor exchange service to employers and job seekers through a network of 1,800 offices throughout the United States. America's Job Bank lists over 1.4 million jobs and posts résumés. No fee; registration required for résumé posting.

Career Magazine. <http://www.careermag.com> (25 January 2000). This Web site is an on-line career magazine with information on job openings, employers, résumé banks, job fairs, and various articles on current topics such as diversity in the workplace. No fee; registration required for résumé posting.

CareerMosaic. <http://www.careermosaic.com> (25 January 2000). This Web site is popular with college students since it has a job database, a "usenet" to perform searches of jobs listed in regional and occupational newsgroups, an on-line job fair, a career resource center, and an international gateway to link to CareerMosaic sites around the world. This Web site strives to be a valuable source to both the employer and the job seeker. No fee; no registration required.

CareerPath.com. <http://www.careerpath.com> (14 February 2000). CareerPath lists approximately 250,000 jobs. You may also access classified ads from over 90 major newspapers—the *Boston Globe, New York Times, Los Angeles Times, Chicago Tribune, Washington Post, San Jose Mercury News,* as examples. No fee; registration required for résumé posting.

Catapult Career Offices Home Pages: Index. <http://www.jobweb.org/catapult/homepage.htm> (25 January 2000). Provides links to the Web sites of college and university career centers.

JobDirect.com. <http://www.jobdirect.com> (25 January 2000). JobDirect connects entry-level job seekers with employers who want qualified applicants. This Web site is designed to help students and recent college graduates find internships, part-time jobs, or career positions. No fee; registration required.

JOBTRAK.COM. <http://www.jobtrak.com/> (14 February 2000). JOBTRAK has job listings for full-time jobs, part-time jobs, temporary jobs, and internships. This site provides an on-line career fair, job search tips, career forums, and a career contact network. Students and alumni from more than 900 colleges and universities may view job listings posted and/or post résumés by obtaining a password from their college or university.

Monster.com. <http://www.monster.com> (25 January 2000). This is one of the most popular Web sites for job seekers. The site offers a variety of hypertext links to job-search resources and connections to job listings. No fee; registration required.

Monster Healthcare. <http://www.medsearch.com> (25 January 2000). This site, formerly MedSearch America, lists job openings and posts résumés for all classifications of positions in the health industry. This site is part of *Monster.com.*

USA TODAY Career Center. <http://findjob.usatoday.com/search.html> (25 January 2000). This site provides job listings accessible by location and career objective. No fee; no registration required.

Yahoo! Business and Economy:Employment:Jobs. <http://dir.yahoo.com/business/employment/jobs/> (25 January 2000). This site provides a listing, brief description, and link to a large number of career resources on the Internet.

Yahoo! Classifieds. <http://classifieds.yahoo.com/employment.html> (25 January 2000). Provides a nationwide listing. Categories are refined by state, major city (includes surrounding area), general field, and keywords. No fee; registration required.

15–18 Other Information Sources

a. Several other kinds of information sources on the Internet that may be of value to persons involved in business, industry, or government are listed below:

All-Hotels.com. All-Hotels, 1999. <http://www.all-hotels.com/> (25 January 2000).

Biography.com. A&E Television Networks, 2000. <http://www.biography.com/> (25 January 2000).

Biztravel.com. Biztravel.com, Inc., 2000. <http://www.biztravel.com/> (25 January 2000). A business travel site.

CEOExpress. CEOExpress Company, 1999. <http://www.ceoexpress.com/> (25 January 2000). Links to hundreds of business resources.

"Country Profiles." *Careers.wsj.com.* Window on the World, Inc. Dow Jones & Company, Inc., 2000. <http://careers.wsj.com/?content=cwc-countries.htm> (25 January 2000). Tips on social and business customs in 26 major countries.

Excite Travel. Excite Inc. and WeatherLabs, Inc., 2000. <http://www.excite.com/travel/> (25 January 2000).

Expedia.com. Expedia, Inc., 1999. <http://www.expedia.msn.com/> (25 January 2000). A popular travel site.

Hotelguide.com. Meggen, Switzerland: Hotelguide.com, 1999. <http://www.hotelguide.com/e_search.cfm> (25 January 2000). A worldwide hotel reservation site.

HotelsTravel.com. WebScope, 2000. <http://www.hotelstravel.com/> (25 January 2000).

The List. internet.com Corp., 1999. <http://thelist.internet.com/> (25 January 2000). Listing of over 8,300 Internet service providers.

Previewtravel.com. Preview Travel, Inc., 1999. <http://www.previewtravel.com/Home/> (25 January 2000).

Rudolph, Dana. *Really Useful Sites: An Online Reference for Fast Facts.* 1999. <http://www.tac.nyc.ny.us/%7Erudolph/useful/> (25 January 2000).

Smith, Mark J. *Virtual Perpetual Calendars.* December 4, 1999. <http://www.mnsinc.com/utopia/Calendar/> (14 February 2000). Provides calendars from 1901 through 2100; holidays from 1990 through 2010.

StockMaster.com. StockMaster.com, Inc., 2000. <http://www.stockmaster.com/> (25 January 2000).

TravelNow.com. TravelNow.com, 2000. <http://www.travelnow.com/> (25 January 2000).

Travelocity.com. Sabre Inc., 1999. <http://www.travelocity.com/> (25 January 2000).

Yahoo! Yahoo!, 2000. <http://www.yahoo.com/> (25 January 2000).

b. **Remember that the Internet is still in its infancy. As this information source continues to grow, new Web sites will emerge as others disappear. Some Web sites will be updated almost daily, some periodically, and others not at all. Not every source contains valid information, so evaluate its contents and origin judiciously.**

Learn to use search engines to gather the information you need. Bookmark those sites that you use frequently or that you feel will be useful to you sometime in the near future. Continually search out those Web sites that will assist you in carrying out your responsibilities.

Chapter 16

Manual and Electronic File Management

Manual and Electronic File Management Solution Finder

Filing Process, The

Indexing and Alphabetizing

Organizing and Maintaining Computer Data Files

The Filing Process

16–1 Purpose of Indexing

You may find that you need to set up communication indexers (telephone, fax, E-mail, address), customer or client files, patient files, vendor files, or some other kind of database involving individual and/or organizational names. To organize names so they can be located easily, you will first need to place the separate words in each name in a sequence to be alphabetized. This process is known as *indexing*. Once placed in the proper order, the units may be alphabetized.

So that filed names may be located easily (retrieved), all names must be indexed and alphabetized in the same manner; that is, you need to follow the same set of guidelines in preparing each name for filing. The most commonly used set of guidelines is called the *Simplified Filing Standard Rules*.

16–2 Simplified Filing Standard Rules

The rules presented here for indexing and alphabetizing individual and organizational names are the Simplified Filing Standard Rules endorsed by ARMA International (Association for Information Management Professionals).[1]

The ARMA International publication for alphabetic filing explains and illustrates accepted deviations from the Simplified Filing Standard Rules but cautions that these deviations must be documented for all users. Otherwise, inconsistencies in indexing records for alphabetizing will lead to difficulties in locating and retrieving records.

The following rules and examples are based solely on the Simplified Filing Standard Rules.

Indexing and Alphabetizing

16–3 Indexing and Alphabetizing the Names of Individuals

a. **To index the names of individuals, arrange the units (words and initials) in each name in the following order:**

(1) Complete last name as written (includes hyphenated last names and *all* prefixes such as *D', Da, De, Del, De La, Della, Den, Des, Di, Du, El, Fitz, L', La, Las, Le, Les, Lo, Los, M', Mac, Mc, O', Saint, San, St., Ste., Te, Ten, Ter, Van, Van de, van Der, Von,* and *Von der*. Many of these prefixes may be written with lowercase letters or combinations of

---

[1]*Alphabetic Filing Rules*, 2nd ed. (Prairie Village, Kans.: ARMA International, 1995), 3–4, 7–9, 17–22. Copies of this publication may be purchased from ARMA International by telephoning (913) 341-3808, Ext. 2117, or (888) 298-9202. Copies are also available at the ARMA International on-line bookstore, which may be accessed through <http://www.arma.org/>.

uppercase and lowercase letters. These variations in capitalization are treated the same.

(2) Complete first name or initial (includes two-word first names such as *Jo Ann, Mary Ellen, John Paul,* and *Billy Bob*)

(3) Complete middle name(s) or initial(s)

Do not use suffixes and titles as filing units unless they are needed to distinguish between or among identical names. Titles and suffixes include the following:

(1) Seniority suffix (rank designated by a Roman numeral or the abbreviation *Jr.* or *Sr.*)

(2) Professional suffix (position designated by a certification such as *CPA, Ph.D.,* or *R.N.*)

(3) Title (such as *Mr., Mrs., Ms., Dr., Professor, Sergeant, Dean,* or *Governor*)

Titles followed only by a first name or a last name are indexed in the order they are written. Examples of such names are *Queen Elizabeth, Brother John,* and *Mr. Damico*.

complete names of individuals placed in indexing order

Last (Unit 1)	*First (Unit 2)*	*Middle (Unit 3)*	*Suffixes and Titles (Unit 4)*
Clark	James	L.	Jr.
Clark	James	L.	Sr.
Hoover	Han Nang	Kim	Mrs.
Hoover	Herb	Michael	Mr.
Clark	William	James	Mr.
Clark	William	James	Dr.
Costellano	Maria Elena	Murillo Lopez	
Hoover	Hannah	Kim	Ms.
Clark	Wm.	Bradley	
Clark-Hoover	Karen	Lynelle	Ms.
Clemson	B.	Thomas	II
Ho	Hung		Mr.
Clemson-Clark	Alice	Marie	
Harper	Mary		Sister
Hoover	BettyBruce	Howard	
Hoover	Betty Lou	H.	Ms.
Hertig	Thomas	J.	Major
De Hertog	Thos.	I.	R.N.
De Hertog	Thomas	James	
Hertig	Thomas	J.	Mr.
Clemson	B.	Thomas	III
Hoover	Herbert	Charles Marsh	Mr.
Hoover	Herb	Michael	M.D.
Debrosian	John	T.	
Delano	Marisa	Torti	Mrs.
Hoover	Billy Bob	Scot	

title with first or last name only

Title (Unit 1)	*First or Last (Unit 2)*
Sister	Mary
Mr.	Hoover
General	Clark

b. **Indexed names are alphabetized in indexing order. In alphabetizing names, place (1) nothing before something, (2) numerals before alphabetic letters, and (3) initials before names beginning with that letter.**

Compound names (those containing more than one word) in an indexing unit are treated as a single word, whether they are hyphenated or separated by a space. All punctuation marks—such as periods, apostrophes, hyphens, and commas—are disregarded.

Abbreviated and shortened names such as *Wm.* and *Sandy* are alphabetized as they are written.

Unit 1	*Unit 2*	*Unit 3*	*Unit 4*
Clark	James		
Clark	James	L.	Jr.
Clark	James	L.	Sr.
Clark	William	James	Dr.
Clark	William	James	Mr.
Clark	Wm.	Bradley	
Clark-Hoover	Karen	Lynelle	Ms.
Clemson	B.	Thomas	II
Clemson	B.	Thomas	III
Clemson-Clark	Alice	Marie	
Costellano	Maria Elena	Murillo Lopez	
Debrosian	John	T.	
De Hertog	Thomas	James	
De Hertog	Thos.	I.	R.N.
Delano	Marisa	Torti	Mrs.
General	Clark		
Harper	Mary		Sister
Hertig	Thomas	J.	Major
Hertig	Thomas	J.	Mr.
Ho	Hung		Mr.
Hoover	BettyBruce	Howard	
Hoover	Betty Lou	H.	Ms.
Hoover	Billy Bob	Scot	
Hoover	Hannah	Kim	Ms.
Hoover	Han Nang	Kim	Mrs.
Hoover	Herb	Michael	M.D.
Hoover	Herb	Michael	Mr.
Hoover	Herbert	Charles Marsh	Mr.
Mr.	Hoover		
Sister	Mary		

16–4 Indexing and Alphabetizing the Names of Organizations

a. Words in business and organizational names are arranged in the order they are written, even the full names of individuals. Each word—including articles, prepositions, conjunctions, and symbols—is a separate unit. Except for the word *The* appearing as the first word, index the words in the order they are written. When the word *The* begins a business or organizational name, consider it the last filing unit.

Spell out any symbols such as & (*and*), $ (*dollar*), or # (*number*). Disregard all punctuation marks such as hyphens, apostrophes, periods, commas, or quotation marks. Close up any letters or words containing punctuation marks, and index them as a single unit.

business names containing articles, lowercase words, and symbols

Business/ Organizational Name	*Unit 1*	*Unit 2*	*Unit 3*	*Unit 4*	*Unit 5*
Fortune $ Saver	Fortune	Dollar	Saver		
Jane Ryan & Associates	Jane	Ryan	and	Associates	
Jane Ryan and Sons	Jane	Ryan	and	Sons	
The Jane Ryan Realty Company	Jane	Ryan	Realty	Company	The
Rings and Things	Rings	and	Things		

business names containing punctuation

Business/ Organizational Name	*Unit 1*	*Unit 2*	*Unit 3*	*Unit 4*	*Unit 5*
Dr. Ryan's Hospital and Clinic	Dr.	Ryan's	Hospital	and	Clinic
Foreman-Ryan Furniture	Foreman-Ryan	Furniture			
In-and-Out Burger King	In-and-Out	Burger	King		
Mark C. Bloom Tires	Mark	C.	Bloom	Tires	
Ryan, Irwin, Kirk, and Janns	Ryan	Irwin	Kirk	and	Janns
Ryan's Automotive Repair	Ryan's	Automotive	Repair		

b. Single letters separated by spaces in business and organizational names are considered separate indexing units. Single letters written without spaces, letters representing the full organizational name (such as *IBM, GM,* and *YMCA*), acronyms (names made from initial letters such as *MADD* and *DARE*), and call letters for radio and television stations are indexed as single units.

letters indexed as separate units

Business/ Organizational Name	*Unit 1*	*Unit 2*	*Unit 3*	*Unit 4*	*Unit 5*
A B C Linen Service	A	B	C	Linen	Service
A to Z Rentals	A	to	Z	Rentals	
H L T Express	H	L	T	Express	

letters indexed as a single unit

Business/ Organizational Name	*Unit 1*	*Unit 2*	*Unit 3*	*Unit 4*	*Unit 5*
ABC Learning Systems	ABC	Learning	Systems		
ARMA International	ARMA	International			
A-to-Z Data Systems	A-to-Z	Data	Systems		
ITT	ITT				
KABC Radio	KABC	Radio			
KNXT Television	KNXT	Television			
TWA	TWA				
ZZZ Freight Express	ZZZ	Freight	Express		

c. **In business and organizational names, all abbreviated words such as *Inc., Co.,* and *Mfg.* are indexed as written. Names of cities appearing in business and organizational names are also indexed as written; however, prefixes (see Section 16–3a) and names appearing together are indexed as one unit.**

abbreviations indexed as written

Business/ Organizational Name	*Unit 1*	*Unit 2*	*Unit 3*	*Unit 4*	*Unit 5*
A & A Paper Co.	A	and	A	Paper	Co.
The Clothing Factory, Ltd.	Clothing	Factory	Ltd.	The	
Mrs. Ryan's Cookies, Inc.	Mrs.	Ryan's	Cookies	Inc.	

cities indexed as written or combined with prefixes

Business/ Organizational Name	*Unit 1*	*Unit 2*	*Unit 3*	*Unit 4*	*Unit 5*
El Centro Produce Market	El Centro	Produce	Market		
Ft. Lauderdale Resorts, Inc.	Ft.	Lauderdale	Resorts	Inc.	
The Kansas City Inn	Kansas	City	Inn	The	
Las Vegas Credit Bureau	Las Vegas	Credit	Bureau		
Los Angeles Flower Exchange	Los Angeles	Flower	Exchange		
New York Stock Exchange	New	York	Stock	Exchange	
Newark Yellow Cab Co.	Newark	Yellow	Cab	Co.	
San Diego Gas and Electric Co.	San Diego	Gas	and	Electric	Co.
San Francisco Travel Agency	San Francisco	Travel	Agency		
South Pasadena Cleaners	South	Pasadena	Cleaners		
St. Louis Flowers and Gifts	St. Louis	Flowers	and	Gifts	
Terre Haute Pharmacy	Terre	Haute	Pharmacy		
West Covina Pet Hospital	West	Covina	Pet	Hospital	
The West Haven Motor Lodge	West	Haven	Motor	Lodge	The
The Westfield Motor Lodge	Westfield	Motor	Lodge	The	

d. **Spelled-out numbers in business and organizational names are treated as any other word in alphabetizing names. Arabic numerals, however, precede all alphabetic letters in arranging indexing units; Roman numerals follow directly after any Arabic numerals—before any alphabetic letters. Arrange the numerals in ascending order, and disregard any ordinal endings such as *st, nd,* or *rd*.**

spelled out numbers

Business/ Organizational Name	*Unit 1*	*Unit 2*	*Unit 3*	*Unit 4*	*Unit 5*
Twelfth Street Cafe	Twelfth	Street	Cafe		
Twentieth Century Insurance	Twentieth	Century	Insurance		
Two-for-One Sundries	Two-for-One	Sundries			

Arabic or Roman numerals

Business/ Organizational Name	*Unit 1*	*Unit 2*	*Unit 3*	*Unit 4*	*Unit 5*
$1 Outlet	1	Dollar	Outlet		
2-for-1 Photos	2-for-1	Photos			
5 Star Realty	5	Star	Realty		
20th Century Realtors, Inc.	20	Century	Realtors	Inc.	
99¢ Store	99	Cent	Store		
A1 Photos	A1	Photos			
Aaron Bros. Art Studios	Aaron	Bros.	Art	Studios	
Pier 1 Imports	Pier	1	Imports		
Pier I Food Imports	Pier	I	Food	Imports	
Sixth Avenue Pharmacy	Sixth	Avenue	Pharmacy		
Star 4 Studios	Star	4	Studios		
Star III Studios	Star	III	Studios		

e. **Names of domestic government entities are indexed first under the level of government: United States Government, (state name) State of, (county name) County of, (city name) City of, and (village name) Village of. These levels are a single indexing unit.[2]**

Departments and agencies of the federal government are first indexed under *United States Government.* The second indexing unit is the main word that identifies the department, bureau, or office. Terms such as *Bureau of* or *Department of* follow the second indexing unit and are placed in parentheses since they are not considered to be indexing units.

Subdivisions of departments and agencies are subsequently indexed according to their order of authority. Again, use main words for the primary indexing units.

[2] *Alphabetic Filing Rules,* 2nd ed. (Prairie Village, Kans.: ARMA International, 1955), 31.

federal government entities

Unit 1	*Unit 2*	*Unit 3*	*Unit 4*	*Unit 5*
United States Government	Agriculture	(Department of)		
United States Government	Commerce	(Department of)		
		Economic	Development	Administration
		International	Trade	Administration
United States Government	State	(Department of)		
		Passport	Agency	
United States Government	Transportation	(Department of)		
		Coast	Guard	
		Federal	Aviation	Administration
United States Government	Treasury	(Department of)		
		Alcohol	Tobacco (and)	Firearms (Bureau of)
		Customs	Service	
		Internal	Revenue	Service

state and local government entities

Unit 1	*Unit 2*	*Unit 3*	*Unit 4*	*Unit 5*
California State of	Consumer	Affairs	(Department of)	
California State of	Employment	Development	Department	
Glendale City of	Building	Permits		
Glendale City of	Community	Development	and	Housing
Los Angeles County of	Animal	Care	and	Control
Los Angeles County of	Disabilities	Commission on		

f. **Index government agencies in foreign countries first by their country. To prevent confusion, use English names. If appropriate, index any additional units in the country name, e.g., *China, Republic of*. States, colonies, provinces, cities, and other such government entities follow, with their names spelled in English.**

Unit 1	*Unit 2*	*Unit 3*	*Unit 4*	*Unit 5*
Belgium	Kingdom of	Taxation	Department of	
China	Republic of	Internal	Affairs	Bureau of
South Korea	Seoul	City of		
Uruguay	Republic of	Public	Education	Secretary of

16–5 Handling Identical and Alternate Names

a. **Use the address to determine the correct filing order of identical individual or organizational names. Compare addresses in the following order: (1) city names, (2) state names, (3) street names (with numbered street names appearing first), and (4) house or building numbers. Use** these address components in the order listed only until the names are distinguished.

Identical Name	*City*	*State*	*Street*	*House*
John R. Smith	Springfield	Connecticut		
John R. Smith	Springfield	Illinois	23rd Street	
John R. Smith	Springfield	Illinois	Dover Avenue	910
John R. Smith	Springfield	Illinois	Dover Avenue	3640

b. Individuals or organizations that are known by more than one name should be cross-referenced. These second (and even third) names are an additional filing entry indexed in the order of the alternate name. When persons look for the entry under the alternate name, the cross-reference entry refers them to the original record.

Cross-referencing is often used for (1) unusual names, (2) persons or businesses having more than one name, (3) abbreviated names, and (4) foreign business names.

cross-reference entry

IAAP

See: International Association of
Administrative Professionals

examples of cross-referenced names

Thomas Howard	See: Howard, Thomas
Hung Ho	See: Ho, Hung
Duncan, Thelma R.	See: Nicklin, Thelma R. Duncan
Yama Motors	See: Matsuyama Motor Imports, Inc.
ABC	See: Association for Business Communication
Bonn Chemische Fabrik AG	See: Bonn Chemical Works Inc.

Organizing and Maintaining Computer Data Files

Computer program files and data files are organized into folders for easy access. These folders may be likened to the folders you will find in a traditional file cabinet and are sequenced automatically in alphabetical order. A Windows program, Windows Explorer, is used by many to manage the files and folders contained on computer hard drives, floppy disks, and CD-ROMs—although most other software applications have data management capabilities too.

16-6 Configurations for Windows Explorer[3]

a. Access Windows Explorer by right-clicking on the *Start* button in the lower left corner of your screen. Left-click on *Explore* to enter the program.

b. The default configurations for Windows Explorer in Windows 95 and Windows 98 differ, but both operating systems offer the same options for configuring this file manager. When configured the same way, Windows Explorer operates identically in Windows 98 and Windows 95.[4]

c. Access the configuration options through the menu bar by clicking on *View* and then selecting *Folder Options*. The following choices are available:

(1) *Web style.* Your computer looks and acts like the Web. All folders and files perform like hyperlinks; that is, a single click opens a folder, and a single click opens a file in the program in which it was created if the program is located on the hard disk or network. See Figure 16-1 below and Figure 16-2, page 498, for screen illustrations of the Web style configuration in Windows 95 and 98.

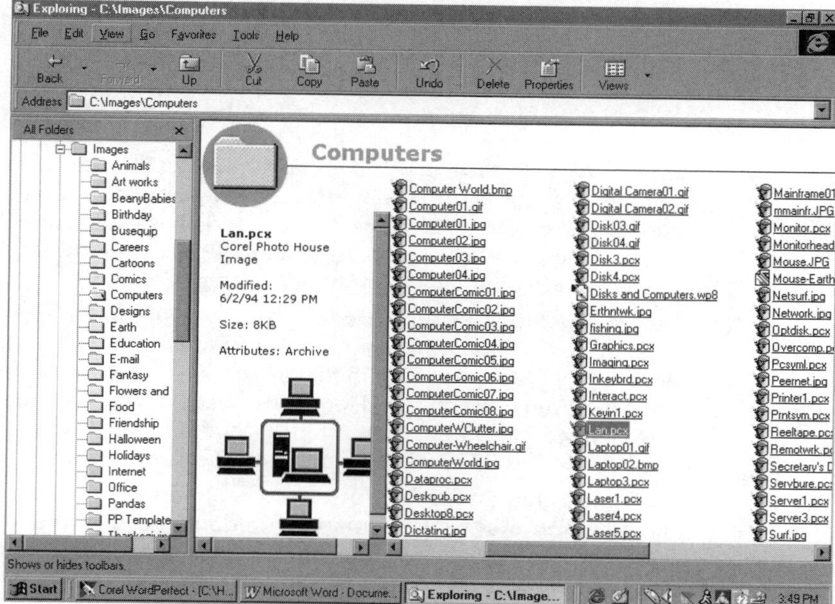

Figure 16-1. Windows Explorer in Windows 95: Web Style **and** Custom Style With Single-Click Setting, View as Web Page

[3]The computer-specific procedures outlined here and in the remaining sections of this chapter are based on Windows Explorer, the version provided in Windows 98 and Windows 95.

[4]Early releases of Windows 95 do not offer the configuration options and operate only in the Classic style. The Windows 95 illustrations shown in this section are screen captures from Releases B and C.

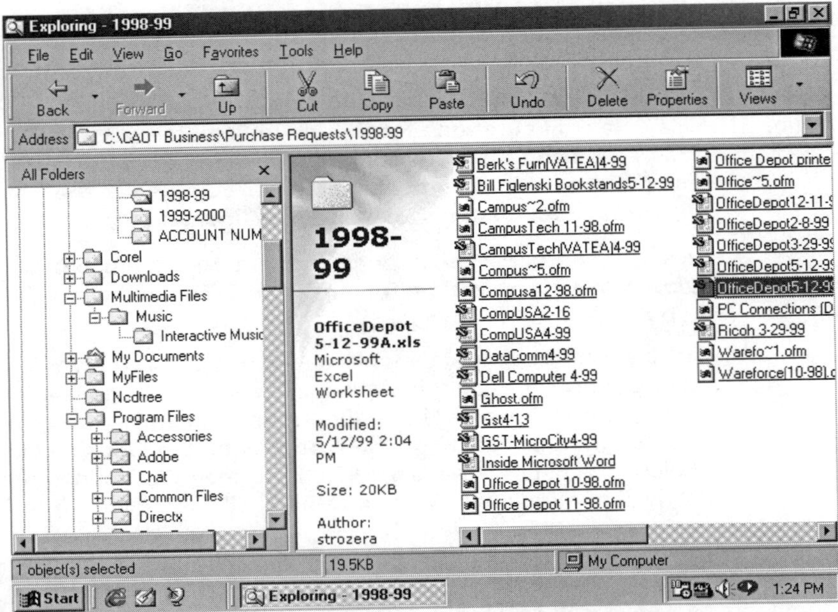

Figure 16-2. Windows Explorer in Windows 98: Web Style **and** Custom Style With Single-Click Setting, View as Web Page

(2) *Classic style.* As the default style for Windows 95, the Classic style operates in the traditional way (the same way as any Windows applications software)[5] to manage folders and files—with double clicks and single clicks. See Figure 16-3, page 499, for a view of a Classic style screen in Windows Explorer, Windows 95.

(3) *Custom style.* The Custom style, the default style for Windows 98, displays a different menu bar and a different toolbar from the ones contained in the Classic style. Both these access bars resemble those contained in a Web browser. See Figure 16-1, page 497, to view the Custom style in Windows 95 and Figure 16-4, page 499, to view the Custom style in Windows 98. You will note that the access menus are the same.

The *Settings* button for the Custom style option permits you to refine this style. You may elect to manage folders and files the traditional way, the same way as you manage Windows applications folders and files—with double and single clicks; or you may elect to manage folders and files in a Web mode—like hyperlinks, with single clicks. Figures 16-4, page 499, and 16-5, page 500, display files managed the same way as Windows applications software files. Figures 16-1, page 497, and 16-2, located above, display files as hyperlinks; notice that the file names are underlined.

The Custom style may be refined even further to resemble a Web page. By selecting *View* from the menu bar and then choosing *as Web*

[5]Windows applications software includes, to name just a few, such programs as Access, Excel, Lotus, PowerPoint, QuickBooks, Word, and WordPerfect.

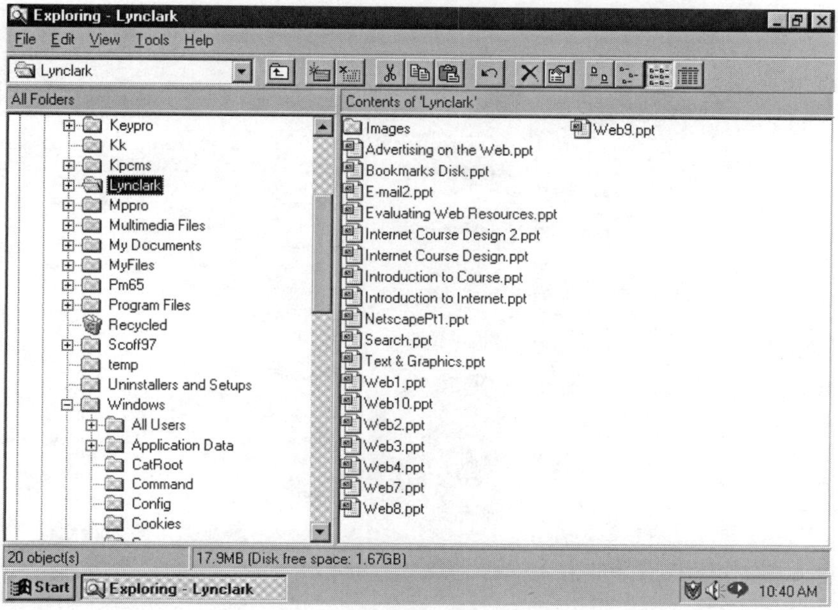

Figure 16-3. Windows Explorer in Windows 95, Classic Style

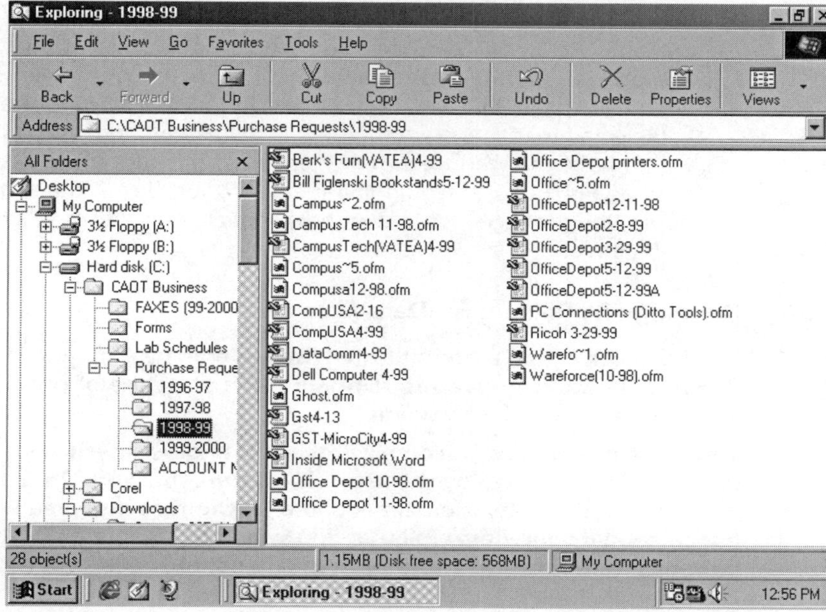

Figure 16-4. Windows Explorer in Windows 98, Custom Style With Double-Click Setting (Default)

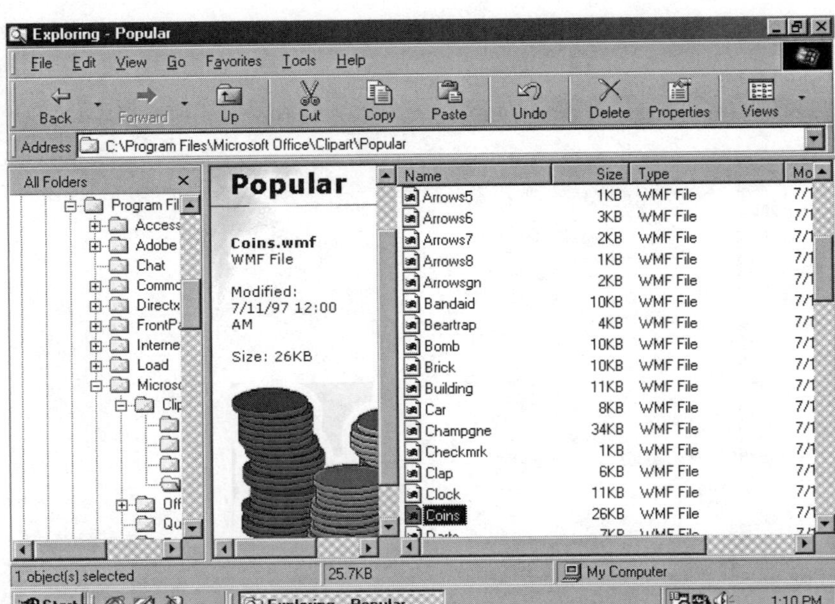

Figure 16-5. Windows Explorer in Windows 98, View as Web Page, Custom Style With Double-Click Setting

page, you can enhance the Custom style to display file attributes and graphic thumbnails. If you had elected the folders and files to perform like hyperlinks, then you would have customized Windows Explorer to operate in the same manner as the Web style (see Figures 16-1, page 497, and 16-2, page 498). If, on the other hand, you had elected to manage your folders and files traditionally, your screen would have the Web feature of displaying file attributes and graphic thumbnails, but you would still manage your files in the same manner as you manage files in Windows applications software (see Figure 16-5 above).

16–7 Creating File Folders for Data Files

Program files install automatically with a hierarchy of folders and files. Rarely does the user need to reorganize the structure of program files and folders to use the software.

Windows automatically comes with two folders specifically for the storage of files created by the user: *My Documents* and *My Files.* If you were to use these two folders to store all the files you created, these folders would soon be so full that you would be unable to locate easily files you might need. Therefore, you need to create your own file cabinet—additional folders—to store your data files.

a. Create file folders for the major categories of information that comprise your data files. Use the following procedures to determine the names and the number of folders you will need:

(1) Make a list of the major categories of information with which you deal. Your categories may be function based, client based, department based, or a combination of major areas for which you are responsible.

(2) Under each major category list any subcategories that would ultimately contain sufficient files to warrant a separate folder.

(3) List under any subcategories additional subcategories that may be appropriate. Attempt to keep your listing hierarchy to no more than three levels.

b. **Access Windows Explorer by right-clicking on the *Start* button in the lower left corner of your screen. Left-click on *Explore* to enter the program. Close any open files by left-clicking on the drive to which you wish to add new folders for your data files. You should then be in the root directory of your selected drive and ready to create folders to store your data files. Follow these procedures to create new folders in the root directory:**

(1) To create a new folder in the root directory, click *File* on the menu bar. Select *New–Folder*. In the name box that appears next to the new folder, key a name that will describe its contents. Use as few letters as possible, but not so few that you will not be able to recognize easily the subject matter of the folder. Begin the name of each folder with a capital letter.

(2) To create a folder within a folder that is in the root directory, you must first open the existing folder. Do so by left-clicking on it (double-click for traditional mode—single-click for Web mode). When the folder is open, you may create additional folders within this major category by left-clicking *File* on the menu bar, selecting *New–Folder*, and naming the new folder with a descriptive title.

(3) To create a new folder within a subcategory folder, first open the subcategory folder by left-clicking on it (double-click for traditional mode—single-click for Web mode). Follow the usual procedure of left-clicking *File* on the menu bar and selecting *New–Folder* to create any additional folders in this subcategory.

c. **As you create files in separate software applications such as Microsoft Word, Excel, WordPerfect, Lotus, Access, etc., be sure to save your file in the folder that best categorizes the information in the file. To do so, use the *File–Save As* command from the menu bar and make sure the *Save in:* box displays the folder name in which you wish to store the file.**

d. **You may manage your files from Windows Explorer or from your applications software. In applications software the file management options are available from the menu bar through the *File–Save As* and the *File–Open* dialogue boxes.**

16–8 Selecting Folders and Files

a. **Selecting a folder permits you to open it, delete it, move it to another location, or copy it to another location. In applications software select**

a folder by left-clicking on it. In Windows Explorer select a folder in one of the two following ways, depending upon your program configuration (see Section 16–6):

(1) *Traditional mode.* Place your pointer on the folder and left-click the mouse. The folder name should be highlighted.

(2) *Web page mode.* Place your pointer on the folder to select and highlight the folder name.

In applications software double left-clicking on a folder opens the folder and displays its contents. In Windows Explorer you may open a folder and display its contents in one of the two following ways, depending upon your program configuration (see Section 16–6):

(1) *Traditional mode.* Place your pointer on the folder and left double-click the mouse to open the folder.

(2) *Web page mode.* Place your pointer on the folder and left-click the mouse to open the folder.

b. Selected files may be deleted, moved to another location, or copied to another location. In applications software select a single file by left-clicking on it. In Windows Explorer if placing the mouse pointer on a file does not highlight it, left-click the mouse to highlight and select it.

c. Multiple folders or files may be selected simultaneously. Use the following procedures to select contiguous and noncontiguous files or folders simultaneously.

Windows Explorer

(1) Contiguous folders or files, those appearing one after another, may be selected simultaneously by placing your mouse pointer on the first folder or file (left-click once if the file is not highlighted), holding down the *Shift* key, and then moving your mouse pointer through the files to be selected until you reach the last folder or file in the series to be selected. Release the *Shift* key and the mouse. The series of selected items will be highlighted.

(2) Noncontiguous folders or files, those not appearing directly one after another, may be selected simultaneously by placing your mouse pointer on the first folder or file (left-click once if the folder or file is not highlighted), holding down the *Ctrl* key, and then carefully placing the mouse pointer (clicking if necessary) only on each folder or file to be highlighted and selected. Release the *Ctrl* key and the mouse when your selection has been completed. All the selected items will be highlighted.

Applications Software

(1) Contiguous folders or files, those appearing one after another, may be selected simultaneously by left-clicking on the first folder or file, holding down the *Shift* key, and then left-clicking on the last folder or file in the series to be selected. Release the *Shift* key. The series of selected items will be highlighted.

(2) Noncontiguous folders or files, those not appearing directly one after another, may be selected simultaneously by left-clicking on the first folder or file, holding down the *Ctrl* key, and then left-clicking on each folder or file to be selected. Release the *Ctrl* key when your selection has been completed. The selected items will be highlighted.

16–9 Deleting Folders and Files

Files and folders that are no longer needed occupy valuable space on the computer hard disk and slow down its operation. Proper maintenance procedures require that any obsolete folders and files be removed. Follow these procedures to delete any unwanted folders or files:

(1) Select the folders or files to be deleted by following the procedures described in Section 16–8.

(2) Place the mouse pointer anywhere in the highlighted selection and press the *Delete* key on the keyboard. You may, as an alternative, right-click the mouse and select the *Delete* option from the drop-down menu.

16–10 Copying Folders and Files

Copying folders or files to another location—in another folder on the hard disk, to a floppy disk, or to a CD-ROM—leaves the folders or files in their original location and places a copy in the designated location. Procedures for copying folders and files to another location are many and varied. The following procedure is just one of many that may be used in Windows Explorer or with applications software. It permits folders and files to be copied to a variety of locations.

(1) Select the folders or files to be copied by following the procedures described in Section 16–8.

(2) Place the mouse pointer anywhere in the highlighted selection and press *Ctrl-C* (the copy command). You may, as an alternative, right-click the mouse and select the *Copy* option from the drop-down menu.

(3) ***Windows Explorer:*** Scroll to the location where the files are to be copied, and left-click (Web mode) or double left-click (traditional mode) on the drive or folder to open the location where the selected items are to be copied.

Applications software: Use the *Look in:* box (in the *File–Save As* or *File–Open* dialogue box) to navigate to the location where the files are to be copied, and double left-click on the drive or folder to open the location where the selected items are to be copied.

(4) Place the pointer on the destination drive or folder and press *Ctrl-V* (the retrieve [paste] command) to place a copy of the folders or files in the opened location. You may, as an alternative, right-click the mouse and select the *Paste* option from the drop-down menu.

(5) Copied folders and files will initially appear at the bottom of the listing but will be sorted correctly once a drive or folder has been closed and reopened. A copied folder is copied with all its contents.

16–11 Moving Folders and Files

Moving folders and files to another location removes the folders and files from the original location and places them in a new drive or folder. Procedures for moving folders and files to another location are many and varied. The following procedure is just one of many that may be used in Windows Explorer or with applications software. It permits folders and files to be moved easily to a designated location.

(1) Select the folders or files to be moved by following the procedures described in Section 16–8.

(2) Place the mouse pointer anywhere in the highlighted selection and press *Ctrl-X* (the move [cut] command). You may, as an alternative, right-click the mouse and select the *Cut* option from the drop-down menu.

(3) ***Windows Explorer:*** Scroll to the location where the files are to be moved, and left-click (Web mode) or double left-click (traditional mode) on the drive or folder to open the location where the selected items are to be moved.

Applications software: Use the *Look in:* box (in the *File-Save As* or *File-Open* dialogue box) to navigate to the location where the files are to be moved, and double left-click on the drive or folder to open the location where the selected items are to be moved.

(4) Place the pointer on the destination drive or folder and press *Ctrl-V* (the retrieve [paste] command) to transfer the folders or files to their new location. You may, as an alternative, right-click the mouse and select the *Paste* option from the drop-down menu.

(5) Moved folders and files will initially appear at the bottom of the listing but will be sorted correctly once a drive or folder has been closed and reopened. A moved folder is moved with all its contents.

Glossary A

Grammatical Terms Used in *A Handbook for Office Workers*

Abbreviation

A shortened form of a word or word group. Examples: *in.* for *inches* and *AMA* for *American Medical Association.*

Absolute adjective

An adjective that cannot be compared because it represents a definite and exact state. Examples: *dead, perfect, unique,* and *full.*

Action verb

A verb that shows or represents movement. Examples: *run, talk,* and *breathe.*

Active voice

A method of constructing sentences that identifies who does what. The person or thing performing the action is the subject of the sentence. Example: The *stockholders* rejected the proposal.

Adj.

Abbreviation of *adjective.*

Adjective

A word or word group that describes a noun or pronoun. It tells what kind, which one, or how many. Examples: *good* investment, *this* bank, and *three* employees.

Adverb

A word that describes a verb, an adjective, or another adverb. It tells when, where, how, or to what degree. Many adverbs end in *ly.* Examples: arrive *early,* come *here,* drive *carefully,* and *too* small.

Adverbial clause

A word group containing a subject and a verb that begins with a subordinating conjunction such as *if, when, since, because,* or *as.* An adverbial clause modifies the verb in the main clause. Example: *If you wish to make an appointment,* please *call* me.

Ampersand

A symbol (&) meaning *and* used mainly in organizational names. Example: We have signed a contract with Robert White & Associates.

Animate object

Any person, any living thing, or any group composed of persons or living things. Compare with **Inanimate object**. Examples: *manager, tree, company,* and *flock of sheep.*

Antecedent

A noun (or an indefinite pronoun) to which a pronoun or any number of pronouns refer. Examples: Our last newsletter asked all *clients who* are interested in bond investment to indicate *their* willingness to attend a free seminar by phoning me. *Anyone* in the office *who* is interested in carpooling should submit *his* or *her* name to our manager.

Apostrophe

A symbol (') used to show noun possession, the omission of letters in contractions, and the beginning and ending of quotations within quotations. Examples: (1) *Carol's* salary; (2) we *haven't*; and (3) He asked, "Have you read my latest article, 'Western Travels'?"

Apposition, Appositive, Appositive expression

A word or word group that renames or explains the noun or pronoun it follows. These descriptive words usually add extra information. Example: Ms. Johnson, *our new manager,* has been with the company for three years.

Article

The words *a, an,* and *the*. These words are used as adjectives. Examples: *a* method, *an* interesting tour, *the* stock market.

Being verb

A form of the verb *to be* when it is used as a main verb, that is, when it appears alone or as the last verb in a verb phrase. These forms are *am, is, are, was, were, be,* and *been*. Examples: (1) Jill *was* here yesterday. (2) He has *been* our client for three years.

Being verb helper

A form of the verb *to be* when it is used in a verb phrase as a helping verb. These forms are *am, is, are, was, were, be,* and *been*. Example: Whitmore appliances *have* not *been sold* in our store for the past three years.

Cardinal number

A number such as 3 (three), 10 (ten), 32 (thirty-two), 541, or 1,856 that is used in simple counting.

Case form

A category used to classify nouns or pronouns in a sentence as subjective, objective, or possessive.

Celestial body

A planet, star, or other heavenly form. Examples: *Mars, North Star,* and *sun*.

Clause

A word group that contains a subject and a verb.

Collective noun

A noun composed of individual persons or things. Examples: *committee, team, jury, herd,* and *class*.

Colon

A punctuation mark (:) used to indicate that the following words explain further the word or word group appearing before the punctuation mark. Example: Our company specializes in the manufacture of the following women's clothing accessories: shoes, boots, handbags, and belts.

Command
A sentence in which the subject *you* is not stated but instead is implied. The sentence directs the understood subject *you* to perform (or refrain from) an action. Examples: (1) (You) Mail this information to me as soon as possible. (2) (You) Do not slam the door as you leave.

Common noun
A noun that does not name a specific person, place, or thing. Examples: *supervisor, building, city council, university,* and *company.*

Common noun element
That part of a proper noun that is not a specific name. Examples: *university* in Rutgers University, *building* in Tishman Building, and *city council* in Miami City Council.

Comparative form
The spelling or form of an adjective or an adverb when it compares two nouns or pronouns or two conditions. Compare with **Superlative form.** Examples: (1) This year's sales are *greater* than last year's. (2) We have progressed *more slowly* in this area than we had hoped.

Complement pronoun
A pronoun that completes a being verb. It follows a form of the verb *to be—am, is, are, was, were, be,* and *been.* Example: The contest winners were *they,* Karen and Bill.

Complete thought
A word group that contains a subject and a verb. The word group must make sense and be able to stand alone as a complete sentence. A complete thought is also known as an *independent clause.* Example: *Mr. Reed agreed to the terms of the contract,* but *his attorney advised him not to sign it.*

Complex sentence
A sentence that contains a dependent clause and an independent clause. Example: As soon as we receive your reply, we will send you a replacement or issue a credit to your account.

Complimentary close
The first closing line of a business letter. Example: *Sincerely yours.*

Compound adjective
Two or more words acting together as a single thought to describe or modify a noun or pronoun. Same as *compound modifier.* Example: *part-time* job.

Compound modifier
Same as *compound adjective.*

Compound noun
Two or more words used as a single unit to name a person, place, or thing. Examples: *sister-in-law, notary public, high school, community college, word processing,* and *income tax.*

Compound number

A number requiring more than one word when written in word form. Examples: *twenty-seven, ninety-eight, one hundred, two hundred fifty.*

Compound sentence

A sentence containing two independent clauses (complete thoughts) joined by (1) a semicolon; (2) a transitional expression (such as *therefore, consequently,* or *nevertheless*); or (3) the conjunction *and, but, or,* or *nor.* Examples: (1) Please call me when the shipment arrives; I will pick it up immediately. (2) The Model 432 cart you ordered has been discontinued; *however,* our Model 434 cart has all the features of the cart you ordered. (3) The manufacturer has promised to send us another shipment of these disks by next week, *and* we will fill your order immediately upon its arrival.

Compound subject

A subject that contains two or more nouns or pronouns joined by *and, or,* or *nor.* Example: *Ellen and Jack* have already reached their quotas for this month's sales.

Compound verb

Two or more words combined to produce a single thought unit that functions as a verb. Compound verbs appear as one word, as two words, or hyphenated. Examples: *upgrade, mark up, double-space.*

Compound-complex sentence

A sentence containing two independent clauses (complete thoughts) and a dependent clause. Example: This suite of offices is currently available for occupancy, and we will release the keys to you as soon as you return the signed lease agreement with a certified check for $3,000.

Conjugation

The various forms of a verb that show person. Examples: I *see,* he or she *sees,* we *see,* you *see,* they *see;* I *am,* he or she *is,* we *are,* you *are,* they *are.*

Conjunction

A part of speech that serves as a connector of words or word groups within a sentence. Examples: *and, but, or, nor, either . . . or,* and *not only . . . but also.*

Conjunctive adverb

An adverb—such as *consequently, however,* or *therefore*—that connects the main clauses of a compound sentence. Example: Most of our advertising budget has already been allocated; *therefore,* we are unable to take advantage of your offer.

Conjunctive pair

A class of connecting words—conjunctions—that link contrasting or dependent ideas. These connectors consist of two parts. Examples: *either . . . or, neither . . . nor, if . . . then,* and *not only . . . but also.*

Consonant

Any letter of the alphabet other than *a, e, i, o,* and *u.*

Contingent expression
An expression that depends upon a similar expression for completion. Example: *The sooner* you take advantage of this offer, *the more often* you will be able to enjoy your personal home movie selections.

Contraction
Shortened forms in which an apostrophe is used to show the omission of letters or numbers. These shortened forms may be applied to certain words, verb phrases, and dates. Examples: *internat'l* for *international, doesn't* for *does not,* and *'01* for *2001.*

Coordinating conjunction
A part of speech (conjunction) that joins equal words or word groups. Examples: *and, but, or,* and *nor.*

Courtesy title
A title used to address individuals. Examples: *Mr., Ms., Mrs., Miss,* and *Dr.*

Dash
A mark of punctuation (— or --) used to precede summary statements or for emphasis in setting off words or word groups. The em dash (—) is used in computer-based and printed copy. In typewritten copy the dash is formed by keying two hyphens consecutively (--); no space appears before, between, or after the hyphens. Examples: (1) Sofas, chairs, bedroom suites, dining room sets—we have a large variety of styles and brands from which you may choose. (2) Three employees--Clyde Jones, Janice Lee, and Dennis Martinez--have agreed to work overtime next week.

Decimal
A small dot (.) used in numbers to separate a whole number from a portion of the next number in the sequence. Examples: *12.5, 0.07, 147.38, 6.75 percent,* and *$1.4 million.*

Declarative sentence
A complete sentence that makes a statement. Example: Our company president announced our merger with Cory Industries yesterday.

Dependent adverbial clause
A word group that (1) contains a subject and a verb and (2) begins with a subordinating conjunction such as *if, when, since, because,* or *as.* An adverbial clause modifies the verb in the main clause. Example: *When the shipment arrives,* we will *call* you immediately.

Dependent clause
A word group that contains a subject and a verb but cannot stand alone as a complete sentence. Same as a *subordinate clause.* Example: John told me last week *that he expects to win this month's sales contest.*

Direct address
The act of calling a person by name, title, or classification in written or oral communication *with that person.* Examples: (1) Thank you, *Ms. Burwell,* for responding so promptly. (2) Yes, *Professor,* we will have this textbook available for use during the spring semester. (3) Only you, *fellow citizens,* can prevent a further decline of schools in this city.

Direct object

A noun or pronoun acted upon by the subject and verb of a sentence. Example: Our accountant mailed the *check* yesterday.

Direct quotation

The exact words spoken or written by a person or group. Example: According to the committee's report, "The property was sold in 1999 for $10,950,000."

Ellipsis

A series of three periods (. . .)—with spaces before, between, and after the periods—used to show omissions in quoted material or hesitations in other printed material. Example: According to his latest journal article, Professor Haley concludes, "Social conditions will continue to improve in this area . . . unless the government withdraws its funding commitment."

Essential subordinate clause

A word group that contains a subject and a verb but cannot stand alone as a complete sentence. The word group is needed to complete the main idea of the sentence by furnishing *who, what, which one, when, why, how, whether,* or *to what degree*. An *essential subordinate clause* is the same as a *restrictive clause,* a *restrictive dependent clause,* or a *restrictive subordinate clause.* Example: Dr. Logan is the professor *who is in charge of preparing the accreditation report.*

Exclamation mark

A mark of punctuation (!) used to show strong feeling or emotion. Example: Take advantage of our free offer today—while this letter is in front of you!

First person

I or *we* used as subjects in writing or speaking. Example: After analyzing the specimen, *we* contacted several contagious disease specialists.

Fraction

A part of a whole number expressed in proportion to the whole. Example: The legislature is proposing a 1/2 percent increase in our state's sales tax.

Future perfect tense

A verb phrase used to express an action that will occur before a certain time in the future. This tense is formed by using the verb helpers *will have* and the past participle of a verb. Example: If donations continue to be made at this same rate, we *will have paid* for this new hospital wing before its completion.

Future progressive tense

A verb phrase used to express an action that will be ongoing in the future. This tense is formed by using the verb helpers *will be* and the present participle of a verb. Example: Our volunteers *will be calling* other alumni during the next month to solicit donations for the newly formed college foundation.

Future tense

A verb phrase used to express an action that will happen in the future. This tense is formed by using the verb helper *will* and the present part of a verb. Example: I *will call* you next week.

Gender

A term used to refer to the sexual classification of nouns, pronouns, and their modifiers. Classifications include feminine, masculine, and neuter. Examples: (1) *Maria* lost *her* purse. (2) *He* sold all *his* stock. (3) The *company* has just purchased dental insurance for all *its* employees.

Gerund

A verb form ending in *ing* that functions as a noun in a sentence. Example: His *refusing* our offer came as a surprise to all of us.

Helping verb

A verb that appears with the present part, present participle, or past participle of another verb to form tenses. Examples: *will* go, *are* planning, *have been* employed.

Horizontal listing

A listing of items that continue across the page like ordinary text. Compare with **Vertical listing**. Example: Check the following sources for current employment opportunities: *classified ads appearing in your local newspaper, postings in your college or university employment office, and listings provided by career centers on the Internet.*

Hyphen

A mark of punctuation (-) used in some word groups to join two or more words that function as a single idea. In typewritten copy this mark is also used to represent *through* when placed between two numbers. Examples: *mother-in-law, up-to-date,* and pages *34-35.*

Hyphenated compound

A word group joined by hyphens that functions as a single thought unit. Examples: *trade-in, self-employment, well-to-do.*

Imperative sentence, Imperative statement

A complete sentence in which the subject *you* is not stated; it is understood. Example: (You) Please mail your check in the enclosed envelope today.

Implied verb

A word group in which an intended verb is not stated. Compare with **Stated verb**. Examples: (1) If possible (If it *is* possible), we would appreciate your shipping this order by July 10. (2) John has more seniority with the firm than I (I *have*).

Inanimate object

A nonliving thing. Compare with **Animate object**. Examples: *computer, lease,* and *pen.*

Indefinite pronoun

A pronoun that does not represent a specific person, place, or thing. Examples: *each, every, either, someone, anyone,* and *something.*

Independent adjective

An adjective that describes a noun without relying on other adjectives to enhance its meaning. Two or more independent adjectives modifying a noun are separated by commas. Examples: an *intelligent, conscientious* student. Note that in the phrase "... printed in *large bold* print ... " the adjectives are not independent and therefore are not separated by commas.

Independent clause

A word group that (1) contains a subject and a verb and (2) can stand alone as a complete sentence. An *independent clause* is the same as a *main clause*. Example: Although he was at first reluctant, *Senator Richards has agreed to seek reelection for a third term.*

Independent phrase

A word group that represents a complete sentence although it is not. Example: *Now to the point.*

Independent question

A word group stated in question format that stands alone as a complete sentence. Example: Who is responsible for closing the office on Friday evenings?

Indirect object

A noun or pronoun acted upon by a subject, a verb, and a direct object. Example: Chris gave *him* the check yesterday.

Indirect question

A statement that describes the content of a question or questions. Example: Several customers have asked whether we will extend our shopping hours for the holiday season.

Indirect quotation

A statement that describes the written or spoken word of another person or source but does not employ the exact words used by that person or source. Example: Sharon said that if she was not promoted within the next three months, she would begin to look for another position.

Infinitive

The present part of a verb preceded by the word *to*. Example: You will probably need *to work* overtime *to finish* this project by its deadline date.

Infinitive phrase

A word group beginning with an infinitive and ending with a noun or pronoun. Example: *To obtain more information,* just mail the enclosed card.

Inside address

The part of a business letter that lists the addressee's name, professional title (if any), company name (if any), street address, city, state, and zip code.

Intransitive verb

A verb that does not have a direct or an indirect object. Compare with **Transitive verb**. Examples: (1) The governor will *campaign* heavily in the southern part of the state next week. (2) Responsibility for the success of this project *lies* with the project manager. (3) Prices *rise* when manufacturers encounter increased costs.

Introductory clause, Introductory dependent clause

A word group that (1) contains a subject and a verb and (2) starts with a subordinating conjunction such as *if, when, since, because,* or *as*. The word group begins the sentence, ends with a comma, and is followed by the main clause. Example: *Because we are unable to obtain this merchandise,* we are returning your check.

Introductory phrase

A word group without a subject and corresponding verb that starts with a preposition, an infinitive, or a participle. Such word groups that begin a sentence and appear directly before the main clause are introductory. Examples: (1) *By this time next year,* we will have moved our home office to Louisville. (2) *To receive your free copy,* simply sign and mail the enclosed card. (3) *Lured by the promise of large profits,* investors poured millions of dollars into this fraudulent development project.

Introductory prepositional phrase

A word group that starts with a preposition but does not contain a subject or a verb. The word group begins the sentence and is followed directly by the main clause. Example: *During this time* we will need to gather more information about the economic conditions of this area.

Irregular verb

A verb that does not form its parts in the usual way, that is, by adding *ed* to the present part to form the past part and the past participle. Examples: *eat, ate, eaten; go, went, gone;* and *sing, sang, sung.*

Limiting adverb

A word or word group that restrains, confines, or negates the meaning of a verb. Examples: *not, barely, scarcely,* and *hardly.*

Limiting expression

A word group that restrains or confines another word group. Example: You may petition for a grade change, *but only for a valid reason.*

Linking verb

A form of the verb *to be* used as a main verb or a form of another nonaction verb. Examples: (1) She *is* a conscientious employee. (2) I *feel* bad that our manager is being transferred.

Lowercase

Refers to the format of alphabetic characters; letters that are not capitalized. Examples: *a, d, m,* and *u.*

Main clause

A word group that (1) contains a subject and a verb and (2) can stand alone as a complete sentence. A *main clause* is the same as an *independent clause.* Example: When we receive your signed contract, *we will order the equipment needed for your installation.*

Main verb

A single verb or the last verb in a verb phrase. Examples: (1) Please *call* me tomorrow. (2) The display *was* too large to fit into a suitcase. (3) Only three candidates have been *called.* (4) Our manager was *disappointed* with the results of the advertising campaign.

Main word

The most descriptive or definitive word in a compound noun. Examples: *mother*-in-law, personnel *manager, notary* public, and vice *president.*

Main words in a heading or title to be capitalized

All words except the articles *a, an,* and *the*; the conjunctions *and, but, or,* or *nor*; and prepositions with three or fewer letters such as *of, for, to, in,* or *out* UNLESS any of these words appear as the first or last word. Examples: (1) Normal Climate Conditions in the Northeastern Part of the United States, (2) Corporate Goals and Strategies for 2002, (3) An Analysis of Marketing Strategies Used by an Independent Mail-Order House.

Modifier

An *adjective* that describes a noun or pronoun. An *adverb* that describes or limits a verb, an adjective, or another adverb.

N.

An abbreviation for *noun.*

Nominative case, Nominative case form

A noun or pronoun used as the subject of a sentence, the complement of a *being* verb, or the object of the infinitive *to be* when this infinitive has no subject. Nouns always maintain the same form; pronouns require a specific form: *I, he, she, you, we, they, who, whoever.* Same as *subjective case, subjective case form.* Examples: (1) *We* called you yesterday. (2) The winner was *she,* Joyce Moore. (3) I would not want to be *he* when the mistake is discovered.

Nonaction verb

A verb that does not demonstrate action. Examples: *am, is, was,* and *were.*

Nonessential subordinate clause

A word group that (1) contains a subject and a verb and (2) starts with a subordinating conjunction such as *if, when, as, after,* or *although* or a relative pronoun such as *who* or *which.* This word group is an additional thought unit that does not change or modify the main clause of the sentence. It is the same as a *nonrestrictive clause* or a *nonrestrictive subordinate clause.* Examples: (1) Our major advertising campaign will begin on November 1, *after all our dealers nationwide have the new product line in their stores.* (2) Jan Davidson, *who has been with our company for three years,* has been placed in charge of the project.

Nonrestrictive

A word or word group that is not essential to the meaning of the main idea.

Nonrestrictive clause

A word group that (1) contains a subject and a verb and (2) appears with a main clause. This word group is subordinate to the main idea and does not alter its meaning. It complements the main idea by adding additional information. A *nonrestrictive clause* is the same as a *nonessential subordinate clause* or a *nonrestrictive subordinate clause.* Examples: (1) This proposal, *as I explained to you earlier,* has not yet been approved by the Board of Directors. (2) The profit and loss statement for this project was shown in our last annual report, *which was distributed to the stockholders on March 1.*

Nonrestrictive phrase

A word group beginning with a preposition, an infinitive, or a participle and ending with a noun or pronoun. This word group does not affect the meaning of the main clause; it adds an additional idea that does not modify the main idea. Examples: (1) You cannot, *in my estimation,* expect a greater return on your investment at this time. (2) Susan and Randy, *to name at least two people,* were among those staff members in our department who were affected by the abolishment of our child care center. (3) Our president, *concerned about the steady sales decline,* has decided to invest more heavily in research and development.

Nonrestrictive subordinate clause
Same as *nonessential subordinate clause.*

Noun
A person, place, thing, animal, quality, concept, feeling, action, measure, or state. Examples: *employee, city, chair, cat, sincerity, democracy, love, swimming, inch,* and *happiness.*

Object
A noun or pronoun acted upon by another part of speech, e.g., a verb or a preposition. Examples: (1) Scott sent *me* the *check* yesterday. (2) For the next three *months,* you will receive a free trial *subscription.*

Object of a preposition
The noun or pronoun that follows a preposition. Examples: of our *clients,* for the last few *months,* from *her,* and through your *efforts.*

Objective case, Objective case form
A noun or pronoun used as the object of a verb, the object of a preposition, the subject or object of an infinitive other than *to be,* or the object of the infinitive *to be* when this infinitive has a subject. Nouns always maintain the same form; pronouns require a specific form: *me, him, her, you, us, them.* Examples: (1) You may *contact me* at this number after 3 p.m. (2) Please send this information *to me* directly. (3) I do not want *to give her* too much information about our new product. (4) I would not want our new *supervisor to be him.*

Open compound
Two or more words used to represent a single idea. The words appear as separate words and are not hyphenated. Examples: *information processing, golf club,* and *vice president.*

Ordinal number
A number form that indicates order in a series. Cardinal numbers such as *3, 10,* and *246* are numbers used in counting; ordinal numbers such as *first (1st), second (2nd),* and *twenty-fourth (24th)* indicate order or position in a series. Example: Our sales report for the *fourth* quarter must be ready by January 15 for inclusion in the annual report.

Parallel structure
Words or word groups used in a similar fashion that are expressed in the same format. Parallel structure applies to words joined by a conjunction, joined by a conjunctive pair, appearing in a series, and appearing in a listing. Examples: (1) Our receptionist's main duties are to *answer the telephone* and *greet office visitors.* (2) You

may order supplies from not only *our standard supply catalog* but also *Kalleen's Computer Supply Catalog.* (3) The whole day was spent *returning phone calls, reading the mail,* and *dictating correspondence.*

Parenthesis
A mark of punctuation signifying the beginning [(] of a side thought and the ending [)] of a side thought. Example: Please request copies of any ancillary materials (at least an instructor's manual and key) that may accompany the text.

Parenthetical element, Parenthetical expression, Parenthetical remark
A word or word group that does not contribute to the meaning of the main clause but merely acts as a transitional thought or provides an additional idea. Examples: (1) *Therefore,* we are returning this order for credit. (2) The meeting scheduled for October 24, *as you probably already know,* has been canceled.

Participial phrase
A word group beginning with a past or present participle. Examples: (1) *Encouraged by last month's increased sales,* our Advertising Department has decided to extend the present campaign another month. (2) *Hoping to sell the property immediately,* Mr. Rice agreed to drop the price $10,000.

Parts of a verb
The forms of a verb that are used to construct tenses, that is, those spellings of a verb used in expressing time periods. The parts of a verb include the *infinitive, present, past, present participle,* and *past participle.* Examples: *to send, send, sent, sending, sent.*

Passive voice
A form of sentence construction in which the doer of the action is not the subject of the sentence. This form is used primarily to deemphasize the person performing the action by focusing instead on the results. The passive voice is constructed by using a form of the verb *to be* as a helper and the past participle of the main verb. Example: These reports *were mailed* last week.

Past part
One of the five verb parts used in constructing tenses. For most verbs this part is formed by adding *ed* to the present part, the form listed in the dictionary. The past part for verbs not following this pattern is shown in the dictionary directly after the main entry. Examples: (1) *called* (call), *discussed* (discuss), and *answered* (answer). (2) *saw* (see), *wrote* (write), and *went* (go).

Past participle
One of the five verb parts used in constructing tenses. The past participle is always used with a helping verb. For most verbs this part is formed by adding *ed* to the present part, the form listed in the dictionary. The past participle for verbs not following this pattern is shown in the dictionary directly after the main entry. Examples: *called* (call), *discussed* (discuss), and *answered* (answer). (2) *seen* (see), *written* (write), and *gone* (go).

Past perfect tense
Used to describe a past action that has taken place before another past action. This tense is formed by using the helping verb *had* and the past participle of the main verb. Example: The applicant *had accepted* another position before he *received* our offer.

Past progressive tense

Used to describe an ongoing action that took place in the past. This tense is formed by using the helping verb *was* or *were* with the present participle of the main verb. Example: Last year our company *was hiring* additional personnel; this year the company is reducing its staff in all departments.

Past tense

Used to report a single past action or occurrence. This tense is formed by using the past part of a verb. Example: We *finished* the report last Friday.

Perfect tense

Describes the present, past, or future by using a form of *have* as a helping verb and the past participle of the main verb. Examples: *have completed, had completed,* and *will have completed.*

Permanent compound

Dictionary entries consisting of more than one word to represent a single idea. Examples: *air-conditioning, high school, community college, up-to-date,* and *full-time.*

Personal pronoun

A word that substitutes for the name of a person or thing. Examples: *I, he, she, it, we, they, you, me, him, her, us,* and *them.*

Phrase

A group of two or more grammatically related words that act upon one another in a modifying, coordinating, or composite relationship. The word group does not have a subject and a verb. Examples: (1) Our sales have increased *during the past few months.* (2) Mr. Lee requested the custodial crew *to wash the windows, vacuum the carpeting,* and *set up the chairs.* (3) Our supply *of printer ribbons* is diminishing rapidly.

Plural

More than one. Nouns, pronouns, and verbs have plural forms.

Plural noun

More than one person, place, or thing. These nouns usually require a special form and appear with a plural verb. Examples: *files* (file), *bosses* (boss), *companies* (company), *curricula* (curriculum), and *potatoes* (potato).

Polite request

A command worded like a question that requests the reader or listener to perform a specific action. Example: Will you please send us your remaining application materials by November 16.

Possessive

A noun or pronoun that shows ownership. Examples: (1) The *company's* liability in this case has not yet been determined. (2) The company awarded all *its* employees a bonus.

Possessive case, Possessive case form

The spelling of a noun or pronoun that shows ownership. Examples: *Sally's* desk, an *accountants'* convention, *his* books, *your* paycheck, and *their* tickets.

Predicate
That part of the sentence that includes the verb or verb phrase and all its modifiers—all parts of the sentence except the complete subject. Example: All parts in this assembly *will need to be replaced within the next few months.*

Prefix
A syllable attached to the beginning of a word that forms a derivative word or an inflectional form. Compare with **Suffix.** Examples: *un*able, *dis*cover, *mis*pronounce, and *ful*fill.

Preposition
A part of speech that links a noun or pronoun to another word in the sentence. Examples: *of, for, behind, in, through, during, around, above, between,* and *except.*

Prepositional phrase
A word group that begins with a preposition and ends with a noun or pronoun. The phrase modifies another noun or pronoun or a verb in the sentence. Examples: (1) Our new line *of office equipment* will be on display at the convention. (2) Do not park your car *between these posts.*

Present part
One of the five verb parts used in constructing tenses. This part is the form shown as the main dictionary entry of the verb. Examples: *call, discuss, answer, see, write,* and *go.*

Present participle
One of the five verb parts used in constructing tenses. For most verbs this part is formed by adding *ing* to the present part, the form listed in the dictionary. The present participle for verbs not following this pattern is shown in the dictionary directly after the main entry. Examples: (1) *calling* (call), *discussing* (discuss), and *answering* (answer). (2) *omitting* (omit), *writing* (write), and *starring* (star).

Present perfect tense
Used to describe an action that began in the past but has continued during the time leading to the present. This tense is formed by using the helping verb *has* or *have* and the past participle of the main verb. Example: We *have sent* this client at least three reminders about his past-due account.

Present progressive tense
Used to describe an action in progress during the present time. This tense is formed by using the helping verb *am, is,* or *are* and the present participle of the main verb. Example: We *are* now *taking* applications for this position.

Present tense
Used to describe an ongoing action or an existing condition. This tense is formed by using the present part of the verb. Examples: (1) Lisa *drives* 20 miles each day to work. (2) Your company *has* too many employees.

Principal parts of a verb
See **Parts of a verb.**

Principal word

The word in a compound noun that describes or defines the noun most explicitly. Examples: *brother*-in-law, *sergeant* at arms, lieutenant *colonel,* and high *school.*

Principal words in a heading or title to be capitalized

See **Main words in a heading or title to be capitalized**.

Professional title

A title related to a person's employment. Examples: *Professor* Scot Ober, *Governor* Joyce Arntson, *Dean* Dolores Denova, *Vice President* Norlund, *General* Rodriguez, and *Mayor* Bradley.

Progressive tenses

Used to describe actions in progress during various time periods. Describes the present, past, or future by using a form of *to be* as a helping verb and the present participle of the main verb. Examples: *are processing, were processing,* and *will be processing.*

Pronoun

A word that functions as the substitute for a noun. Examples: *I, her,* and *they*; *that* and *who*; and *this, each,* and *everyone.*

Proper noun

The name of a specific person, place, or thing. Examples: *Jane Thompson, San Francisco Bay Bridge,* and the *Empire State Building.*

Question mark

A mark of punctuation (?) used to end a word group or complete sentence that is a direct question. Example: Have you received any further information about the proposed project*?*

Quotation mark

A mark of punctuation (") used primarily to set off the exact words spoken or written by another person. Example: The author stated in his article, "As interest rates decline, investments in the municipal bond market become less attractive."

Reflexive pronoun

A pronoun that refers back to and is acted upon by another noun or pronoun in the sentence. Example: *We* can certainly give *ourselves* a pat on the back for this accomplishment.

Regular verb

A verb that forms its parts by adding standard endings to the present form; that is, by adding *ed* for the past part, *ed* for the past participle, and *ing* for the present participle. Example: *check, checked, checked, checking.*

Relative clause

A word group (containing a subject and a verb) introduced by a pronoun that refers back and relates to a noun or pronoun in the main clause. Relative clauses are most commonly introduced by *who, whom, that,* and *which.* Example: Dr. Williams is the physician *who will handle your case.*

Relative pronoun
The noun substitutes *who, whoever, whom, whomever, that,* and *which* used to introduce a clause that refers back and relates to a noun or pronoun in the main clause. Example: The *subsidiary* of our company *that* handles this product is Belegrath Tool & Die.

Relative pronoun clause
A word group containing a subject and a verb that appears with a main clause; it begins with *who, whom, whoever, whomever, that,* or *which.* Example: Heritage Inc. is the real estate agency *that is handling the sale of our Springfield warehouse.*

Restrictive
A word or word group that contributes substantially to the main idea of the sentence and is needed for it to convey the same meaning. Without the word or word group, the meaning of the sentence would be changed or incomplete.

Restrictive appositive
A word or word group used to rename or describe a previous noun or pronoun. The word or word group is needed to identify *which one.* Example: The *book* *The Pentagon Heroes* has been on the best-seller list for the past eight weeks.

Restrictive clause
A word group that (1) contains a subject and a verb and (2) appears with a main clause. Although this word group is subordinate to the main idea, it does clarify, limit, or otherwise affect its meaning. A *restrictive clause* is the same as an *essential subordinate clause,* a *restrictive dependent clause,* or a *restrictive subordinate clause.* Examples: (1) This order will be shipped *as soon as I receive approval from our Credit Department.* (2) The only person *who can approve this request* is the vice president of financial services.

Restrictive dependent clause
Same as an *essential subordinate clause,* a *restrictive clause,* or a *restrictive subordinate clause.*

Restrictive phrase
A word group beginning with a preposition, an infinitive, or a participle and ending with a noun or pronoun. This word group affects the meaning of the main clause by answering such questions as *who, what, which one, when, why, how, whether,* or *to what degree.* Examples: (1) The auction will be held *on Saturday, December 4.* (2) Please mail the enclosed postcard *to obtain further information.* (3) We increased our advertising budget *hoping to increase sales.*

Restrictive subordinate clause
Same as an *essential subordinate clause,* a *restrictive clause,* or a *restrictive dependent clause.*

Return address
The complete address of the person writing a business letter that is not prepared on letterhead stationery. On envelopes prepared for mailing, the complete address of the person mailing the envelope and its contents.

Roman numeral

One of a sequence of numbering based on the ancient Roman system. In business this system is used primarily for numbering the major divisions in an outline, the chapters in a report, and the preliminary pages of a report. Examples: *I, II, III, IV, V* and *i, ii, iii, iv, v*.

Salutation

The opening greeting in a business letter. Examples: *Gentlemen, Ladies and Gentlemen, Dear Dr. Gates, Dear Ms. Howell,* and *Dear Bob.*

Semicolon

A mark of punctuation (;) used primarily to join two complete thoughts in a sentence. Example: We have not received any responses to our advertisement for an administrative assistant*;* therefore, please do not renew our ad in the *Valley Star.*

Sentence fragment

A word group ending with a period, question mark, or exclamation mark that is not a complete sentence or does not represent a complete thought. Example: We are interested in sponsoring a number of spot announcements. *That describe how our services and employees benefit the community.*

Series

Three or more words or word groups that have the same structure within a sentence. Items in a series consist of words, phrases, or clauses. The last item is joined to the others with a coordinating conjunction: *and, or,* or *nor.* Example: You may *telephone, fax, or mail* your orders.

Signature block

In a business letter, the lines that contain the signature of the writer, the typewritten name of the writer, and the title of the writer, if any.

Simple fraction

Any portion of a whole number that is less than *one*. Examples: *1/4* or *one fourth, 2/3* or *two thirds,* and *3/5* or *three fifths.*

Simple noun

The name of a person, place, or thing that consists of one word. Examples: *Mary, state, computer,* and *manager.*

Simple sentence

A word group that contains only one subject and one verb and makes sense. Example: I received the package of materials yesterday.

Simple subject

The single word in the main clause of a sentence that answers *who* or *what* in relation to the verb. Example: All *employees* in our division *have received* copies of the employee newsletter.

Simple tenses

The present, past, and future tenses. Examples: (1) He *writes* well. (2) He *wrote* this letter yesterday. (3) He *will write* the letter tomorrow.

Singular
A mode or form of nouns, pronouns, and verbs signifying *one*. Examples: *truck* (vs. *trucks*), *she* (vs. *they*), and *drives* (vs. *drive*).

Singular noun
The form used to name a person, place, or thing that signifies *one*. Examples: *supervisor, country,* and *bank*.

Slash
A symbol (/) used primarily for expressing fractions and certain expressions. Same as a *solidus* and a *virgule*. Examples: *3 3/4, c/o* (in care of), and *and/or.*

Solidus
Same as a *slash* and a *virgule*.

Stated verb
A verb expressed orally or in written format. Compare with **Implied verb**. Examples: (1) If this *is* so, please *call* me. (2) He *is* older than I *am*.

Statement
A word group that presents facts or ideas. It is concluded with a period. Example: Our company was established in 1973.

Subject
The word or word group in the main or subordinate clause of a sentence that answers *who* or *what* in relation to the verb. Examples: (1) The *stockholders* of the corporation *approved* the merger last month. (2) Both *answers and explanations* for this test *are contained* in the instructor's manual. (3) *We will notify* you when your order arrives.

Subject of a clause
The word or word group in the subordinate clause of a sentence that answers *who* or *what* in relation to the verb. Example: If *you are interested* in this position, please send us your résumé.

Subject complement
The noun, pronoun, or adjective following a being verb (*am, is, are, was, were, be, been*) that either renames or describes the subject. Examples: (1) The former *supervisor* of our department *is* the new *vice president.* (2) The *paintings* in this exhibition *are* exceptionally *valuable*.

Subject of a sentence
The word or word group in the main clause of a sentence that answers *who* or *what* in relation to the verb. Example: As I mentioned in my previous memorandum, any further *delays* in the completion of this contract *will cost* the company thousands of dollars.

Subject of an infinitive
A noun or pronoun that appears directly before an infinitive. Example: I did not expect *him to have* the authority to release this kind of information.

Subjective case, Subjective case form

A noun or pronoun used as the subject of a sentence, the complement of a *being* verb, or the object of the infinitive *to be* when this infinitive has no subject. Nouns always maintain the same form; pronouns require a specific form: *I, he, she, you, we, they, who, whoever*. Same as *nominative case, nominative case form*. Examples: (1) *They* signed the papers this morning. (2) The only person who responded was *he*. (3) I would not want to be *she* when our manager discovers her mistake.

Subjunctive mood

Used to describe events that cannot or probably will not happen and conditions that are not true or highly unlikely. The plural form *were* is used with *if, as if, as though,* or *wish* for singular subjects when the situation described is not true or unlikely. Examples: (1) *If* I *were* you, I would refer this letter to my attorney. (2) During the meeting Tina acted *as if* she, not Ms. Elliott, *were* the department manager.

Subordinate clause

A word group that contains a subject and a verb but cannot stand alone as a complete sentence. Same as a *dependent clause*. Example: Please notify our office *if you need any additional sales literature*.

Subordinating conjunction

A specific kind of conjunction used to introduce a dependent or subordinate word group that contains a subject and a verb. Examples: *if, as, when, because,* and *since*.

Suffix

A syllable attached to the ending of a word or word root that forms a derivative word or an inflectional form. Compare with **Prefix**. Examples: invest*ment,* account*ing,* and fruit*ful*.

Superlative form

The spelling or form of an adverb or an adjective when it compares more than two nouns or pronouns or more conditions than two. Compare with **Comparative form**. Examples: (1) Your firm is the *most* highly *respected* one in the industry. (2) Sales figures for this year are the *highest* in our company's history.

Suspending hyphen

A hyphen following the first word (or multiple words) of a compound adjective in which the last word of the compound appears later with a compatible compound adjective. Examples: (1) This carpeting may be purchased in *10-, 12-,* and 15-foot widths. (2) Most of our automobile loans extend over a *four-* or five-year period.

Syllable

A unit of spoken language used to make up words. Syllables are marked off in main dictionary entries; a small dot separates each syllable. Written words may be divided at the end of a line only between syllables. Examples: *syl•la•ble, di•vi•sion,* and *ir•re•vo•ca•ble*.

Temporary compound

A compound adjective not appearing in the dictionary. This compound is hyphenated only when it precedes the noun it modifies. Examples: (1) These *easy-to-follow instructions* were written by one of our staff members. (2) These *instructions* are *easy to follow.*

Tense

The form of a verb that places an action or a condition in a time frame.

Transitional expression, Transitional words

A word or phrase that does not contribute to the meaning of a sentence but takes the listener or reader smoothly from one concept to another by bridging two ideas or signaling a turn in thought. Examples: (1) You may, *however,* wish to upgrade the memory of your computer to 128 or 256 megabytes. (2) Our supplier is unable to obtain any additional pieces of Harwood china by Lexington; *therefore,* we are returning your deposit.

Transitive verb

A verb that has an object. Compare with **Intransitive verb**. Examples: (1) Mr. Morris *called me* yesterday. (2) Please *place the book* on the table. (3) Our supervisor *gave her* an excellent *rating.*

Uppercase

Capital letters. Examples: *A, M,* and *IBM.*

Verb

A part of speech that shows action or movement or describes a situation or condition. Examples: *write, listen, send, be, appear,* and *look.*

Verb phrase

A verb part combined with helpers such as *was, have, did,* and *will* to form tenses. Examples: *were divided, had reached, does work, will have finished,* and *may be reached.*

Vertical listing

A listing of items in which each item begins a new line on the page. Compare with **Horizontal listing**. The following entries are an example of a vertical listing:

First entry in the listing
Second entry in the listing
Third entry in the listing
Fourth entry in the listing
Last entry in the listing

Virgule

Same as a *slash* and a *solidus.*

Vowel

Letters of the alphabet *a, e, i, o,* and *u.*

Glossary B
Glossary of Computer and Internet Terms

The following listing of terms is only a sampling of words and phrases peculiar to computer applications, computer technology, and the Internet. Specialized dictionaries dealing with computer and Internet terms are available in printed form (see Section 15–1c) and on-line (see Section 15–11). Two additional on-line sources for obtaining definitions and detailed explanations of computer and Internet terminology are *PC Webopaedia* (a search site that locates definitions and explanations of computer and Internet terms)[1] and *Glossary of Internet Terms* (an extensive, up-to-date listing of Internet terms and their definitions).[2]

Access
To open and look into a computer file.

Access time
The amount of time the computer takes to locate (retrieve) a piece of data in its storage system. See also **Megahertz**.

American Standard Code for Information Interchange (ASCII)
A seven-bit code widely used in data communications.

Applications software
Computer programs developed for a specific purpose such as word processing, desktop publishing, graphics, spreadsheets, database management, accounting, telecommunications, and other related functions.

Archiving
The process of transferring data from operating disks or on-line computer storage to permanent storage disks or tape.

ASCII
See **American Standard Code for Information Interchange**.

Auxiliary storage
Storage by using usually either magnetic tapes or disks to supplement the working storage of the computer.

Backup
The duplication of a program or document on a secondary storage device such as a disk to preserve that information in case the primary storage device fails.

---

[1] *PC Webopaedia,* internet.com Corp. and Sandy Bay Software, 1997, <http://webreference.com/services/reference/> (7 February 2000).

[2] Howe, Walt, *Glossary of Internet Terms,* <http://www0.delphi.com/navnet/glossary/> (7 February 2000).

Baud
A unit of measure used to describe data transmission speeds through communication lines.

BBS
See **Bulletin board system**.

Binary numbering system
A numbering system with a base of 2 that uses either 0 or 1 to represent values.

Bit
A binary digit (either 0 or 1).

Boilerplate
A series of standardized paragraphs that can be arranged in any specified order as needed to produce a document.

Bookmark
The process of marking a document or a specific place in a document so that it may be located easily again at a later time. Web browsers contain a bookmarking feature that permits the user to save the address (URL) of a Web page so that the page can easily be retrieved and revisited.

Boolean operators
Phrases and words such as *AND, OR,* and *NOT* that may be used in a search string at an Internet search site to refine or limit a search.

Boot
The process of loading the operating system program into the computer, enabling it to accept and run applications software.

Browser
A graphic interface program that provides user-friendly techniques for searching and viewing World Wide Web Internet sites.

Buffer
The area within a computer or printer memory into which information is read and held until the data are recorded or printed.

Bulletin board system (BBS)
An on-line message system where information on a topic is posted electronically. Once a message is posted, anyone having access to that board may read and respond to the posting.

Byte
A group of eight bits used as a measure of the storage capacity of computers, e.g., 32K = 32,000 bytes of data that can be stored in memory. One byte may be equated to a single letter or space.

Cache
The storage area within a browser that houses the URLs, text, images, and sounds of

Web pages that have been accessed. If the sites are revisited, the pages do not have to be downloaded if they are still resident in the cache.

Cathode-ray tube (CRT)
A television-like screen used with a computer or terminal for displaying data.

CD-ROM
See **Compact disk–read only memory**.

Cell
A specific point in a spreadsheet or table where both the row and column intersect.

Cell address
The code designation such as *A2, C4,* or *G9* that identifies the column and row location of a specific cell in a spreadsheet or table. Columns are labeled with alphabetic characters; rows are numbered.

Central processing unit (CPU)
Components of computer systems that enable processing to occur by controlling the input and output functions.

Chip
A tiny electronic component that enables computers to process and store data.

Communicating computer
A computer that is connected through a modem (or other transmission means) to other computers so that data may be exchanged between or among the terminals.

Compact disk–read only memory (CD-ROM)
A disk that can store up to 650 MB of data, all of which can be made available interactively on the computer's display screen. A CD-ROM disk can be used, for example, to access an entire set of encyclopedias, Merriam-Webster's collegiate dictionary, and large numbers of fonts or clip art images for desktop publishing.

Compatible
The ability of one computer to accept and process data from another computer without conversion or code modification.

Cookie
Cookie technology allows the storage of personal preferences for Internet use through a message given to a Web browser by a Web server. The browser stores the message in a text file called a *cookie file*. Each time the browser requests a page from the server, the message is sent back to the server. Cookie files may be used to (1) personalize Web sites and (2) record information accessed, ads viewed, purchases made, files downloaded, and other preferences. Individuals who view cookies as a privacy problem may purchase *cookie munchers,* software that deletes cookies upon logging off.

CPU
See **Central processing unit**.

CRT
See **Cathode-ray tube**.

CRT screen
See **Monitor**.

Cursor
A highlighted mark on a display screen that shows where the next character will appear.

Cut
A command used to move (1) a section of text, a display of values, or an image from a document; (2) a file or array of files; or (3) a folder or array of folders to a temporary buffer from where they may be deleted or moved to another location. (See also **Paste**.) The process of moving selected items from one place to another is often called *cut and paste.*

Data Processing (DP)
The process of employing computers to store, manipulate, and report on data used by an organization.

Database
A collection of interrelated data composed of fields and records that may be accessed in a nonsequential manner. Information may be sorted, extracted, and summarized.

Default
A setting in a computer, printer, or program that is automatically implemented if no other choice is designated.

Desktop
The opening screen of the operating system that displays shortcuts to frequently used software applications, functions, folders, or files.

Desktop computer
A computer designed to fit on top of a desk. Typically the monitor sits on top of the computer, and the keyboard is in front of the computer. In tower models the computer sits on the floor, and the monitor and keyboard occupy the top of the desk.

Desktop publishing
Combines a laser printer or inkjet printer with a microcomputer and software application programs to create documents that appear as if they have been professionally printed. Desktop publishing permits the use of graphics and a variety of fonts to achieve print quality.

Dialog box
A temporary box that appears on the screen to display information or request input.

Digital camera
A camera that stores images digitally instead of on film. Pictures are stored in image files and may be downloaded to the computer where they may be edited and printed through various software applications.

Directory
A list of files stored on a disk.

Disk
A magnetic storage device on which information can be stored. Disks may be either floppy or hard. Hard disks are internal and have considerably more storage capacity than do floppy disks. See also **Floppy disk**; **Hard disk**.

Disk drive
A computer device that reads data from and writes data to a disk.

Documentation
A set of instructions that enable an operator to run a computer or program.

Domain name
The unique name that identifies an Internet site. Domain names have at least two parts, each separated by a dot (.); e.g., *amgen.com, cbeaonline.org,* and *usps.gov.*

Download
The process of transmitting a file from one computer to another, e.g., the process of transferring a file or files from the Internet (or other on-line source) to the user's computer.

DP
See **Data processing**.

E-commerce
The sale and purchase of goods and services through the Internet.

Electronic mail (E-mail)
A system for the transmission of computer-generated messages and documents from one point to another through the use of telephone lines, satellite, microwaves, or direct cable.

Emoticon
See **Smiley**.

Ergonomics
The science of designing office systems to meet the needs of the human body.

Execute
To carry out an instruction, perform an operation, or run a program on a computer.

External storage
A storage device separate from the computer that stores information.

Facsimile (FAX)
A device used to scan printed pages—including tables, charts, diagrams, photographs, and other graphic data—and transmit copies of these pages electronically to a similar device at another location.

Fiber optics
A technology that uses hair-like glass fibers to enable telecommunications systems to transmit data at high rates of speed.

Field
A defined group or block of data in a database.

File
A named location within a computer disk in which data can be placed and stored.

File transfer protocol (FTP)
A system that enables one computer to transfer files to another without distorting the data during the transfer process.

Floppy disk
A removable, magnetically sensitive disk used as a secondary storage device.

Flowchart
A diagram that graphically illustrates the sequential steps involved in solving a problem.

Folder
An organizational storage unit in the Windows and Macintosh environment that can contain multiple files.

Font
A complete set of characters for a single typeface in one size and one type style.

Footer
Information automatically printed at the bottom of each page of a document.

Format
The organized layout or appearance of data, usually when the data is printed on paper.

FTP
See **File transfer protocol**.

Function keys
The *F1* through *F12* keys on a computer keyboard, which are programmable. Their function depends on the program being used.

Gigabyte
A unit of memory measurement equal to approximately 1 billion bytes or 1,000 megabytes.

Global search
A computer search throughout an entire document for words, characters, or other data that need to be located or changed.

Graphical user interface (GUI)
A program component that uses the graphics capabilities of the computer to make the program easier to use; e.g., icons, dialog boxes, drop-down menus, etc.

Graphics
Information entered into a computer and formatted as graphs, charts, illustrations, and images. These forms may be displayed on the screen or printed on paper.

GUI
See **Graphical user interface**.

Hard copy
A document printed on paper that has been transferred from the document displayed on a computer monitor or a file stored on a computer disk.

Hard disk
A magnetic storage device that has a large data storage capacity. Typical contemporary microcomputers have a permanently installed hard disk that holds from 3 gigabytes (3 billion bytes) to 20 gigabytes (20 billion bytes) of data.

Hardware
A term used to describe the actual equipment, as distinguished from the programs, used in the computing process. (See also **Software**.)

Header
Information automatically printed at the top of each page of a document.

High-capacity disk
A magnetic storage disk that stores from 100 to 120 megabytes of data.

High-density disk
A magnetic storage disk that stores 1.44 megabytes of data.

Home page
An opener that usually outlines the contents of a Web site and provides links to other pages on the site.

HTML
See **Hypertext markup language**.

HTTP
See **Hypertext transfer protocol**.

Hyperlink
On the World Wide Web, graphic images or words appearing in a different color and/or underlined that transport the viewer with a mouse click to a related site.

Hypertext markup language (HTML)
The programming language used to create pages for sites on the World Wide Web of the Internet.

Hypertext transfer protocol (HTTP)
A protocol used to transfer information within the World Wide Web. It prescribes how messages are to be formatted and transmitted and how Web servers and browsers should interact.

Icon
An on-screen graphic symbol that represents a program file, data file, or some other computer entity or function.

Information processing
The movement of words, symbols, or numbers from the origination of an idea to its destination.

Inkjet printer
A nonimpact printer that forms an image by spraying ink from tiny jets.

Input
Data entered into a computer for processing.

Insert mode
Inserted text pushes existing text to the right as information is keyboarded at the point of insertion. (See also **Typeover mode**.)

Interface
The process that connects one component of the computer with another or connects one computer with another.

Internet
An extensive system of connected computers that comprise a vast number of networks made up of millions of host computers. This on-line global network, which is accessible in over 170 countries, has promoted information exchange between virtually every segment of our society.

Internet service provider (ISP)
A company or organization that provides a dial-up or cable connection to the Internet and an E-mail account.

Intranet
An organizational network (usually corporate) based on Internet protocols that look and act like Web pages. An intranet is accessible only to members of the organization and those others given access.

ISP
See **Internet service provider**.

Java
A high-level programming language that permits miniprograms, known as *applets,* to be downloaded and run on Web pages.

Justification
Distributing letters, numbers, symbols, and spaces within lines of text so that the right margin ends evenly.

KB
See **Kilobyte**.

Keyboarding
Using a keyboard to enter data into a computer.

Kilobyte (KB)
A term used to describe the storage capacity of computer memory and storage devices. One *KB* equals 1,024 bytes of memory.

LAN
See **Local area network**.

Landscape orientation
Repositioning the printed page so that text and graphics are printed across the length (the longer dimension) of the page instead of the width. (See also **Portrait orientation**.)

Laptop computer
A portable computer.

Laser printer
A high-speed, high-quality nonimpact printer that employs a narrow beam of electromagnetic light to enable it to print over 20,000 lines per minute.

Liquid crystal display (LCD)
A type of monitor used with many portable computers.

Listserv
A mailing list server that automatically distributes a prepared E-mail to all those addresses on a specified list.

Local area network (LAN)
A computer network that is in one physical location—a building or a group of buildings.

Macro
A recorded set of computer instructions that may be executed with a minimum number of key strokes or mouse clicks.

MB
See **Megabyte**.

Medium
The material on which information is recorded, e.g., magnetic tape or disks.

Megabyte (MB)
A term used to describe the storage capacity of computer memory and storage devices. One megabyte equals 1,024,000 bytes of memory or storage capacity.

Megahertz (MHz)
A measure to describe the speed at which a computer operates to execute commands and process data.

Memory
That part of the computer that holds information for use.

Memory, random access (RAM)
RAM is temporary memory within the computer and is used primarily for loading programs from disk or tape or holding data until it is stored to disk. Data in RAM memory is lost when the computer is turned off.

Memory, read only (ROM)
ROM stores permanent programs that may not be altered. They include the programs that instruct the computer what to do when the power is turned on and how to do various jobs such as loading the operating system and application programs from disk or tape. ROM will not lose its information when the power is turned off.

Menu
A listing on the screen of possible actions an operator may take to perform tasks on a computer.

Merge
A word processing function that allows the data in two prefiled locations to be combined—on screen or during the printing process.

MHz
See **Megahertz**.

Modem
A device attached to computer terminals that allows the transmission of data between terminals over telephone wires by converting digital signals to analog signals at one end and reconverting the analog signals back to digital signals at the other end.

Monitor
A television-like screen that connects to a computer and displays data. The monitor is also referred to as the *CRT screen*.

Mouse
A small device that moves an on-screen arrow to select functions. Clicking a control button on the mouse enables the operator to activate a selected function such as moving the cursor on the screen, opening or closing a file, displaying a menu on the screen, or performing another operation.

Multimedia
The integration of text, graphics, sound, animation, and video in computer applications.

Network
A group of computers (or other devices) connected into a planned system to enable the exchange of files and resources among the members of the system.

OCR
See **Optical character recognition**.

On-line

(1) Computers and/or peripherals are turned on and connected and are ready to send and receive data and (2) computers are connected through an Internet service provider to the Internet.

Operating system (OS)

An integrated collection of service routines for supervising the sequencing and processing of programs by a computer. Operating systems may perform debugging, input-output, machine accounting, compilation, and storage-assignment tasks. Computers will perform no functions until an operating system has been loaded. The most popular operating systems for personal computers include Windows and Macintosh System.

Optical character recognition (OCR)

Text read into a computer by scanning a document electronically.

OS

See **Operating system**.

Paste

A command used to retrieve (1) a section of text, a display of values, or an image from a document; (2) a file or array of files; or (3) a folder or array of folders from a temporary buffer and place the selection in another location. The process of moving selected items from one place to another is often called *cut and paste.* The process of copying selected items from one place to another is often called *copy and paste.*

Peripherals

Equipment such as printers, monitors, and modems that work in conjunction with the computer but are not part of the computer itself.

Pitch

A method of measuring font size by counting the number of characters per horizontal inch. The two most common pitches are 10 pitch and 12 pitch. The higher the number in this method of measuring font size, the smaller the font.

Pointer

An on-screen symbol, usually an arrow, that shows the current position of a mouse.

Points

A font size measurement method that measures the height of a character; 72 points equal one inch. The width is proportional to the height. A 12-point font is 12/72 or 1/6 inch high, and a 24-point font is 24/72 or 1/3 inch high. The higher the number in this method of measuring font size, the larger the font.

Port

An entry/exit opening that connects the CPU with the external devices such as the printer or modem.

Portrait orientation

Positioning the printed page so that text and graphics are printed across the width (the shorter dimension) of the page. (See also **Landscape orientation.**)

Processing
The transformation of computer input to a final product through the execution of program instructions.

Program
A set of instructions designed to provide a computer solution to a problem by directing the computer to carry out a desired sequence of operations.

Programming
Writing instructions to direct a computer to perform a desired process.

Prompt
A symbol or phrase that appears on the screen to inform the operator that the computer is ready to accept input.

Protocol
A set of conventions for the electronic transmission of data including modes, speed, character length, and code.

RAM
See **Memory, random access**.

Record
Represents all the related fields for a single person, company, or thing in a database.

Replace mode
See **Typeover mode**.

Reprographics
The duplication of hard copy usually by employing a computer peripheral such as a high-speed film or photocopier.

ROM
See **Memory, read only**.

Sans serif
Without small cross strokes at the top and bottom of a typeface.

Scanner
A computer peripheral that copies pages in digital format for use in applications software.

Screen capture
The process of copying the current screen display to a file or to the printer.

Scrolling
The process of moving text up or down on a computer screen.

Search and replace
A word processing command that directs a computer to locate a piece of information wherever it occurs in a document and replace it with another piece of information.

Search site
A World Wide Web site that contains software you can use to search and locate a given topic of information on the Internet.

Serif
A typeface with small cross strokes at the top and bottom of the letters.

Shouting
In E-mail messages, placing a series of words in all capital letters.

Smiley
An icon used in E-mail messages that is made up of punctuation marks to indicate the writer's mood; e.g., :-) [smile], ;-) [wink], :-([sad], etc. Also known as *emoticons,* an acronym for e*moti*on *icons.*

Soft copy
Information or data shown on the screen.

Software
Programs written to direct the operations of a computer. (See **Hardware**.)

Sorting
Process of directing the computer to organize information or data in a specific order.

Spam
Unsolicited E-mail, e.g., advertisements.

Split screen
The ability of some software programs to display two or more documents on the screen simultaneously.

Spreadsheet
A computer program similar to an accounting worksheet that displays columns and rows in the form of cells on the screen. When the values in the cells are changed, the result is automatically calculated throughout the worksheet.

Strikeover mode
See **Typeover mode**.

Template
A document or spreadsheet that includes the text or formulas needed for a generic application that needs to be repeated.

Terminal
A configuration connected to the computer for the purpose of entering and retrieving data. The most common computer terminal consists of a monitor and a keyboard.

Tilde
An accent mark produced by the keyboard that is a small horizontal wavy line (~).

Toggle
The process of switching back and forth between two modes by pressing a key. For example, once the *Caps Lock* key is pressed, the keyboard will remain in the all capital letter mode until the *Caps Lock* key is pressed again.

Tool bar
A set of navigational buttons—icons— used in graphical user interface (GUI) applications that perform frequently used related commands.

Typeface
The design of a set of characters. Examples of typefaces are Times Roman, Arial, CG Times, and Univers.

Typeover mode
Inserted text replaces existing text from the point of insertion; also known as *replace mode* or *strikeover mode.* (See also **Insert mode**.)

Type style
The treatment of typeface characters; such as, regular, bold, italic, underline, shadow, outline, and bold italic.

Uniform Resource Locator (URL)
The unique address of each Web page. A World Wide Web address locator that enables the World Wide Web system to search for, locate, and open a site.

UNIX
An operating system for a wide variety of computers (from mainframes to personal computers) that is suited for multitasking and multiuser operations.

URL
See **Uniform Resource Locator**.

User friendly
The degree to which the operations of a computer or software program are made relatively easy to learn through the use of menus, function keys, software, and documentation.

VGA
See **Video Graphics Array**.

Video Display Terminal (VDT)
A television-like screen used with a computer or terminal for displaying data. Same as *monitor.*

Video Graphics Array (VGA)
A color bit-mapped graphics display standard.

Virus
A command or program hidden in an executable file that can cause computer damage or data loss.

Voice-recognition software

An applications software program that recognizes spoken words and prints them on the computer screen as they are spoken.

Windows

(1) A series of Microsoft operating systems. (2) Divisions on a computer screen that enable an operator to view parts of a document or different documents simultaneously. Windows are created on a computer screen through software programs.

Word processing

The use of computerized equipment and software programs to keyboard, edit, produce, and store business documents.

Word wrap

A process by which a word at the end of a line is automatically dropped to the next line if it extends beyond the right margin.

World Wide Web (WWW)

A vast network of computers on the Internet that host documents formatted with graphics, sound, and other media. These documents may be accessed with an on-line connection and appropriate software.

WYSIWYG

A term used to describe on-screen displays that show the appearance of the printed text. An acrynom for the phrase *What you see is what you get,* it is pronounced "wizzy wig."

Index

B

C

D

E

N

O

P

S

T

U

V

Abbreviations of States and Territories

State or Territory	Two-Letter Postal Designation	Standard Abbreviation
Alabama	AL	Ala.
Alaska	AK	—
Arizona	AZ	Ariz.
Arkansas	AR	Ark.
California	CA	Calif., Cal.
Colorado	CO	Colo., Col.
Connecticut	CT	Conn.
Delaware	DE	Del.
District of Columbia	DC	D.C.
Florida	FL	Fla.
Georgia	GA	Ga.
Guam	GU	—
Hawaii	HI	—
Idaho	ID	—
Illinois	IL	Ill.
Indiana	IN	Ind.
Iowa	IA	—
Kansas	KS	Kans., Kan.
Kentucky	KY	Ky.
Louisiana	LA	La.
Maine	ME	—
Maryland	MD	Md.
Massachusetts	MA	Mass.
Michigan	MI	Mich.
Minnesota	MN	Minn.
Mississippi	MS	Miss.
Missouri	MO	Mo.
Montana	MT	Mont.
Nebraska	NE	Nebr., Neb.
Nevada	NV	Nev.
New Hampshire	NH	N.H.
New Jersey	NJ	N.J.
New Mexico	NM	N. Mex.
New York	NY	N.Y.
North Carolina	NC	N.C.
North Dakota	ND	N. Dak.
Ohio	OH	—
Oklahoma	OK	Okla.
Oregon	OR	Oreg., Ore.
Pennsylvania	PA	Pa., Penn., Penna.
Puerto Rico	PR	P.R.
Rhode Island	RI	R.I.
South Carolina	SC	S.C.
South Dakota	SD	S. Dak.
Tennessee	TN	Tenn.
Texas	TX	Tex.
Utah	UT	—
Vermont	VT	Vt.
Virgin Islands	VI	V.I.
Virginia	VA	Va.
Washington	WA	Wash.
West Virginia	WV	W. Va.
Wisconsin	WI	Wis., Wisc.
Wyoming	WY	Wyo.